Exploring the Legacy of the 1948
Arnhem Land Expedition

Exploring the Legacy of the 1948 **Arnhem Land** Expedition

Edited by Martin Thomas and Margo Neale

A book developed from the National Museum of Australia's 2009 symposium Barks, Birds & Billabongs: Exploring the Legacy of the 1948 American–Australian Scientific Expedition to Arnhem Land.

Published by ANU E Press
The Australian National University
Canberra ACT 0200, Australia
Email: anuepress@anu.edu.au
This title is also available online at: http://epress.anu.edu.au/arnhem_citation.html

---

National Library of Australia Cataloguing-in-Publication entry

Title: Exploring the legacy of the 1948 Arnhem Land expedition / edited by Martin Thomas and Margo Neale.

ISBN: 9781921666445 (pbk.) 9781921666452 (eBook)

Subjects: American-Australian Scientific Expedition to Arnhem Land (1948)
Aboriginal Australians--Northern Territory--Arnhem Land.
Arnhem Land (N.T.)--Discovery and exploration.

Dewey Number: 919.4295

All rights reserved. No part of this publication may be reproduced, stored in a retrieval system or transmitted in any form or by any means, electronic, mechanical, photocopying or otherwise, without the prior permission of the publisher.

Cover design and layout by Gaye Reid, Let's Create

Printed by Griffin Press

This edition © 2011 ANU E Press

Contents

Foreword ix
Prologue xi
Acknowledgments. xv

1. Expedition as Time Capsule: Introducing the American–Australian Scientific Expedition to Arnhem Land. . . . 1
   Martin Thomas

Part I. Engagements with Aboriginal Cultures

2. Inside Mountford's Tent: Paint, politics and paperwork. 33
   Philip Jones

3. Nation Building or Cold War: Political settings for the Arnhem Land Expedition 55
   Kim Beazley

4. A Robinson Crusoe in Arnhem Land: Howell Walker, *National Geographic* and the Arnhem Land Expedition of 1948 73
   Mark Collins Jenkins

5. Birds on the Wire: Wild sound, informal speech and the emergence of the radio documentary 87
   Tony MacGregor

6. From Kunnanj, Fish Creek, to Mumeka, Mann River: Hunter-gatherer tradition and transformation in Western Arnhem Land, 1948–2009 113
   Jon Altman

7. Making a Sea Change: Rock art, archaeology and the enduring legacy of Frederick McCarthy's research on Groote Eylandt 135
   Anne Clarke and Ursula Frederick

8. Ecology and the Arnhem Land Expedition: Raymond Specht, a botanist in the field 157
   Lynne McCarthy

9. Piecing the History Together: An overview of the
   1948 Arnhem Land Expedition 171
   Sally K. May

Part II. Collectors and Collections

10. The String Figures of Yirrkala: Examination of a legacy. . . . 191
    Robyn McKenzie

11. The Forgotten Collection: Baskets reveal histories 213
    Louise Hamby

12. Hidden for Sixty Years: The motion pictures of the
    American–Australian Scientific Expedition to
    Arnhem Land 239
    Joshua Harris

13. The Responsibilities of Leadership: The records of
    Charles P. Mountford 253
    Denise Chapman and Suzy Russell

14. Beneath the Billabongs: The scientific legacy of
    Robert Rush Miller 271
    Gifford Hubbs Miller and Robert Charles Cashner

15. An Insider's Perspective: Raymond Louis Specht's
    oral history 283
    Edited and introduced by Margo Daly

Part III. Aboriginal Engagements with the Expedition

16. The American Clever Man (*Marrkijbu Burdan Merika*) 313
    Bruce Birch

17. Missing the Revolution! Negotiating disclosure on the
    pre-Macassans (Bayini) in North-East Arnhem Land 337
    Ian S. McIntosh

18. Aural Snapshots of Musical Life: The 1948 recordings 355
Linda Barwick and Allan Marett

19. Unpacking the Testimony of Gerald Blitner: Cross-cultural brokerage and the Arnhem Land Expedition 377
Martin Thomas

20. The Forbidden Gaze: The 1948 Wubarr ceremony performed for the American–Australian Scientific Expedition to Arnhem Land 403
Murray Garde

21. Epilogue: Sifting the silence 423
Margo Neale

Contributors 437
Index 453

Foreword

This publication is one enduring result of the first major event dedicated to exploring and re-evaluating the legacy of the 1948 American–Australian Scientific Expedition to Arnhem Land. The symposium Barks, Birds & Billabongs was organised and hosted by the National Museum of Australia in November 2009.

The National Museum was ideally placed to undertake this collaborative venture. Initially, the Australian Institute of Anatomy, which had sent a team of biomedical researchers on the Expedition, had custodianship of the Commonwealth's share of the Arnhem Land Expedition collection. In 1984, some 270 ethnographic objects from this collection were transferred to the National Museum. With the opening of the Museum in March 2001, objects from the collection could be displayed.

In 2009, the Museum ventured into a closer examination of the complex cross-cultural, multidisciplinary dimensions of the 1948 Arnhem Land Exhibition.

In mounting Barks, Birds & Billabongs, the National Museum worked closely with the Smithsonian Institution and the National Geographic Society—original partners on the Expedition (with the Australian Government). This symposium was designed to recapture something of the collaborative spirit of the Expedition that was a watershed event in Australia's cultural and scientific history.

This publication has been undertaken by the Australian National University, our neighbour and natural collaborator on projects of intellectual significance.

The Museum is well positioned culturally to engage in this project, with its strong commitment to Indigenous programs and collections. Indeed the Museum's collection has built on the original base and includes an extensive, magnificent and historically significant collection of bark paintings. Our commitment to Indigenous agency and voice informs the management of our Indigenous collection, exhibitions and employment practices. The Museum's continued emphasis upon and dialogue with Indigenous Australia resonates with the strong Indigenous community participation and focus of this international symposium.

Exploring the Legacy of the 1948 Arnhem Land Expedition draws upon the Museum's research commitment. Northern Australia is an area where the Museum has had a long research involvement. The expertise of our staff covers Indigenous and environmental histories, the history of science, biography, archaeological research in the region, the history of conservation and national park programs, and the emergence of a thriving contemporary Aboriginal art movement.

From the perspective of the National Museum of Australia, Barks, Birds & Billabongs was a project that ideally combined our research interests, our deepened understanding of our collection and our capacity and willingness to enter into fruitful partnerships across Australia and internationally.

Andrew Sayers
Director, National Museum of Australia

Project Director, Margo Neale, Council of the National Museum of Australia Chairman, Daniel Gilbert, and the Governor-General of Australia, Quentin Bryce, meeting Manikay performers (left to right) Djangirrawuy Garawirrtja, Manimawuy Dhamarrandji, Djombala Dhamarrandji and Gordon Lanyipi at the Barks, Birds & Billabongs symposium, 2009

Photograph by George Serras

Prologue

The triumphs and travails of the American–Australian Scientific Expedition to Arnhem Land were front-page news back in 1948. In the decade that followed, the release of the official film productions, the widespread display of art, craft and scientific collections in museums and galleries, and high-level coverage in *National Geographic* ensured that a global audience numbering millions of people was exposed to aspects of the Arnhem Land venture. From this high point, its profile inevitably diminished with the passing of the years, to the extent that the Expedition became known for the most part only by specialists. Scholars in fields ranging from ornithology to ethnomusicology would advance their particular projects by making use of the rich collections and documentation assembled in 1948, some only dimly aware that a greater story lay behind the objects. The transnationalism of the Expedition, which did so much to boost its profile in the first instance, now weighed against it. For someone trying to understand the event in its totality, the dispersal of collections, photographs and documents across Australia and the United States presented logistical challenges of a high order.

The extent of these challenges—and the exciting prospects they signalled—became evident to the three of us as we established the steering committee for Barks, Birds & Billabongs, the National Museum of Australia symposium that was the stimulus for this book. Although we had trodden somewhat different paths, we had come to a common conviction that the cross-cultural engagement that distinguished the Arnhem Land Expedition was of enduring significance. Margo Neale, a curator of Aboriginal art, became intrigued by the remarkable paintings on bark and paper amassed by the Expedition, many of which were acquired by Australia's six state art galleries in 1956. They were foundational to the major collections of Aboriginal art that subsequently developed. As an archaeology student in the 1990s, Sally K. May picked up on another thread of the story when she investigated the often fraught politics that influenced the dispersal of the Expedition's ethnographic collections between Australia and the United States. For Martin Thomas, a historian long interested in photography and broadcasting, the Expedition's electronic recordings of Aboriginal music—produced in collaboration with the Australian Broadcasting Commission—were what prompted him to delve into the Expedition story. We all agreed that so large and complex an event deserved to be better understood.

By any standard, the adventures of the 17 men and women who formed the Expedition party make for an intriguing story in their own right. But more than that, the event encapsulates some of the great themes that have come to define our own epoch. In terms of geopolitics, the desirability of a joint scientific project between Australia and the United States was symptomatic of the mood post World War II. The theatrics of the Expedition were a public face to the secret negotiations that resulted in the military alliance that was formalised as the ANZUS (Australia, New Zealand and the United States) Pact in 1951. In terms of the history of science, the interdisciplinary make-up of the Expedition party is indicative of the growing status of ecology post war, and with it the dawning recognition among Westerners that our ecosystems—comprising both natural and human heritage—are resources worthy of protection rather than exploitation. But it is the breadth of the Expedition's interest in Aboriginal society and culture that represents the most prescient aspect of its inquiries. The paradox at work here is intriguing, for the Expedition was initially justified on the grounds that Arnhem Land's Aboriginal cultures, particularly its strong traditions of dance, music and painting, were on a fast track to disappearance. Fortunately, these dire predictions were erroneous. Far from disappearing or assimilating with the wider population, the descendant communities take a lively interest in the way their forebears interacted with the visiting researchers 60 years ago.

Barks, Birds & Billabongs was convened as a way of expanding the scope of what is normally thought of as historical inquiry. We hoped to encourage an understanding of the Expedition and its era, and we wanted to grapple with the many facets of its legacy. Some of these—such as the preservation of wonderful paintings and artefacts—are a source of wonder and pleasure for contemporary Arnhem Landers. Others—such as the removal of human remains—have caused argument and grief. These and many other issues were put on the agenda because we believed that a continuation of the original transnational and cross-cultural conversation was urgently required. This book is a continuation of that dialogue, involving 24 of the scholars who contributed to the original conversation.

Sally K. May, Margo Neale and Martin Thomas
Steering Committee
Barks, Birds & Billabongs Symposium

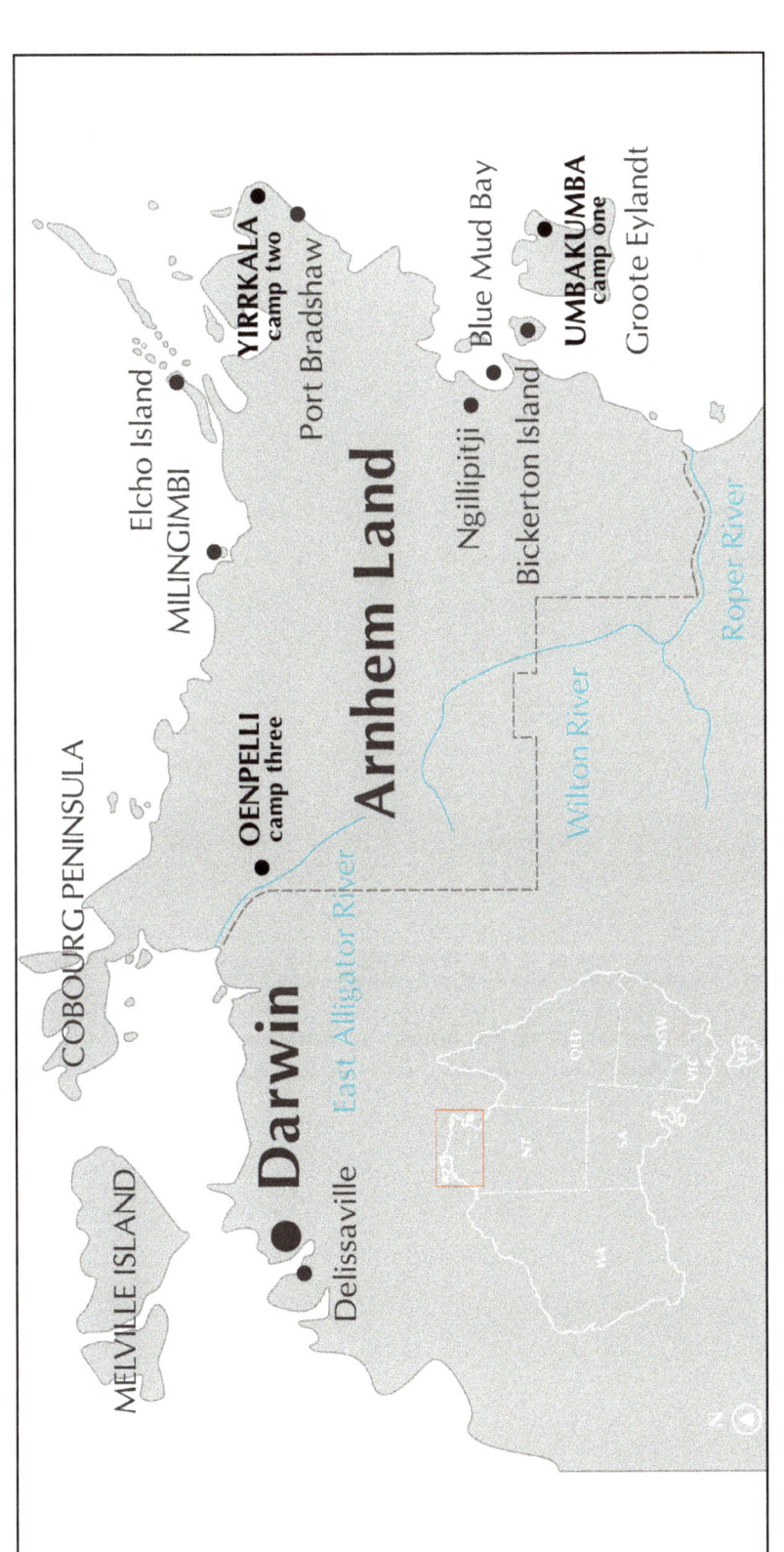

Map showing main sites visited by the Arnhem Land Expedition

NAME	ROLE	INSTITUTION
Charles P Mountford	Leader, Ethnologist and Film Director	Honorary Associate Curator in Ethnology, South Australian Museum, Adelaide
Frank M Setzler	Deputy Leader and Archaeologist	Head Curator, Department of Anthropology, Smithsonian Institution, Washington
Herbert G Deignan	Ornithologist	Associate Curator of Birds, Smithsonian Institution, Washington
David H Johnson	Mammalogist	Curator of Mammals, Smithsonian Institution, Washington
Robert R Miller	Ichthyologist	Associate Curator of Fishes, Smithsonian Institution, Washington
Raymond L Specht	Botanist	Lecturer, Department of Botany, University of Adelaide*
Frederick D McCarthy	Anthropologist	Department of Anthropology, Australian Museum, Sydney
Harrison Howell Walker	Photographer and Staff Writer	National Geographic Society, Washington
Bessie I Mountford	Honorary Secretary	NA
William E Harney	Guide and Liaison Officer	NA
Peter Bassett-Smith	Cine-Photographer	NA
Keith Cordon	Transport Officer	NA
John E Bray	Cook and Honorary Entomologist	NA
Reginald Hollow	Cook	NA
Brian Billington	Medical Officer	Institute of Anatomy, Canberra
Margaret McArthur	Nutritionist	Institute of Anatomy, Canberra
Kelvin Hodges	Biochemist	Institute of Anatomy, Canberra

* Specht held this position in 1956 when this volume of the Records was published.

Members of the Arnhem Land Expedition as listed in volume 1 of *Records of the American–Australian Scientific Expedition to Arnhem Land*, 1956.

Acknowledgments

This volume has benefited from the generous support of many friends, colleagues and institutions. The editors gratefully acknowledge the support of Sally K. May for her input as an advisor and reader in the early stages of this volume. For their editorial and administrative contribution, thanks to Rowena Dickins-Morrison, Sonja Balaga and Katherine Aigner from the National Museum of Australia and Margo Daly and Amanda Harris from the University of Sydney. We are grateful for the copyediting services of Jan Borrie, the indexing of Barbara Bessant, the proofreading of Mark Evans and the cover design of Gaye Reid of Let's Create, who also designed the poster and handbook for Barks, Birds & Billabongs, the 2009 symposium that was the genesis of this book. Thanks to Nicolas Peterson and Karen Westmacott for opening the path to ANU E Press and to Duncan Beard and Nausica Pinar at the press for their care and patience. For their generous feedback, suggestions and practical assistance, special thanks to Emanuela Appetiti and Sarah Bunn. We gratefully acknowledge the generosity of Expedition botanist, Raymond Specht, who willingly responded to all our questions.

Thanks to everyone who attended and contributed to Barks, Birds & Billabongs. We collectively thank the former director Craddock Morton, the staff of the National Museum of Australia, and the many people who supported the symposium as volunteers. Special thanks to Jodi L. Neale, Troy Pickwick, George Serras and Rebecca Richards. Sally K. May played a special role in consulting with communities and assisting with the programming in her capacity as an academic advisor on the steering committee.

The major sponsors of Barks, Birds & Billabongs were: the Department of Families, Housing, Community Services and Indigenous Affairs; the Faculty of Arts, the University of Sydney; the Research School of the Humanities and the Arts, the Australian National University; and the Australian Centre for Indigenous History, the Australian National University. Other sponsoring institutions included the National Geographic Society; the National Museum of Natural History, Smithsonian Institution; and the Embassy of the United States of America in Australia.

The symposium was supported by the Australian Institute of Aboriginal and Torres Strait Islander Studies; the National Library of Australia; the National Film and Sound Archive; the State Library of South Australia; and the Australian–American Fulbright Commission.

We acknowledge the support of the following community organisations: Anindilyakwa Arts and Cultural Centre, Groote Eylandt; Injalak Arts and

Crafts Centre, Gunbalanya; Kunwinjku Language Project, Gunbalanya; Buku-Larrnggay Mulka Centre, Yirrkala; Milingimbi Art and Craft Centre, Milingimbi; and Galiwinku Art Centre, Elcho Island. Thanks to Joy Williams of Croker Island for making available the Adjamarduku Outstation, where interviews on the 'American Clever Man' story were filmed.

For their contributions to the Barks, Birds & Billabongs special events, we thank Yidumduma Bill Harney, Mick Dodson, Robyn Williams, Jack Thompson and Her Excellency Quentin Bryce, the Governor-General of Australia.

Research and editorial work on this volume was made possible by support from the Australian Research Council through Future Fellowship and Discovery Project grants (FT0992291 and DP1096897). Martin Thomas gratefully acknowledges the support of the Smithsonian Institution through its Smithsonian Fellowships program and the personal support of numerous staff, especially Paul Michael Taylor, Adrienne L. Kaeppler, Pamela Henson, Jake Homiak and Robert Leopold.

We thank the many institutions and individuals who have made their collections available to authors and editors. All reasonable efforts have been made to contact copyright holders of pictorial and other material reproduced in this volume.

1. Expedition as Time Capsule: Introducing the American–Australian Scientific Expedition to Arnhem Land

Martin Thomas

Nineteen Forty-Eight brought little of the quietude that a war-weary world might have wished for. The chill winds of the Cold War were blowing; the great postwar migrations had begun. The time line on the '1948' page of *Wikipedia* conveys something of the temper of this formative year—or at least a perception of it, collectively created by contributors to that intellectual common. Burma and Ceylon gain independence. Israel becomes a nation-state. Gandhi begins the year with a hunger strike to protest the violence resulting from the Partition of India. In late January, he is assassinated. The Treaty of Brussels, predecessor of the North Atlantic Treaty Organisation (NATO), is signed. The Communist Party seizes control of Czechoslovakia. The Berlin Blockade begins. The World Health Organization is established. Dutch troops and Indonesian nationalists declare a truce. Truman signs the Marshall Plan. An executive order ends racial segregation in the US Armed Forces. The first monkey is launched into space. The paper proposing big-bang nucleo-synthesis as the origin of the universe is published, as is Kinsey's *Sexual Behavior in the Human Male*.[1] Not mentioned on the '1948' page—although utterly encapsulating the spirit of the moment—is George Orwell on the island of Jura, who has been writing all year. In December, he sends to his London publisher the manuscript that will soon be released as *Nineteen Eighty-Four*, the title a transposition of *four* and *eight*. Nineteen Forty-Eight was nothing if not eventful—and it set the paradigm for many of the most pressing concerns of the present day.

The 17 men and women who officially constituted the American–Australian Scientific Expedition to Arnhem Land were physically quarantined from these events as they went about their research in the far north of Australia. But as this book shows, they, in their way, embodied the zeitgeist, although they did so through participation in a type of activity that is usually associated with the expansion of the European empires, not their falling apart. The Arnhem Land Expedition reminds us that the boundaries between epochs are not always sharply defined; an event constituted on seemingly outmoded principles can be a harbinger of things to come. As much as the expeditionary team was of

---

1 See <http://en.wikipedia.org/wiki/1948> (viewed 22 October 2010).

the moment, enacting a display of trans-Pacific harmony that the Australian Government, in particular, was eager to broadcast to the world, the concept of an expedition through the wilds of Arnhem Land was wildly anachronistic, as Anne Clarke and Ursula Frederick explain in their chapter on archaeology. The 1948 Expedition, they write, was an

> astounding initiative, not only because of the scale, logistics and multidisciplinary scope of its vision, but also because it was a kind of historical re-enactment—a project that performed the investigative urges of an earlier era in modern times. Like the explorers who mapped the continent in the previous century, the Expedition scholars sought to discover and progress knowledge about a particular region in an effort to better grasp a bigger picture of our world.

One of the great problems for the researchers involved in this enterprise was the rate of change in the world they were trying to picture. By 1964, when the fourth and final volume of the lavish *Records of the American–Australian Scientific Expedition to Arnhem Land* (1956–64) was published, the whole project had attained something of a sepia hue. In time, scholars would speak of 1948 as 'the last of the big expeditions'. This did not mean that researchers had abandoned locations such as Arnhem Land as destinations for fieldwork; far from it—as many chapters in this volume attest. The problem was with the concept of an *expedition*, which looked increasingly archaic in a period when decolonisation was forcing revision of the most basic assumptions— especially those relating to the world's indigenous populations, whose rights and equality were being established in international covenants. These shifting values and mores, which have so coloured our current outlook and perceptions, greatly complicate the task of interpreting the Expedition and its impacts. Clarke and Frederick note that changes in scholarly methods and legal frameworks, added to the completely different ethical considerations that now govern research in Aboriginal communities, have rendered the 'expeditionary approach obsolete'. As we will see, this was anticipated at the time by rival anthropologists who, like later historians of science, tended to ignore the Arnhem Land Expedition or deride it as a populist extravagance. In this book, however, we reject this view, and propose that the fusion of nineteenth- and twentieth-century modes of thinking greatly adds to the interest, complexity and ultimate significance of this event.

1. Expedition as Time Capsule

Figure 1.1 Rear view of ichthyologist Robert R. Miller (left) at Yirrkala, with the Expedition camp in the background, 1948

Photograph by Frank M. Setzler. By permission of the National Anthropological Archives, Smithsonian Institution. NAA Photo Lot 36, Box 8.

To get a sense of the world of the Expedition, let us plunge in at the middle. It is July 1948 and the Expedition has reached its fourth month and the second of its three base camps, Yirrkala, on the Gove Peninsula in Arnhem Land's northeast. The clans of this part of Arnhem Land are known collectively as Yolngu, meaning 'people'. The researchers and support team have recently flown in from Groote Eylandt in the Gulf of Carpentaria, where, among the various frustrations that dogged them in those early months, was the delayed arrival of equipment and provisions, owing to the stranding on a reef of their supply barge, the *Phoenix*. At Yirrkala—and at all the Arnhem Land bases—the visitors are referred to as 'Balanda' by the locals. This term for white people, common throughout the linguistically and culturally diverse terrain of the Arnhem Land reserve, is a loan word—a corruption of 'Hollander'—introduced to Australia by traders who came from the port of Macassar on South Sulawesi to harvest the sea slug known as trepang.[2] (Their annual visits to northern Australia predate British occupation, although the introduction of the term Balanda indicates that the expansion of the European empires was to some extent known and discussed in Arnhem Land.) The Balanda of the Expedition have pitched large cottage tents at a site called Balma, where the Yirrkala cemetery is now located, and where the grave of Wandjuk Marika (1927–87), a young man who would

---

2 Macknight, C. C. 1976, *The Voyage to Marege': Macassan trepangers in Northern Australia*, Melbourne University Press, Carlton, Vic.; and Macknight, C. C. 2008, 'Harvesting the memory: open beaches in Makassar and Arnhem Land', in P. Veth, P. Sutton and M. Neale (eds), *Strangers on the Shore: Early coastal contacts with Australia*, National Museum of Australia, Canberra.

serve as one of their main interpreters, can now be found. They are just a stone's throw from the area of the mission known as Beach Camp. With the research and collecting continuing apace, it is a surreal spectacle that the visitors present to the hundred or so people resident at the mission this dry season.

An ornithologist, a mammalogist, an ichthyologist and a botanist are roving the surrounding land and waterways, returning to the camp with bags of specimens. They must preserve them to museum standard, often working until long into the night. Two biomedical researchers have set up a laboratory and are doing their utmost to convince the locals to be pricked and prodded, and to surrender blood, breast milk or faeces to the service of science. Local artists and craftspeople are in overdrive in an effort to satisfy the requirements of three ethnological collectors hungry for paintings, baskets, weapons and other artefacts. The cameras of two photographers snap or whirr as they steadily expose a vast stock of still and moving film. In the middle of the hubbub is the camp kitchen, presided over by a cook who doubles as the honorary entomologist. Like all his colleagues, he is dependent on the input of the local people. A stream of children, whom he refers to as the 'cockroach committee', brings in insects for his collection. Tobacco is the currency for remunerating adults, but the children are paid in sweets.

In his potted accounts of the Expedition's origins, the leader, Charles P. Mountford, always acknowledged the input of three founding fathers.[3] They were Gilbert Grosvenor, celebrated President of the National Geographic Society (NGS) and editor of its universal magazine; Arthur Calwell, Australia's Minister for Information (who also served as Minister for Immigration and went on to lead the Australian Labor Party in opposition in the 1960s); and Alexander Wetmore, Secretary of the Smithsonian Institution. Grosvenor was the enabler of a research grant that seeded the Expedition. Wetmore, who recognised that Smithsonian participation could rectify his institution's deficiency in Australian collections, offered to send a delegation of scientists. Calwell, who saw the possibility of Australian collaboration with these two iconic US organisations as a diplomatic and propagandist opportunity, arranged to sign up the Australian Government as an official partner (see Jones, Beazley, May and Chapman and Russell, this volume). Mountford was generous in crediting this trio, and seems to have gloried in his association with them. His own diaries, however, reveal a more complex story. In reality, there were many others who played central roles in negotiating what would become the Arnhem Land Expedition. Foremost among them was David Bailey, a journalist and Department of Information press officer stationed on Manhattan, who in early 1945 arranged the itinerary for

---

3   See, for example, the acknowledgments page in Mountford, C. P. (ed.) 1956, *Records of the American–Australian Scientific Expedition to Arnhem Land. Volume 1: Art, myth and symbolism*, Melbourne University Press, Carlton, Vic., p. xiii.

Mountford's film screenings and lectures in the United States and organised meetings with mid-level officials at the Smithsonian, the NGS, the American Museum of Natural History in New York, and other institutions supportive of anthropological research.[4]

Figure 1.2 Expedition cook and honorary entomologist, John Bray, with his insect collection, 1948

Photograph by Howell Walker. By permission of the State Library of South Australia. PRG 487/1/3.

---

4 C. P. Mountford, 'A Journey to America 1944–5', vol. 1, PRG 1218/16/1, Mountford-Sheard Collection, State Library of South Australia (hereafter SLSA), Adelaide.

Of Mountford's major supporters, Wetmore was most alert to the pressures and interpersonal dynamics that complicate the progress of an expedition. His passion for all things to do with birds began in boyhood, and he published his first paper, 'My experience with the Red-headed Woodpecker', at the age of thirteen. Regarded as a '20th-century doyen of American ornithology', he never relinquished his research and collecting—the administrative demands of the Smithsonian secretaryship notwithstanding.[5] He kept a paternal eye on officers posted to exotic locations, especially the Arnhem Land Expedition ornithologist, Herbert Deignan, with whom he had shared field trips in America, and archaeologist Frank Setzler, the deputy leader. On 9 July, Wetmore wrote to Setzler from his office overlooking The Mall in central Washington, reflecting on the 'affairs of the Australian Expedition', which had been 'much on my mind':

> The party now has been long in the field, and has had sufficient of the usual mishaps incident to travel in remote places so that care needs to be used in the personal relationships of the leaders with the men. Let me say that I regard this present trip as one of great importance in furthering friendly relations between scientists and government officers in Australia with the Smithsonian Institution. We must do everything that we can to promote the welfare of the work and the relationships that should exist between the Smithsonian and Australian workers. These, for various reasons, have been more tenuous in the past than I have liked.

> Having just celebrated my 62nd birthday I can now look back on nearly 50 years during which I have had active part in many expeditions large and small. I know too well the tensions that develop in the field and the minor incidents that often are magnified by the close contact of individual workers…What I can tell you I wish you would pass on to the three other men in the American party.

> Mountford I am sure has had his difficulties, due probably in part to 'politics' among his own countrymen…I have the feeling that he has been put in a very difficult situation due to the delay in transport of supplies and equipment for which he can hardly be blamed personally…I do not know the personnel of the Australian party. Possibly you may have too much information on the subject. There again the personal element enters and we have to do the best we can.

> The unforeseen delays will undoubtedly curtail the field work but at that I am not surprised since the program was fairly comprehensive. Regardless of this, whatever we get is so greatly to our advantage here

---

5   Oehser, P. H. 1980, 'In memoriam: Alexander Wetmore', *The Auk*, vol. 97, no. 3, p. 608.

> that we should not feel badly. It is always true that a large party has to move more slowly than a small one, which has brought my own personal preference for making most of my own expeditions either alone or with one or two other people. The addition of every new worker means more equipment and more difficulty in transport. As a matter of fact I rather doubt that Mountford through his experience as an anthropologist and photographer realized the extent of the equipment that would be necessary for successful work in other branches when he was developing with me the details of our American party.[6]

Wetmore's letter, so revealing in what it says about the motivations for Smithsonian participation in the Expedition, betrays a suspicion that there was ill feeling towards Mountford, as was certainly the case—and not only among the Americans. Complaints from the Expedition's biochemist and physician, Brian Billington, had reached senior bureaucrats in Canberra.[7] Furthermore, there are indications that Howard Coate, an employee of the Native Affairs Branch who was delegated to help the party at its first base, Groote Eylandt, criticised Mountford in a report to his superiors.[8] Even so, Wetmore, when he penned his shrewd advice to Setzler on 9 July, little imagined that the following day Calwell's Director of the Department of Information, accompanied by the Administrator of the Northern Territory and an American diplomat, would fly into the isolated settlement of Yirrkala to declare Mountford unfit for leadership and appoint Setzler in his place. As Philip Jones explains in his account of the incident in Chapter 2, Setzler was eventually persuaded to decline the promotion after conferring with his American colleagues, but the incident remained an enormous humiliation for Mountford and led to further deterioration of an already strained relationship between the two men.[9] Wetmore, when briefed on these theatrics, confided to Setzler that he was moved to laughter at his earlier 'almost prophetic' letter. Setzler's decision to decline the leadership he thoroughly endorsed; the last thing he wanted was Smithsonian personnel getting bogged down in the trivialities of transport and organisation.

> You were absolutely correct in refusing to take over the scientific administration…Mountford's difficulties are the ones usually found in a country where scientific work is not established as fully as it is

---

6 Wetmore to Setzler, 9 July 1948, General Correspondence 1948–9, Folder 1, Frank Maryl Setzler Papers 1927–1960, Box 7, National Anthropological Archives, Suitland, Md.
7 Correspondence in file titled 'Survey Arnhem Land 1947–8', Institute of Anatomy Records, Series No. A2644/1, Item 50/11 Section 1, National Archives of Australia (hereafter NAA), Canberra.
8 Expedition cook, John Bray, made note in his diary that Coate had complained to Native Affairs about Mountford's leadership. The diary is in the private collection of Bray's son, Andrew Bray, of Canberra.
9 For discussion of how the incident was viewed within the US State Department, see Thomas, M. 2010, 'A short history of the 1948 Arnhem Land Expedition', *Aboriginal History*, vol. 34.

with us. Under such circumstances there is usually more jealousy and contention than cooperation. We had plenty of it in the early days here in the United States.[10]

Wetmore's correspondence shows that to his way of thinking, an expedition of any scale was something of a last resort. So pared back was his own ideal of ornithological fieldwork—a man, a gun, one or two companions—that it was more a bushwalk than an expedition as that term is usually understood. Wetmore was by no means alone in this view. Another sceptic when it came to expeditions was the anthropologist A. P. Elkin—a dominating presence in Aboriginal studies, whose name appears often in this volume. Elkin was the long-serving Professor of Anthropology at the University of Sydney—a position he assumed after his predecessor, A. Radcliffe-Brown, moved to Chicago in 1931.[11] Elkin had no affection for Mountford, who was of working-class origin and essentially self-trained. For many years, his day job was as a telephone mechanic for the Department of the Postmaster General. Highly gifted as a photographer, he had risen to prominence as an authority on Aboriginal society and culture thanks to the mentorship of museum professionals in Adelaide and through his involvement in amateur societies. His lack of formal credentials was unimpressive to the Chicago-trained Setzler, and it certainly irked Elkin, whom Mountford—with some justification—regarded as his nemesis. Archival records reveal that Elkin waged a sustained campaign against Mountford over many years. He torpedoed a Carnegie grant that Mountford would otherwise have received in 1940 (see Jones, this volume) and in 1947 he queried the award of a Commonwealth Literary Fellowship to Mountford, who proposed writing a book on 'the life and customs of Aborigines of Western Australia'. Elkin wrote to the secretary of the fund that he was 'always a bit suspicious of a title "life and customs"; it savours too much of the travelogue descriptions of the 1880's by untrained observers. These days we look for sociological studies by highly trained men or women.'[12] When news of the planned Arnhem Land Expedition broke in the Australian press in May 1945, Elkin immediately wrote to the NGS, urging the appointment of 'a trained social anthropologist' and again querying the credentials of Mountford, whom he described as 'a good photographer, especially of still subjects'. Mountford was given a copy of this missive, which he annotated: 'Elkin's letter to National Geographic. Nice man.'[13]

---

10   Wetmore to Setzler, 10 August 1948, General Correspondence 1948–9, Folder 1, Frank Maryl Setzler Papers 1927–1960, Box 7, National Anthropological Archives.
11   Wise, T. 1985, *The Self Made Anthropologist: A life of A. P. Elkin*, Allen & Unwin, Sydney.
12   Elkin to H. S. Temby, 13 March 1947, Commonwealth Literary Fund Records, Series A463, Item 1948/603, NAA.
13   Elkin to Secretary of NGS, 30 May 1945, Correspondence, 1945–1949, p. 12, PRG 1218/17/4, Mountford-Sheard Collection, SLSA.

The struggles between Mountford and Elkin expose disciplinary fault lines that were a defining characteristic of anthropology in this formative period. This is just one of the ways in which the 1948 Expedition provides insight into the world of which it was part. Elkin was undoubtedly thinking of Mountford when he wrote to Setzler in 1950, by which time the American was home in Washington, DC, accessioning the material he had collected in Australia and writing up his reports. Among other business, Elkin mentioned his own trip into southern Arnhem Land the previous year, explaining that he 'took an expedition which normally I severely refrain from doing, but in addition to studying social organisation and ritual I got recordings of native chants, secret and public'.[14]

Elkin's preferred model of fieldwork, which became ever more standard among social anthropologists after World War II, required the researcher to live in a community for an extended period and hopefully become conversant in the language. For many who did this, the experience of social immersion was the prelude to a lifelong commitment to those communities. Jones in this volume likens the long-term approach to 'careful angling across several seasons', in contrast with Mountford's expeditionary method, which 'was more like an afternoon's intensive trawling'. Yet as Elkin himself realised, the driftnet could be useful on occasion, not only because it allowed for rapid and diverse results, but because the collaboration of a range of experts would—in theory at least—result in productive synergies. In addition, the expeditionary approach, which often involved professional filmmakers and photographers, allowed an academic such as Elkin to compete for the substantial audience— interested in Aboriginal issues—that maligned 'amateurs' such as Mountford were doing much to cultivate. Collaborators in Elkin's 1949 venture included 'my Linguist, Dr. Capell', the archaeologist N. W. G. Macintosh, and Jesse Buffum, an American photographer who 'gave me some beautiful movies'. Bill Harney, the bushman, writer and retired Native Affairs patrol officer who had served as guide for Mountford from July to November 1948, helped liaise with Aboriginal groups and managed the camp.[15] The recording of 'native chants' was overseen by another participant, poet and broadcaster John Thompson, the adoptive father of actor Jack Thompson and a distinguished radio producer for the Australian Broadcasting Commission (ABC; now Corporation). This was a mutually beneficial arrangement, with the ABC acquiring unique ethnographic material that it put to immediate use in a documentary feature and then retained in its sound effects library for future productions. In return, the ABC supplied a producer, technician and recording equipment, and allowed Elkin to publish songs on vinyl as a resource for other researchers (see Barwick and Marett, this volume).

---

14   Elkin to Setzler, 1 June 1950, General Correspondence 1950, Frank Maryl Setzler Papers 1927–1960, Box 8, National Anthropological Archives.
15   Ibid.

Expeditions were an old idea, but new media permitted a partial reconfiguration of what they were about. Portable sound recording, smaller 16 mm cameras, colour photography and cheaper methods of reproducing it resulted in interesting alliances between scientific and media organisations.[16] *National Geographic* was the pioneer in this regard, for it had had a foot in both media and science since 1899 when the young Gilbert Grosvenor was recruited as editor and rapidly transformed it from a learned journal to a popular pictorial magazine. Mark Collins Jenkins in his chapter on Expedition photographer, Howell Walker, explains how the popular geography promoted by *National Geographic* was made possible by channelling the proceeds from magazine subscriptions into NGS expeditions and other ventures—ostensibly intended at scientific advancement although very much concerned with the generation of future content. Examination of Elkin's papers suggests that the idea of harnessing the ABC's technical resources was a direct result of him listening to the new genre of radio documentary, and discerning its ethnographic possibilities.[17] That is to say, Elkin did not directly emulate his despised rival. Nevertheless, Elkin's collaboration with Thompson in 1949 was very similar to that between Mountford and the ABC's Colin Simpson the previous year. Simpson met up with the Arnhem Land Expedition at its third base, Oenpelli (now known as Gunbalanya). Working with technician Ray Giles, he initiated a program of audio recording that included documentation of song, ceremony, environmental ambience and interviews with the Expedition members. To advance scholarship on Aboriginal culture, while communicating with a national audience, was seen as highly beneficial to the researchers and, as Tony MacGregor observes in his chapter on Simpson, was concordant 'with the state broadcaster's sense of high national purpose'.

MacGregor provides in-depth analysis of Simpson's audio documentary *Expedition to Arnhem Land*, which was first broadcast in late 1948 and quickly repeated the following year in a new weekly timeslot called *Australian Walkabout*. In a departure from the studio-made product that had dominated the airwaves since the inception of radio, advertisements for the program promised listeners the novelty of hearing 'Actual Voices of Australian Personalities' recorded on location. Documentary was a rapidly emerging genre at this time; Expedition cinema-photographer, Peter Bassett-Smith, noted in his oral history that before the war he had never heard the word 'documentary', despite his passion, dating from boyhood, for filming

---

16 For an account of the effect of technological change on documentary making, see Musser, C. 1966, 'Engaging with reality', in G. Nowell-Smith (ed.), *The Oxford History of World Cinema*, Oxford University Press, UK.
17 Thomas, M. 2007, 'The rush to record: transmitting the sound of Aboriginal culture', *Journal of Australian Studies*, no. 90, p. 109.

actuality.[18] The rise of documentary, which was greatly enabled by the spread of television, transformed the representation of adventure to exotic places, just as it influenced the organisation and financing of this type of travel. The 1953 ascent of Mount Everest by Edmund Hillary and Tenzing Norgay—who used bottled oxygen at the higher altitudes—is emblematic of what happened to the concept of the expedition in the postwar era. 'Blank' spaces on maps were now so scarce that the rhetoric of geographic exploration and discovery became increasingly implausible. Enabled by such innovations as cylinder oxygen, synthetic ropes and fabrics, and improved survival equipment, expeditions morphed into something approximating an extreme sport. It is notable that the word 'expedition' was little used when the drive for exploration took its most extreme turn by abandoning the Earth altogether. In its quest to reach the heavens, the space race required a religious terminology. Astronauts go on *missions*, not expeditions.

Even as the space race rumbled into action, the documentation of terrestrial travel—much of it carefully staged for the camera—remained important to the way nations made images of themselves, whether they be for distribution abroad or domestic consumption. Cinema spawned the Arnhem Land Expedition, for it was Mountford's films of Central Australia, shot in the early 1940s, that aroused the interest of American backers when he toured the United States in 1945. Cinema kept the Expedition story alive in the 1950s and after, in part through the NGS silent film production, shot by Howell Walker, to which Setzler lectured before audiences of thousands (see Harris, this volume), and through four Australian productions, based on Bassett-Smith's footage and released by the Commonwealth Film Unit. The titles included *Arnhem Land*, a celebratory chronicle of the Expedition and its achievements, and the nature film *Birds and Billabongs* (which suggested the title for the symposium that inspired this volume).

---

18 Peter Bassett-Smith in interview with Sally K. May and Martin Thomas, 12 February 2006, Kangaroo Ground, Vic., ORAL TRC 5655, National Library of Australia Oral History Collection (hereafter NLAOHC), Canberra.

Figure 1.3 Advertisement for Mountford's 1945 film and lecture tour of the United States, inserted in his diary

By permission of the State Library of South Australia. PRG 1218/16/2.

The short production time of radio feature making allowed the Australian national broadcaster to carry the first documentary on the Expedition. Simpson's program first went to air on 30 November 1948, less than four weeks after the party's departure from its final base, when much of the film stock had yet to be processed. The production opens not with 'actual voices', but with a heady dose of orchestral fanfare. It is film music, 1940s-style. Trumpets blare; strings and percussion stamp out a rhythm that conjures a vision of pith-helmeted white men leading native carriers through fake jungle. A most un-Australian voice announces: 'Expedition to Arnhem Land—an ABC feature program.' Perhaps it is all a little tongue-in-cheek, for at this moment a cross-fade occurs and the studio-confected journey into the heart of darkness is suddenly replaced with music from Western Arnhem Land: a beautiful ensemble performance involving singers accompanied by clap sticks and didjeridu.[19] That staged transition from 'artifice' to 'reality' is highly prescient. In compressed form, it seems to register the shift from prewar to postwar mind-set, anticipating the broader concern for Aboriginal heritage that the Expedition helped foster—partly through Simpson's own travel writing, particularly his bestselling book stimulated by his 1948 experience, *Adam in Ochre* (1951), which argued for the legitimacy of Aboriginal culture and made withering critique of white Australia's treatment of the people it dispossessed. The didjeridu we now regard as a quintessentially Australian sound—as iconic to the nation as the gum tree or the kangaroo. So it is salutary to realise that this became possible only because of specific collaborations involving Aboriginal musicians and non-Aboriginal recordists.[20] For the majority of listeners to Simpson's program, it was their first hearing of the instrument. By MacGregor's reckoning, it was only the second time that a didjeridu recording had been broadcast (see MacGregor, Note 39).

Expedition to Arnhem Land contains interviews with most of the researchers, commencing with Mountford, who explained the purpose of the mission:

> SIMPSON: And the nature of this expedition, Mr Mountford, it's not an exploring expedition is it, going into darkest Arnhem Land to contact savages who don't exist any more? It is a scientific expedition, is that right?
>
> MOUNTFORD: That is so. This is not an exploring party, its objects are purely scientific and that is to increase our knowledge of the natural history and the Aborigines of Arnhem Land.

Mountford's deflection of Simpson's scepticism is revealing. In Western cartographic terms, Arnhem Land was for the most part mapped and 'known'. Topographical charts and large aerial photographs were made available to the researchers long before they began their journey (see McCarthy and Daly, this volume). Relieved of the challenges of terrestrial exploration, Mountford's

---

19 Simpson, C. 1948, *Expedition to Arnhem Land*, ABC documentary, first broadcast 30 November 1948, Australian Broadcasting Commission, Sydney.
20 For discussion of the origins and history of the didjeridu, see Moyle, A. M. 1981, 'The Australian didjeridu: a late musical tradition', *World Archaeology*, vol. 12, no. 3; and Neuenfeldt, K. 1997, *The Didjeridu: From Arnhem Land to the Internet*, John Libbey and Perfect Beat Publications, Sydney.

interest in penetrating the unknown was readily channelled to the frontier of knowledge. The 'natural history and the Aborigines'—a most telling conflation—were presented as terra incognita.

The decision to combine anthropological and environmental study was a significant departure from the academic anthropology of mid-twentieth century Australia, and it is key to the uniqueness of the Arnhem Land Expedition. As Jon Altman explains in his chapter on the work of nutritionist Margaret McArthur, the Expedition's study of food gathering in relation to environmental and seasonal influences would mark its most pronounced contribution to social anthropology. An indication of why the Expedition's ethnological inquiries were steered in the direction of environmental study is revealed in Mountford's US diary for 6 February 1945, where he describes a lunch at the Cosmos Club in Washington, DC, attended by personnel from the Smithsonian's Bureau of American Ethnology. Also present was the Harvard anthropologist and racial theorist Carleton S. Coon, who in 1954 would go to Australia and participate for a time in Mountford's NGS-sponsored research on Melville Island. Coon arrived early at the club and spoke to Mountford about problems he discerned in Australian anthropology. He criticised the work of both Elkin and W. Lloyd Warner, a prominent Chicago anthropologist who had made his name with work in Arnhem Land in the late 1920s. According to Mountford's record of the conversation, Coon believed that

> how a people should be studied is to examine them in relation to their environment, the foods they eat, their method of gathering it, obtaining the necessities of life, the design of their laws to prevent disturbances and when they do occur, how they are righted.
>
> He condemned what he called the Elkin–Warner complex, which based everything on the social organisation. That, Coon claimed was secondary. The relationship of the man to his surroundings, physical and spiritual was all important.
>
> That coincides with my idea, although I could not put it as well as he did. We are inclined not to see the wood for the trees. We've always worked from the outside in, not the inside out, an outlook which I think my study of the legends has given me.[21]

The conversation at the Cosmos Club continued with the arrival of other lunch guests, among them William N. Fenton, the distinguished Iroquois specialist—'a young chap who has read a deal of Australian ethnology, but then considers he knows little about it'—who was then working for the Bureau of American Ethnology. While the prospect of NGS funding for an Australian expedition had

---

21   C. P. Mountford, 1944–45, A Journey to America 1944–5, vol. 2, pp. 88–91, PRG 1218/16/2, SLSA.

already been raised, and was discussed during the luncheon, the possibility of direct Smithsonian funding, probably for a project in Central Australia, was also on the table. This idea went no further when planning for the Arnhem Land Expedition took off. As always, Mountford was attuned to the academic machinations within his own country. 'Politically, it's all very complex because the moment they [the Smithsonian Institution] ask, the Commonwealth Government will go to Elkin, and that will scotch my chance.'[22] Mountford's account of the luncheon is intriguing for what it reveals about the fault lines extant in American anthropology, and how they intersected with those in Australia. Coon's criticism of Elkin was music to the ears of Mountford, and the suggestion that environmental study would mark a progressive departure from Elkin's brand of social anthropology was subtly incorporated into his application for NGS funding. The topographical diversity of Arnhem Land was emphasised and Warner was mentioned only as having 'dealt largely with social organization' and 'ceremonial observances'.[23]

The Bureau of American Ethnology—a division of the Smithsonian Institution that lasted (under various names) from 1879 until 1965—was famous for its anthropological studies of Native American culture, which were published in annual reports and regular bulletins. Despite an archaeological focus in its early decades, it had come to put 'greater emphasis on linguistics and ethnography' by the early twentieth century.[24] The Smithsonian also had a quite separate Department of Anthropology within the US National Museum (now the National Museum of Natural History), and, almost inevitably, there was rivalry between the two. Mountford's personal contact with Fenton and Henry B. Collins, another bureau employee, made it likely that one of them would have gone to Arnhem Land once the NGS funding was approved and the Smithsonian committed itself to the Expedition. Fenton related in his 2007 memoir that he 'had been slated' to go to Arnhem Land, but that Wetmore decided to 'replace me with Frank Setzler [of the US National Museum], whom Wetmore had elevated to head curator, thereby creating an uproar'.[25] The appointment of Setzler to the Expedition was highly significant. Fenton was a cultural anthropologist with a distinguished record of collaborative involvement in Native American communities. That he might have brought this experience to Australia is a tantalising thought. Setzler was an altogether different figure. Although trained in anthropology, he was by disposition an archaeologist.[26] Many of his publications concerned the

---

22 Ibid., p. 91.
23 Application to Chairman of the Research Committee, National Geographic Society, 5 March 1945, Correspondence 1945–49, vol. 1 1945–47, PRG 1218/17/4, American–Australian Scientific Expedition to Arnhem Land 1948 Records, SLSA, p. 4.
24 Woodbury, B. and Woodbury, N. F. S. 1999, 'The rise and fall of the Bureau of American Ethnology', *Journal of the Southwest*, vol. 41, no. 3, p. 286.
25 Fenton, W. N. 2007, *Iroquois Journey: An anthropologist remembers*, University of Nebraska Press, Lincoln, p. 135.
26 Davis, M. 2007, *Writing Heritage: The depiction of Indigenous heritage in European–Australian writings*, Australian Scholarly Publishing, Kew, Vic. See also Clarke and Frederick, this volume.

Hopewell mounds of the north-eastern and mid-western United States. With no real interest in ethnography, his reputation as a fieldworker was founded on his many excavations of Native American sites. These included a number of burial sites—experience that he would put to use in Arnhem Land.[27]

Setzler's leanings towards archaeology and the collecting of material culture dovetailed with Mountford's own preoccupation with bark paintings, to the extent that competition for collections drove a wedge between them. While Mountford argued in his grant application for a synthesis of ethnological and ecological study, he never abandoned his basic commitment to the collection of objects, inculcated during his long association with the South Australian Museum, as is apparent in his essay 'The Story of the Expedition', which opens the first volume of the records:

> The results of the expedition could hardly have been richer, both from the standpoint of human companionship and scientific results…The gross results of the collections, too, were impressive: 13,500 plant specimens, 30,000 fish, 850 birds, 460 animals, several thousand aboriginal implements and weapons, together with photographs and drawings of a large number of cave paintings…There was also a collection of several hundred aboriginal bark paintings and two hundred string figures. In addition to the physical collections of natural history and ethnological specimens, each scientist had written extensive field notes as a basis for his scientific papers. There were also many hundreds of monochrome and coloured photographs as well as several miles of colour film on aboriginal life and natural history.[28]

Mountford championed their success not in terms of new theories or ideas, but in numbers of specimens. As a contribution to science, the Expedition was measurable by the ton or the yard. As Robyn McKenzie observes in her chapter on string-figure collecting, the preoccupation with metrics was 'a currency' shared by nearly all team members: it was 'the measure of their work both for themselves and others'. This stockpiling of objects to be warehoused in museums for future study connects the 1948 Expedition with the well-established assumption that the collecting and categorising of objects inevitably results in the advancement of knowledge. This confidence in the equation that taxonomic achievement equals scientific advancement makes the 1948 project a latter-day example of a tradition that became entrenched with key explorations of the Enlightenment period, of which Cook's voyages are paradigmatic. In mounting and laboriously promoting his high-profile venture, Mountford was consciously

---

27   Information drawn from Frank M. Setzler Biographical File, RU 7098, Smithsonian Institution Archives, Washington, DC.
28   Mountford, *Records of the American–Australian Scientific Expedition to Arnhem Land*, vol. 1, p. xxx.

connecting himself with this heroic history. The hubris that is almost endemic to the expeditionary model is evident in Mountford's more hyperbolic rhetoric, which memories of those who conspired against him would sometimes unleash. In a 1966 interview, he recalled having 'a lot of trouble getting the expedition through, because here was I with the status of little more than a telephone mechanic, taking out the biggest scientific expedition in history, and what the academic world tried to do to me was nobody's business!'.[29]

Figure 1.4 Cinema-photographer Peter Bassett-Smith demonstrating the Expedition radio to an unidentified boy, 1948

Photograph by Howell Walker. By permission of National Geographic Stock.

---

29 Mountford in interview with Hazel de Berg, 28 October 1966, Hazel de Berg Collection, Oral DeB 189, NLAOHC.

As I note in my chapter on Gerald Blitner, who was a guide and translator to the Expedition on Groote Eylandt, Mountford and his team produced a plethora of photographs and other images 'where Aboriginal performers have their voices recorded or watch with fascination as the visiting scientists go about their work, busy at the technological forefront'. The researchers themselves are on display in these images; science must not only be done, but seen to be done by as large an audience as possible. All of this is a reminder (if any is needed) that the *expedition* is a uniquely Western mode of moving through space and acquiring knowledge. Indeed, given its centrality to empire building in the exploratory phases, the notion of the expedition is central to the very construction of the idea of 'the West' and the claimed advancement of Western over other societies. An expedition is by definition much more than a journey. To qualify as such, an expeditionary party must leave more than footprints. Typically, it will dislocate living or non-living objects from the environment it traverses, transforming them into specimens; invariably, it will produce maps, pictures or written documents. In a highly formalised way, the expedition fuses travel and textual production.

Given that the traversing of 'unknown' territory nearly always involves contact with peoples of different cultures, there is a highly performative aspect to an expedition. This makes it the subject of observation, as much as it is a vehicle from which to observe. That is part of the reason why hierarchical display is pivotal to the expedition as an expression of power. At the peak is a leader whose name is often immortalised through attachment to the expedition. Below him (my gender specificity is intentional) is a deputy and then the middle ranks, and at the bottom the typically anonymous—and very often indigenous—guides and carriers, on whom it all depends. Consciously or unconsciously, the expedition cultivates a microcosm of the society it represents, projecting it into foreign territory. An expedition is a type of activity, but it is also a *genre*; it is a distinctive and self-perpetuating mode of moving, acting, organising and writing. It is not surprising that the ethnographers in the 1948 team took with them copies of Warner's *A Black Civilization*—the most significant contribution to Arnhem Land anthropology then published—and other texts about the region they were visiting (see Hamby and Thomas, this volume). Processing the current journey through the lenses of earlier travellers-cum-authors is crucial to the ongoing life of the genre.

Of course, the expedition-as-microcosm is always a selective depiction of the society that produced it. That is part of its fascination. The competing demands of sponsors and host institutions, and conflicting desires and expectations within the expeditionary party, create estrangements and entanglements that expedition members must deal with in the course of the journey—and often, as is the case here, for years after it is over. That is why an account of the Arnhem

Land Expedition involves so much more than those months in the field. We must seriously engage with the forces that shaped it. In so doing, we obtain a rich perspective on the historical context of this extraordinary event. From various points of view, these influences are scrutinised in the chapters ahead. Kim Beazley, whose father served in Chifley's government and who himself is a veteran of Labor politics, connects the Arnhem Land Expedition with the vision of postwar nation building held by Ben Chifley's government, for whom scientific advancement and the fostering of a home-grown research culture were crucial. Related developments include the establishment of the research-focused Australian National University in 1947. Beazley describes how the pressures of the Cold War, the looming possibility of an alliance with the United States, the rethinking of the relationship with Britain, and the tussles between the pro-American Calwell and the internationally minded Minister for External Affairs, H. V. Evatt, left their imprint on the Arnhem Land Expedition.

Born of strategic considerations, the Expedition made its own transit through a range of political contexts. If its genesis was in the lofty realm of international relations, its destination was the parochial world of the Northern Territory, where Arnhem Land is located. At the time of the Expedition, the Territory had a very new Legislative Council, partly appointed and partly elected. It met for the first time in February 1948. In the small town of Darwin, where the researchers congregated in March and waited for weather sufficiently calm to allow them to fly to Groote Eylandt, the Administrator, A. R. Driver, wielded considerable authority. The administration's file on the Expedition has recently come to light, and it reveals a bureaucracy indignant at having to deal with this oversized inconvenience, thrust upon them by distant masters.[30] Out in the field, Mountford and his company confronted another sphere of white authority: the people who ran the official Aboriginal settlements. Mountford had championed Arnhem Land as a suitable locale for research because it was a 'Stone-Age' world that the twentieth century had bypassed.[31] Yet two of their three bases were Christian missions (Yirrkala and Oenpelli), while the other, Umbakumba on Groote Eylandt, was a less orthodox set-up: a 'native settlement' privately established and operated by the expatriate Englishman Frederick Gray (see Thomas, this volume). Gray was an honorary Aboriginal Protector and his settlement had the reluctant blessing of Native Affairs, the Commonwealth bureaucracy responsible for Aboriginal welfare in the Northern Territory. At each of these locations, Mountford was required to deal with the quixotic array of individuals in positions of authority. It was a latter-day frontier situation, where Balanda—or in the case of Yirrkala, Fijian—missionaries dictated the

---

30 File titled 'Scientific Expedition to Arnhem Land & NT—C. P. Mountford', Series F1, Item 1945/151, NAA, Darwin.
31 Thomas, M. 2010, 'A short history of the 1948 Arnhem Land Expedition', *Aboriginal History*, vol. 34, p. 148.

daily routine of residents, wielding in many instances an extraordinary level of power. The researchers had to pick their way around these obstacles and at the same time negotiate the most complex transaction of them all: the cross-cultural one. To have any chance of fulfilling its stated objectives, the Expedition needed to establish collaborative partnerships with the traditional owners of the country they were visiting.

So we find in the Expedition an event thickly inscribed with the political complexities of its epoch. It occurred at a seminal moment post World War II and was directly influenced by the shifting geopolitics of the period. In its organisational structure, it carried the residue of earlier imperial ambitions, yet it embodied the contemporary moment by embracing new media and by anticipating shifts in the natural sciences, particularly the more holistic outlook of ecological thinking. As Lynne McCarthy emphasises in her chapter on botany, exploring the relationship between people and their environment is axiomatic to an ecological approach. The Expedition was at odds with mainstream values in treating the Aboriginal cultures of northern Australia as valid knowledge systems, worthy of greater understanding.

For these reasons, the Arnhem Land Expedition can be thought of as a time capsule. The metaphor is particularly appropriate given its basic concern with the amassing of objects. At the kernel of our time capsule is that vast array of collections—ranging from bottled fish to works of art—headily described by Mountford in his summation of their accomplishment. Admittedly, the contents of the capsule are anything but concentrated. The location of the collections reflects the plethora of interests that had a stake in the venture and therefore a claim to its material rewards—an often disputed process, as Sally K. May has shown.[32] Substantial holdings of natural-history specimens and ethnographic objects are held in the National Museum of Natural History at the Smithsonian Institution. Insects, bark paintings, string figures and other examples of Aboriginal material culture are held in the Australian Museum, Sydney. The South Australian Museum and the National Museum of Australia in Canberra have ethnographic holdings. The art galleries of all six Australian states possess ochre paintings on bark and paper, while botanical collections are held by some of the world's leading herbaria. When we add to these varied riches the films, photographs and sound recordings, and the vast written record kept by Expedition members and others, many of whom were fastidious note takers, letter writers and diarists, the full significance of the Expedition-as-time-capsule becomes apparent—as does the daunting task of trying to decode it.

---

32   May, S. K. 2010, *Collecting Cultures: Myth, Politics, and Collaboration in the 1948 Arnhem Land Expedition*, Altamira Press, Lanham, Md.

The size of the collections—and their dispersal across two continents—explains why the Arnhem Land Expedition has tended to defy interpretation as a whole. Sally May's book *Collecting Cultures* (2010), launched during the Barks, Birds & Billabongs symposium, marks the first attempt to synthesise data from the US and Australian collections. Overall, the amount of scholarship on the Expedition has been incommensurate with the scale and significance of the event. While this book—to which more than 20 writers have contributed—is a substantial unpacking of the capsule, all of us would acknowledge that the work of interpretation has only begun. Just as a time capsule betrays the mindset of those who packed it, the readings of the Expedition that make up the following pages reveal the predispositions of the unpackers. Offered here is a dialogue, with continuities between past and present forming one strand of the discussion. Disjunctions are another. The latter become particularly prominent in the later chapters where the effects of the Expedition upon Arnhem Land cultures, past and present, are considered. When Mountford argued for the benefits of the Expedition, its impact (positive or negative) upon the people who would provide the intellectual capital was not considered for a moment. Many friendships developed between researchers and members of host communities, but their hopes, feelings and aspirations were, in the broader scheme of things, largely ignored. Murray Garde and Ian McIntosh take up this issue in their discussions of secret-sacred ceremony and objects, which the Expedition made public in films, exhibitions and still photographs. At best, the public use of this footage was not negotiated with traditional owners. Gerald Blitner claimed more controversially that senior men sanctioned filming of the secret ceremony on Groote because Mountford promised that it would be used for research purposes only (see Thomas, this volume). Notably, Mountford never challenged the most controversial activity that occurred under his leadership: the removal by Frank Setzler of human remains from mortuary caves and burial sites. The collection of skeletal material was not advertised in Mountford's inventory of trophies—a revealing omission. Nearly all the bones were exported to the United States, where they were accessioned into the collection of the Smithsonian's US National Museum. Bone collecting was never mooted in the build-up to the Expedition, and, in contrast with the collecting of native fauna, for which permits were required, no arm of government approved the harvesting of graves. These remnants of human beings are—or were—a crucial element of the Expedition-as-time-capsule. The issue has caused sadness, anger and bewilderment in Arnhem Land, and deep frustration among certain personnel at the Smithsonian, owing to resistance to a decision to repatriate the remains after extensive lobbying by Australian officials. They pointed out that early in the planning of the Expedition, the Smithsonian Institution and the Department of Information came to an agreement that two-thirds of all specimens collected should remain in Australia. The Smithsonian eventually accepted this, and, in 2008, the institution returned this proportion of its holdings of Arnhem

Land human remains to a delegation of traditional owners. Requests that the remaining third should also be returned were resisted by the Department of Anthropology. Lobbying by the Australian Government continued, and, in July 2010, in the wake of the Barks, Birds & Billabongs symposium and an embarrassing media report on the Smithsonian's intransigence over this issue, the rest of the human remains were released to three traditional owners from Arnhem Land. The handover was formalised at a moving ceremony held in the Cultural Resources Center of the Smithsonian Institution's National Museum of the American Indian.[33]

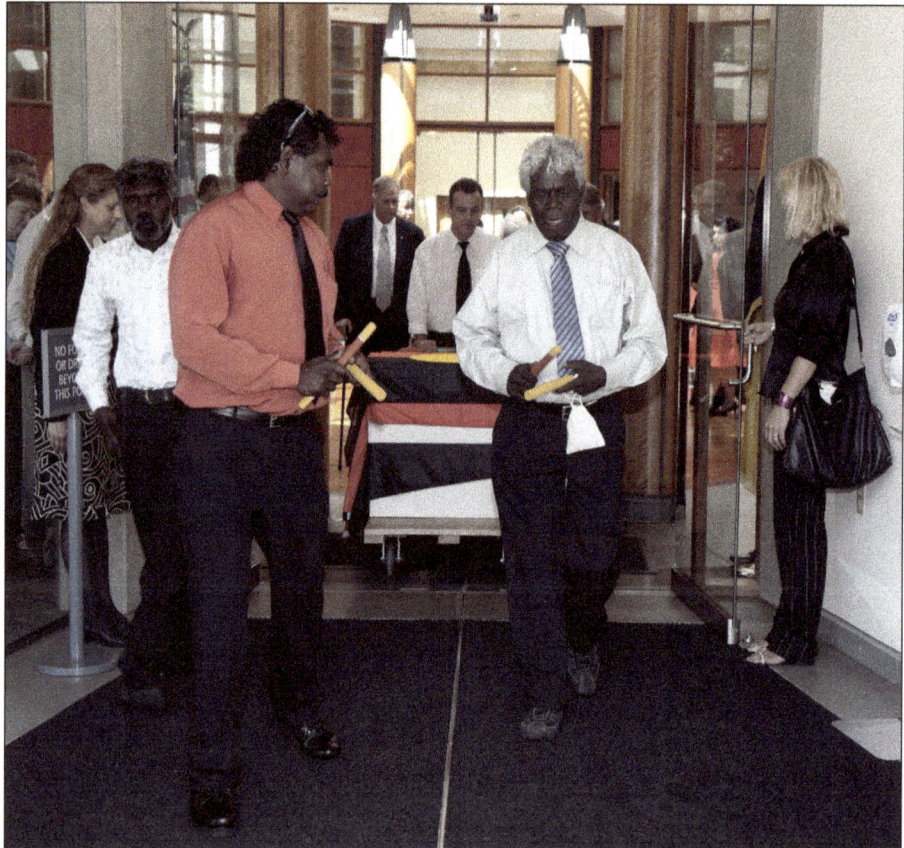

Figure 1.5 Victor Gumurdul of Gunbalanya (left), Thomas Amagula of Groote Eylandt and Joe Gumbula of Galiwinku (right) escorting the Arnhem Land human remains as they leave the Smithsonian Institution, 2010

Photograph by Adis Hondo

---

33   This account is based on personal discussions with officials involved in the case. A report by the ABC journalist Danielle Parry is likely to have caused particular embarrassment to the Smithsonian Institution. See <http://www.youtube.com/watch?v=oB-Oqe9Fxes> (viewed 20 December 2010).

*

Just as the 1948 Expedition had many precedents, this study of it contributes to an enormous literature. Explorations and expeditions have long been fodder for historians. In national-history writing, the narratives concerning them were often conspicuous for their triumphalism. These days, we can expect a more critical and reflective analysis. Since the 1990s, scientific and anthropological fieldwork have been put under the microscope in a multitude of ways. Among the influential edited collections that appeared in that decade were *Darwin's Laboratory* (1994), a study focused on fieldwork in the Pacific and its impact on science, edited by Roy MacLeod and Philip F. Rehbock.[34] In the United States, Edward C. Carter's *Surveying the Record: North American Scientific Exploration to 1930* (1999), based on a conference at the American Philosophical Society, provided a comparative approach to science in the field.[35] The centenary of the Cambridge Expedition to the Torres Strait inspired a 1998 volume edited by Anita Herle and Sandra Rouse, while the 1894 Horn Scientific Expedition to Central Australia was the subject of a substantial collection of essays co-edited by D. J. Mulvaney, the most influential historian of early Australian anthropology.[36] These accounts are relevant here because the multidisciplinary Cambridge and Horn expeditions were important precedents for Mountford's 1948 initiative. Studies of individual expeditions have provided one way of investigating scientific study and collecting in cross-cultural contexts. Major studies of this nature are occurring within the Smithsonian Institution, as is evident, for example, in Paul Michael Taylor's web-based publication *By Aeroplane to Pygmyland* on the 1926 Dutch and American Expedition to New Guinea.[37]

Other investigations have focused on individuals or particular partnerships. Mulvaney's work on Baldwin Spencer, including the major biography and, more recently, collections of Spencer's correspondence from Francis Gillen and other outback collaborators, is a foundational contribution to the history of anthropology.[38] Queensland ethnographer Walter Edmund Roth and his

---

34   MacLeod, R. and Rehbock, P. F. (eds) 1994, *Darwin's Laboratory: Evolutionary theory and natural history in the Pacific*, University of Hawai'i Press, Honolulu.
35   Carter II, E. C., (ed.) 1999, *Surveying the Record: North American scientific exploration to 1930*, Memoirs of the American Philosophical Society, vol. 231, Philadelphia.
36   Herle, A. and Rouse, S. (eds) 1999, *Cambridge and the Torres Strait: Centenary essays on the 1898 anthropological expedition*, Cambridge University Press, UK; and Mulvaney, D. J. and Morton, S. R. (eds) 1996, *Exploring Central Australia: Society, the environment and the 1894 Horn expedition*, Surrey Beatty & Sons, Chipping Norton, NSW.
37   Taylor, P. M. 2006, *By Aeroplane to Pygmyland*, viewed 10 November 2010, <http://www.sil.si.edu/expeditions/1926/index.cfm>
38   Mulvaney, D. J. and Calaby, J. H. 1985, *'So Much That is New': Baldwin Spencer, 1860–1929. A biography*, Melbourne University Press, Carlton, Vic.; Mulvaney, J., Morphy, H. and Petch, A. (eds) 2001, *My Dear Spencer: The letters of F. J. Gillen to Baldwin Spencer*, Hyland House, Melbourne; Mulvaney, J., Morphy, H. and Petch, A. (eds) 2000, *From the Frontier: Outback letters to Baldwin Spencer*, Allen & Unwin, St Leonards, NSW.

remarkable family were the subjects of a conference and book, while the ethnolinguist and material culture collector T. G. H. Strehlow is the subject of a major biography by Barry Hill.[39] An important comparative study of individual collectors, developed from a conference at the Museum of Victoria, was published as *The Makers and Making of Indigenous Australian Museum Collections* (2008).[40] My own work on early Australian anthropologist R. H. Mathews developed concurrently with these conferences and publications.[41]

Among the scholars of Arnhem Land, Ronald and Catherine Berndt, who were contemporaries—and rivals—of Mountford, and who likewise hailed from Adelaide, are historically the most influential. But it is the anthropologist Donald Thomson who has to date received the most sustained attention, most recently for the inspiration of his work upon the film *Ten Canoes* (2006).[42] Thomson, who was in Arnhem Land before and after the 1948 Expedition, assembled outstanding material culture collections and was an exquisite photographer. The contemporary anthropologist Nicolas Peterson has played a particular role in investigating Thomson's legacy and encouraging debate about his work.[43] Thomson—another individual whose career was sabotaged by Elkin—has come into his own in recent years because the visual ethnographic record he excelled in making has had particular impact on Arnhem Land cultures today. Since the 1990s, it has become increasingly standard in Aboriginal studies to take historical source material, including film and photographs, back to the places of origin for interpretation. In the 1990s, the visual anthropologist Roslyn Poignant repatriated to the Arnhem Land community of Maningrida photographs taken by her late husband, Axel Poignant, in the early 1950s. Her account of this process is a compelling study of how the medium of photography has been incorporated into Aboriginal knowledge systems, and it has provided inspiration to many subsequent researchers.[44]

---

39 Hill, B. 2002, *Broken Song: T. G. H. Strehlow and Aboriginal possession*, Knopf, Milsons Point, NSW; McDougall, R. and Davison, I. (eds) 2008, *The Roth Family, Anthropology, and Colonial Administration*, Left Coast Press, Walnut Creek, Calif.
40 Peterson, N., Allen, L. and Hamby, L. (eds) 2008, *The Makers and Making of Indigenous Australian Museum Collections*, Melbourne University Publishing, Carlton, Vic.
41 Thomas, M. (ed.) 2007, *Culture in Translation: The anthropological legacy of R. H. Mathews*, ANU E Press and Aboriginal History Incorporated, Canberra; Thomas, M. 2011, *The Many Worlds of R. H. Mathews: In search of an Australian anthropologist*, Allen & Unwin, St Leonards, NSW.
42 See Davis, T. 2007, 'Remembering our ancestors: cross-cultural collaboration and the mediation of Aboriginal culture and history in *Ten Canoes* (Rolf de Heer, 2006)', *Studies in Australasian Cinema*, vol. 1, no. 1; Thomas, M. 2010, 'The crackle of the wire: media, digitization and the voicing of Aboriginal languages', in N. Neumark, R. Gibson and T. Van Leeuwen (eds), *Voice: Vocal aesthetics in digital arts and media*, MIT Press, Cambridge, Mass.
43 Thomson, D. F. 1983, *Donald Thomson in Arnhem Land*, (Compiled and introduced by N. Peterson), Currey O'Neil, South Yarra, Vic.; Rigsby, B. and Peterson, N. (eds) 2005, *Donald Thomson: The man and scholar*, The Academy of the Social Sciences in Australia, Canberra.
44 Poignant, R. with Poignant, A. 1996, *Encounter at Nagalarramba*, National Library of Australia, Canberra.

The recognition that expeditions and other types of cross-cultural research can be of service to Indigenous communities is the most critical distinction between the approach taken in this book and much of the earlier literature on fieldwork and exploration (including great swathes of post-colonial critique, where the views of colonised people are considered only from a theoretical point of view). That distinction is fully evident in the chapter by ethnomusicologists Allan Marett and Linda Barwick, who, during long careers of recording and studying Aboriginal music in northern Australia, have helped get computers into communities and loaded them with archival song recordings and other historical material. They movingly describe how Colin Simpson's radio feature about a funeral rite at Delissaville (now Belyuen) was subtly alluded to in the choice of movements by dancer David Rankin during a recent funeral at which Barwick was present and in which Marett participated by singing. Significantly, this allusion did not involve a straightforward emulation of the historical material. Rather, the documentation provided 'a locus for the generation of new stories and narratives'. Marett and Barwick suggest that the internalisation of Simpson's recordings by Rankin and others in the community 'played a part in generating the shared understandings' that allowed them, as outsiders, to be drawn more deeply into the ceremony. This is part of a larger cultural shift within Arnhem Land today. Barwick has written elsewhere about the effect of digitisation on ethnographic archives, transforming them from institutions that serve researchers into ones that service the original knowledge holders or their descendants.[45] This has resulted in significant initiatives within communities, aimed at the education of young people among other agendas. Yirrkala, for example, has the Mulka Centre, a community database for the storage and accessing of digitised photography, recorded sound and moving image.[46] It is an outstanding example of how the ethnographic record can serve the interests of relevant knowledge holders. In this fast-moving environment, films and photographs—sometimes dismissed as the ephemera of the anthropological enterprise—acquire a wholly different value. It is in this context that the vast, if disputed, legacy of Charles Mountford—including the Arnhem Land Expedition—has come to attention.

Not only did the Expedition study what for its members were exotic cultures, it created a micro-culture of its own. Despite some notorious internal tensions, especially between Mountford and Frederick McCarthy, lifelong friendships developed. Membership was a badge of distinction for all involved. A commonality of experience bound the veterans of the Expedition. Many stayed in touch with one another and reunions were organised for the major anniversaries.

---

45 Barwick, L. 2004, 'Turning it all upside down…: imagining a distributed digital audiovisual archive', *Literary and Linguistic Computing*, vol. 19, no. 3. See also Thomas, M. 2007, 'Taking them back: archival media in Arnhem Land today', *Cultural Studies Review*, vol. 13, no. 2.
46 See <http://www.yirrkala.com/mulka/index.html> (viewed 1 December 2010).

Both Setzler and ichthyologist Robert Miller made the long journey across the Pacific to attend such events in Australia. Their numbers inevitably diminished as the decades passed. The surviving members ate, drank, reminisced, and sang some of the comic songs that they had first performed around the campfire (for an example, see May, this volume). Most of the planning and preparation for the symposium that inspired this book occurred in 2008—the sixtieth anniversary. The symposium itself was in late 2009. We were consciously building on the earlier tradition of anniversary celebrations, and the event was attended by Expedition botanist, Raymond Specht, and relatives of many other participants. Sadly, ill health prevented Peter Bassett-Smith, the other surviving Expedition member, from attending. Some observers from afar assumed that celebration was the sole motive in organising the event. That is simplistic—although all the organisers, of whom I was one, felt there *were* things to celebrate in the Expedition's legacy, particularly its contribution to greater cross-cultural understandings. Many Arnhem Land people of my acquaintance have similar views. The original appeal for scholarly papers noted that, with the passage of six decades, it would be timely 'for celebration, re-evaluation, and renewed collaboration between the individuals, institutions, and countries touched by this formative research venture'. As the contents of this book reveal, we received a multitude of responses from around the world—more than could possibly be included in the program. It is a casual reader indeed who would claim that this study of the Expedition is a panegyric. In working with the contributors, and seeing the spoken papers develop into the chapters of this book, I have come to think that the tripartite objectives of celebrating, evaluating and collaborating have been thoroughly pursued, and that they create an interesting internal tension within the volume.

That we achieved this is due to the truly seismic distinction between our public event that was Barks, Birds & Billabongs in 2009 and the private anniversaries of previous years. Here I refer to the substantial representation from the main Aboriginal communities visited by the Expedition. Any thought that this would be a standard academic conference was utterly dispelled by this reality, and I hope that its effects are registered in the book. It should be noted that the contributions of Arnhem Land delegates did not include the giving of papers in English. In that respect, this book—a representation of the more academic component—is a partial record. The people from Arnhem Land, many of whom were visiting Canberra for the first time, have as their first language Bininj Kunwok, Iwaidja, Anindilyakwa or one of the clan-based languages known collectively as Yolngu Matha. Paper writing is *not* their cultural form. Their participation took the form of community panels, where issues such as the theft of human remains were movingly addressed. Film and photography were interpreted, and magnificent performances were given, including the epic *Currents from a Distant Shore: Birrkili Yolngu songs of Makassan contact in*

Northeast Arnhem Land, led by Djangirrawuy Garawirrtja of Milingimbi and produced by musicologist Aaron Corn. Recordings and documentation of much of the event are permanently available on the National Museum of Australia's web site.[47] Arnhem Landers made behind-the-scenes visits to the National Museum's off-site storage and other collections, while many pursued business among themselves. As those of us who work in Arnhem Land are aware, the symposium itself has left an enduring imprint on many who participated, as Margo Neale explains in her Epilogue.

When arranging the volume, and identifying common themes in the disparate chapters, it became apparent that they fall into three (admittedly overlapping) categories, each of which has become a section of the book. The first, 'Engagements with Aboriginal Cultures', positions the Expedition narrative in the context of Western structures, institutions and fields of knowledge. In this, it makes a compelling argument about the interest of Westerners in Australia's Aboriginal cultures, and how the engagements resulting from that interest affected modernity in the postwar era. There are eight chapters, bracketed between Philip Jones's account of Mountford and Sally May's description of the Expedition's origins, bases and activities. Jones provides a considered evaluation of the Expedition from Mountford's point of view. In sketching the background, he gives an illuminating account of Mountford's participation in the Board of Anthropological Research expeditions that went north from Adelaide in the 1930s. They were Mountford's introduction to the expedition experience and they opened a door to the living cultures of Aboriginal art that preoccupied him for the remainder of his life. Mark Collins Jenkins, formerly a historian for the NGS, gives a portrait of the Expedition's chief photographer, and in the process turns the lens upon a golden age at *National Geographic*. Kim Beazley also gives an inside perspective, opening up the political scene of Chifley, Calwell, Evatt and Menzies, and exploring the remarkable and highly confessional correspondence between Calwell and Setzler, which lasted long into the Cold War. Tony MacGregor's evaluation of Simpson as a broadcaster and writer is an important contribution to the study of radio and to the writing of Simpson, whose world view was significantly altered by his stay in Arnhem Land. The Expedition's effect on the disciplines of anthropology, archaeology and botany are considered in separate chapters. Jon Altman pursues the legacy of nutritionist Margaret McArthur, whose paper 'The Food Quest and the Time Factor', published in Volume 2 of the records, proved to be the Expedition's most enduring impact on anthropological theory when it was taken up by Marshall Sahlins to support his notion of the 'original affluent society'. Altman—like

---

47 <http://www.nma.gov.au/research/centre_for_historical_research/conferences_and_seminars/barks_birds_billabongs/> (viewed 20 December 2010).

Clarke and Frederick in their study of McCarthy as archaeologist—explains how the Expedition's legacy informed his own approach to fieldwork over a sustained period.

The second section—on collectors and collections—is integral to any study of the Expedition, for reasons already explained. The contributors offer a catholic range of responses to the subject. Archival collections are dealt with through the example of Walker's films and Mountford's papers. Louise Hamby, in her work on baskets and other fibre objects, and Robyn McKenzie, in her study of string figures, provide a significant corrective to the preoccupation with bark paintings that dominates popular perceptions of the Expedition. Both writers are informed by their own fieldwork experiences, where Expedition collections provide a stimulus for discussion at Milingimbi and Yirrkala respectively. Raymond Specht explains his approach to botanical collecting in an oral history, while the fish collections of Robert Rush Miller are considered in an elegant portrait by Gifford Hubbs Miller and Robert Charles Cashner (the son and son-in-law of the Expedition ichthyologist).

Five chapters make up 'Aboriginal Engagements with the Expedition'—the third and final section of the book. Here, the focus is on the Expedition's effect on the communities it visited. Some of these were rapid, as we see in Ian McIntosh's contribution, 'Missing the Revolution!', which addresses an astonishing event on Elcho Island, made famous to the world of anthropology through Ronald Berndt's classic monograph *An Adjustment Movement in Arnhem Land* (1951). For the secret-sacred culture of the Yolngu, the 'adjustment movement' signalled a revolutionary transformation by which formerly esoteric ceremonial objects, known exclusively to male initiates, were made public as an offering to non-Aboriginal Australia in the expectation that the nation would reciprocate by sharing money, educational resources and material goods. Berndt claimed that it was a screening of an Arnhem Land Expedition film production showing secret ceremony—and thus indicating to Yolngu that their most cherished secrets had already been disclosed—that was the impetus for this development. McIntosh, who in the 1980s came under the mentorship of David Burrumarra—a protagonist in the adjustment movement—gives a rereading of the Expedition's ethnographic work in North-East Arnhem Land, based on what Burrumarra told him about the Bayini: an ancestral group of white people, said to predate the Macassans. Bayini narratives, according to McIntosh, provided a prism through which 'visitors to Arnhem Land since the beginning of time—including random and unplanned Indonesian visitors, explorers, trepanging Macassans, Japanese pearlers and Europeans (of all descriptions)—were explainable'. The interface between the esoteric world of Aboriginal religion and the putatively 'open' culture of scientific investigation is also at issue in Murray Garde's study of the Expedition's documentation of the Wubarr, a male initiation rite indigenous to Western Arnhem Land. Garde also writes of the offence caused by screenings of Expedition films, as happened at Gunbalanya before a mixed audience without prior consultation. But he also paints a more sanguine picture of the Expedition's documentation of culturally restricted material when it is repatriated in a consultative manner. He describes the joy with which the late Lofty Bardayal Nadjamerrek and other senior men received film and audio footage of this cherished ritual that has, since the 1970s, fallen into abeyance.

My own chapter on Gerald Blitner concerns his penetrating observations of the Expedition, recounted in the last year of his life during several days of oral-history interview, and traces in his life story how encounters with Fred Gray, Mountford and other outsiders helped in the development of a political style that empowered him in his later negotiations with the Balanda world. The issue of how Aboriginal people engaged creatively with their new historical conditions is taken up in a very different way by Barwick and Marett in their fine-grained analysis of Simpson's song recordings from Oenpelli and Delissaville. From the mixture of genres and styles represented in these 'musical snapshots', they show how people were coping with the new social environments of missions and pastoral stations, where many were dislocated from ancestral country. The result was not cultural breakdown—as many outsiders have assumed—but innovation and collaboration between 'people from a number of different language groups, providing a rich multilingual social fabric in which marriage laws maintain diversity by demanding that people marry outside their own clan or language group'. Connections to traditional country were preserved in song, while 'ongoing attachments to their current residence' were also fostered.

A further and truly remarkable engagement with the Expedition is described in 'The American Clever Man' by Bruce Birch, a linguist who specialises in Iwaidja, traditionally spoken on the Cobourg Peninsula north of Gunbalanya, and now the dominant language on Minjilang (Croker Island). Birch recounts and analyses a story told to him by senior figures on Minjilang concerning an American scientist who visited the area, shot mammals and birds and then reanimated them, and who stole a deceased man by the name of Marrarna, whom he took home to America and brought back to life. The story was undoubtedly inspired by the Smithsonian's mammalogist David Johnson, who was a superb marksman and taxidermist, and whose epic solo walk through the Cobourg Peninsula was celebrated as one of the great feats of the Expedition. The scientist of this story is probably a fusion of various Expedition members. The documentary evidence indicates that it was Setzler, not Johnson, who robbed burial caves. Even so, the story is evidence of the concern raised by the theft of human remains and, as Birch writes, it gives compelling insight into how 'Indigenous people… tried to make sense of the activities of an alien culture in their midst', just as it emphasises how 'observation and analysis during the course of the Expedition were inevitably reciprocal in nature, the result of the interaction of two distinct culturally reinforced world views'.

The Arnhem Land Expedition's capacity to encourage thinking and empathy across cultures is the reason it retains relevance today. Peter Bassett-Smith recalled in an interview how Mountford often interrupted him when he was filming with the warning: 'Widen your scope!' It became a signature phrase within the Expedition party, and Peter wove it into at least one of his campfire songs. Comedy aside, engaging with the time capsule that is the 1948 Expedition is indeed a scope-widening experience. In illuminating a past event, it opens a conversation about the future.

Part I
Engagements with Aboriginal Cultures

2. Inside Mountford's Tent: Paint, politics and paperwork

Philip Jones

Figure 2.1 Charles Pearcy Mountford (1890–1976) at Uluru, ca. 1960

Photograph by M. Lamshed 1972. From Lamshed, M. 2972, *Monty. The biography of Charles Mountford*

Photographs of Charles Mountford suggest few of those qualities of refinement and discerning judgment generally associated with internationally known art historians or ethnographers. Indeed, Mountford's bluff demeanour and his utter lack of pretension better match the careers he transcended—those of the farmer, the tram conductor and the telegraph technician. His own nickname, 'Monty', seemed to confirm his place outside the academy, reflecting the style of his more popular publications, such as *Brown Men and Red Sand* (1948). Indeed in later life, Mountford was characterised more than once as a bumbling, opportunistic amateur with a tin ear, hardly capable of making sense of the rich anthropological data he gathered. Yet, with all their defects, Mountford's *Nomads of the Australian Desert* (1976) and *Art, Myth and Symbolism* (1956) are works of substance and scholarship, and his extraordinary career as a discoverer and promoter of Aboriginal art is overdue for reassessment.[1]

Mountford's original manuscripts have been little studied, and contain rich insights. Among the most telling documents in terms of defining his role is a letter he received in January 1956 from a young anthropologist who would become one of the most influential specialists in Aboriginal art, laying the basis for much of its contemporary academic interpretation. Nancy Munn had arrived in Canberra during late 1955 and was soon to begin her extended, intensive fieldwork at Yuendumu. She laid out her research proposal for Mountford and wrote, a little plaintively: 'There is noone here who both understands the problem of Aboriginal art (and of art in general) and who knows the Australian field; thus I am relying upon your knowledge and interest for guidance.'[2] Significantly, Munn's letter, written early in 1956, arrived shortly before Mountford published his extensive work *Art, Myth and Symbolism*—the first of the four volumes of the *Records of the American–Australian Scientific Expedition to Arnhem Land*. Her appreciation was founded on Mountford's 1930s journal articles analysing the symbolism and mythology associated with Western Desert art.[3]

---

1   Mountford's life and career has been only partially assessed by biographers—by M. Lamshed (1972, *Monty: The biography of C. P. Mountford*, Rigby, Adelaide) and by Philip Jones (2000, 'Mountford, Charles Pearcy (1890–1976)', Australian Dictionary of Biography. *Volume 15*, Mebourne University Press, Carlton, Vic., pp. 431–3).
2   N. Munn to C. P. Mountford, 5 January 1956, Correspondence, vol. 14, PRG 1218/28/14, pp. 1–2, in Mountford-Sheard Collection, State Library of South Australia (hereafter SLSA).
3   These articles included: Mountford, C. P. 1937, 'Aboriginal crayon drawings: relating to totemic places belonging to the northern Aranda tribe of Central Australia', *Transactions of the Royal Society of South Australia*, vol. 61, pp. 81–95; Mountford, C. P. 1937, 'Aboriginal crayon drawings from the Warburton Ranges in Western Australia relating to the wanderings of two ancestral beings, the Wati Kutjara', *Records of the South Australian Museum*, vol. 6, pp. 5–28; Mountford, C. P. 1938, 'Aboriginal crayon drawings III: the legend of Wati-Jula and the Kunkarunkara women', *Transactions of the Royal Society of South Australia*, vol. 62, pp. 241–54; Mountford, C. P. 1938, 'Contrast in drawings made by an Australian Aborigine before and after initiation', *Records of the South Australian Museum*, vol. 6, pp. 111–14; Mountford, C. P. 1939, 'Aboriginal crayon drawings, IV: relating to every-day incidents of the Ngada tribe of the Warburton Ranges of Western Australia', *Transactions of the Royal Society of South Australia*, vol. 63, pp. 1–13; Mountford, C. P. 1939, 'Aboriginal crayon drawings, Warburton Ranges, Western Australia', *Oceania*, vol. 10, pp. 72–9.

Another letter has a bearing on this question. It was written by the person to whom a young and brilliant anthropology student of the 1950s, such as Munn, might have been expected to defer: Mountford's old enemy, A. P. Elkin. It was Elkin who had apparently vetoed Mountford's otherwise successful application during 1940 for a Carnegie Fellowship to pursue his study of Aboriginal art in the Western Desert.[4] In May 1945, hearing of Mountford's appointment as leader of the Arnhem Land Expedition, Elkin wrote to the Secretary of the National Geographic Society in Washington, DC, urging that an anthropologist be appointed. 'Mr Mountford', he wrote, 'who is a good photographer, especially of still subjects, and who has done valuable work in the recording and copying of native art, is not a trained social anthropologist, much to his own regret'.[5]

What was it that annoyed Elkin so much about Mountford? Was it that he was a self-taught dilettante, whose dabbling in art and populist lectures, films and publications threatened to overshadow the fragile and complex plant Elkin was nurturing in the hothouse atmosphere of the Sydney University anthropology department? Perhaps Mountford's robust approach to anthropology and art, untutored and unconstrained by theory, and founded on direct transactions with the artists themselves, exposed insecurities in the new discipline. Mountford's close alignment with the 'Adelaide school' of anthropology—scorned by Elkin for its superficial, data-oriented approach—was certainly a factor. This chapter explores some of the background to Mountford's emergence as leader of the 1948 Arnhem Land Expedition and examines this leadership under pressures that were, in part at least, fuelled by his feud with Elkin.

Mountford was encouraged by Adelaide anthropologists and ethnographers such as J. B. Cleland, T. D. Campbell and (at least until the mid-1930s) N. B. Tindale, whose collaboration on the Board for Anthropological Research resulted in an intensive team methodology—distinctly at odds with Elkin's individual model of participant observation.[6] During the 1930s, Mountford had participated in three of the annual Board for Anthropological Research expeditions to Central Australia. As a recorder of Aboriginal art and motifs, he had become familiar with the workings of a multidisciplinary expedition composed of diverse professionals, qualified in the fields of physical anthropology and natural history. During a packed fortnight, they interacted closely with a large group of Aboriginal people, person by person, obtaining sociological data and physical measurements according to the scientists' specialisations, recording songs and ceremonies and material culture processes with notebooks, 16 mm film and

---
4 This claim was made by Mountford himself, within his correspondence, and has not been verified.
5 A. P. Elkin to Secretary of NGS, 30 May 1945, Correspondence, 1945–1949, p. 12, PRG 1218/17/4, Mountford-Sheard Collection, SLSA.
6 See Jones, P. G. 1987, 'South Australian Aboriginal history: the Board for Anthropological Research and its early expeditions', *Records of the South Australian Museum*, vol. 20, pp. 71–92.

wax-cylinder recorder, collecting artefacts and, in the case of Tindale and Mountford, obtaining hundreds of crayon drawings on large sheets of brown paper, depicting mythological routes and sites.

In contrast, Elkin's fieldworkers were trained to work alone, becoming accepted by an Aboriginal group, learning the language, and applying specialised anthropological skills to analyse a social network essentially undisturbed by their presence. If this could be described as careful angling across several seasons, the South Australian approach was more like an afternoon's intensive trawling. That said, the bounty of those Board for Anthropological Research expeditions—including thousands of artefacts, photographs, genealogies, film and sound recordings—is certainly more tangible, and perhaps more useful today, both to Aboriginal descendants and to researchers, than relatively arcane data concerning kinship and social relations. The crayon drawings gathered by Tindale and Mountford not only represent the precursors of the Western Desert art movement; they have also been deployed as documents of traditional knowledge and landownership.

Figure 2.2 Unidentified man drawing on brown paper sheet during Mountford expedition to Central Australia, probably 1940

Photograph by C. P. Mountford. From M. Lamshed 1972, *Monty. The biography of Charles Mountford*, p. 137.

The crayon drawing technique had been pioneered by Daisy Bates and Herbert Basedow as a means of delineating tribal territories, and was refined by Tindale during his long career as a curator at the South Australian Museum. The idea was to make sheets of brown paper and crayons available to Aboriginal men (and to a lesser extent, women), with the suggestion that the artists depict their key waters or ritual sites. These sites and their connections to important mythological trajectories were later annotated and documented in English and relevant Aboriginal languages with advice from the artists, assisted by an interpreter. Aboriginal people participated enthusiastically and the technique resulted in a rich haul during the 1930s. In no case, it seems, did Tindale and Mountford ever encounter blank sheets. Tindale's comment during the 1934 Ooldea expedition that 'the natives seem to be tireless in their interest in their own drawings…each intent on his own subject and apparently oblivious to the efforts of others' is equally applicable to Mountford's experience.[7] Later, following the expedition's return, the drawings would be assembled and analysed in relation to territorial boundaries or mythological trajectories, and placed in context by reference to texts, songs or ceremonies recorded by expedition members. In other words, what might appear now to have been a rapid and cheap method of gathering a priceless art collection was in fact an innovative research tool, with multiple possible outcomes. For Tindale, these had much to do with his tribal boundary and mapping project, helping him to adjust or redefine the data he had gleaned in the field or from secondary sources, resulting in a series of articles and his grand synthesis of Australian data, published in 1974.[8] For Mountford, it became an intertwined investigation of mythology and art, in which his field documentation of narrative was combined with an analysis of motifs. By 1948, this research methodology was more sophisticated, integrating evidence from primary sources (the bark paintings themselves) with data from his own field observations as well as those of Elkin, Ronald and Catherine Berndt, and, most especially, W. Lloyd Warner. In 1951, Mountford wrote to Warner at the University of Chicago, praising his book *A Black Civilization* (1958) ('by far the high point of any piece of research work done on any Australian tribe'), and explaining how much he had relied on it in 'searching for details on some of the fragmentary myths that I had collected in connection with the bark paintings' acquired during the Arnhem Land Expedition.[9]

---

7 N. B. Tindale, Journal of a visit to Ooldea to study the Aborigines, November 1934, p. 185, AA338/1/13, South Australian Museum Archives.
8 Tindale, N. B. 1974, *Aboriginal Tribes of Australia: Their terrain, environmental controls, distribution, limits and proper names*, The Australian National University Press, Canberra. See bibliography for Tindale's articles on Western Desert art and crayon drawings.
9 C. P. Mountford to Lloyd Warner, 2 April 1951, Correspondence, vol. 10, pp. 120–1, PRG 1218/28, Mountford-Sheard Collection, SLSA. Mountford was referring to Warner, W. L. 1937, *A Black Civilization: A social study of an Australian tribe*, Harper and Brothers, New York.

Mountford's first expedition involving the crayon drawing technique took place in 1935 with Tindale and Cecil Hackett, among Ngadadjara people of the Warburton Range. Later that year he collected drawings from Luritja and Anangu people at and near Uluru. After almost 10 years spent locating and describing rock art for which there was no surviving Aboriginal knowledge, this form of evidence was a revelation for Mountford. It enabled him to test propositions about art, myth and symbolism to a degree unimagined by his international correspondents, such as the English art historian and critic Herbert Read or the American art historian Carl Schuster, co-founder of New York's Museum of Primitive Art and author of the 12-volume *Social Symbolism in Ancient and Tribal Art* (1966).[10]

Figure 2.3 Yattalunga rock shelter paintings, near Gawler, South Australia

Photograph by C. P. Mountford, 1920s. By permission of South Australian Museum Archives. AA228.

---

10   Schuster's mammoth work of synthesis, intended only for museums and libraries, was condensed and published in 1996 with Edmund Carpenter as co-author, as *Patterns That Connect: Social symbolism in ancient and tribal art* (Harry Abrams, New York). Mountford's extensive correspondence with Read, Schuster and other international art historians is preserved in the Mountford-Sheard Collection, SLSA, Adelaide.

Figure 2.4 Mountford's photograph of rock engravings at Panaramittee, north-eastern South Australia, ca. 1930

By permission of South Australian Museum Archives. AA228.

Mountford had previously resisted the temptation to speculate about the meaning of rock-art motifs that he had documented in his surveys of South Australia's mid-north, Flinders Ranges and north-east, but now he encountered a flood of authoritative data directly from Aboriginal artists of the Western Desert. With their guidance, he was able to link motifs not only with their immediate, symbolic meanings, but with elaborate and lengthy mythological itineraries. Like Tindale, Mountford soon became aware of the risks associated with generalised interpretations. 'By far the greatest number of designs in use', he observed in 1937, 'are so highly conventionalized as to be indecipherable without the assistance of the artist who produced them'.[11] The skills required to successfully document links between motifs and meaning and to analyse the art's formal characteristics derived from Mountford's experience as a meticulous recorder of rock art and his abilities as a clear and engaging writer. As a result, by 1948, he neither needed anthropological training nor regretted its lack.

At the same time, Mountford displayed the limitations of an ethnographer of his day. His acceptance of the imminent demise of traditional beliefs and cultural practices was widely shared during the early and mid-twentieth century; it fuelled the sense of urgency that drove both the Board for Anthropological Research expeditions and Elkin's research program. Mountford's 1945 assertions that 'the simple art of these people would be the first aspect of their culture to disappear', and that by obtaining more than 1500 documented crayon drawings from Central Australia he had 'saved the art of the Central Australian from extinction', might seem apocryphal, even arrogant, today.[12] But they were unexceptional for their time. Indeed, even by 1956, when *Art, Myth and Symbolism* was published, Mountford had no way of knowing that his own promotion of Aboriginal art would help to stimulate an unprecedented renaissance in its production, in both Arnhem Land and Central Australia. This renaissance would lead ultimately to the upending of a time-honoured paradigm that Aboriginal art was an iterative, unchanging form in which artists were restricted to traditional motifs and a three- or four-colour palette. The transformed paradigm became that of an innovative, adaptive culture, distinguished by brilliant individual artists with expanding reputations across a range of media—an outcome barely imaginable for Mountford and other 'salvage ethnographers' during the 1940s.

The collegial partnerships behind the Board for Anthropological Research expeditions of the 1930s had meant that little formal leadership was required. Each scientist knew his role and each contributed to the camp organisation. Mountford knew that the 1948 Expedition posed a much greater organisational challenge, with formidable responsibilities and an untested team of strangers, but he assumed that as independent professionals their daily research activities would not require close direction, leaving him sufficient time to pursue his own research. His 1930s experience had given him a straightforward technique for realising those objectives. Preparation for the Board for Anthropological

---

11 Mountford, 'Aboriginal crayon drawings from the Warburton Ranges in Western Australia relating to the wanderings of two ancestral beings, the Wati Kutjara', p. 21.
12 Mountford, quoted in May, S. K. 2003, 'Colonial collections of portable art and intercultural encounters in Aboriginal Australia', *Before Farming*, vol. 1, no. 8, pp. 1–17, at p. 2.

Research expeditions had involved simply laying in a stock of brown paper and crayons. For the 1948 Arnhem Land Expedition, he needed to organise the cutting of sufficient bark in the wet season, well ahead of commencement, and to be sure that there were sufficient quantities of ochre. The Australian Museum archaeologist Frederick McCarthy was also aware of this requirement, and he and Mountford collaborated to secure a supply of bark through the Darwin Native Affairs Administration office.[13] One hundred sheets of bark (of unspecified dimensions) were cut by Milingimbi staff during a visit to Roper River in February 1948, and were sent to Groote Eylandt for the Expedition's use.[14] It is likely that these sheets were further divided, and were used at Yirrkala. Mountford was supplied with a further 100 bark sheets at Oenpelli (now Gunbalanya). The small size of the Expedition barks from the three Expedition stations (barely one-fifth the size of those Donald Thomson had collected during 1941) can probably be attributed to the limited supplies of cut bark.[15] So also could Mountford's decision to provide paper to artists at Yirrkala and Oenpelli. Mountford wrote: 'As the supply of prepared sheets of bark at Yirrkala and Oenpelli became exhausted, I provided the artists with sheets of rough-surfaced dark grey and green paper.'[16]

Mountford also planned ahead in the matter of pigments. He corresponded with the Board for Anthropological Research cinematographer E. O. Stocker (who also directed a paint company in Sydney) to order a stock of red ochre, yellow ochre, graphite, kalsomine and binding agents and to seek advice on paint binders.[17]

---

13 F. D. McCarthy to C. P. Mountford, 16 January 1948, PRG 1218/17/4, Mountford-Sheard Collection, SLSA. McCarthy's observation to Mountford that '[y]ou will require some hundreds I suppose' suggests that McCarthy's interest in acquiring bark paintings emerged only after joining the expedition.

14 Native Affairs patrol officer Coate informed Mountford on 27 April 1948 that 'Mr T. H. Hanna of the Methodist Overseas Mission, Milingimbi, has advised that he has procured on your behalf 100 sheets of bark' (Coate to Mountford, 27 April 1948, PRG 1218/17/4, Mountford-Sheard Collection, SLSA). Mountford noted that these sheets were forwarded to Groote Eylandt.

15 The Thomson barks were displayed in the exhibition *Ancestral Power and the Aesthetic* at the Ian Potter Gallery, University of Melbourne, June to August 2009, curated by Dr Lindy Allen. See: <http://www.art-museum.unimelb.edu.au/art_exhibitions_detail.aspx?view=156>

16 Mountford, C. P. (ed.) 1956, *Records of the American–Australian Scientific Expedition to Arnhem Land. Volume 1: Art, myth and symbolism*, Melbourne University Press, Carlton, Vic., p. 13, fn. 47. At Yirrkala, the prepared bark supply ran out in mid-August, according to Bessie Mountford's journal entry of 31 August 1948: 'Perhaps all to the good. The paper is proving an easy medium, and the drawings grow more interesting. Besides drawings on paper can be stored so easily, right at the bottom of one's large trunk' (Bessie Mountford diary, PRG 187/1/3, Mountford-Sheard Collection, SLSA). For another perspective on this issue, see also May, S. 2010, *Collecting Cultures: Myth, politics and collaboration in the 1948 Arnhem Land Expedition*, Altamira Press, Lanham, Md, pp. 161–2.

17 See, for example: E. O. Stocker to C. P. Mountford, 14 January 1947; 2 January 1948; and Mountford's own letter to Stocker of 11 December 1947, inquiring whether it would be possible to premix Stocker's 'Wesco' powdered binder with dry colours (Correspondence, 1945–49, PRG 1218/17/4, Mountford-Sheard Collection, SLSA). Stocker indicated that the red and yellow ochres would be from mines 'north of the MacDonnell Ranges'.

None of the Expedition publications or records so far examined offers clues as to whether these pigments were actually used during the Arnhem Land Expedition; ochre provenancing and other analytical projects might provide answers.[18]

Mountford gained something else through his association with the Board for Anthropological Research. Its members were accustomed to rapid publication through specialist medical or scientific journals, or through the *Transactions of the Royal Society of South Australia* and the *Records of the South Australian Museum*. Publication helped to assure access to a small pool of research funding available through the University of Adelaide or the Australian National Research Council. From 1926 until 1939, approximately 110 scientific papers by board members on the results of the expeditions were published, including nine papers by Mountford. He published another 21 papers on diverse topics, including Aboriginal art, during the same period.[19]

Mountford also took the lead from Tindale and began contributing newspaper articles, using the earnings to support his own research. This popular style of writing suited Mountford and he used it more broadly, particularly as his ethnographic films began finding a wide audience during the early 1940s. But Mountford's publications were not merely descriptive. He had grasped a central fact about Aboriginal art: it linked place, story and identity, and the art of each cultural region comprised an essentially fixed corpus of symbols and motifs, expressed differently by individual artists, but held as shared heritage and revealed to each generation in conjunction with song and ceremony. Indeed, it could be said that Mountford's special gift was to grasp this key idea, and to relay it to a broader public, laying the basis for an unfolding appreciation of Aboriginal art and culture during ensuing decades. These insights, which Mountford took to Arnhem Land, allowed him to begin recording mythological details for bark paintings systematically from the moment of the Expedition's arrival on Groote Eylandt. Colin Simpson's observation that each evening at Oenpelli Mountford could be seen in his tent 'surrounded by bark paintings, writing up his notes' applied also on Groote Eylandt and at Yirrkala, even if the pressure of administrative duties and the controversy over leadership at Yirrkala in particular meant that both the quantity and the quality of his record declined markedly after the Groote Eylandt camp.[20]

---

18 The author is a co-investigator on a current Australian Research Council (ARC) funded project with the aim of arriving at chemical signatures to match ochres in museum collections and ochre mines. In a survey of the Expedition's works on paper, Sarah Bunn, conservator at the Art Gallery of New South Wales, has detected the presence of crayon in a small number of paintings (M. Thomas, Personal communication, 7 October 2010; S. Bunn, Personal communication, 23 November 2010).

19 See Jones, P. 1987, 'South Australian anthropological history: the Board for Anthropological Research and its early expeditions', *Records of the South Australian Museum*, vol. 20, pp. 71–92; Stone, W. W. (ed.) 1958, 'Charles Pearcy Mountford. An annotated bibliography, chronology and checklist of books, papers, manuscripts and sundries, from the library of Harold L. Sheard', *Studies in Australian Bibliography No. 8*, Stone Copying Company, Cremorne, NSW.

20 Simpson, C. 1951, *Adam in Ochre: Inside Aboriginal Australia*, Angus & Robertson, Sydney.

Mountford's immersion in Aboriginal art was more intense than that of any of his anthropological colleagues in Australia. It occurred well before a market had emerged, and well before the phenomenon of known, let alone collectable, Aboriginal artists. Notably, Mountford's acquisition of knowledge in a field that rapidly became appealing to academic anthropologists for its potential in linking mythology, place and totemic identity also placed him on a collision course with Elkin and the Berndts. In the meantime, the relative anonymity of Aboriginal artists predisposed Mountford to think in terms of a universal artistic impulse, shared with artists from all cultures—indeed presumably with Mountford himself, for he had won prizes for artistic photography as early as 1923, when he had worked for the Postmaster General in Darwin.[21]

Figure 2.5 Mountford's photograph of a 'Sunday afternoon corroboree, Katherine River', entered in a Darwin photographic competition during his employment there, 1920–23

By permission of South Australian Museum Archives. AA228.

---

21 Mountford won prizes in six sections in the 1923 Northern Territory Photographic Competition, including for 'Original or Imaginative Study…A very clever manipulation of a curling column of smoke arising out of a bowl, the smoke taking the shape of a human face' (*Northern Territory Times and Gazette*, 4 September 1923, p. 7).

Untrained in social anthropology, Mountford wanted the Aboriginal artistic impulse to float free of totemic obligation—or free enough to transcend the parameters of customary relationship as delineated by academic anthropologists such as Ronald Berndt and Elkin. In the introductory chapter to *Art, Myth and Symbolism*, Mountford conceded that Arnhem Land art comprised several categories indicating specific purpose and function, such as 'sacred art', 'magical paintings, by means of which the aborigines believe they can control nature, punish enemies, and increase the supply of the food animals', and 'didactic bark paintings', but he nevertheless concluded that Aboriginal art 'is predominantly non-magical, that is, the aborigines paint because they want to, and not for some material advantage'.[22] Surprisingly perhaps, Mountford did not use the observable talent of key individual artists to advance this argument. His push for international recognition of Aboriginal art saw him negotiating as early as 1938 with the Museum of Modern Art to host an exhibition in New York. Had it gone ahead we might be certain that it would have promoted Aboriginal art as a 'corporate' contribution to world culture, rather than elevating individual, named Aboriginal artists. For Mountford, as for many collectors and recorders until the late twentieth century, Aboriginal art's reiterative and tradition-bound character necessarily overshadowed, if not subsumed, individual artists' identities. Albert Namatjira, the subject of a book by Mountford (published in 1944, followed by Lee Robinson's 1947 film, which Mountford helped produce), constitutes the rule-proving exception, for the very reason that Mountford judged the Arrernte artist's painting to be hybrid in its origins and influences. To Mountford, Namatjira's individual artistic success reflected his liberation from traditional mores.[23]

By the time of the 1948 Expedition, Mountford's looser interpretation—bordering upon the notion of 'art for art's sake'—had begun to appeal to a wide international community of art historians, particularly Herbert Read, Carl Schuster, Leonhard Adam, Madeline Rousseau and even the doyen of rock-art investigators, Abbé Henri Breuil. These scholars were all concerned to trace universal themes in art history and all corresponded with Mountford. These contacts, and others with diverse anthropologists and curators, gave Mountford a sense of credibility and purpose that expunged the amateur's taint—at least in the eyes of those viewing the Expedition in a positive light. In stark contrast with his standing with A. P. Elkin and the Berndts, Mountford had become an international authority in an emerging, exciting field.

---

22 Mountford, *Records of the American–Australian Scientific Expedition to Arnhem Land*, vol. 1, p. 6.
23 For further analysis of this proposition, see Jones, P. G. 1992, 'Namatjira: traveller between two worlds', in J. Hardy, J. V. S. Megaw and R. Megaw (eds), *The Heritage of Namatjira. The watercolourists of Central Australia*, Heinemann, Melbourne, pp. 97–136.

Once the Expedition began, Mountford knew that most of his days would be spent on paperwork and administration, organising supplies, signing cheques and smoothing out difficulties. The pressure was relieved considerably by his gifted and patient wife, Bessie, who undertook secretarial duties in her own, adjoining tent, redrafting and typing his official correspondence, checking the accounts, and providing—in Bill Harney's words—'the backbone to the party'.[24] Largely confined to the camp itself, Mountford needed a contained and efficient strategy for his main professional objective: obtaining and documenting artworks. His method was essentially the same as that employed during the 1930s Board for Anthropological Research expeditions: 'to ask the men to make bark paintings for me, seldom suggesting subject. At the end of the day, the artists brought the work to my tent, related the associated myth, and explained the meanings of the designs.'[25]

Mountford's Groote Eylandt journal contains the fullest exposition of his bark-painting documentation. For its time, it represents the most detailed set of documentation of individual artworks collected by a field ethnographer in Australia, if not internationally. Headed with the artist's name and moiety, each entry contains a simple diagramatic sketch laying out the main elements of the painting, followed by Mountford's unfolding narrative of the relevant myth as it evokes the events and sites represented.[26]

Mountford's strategy at each of the three Expedition camps was to engage a group of Aboriginal men as general workers who would not only fetch and carry provisions as required, but also remain on the payroll as artists. On Groote Eylandt, this pool of workers corresponds neatly with the artists documented in Mountford's journal. At Yirrkala and Oenpelli, this correspondence is less obvious, but discernible nevertheless. The pool of workers and paid artists at those camps is also identifiable from the published records, but by the time the Expedition struck camp on Groote Eylandt at the end of the first week of July, Mountford's capacity to fully document the bark paintings had become severely compromised.[27]

---

24 Harney to C. P. Mountford, 24 May 1950, Correspondence, vol. 8, pp. 93–4, PRG 1218/28, Mountford-Sheard Collection, SLSA.
25 Mountford, *Records of the American–Australian Scientific Expedition to Arnhem Land*, vol. 1, p. 13. Sally May has suggested that Mountford's published assertion that he seldom suggested subjects to the bark painters is contradicted by his diary entries in which several such suggestions are documented (May, 'Colonial collections of portable art and intercultural encounters in Aboriginal Australia', p. 12). My conclusion is that these entries (and other, published references, such as Mountford, *Records of the American–Australian Scientific Expedition to Arnhem Land*, vol. 1, p. 73) constitute the very exceptions allowed for by Mountford's published statement.
26 See particularly: C. P. Mountford, Expedition to Arnhem Land, 1948, Art of Groote Eylandt, vol. 1, April 11 – July 7 1948, PRG 1218/17/18, Mountford-Sheard Collection, SLSA.
27 See, for example, AASEAL Correspondence, vol. 5, March–July 1948, pp. 421–36, PRG 1218/17/8, Mountford-Sheard Collection, SLSA.

Figure 2.6 Charles Mountford taking notes as Mawalan Marika explains details of a painting, while two other Yolngu artists (so far unidentified) look on, Yirrkala, 1948

Photograph by Howell Walker. By permission of *National Geographic* magazine, December 1949.

Mountford's apparent lack of attention to the vital details of artistic attribution at Yirrkala and Oenpelli has puzzled researchers examining the 1948 Expedition, and has tended to reinforce the orthodox view of his status as an amateur. Mountford's apparent bias towards the mythological content of bark paintings—transmitted through corporate ownership, rather than through individual artistic creativity—suggests one explanation. Howell Walker's photograph of Mountford discussing a painting with Yirrkala artists supports this interpretation; any or all of the Yolngu men surrounding Mountford might have painted the picture being discussed, or, at least, held particular sacred knowledge relevant to it. Undoubtedly, this factor might have blurred a work's attribution, especially if it had been painted hours earlier, out of Mountford's sight. But the real reason for Mountford's diminished capacity to capture the same standard of documentary detail as the Expedition moved from Groote Eylandt to Yirrkala and Oenpelli lay in the complex politics of the Expedition itself. Circumstantial evidence suggests that those tangled strands extended even to Elkin's indirect role in the leadership coup, which occurred in Mountford's tent at Yirrkala, following the party's arrival from Groote Eylandt.

Figure 2.7 The cartoonist Eric Jolliffe visited the Expedition for long enough to capture a playful sense of the cultural distance between the party and the 'natives'

By permission of State Library of South Australia. Mountford-Sheard Collection.

If the Expedition is regarded as a three-act play, its crisis was reached early in the second act, at Yirrkala. The precipitating event was the non-arrival and eventual stranding upon a reef of the *Phoenix*, the barge carrying the party's supplies and equipment to Groote Eylandt. The resultant uncertainty and the breakdown of the Expedition's inadequate radio obliged Mountford and a small party (including anthropologist Frederick Rose) to hike 50 km eastwards across the island from the Umbakumba camp through floodwaters to the Angurugu mission, to organise alternative supplies. Despite his efforts, Mountford became the focus of discontent as key allegiances were forged between Expedition members. Given the size and complexity of the Expedition party, this was likely to occur with any leader. It was not surprising that the chief American scientist, anthropologist Frank Setzler, formed a close working relationship with Frederick McCarthy. McCarthy already had an independent brief to obtain bark paintings for the Australian Museum, and was soon on a collision course with Mountford. The ruction ultimately surfaced during later negotiations over publication and distribution of the collection, in which McCarthy accused Mountford of asserting ownership over part of the collection and directing a proportion of it to the South Australian Museum.[28]

Australian scientific and exploration expeditions had often experienced conflict between members, most notably during the Burke and Wills Exploration Expedition of 1861–62 and the Elder Scientific Exploration Expedition of 1891–92. But this was the first major expedition in which members could communicate directly with organisers and backers, independently of the leader.[29] The result was that the National Geographic Society in Washington, DC, the Native Affairs Department in Darwin, the Department of Information in Canberra, and probably A. P. Elkin in his University of Sydney department were aware of the Expedition's initial difficulties with the stranded *Phoenix*, soon after the first camp was established at Groote Eylandt, and subsequently formed a picture of a disorganised expedition under the leadership of a man overly preoccupied with Aboriginal art.

On Groote Eylandt, the key intermediary between the Expedition and the Native Affairs branch was Howard Coate, a patrol officer who had been deputed to the Expedition from Darwin at Elkin's request and against Mountford's advice. A few months earlier, Coate had already undertaken his own research into Aboriginal art under Elkin's supervision, successfully relocating the remarkable Wandjina rock paintings reported by George Grey in the Kimberley during his 1838 expedition.[30] Elkin's friendship with Coate extended over a 40-year period,

---

28 It should be noted here that even now, more than six decades later, it is unclear just how many of the 1948 barks are contained within the South Australian Museum collection. Mountford revisited Arnhem Land during 1949 and 1951 and it is clear that on the latter trip he commissioned a number of barks to 'replace' those that he had been unable to retain in his possession long enough to include in his preparatory research for the 1956 records volume. Several of Mountford's Yirrkala barks in the South Australian Museum collection, published as 1948 barks in the records volume, were undoubtedly collected during 1951.

29 Discussed in Jones, P. 1996, 'The Horn Expedition's place among nineteenth century inland expeditions', in S. R. Morton and D. J. Mulvaney (eds), *Exploring Central Australia: Science, the environment and the 1894 Horn Expedition*, Surrey Beatty & Sons, Sydney, pp. 19–28.

30 Grey, G. 1841, *Two Expeditions of Discovery in North-Western and Western Australia During the Years 1837, 1838 and 1839*, (2 vols), T. & W. Boone, London, vol. 1, p. 214. Coate's findings were published by A. P. Elkin (1948, 'Grey's northern Kimberley paintings re-found', *Oceania*, vol. 19, no. 1, pp. 1–15).

and it is reasonable to conclude that they continued to communicate during the course of the Arnhem Land Expedition. Coate later admitted, without denying the charge, that Mountford had regarded him as 'a "spy" for Elkin'.[31] In fact, Coate's official role, as specified by the Department of Native Affairs, was 'purely an observer', prompting a wry journal entry by Mountford: 'we have another less pleasant name for men like that.'[32] On Groote Eylandt, Coate's first allegiance was to the Native Affairs office, which reported in turn to Canberra-based Department of Information officers, whose primary concern was the Expedition's success at generating favourable publicity. In the eyes of these bureaucrats, Mountford had been appointed for his capacity to make promotional films about Australia, incorporating ethnological and natural-historical themes. Disturbing reports of his consuming passion for collecting and recording Aboriginal art, together with allegations of poor management, began to reach the Darwin and Canberra offices. Mountford's artistic enthusiasms could readily be interpreted as a fundamental distraction from the Expedition's stated scientific objective: to understand how the Arnhem Land Aborigines made their living from the land.

Coate's presence became a critical factor. Mountford had worked hard to have Bill Harney, the celebrated bushman-writer and patrol officer, appointed to the Expedition as a representative of the Commonwealth's Native Affairs branch. Prior to the Expedition, Harney had kept Mountford informed about the activities of the Berndts and Elkin in Arnhem Land, reassuring him that they and other visitors had not 'touched the main things of importance' and that there was plenty of art left to investigate.[33] During early 1947, Mountford had even asked Harney to have some of the older men at Yirrkala make drawings on paper 'similar to the bark paintings', to 'give me a start on what to expect next year'.[34] Harney eventually joined the party at Yirrkala, replacing Coate. Harney's contribution to the Expedition was significant in terms of his logistical support and his informal gifts as a storyteller and bushman. Unlike Coate, who was omitted altogether, Harney appears as 'guide and liaison officer' in the full listing of Expedition participants published by Mountford in the official records.[35]

---

31 McGregor, W. (ed.) 1996, *Studies in Kimberley Languages in Honour of Howard Coate*, Lincom Europa, Munich, p. 7. Bessie Mountford's diary entry for Saturday, 31 July 1948 reads: 'We are more than ever convinced that friend Coate is the cause of most of our trouble. He is apparently an over zealous reporter to an unfriendly Govt Dept. Though why a C/wealth Dept should set out to be unpleasant to an officer of another C/wealth Dept makes little sense' (Bessie Mountford diary, p. 324, PRG 187/1/1, Mountford-Sheard Collection, SLSA).
32 Mountford diary entry, 23 May 1948, p. 308, PRG 1218/17/12, Mountford-Sheard Collection, SLSA.
33 Harney to C. P. Mountford, 6 June 1947, AASEAL Correspondence, vol. 1, 1945–47, PRG 1218/17/4, Mountford-Sheard Collection, SLSA.
34 C. P. Mountford to Harney, 5 February 1947, AASEAL Correspondence, vol. 1, 1945–47, PRG 1218/17/4, Mountford-Sheard Collection, SLSA.
35 Mountford, *Records of the American–Australian Scientific Expedition to Arnhem Land*, vol. 1, pp. xi and 21. Coate is unmentioned throughout the volume.

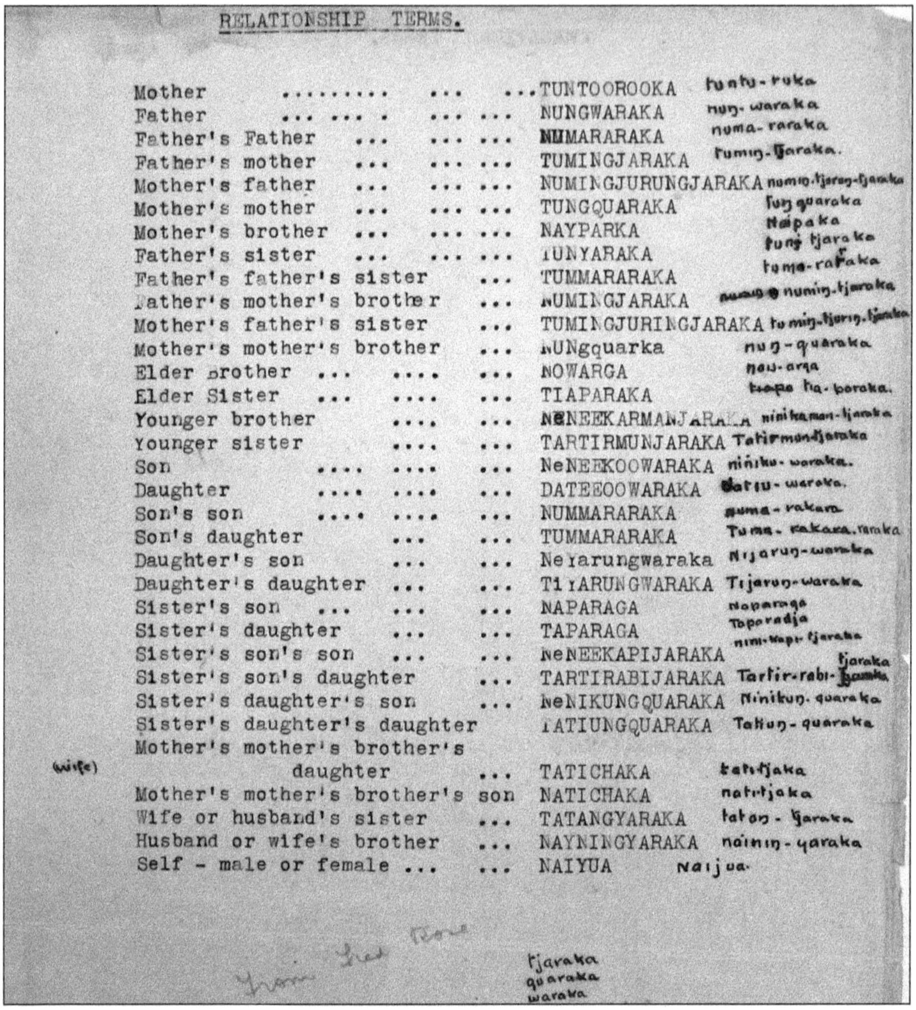

RELATIONSHIP TERMS.		
Mother	TUNTOOROOKA	tuntu-ruka
Father	NUNGWARAKA	nuŋ-waraka
Father's Father	NUMARARAKA	numa-raraka
Father's mother	TUMINGJARAKA	tumiŋ-tjaraka.
Mother's father	NUMINGJURUNGJARAKA	numiŋ-tjaroŋ-tjaraka
Mother's mother	TUNGQUARAKA	tuŋ quaraka
Mother's brother	NAYPARKA	Naipaka
Father's sister	TUNYARAKA	tuŋ tjaraka
Father's father's sister	TUMARARAKA	tuma-rafaka
Father's mother's brother	NUMINGJARAKA	numiŋ.tjaraka
Mother's father's sister	TUMINGJURINGJARAKA	tumiŋ-tjuriŋ.tjaraka
Mother's mother's brother	NUNgquarka	nuŋ-quaraka
Elder brother	NOWARGA	nou-arqa
Elder Sister	TIAPARAKA	tiapa tia-poraka.
Younger brother	NeNEEKARMANJARAKA	ninikaman-tjamka
Younger sister	TARTIRMUNJARAKA	Tatirmondjamka
Son	NeNEEKOOWARAKA	niniku-waraka.
Daughter	DATEEOOWARAKA	datiu-waraka.
Son's son	NUMMARARAKA	numa-rakara
Son's daughter	TUMMARARAKA	Tuma-rakara.raraka
Daughter's son	Neyarungwaraka	Nijaruŋ-waraka
Daughter's daughter	TIYARUNGWARAKA	Tijaruŋ-waraka
Sister's son	NAPARAGA	Naparaga
Sister's daughter	TAPARAGA	Toparadja
Sister's son's son	NeNEEKAPIJARAKA	nini-kapi-tjaraka
Sister's son's daughter	TARTIRABIJARAKA	Tartir-rabi-tjaraka
Sister's daughter's son	NeNIKUNGQUARAKA	Ninikuŋ-quaraka
Sister's daughter's daughter	TATIUNGQUARAKA	Tatiuŋ-quaraka
Mother's mother's brother's daughter (wife)	TATICHAKA	tatitjaka
Mother's mother's brother's son	NATICHAKA	natitjaka
Wife or husband's sister	TATANGYARAKA	tatoŋ-Yaraka
Husband or wife's brother	NAYNINGYARAKA	nainiŋ-yaraka
Self - male or female	NAIYUA	Naijua.

from Fred Rose
tjaraka
quaraka
waraka

Figure 2.8 Anthropologist Fred Rose's list of Groote Eylandt relationship terms, annotated by Mountford

By permission of State Library of South Australia. Mountford-Sheard Collection.

In the meantime, Mountford was lucky to have had anthropological guidance on Groote Eylandt from Frederick Rose, a good friend of Fred Gray, the superintendent of Umbakumba Aboriginal Settlement (see Thomas, this volume). Rose had written to Mountford as early as 1945 with a request to join the Expedition, and later made it plain that he shared Mountford's distrust of Elkin.[36] The pair had met in Sydney during 1947. Rose gave Mountford his own

---

36 Rose to Mountford, 24 June 1945, AASEAL Correspondence, vol. 2, 1945–1948—Applications, p. 3, PRG 1218/17/5, Mountford-Sheard Collection, SLSA. Two years later, Rose recommended a female graduate (Pamela Beasley) to Mountford, assuring him that 'I can vouch in no uncertain terms for the fact that she is anti-Elkin (although for obvious reasons her tongue is in her cheek until her M.A. is finished this term) and anti-functionalist and pro-evolutionist' (Rose to Mountford, 6 October 1947, ibid., p. 29).

notes on Groote Eylandt social organisation and totems, and negotiated with key elders for the performance of the ceremonial cycle, which absorbed Mountford's attention during the Expedition's last weeks on the island. But Mountford's role in organising, provisioning and documenting these ceremonies through film and sound recordings was exposing him to further criticism.

Figure 2.9 Mountford recording ceremonial songs with the Groote Eylandt man known as 'India', near site of ceremonies. Mountford's journal confirms that he played a major role in recording during this cycle of ceremonies, June 1948

Photograph by Howell Walker. By permission of *National Geographic* magazine, December 1949.

It was always risky to hold ceremonies close to a mission, as Mountford himself had discovered during Adnyamathanha ceremonies held at his instigation at Nepabunna in South Australia's Flinders Ranges during 1937. The sudden endorsement of traditional ritual not only compromised the missionary who had otherwise sought to suppress it; it also triggered tensions within the Aboriginal group, particularly between older ritual leaders and younger men who were beneficiaries of the missionary's new order. Mountford later observed that there had been 'some opposition by the local residents of Groote Eylandt to the performance of this ceremony, the missionaries objecting because they considered that the ceremony was evil, and the superintendent of the Umbakumba settlement [Gray] because it interfered with the planting of his garden'.[37] Both Mountford and Expedition cook, John Bray, made observations and diary entries indirectly indicating that Coate (a lay-missionary) was the

---

37 Mountford, *Records of the American–Australian Scientific Expedition to Arnhem Land*, vol. 1, p. 21.

source of rumours that the Groote Island Arawaltja ceremonies would result in ritual killings and payback. As it happened, Mountford's decision to proceed with the ceremonies almost resulted in physical violence between young men of the Umbakumba camp and those attached to the Church Missionary Society mission on the east coast, and he was obliged to shift the ceremonial ground.[38] Bessie Mountford documented other tensions surrounding this event, such as the resistance to their fate of two young wives who had been promised to older men, but who preferred younger men: 'the whole population is involved as families take sides—the girls for them, the husbands against.'[39] Mountford's management of these difficult circumstances was adroit enough, but the Expedition's progress was being reported rather differently to Darwin and Canberra. Tensions between members were rising to the surface and, as Bessie Mountford observed of her husband, 'the continued stress of an organisation that will not function completely is beginning to wear him down'.[40]

Figure 2.10 Arnhem Land Expedition at the third camp, Oenpelli (now Gunbalanya), 1948

Photograph by Howell Walker. By permission of *National Geographic* magazine, December 1949.

Matters came to a head immediately after the Expedition arrived at its second camp, among the Yolngu at Yirrkala. On 10 July, the Administrator of the Northern Territory, Arthur Driver, and the Acting Director of the Department of Information, Kevin Murphy, flew in, accompanied by the US Consul in Adelaide, Elvin Seibert. Mountford's tent was the venue for a meeting between himself, Setzler, Driver and Murphy, during which, as the other scientists

---

38 See Mountford to Director-General of Information, 29 July 1948, Correspondence, vol. 5, March–July 1948, p. 462, PRG 1218/17/8, Mountford-Sheard Collection, SLSA; Diary entry by John Bray for 12 June 1948, pp. 64–5 (M. Thomas, Personal communication, 7 October 2010).
39 Bessie Mountford diary, 7 May 1948, p. 116, PRG 187/1/1, Mountford-Sheard Collection, SLSA.
40 Ibid., p. 118.

observed, voices were raised. Mountford was informed that he was relieved of the leadership, which would pass to Setzler, and that he was to confine his activities to photography and to producing the films required by the Department of Information. The delegation flew out that afternoon and the camp remained eerily quiet as the news circulated. But within 24 hours the situation was reversed. The Americans met the following morning, and Setzler was informed by his colleagues, led by ornithologist Bert Deignan, that they still considered Mountford the rightful leader. Setzler was forced to renounce the leadership by telegram and to apologise to Mountford. McCarthy and Coate remained silent, but they were regarded by Mountford as complicit, if not instrumental, in the attempted coup. Within a day or two, Mountford received the following cable from the executive officers of the Smithsonian Institution and the National Geographic Society:

> Glad know Yirrkala new base established. Congratulate you as leader expedition and your associates on results reported to date. Best wishes continued progress under your able leadership.[41]

From that point, Mountford's leadership was fundamentally accepted, but the pressures of administration continued to mount. He was the first to recognise that he could no longer meet the standard of documentation set on Groote Eylandt. Shortly after this event, he wrote in the following terms to his friend Alexander Wetmore, Secretary of the Smithsonian Institution:

> The prohibition, by the Department of Information, on my carrying out of research on the primitive art of the native peoples is indeed a sad blow, though I am still doing odd research work. My allotted duties are those of leadership and film director. So you will see my enemies, of whom you have already had some knowledge, are still active and powerful.[42]

Mountford's pared-down art-collecting methodology, giving precedence to mythological content over artistic provenance, became his only means of continuing research. That methodology—supplemented by Mountford's fieldwork and strategic collecting during subsequent visits to Arnhem Land (particularly that of 1951)—formed the backbone of *Art, Myth and Symbolism*.

---

41 Cablegram reproduced in AASEAL Correspondence, vol. 5, March–July 1948, p. 552, PRG 1218/17/8, Mountford-Sheard Collection, SLSA. By the time of the publication of the expedition records in 1956, Mountford was able to treat the matter with irony, writing: 'The day after reaching Yirkalla, we received a pleasant surprise in the form of a visit from the American Consul for South Australia, Mr E. Seibert, who had made the journey to see his American colleagues; the Administrator for the Northern Territory, Mr A. R. Driver; and the Director-General of Information, Mr Kevin Murphy' (Mountford, *Records of the American–Australian Scientific Expedition to Arnhem Land*, vol. 1, p. xxvii).
42 Mountford to Wetmore, 29 July 1948, AASEAL Correspondence, vol. 5, March–July 1948, p. 464, PRG 1218/17/8, Mountford-Sheard Collection, SLSA.

Surprisingly, even Mountford's fiercest critics—Elkin, McCarthy and the Berndts—failed to notice that the volume drew on research and bark paintings collected after the 1948 Expedition. Nevertheless, it remains one of the most detailed and accurate records of an Aboriginal art and material culture collection to be published in Australia. That Mountford was able to produce this work at all, given the obstacles facing him during the 1948 fieldwork, was a notable achievement. His considerable experience in the field, both with Aboriginal people and with fellow researchers, undoubtedly equipped Mountford to survive the vagaries and pitfalls of a seven-month scientific expedition—the most complex and successful venture of its kind in Australian history.

These events and undercurrents, interlocking with the distinctive island, seashore and lagoon landscapes encountered by the researchers, not to mention the contrasting cultural groups of Aboriginal people and the three varying sets of mission practice and personnel at Angurugu, Yirrkala and Oenpelli, make the Arnhem Land Expedition triptych a fascinating object of study. Mountford's resilience as a fieldworker (sustained cheerfully by his wife and most of his colleagues despite being undermined before, during and after the Expedition) and his dogged commitment to obtaining a rich and durable record of Arnhem Land art make him a compelling central character in this historic tableau of Australian art and science.

3. Nation Building or Cold War: Political settings for the Arnhem Land Expedition

Kim Beazley

Frank M. Setzler, the Deputy Leader of the Arnhem Land Expedition and its senior American, described in his diary the Expedition's chief Australian political patron, Arthur Calwell, after their first meeting:

> Met Mr Arthur Calwell, Minister of Immigration and Information, who is a most delightful politician with a sharp tongue, quick wit, and keen mind. He has red hair and talks out of the side of his mouth. He has cousins and has visited them here in the US (Pennsylvania).[1]

In a sentence, Setzler captured the attributes that would take Calwell to the leadership of the Australian Labor Party (ALP), but which also killed his political career when, a generation later, telegenic requirements either advanced or impaired a political career. Setzler was documenting a meeting with the minister on 25 February 1948 at the outset of their pre-expedition meetings in Canberra. Later he described a convivial Arthur Calwell at a cocktail party at the American Embassy, and the next day at an equally lubricated gathering hosted by the minister in Parliament, also attended by Opposition Leader, Robert Menzies.[2]

These functions were a peaceful social interlude at the beginning of two of the most bitter years in Australian politics, which were the prelude to the longest-serving government in Australia's history, led at the outset by the man who introduced Setzler to sparkling Porphyry Pearl at the gathering mentioned above: R. G. Menzies.

The Expedition—arguably the most dramatic manifestation of Australian–American scientific collaboration—was a quiet backdrop to an intense debate that went to the heart of Australian political culture at the onset of the Cold War. As the Expedition proceeded, a reluctant government was drawn into the Cold War vortex, symbolised by the creation of the Australian Security Intelligence Organisation (ASIO), which was a necessary security measure to cement much broader allied collaboration in an era of great mistrust. At the same time, Menzies' Liberal Party honed an argument that was decisive in

---

1 Diary of Frank M. Setzler, Deputy Leader, Arnhem Land Expedition, Australia 1948, vol. 1: New York to Groote Eylandt, p. 20, MS5230, National Library of Australia, Canberra.
2 Ibid., pp. 22–3.

the subsequent election in 1949. The Liberals argued that despite the Chifley government's security measures, including its support for the Allied side in the 1948 reaction to the Soviet blockade of Berlin and its crushing of the communist-led coalminers' strike in New South Wales the following year, the ALP was not to be trusted with national security, and Chifley's socialism was on a slope, at the bottom of which was Stalin. 'Socialists and controls or the Liberals and Freedom'[3] was as potent a slogan in 1949 as 'We will decide who comes to this country and the circumstances in which they come' more than 50 years later.[4]

It was a bewildered ALP that went into its long drought in 1949. As Calwell told the Parliament in September 1949, 'the people of Australia, I believe, are satisfied with this government'.[5] Labor believed it had the model domestic and foreign policies to deal with that generation's most recent traumas: depression and a war close to home. Labor had immense self-confidence in its focus on planning. It had seen Australia emerge from World War II as a massive Allied supply dump as well as a geographical anchor for the southern tier of the fight back against the Greater East Asian Co-Prosperity Sphere. Chifley drew out of the wartime experience a conviction that Australia could create a new manufacturing industry within the Sterling area, using the new tools for the management of trade in the Bretton-Woods agreement, as Australia segued out of war production to meeting civilian needs.

Nation building took the form of grand schemes such as the Snowy Mountains Hydro-Electric Scheme and a new focus on scientific research and educational attainment. The Australian National University was established. Above all, immigration was perceived as the key to renewal. The unions were persuaded that a postwar economy could sustain a massive population increase. As Immigration Minister, Arthur Calwell was at the centre of this aspect of nation building.

An enthusiasm for social democratic ideology underpinned this position. A combination of nationalism and social democracy informed the ALP's foreign outlook, which was confident in the efficacy of Franklin Delano Roosevelt's liberal internationalism. This sought to uphold international order with a system of collective security, managed decolonisation and economic development as an antidote to Marxist insurrection. Liberal internationalism did not obviate realism when it came to Australia's own defences, however. Regional arrangements that

---

3   Lowe, D. 1999, *Menzies and the 'Great World Struggle': Australia's Cold War 1948–1954*, UNSW Press, Sydney, p. 32.
4   Howard, J. 2001, Transcript of the Prime Minister the Hon. John Howard MP Address at the Federal Liberal Party Campaign Launch, Sydney, 28 October 2001, viewed 20 October 2010, <http://parlinfo.aph.gov.au>
5   Kiernan, C. 1978, *Calwell: A personal and political biography*, Nelson Publishing, Melbourne, p. 153.

included the United States and the United Kingdom were actively sought for the Pacific whilst Australia was prepared to offer a substantial effort of its own in the South Pacific.

Scientific expeditions were easy to fit into this model. Science was seen as being at the heart of Australia's industrial renewal. For example, in the 1947 five-year defence budget of A£250 million, defence research and development received a massive A£33 million.[6]

Labor underestimated its opponents. Menzies was perceived by the Chifley government ministers as a failed wartime prime minister, out of touch with ordinary Australians and easily defeated in the 1946 election. The burgeoning Cold War notwithstanding, Liberal anti-communism was seen as politically self-serving by the ALP, and based on no real experience of dealing with communists politically. Labor politicians, particularly those with a union background, had cut their teeth on struggle with communists for control of the Labor movement. Labor acted, Liberals talked.

The ALP's was a powerful paradigm for members who had fought internal battles and were hardened by the experience of brutal defeat during the Depression and hard-won victory during the war. Convinced of the power of their arguments, Labor's leaders were unable to understand the postwar drift of public opinion. Genuine public concern at the ALP's proposals to nationalise the banks and persist with rationing, together with growing public fear of international communism (shown in rudimentary opinion polling), was seen as only the manifestation of a routinely self-serving, hostile capitalist press.[7] Labor became relatively easy for its Liberal opponents to define. This was a considerable change from the 1943 and 1946 elections when the ALP had been able to portray the Liberals as the party of defeat, disunity and incompetence.

The American alliance has been enduringly popular in Australian domestic politics for the lifetime of most of this generation of Australians. Both sides of Australian politics like to claim a creator's role. The ALP stresses Curtin's 1941 New Year message in which he turned Australia to the United States 'free of any pangs as to our traditional links or kinship with the United Kingdom'.[8] Liberals stress the 1951 conclusion of the Australia, New Zealand, United States (ANZUS) Security Treaty as the originating point. The reality is more complex.

Certainly, in World War II, one strand of American opinion saw Australia as geographically useful for American strategic purposes. Roosevelt was prepared

---

6 Lee, D. 1995, *Search for Security: The political economy of Australia's postwar foreign and defence policy*, Allen & Unwin, St Leonards, NSW, p. 76.
7 Lowe, *Menzies and the 'Great World Struggle'*, p. 20.
8 Curtin, J. 1941, 'The task ahead', *The Herald* [Melbourne], 27 December 1941.

to back Douglas MacArthur as commander of the South-West Pacific area as one basis for a fight back against Japan. The US Navy did not share the enthusiasm for this position, seeing the fight back as more appropriately focused on the central Pacific. The result was that it was not until 1944, when Roosevelt approved MacArthur's plan to resecure the Philippines, that he placed more American soldiers under his command than Australians. It was not until then that aircraft carriers were assigned to his authority. Much of MacArthur's highly successful campaign of isolating Japanese formations by bypassing them and mopping them up later—'hit 'em where they ain't'—was driven by the necessity of creating land bases for aircraft in the absence of sea platforms as he sought to bring air power to his campaigns.

Australia's geographic value—contested in World War II—disappeared altogether in its aftermath. The Australian political commitment was welcome during the Cold War but Australia's geographic position was not militarily significant for the United States until the 1960s. The first ANZUS Council meeting was held in Hawai'i. That was the closest it got to Australia until 1962 when the United States was seeking support in Vietnam. More significantly in this period, the United States discovered in Australia an important ground station location for communications, intelligence, early warning surveillance and reconnaissance technologies. From that point, Australian and American militaries intertwined, as intensively as was the case in 1942.[9]

Relative American indifference, however, was not matched by a lack of Australian enthusiasm. Despite highly divergent views between the ALP and the Liberals on national security policy in the late 1940s, both sides eagerly sought a relationship with the United States—for very different purposes. The Arnhem Land Expedition had its origins within the framework of one perspective. The Expedition was conducted as the Cold War intensified and it became part of a catalogue of initiatives through which Australia was slowly enmeshed in a Cold War alignment. By the time the articles, films, sound recordings and reports of the Expedition were ultimately released in the mid-1950s, Australia's national security debate revolved around Cold War issues and perspectives.

Through this period, Setzler and Calwell formed a bond, founded on the Expedition and reflected in a delightful correspondence in which they asserted a cousinly relationship between them. The historian Martin Thomas has kindly shared with me this correspondence, which came to light during a fellowship he held at the Smithsonian Institution. The correspondence shows that they shared a particular strand of Cold War thinking, slightly off the centre of its most virulent forms. Setzler was a liberal American type. Patriotic and anti-

---

9   Beazley, K. 2008, 'The Coral Bell Lecture 2008', in *Thinking Security: Influencing national strategy from the academy, an Australian experience*, The Lowy Institute for International Policy, Sydney.

communist, he nevertheless had a profoundly diplomatic persona, and a commitment to liberal democratic principles. Arguably, during the Expedition this led him to smooth over differences between members and the Australian leader, Charles P. Mountford. He firmly rejected the notion that he should take the leadership from Mountford, considering it the prerogative of an Australian to lead an expedition in Australia.[10]

Calwell, on the other hand, though radical and by self-definition a committed socialist, was also anti-communist and more sceptical than his colleagues of prevailing public and political identification with the interests of the British Empire. He was emphatic that the miners' strike was a communist conspiracy and not legitimate industrial action.[11] Chifley, though ultimately vigorous in suppressing it by deploying troops into the mines, was motivated more by anti-inflationary concerns with the deviation from centralised wage-fixing that the strike represented.

Though contemporary language required sensitivity to British concerns, including in immigration policy, Calwell gloried in his American and Irish antecedents, and shared Catholic concerns about communism. He was, as I will discuss later, fascinated by the American social model. A statement he made shortly after his electoral defeat in 1949 rested more easily with prevailing public sentiment than the views of most of his colleagues:

> We belong to the defence of the Pacific, and we are therefore in the orbit of America. Our hope of continuing as a portion of the British Commonwealth of nations in the Pacific lies in our willingness and readiness to cooperate with America. If we do not want to do that, then we cannot expect to get similar assistance as in World War II, if the conflagration spreads to Communist-minded people of South and South-East Asia—some of them within 24 hours flying time of Australia.[12]

Setzler and Calwell readily accepted the Cold War paradigm. Neither, as their correspondence shows, could accept a transition into McCarthyism. Part of countering communism was upholding liberal democratic values, not trashing them for narrow politics. They were firmly in the liberal-realist camp.

---

10 Thomas, M. 2010, 'A short history of the Arnhem Land Expedition', *Aboriginal History*, vol. 34.
11 Lowe, *Menzies and the 'Great World Struggle'*, p. 23.
12 'Concentrate on Pacific says Mr Calwell', *The Canberra Times*, 25 July 1950, p. 1, viewed 21 October 2010, <http://nla.gov.au/nla.news-article2790269>

Australia's international political engagement from post-World War II to the 1950s, covering the time of the Expedition, has been well analysed elsewhere.[13] A short summary of the debate and the government's motivations is, however, necessary here to see how the Expedition fitted broader policy thinking.

1946–1950: Spiralling into the Cold War

Of the Western World War II Allies, the Australian Government was the slowest to accept the changing framework of international politics from the optimism that marked wartime collaboration and the postwar establishment of the United Nations to the anxious creation of two armed camps: East versus West. In the process, the Australian Government deeply annoyed its American and British counterparts. Despite the Chifley government's efforts in 1948–49 to mollify its wartime allies, Chifley's demise was satisfying to American and British interests—including their diplomatic representatives in Australia.

John Spender would become Menzies' Minister for External Affairs in late 1949, when he negotiated the ANZUS Treaty. In February that year, in a debate with Minister for External Affairs, H. V. Evatt, Spender claimed:

> This debate…has thrown into highlight two matters, one that the government's policy is based solely on the United Nations, and the other that the Opposition, which directs itself to the realities of the situation, wants some support other than that of the United Nations in facing the difficulties that lie ahead…In my view, he [Evatt] has been so carried away by his internationalism, that either he has lost sight of or is unmindful of the strategic and vital considerations that affect Australia.[14]

Spender was arguing for wholehearted support for the Atlantic Pact, negotiated on British initiative, and an attempt to emulate it in the Pacific. He was implicitly accepting a strategy that saw the principal flash points in the international system as Europe and the Middle East, where the British and Americans perceived a Soviet political and maybe military thrust to interdict Western access to oil. This position also accepted an incorporation of Japan into the Western alliance and a Pacific pact, effectively condoning the status quo in various empire positions in the Asia-Pacific. As is often the case in political debates, the Liberals' argument effectively cartooned real government policy,

---

13   See, for example: Lowe, *Menzies and the 'Great World Struggle'*; McLean, D. 1990, 'ANZUS origins: a reassessment', *Australian Historical Studies*, vol. 24, no. 94 (April), pp. 64–82; Meaney, N. 1992, 'Australia, the great powers and the coming of the Cold War', *Australian Journal of Politics and History*, vol. 38, no. 5, pp. 316–33.
14   Lee, *Search for Security*, p. 100.

but its positioning had the strength of being on song with the Americans, the British and, within the Australian structure, the defence chiefs. It also had the political virtue of simplicity.

Government policy emanated from a more self-confident approach to the possibilities in the emerging international system for middle-power influence and a determination to answer half-a-century's worth of Australian strategic conundrums—principally, how to secure Australian interests in its own region when the strategic perspectives of allies drew them in directions that rendered Australia vulnerable. The government had before it the experience of 40 years' worth of concern that Anglo-Japanese relations before World War II had, in the first instance, outsourced imperial defence in the Far East to the Japanese and then, as the storm clouds brewed, seen imperial policy in the Far East undermined by the necessity for Britain to concentrate on threats in Europe. Then in World War II, Australia's Anglo-American allies evolved a 'beat Hitler first' strategy, implying a holding operation in Australia's region. In all instances, Australia's focus on Japan and its priorities had been subordinated to wider strategic goals. The Australian experience was that it had little influence in allied councils.

There were many subsets of this assessment. First, it did not involve a rejection of the value of British imperial defence. Rather it sought to control the direction of imperial policy in the Australian region. It is interesting that Curtin's primary effort to turn around the ALP's prewar scepticism about imperial security arrangements during the war—manifest at the party's 1943 Federal Conference—had not been to build an American alliance but to reinvigorate imperial defence. The catch was that imperial policy in the Pacific was to shift towards Australian perspectives not British ones.[15]

Throughout the 1946–49 period, Chifley sought to strengthen the British economy and the trading position of the Sterling area, going so far as providing the British with a A£25 million grant in 1947, from a hard-pressed Australian budget, followed by A£10 million in both 1948 and 1949.[16] This had the paradoxical effect of keeping postwar rationing going—a situation the Liberals exploited in the 1949 election.

Proximity to Britain and sympathy for the Attlee government did not mean identification with British perspectives and goals. Emerging Cold War strategic assumptions seemed to foreshadow precisely the old direction away from Australian strategic interests, drawing Australia into Britain's priorities, and undermining both Britain's and Australia's capacity to advance Australia's own.

---

15   Curran, J. 2009, '"An organic part of the whole structure": John Curtin's empire', *Journal of Imperial and Commonwealth History*, vol. 37, no. 1, pp. 51–75.
16   Beazley, K. E. 1961, Caucus as an instrument for determining the policy and tactics of the Federal Parliamentary Labor Party in the Commonwealth Parliament 1901–1960, MA thesis, The Australian National University, Canberra, p. 93.

The Chifley government assumed it would see more clearly than the British the consequences for Australian interests of approaches to both colonial policy and the postwar fate of Japan. Communist threats in South-East Asia could be better handled by transitioning colonies to moderate nationalist-controlled independent nations. Priority given to economic development would keep revolutionaries at bay. The Chifley government strongly supported Indonesian independence against a revived Dutch Empire.

Both in relation to former colonies and on governance more generally, the Chifley government was inclined to be suspicious of support for a regime merely because it was anti-Soviet. It believed dictatorial regimes were in the long term unstable and encouraged domestic communist-led revolt.

Second, policy towards Japan also needed an Australian perspective; the government's hand was strengthened by a status that saw it play a leading role in determining empire policy in the Pacific. The Chifley government feared US policy—motivated by narrow anti-Soviet concerns—would lose focus when it came to preventing a future Japanese military recovery.

Third, the United States was important in all of this and a Pacific pact involving the United States was desirable. In 1945–46, the government tried hard to talk the United States into a military bases deal involving reciprocal rights at each other's bases in the South and central Pacific.[17] The United States had no interest in this zone once the war ended and was not impressed with Australia's military strength. The Chifley government continued to try to draw the United States into a Pacific pact associated with an anti-Soviet direction but which was implicitly anti-Japanese. The proposition did not fit well with the direction of US policy, and the administration found its underlying assumptions annoying.

Fourth, while it acknowledged the possibility of a future war with the Soviet Union, the Chifley government did not see it as inevitable. Communist subversion was real but it demanded a governance and economic response in threatened areas. As the decade progressed, the Chifley government combined opposition to perceived communist and Soviet initiatives such as the blockade of Berlin, and insurrection in Greece, with an effort to get the issues mediated in the United Nations. Western allies believed, however, that mediation implied some legitimacy to the Soviet position. The advent of a communist China made action more urgent.

In the context of this point and the previous one, the Chifley government's focus on the United Nations was not simply a product of idealism. The United Nations provided a tool for mediation and development, and, when the Security Council

---

17   Bell, R. 1973, 'Australian–American discord: negotiations for post-war bases and security arrangements in the Pacific 1944–1946', *Australian Outlook*, vol. 27, no. 1, pp. 12–33.

froze on the veto of a great power, the UN General Assembly could be used. Above all, it was a forum where a small power such as Australia could be heard. It had no other forum, particularly when the Far East Commission around the Japanese occupation appeared to be sidelined by MacArthur's Headquarters. The United Nations provided a way to talk back into empire policy and to the United States.

Finally, Australia's best defence lay in the rapid economic development of the continent. Since Australian Federation, a body of alarmist literature had been built up around the vulnerability of Australia's undeveloped north.[18] Likewise, Australian economic, industrial and scientific immaturity needed to be addressed if Australia was to enhance its self-reliance. The Chifley government enthusiastically pursued defence science collaboration with the British, negotiating rocket-testing facilities in South Australia. Defence concerns lay at the heart of immigration policy as the government sought to increase the population base to confront the challenges that post-imperial changes would bring to the region. A larger population, the government believed, would accelerate economic development and industrialisation and provide for larger armed services.

At the best of times, these perspectives were met with limited approval by Australia's British and American allies. Pursued in the emerging Cold War context, they suggested that Australia was obtuse at best and, at worst, might have been induced by an excessive influence of radical, pro-Soviet thinkers. Even when sympathetic to Western goals and critical of Soviet motivations, as the Chifley government was, the determination to pursue policy in increasingly mistrusted forums such as the United Nations could appear to be a product of the naive or the sinister.

As Foreign Minister and as Chifley's successor to the ALP leadership, Evatt was actively detested by his British and American counterparts. The secretary of his department, John Burton, was widely perceived as a fellow traveller. How absurd this proposition is can be seen in a piece of advice he gave Chifley's Defence Council in 1948, issued, coincidentally, as the Arnhem Land Expedition was proceeding, and before a final communist takeover in China:

> Whatever government is in power in China…Chinese policy and interest in South East Asia will not change. Any open conflict between North and South China, or any involvement in a broader global conflict, will lead to increased interest in South East Asia. A Communist-dominated China, which would result from the present confused political situation

---

18 See, for example: Stanley, P. 2008, *Invading Australia: Japan and the battle for Australia, 1942*, Viking, Camberwell, Vic. Chapters 1 and 2 detail the widespread fear of Japanese invasion in Australian popular culture dating from the late 1890s onwards, and the specific concerns of invasion in the 'empty north'.

in China, and which could follow quickly on the commencement of an East-West conflict, would certainly aim at acquiring the use of the resources of South East Asia, not by military action, as was the case with Japan, but by internal action, using Chinese populations and the already organised political groupings of secret societies.[19]

The emerging threat from China and the possibility of a renewed Japanese threat were what focused the Chifley government. These were seen as more problematic for Australia than the emerging tensions with the Soviet Union.

By the time the Expedition commenced, the Chifley government could see that as far as potential allies were concerned, the Cold War paradigm had overwhelmed them. If the United States and the United Kingdom were to be engaged for defence purposes on scientific intelligence or industrial collaboration then Australia would have to engage with their issues. The Australian Government supported the Berlin airlift, criticised the Soviet Union's military occupation of northern Iran and its hand in communist activities in Greece, sent military equipment to Malaya in support of the British against the communist insurrection and created ASIO to enhance domestic security. It was finally drawn into the Cold War agenda but not so convincingly that it did not need as many examples of allied collaboration as it could find. The Expedition was a chance to show that collaboration was possible. Its location was very useful in drawing international attention to Australia's perceived vulnerable reaches, and expanding understanding of that region.

The Expedition as Positive PR: Scientific collaboration and a nascent alliance

At its conception, the Expedition was a product of an aggressive Australian information campaign among its allies. At its onset, it embellished prevailing Australian developmental and defence concerns. At its reporting stage, it was enmeshed with increasing Australian focus on its American partner in the Cold War. Throughout its operation, it was in the hands of the one senior minister most culturally attuned to the United States: Arthur Calwell.

In the Australian public historical mind, Arthur Calwell is remembered as a devotee of the White Australia Policy—both while he was a minister and long after it was discarded in the 1960s. Beyond that he is remembered as a leader of the ALP who dramatically lost the 1966 election on Vietnam, as a result of

---

19 Lowe, *Menzies and the 'Great World Struggle'*, p. 35.

his opposition to conscription for military service and his fight as a last-ditch defender of the left-controlled Victorian Branch against E. G. Whitlam's attempts to reform the party.

Arthur Calwell was a much more substantial figure than these nevertheless factually based perceptions indicate. He was also the architect of Australia's modern immigration program (non-European component excluded). In fashioning the program with its heavy focus on continental European migrants and generous attitude to Jewish refugees, he had in mind the creation of a polyglot community such as that in the United States. As one of his biographers has suggested, this approach would provide 'both a model for Australia and an assurance that a democratic society did not have to be just like Britain'.[20]

On a visit to the United States in 1947, he called for a million American migrants.[21] He was not, however, completely overwhelmed by American enthusiasm. He records in his autobiography an interchange on that trip with a CBS reporter, in which the latter asked, 'Why do you want people to leave this great country to go to faraway Australia?' He replied: 'Because Australia is God's own country.' When the correspondent suggested Calwell talked like an American, he responded, 'I think we have better reasons for calling Australia God's own country than you have for giving that title to America.'[22]

He was more deeply impressed than most of his colleagues with General Douglas MacArthur (and they were very impressed). He did not share enthusiasms for the revival of the British Empire and saw his efforts to populate Australia as a more effective substitute for MacArthur in defending Australia from threats from the region. In his autobiography, he expressed immense pride at having persuaded Menzies to record MacArthur's death in Australia's parliamentary proceedings. He concluded with his own remarks:

> Now he is dead. There is neither rank nor station nor prerogative in the democracy of the dead or the republic of the grave. For us, however, Douglas MacArthur belongs to the immortal dead. But he belongs forever in the hearts and history of the Australian people. In the words of the poet, this country, as does his own, owes him 'the debt immense of endless gratitude'.[23]

Evatt was not one of Calwell's enthusiasms, even though he served as Evatt's deputy after Chifley's death. In his remarkably frank correspondence with Setzler in the decade after the Expedition, Calwell said of the infamous Petrov

---

20   Kiernan, *Calwell*, p. 122.
21   Ibid., p. 127.
22   Calwell, A. 1972, *Be Just and Fear Not*, Lloyd O'Neil Publishing, Melbourne, p. 106.
23   Ibid., p. 240.

case: 'Fortunately, the Petrov incident is fading into history and would never have been the cause celebre which it became but for Dr Evatt's foolishness in seeing conspiracies where there were none, and in behaving so strangely as to discredit both himself and the Labor Party.'[24]

The Expedition was a direct product of Calwell's drive to entwine the two societies through the activities of his Information Directorate when that was his sole ministry, and then through his dual departments of immigration and information. The depth of this engagement is obvious in Calwell's reports to Parliament, and predated the end of World War II hostilities. For example, on 8 March 1945, Calwell reported the engagement of one Frank Goldberg, an advertising executive, to tour the United States scoping the possibilities for an Australian information campaign. He read his letter to Goldberg:

> I have great pleasure in inviting you, during your forthcoming visit to the United States and Canada, to investigate on my behalf the use and availability of commercial advertising media in those countries for presenting in the post war period the case of Australia in relation to tourist traffic, trade possibilities, migration advantages and allied subjects…We realise that there is still a very big task to be accomplished in making known abroad Australia's urgent need of greater population, the opportunities that it can offer to new citizens, the possibilities that our national post war development will cater for a big expansion of our international trade, and the amazing untapped resource of interest that Australia can offer to tourists seeking relaxation from their ordinary normal spheres of activity.[25]

Goldberg's activities were a small part of the 'full court press' by Calwell's department on the United States. Charles Mountford's lecture tour, which included a presentation to the National Geographic Society that year, was another. When Mountford's lecture provoked the society's interest in supporting research into a little-known part of Australian territory, Calwell seized the opportunity with both hands—as the records of the Expedition explain:

> Realising that such an expedition afforded a great opportunity both to better the good relations between Australia and the United States, and to investigate one of the least known parts of Australia, the Minister for Information arranged for the party to be much more comprehensive, consisting of both American and Australian naturalists and ethnologists.[26]

---

24 Letter from Calwell to Setzler, 17 December 1954, Setzler Papers, Box 24, Hon. Arthur A. Calwell correspondence, National Anthropological Archives, Suitland, Md.
25 House of Representatives, *Hansard*, 8 March 1945, pp. 469–70.
26 McLaren, W. 1956, 'Introduction', in C. P. Mountford (ed.), *Records of the American–Australian Scientific Expedition to Arnhem Land. Volume 1: Art, myth and symbolism*, Melbourne University Press, Carlton, Vic., p. ix.

Calwell had much more on his plate than just the Expedition. In his report to Parliament on budget estimates for 1948/49, he opened the discussion of his department's activities with descriptions of efforts in the United States:

> Large quantities of descriptive booklets and maps are sent to school teachers, children, universities, colleges and libraries. In many American schools classes are doing regular studies on Australia. Requests from American schools often total 500 a month, and requests of a general nature about Australia's arts, sciences, industries, sports and other activities run at the same high rate. The Department's documentary films for publicizing Australia abroad are popular in America. The cost of production is now being offset by increasing revenues from rentals. Television has opened up new avenues for publicising Australia. Programme organisers have already featured much Australian material from films made by the department. We expect more placements in this direction as television expands.[27]

These efforts, Calwell reported, had produced 1000 American migrants. Shortly before this parliamentary speech, Calwell had been pleased to inform the Australian public about the fruit of an earlier activity of his department: the discovery by the Expedition of previously unrecorded bird and fish life. He also reported on intensive archaeological work.[28]

Though the connections were rarely directly made, the political atmospherics around the Expedition contributed to broader discussion and calculations of Australia's national security issues. On one level, here was scientific collaboration of relevance to defence. An understanding of Australia's north was a critical component of defence thinking given the importance the region had played in Australia's war effort—important again in an era when new challenges were being identified to Australia's north. As one of Calwell's biographers has written: 'Calwell backed the development of the north of Australia, which he visited on several occasions, hoping that it would provide space for an increased population and a defence against possible Indonesian or Japanese aggression.'[29]

At another level, when evidence of Australian–American collaboration had thinned, it was a subliminal reminder to the Australian people that the government had been able to manage alliance relationships when it counted. Too much should not be claimed for this, because, as the 1949 election result demonstrates, the Labor Party was making heavy weather of the argument. But for Arthur Calwell—an influential figure in Labor circles who had the satisfaction

---

27 House of Representatives, *Hansard*, 6 October 1948, pp. 1295–304.
28 'Rare fish and birds found at Arnhem Land', *The Canberra Times*, 1 October 1948, p. 4, viewed 21 October 2010, <http://nla.gov.au/nla.news-article2768612>
29 Kiernan, *Calwell*, p. 114.

of seeing five other government departments support the Expedition—it reinforced his confidence that his side of politics could handle an emerging core element of Australian national security policy. A Labor government would be a reliable American ally in troubled times and could be perceived as such by the Australian electorate.

A Meeting of Minds

The delightful and extensive correspondence made available to me by Martin Thomas shows that Arthur Calwell and Frank Setzler wrote to each other for more than a decade after the Expedition's completion. 'Dr Setzler' in the early correspondence rapidly became 'Cousin Frank', and 'Mr Calwell', 'Cousin Arthur'. Much of the interchange contained reference to personal family matters. Of more interest to a wider audience was the equally extensive interchange of political information for use and circulation (mostly) to a wider audience. In it, Calwell—in the 1950s an even more powerful figure in ALP circles than he had been in the 1940s—revealed a deal of his thinking on foreign policy matters in line with his readier adjustment to the Cold War ambience referred to earlier.

For example, in a letter of 23 July 1951, after the 1951 election, Chifley's death and Calwell's accession to the deputy leadership, Calwell wrote:

> Since your letter arrived the Korean War has been halted by truce talks, while MacArthur's dismissal created almost as great a sensation in this country as it did in America, and the after effects are still being felt. The Persian oil crisis has come and, whilst not yet over, I doubt if it will be the starting point of the third World War. On the whole it looks as if there will be no war in Europe this year. If we get past August and September, there should be no major conflict before August or September of 1952, if at all. And then by 1953, the United States will be so powerful, and the allied western democracies will be helped by her to become much more powerful than they are today, that World War III may be avoided for a considerable period, if not altogether.[30]

The letters are an authentic Cold War correspondence between two liberal anti-communists. Neither is in doubt about the necessity of American power, nor of Australia's alignment with it. Both are fearful that each manifestation of conflict might lead to a wider war but hope wisdom will prevail. They are classic 'containment' advocates in a debate that at the time revolved around whether a more aggressive strategy should be pursued against the Soviet Union. They share the Australian sense of its unique isolation and vulnerability in a

---

30   Calwell to Setzler, 23 July 1951.

culturally alien and potentially hostile Asian environment. Both hope for an ALP victory in the various elections in the period. Both are confident that such an event will not change Australia's alignment but will temper necessary anti-communism with social justice. Both are alive to democratically debilitating paranoia in the fraught Cold War ideological environment.

A few examples of the interchange highlight these perspectives, such as Frank Setzler's letter to Calwell of 13 April 1954:

> It would seem we cannot expect the world to be without a serious crisis. First Korea and now Indo-China. To me the latter is more serious. Moreover, the spreading Red tide comes closer to my adopted land. Sometime, somewhere we must call a halt and build a wall of Christian faith that cannot be penetrated, and more powerful than the iron curtain.

Arthur, however, is the man for the job. Setzler replied: 'With you at the helm I shall feel more secure. Perhaps history will repeat itself as it did with the Japs, when our combined efforts stopped them at the threshold.'[31]

When Calwell replied to that letter, written before the 1954 election, he had to report the disappointment of electoral defeat, despite the ALP obtaining a majority of votes. His response to Setzler's foreign policy concerns reflected the identified themes:

> We are wondering what is going to happen at Geneva and whether the world is moving towards peace or war. In this part of the Pacific, surrounded by a thousand million Asians within twenty-four hours flying time of our shores, we do not feel exactly happy about the future.[32]

Calwell was referring to discussions on the French exit from Indochina.

By 1954–55, Arthur Calwell, never an admirer of Evatt, had become seriously concerned about his judgment. Evatt's handling of the Petrov affair and his role in the Labor split at the Hobart conference of the ALP enraged him. Apart from its effects on party unity, Calwell feared Evatt was permitting the ALP to be portrayed as unreliable in a Cold War context. As letters and clippings were exchanged on these matters, however, and with Calwell confident of Setzler's discretion, they did not allow foolishness on the left to blind them to paranoia on the right.

Setzler, writing on 17 June 1954, thanking Calwell for parcels of newspaper clippings on the Petrov affair and detailing Calwell's criticism of Evatt, replied:

---

31 Setzler to Calwell, 13 April 1954.
32 Calwell to Setzler, 2 June 1954.

I could well imagine the excitement in Darwin and clearly picture every action that was made, even to the excellent view Mrs Petrov would have had from Government House. I marvel at the more conservative method of handling such a case as in contrast to what might happen here. Our McCarthy Army case relating to hypothetical 'commies' is due to go off the television air today. Such a thing would only happen here. Now the housewives can get back to their chores.[33]

Calwell's response on 17 December continued the theme of middle-of-the-road anti-communism. Referring to the infamous Army—McCarthy hearings of 1954, Calwell observed with pleasure that McCarthy is 'well on the way to oblivion after the Senator got a flea in his ear from his colleagues in the Senate, and one that he was well entitled to expect'.[34]

Setzler's reply confirmed his hopes for a liberal anti-communist stance: 'I am pleased you have made a definite stand with regard to the Leader. If men like yourself can control future governments, the spread of Communism will be checked and perhaps territorially reduced.'[35]

Calwell's high hopes for government earlier in the decade had now receded. He could not see victory possible without a return to the ALP of those who supported the anti-communist Democratic Labor Party, the offshoot born of the tumultuous Hobart conference in 1955. He existed in a state of internecine cold war with Evatt until the latter's retirement in 1960, when Calwell replaced him.

Setzler could at last write: 'It has taken several years but I have never lost faith in your ability to lead the party. Now we must await your next general election so that you can visit the U.S.A as the next Prime Minister.' Setzler enclosed an article on Australia from *Time* magazine and suggested that many of 'the social advances seem to be the very things you were advocating twelve years ago. I shall always remember how they criticised you when you advocated an independent Australian passport. Everyone should thank you for your farsighted immigration program.'[36]

Setzler was thoroughly aware that the Arnhem Land Expedition was potentially embroiled in Australian domestic politics in a Cold War context. As he became aware of the detail of Australian politics, he hoped it would advance the position of that strand of liberal anti-communist sentiment he espoused. He hoped that as publications emerged—in particular, the Expedition reports—they would advance the pro-American credentials of the man who had launched it. As he

---

33   Setzler to Calwell, 17 June 1954.
34   Calwell to Setzler, 17 December 1954.
35   Setzler to Calwell, 19 April 1955.
36   Setzler to Calwell, 11 April 1960.

wrote to Calwell in 1955, '[a]ll of us are anxiously awaiting the publication of the Arnhem Land Expedition reports. Their timely publication should bring credit to the 1948 leaders of the Party. Who knows, their publication may even assist in a future election.'[37]

The Expedition of course should be viewed primarily in the context of its scientific, anthropological and archaeological achievements. To a contemporary generation, its political value is most heavily weighted to an understanding of historical aspects of Indigenous issues. Nevertheless, it throws light on the complexities of the internal debate at the time on Australia's national security policy. The Expedition was a product of contemporary views on nation building and an effort to continue and deepen the wartime engagement with the United States, pushing Australia beyond the boundaries of a British Empire paradigm. As such, however, it was inevitably drawn into what was increasingly the predominant issue in Australia's political debate: the Cold War.

---

37   Setzler to Calwell, 19 April 1955.

4. A Robinson Crusoe in Arnhem Land: Howell Walker, *National Geographic* and the Arnhem Land Expedition of 1948

Mark Collins Jenkins

'A tall, dark, handsome stranger has come into my life—and gone', a California newspaperman once jocularly wrote in the early 1950s. 'Now what nationality would you say that man was?' he reported a friend of his asking.[1]

That cultured accent, that refined deportment, and those Cary Grant good looks that suggested a citizen of the world belonged to a correspondent named Harrison Howell Walker, who happened to be travelling in California on a *National Geographic* magazine assignment. Yet the newspaperman's reaction was scarcely unique, for Walker left the same impression on nearly everyone he met. In December 1953, for instance, he and a *Geographic* colleague were covering the royal visit of Queen Elizabeth II to Fiji and Tonga. In Fiji, the members of the press were all shacked up in one large tent. One morning, Eliot Elisofon of *Life* magazine awoke, pushed back his mosquito netting, looked around him, and declared, 'Well, here we are, all 21 of us—19 journalists and two gentlemen from the Geographic.'[2]

He might have been the *National Geographic*'s 'parfit gentil Knight', as one Chaucerian-minded colleague dubbed him, but when Howell Walker strolled back into the camp of the American–Australian Scientific Expedition to Arnhem Land after having been 'lost' for days in the Northern Territory's stormy Gulf of Carpentaria, he became its 'intrepidest' explorer as well. Both gentleman and adventurer, he was the epitome of the *Geographic*'s foreign editorial staff— those dexterous individuals who, as representatives of a non-partisan scientific and educational organisation, were in journalism but not of it. Unaided, each could write articles, take still pictures, and make a 16 mm motion picture while wandering about the world, though always following the high road.

---

1 Clippings: 'Walker, Howell', Library News Collection, National Geographic Society Library, Washington, DC.
2 Hunter, C. 2003, 'Howell Walker', *National Geographic TimeLine Biography*, National Geographic Archives, Washington, DC.

No examination of the legacies of the 1948 Arnhem Land Expedition would be complete without a glance at the role played by the *National Geographic* and its intrepid representative. Founded in 1888 to 'increase and diffuse geographic knowledge', the National Geographic Society had by the 1940s become a dignified, almost hallowed, and thoroughly American institution, its famous oak-and-laurel trimmed magazine sent each month to more than one million members—90 per cent of whom lived in the United States. Behind the Arnhem Land Expedition one might glimpse how it was that the National Geographic Society of that era went about its business, how it construed its mission as both a sponsor of science and a populariser of 'humanised geography', and how central was the role of photography in its activities. Howell Walker, the society's roving writer-photographer, strayed through Arnhem Land constrained on the one hand by the demands of popular Kodachrome travelogues, whether printed or projected, and on the other by America's hunger for images of the faraway and exotic. 'In an unruffled and Princetonian way', the California newspaperman continued, 'Walker investigated and reported on far-off, rugged places, in the National Geographic manner'.

Figure 4.1 Howell Walker from the National Geographic Society photographing at Umbakumba, 1948

Photograph by Charles P. Mountford. By permission of the State Library of South Australia. PRG487/1/2/209/1.

Figure 4.2 Howell Walker during the Arnhem Land Expedition, 1948

Photograph by Charles P. Mountford. By permission of the State Library of South Australia. PRG1218/34/2859.

*

That manner was made not born. What was born that drizzly winter night in January 1888 in the old Cosmos Club one block from the White House was but another scientific and professional association to be caught up in the social whirl of late nineteenth-century Washington, DC. It was tentatively called the 'Society of Geography', and its founders voted to call themselves the National Geographic Society because, first, an American Geographical Society had already existed in New York since 1851, and second, it aspired to be not merely a local, Washington-based society, but to attract members from all over the United States.

Yet it was undeniably local and thoroughly professional. The majority of its 33 founders were government scientists working for such great and growing Washington-based bureaus as the US Geological Survey and the US Coast and Geodetic Survey; tellingly, only one was a journalist. But Washington for the most part was only their winter home. These geologists and mapmakers spent their summers in the field, dispersed all over the continent, converging back upon the capital each autumn to write their reports, dispose of their collections, and of course socialise with one another through the city's numerous clubs and organisations. They might have worked for competing and sometimes mutually hostile agencies, but they were, in their own way, companions in geography, for that was the metier they shared.

If not yet a national institution, the society quickly became a Washington one. It was no Smithsonian, of course; rather it resembled a local history society or garden club. It had no such thing as paid staff or a permanent headquarters. Its officers were elected by the membership at large and worked on society matters in their free time. The organisation was social as well as professional; it held popular annual field trips to such nearby points of geographical interest as Civil War battlefields. It threw grand parties and receptions honouring visiting explorers and dignitaries. It mounted a lecture program, held in various venues in the city each winter, although the 'excessive use of picture and anecdote', as one society officer in the 1890s declaimed, 'is discouraged'.[3] Such bleakly austere addresses were then printed in a slim, brown-backed journal of proceedings, issued sometimes quarterly, sometimes irregularly, and finally monthly, called the *National Geographic* magazine. Often on such laudable topics as orogeny, physiography or hydrology, these articles were sometimes so impenetrably dense that they were read only by experts—'diffusing geographic knowledge', as one wag put it, 'among those who already had it and scaring off the rest'.[4]

The upshot was that after its first president and chief patron, Gardiner Greene Hubbard, died in December 1897, the fledgling National Geographic Society found itself teetering on the brink of bankruptcy. The board, casting around for his replacement, persuaded Hubbard's son-in-law, who did not want the job, to take it anyway. His name was Alexander Graham Bell.

In the five years (1898–1903) that the famous inventor of the telephone was President of the National Geographic Society, he planted the seeds of a new conception of it—one that ultimately steered it in a direction perhaps radically different from its founders' original vision. Though he virtually abandoned the

---

3 Bryan, C. D. B. 1987, *The National Geographic Society: 100 years of adventure and discovery*, Harry N. Abrams, New York, p. 33.
4 Ibid, p. 28.

society during his first year in the post, the corpulent, insatiably curious Bell eventually girded up his substantial loins and applied himself to the task of making the society successful.

In order to make the National Geographic Society truly national, he concluded, he had to expand its base of membership. According to Bell—who was no geographer—in order to swell its membership ranks, the society would have to reach beyond its narrow circle of professional geographers and invite ordinary people to enlist on its rolls. The way to do that was precisely through the excessive use of picture and anecdote. And the vehicle for that should be the *National Geographic* magazine, made so bright and engaging and inviting that many people should find it irresistible; however—and this was a key part of the strategy—it could be obtained only through membership in the National Geographic Society, of which it was the official journal. But unlike the Smithsonian Institution, for instance, which grew out of a substantial bequest to 'increase and diffuse knowledge' and which first operated as a research institution, then as a series of museums (and only in the mid-twentieth century invited a popular membership through its magazine), the National Geographic Society was born without a cent to its name.

What happened next is part of magazine publishing legend. In 1899, Bell hired the society's first full-time employee—paid out of his own pocket—to help put his ideas into action. Twenty-three-year-old Gilbert Hovey Grosvenor had been courting Bell's daughter. He would also prove to be an editor of genius. Spurred by Bell's ideas, he swiftly transformed the society's dowdy journal into a magazine of wide appeal by publishing as many photographs of exotic corners of the globe as he could lay his hands on. His pictorial eye had been sharpened early in life, for he had been born and reared in Constantinople. In the last quarter of the nineteenth century, the capital of the Ottoman Empire was a crossroad for every picturesque tribe in the Near East—at least as they surely appeared to stiff dyed-in-the-wool New Englanders such as the Grosvenors. Moreover, Grosvenor adopted colour photography at an early stage in its development, when it was still a demanding technique mastered only by a few practitioners. It was extremely expensive to engrave and print in magazines, and even then the results were hardly convincing. Nevertheless, Grosvenor stuck with it. Through colour, he would open a window on the world for his members, and colour photography soon became the signature of *National Geographic*.

He was successful almost certainly beyond his wildest dreams. If Bell was the architect of today's National Geographic Society, as has been said, Grosvenor was its master builder. He laboured away at it for more than half a century (from 1899 until 1954), watching the membership grow from something less than 1000 when he first arrived, to half a million by 1916, and to more than one million by the 1920s—the 'first million', as a tagline in the magazine used to put it, for Grosvenor was not only a born editor but a born promoter, too.

Geography at the society thus became geography broadly construed—'the world and all that is in it', in Bell's famous phrase. That meant plants and animals joined the long parade of quaintly costumed humanity, marching, creeping, swimming or flying through the magazine's pages. Though it changed the character of the institution forever—gone were the articles on orogeny or hydrology; while such relentless popularisation drove off many of the academic or professionally oriented original members—it did allow, ironically, a fuller realisation of the stated mission to 'increase and diffuse' geographic knowledge. That seemed conventional enough. The Smithsonian, after all, was founded for the 'increase and diffusion of knowledge' and the Carnegie Institution of Washington for the 'increase and diffusion of knowledge among men'. Yet by swelling the ranks of the National Geographic Society with middle-class members who dreamed of faraway places and pored over the magazine's pictures of the exotic 'Other', Grosvenor was able to fill the organisation's coffers to overflowing in a remarkably short time. This allowed it to start sponsoring expeditions of exploration and discovery.

Although the society had been lending its name to such field expeditions since 1890, that was about all it lent; it had not a dollar to spare. By 1906, however, it had amassed enough funds to put its money where only its seal had previously been. Its first such expedition was Robert E. Peary's to the North Pole. Soon the society was supporting expeditions large and small to the far corners of the New World—from Alaska's Valley of Ten Thousand Smokes to the fabulous ruins of Machu Picchu in Peru. Often it teamed up with the Smithsonian Institution—excavating the ruins of Chaco Canyon in New Mexico during the 1920s and virtually uncovering the vanished Olmec civilisation in tropical Mexico during the 1930s and 1940s. A pattern arose out of such partnerships: the Smithsonian, say, or the American Museum of Natural History in New York, or Yale University would get the physical collections, while the *National Geographic* would get the pictures and first publication rights. The engine that drove the society—the two-piston beat of increase and diffusion—was finally operating at maximum efficiency. Not only was the incredible success of *National Geographic*'s middlebrow presentation of the world funding its scientific expeditions, those expeditions were chosen by the society's Research Committee with one eye on their appeal to their far-flung membership. An appealing expedition would then provide ample fodder for the magazine, thus closing the feedback loop.

Grosvenor might have been a master builder, but he had Edwardian notions of propriety. Though many of the contributors on whom he depended might never be welcome into a middle-class parlour, he needed his magazine to become a fixture there. So as he built the National Geographic Society into the organisation we still recognise today, he cultivated dignity and respectability and projected that image not just to the membership but also to the wider world. And when about 1915, tired of chasing down articles and pictures from a shifting and sometimes unreliable cast of diplomats, military men, wealthy travellers and gadabout rogues, he decided to build his own staff, he demanded of them gentlemanly behaviour above all. Those staff men who worked abroad were the 'foreign service' of the society, representing its interests and spreading its good name around the globe.

Thus was made that National Geographic 'manner'. By the 1930s, it was embodied in stone and marble in another 'manor': the society's Washington, DC, headquarters. Located only six blocks from the White House, it had Italian Renaissance detailing, panelled offices, and segregated dining rooms—the women in one, the men in the other—because it was feared the men might tell off-colour jokes in the presence of the ladies. Those ladies had to wear white gloves, and those gentlemen could not walk down the hall without donning their jackets. Ties, needless to say, were obligatory.

Yet it was a fitting headquarters for an institution that could now pride itself on having achieved a venerable status. With more than one million members, the National Geographic Society billed itself as the 'largest scientific and educational organization in the world'. Its magazine was found in every school and doctor's office in the United States. Always referred to with a capital 'M' within those hallowed halls, the magazine, too, enshrined that sense of dignity on the one hand and exotic adventure on the other. Both were hinted at in the classic oak-leaf cover that identified it from 1910 to the end of the 1950s. The border of oak leaves and acorns, it was said, represented the origins and sturdy growth of the society; the garland of laurel at the top was the traditional crown of achievement in the arts. The hemispheres—northern, southern, eastern and western—at the cardinal points suggested that the contents were indeed constrained only by 'the world and all that was in it'.[5]

So established in the hearts of its members was this design that when in 1959 photographs first erupted onto the cover, an Englishman was reported to have written: 'If God had intended a picture on the cover of the *National Geographic*, he would have put one there in the first place.'[6]

---

5   Jenkins, M. C. 1999, 'Birth of a classic: the 1910 oak-and-laurel cover', *National Geographic TimeLine*, National Geographic Archives, Washington, DC.
6   Jenkins, M. C. 2003, '1959: pictures erupt onto the cover', *National Geographic TimeLine*, National Geographic Archives, Washington, DC.

*

This, then, was the *National Geographic* that Howell Walker grew up with.

Born Harrison Howell Dodge Walker on 4 August 1910, he came from an old and established Georgia family on his father's side and a New York one on his mother's. He was educated at St Alban's School in Washington, DC, and the Berkshire School in Sheffield, Massachusetts, before enrolling at Princeton University, where he was a track star as well as a 1933 graduate in languages.[7]

While other members of his class went on to become captains of industry and leaders of finance, Walker opted instead to be a walkabout magazine correspondent—a professional globetrotter. Of course, he did not just stroll in and get the job. He was told when he first stepped into the *Geographic*'s marble foyer to go away, he had no experience.

So, he went away and got some, spending the better part of the next three years travelling around the world. And as he wandered he wrote, occasionally sending material back to *National Geographic*. The editors apparently liked what they saw. They conferred with the chief of the photo lab, who declared that the young man might be made into a passable professional photographer. Persistence paid off. On 2 March 1936, Howell Walker, aged twenty-five, was hired on a three-month trial basis in the photo lab, the place where all aspiring young writer/photographers started—wearing a smock with his name embroidered over the left-hand pocket, mixing chemicals in earthenware crocks.

He quickly proved himself in the field, though, and soon joined that elite corps of *National Geographic* 'triple threats', as they were called: those foreign editorial staff men—and they were all men at this time—who could take the pictures, write the story, and make the 16 mm travelogue film for the society's popular lecture series. Walker might have made a career producing such late 1930s period pieces as his early 'Adirondack idyls' and 'Gentle folk settle stern Saguenay' (alliteration being much favoured at the time), were it not for World War II. In early 1941, he was sent to cover the war effort in Australia; it was the luck of the draw as it might just as easily have been Greenland, where one of his colleagues was posted. The next five years proved to be the most pivotal of his life.

Initially, Walker was the well-behaved correspondent, writing articles such as 'The making of an Anzac' and 'Life in dauntless Darwin' for the magazine. Soon, he grew restless, and began peppering his dispatches with the phrase 'big yellow full moon' so as to goad the censors; they would always delete it, despite

---

7   Clippings: 'Walker, Howell', Library News Collection, National Geographic Society Library; and Z News Service Biographies: Walker, Howell, 38-1.153, National Geographic Archives.

the fact that the same big yellow full moon shone on the Japanese as it did on the Allies.[8] Finally, after a month's tour with US Army Air Forces, he joined up. In April 1943, in Brisbane, he was commissioned a second lieutenant, serving thereafter as an intelligence officer with the Fifth US Air Force from Australia to New Guinea and the Philippines, eventually rising to the rank of captain.

The war was not his only Australian complication. Sheila Gordon Anderson was the daughter of a prominent Sydney businessman and retired brigadier general. Howell met her in 1942, and before the year was out they were married. After the war he brought his bride to Washington and resumed his life as a *National Geographic* roving correspondent. Only now he had a beat. Whereas the magazine already had its 'Latin America man' and 'Middle East man', Howell now became its 'Australia man'. And it was not long before he returned Down Under.

The war had not yet ended when Charles Mountford toured the United States, lecturing and showing his films on Aboriginal life. Grosvenor and his editors found the films enchanting and thought that the Australian himself made an engaging figure. With unerring instinct, they realised their broad membership would also find his work appealing, and the upshot was that they invited Mountford to apply for a National Geographic Society research grant. Expeditions might have many beginnings, but that was certainly an important one for what became the Arnhem Land Expedition. Furthermore, the Secretary of the Smithsonian Institution, Alexander Wetmore, who happened to be a corresponding member of the Royal Australasian Ornithologists Union, was also a long-serving member of the National Geographic Society's board of trustees and a pillar of its Research Committee. That cosy relationship helped ensure joint backing of the proposed expedition. The Smithsonian would get its share of the collections, while the *National Geographic* would get the pictures. That meant sending Howell Walker back to Australia.

Of the tonnes of equipment the American Expedition members brought, Walker's share—except for the better part of 8 km of colour film—was low for the most part. Cases of still film and a battery of cameras—including large-format Linhofs and Graflexes, medium-format Rolleiflexes, and the 35 mm Leicas that the magazine used almost exclusively for colour—were the common kit of the era.[9] Peter Bassett-Smith, Mountford's filmmaker, used the popular Bolex, but Walker sported the big Kodak Ciné-Special movie camera. Last but not least, of course, he brought a portable typewriter.

---

8   Z News Service Biographies: Walker, Howell, 38-1.153, National Geographic Archives.
9   Jenkins, M. C. 2008, 'Luis Marden', in *Odysseys and Photographs: Four* National Geographic *field men*, National Geographic Society, Washington, DC, pp. 78–83. For details about various editorial demands and constraints on field photographers, I am indebted to personal conversations with the late Luis Marden.

With his typewriter, Walker filed dispatches back to the office whenever he could. But news of Expedition mishaps—not all of it accurate—filtered out even when he could not. 'Five D.C. scientists reported marooned on primitive isle' ran the headline of the 21 April 1948 *Washington Post*, when the rains and floods on Groote Eylandt were at their worst.[10] The only problem was, three of those five—David Johnson, Herbert Deignan and Howell Walker—were nowhere near Groote Eylandt; they were instead marooned on the 200-tonne supply ship, the *Phoenix*, stranded on a reef.

Eventually, they were rescued, of course, and, a few months later, after the Expedition had moved on to Darwin, Walker remained behind on Groote Eylandt to catch up on photography. In August, he clambered aboard the ketch *Wanderer II*, owned by the superintendent of Umbakumba Aboriginal Settlement, Fred Gray—and promptly went missing again. A search and rescue mission by the Royal Australian Air Force finally located *Wanderer II* holed up in an obscure harbour due to rough seas. That also landed on the front page of the Washington papers. 'I feel genuinely sorry and not a little sheepish about the reported-missing incidents', Walker wrote back to headquarters.[11] But in those marble halls, unknown to him, he was already being dubbed the 'intrepidest explorer' because he had been twice listed as missing. No other *Geographic* man, it seems, had gone missing more than once.[12]

Wherever and whenever he did manage to catch up with the Expedition, Walker of course had plenty of work to do. Editors had 'shot lists' the photographers were supposed to follow. Though the bulk of the photography was in black and white, there were 'establishing shots', for instance, which needed to be saturated with what was called 'scenic colour'. A number of pictures were taken of the camp at Oenpelli (now Gunbalanya), for instance. Clearly, a morning was given over to posing for photographs. Move a few crates around, repose the people, make the cook wear his get-up, and switch over the Australian and American flags for a National Geographic Society flag that dwarfs them both combined—and you have the version the magazine published. Grosvenor never missed a chance to get that flag into the magazine—the brown stripe symbolised land, the green one sea, and the blue one sky, meaning the 'world and all that is in it'—because it served to remind the members that here was their society hard at work.

Such colour pictures were often posed not so much because imaginations were stilted as because early Kodachrome was slow: it had an ASA rating of eight (modern films and digital cameras are often at least ten times as fast). Although

---

10 Z News Service Expeditions: Australia Northern Territory Arnhem Land, 38-2.
11 Ibid.
12 Hunter, 'Howell Walker'.

Walker could and did take hand-held action shots, the slow film often meant he put the 35 mm Leicas on tripods in order to ensure the sharp exposures necessary for proper colour engraving—always a tricky business at this time. That in turn necessitated set-ups or at least a pause in the action.

The dependence on Kodachrome imposed another constraint—this one more stylistic than technical. The *National Geographic*'s editors also wanted landscape shots—sometimes derided as 'postcard views'—but the age of mass travel had yet to dawn and most Americans wanted to see what faraway places looked like. Grosvenor and the editors, however, demanded that people appear in the scene to give scale to geography. They even called it 'humanised geography'. Those people were usually garbed in red—red shirts, red scarves, red sweaters—because when Kodachrome was first released in the mid-1930s, it was believed that the inclusion of some red in a picture helped make colours 'pop'. That, unfortunately, might have been taken to extremes at the *Geographic*, where photographers were instructed to carry red scarves and sweaters in their kit, giving rise to what later was sneeringly called the 'red-shirt school of photography'. Thankfully, Walker must have left those red scarves and sweaters behind, for they would have been decidedly out of place in 'Stone Age' Arnhem Land.

It was said that the 'Geographic man' always travelled first class, stayed in the finest hotels, and, because he was expected to be a gentleman, always carried a black tie.[13] No doubt Walker had a twinkle in his eye when he set up the shot eventually printed on page 777 of 'Exploring Stone Age Arnhem Land', the major article on the Expedition, published in December 1949. There, for American eyes, was the *Geographic* gentleman in distant Australia, under the lee of Injalak Hill near Oenpelli. 'A Robinson Crusoe in Arnhem Land', states the caption. And the image does have an idyllically self-reliant quality. There is Walker, shirtless, at work in his improvised alfresco office; there is his rustic bed, his rolled-up mosquito net, his satchel, his portable typewriter, his rigged-up lamp. There is even some rock art to gaze at on the ledge above him. In this outdoor bedroom, with the rains long past, Walker could fall asleep each night with the Southern Cross etched on his fluttering eyelids.

To his colleagues back at headquarters, however, it was an image that evoked freedom—not only freedom from the strictures of society, but from those of one society in particular. At the clean-cut *National Geographic*, where all the ladies wore white gloves and even moustaches were frowned upon, here was its Cary Grant: Howell Walker, with a beard.

---

13 Jenkins, 'Luis Marden', pp. 78–83.

Of course he was out on expedition. But it is hard to imagine today, when beards are commonplace, how much attention they once attracted. The caption writers of the day could never resist pointing out, tiresomely, the deficiencies of barbering in faraway places. The picture was even used in an advertising appeal a year or so later. Under the title 'Have Typewriter, Have Traveled', the circular stated that eight months in Arnhem Land 'can't help but bring out a flair for improvisation in anybody'.[14]

Even today, for those few people at the National Geographic Society who still recognise the name Howell Walker, it is this image that comes to mind.

In subsequent years, Walker often returned to Australia. In 1954, he journeyed to Melville Island with Mountford in a kind of sequel to the Arnhem Land Expedition. Before his retirement in 1975, he wrote at least five more *National Geographic* stories on various Australian topics. By then, of course, times had changed at the society. Old Dr Gilbert H. Grosvenor had retired in 1954, after an impressive half-century at the helm. He was eventually succeeded, in 1957, by his son, the energetic Melville Bell Grosvenor, who promptly propelled the staid National Geographic Society in a multitude of exciting new directions. Throughout the golden years of the 1960s and 1970s—the era of Louis Leakey and Jane Goodall and Jacques Cousteau—the society's books and atlases and globes, and above all television documentaries, increasingly supplemented the *National Geographic* magazine in the public eye. Furthermore, an age of specialisation had set in. Gone were the days when the magazine depended on a foreign editorial staff composed of adroit 'triple threat' men who could do a little of everything in the field and do it reasonably well. Writers now became full-time writers and a corps of young Nikon-toting photojournalists—benefiting from faster films and eschewing posed set-ups, and including talented women—displaced the Leica-loving gentlemen of the previous generation. Howell Walker—his hair gone silver—ended his *Geographic* days in a cosy and decidedly conventional office, where behind his typewriter he mostly edited other people's manuscripts. Nevertheless, in a poll among the secretaries, he was still voted 'the man with whom they would most like to be stranded on a desert island'.[15]

He must have left them disappointed, because after he did retire, he and Sheila settled permanently in Australia, spending the last two decades of their lives together in an art-filled home in Woollahra, Sydney. Old friends who visited returned with the report that, before he died at the age of ninety-two on 26 January 2003, Howell Walker, once the epitome of the *Geographic* gentleman, was sporting a bushy white beard.

---

14   Z News Service Expeditions.
15   Hunter, 'Howell Walker'.

Acknowledgments

The author wishes to thank his former colleagues Renee Braden, manager of the National Geographic's Archives and Special Collections, and Cathy Hunter, chief archivist, for help and assistance.

5. Birds on the Wire: Wild sound, informal speech and the emergence of the radio documentary

Tony MacGregor

Sound Effect (SFX): The sound of a needle being placed into the groove of an old and worn 78 rpm disc. A low-level rumble, and the hiss and scratch of surface noise, and then the sound of birds—exotic whistles and cluckings, a cacophony of magpie geese and plovers and a dozen species besides.

Voice, Sound, Context

On 18 January 1949, on the *Australian Walkabout* program, the national service of the Australian Broadcasting Commission (now Corporation; ABC) broadcast a radio documentary feature on the American–Australian Scientific Expedition to Arnhem Land. The title might have lacked imagination—it was called 'Expedition to Arnhem Land'—but it marked a critical moment in Australian media history, and an informed audition of this all-but-forgotten 'text' allows us to hear something of the way in which the Expedition was culturally located in postwar Australia.[1] Most importantly (for this writer), it allows us to see and hear how a significant cultural actor of the day, the journalist Colin Simpson, grappled not only with the issues or 'problems' thrown up by the Expedition and his role in reporting it (not the least of these being the representation of Aboriginal culture), but also how an independent writer or journalist might position himself in relation to the ABC as a state-owned public cultural institution at a moment when those relationships were very much in active negotiation. In particular, this chapter explores the uneasy and, at the time, ill-defined relationships between writing and recording, between 'free' and written speech, and between the voice and other sound, in reporting and documenting events.

In this context, the 'wild sounds'—those being the sounds of the environment (both natural and human) recorded and incorporated into this documentary by Simpson—should be read as signal moments in Australian media history. With the exception of some extraordinary war reporting in the preceding

---

1 This was a repeat broadcast. The first took place on 30 November 1948.

five years, sounds such as the recording labelled 'Bird life on a swamp on [sic] Arnhem Land 1948', the sound effect or 'SFX' invoked in the opening to this chapter (and referred to hereafter as 'Bird life'), had rarely been included in a documentary feature as 'texts'—as syntactical elements in a narrative—let alone as autonomous sonic objects. While today a sound recordist (working with a film crew, say) will refer to the ambient environmental sound that must be recorded on site after an interview or dialogue has been recorded as 'wild sound', in this discussion a more critically inflected idea is at play, as evoked by the radio-maker and sound studies scholar Virginia Madsen in her essay 'The call of the wild':

> Sounds seem to rise up out of the depths and chaos of noise, mysteriously calling, summoning us to respond. Sound is a paradox. It is both *effect* and *fact*, both a virtuality (in the sense of a force) and an actuality—the consequence of movement in space; in an atmosphere, a milieu; of a source. Source and milieu cannot be separated…The being of sounds—their coming into presence—leads us to their mystery, their ability to act as marked figures within the noise of acoustic space, while at the same time appearing as if they are free of this space—purified, disembodied and metaphysical. Sound is, by nature, a detaching and transforming event, a mix between figure and ground, a re-sounding which always implies a medium: a 'flux in which figure and ground rub up against and transform each other' [as Marshall and Eric McLuhan described it].[2]

Madsen's discussion of the 'virtuality' of recorded 'wild sound' is founded in a notion of fidelity that would not be achievable for a good 10 or 15 years after the 'Bird life' recording. So the audio documentation described here was made on the cusp of these developments, and is all the more important as a consequence. Their resonance, if you like, goes well beyond their indexical functionality.

In 1949, the radio 'documentary feature' was a novel formal category. Scripted 'talks' and various forms of radio drama had been core elements of ABC programming almost from the inception of the commission in 1932.[3] But the 'documentary feature'—particularly the type of program discussed here, involving recordings made in the field—was, in 1948, an almost new category. Indeed, it was only that year that a separate Features Department had been established within the ABC. The *Australian Walkabout* series was inaugurated in 1947 by Colin Simpson.[4] Its defining quality was its reliance on facts; as the advertising explained, the program was 'Built upon Factual Happenings of

---

2 Madsen, V. 1999, 'The call of the wild', in M. Thomas (ed.), *Uncertain Ground: Essays between art and nature*, Art Gallery of New South Wales, Sydney, pp. 34–5.
3 For a comprehensive overview of the ABC's early development, see Inglis, K. 1983, *This is the ABC: The Australian Broadcasting Commission 1932–83*, Melbourne University Press, Carlton, Vic.
4 Ibid., p. 164.

Yesterday and To-day'.[5] While 'Expedition to Arnhem Land' was researched and presented by Simpson, the credit of producer went to John Thompson, the other pioneering figure in the development of 'the feature'. Simpson recorded actuality for the program when he spent a fortnight at the Oenpelli (now Gunbalanya) base camp of the Expedition in late September and early October 1948.[6] Simpson was accompanied on his Arnhem Land foray by Ray Giles, a sound engineer employed by the Postmaster General's Department (PMG), which, until 1964, provided technical services to the ABC.

Figure 5.1 Recording session at Oenpelli (now Gunbalanya). Colin Simpson (far right), Raymond Giles and five unidentified men around the Pyrox Wire Recorder, 1948

Photograph by Howell Walker. By permission of the National Library of Australia. NLA MS5253, Box 99, Bag B.

---

5 Advertisement, *ABC Weekly* [Sydney], 27 November 1948, p. 14.
6 Elsewhere in this volume, Barwick and Marett and Garde draw upon the work of Simpson and the material he gathered in Arnhem Land working with Ray Giles.

An Effect

Spinning at 78 rpm, 'Bird life on a swamp on Arnhem Land 1948' is a bakelite rendering of an acoustic event, previously recorded onto a strand of magnetised steel wire. Simultaneously, it is an object of nostalgia and its opposite: an irruption of pure noise, a moment of lived experience. In *play* (spinning), it stands as a lacuna of wild sound, a moment of *then* opening onto the *now*, almost (but not quite) managing to be the moment it claims for itself. But listening carefully beyond the birds caught on the wire, we might also discern not simply the fleeting 'being something' of another place and another time, but also a media practice in transition.

The 'Bird life' recording is one of the many field recordings made by Giles under Simpson's direction whilst the duo was 'up north', only three of which were of environmental sound. The remainder (23 'sides' of 78 rpm discs) were of Indigenous music and song. Elsewhere in this volume, Allan Marret and Linda Barwick address the music recordings and Murray Garde analyses the ceremony in detail. My concern is with the non-music recordings (including the broadcast feature itself), which I think of as a kind of archaeological site. Digging down, we might be able to show, or at lest infer, the critical significance of these recordings in Australian media and cultural history.

Through close audition of this recording—a *sounding*, if you like, to borrow a metaphor from marine navigation—we might perform a type of cultural mapping. In so doing, we can gain insight into a largely unexamined moment—the moment when an emerging media technology enabled the voice to displace the authority of the written word in broadcast media. Inter alia, I want to locate that moment biographically, and to reflect on some ideas about the national broadcaster and the construction of national identity in relation to the 1948 Expedition.

I hope to demonstrate the extraordinary impact Arnhem Land had on Colin Simpson, who found in it a kind of 'souvenir' of a paradise lost—a memento from an Edenic landscape, which he understood to be at risk of vanishing. I also want to suggest that the recording might serve as a souvenir of another kind of loss: the loss of a writer's 'voice'. The recording marks the moment when the authenticity of reportage is guaranteed not by authority of the witnessing writer, but rather by his (or her) capacity to refer to the recording.

Setting Out/Coming Home

After his fortnight with the Expedition, Simpson went on to Melville Island, where he recorded a local ceremony, the Yoi, that formed the subject of another *Australian Walkabout* feature titled 'Island of Yoi', first broadcast on 4 January 1949—a fortnight before the repeat of the Arnhem Land program. Simpson later wrote *Adam in Ochre* (1951), a best-selling book based on these experiences, which covers much of the same territory as the radio feature and comments extensively upon the recording process.[7]

We thus have three documents to work between: the field recordings, the feature program, and the book. We can 'hear' Simpson's voice in each of its different registers—the voice of the independent writer and the voice of the contracted state broadcaster—and it is possible to trace the lines of authority accorded to voice, sound and written word. Through this triangulation of auditory and written texts, we can track the course of the recordings through the static of history.

Three copies of the complete set of recordings are known to exist: one is held by the University of Sydney, a second set is held by the Australian Institute of Aboriginal and Torres Strait Islander Studies (AIATSIS), and the third is kept in the Sound Effects Library of ABC Radio. They can be simultaneously regarded as objects of scholarly inquiry and research; as a cultural record; and as a set of working tools for the radio producer.

The distribution of the recordings into research collections alerts us to the ABC's self-consciousness as a state institution with expressly pedagogic and cultural responsibilities, created 'to develop a service to meet national needs and foster a national culture', an organisation that, in 1939 (after seven years of existence), could claim to have had 'beneficial influence upon Australian standards of thought'.[8] In the pages of the *ABC Weekly*, the Arnhem Land Expedition is discussed in terms of its scientific and national benefit. In addition to previewing the radio feature ('Scientists tell A.B.C. unit of curious findings in expedition to Arnhem Land'), there are several articles written by the members of the expedition detailing their activities.[9] The ABC is not simply documenting or reporting upon a scientific expedition, but participating in the process of collecting, discussing and archiving materials for further study.

---

7 Simpson also prepared a script for another feature, describing the performance of key elements of the Wubarr ceremony, which on the advice of A. P. Elkin was never produced and broadcast. See Garde in this volume.
8 Australian Broadcasting Commission (ABC) 1939, *The ABC Annual*, Australian Broadcasting Commission, Sydney, pp. 6–7.
9 *ABC Weekly*, 27 November 1948.

Going Walkabout

The first edition of *Australian Walkabout* went to air on 15 May 1947, two weeks prior to the inauguration of the ABC's independent news service on 1 June. A full-page advertisement for *Australian Walkabout* in the 21 June edition of *ABC Weekly* runs: 'Meet Old Pioneers…Hear Actual Voices of Australian Personalities…Hear Exciting Incidents from Australia's Past and Present.' In its publicity, the ABC describes 'Expedition to Arnhem Land' as 'the authentic story of the Mountford Expedition'.[10]

The claim to the authenticity and factuality of the ABC's feature programs was made repeatedly at this time—on air (in program presentation), in promotional material and in corporate reporting. Given the frequency with which 'authenticity' is invoked, it is difficult not to read into it some corporate anxiety as to the legitimacy of the claim. It might, however, also reflect the habits of Colin Simpson as a journalist best known for his previous role as editor of *Fact*, the weekly feature supplement of the Sydney *Sun* newspaper, in which role he had been instrumental in exposing the Ern Malley literary hoax in 1944—a fact that might be seen to add particular poignancy to Simpson's negotiation of 'authenticity'.[11]

The stated objective of *Australian Walkabout* was to portray 'the life and history of important Australian towns and districts against the background of national development'.[12] The ABC was at pains to assure listeners 'that the greatest care was taken to see that every detail was authentic, the material gathered at first hand by the special writers concerned'.[13] Before moving to briefly consider the meanings of 'authenticity' in this context, it is important to look at the program series in which this feature was broadcast.

Today the term 'walkabout' seems to be used only by 'outback' tour operators and in describing the brief meet-the-people street walks of visiting royalty. While it might well be the case that 'to go walkabout' has lost much of its 'racist or disparaging overtones', applied to Indigenous Australians today, it would seem at best archaic and inadvertently offensive.[14] In the 1940s and 1950s, it was a term that, despite its 'disparaging overtones', had significant cultural resonance. While describing the necessary peregrinations of Aborigines—to

---

10   *ABC Weekly*, 3 January 1949.
11   The story of the hoax was, fittingly, the subject of a 1959 radio documentary feature by John Thompson, in which Simpson appeared briefly. The full transcript can be found in *Jacket*: <http:jacketmagazine.com/17/ern-thom.html>
12   Australian Broadcasting Commission (ABC) 1948, *Annual Report*, Australian Broadcasting Commission, Sydney.
13   Ibid.
14   Wilde, W. H., Hooton, J. and Andrews, B. (eds) 1994, *The Oxford Companion to Australian Literature*, Oxford University Press, Melbourne, p. 780.

take part in ceremonial activity for instance—it carries with it the implication of unreliability, a casual attitude towards work and settlement. 'Walkabout' stands in contradistinction with settlement, with civilised life. Aborigines 'on walkabout' ceased to be stockmen or domestic help and became tribesmen and women—natives. While frequently invoked in this negative sense, it also implied the recognition of cultural difference: the recognition by white Australia that there were things that Aboriginal people did—and *had* to do—that 'we' did not understand. They were prepared to give up a job, reliable sources of food, the meagre comforts of the station settlement, to go off and do mysterious things: sorry business, men's business, women's business. 'Walkabout', then, hinted at a deeper way of knowing the country and its workings. The *Macquarie Dictionary* definition makes explicit the conflicts between white Australian culture and Aboriginal ways of knowing, describing walkabout 'as a period of wandering as a nomad, often as undertaken by Aborigines who feel the need to leave the place where they are in contact with white society, and return for spiritual refreshment to their traditional way of life'.[15]

'Going walkabout', then, was seen as an expression of authentic Aboriginal culture, albeit that aspect of Indigenous culture that prevented 'them' from ever really settling down and being like 'us'. And as an authentic reflection of Aboriginality, 'going walkabout' was never fully explicable. In its vernacular use by white Australia, the idea of 'going walkabout' has also acquired a set of seductive and subversive meanings derived from its application to the nomadic habits of Indigenous Australians. Loading up the station wagon with swag and billy, suburban man and his family leave the bitumen (and civilisation) and head off 'outback'. Several weeks or months later, our happy wanderers return from this unstructured journey into the interior more knowledgeable, more at home with the country and with themselves, 'spiritually refreshed'. So, while there were numerous cartoons that depicted shifty blacks slinking back from walkabout, the word was affixed as a title to books and films with the connotation of journeying beyond the civilised world, travelling overland into knowledge. The international success of C. P. Mountford's 1941 ethnographic documentary *Walkabout* provided the kudos and contacts that enabled him to assemble and lead the 1948 Expedition to Arnhem Land.[16]

In choosing to name their new program *Australian Walkabout*, Colin Simpson and his colleagues in the newly formed Features Unit would have been aware of the multiple meanings and iterations of the term then in circulation. Indeed, the full-page advertisement referred to earlier uses of the image of a swagman

---

15 *Macquarie Dictionary*, 1991, (Second edition), The Macquarie Library, Sydney.
16 'New light on native art in Australia', *Sydney Morning Herald*, 21 August 1949, p. 2. See also May, this volume.

as its logo.[17] The 'swaggie' is the white Australian on perpetual walkabout, an unkempt if generally benign itinerant, restlessly on the move, avoiding settlement, shy of regular work. As a symbol of intractable independence, the swagman is a peculiarly Australian figure, entering national mythology via a song that has him stealing a sheep and, to avoid punishment, drowning himself.

As he is depicted in the advertisement for *Walkabout*, the swaggie, waltzing his 'matilda' (a vernacular term for his meagre bundle of possessions), is a nostalgic figure, a relic from the days of the gold rushes and pioneers. At the same time, it is difficult to imagine that Simpson would not also have been familiar with a more recent and less romantic image of the itinerant: the many thousands of men (and women) who took to the road ('on the wallaby') in search of work during the Great Depression.

Waltzing the Wire Recorder

The portability and reliability of recording equipment in the immediate postwar years enabled the program maker not simply to get out of the studio (they had been doing that for years) but to venture forth into remote places with relative ease. The idea of reporting the richness and complexity of life in the wide brown land obviously met with the state broadcaster's sense of high national purpose. This was congruent with an invigorated sense of national development—especially of the remote and sparsely populated north—in the aftermath of the Pacific War.

But there is also, I suspect, a hint of the feckless in calling this roving 'features' program *Australian Walkabout*. One of the implications of getting out and about is that we will hear the unruly voices of ordinary Australians talking about their extraordinary, yet to them ordinary, lives. But, the ABC assures us, every detail is bona fide; the risks of 'going walkabout' could be justified only by the resulting program's claim to authenticity. Listeners could be assured that not a lot of 'wild talk' would be allowed to leak out of the wire. After all, ABC announcers still wore evening dress, and speaking proper was all the go. Parcelled up with the dangerous suggestion of feral authenticity is an ambiguous gesture towards the Indigenous, partly as recuperation of the Aboriginal need to walk the land into being, and partly as a new claim on the part of white Australia to share in this ancient, nomadic way of knowing, to appropriate (or at least partake of) authenticity through the act of recording 'on walkabout'. That we might 'go walkabout' with the ABC in the name of national development

---

17   The *Macquarie Dictionary* cites the wanderings of the swagman as an instance of 'going walkabout'.

further complicates the picture. There is no record of who actually came up with the name of the program, but the mix of the populist and the romantic with a slightly subversive subtext seems particularly 'Simpsonesque'.

The mixed signals about the nature and purpose of *Australian Walkabout* are audible in the opening sequence of 'Expedition to Arnhem Land': the tone of self-importance and cautious reassurance from the announcer, and then, from Charles Mountford, with his insistence upon the scientific purpose of the Expedition and the solemn invocation of the Commonwealth Government. The announcer enters on the back of a pompous and extended orchestral fanfare that cross-fades with the sound of didjeridu (one of the earliest known broadcasts of this instrument). The announcer notes that this exotic music was recorded in remote Arnhem Land, and then enjoins his listeners to attend to this authentic account of the 'joint Commonwealth and National Geographic Society Expedition' and of 'what the scientists did', which is presented in a 'not too formal account'. The announcer throws to Simpson, who proceeds in a tone of weary seriousness (a tone at odds with the words he uses) to evoke beautifully the magical scene that greeted him at Oenpelli, before introducing a recording of an 'interview' with the expedition's Australian leader, C. P. Mountford. Asked to explain the purpose of the expedition, Mountford launches into a statement that is almost certainly read, in which he outlines the scientific brief of the Expedition (to collect samples of the flora and fauna and to study the habits of the natives) and its explicit nature as a government-backed venture, financed in part by the Department of Information. What Mountford does not make explicit is his status as a Department of Information employee, working in the department's Film Unit.

I might also note here that if not actually read (as I believe Mountford's responses are) then the answers to Simpson's questions were at least well rehearsed, as is made plain in an entry for 24 October 1948 in the journal of the Expedition's entomologist, John Bray:

> Made my first recording for…the A.B.C. The two chaps, Colin Simpson, who does the spruiking, and his technician Ray Giles, are both very decent types. The b/cast takes the form of a question and answer business, with all the answers well known beforehand, but not the actual question, so one has natural pauses to collect one's thoughts, but not much time.[18]

Bray goes on to note: 'Anyway, I had a good three minutes, mainly on insects, but a bit on walkabouts.'

---

18 J. E. Bray, 1948, Arnhem Land Expedition Journal, collection of Andrew Bray. I am grateful to Martin Thomas for drawing this to my attention.

Exploring the Legacy of the 1948 Arnhem Land Expedition

Recording Eden

> The greatest care was taken to see that every detail was authentic, the material gathered at first hand by the special writers concerned.
>
> — ABC *Annual Report*, 1949

The very public insistence by the ABC in its *Annual Report* on the 'greatest care' being taken by 'special writers' underscores both the importance the ABC placed on ensuring its feature programming was accurate and the privilege it accorded the writer—and writing—in vouchsafing its much vaunted authenticity. That privilege extended to being able to undertake extensive field trips far from the formalities of the ABC's offices in Sydney. It is easy to imagine Simpson's pleasure and sense of excitement as he made the journey north. With portable wire recorder in tow and notebook in hand, the ABC's 'special writer' was finally out of the office, on walkabout, to meet up with an international scientific expedition, the composition of which was an expression of the new postwar relationship with the United States. The authority of his reporting was affirmed by his reputation as a writer/reporter—an author. It would be several more years until the authorship of the radio documentary feature passed from the *writer* to the *radio producer*—a manipulator of recorded sound. This was the 'new kind of feature' pioneered by Simpson's colleague John Thompson.[19]

In many respects, this later development was made possible by another technical innovation. With the advent of audiotape in 1950, it became possible to edit sound recordings in much the same way as film. Wire recordings were not nearly as tractable and editing them was crude and imprecise. What role, then, for the sound recording in 'Expedition to Arnhem Land'?

There is no single answer to this question, for a set of conflicted relationships between writing and sound recording, and between writer and speaker, becomes evident in the opening moments of Simpson's feature. Questions of authority, authorship and authenticity are raised constantly, especially when we move from listening to 'Expedition to Arnhem Land' to reading *Adam in Ochre*.

Before returning to questions of recording and writing, it is necessary to expand upon the idea of the authentic, and to reflect upon our desire for it. One assumes the ABC had something like the dictionary definition of authenticity in mind: 'Real, actual, genuine: original, first-hand; really proceeding from its stated source, author, painter, etc.'[20] Yet authenticity is a much more culturally determined idea than the dictionaries suggest. The question of Indigenous authenticity, for instance, is one of Simpson's concerns, even though in the

---

19   Inglis, *This is the ABC*, p. 165.
20   *The Shorter Oxford English Dictionary*.

radio feature Aborigines are present in the feature only as 'wild sound' leaking into the official discourse of the Expedition. In the book, the experience of Aboriginal authenticity is the organising principle, and the activities of the Expedition largely a means towards fulfilling a more ambitious pedagogic and personal goal: that of telling an original and originary story for contemporary Australia. Simpson writes: 'Not so much has been written about the northern tribes as, for instance, about the Arunta of the Centre; which is one reason for writing this book. Yet the Arnhem Lander can represent the prototype, the first man, the Adam of this land.'[21]

Here authenticity in the sense of the original is invoked, but, by extension, so is the post-Edenic state, the Fall into civilisation. But who has fallen from grace in Simpson's Eden? If 'Bird life on a swamp on Arnhem Land 1948' is in fact a souvenir from a lost paradise, the expulsion from paradise cannot be ignored.

Simpson was making a contribution to a vigorous public debate at a time when legislatures, experts (such as A. P. Elkin), and a diversity of interest groups negotiated the postwar shift in policy towards Aborigines, essentially from protection to assimilation. A changing sense of nationhood was part of the equation; the 1949 amendments to the *Commonwealth Electoral Act* gave the vote to Aboriginal and Islander servicemen and women, and, a fortnight after Simpson's documentary went to air, the *Nationality and Citizenship Act* came into effect, creating, for the first time, Australian citizens.

While assimilation was the clear thrust of government policy (as explicitly stated by Paul Hasluck, the new Minister for Territories, in 1951), the debate was by no means cut and dried. As the historian Anna Haebich and others have demonstrated, there was in this period considerable discussion about the practice of removing Aboriginal children from their families.[22] While the idea of assimilation was strongly endorsed by bureaucrats and academics, the exact meaning of the term was also being discussed in the press and the legislature. There was a growing interest in Aboriginal art and culture in this period. In the public discourse, a clear division was emerging in the way Aborigines were imagined. On one hand, there were the 'real Aborigines'—'full bloods' living more or less traditional lives in the remote north and centre of the country; and on the other, the 'half-castes' who lived in the settled districts (see Thomas on Gerald Blitner, this volume). One of the ironies of this bifurcation is that popular opinion denied 'real' (authentic) Aborigines citizenship while acknowledging their cultural integrity and the right to control their destiny on their traditional lands, while the 'half-castes'—the inauthentic Aborigines—might be granted

---

21 Simpson, C. 1951, *Adam in Ochre: Inside Aboriginal Australia*, Angus & Robertson, Sydney, p. 7.
22 See Haebich, A. 2000, *Broken Circles: Fragmenting Indigenous families 1800–2000*, Fremantle Arts Centre Press, WA, chs 7 and 8.

full citizenship, but denied their Aboriginality. This view enjoyed the support of political figures, of academics including Elkin, and of many supporters of Aboriginal rights.[23] The Secretary of the Australian Aboriginal League argued in the *Sydney Morning Herald* that

> the use of the term 'aborigines' confuses in the public mind the problem of the persons of mixed blood, who should be granted the privileges of the full citizens, with the problem of the real aborigines, those thousands of persons of full blood who are still living in tribal land under near-tribal conditions.[24]

Simpson's take on this debate is complex. When broaching the subject in *Adam in Ochre*, he begins by asking if the Aborigines have fallen from grace. Has their contact with white society diminished their originality? At first, he assumes this is the case, but his later experience makes him question his initial impressions.

> The old men Mountford brought back to the tent had been hoeing the mission's melon patch. They looked unimpressive, they looked dreadful in cast-offs of clothing and shapeless relics of felt hats. They sat down on the grass, folding themselves down in that slow and diffident way they have with white men, one wringing his nose out with his fingers, another coughing. I thought to myself, 'Nothing much can come of this'. I was judging by appearances, presuming that the old men had shed their validity as aborigines and put off their old culture because they had put on rags of white-man clothing and were taking hand-outs from the mission.
>
> It was these old men and others they mustered who, transformed with paint and fervour, gave us the unforgettable performance of the... corroboree a few days later.[25]

In *Adam in Ochre*, Simpson essays a number of ways of approaching Aboriginal culture and the so-called 'Aboriginal problem'. From this distance, his attitudes can appear contradictory—he can be patronising while asserting the cultural and intellectual equality of white and black Australians—but his underlying commitment is clearly to encourage his fellow citizens to recognise the diversity and complexity of aboriginal culture, and to see the fundamental importance to Australian society of coming to terms with the history of Indigenous displacement and cultural destruction by European settlement.[26]

---

23 Elkin, A. P. 1949, 'Australia and the Aborigines', *Sydney Morning Herald*, 29 January.
24 Groves, H. S. 1949, 'Tribal life menaced', Letter to the Editor, *Sydney Morning Herald*, 8 September.
25 Simpson, *Adam in Ochre*, pp. 6-7.
26 Simpson claims credit for bringing together the composer John Antill and the painter William Constable with the idea of having a ballet created on an Aboriginal theme. The resulting *Corroboree* was a disappointment to Simpson: 'Through a lack of understanding and plain lack of knowledge, the choreographer completely missed the spirit of the real thing in a riot of baseless representationalism, full of incongruous and extraneous elements' (ibid., p. 607).

To return to the Fall and the question of authenticity: the authentic being of the Arnhem Land Aborigines serves to remind us—the listener, the reader, the author—of the *inauthentic* nature of white, urban, civilised existence. Although never stated explicitly, this confrontation with our own inauthentic nature—and the possibility of redemption through encountering the authentic in the landscape—is the key subtext of the book.

Entering Eden

In both the book and the radio documentary, Simpson's introduction evokes the idyllic setting in which he first encounters the Expedition members: the lagoon with its water lilies, the sacred mountain behind, the natives fishing at one end, the naked scientists bathing at the other. It is a scene sketched with great economy and skill, and Charles Mountford's rehearsed bureaucratic banalities (in the radio documentary) bring us down to earth with a thump. In the book, Simpson can tell the story his way, and he completes an extended version of the same introduction as follows:

> In the lagoon at evening, when the last glow of the sun made satin of the water and the wind stood still, was the day's best hour. Down there at the big billabong mirroring Inyaluk, shared with the natives and the near birds no one turned to hunt, there was a feeling of being part of a quest that was wider and *more real than anything you could seek for in a city* [my emphasis], and there was no sense of urgency in need or time. There was a balm and essence I have not felt before or since. Others felt it, too. I remember Bob Miller, the ichthyologist, standing out there in the quiet water the evening before he had to leave Oenpelli and return to America, saying, 'This I am going to miss a great deal…'.[27]

This is Eden invoked and evoked at a time when Arnhem Land 'bore a sinister reputation and was shunned by white men except for a few buffalo hunters, traders, missionaries, patrol officers and anthropologists'.[28]

Simpson is equally romantic but more sentimental as he seeks to instruct his (primarily) white, urban readers in their own inauthenticity. *Adam in Ochre* recounts a personal journey that at least suggests the possibility of individual redemption or recuperation of an authentic being. One section of the book is a novella called 'Kakadu naked', which tells the story of 'Najanja, man of the Kakadu people' and his children. It is a love story that turns into a tragedy, told from an Aboriginal perspective. It concludes with the careless debauching

---

27 Simpson, *Adam in Ochre*, p. 10.
28 'Expeditions begin assembling', *Sydney Morning Herald*, 26 February 1948.

of a young Kakadu woman by a white adventurer. We are presented with a truly nasty encounter between white and black Australia distinguished by hypocrisy and cruelty, and asked to judge the quality of civilised man against his (feminised) opposite, the primitive.

Sounding Bloody

In the book, Simpson makes clear both the personal impact of his journey and his central concern with coming to terms with the Aboriginal situation. How is this reconciled with his role as an ABC employee, a state functionary, out there reporting on this official Commonwealth-sponsored Expedition in the service of nation building? Something of the conflict that Simpson negotiates is discernible in the shift in the tone of his voice between Simpson-in-the-field and Simpson-in-the-studio. The effect is no doubt accentuated by the slippage in playback and recording speeds: the light, easy voice of the man on walkabout; the altogether more solemn, deliberate tones of the pipe-smoking narrator on duty in the studio. Simpson's studio script is economical, but his more lyrical reflections are suborned to the imperative to recount 'what the scientists did'. And what the scientists did is, by and large, less than riveting. Each interview adheres to much the same formula: description of task—'I collect fish'; summary of findings—'there are lots of fish'; and an anecdote—'I found a funny fish'. On location, Simpson is enjoying himself, but also working to rule. He is interested, but the real work is going on in his head and in his diary, finding its fullest expression in the nuanced complexity and descriptive richness of the book.

And so the question again: what role for the sound recording? The wire recorder had allowed the writer to roam far and wide, to talk to real people, to capture the 'authentic' sounds of Australia, but the feature was still authored by writing, not by recording. In 'Expedition to Arnhem Land', we listen on the cusp between the authority of writing and the authenticity of (recorded) actuality. This is the moment when the contemporary radio feature is being born. Simpson was still essaying the written word; it was another 20 years until a distinctively 'radiophonic' essaying found its way onto the Australian airwaves.[29]

Let us attend more closely to the sound of Simpson in the studio—the 'inauthentic' Simpson perhaps—before turning to 'Bird life', and further exploration of the relationship between writing and recording.

On the radio, Simpson introduces his interview with the deputy leader of the Expedition, the American archaeologist Frank Setzler, by describing it as 'the

---

29   See Madsen, V. 2009, 'A *radio d'auteur*: the *documentaire de creation* of Kaye Mortley', *Scan*, vol. 6, no. 3, viewed 12 December 2009, <http://scan.net.au/scan/journal/display.php?journal_id=142>

liveliest of our recorded interviews'. We then cut to the field recording: Simpson is describing Setzler entering the tent at the end of the working day, covered in dust, and emptying a haversack of found objects onto his work table. It is all done 'as live': 'here's Dr Frank Setzler now, he's covered in dust, he looks as black as his native helpers…he's emptying his bag of finds onto the table…[SFX: clattering stones].'

Then Simpson asks Setzler what he has been up to, and Setzler replies: 'wait a moment Colin, until I get this dust off.' It all sounds bright and enthusiastic.

But to the contemporary listener, there is something odd about this, the 'liveliest of our recorded interviews'. The quality that jars for our ears is that it is clearly rehearsed. You can imagine the scene: Simpson says to Setzler, 'First, I'll describe you coming in, then you put down the knapsack, and I'll ask you what you've been doing', and so on. In some cases, as with Mountford's recitation of the Expedition's history, Simpson's interview subjects read from prepared texts. I have no doubt that Simpson's reporting of the scenes is accurate, and the material he recorded on the wire proceeds from his inquiries. Simpson has simply chosen the best bits (or at least, those most appropriate to the needs of his ABC mission) from his conversations with people, and asked them to repeat them for the wire recorder. In effect, these semi-scripted re-enactments constitute a kind of 'writing for the recorder'. Simpson was by force of habit and faith a writer. Mostly, Simpson treats the recorder as something like a typewriter, a tool with which the writer transcribes his rough notes, turning them into reportage for public consumption. He does not appear to trust the recorder as an observing device in its own right, as capable of hearing beyond his own listening. He would not appear to acknowledge that he might in fact *work with the wire* (recording) in the same manner as he might rework his notes.

Curiously, it is precisely Simpson's treatment of the tape recorder as a notebook, which he later transcribes and then reworks as a writer, that allows us to explore the ambivalent nature of the author's relationship to the sound recording—and to the recording machine itself. An event described in great detail in the book—but not included in the radio feature—serves to illustrate the point.

Simpson goes on a buffalo hunt with a number of Aborigines. Also present are Len Hillier, a professional buffalo hunter employed by the Oenpelli mission, and Aub Dunkley, one of the white mission employees. In *Adam in Ochre*, the hunt is described almost exclusively through quotation from, and comment upon, the recordings Simpson and Giles made. It is a story about recording and radio as much as it is about buffalo hunting. First, they set up to record the hunt:

> We went across a narrow stretch of plain into a clump of paperbarks that came out like a peninsula on a sea of green rice-grass…Ray would

stay on the truck with the wire recorder…I picked a paperbark…and from its fork I could see right out over the plain where some buffaloes were already grazing. We ran the microphone lead through a few tree tops to the tree I was in. I looped the mike on to a limb where I could let it hang…A wind was blowing, so I tied a handkerchief over the front of the mike, otherwise the wind comes in a low roar. Then I tested with Ray and, settling myself back in the fork of the paperbark, waited for the shoot-boys to come in sight with that good feeling of anticipated excitement. Maybe we'd get a recording that would have the listeners in the suburbs gripping the Genoa velvet of their lounge chairs. But it wasn't our day.[30]

The buffalo refused to come crashing through the paperbarks, so Simpson had no recourse but to provide a running commentary from his vantage point of the hunt taking place out on the plain. In the book, Simpson directly transcribes the recording, but inserts a number of observations that can be seen as Simpson-the-writer admonishing Simpson-the-speaker. In the book, he puts this commentary on his own speech in italics:

Ah. Over here—er—well, a shot buffalo is not down—he's charged at a horse—the horse jumps aside. The wounded buffalo stops, even from here he looks bullet stricken and bewildered. The horseman rides away, just a calm canter, about fifty yards, looking over his shoulder at the bull, still standing there. Now the shooter has dismounted, he's on foot (*of course he's on foot, mug, if he's dismounted*). The shooter walks towards the buffalo and now the buffalo (*keep your voice down!*) walks toward him, head lowered and—his—the shooter's rifle goes up—and he drops the buffalo with a shot between the eyes. (*How the hell do you know at this distance whether it was between the eyes? Well where else… Get on with it! But there's nothing doing, except that the other buffaloes have got away*). The rest of the buffaloes are racing for the paperbarks on the right—they'll make the timber—while all the shooters are across on the left…OK Ray, cut, you can switch off now. Was I working too close to the mike again and how did it sound—bloody? I'm coming down now, you can tell me. Sorry you couldn't see it from where you are.[31]

At one level, Simpson is simply allowing us behind the scenes, unveiling the clunky machinery of recording and the frailties of the reporter. But it is a passage that also seeks to undermine the authority of the 'live' recording and

---

30   Simpson, *Adam in Ochre*, p. 30.
31   Ibid., p. 31.

Simpson's 'wild talk', his unwritten self. This spontaneous commentary might be authentic, true to the moment, but it lacks the authority of the written word, committed to paper after considered reflection.

Coming into it Like a Child

There is an incident later in the buffalo hunt that perfectly captures Simpson's acute ambivalence about the function of the recorder as a source of authority, a moment when that which is unrecordable—unsayable—is able to be written; a sharp illustration of the division between speech and writing, utterance and text. It also reveals the extent to which Simpson attributes to the recorder an element of agency, in much the same way we attribute agency to a gun in saying it 'goes off'.

Back to our buffalo hunt.

Given the extreme heat, the shooters prefer to cripple rather than kill the buffalo outright. They then leave the animal lying there, in the heat and in pain, until they can come back to skin it—in some cases, overnight. The buffalo is finally killed just before skinning: it is easier to skin a freshly killed carcass, and there is no risk of the beast rotting in the heat; a rotten skin is of no commercial value. Simpson finds the practice repugnant, and is determined to expose it as cruel.

> When we got back to the waterhole near the camp Aub superintended the washing of the hides. They were dragged off the truck and into the water and left there to soak off the mud and the blood, and then they would be liberally salted to keep them. I got Aub to explain that on to the recorder which was on the truck, working off two six volt batteries.
>
> 'We'll go straight from there with a snap start,' I told Ray. I didn't like what I was going to do next, as I went ahead on [Ray's] nod.
>
> 'Mr Dunkley,' I said, 'have you lost any hides today in the heat?' I turned the mike to Aub.
>
> 'Yes, we've lost one that was left too long before skinning,' he said, coming into it like a child.
>
> I lowered the mike and told Ray to cut, I couldn't do it cold.
>
> 'Aub, I'm going to ask you about leaving them alive until the next day. You represent the mission out here…' I looked at Len sitting in the truck.
>
> 'You can't ask him that,' Len said. There was no rancour in his voice.

'No,' I said. 'I'll think that'll do, Aub. Thanks.' I told Ray to finish. I felt grateful to Len. It was as though he had knocked up my rifle when I was going to blast a sitting bird.[32]

It is an interesting moment, and our inquiry might take off in any number of directions. Let us follow the hunting metaphors for a moment. What starts off as entrapment, with the intention of capturing wild talk ('coming into it like a child') suddenly takes on the character of an act of unsportsmanlike aggression: 'It was as though he had knocked up my rifle when I was going to blast a sitting bird.' It is as though the act of recording Aub's unprepared answer parallels leaving the wounded buffalo out on the plain—an act of unnecessary cruelty. And yet Simpson the writer has little hesitation in giving us exactly the same information he could not bring himself to 'capture' on tape by interviewing Aub Dunkley.

Why?

Issues of journalistic ethics aside, I think the answer lies in Simpson's recognition of the fact that the recorder is indiscriminate in capturing 'raw speech'. Like the authenticity of the Aborigines, it approaches a state of nature, unmediated and preliterate, and at odds with his own belief in, and commitment to, the authority of writing and the civilising effect of the written word. It is an appropriately complex moment: contradictory, intensely felt, revelatory. The paradise of authenticity he evokes at the beginning of *Adam in Ochre* has its limits—nowhere more evident than when he writes that 'pre-literate people are sickeningly insensitive to animal suffering, and the first thing expected of any mission is that it should counteract cruelty, not countenance it as a means to an end—the end, in this case, being to earn funds to carry on its work of Christianising'.[33]

I think here we find a key to understanding Simpson's ambivalence towards the sound recorder. The writer can choose his words, but the recorder is insensible to desire. Indiscriminate and amoral, it captures everything, unrestrained. It is a strangely primitive tool that the writer must keep continually in check, lest it reveal the violence in paradise—the violence of preliterate speech, of utterance. The risk of 'going walkabout' with the recorder is that the unsayable will be said, promiscuously authenticating the real with no care for the civilising effect—the discipline—of the (written) word.

While Simpson's abhorrence of what he perceives as cruelty delineates the limits of his romance with the real and original, it would be wrong to see him as some reactionary who resists sound recording—a kind of media Luddite. Instead, he

---

32   Ibid., p. 36.
33   Ibid., p. 39.

is grappling with the problem of authorship in an emerging medium. Indeed, he continually reminds his reader that the writing of *Adam in Ochre* owes everything to the act of recording.

Simpson is also mindful of the way in which the recorder is fundamentally an extension of a larger cultural institution, which, in the immediate postwar years, was directly implicated in the task of 'national development'. There is a wonderful celebratory passage in *Adam in Ochre* where he looks 'back on the cavalcade of people I have seen carrying A.B.C. recording equipment':

> I see the recorder-box and the label-gaudy Globite cases of mikes and vibrators and wires and spare parts being passed from an Indian taxi-driver in Singapore to a Dusan or a Murat carrier in North Borneo who puts some of it in a round bark basket called a *boongen* and hoists it on his back.

The recorder passes from hand to hand through Asia and across Australia, until finally a 'Canberra technician sets it up before the Prime Minister'.[34]

This makes a neat summary of Simpson's ABC career: a series of journeys to exotic places, ending in an audience with the Prime Minister. Simpson joined the ABC in 1947 to help establish the Features Department, and left in 1950, after the commission (somewhat regretfully it would appear) failed to renew his contract, choosing instead to spend the money on purchasing freelance contributions.[35] *Adam in Ochre* was published the following year. Simpson parlayed his ABC experience into a very successful career as a writer of highly regarded travel and history books, the first three of which (the *Adam* series) draw directly upon his ABC travels—and, critically, on the recordings he made 'on duty'.

Institutional Speech

'All speech is on the side of the Law', writes Roland Barthes. The speaker/teacher either accepts his role as authority—speaking clearly—or attempts to subvert it by 'speaking badly', correcting, adding, wavering. Finally, he argues, 'the choice is gloomy: conscientious functionary or free artist'.[36] We might hear the broadcast speech or radio talk of the period under discussion (when a 'talk' was given from a written text) as both confirming and complicating Barthes' assertion that 'writing begins at the point where speech becomes impossible'. The voices we hear can be either reading from prepared scripts or extemporising.

---

34 Ibid., p. 137.
35 Inglis, *This is the ABC*, p. 164.
36 Barthes, R. 1984, 'Writers, intellectuals, teachers', in *Image, Music, Text*, (trans. Stephen Heath), Flamingo, Oxford, p. 192.

In either case, the voice is framed—authorised—by its institutional context: in this case, the ABC. The Simpson we hear in 'Expedition to Arnhem Land' and read about in *Adam in Ochre* is the writer negotiating the paradoxes of recording, but he is also attempting to reconcile his role as a broadcaster within an expressly pedagogic national institution—a role defined (until that moment) by formal speech—with his more strictly independent role as a writer. One of the paradoxes of the move from writing to extemporaneous speech initiated by *Australian Walkabout* is that it seeks to reverse the power relations sketched by Barthes. In letting Australians speak freely (more or less), the authority of the written talk is diminished. Australians talk back to the lecturer, albeit within a highly regulated context.

These are the paradoxes Simpson negotiates in his attempt to record (in writing and sound) the authentic experience of his journey to Arnhem Land. At Oenpelli, Simpson is almost the 'free artist', the writer 'on walkabout' from the ABC, but the Pyrox wire recorder is both his excuse for being there and the source of his authority as agent of the state. It has an almost living presence. Is Simpson accompanying the recorder, or is the recorder accompanying Simpson?[37]

The Morning of the Birds

I have sought to locate Simpson in the midst of complex cultural and historical forces. We see and hear him negotiating competing discourses of authenticity and conflicting notions of authority; attempting to reconcile writing with speaking; and confronting the dilemma of Aboriginal existence in the Australia of 1948.

As is evident in his writing, all these problems engage him very personally. Yet this experience is largely inaudible in the radio program—heard only in the reluctance evident in Simpson's voice as he reads his narration, which might be read as discomfort with his role in the nation-building functions of *Australian Walkabout*. (On close listening to the studio presentation, you can detect the sound of traffic on the street outside the studio. This sonic leakage of the 'outside' into the acoustic sanctum of the studio would be regarded as intolerable in contemporary practice, but in this context it has a strongly poignant effect, placing Simpson behind a desk in a banal Sydney office, far from the exotic doings of his freer, recorded self.) Similarly, in the field recordings, Simpson might be enjoying himself in his rehearsed interviews with the scientists, but he is not giving much away either. Only in those brief moments when the recording breaks with the word and allows 'wild sound' to burst through do we

---

37 Simpson includes a description of the recorder, and its cost, in his extensive glossary to *Adam in Ochre*—a self-consciousness unlikely in contemporary radio reportage.

begin to approach the effect Simpson sought when he described the 'listeners in the suburbs gripping the Genoa velvet of their lounge chairs'. These are the moments when recording takes over from writing—those rare radiophonic moments when Simpson allows sound, not scientists, to speak.[38]

The presentation (in the radio documentary) of the scene represented in the 'Bird life' recording is one such moment. Why does Simpson include it? Superficially, it is consistent with the program's pedagogic intent, and it provides audible evidence of the exotic location. But clearly it is not intended to engender the virtual presence that attends contemporary environmental sound recording. Such recordings depend for their effect upon both high fidelity and extended durations.[39]

In introducing the recording in his radio program, Simpson is restrained, despite offering a detailed description of the location and the mass of birds. He opens with the observation that '[t]he bird life in Arnhem Land is amazing'. This is in contrast with *Adam in Ochre*, in which the same scene is presented as the apotheosis of his Arnhem Land experience. He describes it in great detail in 'The morning of the birds'—a chapter close to the middle of the book.

One morning before dawn, Simpson sets off with four Aboriginal men towards the lagoon. The recording gear has already been set up in a hide at the water's edge the previous night:

> The babel of birds came to us before we reached the nearest edge of the mile-long marshy lagoon. I have never seen such a sight as it was that morning. An empty stretch of water can be beautiful, but this was something beautifully alive. The multitude of birds across the expanse of water left few patches where they were not feeding or swimming or alighting or taking off. Yet, with all their movement, and all their cries and murmur vibrant in the air, there was serenity, as of a park pond made enormous, a sanctuary limited only by the flank of sandstone on our right and the far tall trees of the paperbark belt. Veils of mist were rising and wreathing away. The sky was pearly and the far scarps of sandstone beyond the trees stood up like unsubstantial walls in the soft light that made them mauve. There was no flush of sunrise yet across the water.

After some trepidation about leeches and the possibility of encountering crocodiles, Simpson and the Aborigines enter the water and begin slowly driving birds within range of the microphone.

---

38   Another such moment is the recording of the didjeridu. As far as I have been able to ascertain, this was the second time the sound of the didjeridu had been broadcast.
39   Madsen, V. 1995, 'Notes toward sound ecology', *Essays in Sound*, no. 2.

The sun was coming up now and the water was shining. The sun gave the birds shadows and reflections. I was nearly out in the centre of the lagoon then and, more than ever, the air was alive with the sound. I waded on through the sunrise colours in the water, the birds rising before me, knowing that it was a morning that would be with me as long as I lived.

It was almost seven o'clock when I waded up to a little rocky islet, rolled a cigarette, and wrote some of it down...[I'm glad I did] because the notes have fixed impressions that might have blurred. For all [the birds] that had been flushed to the upper reaches there were still thousands down the lagoon and on either side. The top end had been crowded with birds for the best part of an hour. Ray should have some good sound. It was time to go right up and create the final sound we hoped would make a fine climax.

As I started wading the last stretches there were necks up everywhere; the geese, talking, talking, talking—here was that man again. If I wanted photographs, and I did, this was the time to use the camera, or it would be too late. I took it out of its case, the little Nagel that fits in the palm of my hand, and waded on a few more yards. I was raising the camera to shoot when my right sandshoe went *slip* in the mud and as I saved myself from falling the camera slipped out of my hand and plopped into the water. I whipped it straight up from the muddy bottom. I looked at it and the picture in front of me, a picture such as I shall never get again. Raising the dripping camera I looked at the picture through the viewer. Geese were rising in hundreds just in front of me, and the water was full of the reflections of geese flying. Knowing it was senseless to do so, I clicked the sodden shutter. I swore, but mechanically. The cursing chagrin I felt I should feel just wasn't there. The morning was too big for a thing like that to spoil. To complete the sound picture, which was the important thing, I quickened my pace. The thousands of birds between me and the hide all began to take the air, flapping and honking and calling and crying. More than I had ever anticipated was the surge of sound as their wings beat the air, almost a thunder of sound, a noise like a great cacophonous aerial host, still mounting to a crescendo beyond any crescendo expected as all the flocks wheeled back over my head and the sky was gone in a rushing, breath-taking pattern of black and white.

When it was over I walked out through the ankle deep shallows. The piping of the plovers at the edges and the little running snipe was like a twitter of sound underscoring a silence. I went up to the hide and Ray Giles came crawling out to meet me.

'Did you get it all mate?'

'All you'll ever want and more,' he said. 'Come and listen to a bit of it back. It's wonderful.'

It was, too, even if we say so ourselves. We played back enough of the recording to know it was all there. The take-off was terrific.[40]

Compare that euphoric riff with his comment in the radio narration, where his joy at the crescendo of sound is reduced to 'toward the end of this recording you will hear hundreds of birds take off from the water'.

There are many things that could be said about the written narrative Simpson weaves around the moment of this recording. We might ponder the fact that although his camera has been destroyed, he must complete the ritual of the snapshot. It might appear that the sound recording is not a reliable witness to dawn in paradise. But we must also note that the whole sequence is articulated by—and through—the act of recording. The reader is in the end reminded that she cannot hear what Ray Giles and Simpson hear (or imagine they hear) off the wire: 'Come and listen…it's wonderful.'

There is a radical disjunction between the actual recording and the narrative Simpson weaves around it. A wire recording from 1948 is technically incapable of conveying the auditory richness and depth of Simpson's experience; it will not measure up to his memory. And it is precisely this fundamental inadequacy that defines 'Bird life on a swamp on Arnhem Land 1948' as a souvenir, rather than a 'true record' or document. As Susan Stewart writes, the 'souvenir must remain impoverished, and partial so that it can be supplemented by a narrative discourse, a narrative discourse which articulates the play of desire [without which] it would not function, that both attaches to its origins and creates a myth with regard to those origins'.[41] Stewart then goes on to argue that

> the nostalgia of the souvenir plays in the distance between the present and an imagined, prelapsarian experience, experience as it might be 'directly lived'. The location of authenticity becomes whatever is distant to the present time and space; hence we can see the souvenir as attached to the antique and the exotic.[42]

---

40 Simpson, *Adam in Ochre*, pp. 70–3.
41 Stewart, S. 1993, *On Longing: Narratives of the miniature, the gigantic, the souvenir, the collection*, Duke University Press, Durham, NC, p. 136.
42 Ibid., p. 140.

Notionally included to illustrate the prolific nature of the bird life in Arnhem Land, the recording functions as a souvenir of Arnhem Land's prelapsarian state, but also of the impossibility of Simpson's return to that state, figuratively and literally.

There is, however, another reading (hearing) of 'Bird life' that we might approach through attending to the difference between the way the recording is presented by the writer and by the state broadcaster. In *Adam in Ochre*, Simpson weaves an elaborate nostalgic narrative, a myth, around a recording that he presents to his radio audience with little more than the perfunctory 'the bird life in Arnhem Land is amazing'. Of course, the on-air Simpson is simply acting out his role as the narrator of a scientific documentary, broadcast with due authority by the ABC. But perhaps Simpson's restraint is also an acknowledgment of the failure of the recording to live up to his memory of the experience, a fear that by the time it passes through the ether and emerges from the speakers of Radiograms and Radiolas around the country, this recording too will fail to 'have the listeners in the suburbs gripping the Genoa velvet of their lounge chairs'. If this is Simpson's fear, he was both right and wrong.

In a radio program constructed almost entirely from various types of writing, the sudden opening onto the natural world represented by 'Bird life' is the exception, the irruption. Its brief presence serves to subvert the carefully constructed discourse of scientific inquiry. Its signal *is* its noise—not just the noise of all those birds, but the noise of the wire recorder itself, and the disc cutter and the playback turntable. The recording lacks the fidelity Simpson heard listening back to the original recording with Ray Giles ('it's wonderful'), and it lacks the authorising (and organising) narrative of the interviews. Almost despite himself, Simpson has offered something more than a nostalgic souvenir of the 'real' world to which words—culture—can only refer. Because it is only sound, not 'writing-with-the-recorder', 'Bird life'—a recording of birds and other noise—becomes an instance of the 'becoming', the *being in real time* that is sound. We hear it as an irruption of the 'now' into a carefully ordered assembly of (written) sound documents. As a sound effect, 'Bird life' *refuses* to be a souvenir because of its presence in the real time of now; sound is inherently incapable of being souvenired because it is only ever in the present. Referred to in a book, the recording is the occasion for a glorious evocation of dawn in paradise. Replayed in a studio, it fails to measure up to the myth and insists on its presence in the moment of audition.

'Bird life on a swamp on Arnhem Land 1948' also momentarily resolves the dilemma of speaking on the radio for the writer: it blows away all speech. And in doing so, it is the one moment when Simpson manages to step aside from Barthes' 'gloomy choice' between 'conscientious functionary or free artist'. Perhaps if he had had the opportunity to explore the 'sound effect', Simpson might have found himself relying less on the words and more on the sound. Certainly, his (very successful) post-ABC career is a reminder that the happy life of the 'free artist' is more usually built upon compromises. After completing his *Adam* series, Simpson went on to write popular guides to exotic cultures and difficult countries—roaming from Japan to the remote republics of the USSR. Even this market-driven independence was provisional: he wrote a sponsored history of the Ampol oil company, *Show Me A Mountain*, and between book projects worked in advertising.

There is, however, another sense in which 'Bird life' is indeed a souvenir of a 'lost Eden', not so much of Simpson's much desired state of authenticity, but from a point when the authority of reporting shifted from the writer to the recorder. Going on 'walkabout' with the wire recorder, Simpson inadvertently became the author of another kind of loss: while radio listeners began to hear the sounding world in all its acoustic richness, radio writers ceded (at least some of) their authority to the recorder. It was more than a decade until John Thompson and those who followed began to fully understand the critical and creative possibilities of 'writing on tape'. In the meantime, Colin Simpson left the sound recorder behind and stayed with what he knew best: the written word.

Despite his ambivalence about it, the recording that Simpson brought back was also a souvenir from the future—a crude pre-echo of the extended, highly accurate environmental recordings that are now the stock in trade not only of documentary makers but also of whole new categories of 'earwitnesses': sound designers, audio artists, composers of ambient music.[43] Enter any Australian Geographic store and you will be immersed in richly detailed environmental sound. As likely as not, the landscape thus evoked will be that of some remote northern wilderness—dawn on a lagoon perhaps?

---

43 See Madsen, 'The call of the wild'.

6. From Kunnanj, Fish Creek, to Mumeka, Mann River: Hunter-gatherer tradition and transformation in Western Arnhem Land, 1948–2009

Jon Altman

Introduction

Research undertaken along Fish Creek in 1948 has provided a baseline for an unusual long-term data set on utilisation of wildlife across Western Arnhem Land in the tropical savanna by people who speak a number of commonly understood dialects across the regional pan-dialectical language Bininj Gunwok.[1] The title of this chapter refers to two camping localities on fresh waterways in this region. The first, Kunnanj, is on Fish Creek about 20 km north-east of Gunbalanya (formerly Oenpelli); the second is at Mumeka on the Mann River some 50 km south-west of Maningrida. The two places are about 100 km apart.

In October 1948, Margaret McArthur and Frederick McCarthy resided at Kunnanj with a small group of Aboriginal people from Western Arnhem Land and carefully recorded their economic activity and food consumption over 14 days. The people they camped with were not the landowners of that place; they had migrated to the Gunbalanya region from further east.[2] But for the first time in Australia, Western scientific quantification and participant-observation techniques were used to record an Aboriginal group's food-gathering activities, the time spent in the food quest and patterns and levels

---

1 Evans, N. 2003, *Bininj Gun-Wok: A pan dialectical grammar of Mayali, Kuninjku and Kune*, Pacific Linguistics 541, Research School of Pacific and Asian Studies, The Australian National University, Canberra. Evans identifies six dialects in the Bininj Gunwok dialect chain. The two key dialects referred to in this chapter are Kunwinjku, spoken near Gunbalanya, and Kuninjku, spoken in the Mann–Liverpool rivers region. When I refer to Kunwinjku or Kuninjku people, I am referring to members of these dialect-sharing communities.
2 With the assistance of Murray Garde and Peter Cooke, I have identified these people as members of Durlmangkarr (country Kunburray), Djorrolom (Ngaldjun), Bularlhdja (Dolomyih), Bolmo (Marlkawo) and Bordoh (Ngolkwarre) clans and speakers of Gun-dedjnjenghmi and Kune Narayek dialects of Bininj Gunwok, and possibly also speakers of the neighbouring Dalabon language. See map in Evans, *Bininj Gun-Wok*, p. xxix and Figure 1. Kunnanj is part of the estate owned by members of the Murrwan Mengerrdji clan (M. Garde, Personal communication, 29 June 2009).

of consumption of naturally occurring foods. This was path-breaking research that, while highly experimental, had major consequences for our thinking about the way hunter-gatherers lived in tropical savannas during pre-colonial and colonial times. From October 1979 to November 1980—some 30 years later—I resided at Mumeka outstation and undertook research on a less experimental basis during a period that was arguably post-colonial. In the subsequent 30 years, I have returned to this region regularly and continued working with speakers of the Kuninjku dialect residing at the eastern end of the Bininj Gunwok region (see Figure 6.1).

This chapter focuses on Western Arnhem Land because a continuity of research in this region over a 60-year period provides an unusual opportunity for comparative observations over time with people who share a linked linguistic, ceremonial and cultural identity. I begin by outlining the research undertaken by McArthur and McCarthy at Fish Creek on hunter-gatherer economic life. I discuss the wider implications for anthropological thinking about human evolution, gender and environmental relations of this research, especially in its broader theoretical framing by Marshall Sahlins in *Stone Age Economics* in 1972. I then briefly outline some findings from my own work in 1979–80 and again in 2002–03 on similar issues, before discussing continuity and change in wildlife harvesting over the past 60 years. In this discussion, I engage critically with Sahlins' interpretation of the data from Fish Creek and his more recent views on the resilience of non-capitalist indigenous economies in the highly globalised twenty-first century.

Identifying key moments of epochal change is never easy. Arguably, the immediate postwar period was such a moment of transition when nomadic hunter-gatherers in Western Arnhem Land were increasingly centralising—first at the mission at Gunbalanya, or Oenpelli as it was then known, and later at the trading post established at Maningrida for a year in 1949. (Maningrida was formally established as a government settlement in 1957.) In 1948, the outstations movement of the early 1970s could not have been foreseen. Today, there are many people who live on their ancestral lands, but in a different way to that observed by the Expedition. Now they are again subject to policy pressures to centralise. The chapter ends by reflecting on some of the intended and unintended legacies and lessons to be taken from the path-breaking work of McArthur and McCarthy in 1948.

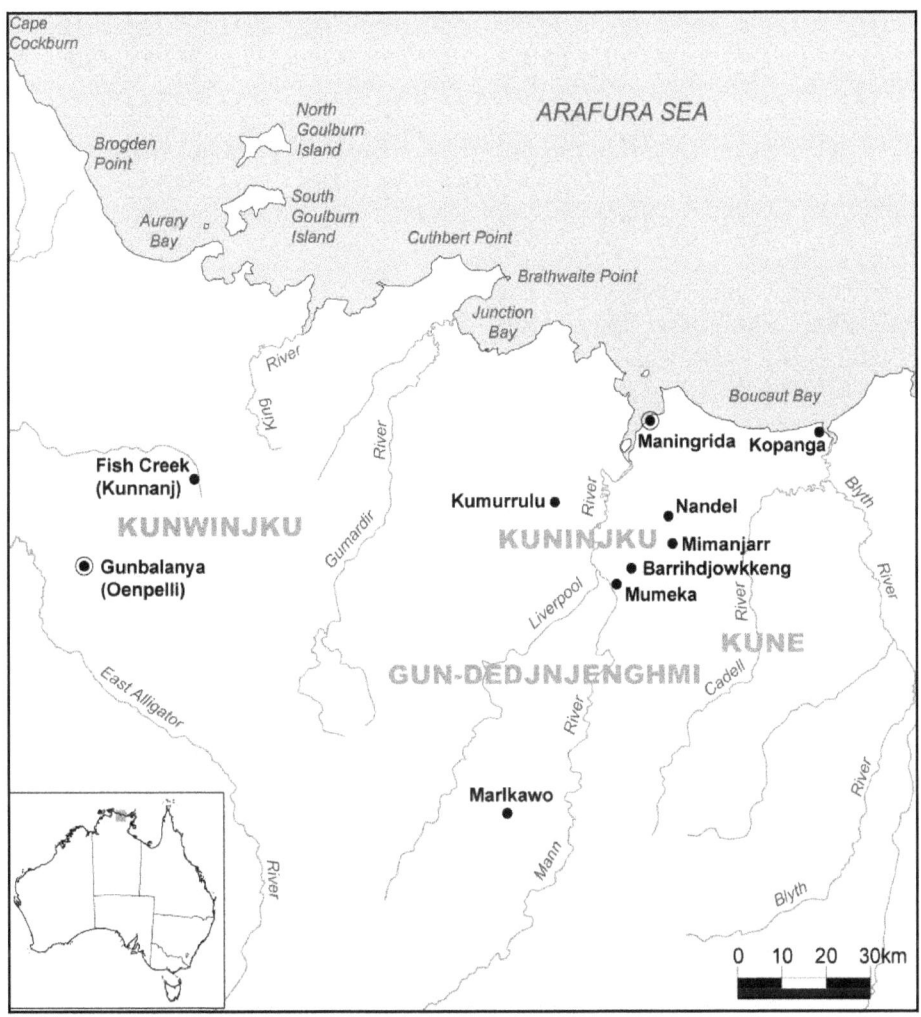

Figure 6.1 Map showing approximate distribution of the Bininj Gunwok language

The Customary Economy at Kunnanj, Fish Creek, 1948

Martin Thomas outlines the ambitious nine-point agenda for the 1948 Arnhem Land Expedition that included: to study and record Aboriginal patterns of life in relation to terrestrial and marine resources; to examine food consumption to see how well people could live off the land; to undertake a nutritional health survey; and to determine the food resources of the land and the sea.[3] Much of

---

3 Thomas, M. 2010, 'A short history of the 1948 Arnhem Land Expedition', *Aboriginal History*, vol. 34. See also Lamshed, M. 1972, *Monty: The biography of C. P. Mountford*, Rigby, Adelaide, pp. 143–4.

this research was left to the Nutrition Unit's Margaret McArthur—at that time a young nutritionist working at the Australian Institute of Anatomy and with a background in biochemistry and bacteriology.[4]

A little needs to be said about McArthur because she was quite a remarkable figure. Among the Expedition's official membership of 17, she was the sole woman scientist. Charles Mountford's wife, Bessie, the only other female on the Expedition, worked in the role of 'honorary secretary'.[5] McArthur was then twenty-nine years old and had already undertaken fieldwork in New Guinea, where she had studied the diet and health of native groups. Her role was to focus on food gathering—an activity assumed to be undertaken predominantly by women. Even at that time, there was emerging recognition that since such activity was highly gendered, data collection might be affected by the gender of the researcher.

The research on food resources was published as an eight-section 'Report of the Nutrition Unit', edited by McArthur in Volume 2 of the *Records of the American–Australian Scientific Expedition to Arnhem Land* (1960).[6] The volume also contains a separate, but linked, chapter titled 'The food quest and the time factor in Aboriginal economic life', co-authored by McArthur and Frederick McCarthy, who was Curator of Anthropology at the Australian Museum.[7] Interestingly, McCarthy was a material culture specialist and the direct ethnographic work he undertook at Fish Creek with McArthur was uncharacteristic of his overall career.

As McArthur explains in her introduction, the Nutrition Unit worked at three settlements: Yirrkala in North-East Arnhem Land, Umbakumba on Groote Eylandt and Oenpelli (now Gunbalanya) in Western Arnhem Land.[8] Each of these localities had experienced a degree of external impact heavily mediated by the passage of the Aboriginals Ordinance in 1918 that restricted unregulated entry onto reserved lands, and the declaration of the Arnhem Land Reserve in 1931. McArthur notes, however, that these were hardly pristine pre-colonial circumstances. Aboriginal people were largely centralised at state-supported settlements where the majority participated in Western forms of work.

---

4   De Lepervanche, M. 2002, 'Obituary: Annie Margaret McArthur 1919–2002', *The Australian Journal of Anthropology*, vol. 13, no. 22, pp. 230–1.
5   Thomas, 'A short history of the 1948 Arnhem Land Expedition'.
6   I focus here on just three sections of this report: McArthur, M. 1960, 'Introduction', in C. P. Mountford (ed.), *Records of the American–Australian Scientific Expedition to Arnhem Land. Volume 2: Anthropology and nutrition*, Melbourne University Press, Carlton, Vic., pp. 1–13; McArthur, M. 1960, 'Food consumption and dietary levels of groups of Aborigines living on naturally-occurring foods', in ibid., pp. 90–135; and Anon. 1960, 'Conclusions and recommendations', in ibid., pp. 139–43.
7   McCarthy, F. D. and McArthur, M. 1960, 'The food quest and the time factor in Aboriginal economic life', in Mountford, *Records of the American-Australian Scientific Expedition to Arnhem Land*, vol. 2, pp. 145–94.
8   McArthur, 'Introduction', pp. 1–13.

She notes that in Western Arnhem Land, white contact dated back more than 50 years (prior to 1948) to the late nineteenth century, when buffalo shooter Paddy Cahill began operating in the region. Cahill set up his residence at Oenpelli in 1906, established a farm, and employed Aboriginal labour in his buffalo and farming operations. In 1915, Oenpelli was chosen as the site for an experimental dairy farm that subsequently closed when exports of butter were boycotted by Darwin unionists because of production by black labour.[9] In 1925, the Anglican-run Church Missionary Society established a mission at Oenpelli on the western extremity of the Arnhem Land Reserve. The Expedition was based at Oenpelli in September and October 1948. Importantly, there was also a significant population east of Oenpelli, who were still living in a fundamentally pre-colonial manner, despite sporadic external contact during the war years.[10] Arguably, the Arnhem Land Expedition should have gone further east.

The research that I focus on here reported on two aspects of Aboriginal economic life: the *quantity* of naturally occurring foods consumed by a group of nine adults camped at Kunnanj, from where they walked to hunt, fish and gather in the immediate area (see Figure 6.1); and the *time* these people spent on food collection in relation to all other activities. This was unusual research on two counts. First, McArthur, assisted by McCarthy, John Bray (Expedition cook and honorary entomologist) and two local interpreters, identified only as Joshua and Dorcas, directly observed and recorded all activities over 14 days, although food consumption was reported for 11 days only.[11] Second, the participants were asked to participate in the research on an experimental basis so they were required not to consume any Western foods to which they had limited access via the mission.[12] Although the Fish Creek group was the only inland group studied, it was the one scrutinised in greatest detail. The observations were probably more streamlined than at coastal Hemple Bay, where a similar exercise had been undertaken with a slightly larger, but more dispersed, group over seven days in May 1948.

---

9   Clinch, M. A., 1979, 'Cahill, Patrick (Paddy) (1863?–1923)', Australian Dictionary of Biography. Volume 7, Melbourne University Press, Carlton, Vic., pp. 521–2.
10   G. Sweeney, 1939, Report of patrol in the Junction Bay, Liverpool River and Tomkinson River areas, July–August 1939, Typescript, Australian Archives File 64/2231; Kyle-Little, S. 1957, *Whispering Wind, Adventures in Arnhem Land*, Hutchinson, London.
11   It is noteworthy that McCarthy and McArthur do not mention three other Aboriginal people who were at Fish Creek. For the entire time, Mary, the seven-year-old daughter of Joshua and Dorcas, was at Fish Creek, while for the first four days two other people, Wendy and Jerrimin-min, also accompanied the interpreters, mainly it seems to act as social mediators with the group that was unfamiliar with Joshua and Dorcas. There could have also been other Aboriginal visitors to Fish Creek. This information has come to light only recently in the diary of Expedition cook, John E. Bray (Arnhem Land Expedition 1948: private journal, Private collection of Andrew Bray, pp. 170, 174). Interestingly, I interacted with the same (now deceased) Jerry Jerrimin-min in 1979 and 1980 when he resided at Kurrhkurr (Table Hill) outstation on his Marin estate.
12   At one point, on 12 October 1948, two of the Aboriginal men at Fish Creek walked nearly 20 km to Oenpelli and back so as to access flour and rice. On their return, they were requested to refrain from consuming these foods until 21 October (McCarthy and McArthur, 'The time factor in Aboriginal economic life', p. 147).

The nature of the interactions between the observers and the observed is only sketchily outlined in McCarthy and McArthur's paper, but indicates that in the interests of science the researchers did not share their own food with the subjects of observation and vice versa during the experimental period. McCarthy and McArthur note that they did not question the subjects of the research about their motivations or choice of activity.[13] This was justified as an attempt to be as rigorous as possible and might be regarded as a little unusual today.

The direct form of observation, participation and quantification was extraordinarily innovative for that time. This was especially the case for the time-allocation study, but unfortunately no explanation is provided for its undertaking (by a nutritionist and an archaeologist) except to note that no quantitative measure of time had previously been collected in Australia on hunter-gatherer work effort, so the chance to pioneer in science might have been the motivation. McCarthy and McArthur note that the absence of time-allocation studies was a global shortcoming, referring to an article by Adrian Digby published after they had completed their fieldwork that makes this point.[14]

The results of the research can be summarised as follows. In her report on consumption of naturally occurring foods, McArthur carefully records the species utilised (including botanical genus and local names) and the weights of food consumed. At Fish Creek, this amounted to a total of 28 lbs (12.7 kg) of vegetables, 5.5 lbs (2.5 kg) of fruit, 7.5 lbs (3.4 kg) of honey, 116.5 lbs (53 kg) of fish, 360 lbs (163 kg) of macropod and 16.5 lbs (7.5 kg) of offal—a total of 534 lbs of food or just on 243 kg at the average rate of nearly 2 kg per capita per day. McArthur then carefully converts all this to mean daily consumption of nutrients, taking into account the participants' gender, weight and activity levels. She found that at Fish Creek mean daily consumption was protein and calcium rich (at 5.4 and 3.6 times the daily recommended allowances respectively). The diet studied was almost optimal in terms of calories, but surprisingly (given meat-consumption levels) deficient in iron (0.3 times) and ascorbic acid (0.5 times). Overall, she notes, 'the diets which were seen at the four camps in Arnhem Land were well balanced and they provided amounts of most nutrients comparable with the recommended daily allowances'.[15] The application of such comparative measures to 'native populations' says something about the Expedition's commitment to a rigorously scientific approach.

---

13   McCarthy and McArthur, 'The time factor in Aboriginal economic life', pp. 146, 191.
14   Ibid., p. 145; Digby, A. 1949, 'Technique and the time factor in relation to economic organization', *Man*, no. 12, pp. 16–18.
15   McArthur, 'Food consumption and dietary levels of groups of Aborigines living on naturally-occurring foods'.

The results of the research on work effort were reported in the stand-alone chapter co-authored with McCarthy. This chapter provides important genealogical information about people at Fish Creek, a careful diary of all activities, some information on the sharing of large game, and then a summary of time occupied in various activities for all members of the group distinguished by gender. At Fish Creek, men worked an average three hours and 50 minutes per day and women three hours and 44 minutes per day in the food quest, or about 27 hours per week. At Hemple Bay, the work effort was somewhat higher at five hours and seven minutes per day for men and five hours and nine minutes for women, or about 36 hours per week.

Their analysis of these data is heavily and very properly qualified. They note that in evaluating their results, the presence of researchers and interpreters, the lower pressure on resources (owing to fewer people living in the bush), seasonality, and the unusual demographic composition of the group must all be considered.[16] They also note that women's work effort in the production of utilitarian artefacts (such as mats, netted baskets and string bags) had declined owing to the availability of tins and cloth from the mission.[17] They emphasise that it is hard to tell how typical their groups might be, for nearly all participants had mission or other external contact, although people did return to bush living intermittently at that time, owing to lack of food at missions or because they were seeking refuge from social or political disputes in the larger settlements. But they emphasise that their findings *are* valid for the groups that they actually studied, which, given their thoughtful qualifications, seems indisputable.

Some of their interesting findings are that returns from hunting especially are linked to individual ability, with hunters possessing impressive stalking skills when targeting kangaroos and dexterity in using spears and spear-throwers. Much of their emphasis is on gender differences: women fished or gathered every day, while men hunted less regularly, on every second day. This might have been linked to the issue of 'work density' (how hard people actually worked), since the observations at Fish Creek were undertaken during the hottest late dry season (*kurrung*). McArthur and McCarthy note that men's daily activity, especially the hunting of macropods, is apt to cause fatigue, mainly because of effort expended in stalking, chasing and then carrying heavy game back to camp. They also note the role of luck in men's hunting of mobile game compared with the greater predictability of women's harvesting of stationary plant foods. Detailed information is also provided on the rules for sharing game to meet kinship obligations.

---

16   McCarthy and McArthur, 'The time factor in Aboriginal economic life', p. 146.
17   Ibid., p. 193.

McCarthy and McArthur reveal the gendered nature of work patterns, but they highlight the small difference in work effort between the sexes. They note: 'This study illustrates well the perfect co-operation that exists between the men and women in their economic life.'[18] This was a theme picked up by Colin Simpson in a chapter, 'Margaret sees no slaves', in his book *Adam in Ochre*.[19] Overall, though, McCarthy and McArthur were cautious with their findings, suggesting that a 'survey of a group throughout the year on the lines of the present study would throw a great deal of light on the economic life of the men and women, and upon the theoretical problems involved in the two patterns and their relationship'.[20]

This path-breaking research was hardly used within Australia for a long time, in part because there was a delay of 12 years between data collection and publication. But even after its publication in 1960, this research was largely ignored. For example, in their 1970 book about Kunwinjku people, Ronald and Catherine Berndt make only fleeting reference to botanical names for species listed by Margaret McArthur and no reference to her work on the time factor.[21] Such disregard and lack of interest reflected antipathy within the Australian anthropological establishment of the time, especially on the part of A. P. Elkin (a powerful patron of the Berndts), who regarded Mountford as an unscientific amateur.[22] McArthur's work was tarred by association. Somewhat ironically, after her work as a nutritionist in Arnhem Land and clearly inspired by participant observation, she retrained as a social anthropologist and, in 1965, was the first woman appointed to a tenured post in the Department of Anthropology at the University of Sydney, where Elkin had reigned supreme in earlier decades.[23]

So it came to pass that the renowned American anthropologist Marshall Sahlins, working outside the Australian scene, was the first to recognise the enormous value of this Arnhem Land research and he used the work effort and foodstuff consumption data as the factual cornerstone for his now famous proposition that hunter-gatherers were 'the original affluent society'.[24]

Sahlins' important theoretical corrective was that it was evolutionary thinking rather than empirical evidence that depicted hunter-gatherers as either living on the subsistence margin or constantly engaged in the food quest. While Sahlins acknowledged that McArthur and McCarthy's data were collected

---

18 Ibid., p. 194.
19 Simpson, C. 1951, *Adam in Ochre: Inside Aboriginal Australia*, Angus & Robertson, Sydney, pp. 52–6.
20 McCarthy and McArthur, 'The time factor in Aboriginal economic life', p. 194.
21 Berndt, R. M. and Berndt, C. H. 1970, *Man, Land & Myth in North Australia: The Gunwinggu people*, Ure Smith, Sydney, p. 36.
22 Gray, G. 2007, *A Cautious Silence: The politics of Australian anthropology*, Aboriginal Studies Press, Canberra, pp. 191–5. See also chapters by Jones and May, this volume.
23 De Lepervanche, 'Obituary'.
24 Sahlins, M. 1972, *Stone Age Economics*, Aldine and Atherton, Chicago, pp. 1–39.

under artificial circumstances in colonial, rather than pristine, circumstances and with demographically unrepresentative groups, he threw caution to the wind somewhat in his interpretation—as is often the case in the nature of major theoretical correctives. Interestingly, Sahlins followed McCarthy and McArthur in noting the differences between Fish Creek and Hemple Bay, suggesting that a key distinction might have been the five young dependents who needed to be supported in the latter context. At Fish Creek, there were no recorded dependents, neither young nor old. McArthur, McCarthy and Sahlins all suggested that Fish Creek was a more inhospitable environment and that the late dry season was a less productive time in the seasonal cycle than the early dry (when the Hemple Bay fieldwork was conducted). Even so, people worked fewer hours at Fish Creek.

Most significantly, perhaps, Sahlins in his comparative analysis with industrial society failed to take into account that workforce participation rates in Arnhem Land were 100 per cent (all adults were workers), compared with the national rate at that time of a much lower 60 per cent, according to the 1947 Census of Population and Housing.[25] Taking these participation rates into account, the 27 hours at Fish Creek converts to a comparative 45 hours per week and the 36 hours at Hemple Bay into 59 hours. This means work levels were comparable, if not higher, for Arnhem Landers. Interestingly, in 1947, only 28 per cent of Australia's working-age females were in the workforce (persons engaged in unpaid home duties were included under the 'inactive' population), compared with the more equitable gender distribution of work in Arnhem Land. These observations are arguably minor quibbles to Sahlins' broad corrective about how we view hunter-gatherers—a view that still holds considerable sway, even though it is hotly debated.[26]

Extremely surprising, however, are the unattributed recommendations that the Nutrition Unit made, drawing from these studies.[27] McArthur had established that naturally occurring foods were nutritious and that people could sustain themselves adequately without excessive work effort. And yet the recommendations were assimilationist, arguing for the production of agrarian food and animal husbandry if Aborigines were to be given a good diet and greater employment at settlements rather than in the bush. This focus on Western food production and its distribution does not resonate with the descriptions of the harvesting of fresh food out bush and its distribution along kinship lines. One wonders if in making these recommendations the

---

25   Commonwealth Bureau of Census and Statistics 1952, 'Statisticians report', *Census of the Commonwealth of Australia, 30th June 1947. Volume III*, Commonwealth Bureau of Census and Statistics, Canberra.
26   Kaplan, D. 2000, 'The darker side of the "original affluent society"', *Journal of Anthropological Research*, vol. 56, no. 3, pp. 301–24. Interestingly, the issue of labour-force participation that I raise here has often been overlooked in efforts to debunk or dilute Sahlins' corrective.
27   Anon., 'Conclusions and recommendations', pp. 139–43.

Nutrition Unit was politically influenced by the emerging postwar policy focus on the inevitability of assimilation and whether there was interference in interpretation by the Institute of Anatomy in Canberra. While McArthur edited the 'Report of the Nutrition Unit', she clearly did not want to take ownership of the recommendations, unless the absence of authorship is just a typographical error—something that I doubt. Certainly, these recommendations indicate that reliance on bush food had no future in the mind of the bureaucracy, and were based on casual observations from the missions rather than scientific quantification from the bush camps.[28] Such is the political nature of knowledge production and policy recommendations.

The Hybrid Economy at Mumeka, Mann River, 1979–1980

In 1979 and 1980, I lived with a group of Kuninjku speakers whose home locality was Mumeka outstation on the Mann River.[29] I was undertaking research on the structure and functioning of the contemporary Kuninjku economy. My background was in economics, but I was in the process of training to be an anthropologist. In this research, my principal residence was at Mumeka, but I accompanied people from the outstation when they moved elsewhere to seasonal camps or ceremonies. During a year-long seasonal cycle, I resided at 15 locations in addition to Mumeka. My research methods included the gathering of quantitative information on productive activity in the three sectors of the local economy. At the time, I termed them 'subsistence or non-market', 'arts and crafts', and 'social security'. I now term them 'customary', 'market' and 'state sectors' of the hybrid economy.[30] Quantitative data were collected in a number of ways: by taking a daily population count; by recording work effort using time-allocation techniques; by recording all hunting, fishing and gathering returns and arts and crafts produced mainly for sale; and by recording all income received.[31]

The group I resided with at Mumeka outstation had a prolonged and chequered encounter with the colonial state. Located deep in Western Arnhem Land, they had experienced a less intense contact with missionaries, the state and

---

28   Further archival research is clearly needed to seriously test this possibility. It is important to note though that by the time this research was published in 1960, assimilation had been Commonwealth policy for nine years.
29   On Kurulk clan estate and with others mainly from Kardbam and Dangkorlo patri-clans.
30   Altman, J. 2005, 'Development options on Aboriginal land: sustainable Indigenous hybrid economies in the twenty-first century', in L. Taylor, G. K. Ward, G. Henderson, R. Davis and L. A. Wallis (eds), *The Power of Knowledge, The Resonance of Tradition*, Aboriginal Studies Press, Canberra, pp. 34–48.
31   Altman, J. 1987, *Hunter-Gatherers Today: An Aboriginal economy in north Australia*, Australian Institute of Aboriginal Studies, Canberra.

the market, although many had lived at Gunbalanya in the postwar period. In 1979, there were many who knew the people who had worked with McArthur and McCarthy at Fish Creek 30 years earlier. In the 1940s and 1950s, many people continued to live in the Liverpool–Mann–Tomkinson rivers region, as indicated by surveys undertaken on foot by government patrol officers. From 1957, Kuninjku people increasingly moved to live at the government settlement established at Maningrida—a process hastened in 1963 by the blazing of a vehicular track through the savanna woodlands by a patrol from the Welfare Branch of the Northern Territory Administration.[32]

After a desperately unsuccessful decade of living in Maningrida, where Kuninjku people failed to adapt to the state project of improvement predicated on centralisation and sedentarisation, many went back to live on their country as part of what is now termed the outstations or homelands movement. This move was associated with a different form of economy that is partially underwritten by access to state support, production of art for sale, and engagement in hunting, fishing and gathering for self-provisioning. It is noteworthy that a similar outstations movement occurred from Gunbalanya. The mission phase observed by the Arnhem Land Expedition was not as enduring as might have been assumed in 1948.

My research was undertaken in a similar tropical savanna inland environment to Fish Creek. The people residing there are from a social network that is part of the Bininj Gunwok linguistic block, sharing kinship and ceremonial linkages. I focus here on two comparative aspects of research with that undertaken at Fish Creek. My first focus is on consumption of food and time spent in productive activity, with the proviso that my research was undertaken under everyday, not experimental, conditions with a group that contained all age grades including children and the elderly. I observed and recorded intake of all foods, from harvesting as well as purchase, and recorded all activity undertaken, in the food quest, as well as for market exchange. My dietary analysis was undertaken over 296 days and my time-allocation study over 256 days, thus covering an annual seasonal cycle. My mode of participant observation involved active participation in activities and sharing of food with members of the group whose economic life was being recorded.

---

32 Altman, J. and Hinkson, M. 2007, 'Mobility and modernity in Arnhem Land: the social universe of Kuninjku trucks', *Journal of Material Culture*, vol. 12, no. 2, pp. 181–203.

Figure 6.2 Celebrating hunting success, Barrihdjowkkeng, 1980

Photograph by Jon Altman

Using direct and indirect methods, I estimated that a total of 4777 kg of naturally occurring bush food was produced, with an additional 4511 kg of shop food purchased. In total, I estimated that just on 9288 kg of food was consumed by an average population of 31 people, or just on 1 kg per capita per day.[33] Of this about half was produced, half purchased. While not a nutritionist, I, like McArthur, sought to estimate the average dietary intake for the group observed, adjusting for gender, age and weight against estimated energy and protein requirement benchmarks. Over the year, energy intake was estimated at 114 per cent of recommended requirements and protein intake at 203 per cent. Forty-six per cent of energy and 81 per cent of protein came from bush foods.[34] I collected information on all naturally occurring foods observed—90 faunal and 80 floral species—during my research.[35]

On work effort, I used a slightly different time-allocation technique and estimated that over the seasonal cycle men worked an average 3.8 hours and women 3.4

---

33 It is noteworthy that I estimated a net proportion of gross weight of both bush and bought foods for all varieties of food (Altman, *Hunter-Gatherers Today*, p. 44). Detailed data are presented in Altman, J. 1982, 'Appendix III Momega outstation: foodstuff consumption data', in Hunter gatherers and the state: the economic anthropology of the Gunwinggu of north Australia, PhD thesis, The Australian National University, Canberra, pp. 464–74.
34 Altman, *Hunter-Gatherers Today*, pp. 31–45.
35 Altman, J. 1983, 'The dietary utilistion of flora and fauna by contemporary hunter-gatherers at Momega outstation, north central Arnhem Land', *Australian Aboriginal Studies*, vol. 1984/1, pp. 35–46.

hours per day, with a total average of 3.6 hours. Of this time, 2.6 hours were spent in the food quest, 0.8 hours in production for market exchange and 0.2 hours in miscellaneous production. Gender differences were very limited; men spent a little more time in the food quest, and women a little more time in production for market exchange.[36]

I make three brief comments comparing work at Fish Creek in 1948 with mine along the Mann River three decades later.

First, Margaret McArthur's nutritional survey work greatly influenced the approach taken by Betty Meehan in her research with a coastal group of Anbarra living at Kopanga outstation on the Blyth River in 1972 and 1973, as reported in her book *Shell Bed to Shell Midden* (1982),[37] and in my later work at Mumeka.[38] Using similar methods, both Meehan and I highlighted seasonal variations in the availability of bush foods, as anticipated by McArthur, with our research indicating that the wet season was the most difficult time. Meehan showed that even with access to bought foods, in January 1973 mean daily energy intake fell below recommended levels at Kopanga, while my research showed a similar sharp dip in availability of bush foods during the taxing mid wet season.

Second, at Fish Creek, McArthur found that what she termed vegetable foods made a small (8 per cent by weight) contribution to the diet and she suggested this was due to locational and seasonal factors. My research at Mumeka similarly found that the bush diet was made up mainly of birdlife, fish and mammals and that floral resources made a negligible contribution to the diet today, at least in terms of energy contributions (less than 5 per cent of intake from bush foods), although some species were an extremely important source of vitamins. From information collected on utilisation of floral species over the seasonal cycle, I was able to confirm McArthur's observation that the late dry season was the worst for availability of bush fruit and vegetables.[39]

Third, while the data on work effort were remarkably similar at just more than 25 hours per week, this figure was the average for all adults, as was the case at Fish Creek. Taking into account the 60 per cent labour force participation rate reported in the 1981 Census, it appears that Kuninjku adults at Mumeka worked just as long as other Australians—it is just that their productive work

---

36 Altman, *Hunter-Gatherers Today*, pp. 71–95.
37 Meehan, B. 1982, *Shell Bed to Shell Midden*, Australian Institute of Aboriginal Studies, Canberra. Meehan undertook a major study of Anbarra foraging based at the coastal outstation of Kopanga during 1972–73. Her research is of greater comparative relevance to the data collected by McArthur at coastal camps on Groote Eylandt, but that is another analysis that cannot be undertaken here.
38 This was overlooked by Raymond Specht when he suggested that McArthur's nutritional research is virtually unknown today. See Specht, R. 2002, 'Margaret McArthur Oliver', *Australian Aboriginal Studies*, vol. 2, pp. 122–3.
39 Altman, 'The dietary utilisation of flora and fauna by contemporary hunter-gatherers at Momega outstation, north central Arnhem Land', p. 39.

effort outside the home was more evenly shared by all adults. Importantly, while gendered work effort at Fish Creek and Mumeka remained remarkably similar between 1948 and 1979–80, in the wider society there was a rapid growth in female workforce participation and a complementary decline in male workforce participation.[40]

The combination of these three findings led me to re-examine Sahlins' 'original affluent society' proposition. Using my data, I argued that if affluence is measured in hours worked then it is likely to be a contemporary rather than a pre-colonial condition since energy-intensive foods, which would have been gathered mainly by women, are now purchased. If workforce participation rates are also taken into account then, at a societal level, work effort outside the home appears remarkably similar for Aboriginal people in Arnhem Land and the rest of the Australian population as measured in official statistics.[41]

Figure 6.3 Butchering a kangaroo, Midjadukkdor, 1980

Photograph by Jon Altman

---

40   In the 1947 Census, 93 per cent of males of working age and 28 per cent of females were in the workforce; by the 1981 Census, these proportions had changed to 77 per cent for males and 46 per cent for females.
41   Altman, J. 1984, 'Hunter-gatherer subsistence production in Arnhem Land', *Mankind*, vol. 14, no. 3, pp. 179–90. In this article, I erroneously question McCarthy and McArthur's time-allocation study (at p. 185) when I am in fact taking issue with Sahlins' interpretation.

6. From Kunnanj, Fish Creek, to Mumeka, Mann River

Tradition and Transformation, 1948–2009

Clearly, a comprehensive assessment of tradition and transformation in Western Arnhem Land is beyond the scope of this brief chapter. What I want to do here is focus on just a few select elements of the regional Aboriginal economy that are amenable to some comparative analysis. This is despite the fact that today people use vehicles and guns that were not available to them at Fish Creek and have access to other market commodities.[42] The material presented can be interpreted using an analytical model that I have devised to explain the contemporary hybrid economy in this part of the world. This model represents the productive economy as being made up of three interlinked sectors—the market, the state and the customary—that in combination generate cash and imputed (non-market) income.[43] I use this approach to briefly outline economic continuity and change initially from 1948 to 1980—a 30-year slice of time; and then from 1980 to the present—another slice of time of 30 years. I then look to the future.

1948 to 1979–80

In pre-colonial times, almost all production was undertaken in the customary sector, since there was no market institution or state sector, although there was some exchange whereby goods and services were traded both with Macassans and between Aboriginal groups across Arnhem Land. There is some debate in the literature about whether this trade was principally a social or an economic institution. By 1948, both the market and the state had partially penetrated Western Arnhem Land and a mission had been established at Gunbalanya to mediate and ameliorate this contact.

The survey at Fish Creek aimed to experimentally recreate the customary economy but post-colonial transformation had already occurred. The nine Aboriginal people at Fish Creek had migrated to the region from the Arnhem Land Escarpment and a number had employment experience outside Arnhem Land, mainly in the war economy. Their food-gathering equipment was influenced by post-colonial circumstances—for example, the spears used for hunting had metal heads and the digging sticks were made of iron. Nevertheless, people had clearly retained pre-colonial hunting and gathering skills, as documented by McArthur and McCarthy. All the activity they recorded at Fish Creek occurred in the customary sector.

---

42   For a discussion of contemporary Kuninjku use of vehicles and associated transformations, see Altman and Hinkson, 'Mobility and modernity in Arnhem Land'.
43   For discussion of the hybrid economy model, see Altman, 'Development options on Aboriginal land'.

Thirty years later, Kuninjku people at Mumeka were among several hundred people who had returned to live at outstations. There was strong continuity in tradition, as the mainstay of the economy continued to be the customary sector. Using social-accounting methodology to give market replacement values to harvested bush foods, I estimated that the customary sector accounted for 64 per cent of the Mumeka economy. But there was also significant transformation, so that people engaged in market exchange to earn cash (10 per cent of income) and also received transfer payments from the Australian state (26 per cent of income). Cash was used to purchase Western foods as well as guns and vehicles, and outstation residents were benefiting from a limited range of services provided from the township of Maningrida and underwritten by the Australian state.[44]

The shift from the experimental customary economy at Fish Creek to an everyday hybrid economy at Mumeka was precipitated in part by changes in legal arrangements: in the 1970s Aboriginal people in Arnhem Land were granted land rights and citizenship entitlements to welfare, while the policy of self-determination facilitated a return to living on country. A market sector was established at outstations by the sale of arts and crafts for cash, brokered by a new government-subsidised arts-collection agency: Maningrida Arts and Crafts. But most importantly, Kuninjku people exercised agency in choosing to return to live on their ancestral lands rather than in the township of Maningrida.

1979–80 to 2009

Just as 1948 provided a quantitative baseline against which to measure change 30 years later, so my work at Mumeka has become historical and provides a new baseline against which to assess subsequent economic change in Western Arnhem Land. This is especially the case because information was collected over the entire annual seasonal cycle, locally divided into six seasons, and for all three broad sectors of the economy. Some updating of my work at Mumeka was undertaken nearly 20 years later, in 1996–97, by a team of biophysical scientists, although their focus was on wildlife utilisation rather than local consumption or work effort.[45]

In 2002 and 2003, I had the opportunity to collaborate with another team of biophysical and social scientists to survey wildlife utilisation at five localities in Kuninjku country, working with many of the same people who were at Mumeka in 1979–80.[46] This research was undertaken on an experimental basis at Mumeka, Nandel, Mimanjarr, Kumurrulu and Barrihdjowkkeng in July 2002, at Mumeka in January 2003, and at Mumeka and Kumurrulu in August 2003.

---

44 Altman, *Hunter-Gatherers Today*, pp. 47–57.
45 Vardon, M. J, Gaston, S. M., Niddrie, J. and Webb, G. J. W. 1999, 'Wildlife use at Momega, north-central Arnhem Land', *Australian Biologist*, vol. 12, no. 1, pp. 15–22.
46 The collaborators in July 2002 were Tony Griffiths, Jennifer Koenig, Joe Morrison and Guy Pardon; in January 2003, Melinda Hinkson and Tony Griffiths; and in August 2003, Tony Griffiths and James Smith from Charles Darwin University and The Australian National University.

Survey periods varied from 10 to 14 days, and were thus of similar duration to McArthur and McCarthy's fieldwork at Fish Creek, but now they could be matched against my earlier records from nearby localities at similar periods in the seasonal cycle some 23 years earlier.

Figure 6.4 Returns from a magpie-goose hunt, Nandel, 2002

Photograph by Tony Griffiths

Figure 6.5 Returns from a barramundi drive, Nandel, 2002

Photograph by Tony Griffiths

This research indicated three key continuities. First, actual wildlife harvesting practices were remarkably similar in both periods, despite the passing of more than two decades. This indicates inter-generational skills and knowledge transfer. Second, the quantum harvested was of a similar magnitude. And third, while the range of species harvested was similar, there was some decline in reptile exploitation owing to the arrival in the region of the poisonous cane toad and an increase in hunting of the feral pig—also a relatively recent arrival in the region.[47]

There have also been some major changes. In overall terms, using the hybrid economy framework, the significance of the customary sector had declined—in part because people were receiving more monetary income from engagement with the visual-arts sector and from payment of income under the Community Development Employment Projects (CDEP) scheme—so the market and state sectors had grown, as had the articulations between them. For Kuninjku, the greater inter-sectoral linkages were evident in more fine-art production, a greater engagement of the local with the global, and more discretionary income to purchase vehicles, which resulted in increased mobility between Maningrida township and the bush. The nature of customary engagement has also changed. It is now more variable and there is far more short-term visitation onto country for hunting using vehicles and guns, and far more focus on harvesting particular large species such as introduced feral water buffalo, which are widely shared. The significance of bush fruit and vegetables—already limited according to earlier research at Fish Creek and at Mumeka—has declined further and is now negligible.

Another significant transformation has seen people in Western Arnhem Land engage more formally in natural resource management activities as community rangers over the past decade. In 2007, the Australian Government introduced a new program, Working on Country, that pays community rangers a proper salary rather than the more limited benefits available under the part-time CDEP scheme. People now engage in a range of activities that utilise customary knowledge integrated with Western scientific knowledge and technology to manage environmental threats as well as to abate carbon emissions by seasonally managing fire regimes at a landscape scale across Western Arnhem Land.

---

47   Altman, J. 2003, 'People on country, healthy landscapes and sustainable Indigenous economic futures: the Arnhem land case', *The Drawing Board: An Australian review of public affairs*, vol. 4, no. 2, pp. 65–82.

Figure 6.6 Children with barramundi and feral pig, Nandel, 2008

Photograph by Jon Altman

Figure 6.7 Transporting feral pig carcasses, Nandel, 2008

Photograph by Jon Altman

Hunter-Gatherers Yesterday, Today—What About Tomorrow?

The analysis undertaken here indicates that while there have been significant regional transformations over the past 60 years, people in Western Arnhem Land still engage in hunting and gathering, ensuring that it remains of economic and cultural significance. Even though the overall significance of the customary sector has declined, it is environmentally sustainable. Part of the decline has been linked to reduced utilisation of floral species and a heightened focus on hunting and fishing, so the pre-colonial hunter-gatherers might be referred to today more accurately as hunter-fishers. The utilisation of wildlife continues in the late modernity of twenty-first-century Australia, but it is now part of a more complex hybrid economy.

It is apposite, perhaps, to frame this discussion of continuity and change within the framework proposed in a recent survey article by Marshall Sahlins, in part because it was his 'original affluent society' theory that placed Fish Creek on the world stage of scholarship. In his 1999 essay 'What is anthropological enlightenment?', Sahlins surveys recent ethnographies of indigenous modernities and finds the predictive powers of anthropology wanting. He suggests that counter to what he terms 'despondency theory', less powerful people are not destined to lose their cultural coherence. On the contrary, local indigenous societies look to organise the forces of late capitalism and the state according to their own value systems with varying degrees of success, and hunter-gatherer engagements with the global economy and modern nation-states have not fundamentally altered customary organisation of production and social and spiritual relations to nature. Rather, Sahlins refers to the indigenisation of modernity and parallel processes of global homogenisation and local differentiation. In all of this, Sahlins is not suggesting that there has been no change, but rather that despite change something distinctly indigenous remains and that 'indigeneity' has itself changed the face of modernity.[48]

As with his original affluent society corrective, there is something intuitively appealing about this new corrective, although again Sahlins overstates the case by overlooking the structuring force of the powerful state and market. Having looked back over 60 years at Fish Creek and then on the Mann River and seen a degree of resilience, if not triumph, of hunter-gatherers in Western Arnhem Land to date, what are the prospects for the future?

---

48   Sahlins, M. 1999, 'What is anthropological enlightenment? Some lessons of the twentieth century', *Annual Reviews in Anthropology*, vol. 28, pp. 1–23.

Despite Sahlins' optimism based on late twentieth-century history, prospects remain especially hard to predict given the current uncertainty around climate change, which will inevitably impact on biodiversity and naturally occurring foods. The immediate challenge, however, appears to be early twenty-first-century despondency in Australian Indigenous affairs that is seeking to revisit the failed state project of improvement—now termed more benignly 'Closing the Gap' or normalisation—that focused on centralisation and assimilation in the 1960s, and that was rejected by those who returned to live at outstations. Despite a growing body of evidence used to contend that people living on country enjoy better health status [49] and have more robust hybrid economy livelihoods than others,[50] the Australian state seems committed to limiting support for outstations and abolishing flexible income-support arrangements that underpin outstation living. While there is a growing instrumental state view that Aboriginal people in Western Arnhem Land can provide environmental services in the national interest, the connection of such a provision with living on country seems to be oddly absent from policy thinking.

Conclusion

This chapter has revisited path-breaking research undertaken at Fish Creek that demonstrates the powers of quantification and participant observation in generating quantitative and qualitative data. These data showed that under experimental conditions Aboriginal people in 1948 could meet their dietary needs, consuming only naturally occurring foods with reasonably modest labour input. This has provided a baseline and broad methodological approach that remains of value today. The information collected, however, had greater theoretical than applied application: it was used by Marshall Sahlins to promote his theory of hunter-gatherers as the original affluent society. Recommendations by the Arnhem Land Expedition, based on this information and reflecting the policy environment of the time, promoted dietary improvement utilising Western foods and production techniques, rather than customary practices, which were shown to be highly effective. Some time later, Sahlins used the same data to challenge the supposed superiority of modernity over the 'stone age'—a conceit embedded in the very rationale for the Arnhem Land Expedition.

---

49   Burgess, C. P., Johnston, F. H., Berry, H. L., McDonnell, J., Yibarbuk, D., Gunabarra, C., Mileran, A. and Bailie, R. S. 2009, 'Healthy country, healthy people: the relationship between Indigenous health status and "caring for country"', *Medical Journal of Australia*, vol. 190, no. 10, pp. 567–72; Garnett, S. T., Sithole, B., Whitehead, P. J., Burgess, C. P., Johnston, F. H. and Lea, T. 2009, 'Healthy country, healthy people: policy implications of links between Indigenous human health and environmental condition in tropical Australia', *The Australian Journal of Public Administration*, vol. 68, no. 1, pp. 53–66.
50   Altman, 'People on country, healthy landscapes and sustainable Indigenous economic futures'.

Since 1948 there has been significant economic transformation throughout Western Arnhem Land, but Aboriginal people remain determined to engage in customary activity and to harvest wildlife for sustenance. There is growing evidence that engaging in the customary sector generates health and livelihood benefits. This evidence base, as in 1948, appears to have little impact on policy makers, who disregard such options. The current one-dimensional fantasy for the people of Western Arnhem Land is communities re-centralised in what are now to be called 'Territory Growth Towns'. It will be interesting to see how Aboriginal people engage with this new state project of improvement and what impacts this policy shift has on a customary sector that has remained remarkably resilient in this region over the past 60 years.

Acknowledgments

I would like to thank Geoff Buchanan for research assistance, especially in locating 1947 Census material, assisting in summarising harvesting data from 2002 and 2003 and for comments; Marie de Lepervanche for her recollections in two short interviews about Margaret McArthur; Gillian Cosgrove for drawing the map; and Murray Garde and Peter Cooke for assisting in locating the country and clan affiliations of residents at Fish Creek in 1948. I would also like to thank Martin Thomas, Bill Fogarty, Melinda Hinkson, Nicolas Peterson and Murray Garde for their input, and helpful comments from anonymous refereeing.

7. Making a Sea Change: Rock art, archaeology and the enduring legacy of Frederick McCarthy's research on Groote Eylandt

Anne Clarke and Ursula Frederick

Introduction

The 1948 American–Australian Scientific Expedition to Arnhem Land was an astounding initiative, not only because of the scale, logistics and multidisciplinary scope of its vision, but also because it was a kind of historical re-enactment—a project that performed the investigative urges of an earlier era in modern times. Like the explorers who mapped the continent in the previous century, the Expedition scholars sought to discover and progress knowledge about a particular region in an effort to better grasp a bigger picture of our world. One respect in which the Arnhem Land Expedition differed from past exploratory ventures is that it advanced the science of archaeology as a field of study.

Frederick McCarthy, the Curator of Anthropology at the Australian Museum in Sydney, was one of two archaeologists involved in the Expedition, and early in 1948 he spent 14 weeks on Groote Eylandt surveying and recording rock art sites and carrying out excavations.[1] Along with his American colleague Frank Setzler (Head Curator of Anthropology at the Smithsonian Institution), McCarthy set out to explore the archaeological signature of Arnhem Land. As part of this effort, they surveyed for sites on Groote Eylandt, and in the process McCarthy recorded some 2400 rock art motifs at three key complexes: Chasm Island, Angoroko and Junduruna.[2] This body of work still constitutes the most detailed recording of Groote Eylandt rock art published to date. The rock art recordings enabled McCarthy to provide descriptions of the motifs and to propose a schema of stylistic changes in the art over time. His application of a systematic

---

1   Mountford, C. P. 1956, 'The story of the expedition', in C. P. Mountford (ed.), *Records of the American–Australian Expedition to Arnhem Land. Volume 1: Art, myth and symbolism*, Melbourne University Press, Carlton, Vic., pp. xxi–xxx.
2   McCarthy, F. D. 1960, 'The cave paintings of Groote Eylandt and Chasm Island', in C. P. Mountford (ed.), *The American–Australian Scientific Expedition to Arnhem Land. Volume 2: Anthropology and nutrition*, Melbourne University Press, Carlton, Vic., pp. 297–414, Figure 1, p. 301.

field methodology to record the art and his subsequent interpretations mark a definitive period in the development of rock art research in Australia.[3] It is in this context that McCarthy's involvement in the Expedition can be seen as both a contribution to the scientific understanding of Groote Eylandt and a reflection of an emergent Australian discipline.

In this chapter, we revisit McCarthy's archaeological research on Groote Eylandt in order to place our own more recent recordings, analyses and excavations of rock art sites on the island in their historical context (see Figure 7.1). We present the rock art and archaeology from one rock shelter site called Angwurrkburna to assess the ongoing relevance of McCarthy's research and to illustrate how our own field project based on Groote Eylandt is tied into a trajectory of theory, method and practice in archaeology in Arnhem Land that both builds on and substantially departs from McCarthy's legacy.

The Archaeology of Arnhem Land in 1948

We have noted that the presence of an archaeological team with specific archaeological objectives was an important aspect of the Expedition's originality. This is all the more remarkable because, at the time of their research, Australian archaeology was in its infancy. By 1948 very little specialised archaeological research had been undertaken and only two sites—Devon Downs in South Australia and Lapstone Creek in New South Wales—were regarded as having been systematically excavated.[4] In northern Australia, the only previously reported excavations were those carried out by anthropologist W. L. Warner in 1927 at two shell mounds in the Milingimbi region.[5] One of his excavations included the Macassar Well shell mound at Milingimbi. The brief account by Warner did not make clear his methods of excavation or provide any detail of his findings, but his statement—that he found a large collection of 'native artefacts' in 8 ft (2.5 m) of shell deposit—was sufficient to draw McCarthy and Setzler back to conduct their own large-scale excavation.[6]

---

3   Clarke, A. and Frederick, U. 2008, 'The mark of marvellous ideas: Groote Eylandt rock art and the performance of cross-cultural relations', in P. Veth, P. Sutton and M. Neale (eds), *Strangers on the Shore: Early coastal contacts with Australia*, National Museum of Australia, Canberra, pp. 148–64.

4   McCarthy, F. D. 1948, 'The Lapstone Creek excavation: two culture periods revealed in eastern New South Wales', *Records of the Australian Museum*, vol. 22, no. 3; and Hale, H. M. and Tindale, N. B. 1930, 'Notes on some human remains in the lower Murray Valley, South Australia', *Records of the South Australian Museum*, vol. 4.

5   Warner, W. L. 1969, *A Black Civilisation. A social study of an Australian tribe*, (Revised edition), Peter Smith, Gloucester, Mass., p. 455.

6   McCarthy, F. D. and Setzler, F. M. 1960, 'The archaeology of Arnhem Land', in Mountford, *Records of the American–Australian Expedition to Arnhem Land*, vol. 2, pp. 215–95.

When McCarthy and Setzler jointly published their chapter, 'The archaeology of Arnhem Land', in 1960, they stated that the primary aim of their research was 'to determine the origin, or at least the prehistory of the Australian aborigines in Arnhem Land'.[7] At the time of their fieldwork, there were no methods for measuring past chronologies and they were reliant on creating timelines based on relative dating by establishing stratigraphic sequences of artefact types. McCarthy and Setzler noted further that the contact Indigenous people had experienced with other 'outside' cultures might prove to be a useful temporal indicator and that 'by recovering datable objects of "Malay" [that is, Macassan] or European origin in direct association with an aboriginal horizon, some specific time sequence might be established'.[8]

Despite their efforts to locate and excavate as many stratified archaeological sites in Arnhem Land as possible, McCarthy and Setzler struggled with the low numbers of artefacts in the excavated deposits, the lack of organic objects and thus a correlation with the range of material culture they observed contemporary Indigenous people using and what appeared to be the absence of evidence of a process of linear cultural evolution.[9] They wrote: 'In other continents of the world one can trace the line of development from a simple hunting-fishing-gathering culture through various stages leading to at least a partially sedentary agricultural subsistence.'[10] Chronology proved elusive and they noted that the excavated deposits appeared to be relatively recent, which they found surprising given that they expected Arnhem Land to contain evidence of the oldest occupation of the continent.

In the conclusion to 'The archaeology of Arnhem Land', McCarthy and Setzler adopted a culture-historical framework that attempted to create named prehistoric cultures based on the presence of specific artefact types, such as 'Pirrian' (designated by the presence of pirri points) or 'Mudukian' (recognised by the presence of a bone-point type called a *muduk*). The aim was to explain how particular cultural traits diffused across both time and space. This approach had been successfully applied in North America, and, most famously of course, by Vere Gordon Childe, to classify European prehistoric cultures.[11] McCarthy and Setzler's quest for stone tool types and industries that would represent the

---

7   Ibid., p. 215.
8   Ibid.
9   Ibid., p. 216.
10 Ibid., p. 217.
11 Kidder, A. V. 1924, 'An introduction to the study of southwestern archaeology', *Papers of the Southwestern Expedition*, Phillips Academy, no. 1, New Haven, Conn.; McKern, W. C. 1939, 'The midwestern taxonomic model as an aid to archaeological culture study', *American Antiquity*, vol. 4, pp. 138–43; Wiley, G. R. and Phillips, P. 1958, *Method and Theory in American Archaeology*, University of Chicago Press, Ill.; Childe, V. G. 1925, *The Dawn of European Prehistory*, Kegan Paul, London; Childe, V. G. 1929, *The Danube in Prehistory*, Oxford University Press, UK; Trigger, B. G. 1989, *A History of Archaeological Thought*, Cambridge University Press, UK, pp. 148–206.

diagnostic markers of cultural phases was not successful and the frustrations of this approach are articulated in their summary statement about the archaeology of Oenpelli (now Gunbalanya), where 'we obtained a mixed industry consisting of Bondaian, Eloueran, Kimberleyan, Pirrian, Mudukian and Murundian elements'.[12]

Over the course of the eight months of the Expedition, McCarthy and Setzler carried out excavations at 24 archaeological sites across Arnhem Land. These included 15 rock shelters around Oenpelli, a cave and Macassan trepang site at Port Bradshaw, three shell mounds at Milingimbi and a Macassan grave site on Winchelsea Island. Numerous surface collections of artefacts were made and McCarthy also carried out a detailed rock art study on Groote and Chasm Islands. The scale of their project was enormous and has never been repeated, nor could it be today in that time frame. The changes in archaeological methods and professional standards, the legislative frameworks governing practice, and the ethical issues involved in working with Indigenous communities have rendered this extraordinary expeditionary approach obsolete. In this sense, we can view 'The archaeology of Arnhem Land' as both a relic of an earlier era of research and pioneering in its establishment of archaeology as a legitimate academic discipline, separate to that of anthropology.

Archaeology on Groote Eylandt in 1948

Groote Eylandt was the first location for the Expedition and the archaeological research project. Their investigations included excavating a Macassan burial site on Winchelsea Island, digging 'several' trenches in a shallow shell deposit on Winchelsea Island near the Macassan site, collecting skeletons from Bartalumba Bay, trenching a shell deposit at Thompson Bay, examining surface camp sites in Hemple Bay and at Amalipa, and extensive recording of rock art sites.[13]

Yet the archaeological record they encountered on Groote Eylandt did not fulfil their aims. They stated: 'No sites suitable for excavation were found on the island…[and] none of the rock shelters containing paintings at Amalipa, or at Angoroko, or on Chasm Island has any floor deposit apart from very shallow and scattered patches of shells and pandanus nuts.'[14] Shell middens and indeed many shallow floor deposits have subsequently become key elements of archaeological research with the advent of radiocarbon dating, technological approaches to the analysis of stone artefacts, and analysis of organic remains such as shellfish and bone. In 1948 on Groote Eylandt, however, '[s]urface middens generally were

---

12 McCarthy and Setzler, 'The archaeology of Arnhem Land', p. 286.
13 Ibid., pp. 215–23 and 297–414.
14 Ibid., p. 219.

noted to be shallow and not concentrated in mounds and heaps. All the sites examined suggested a comparatively short period of occupation of the island by the aborigines.'[15]

Setzler and McCarthy found few of the stone artefact types they were seeking and mention only some pink quartzite flakes, rough hammer stones and mortars. Overall, we get little picture of the Indigenous archaeological record on Groote Eylandt and there is no attempt to interpret their findings except in terms of the likely recent occupation and paucity of material.

The one element of the archaeology of Groote Eylandt that does engender a more detailed discussion is the material recovered from the Macassan site on Winchelsea Island. The excavation of the Macassan graves is described in some detail. McCarthy and Setzler note that they collected an unspecified number of pottery shards from a trepang-processing site to the east of the graves. These shards, together with examples from Port Bradshaw, Melville Bay and Milingimbi, are discussed at length in the concluding section of the report.[16] Over the course of the Expedition, they collected 'hundreds' of pottery shards from the beaches of Arnhem Land.[17] They planned to undertake spectroscopic analyses of the clay and tempers from the Macassan shards to determine whether pots were made locally or overseas—a response to Ronald and Catherine Berndt's proposition that Aboriginal people had learnt pottery making from the Macassans.[18] On his return to the United States, Setzler had some shards analysed by Kamer Aga-Oglu at the University of Michigan. She concluded that the earthenware was of a type common across Indonesia and similar to red earthenware found in the Philippines. These were said to date to anywhere from 208 BC to 906 AD. The stoneware and porcelain shards were regarded as Chinese in origin and dating anywhere from 1368 to 1912 AD.[19] McCarthy and Seztler were disappointed in these results as they felt the date range to be too wide for interpretation. 'If we could limit this to a few centuries after A.D. 1000, we would be able to narrow more precisely the period when these fishermen came into contact with the aborigines.'[20] This statement is a precursor to a debate that continues to this day in Australian archaeology.[21]

---

15 Ibid., p. 219.
16 Ibid., pp. 287–94.
17 Ibid., p. 287.
18 Berndt, R. M. and Berndt, C. H. 1947, 'Discovery of pottery in north-eastern Arnhem Land', *Journal of the Royal Anthropological Institute of Great Britain and Ireland*, vol. 77, pp. 133–8.
19 McCarthy and Setzler, 'The archaeology of Arnhem Land', pp. 293–4.
20 Ibid., p. 294.
21 Clarke, A. 2002, '"The Moormans trowsers": Aboriginal and Macassan interactions and the changing fabric of Indigenous social life', in S. O'Connor and P. Veth (eds), *East of Wallace's Line. Modern quaternary research in Southeast Asia 16*, A. A. Balkema, Rotterdam, pp. 315–35; MacKnight, C. C. 2008, 'Harvesting the memory: open beaches in Makassar and Arnhem Land', in Veth et al., *Strangers on the Shore*, pp. 133–47.

McCarthy and Rock Art on Groote Eylandt

In contrast with the apparent dearth of archaeological deposits, a large number of rock art sites were investigated by Frederick McCarthy.[22] His recording and analysis of the rock art are based upon a classification system he developed specifically for the Groote Eylandt and Chasm Island rock art assemblages. His methods were both physically demanding and original, and he realised, even then, that they would set a new, impressive standard:

> [W]e made a sapling grid 7 x 4 ft in size & placed it against the paintings with the aid of forked saplings…I began recording at 9.30 am and managed to almost complete recording the first cave by 5.30 pm… drawing hundreds of figures at ½ inch to a foot scale…it is, I think, the first scale chart made of a northern Australian painting site & it will cause some admiration (wh. will tickle my vanity a little).[23]

Three features form the basis of McCarthy's classificatory schema: the subject of the art, the colour of the pigment used and the 'style' in which the subject is rendered. These 'styles' reflect McCarthy's individual logic in so far as they combine a variety of different features, such as the formal attributes of shape and line, the colour and tonal contrast of the pigments used and the manner in which the pigment was applied.

McCarthy noted that the rock art of Groote Eylandt displays a wide range of styles and colour and he developed a three-phase sequence. Notably, it is defined almost exclusively on the basis of technology and the identification of specific objects of material culture in the art—namely, the axe and the canoe. As such, these phases are established on the basis of contact with outsiders— namely, Macassans and Europeans. Accordingly, the earliest stage of painting is defined as 'the early stone axe and bark canoe period' as differentiated from 'the intermediate Macassan period with the dugout canoe and metal axe', which was followed by the 'recent European period with another type of metal axe'.[24] On the basis of the dugout canoe and its relative prevalence in the art, McCarthy suggested that the majority of Groote Eylandt art was produced during the several hundred years of cross-cultural interaction with Macassan 'outsiders'.

McCarthy drew a number of conclusions on the basis of his recordings, analysis, the opinions of his Groote Eylandt co-workers and his experience elsewhere in Australia. The following points are key features of his interpretations.

---

22   McCarthy, 'The cave paintings of Groote Eylandt and Chasm Island', pp. 297–401.
23   McCarthy, F. D. 1948, Field notes Groote Eylandt, Diary 2, 9–11 June, Library of the Australian Institute of Aboriginal and Torres Strait Islanders Studies, Canberra.
24   McCarthy, 'The cave paintings of Groote Eylandt and Chasm Island', p. 387.

- '[T]he subjects in the caves indicate that the paintings date back to the earliest occupation [of the archipelago]…but this date is unknown.'[25]
- '[T]he economic field was the major inspiration for this art.'[26]
- 'Fishing groups, with bark and dugout canoes, fishing gear and fish…[are] the principal subject depicted throughout the forty-five sites…850 paintings or one-third of the total.'[27]
- The majority of human figures are men 'participating in hunting, fishing and dancing activities',[28] and on the basis of the subject matter the 'paintings are essentially the work and interest of men'.[29]
- There are 'no cults illustrated by large anthropomorphs'.[30]
- A limited number of weapons and ritual articles are represented.[31]

Another important conclusion of his work concerns the relationship of the rock art sites to other archaeological material. Despite his desire to dig, McCarthy was unable to find a rock art site with a deposit suitable for excavation, having observed that no stone implements or any cultural deposits were found in direct association with the cave paintings. McCarthy's results present a picture of rock art sites appearing in relative isolation, outside the day-to-day lives of Groote Eylandt's Indigenous clans.

Archaeology and Rock Art on Groote Eylandt in the 1990s and Beyond

In 1990, Anne Clarke went to Groote Eylandt to carry out a culture-historical study of the sort that was, at the time, a fairly conventional approach to fieldwork in Australian archaeology.[32] Underlying the original research design was the notion that one or two key rock shelter sites would be found and excavated to set up a long chronological and cultural sequence of human occupation much in the vein of Carmel Schrire's pioneering research in Western Arnhem Land in the 1960s.[33] The choice of Groote Eylandt as the focus of the research was part of this traditional approach. Very little systematic archaeological research had

---

25   Ibid., p. 398.
26   Ibid., p. 389.
27   Ibid., p. 388.
28   Ibid., p. 387.
29   Ibid., p. 389.
30   Ibid., p. 399.
31   Ibid., p. 388.
32   Murray, T. and White, J. P. 1981, 'Cambridge in the bush: archaeology in Australia and New Guinea', *World Archaeology*, vol. 13, no. 2, pp. 255–63.
33   Schrire, C. 1982, *The Alligator Rivers: Prehistory and ecology in Western Arnhem Land*, Terra Australis 7, Department of Prehistory, Research School of Pacific Studies, the Australian National University, Canberra.

been carried out on Groote Eylandt and there were no radiocarbon dates for Indigenous occupation. In this sense, the preliminary research aims fell squarely into line with what McCarthy and Setzler had set out to achieve all those years ago, albeit aided by modern methods and dating techniques.

As described in detail elsewhere,[34] however, the process of working with Indigenous families transformed the project from one concerned with deep time and cultural sequences to one focused on community-based approaches to archaeological research and the material record of cross-cultural interactions or 'contact' in the recent coastal landscape.[35] This transformation occurred primarily as a result of working with Indigenous families who presented Anne Clarke with accounts of their own cultural and historical landscape of old peoples' camping places, identified through cultural practice and memory. This produced different results to those that would be expected by a more traditional archaeological approach, orientated towards those parts of the physical landscape where rock shelters and other stratified deposits might be located. Consequently, Clarke redirected the focus of her study to the many shell middens and rock shelters that contained evidence of Indigenous interaction with Macassans and Europeans. A study of the rock art was added to the field research in 1995 and 1996 when Ursula Frederick joined the project. A specific aim of the rock art project was to investigate the ways in which Indigenous artists were choosing to represent their interactions with outsiders through their rock art.[36] This focus on the art and archaeology of cross-cultural interactions, the development of a community-based approach to the archaeology, and the use of contemporary social theories of agency, performance and cultures of the everyday are the key points of departure from the pioneering research of McCarthy and Setzler in 1948.

Angwurrkburna: The excavation

During a preliminary exploration in 1992 while working with a Yantarrnga man (now deceased) and his family, we found a small rocky outcrop containing a painted rock shelter in an area called Angwurrkburna. This small rock shelter

---

34 Clarke, A. 2000, 'Time, tradition and transformation: the archaeology of intercultural encounters on Groote Eylandt, Northern Australia', in R. Torrence and A. Clarke (eds), *The Archaeology of Difference: Negotiating cross-cultural engagements in Oceania*, One World Archaeology 38, Routledge, London, pp. 142–81; and Clarke, A. 2002, 'The ideal and the real: cultural and personal transformations of archaeological research on Groote Eylandt, Northern Australia', *World Archaeology*, vol. 34, no. 2, pp. 249–64.
35 Clarke, A. 1994, Winds of change: an archaeology of contact in the Groote Eylandt archipelago, Northern Australia, PhD thesis, the Australian National University, Canberra; Clarke, '"The Moormans trowsers"', pp. 315–35; Clarke, 'Time, tradition and transformation', pp. 142–81.
36 Clarke, A. and Frederick, U. 2006, 'Closing the distance: interpreting cross-cultural engagements through Indigenous rock art', in I. Lilley (ed.), *Archaeology of Oceania: Australia and the Pacific islands*, Blackwell, Oxford, pp. 116–33; Clarke and Frederick, 'The mark of marvellous ideas', pp. 148–64; and Frederick, U. and Clarke, A. 2006, Signs of contact: Groote Eylandt rock art and cross-cultural exchange, Picturing Relations (Groote Eylandt Barks Symposium), Ian Potter Museum of Art, University of Melbourne, <http://www.art-museum.unimelb.edu.au/events_transcripts>

is located close to the south-eastern shore of Angurrkwurrikba or Salt Lake on the eastern coast of Groote Eylandt (Figure 7.1). It is part of the Yantarrnga clan lands, which extend south along the coast from Mamalimanja Point (Picnic Beach) to the northern portion of Dalumbu Bay and inland to encompass a large portion of the sandstone country around Yantarrnga (Central Hill). In 1991–92 and again in 1995–96, we worked with the one Yantarrnga family for all of our fieldwork in this area, bush camping for weeks at a time around the shores of Salt Lake.

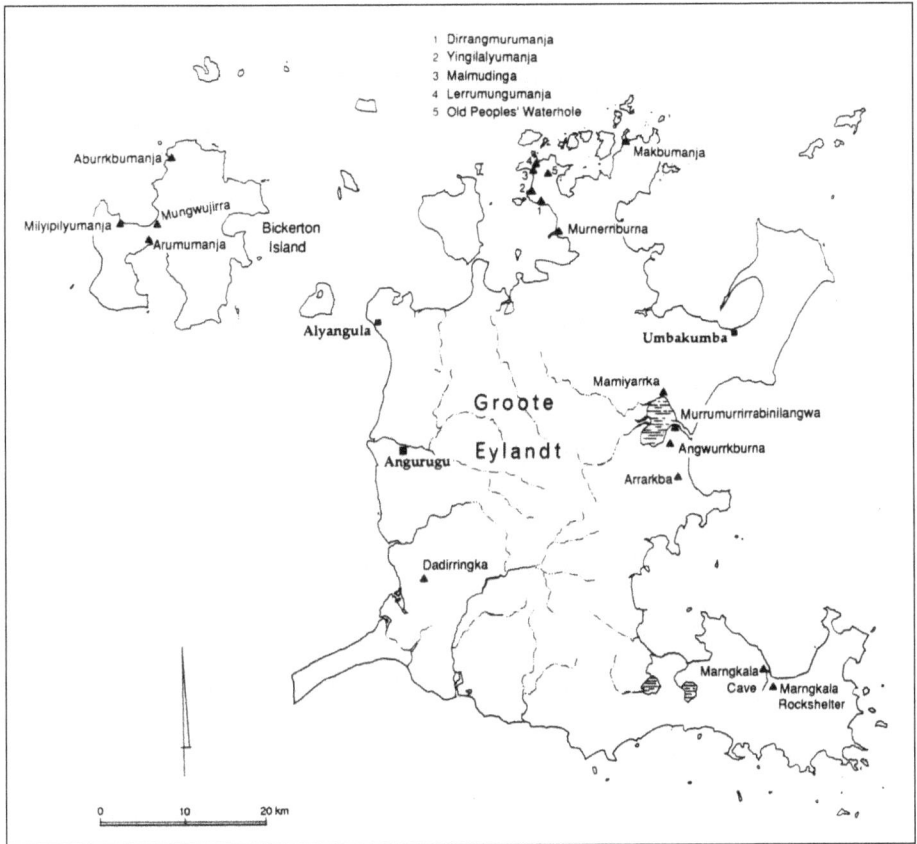

Figure 7.1 Location map of sites excavated by Clarke, 1994

Illustration by Winifred Mumford

The rock shelter is located 500 m south of the lake shore and 3.5 km from the coast to the east. Today this area is visited only to hunt wallabies or to look for yams, and the heavy vegetation growth around the outlier suggested that the area had not been visited or fired for a considerable period. The walls and ceiling of the rock shelter are densely painted and the rock shelter floor has an area 8 m long and 2 m wide. This floor deposit is sandy with marine shells (*Terebralia palustris*) and old firewood is visible on the surface. The site is split into two halves with the southern end being under a roof some 3 m high and the northern portion being under a very low overhang only 1 m in height (Figure 7.2). At the southern end of the shelter, there is a large rock, which contained a smooth grinding patch with red staining, indicating that it had been used for grinding ochre.

Figure 7.2 View of Angwurrkburna rock shelter, facing east, 1995

Photograph by Anne Clarke

The Excavation

In conjunction with our Indigenous co-workers, a Yantarrnga man (now deceased) and his wife, Polly Mamarika, we mapped, photographed, excavated and sketched the Angwurrkburna shelter during two field seasons, in 1992 and in 1995. In 1995, on a return visit to the site, Ursula Frederick also recorded the rock art. In all, three 1 m excavation squares were dug into the deposit. The first (H1) was very shallow and terminated on bedrock after only 15 cm of deposit had been removed. This shallow deposit consisted of a sandy soil mixed with leaf litter. With the exception of some green bottle glass recovered from the base of this square, very little cultural material was found. In comparison, the other two squares, C1 and D1 (only the material from C1 is discussed here), were excavated to a depth of 50 cm and were terminated when rock fall made excavation too difficult to continue. The deposit in these two squares comprised two units: an upper, dark-grey, sandy deposit containing some midden materials and a lower red/brown unit containing greater quantities of sandstone and lateritic rubble. The upper unit was 26 cm deep and the lower unit was 24 cm deep (Figure 7.3).

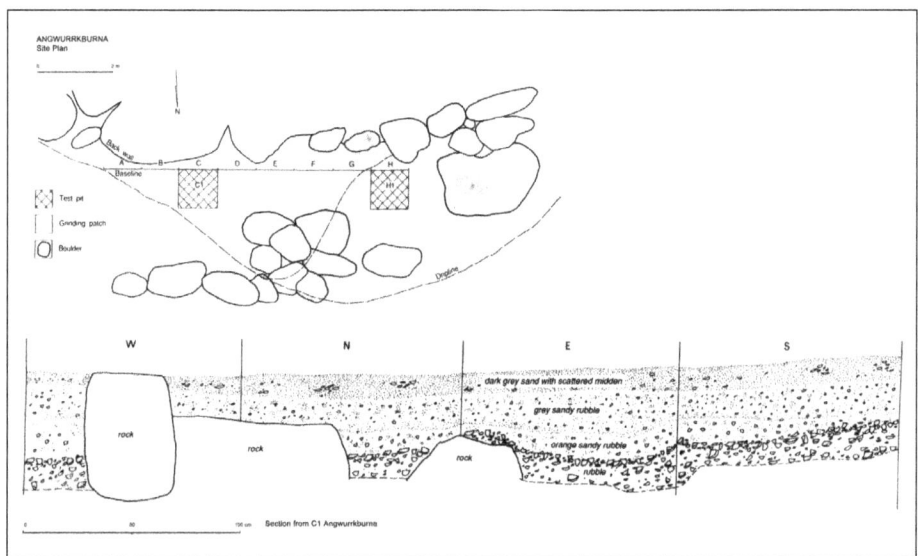

Figure 7.3 Site plan and section drawing from Angwurrkburna

Illustration by Winifred Mumford

Three charcoal samples were submitted for radiocarbon dating (Table 7.1). These dates indicate that the rock shelter was first occupied somewhere between 2700 and 1900 years ago and continued to be visited and used as a shelter until some time in the mid twentieth century.[37]

Table 7.1 Radiocarbon dates from Angwurrkburna*[38]

Laboratory number	Excavation square and spit	Depth below surface (cm)	Radiocarbon date	Calibrated date(2δ 95.4% cal. age range)
ANU-8987	H1-1	15	98.7+/-0.9% modern	130 – 3
ANU-8986	C1, Spit 5	26	1650+/-70 years	1691–1339
ANU- 8985	C1, Spit 9	50	2260+/-140 years	2698–1872

* The radiocarbon ages were calibrated to 2 sigma using CALIB 5.0.1.

Site Contents

The cultural material excavated from Angwurrkburna consists of bone, shell, stone and ochre (Table 7.2). Very little shell or bone was preserved because of

---

37   Brockwell, S., Faulkner, P., Bourke, P., Clarke, A., Crassweller, C., Guse, D., Meehan, B. and Sim, R. 2009, 'Radiocarbon dates from the Top End: a cultural chronology for the Northern Territory coastal plains', *Australian Aboriginal Studies*, vol. 1, pp. 54–76.
38   Ibid., p. 59.

the acidic soil conditions and much of this was too fragmentary to identify to species level. The few identifiable fragments of bone, however, included fish, shark, mammal, crab and reptile. Most of the marine shell is *Terebralia palustris*, a mangrove gastropod used today for bait and as a snack food.

Table 7.2 Weights of stone artefacts, ochre and ground-stone fragments excavated from square C1

	Angwurrkburna (SL/Ang/92-C1)					
Spit	Depth below surface (cm)	Wght 6 mm lithics (g)	Wght 3 mm lithics (g)	Wght 6 mm ground stone (g)	Wght 6 mm ochre (g)	Wght 3 mm ochre (g)
1	3	6.61	3.07	70.56	0.00	0.63
2	7	5.09	6.39	5.96	29.93	1.30
3	12	9.69	4.86	0.00	19.10	2.05
4	19	24.13	7.53	0.00	52.82	4.77
5	26	62.86	4.86	10.70	70.96	9.92
6	30	110.84	9.66	30.27	152.65	12.48
7	39	127.38	6.71	0.00	101.28	10.10
8	44	235.34	10.88	0.00	43.79	4.58
9	50	257.66	10.03	0.00	44.65	6.54
Totals	**50**	**839.60**	**63.99**	**117.49**	**515.18**	**143.27**

In total, 133 chipped stone artefacts were recovered from square C1. Most of the artefacts were made from quartz (which is a locally available raw material), but a few artefacts were manufactured from chert and fine-grained pink silcrete. A fine-grained silcrete from the Walker River (Ngilipitji) area of the mainland is known from the ethnography to have been imported onto Groote Eylandt.[39] There is one unifacial point made from a good-quality, fine-grained silcrete and this material could indeed have come from that mainland locality. One-third of the stone artefacts show evidence of pebble cortex—the weathered 'skin' from rounded stones. This indicates that pebbles and cobbles eroded from beds of sandstone conglomerate are most likely to have been the primary source for the raw material used to make stone artefacts at Angwurrkburna.

---

39   Tindale, N. B. 1925–26, 'Natives of Groote Eylandt and of the west coast of the Gulf of Carpentaria, parts 1–2', *Records of the South Australian Museum*, vol. 3, p. 98.

Of the 133 artefacts present, only four pieces of chipped stone have been retouched into recognisable tool types, the remainder being waste flakes (Table 7.3). There was one unifacial silcrete point, a small chert adze flake, a notched silcrete scraper and one piece of quartz with a retouched edge. This is obviously only a negligible proportion of the excavated assemblage and this low number of recognisable stone tools is in keeping with the findings from the 1948 excavations. The assemblage of stone artefacts also contains 33 cores—the blocks of stone from which flakes and tools are removed. The presence of worked cores in the deposit is evidence that stone knapping occurred at the rock shelter. Interestingly, there are more artefacts in the lower unit than in the upper unit, indicating changes in the way the rock shelter was used over time.

Table 7.3 Numbers of stone artefacts and raw material types from C1 at Angwurrkburna

Angwurrkburna (SL/Ang/92-C1)				
Raw material	No. quartz	No. quartzite	No. silcrete	No. chert
Spit				
1	6	0	0	0
2	8	0	1	0
3	12	2	1	0
4	16	1	2	0
5	35	6	2	0
6	31	5	4	3
7	38	4	5	2
8	83	12	18	7
9	102	6	18	7

A large quantity of worked ochre was recovered from square C1. Almost 20 per cent of it has evidence of use in the form of ground facets and striations. This used ochre was particularly prevalent towards the base of the deposit. Similarly, the total number, weight and raw material diversity of ochres increases in the lower unit. Red ochre is the main pigment present in the deposit (Table 7.4) and varies in colour and fabric from coarse-grained nodules of laterite to very fine-grained, soft ochres. Other pigment colours recovered in the lower deposit include yellow, purple, red/yellow and white.

Table 7.4 Numbers of ochre pieces from Angwurrkburna

Angwurrkburna (SL/Ang/92-C1)						
Spit	No. red	No. yellow	No. purple	No. white	No. red/yellow	No. with facets
1	0	0	0	0	0	0
2	18	0	0	0	0	3
3	13	0	0	0	0	1
4	16	1	0	0	0	0
5	29	9	1	0	0	3
6	45	4	1	1	2	12
7	30	1	0	0	0	9
8	26	9	1	0	0	9
9	22	7	0	1	2	6
Totals	218	31	3	2	5	43

Angwurrkburna: The rock art

Rock art covers much of the walls and ceiling of the Angwurrkburna shelter. It varies in size, subject and style from schematic human figures to the compelling centrepiece on the shelter's ceiling: a depiction of a Macassan prau complete with crew and provisions and composed in three colours with an X-ray view into the interior hull (Figure 7.4). We classified the Angwurrkburna art assemblage according to technique, subject, the number and colour of pigments used, and the formal characteristics the motif displayed. In terms of the spatial aspects of the site, we noted the position of the motifs within the shelter and their relation to one another.

Our recording of the site revealed 47 rock art motifs, amongst other pigment stains and indeterminate forms. Three techniques were used in the production of the art—stencilling, painting and drawing—but the majority (in excess of 90 per cent) of the assemblage was composed of paintings. Seventy-five per cent of these paintings were produced using one pigment colour, 22 per cent using two pigments, and only one recorded painting was composed of three colours. The most frequently employed colour was red, followed by white, then yellow and brown.

The majority of paintings could be described as figurative motifs. A number of these motifs might be considered as single subjects but there are several that appear to be grouped in compositions of stylistically related forms. The majority of such 'grouped' motifs incorporate human figures—often in combination with objects and fauna. Amongst the subjects present, human figures dominate the assemblage. Many of these anthropomorphs are arranged in compositions, such as a group of dancers or people fishing from a dugout canoe. More unusual arrangements include several camping scenes, depicting families sleeping inside bark shelters. This latter interpretation was offered by our Groote Eylandt colleague (a Yantarrnga man) and reflects a more intimate view of the everyday lives of Indigenous families (Figure 7.5). But amongst these domestic scenes there are also representations of marine and terrestrial fauna including turtles, fish, crocodiles, lizards and dogs. There are few representations of material culture with the exception of two dugout canoes and a large prau. There are no wallabies, which were highly prevalent in McCarthy's data.

Figure 7.4 Macassan prau painting at Angwurrkburna, 1992

Photograph by Anne Clarke

We identified a number of superimpositions that go towards defining a sequence at Angwurrkburna (Figure 7.6). Aside from examples of multiple rock art layers, there are numerous single-layer superimpositions. On the basis of these observations, it appears that red silhouette and a purple-red linear infill style are amongst the earliest discernible art. Silhouettes and line paintings of human figures were continued until the most recent episodes of painting. Bi-chromatic paintings in red and yellow have been partially obscured by subsequent paintings employing a white pigment. It is clear that white was the most recent colour used in the art (most often it was in a silhouette style). Examples include a canoe with sail, a turtle with tracks or scrape, and numerous human figures.

Figure 7.5 Rock painting of family group (detail of white pigment digitally enhanced for publication), 1995

Photograph by Ursula Frederick

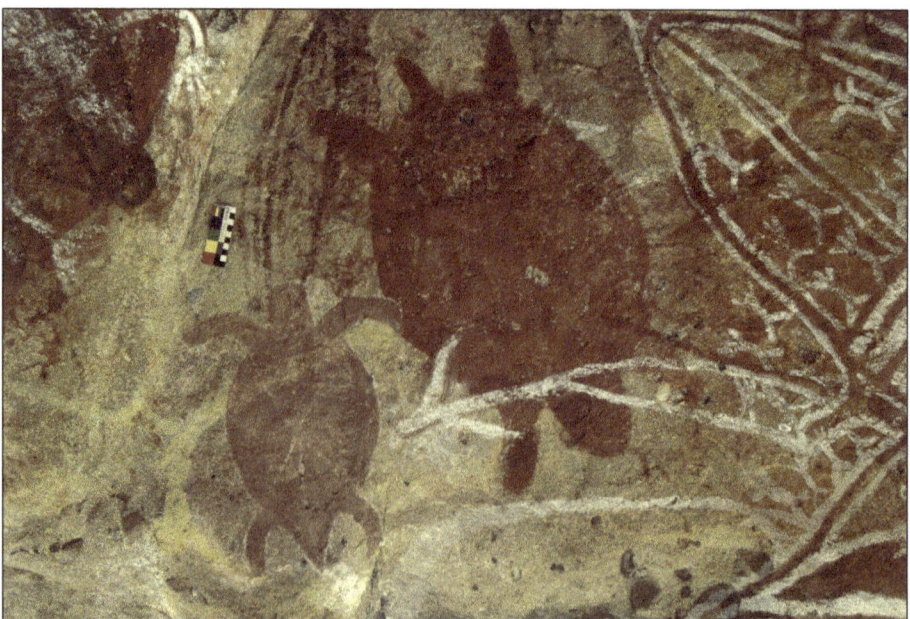

Figure 7.6 Detail of Angwurrkburna ceiling showing superimposed paintings, 1995

Photograph by Ursula Frederick

The superimposing of art at Angwurrkburna enabled us to consider McCarthy's relative sequencing of the art in the context of new data and to revisit a number of his interpretations. If we were to adopt McCarthy's chronology, Angwurrkburna might best fit the intermediate period when he suggests much of the art on the island was made. It is a period that he believes corresponds with contact with the Macassans but for which he ascribes no firm time frame. The impressive prau and the dugout canoes at Angwurrkburna are clearly associated with a contact tradition. Research based on historical records suggests a conservative date of 1780 AD for the inception of contact with Macassans.[40] There are some arguments for an earlier time frame for contact with outsiders[41] —perhaps about 1100 or 1200 AD based on the presence of one small pottery shard at the rock-shelter site of Dadirringka on the west coast of Groote Eylandt in a spit 7 cm below one with a radiocarbon date 930 +/- 60 BP (ANU-8984). This date, when calibrated to a calendar date, falls somewhere between 1026 and 1264 AD.[42]

For the most part, Angwurrkburna conforms to McCarthy's summation that silhouettes are the dominant style of Groote Eylandt art. Indeed, paintings of this kind make up more than 40 per cent of the total at Angwurrkburna. Outline and line design styles are also common at Angwurrkburna, as McCarthy noted generally across the archipelago. Stencils, however, do not occur with the frequency he recorded and are only a minor part of the assemblage. In terms of subject matter, Angwurrkburna reveals some remarkable contrasts with McCarthy's Groote Eylandt data. Foremost is the large number of human figures. Almost half (47.8 per cent) of the identified motifs depict anthropomorphs, either as solitary figures or in groups. This is in keeping with the high proportion of human figures McCarthy recorded, but at odds with his suggestion that 'the human figure does not feature so prominently'.[43] Two of the Angwurrkburna figures are large and occupy a commanding position—a point that further challenges McCarthy's conclusion that there are 'no cults illustrated by large anthropomorphs'.[44] Both examples are painted in silhouette with arms and legs outstretched. One is notable because it appears to re-mark the features of an earlier anthropomorphic painting. Many of the other anthropomorphs are small in size, especially when they are composed as part of a scene.

In several other respects the art at Angwurrkburna departs from McCarthy's analysis and general conclusions. The dominance of white pigment at Angwurrkburna is one key difference with McCarthy, who reported that it occurred infrequently. Another example is the outstanding prau, which has no comparison in McCarthy's data. The painting incorporates three colours—red,

---

40   MacKnight, 'Harvesting the memory'.
41   Clarke, Winds of change, p. 399; Clarke, 'Time, tradition and transformation'.
42   Brockwell et al., 'Radiocarbon dates from the Top End', pp. 64–73.
43   McCarthy, 'The cave paintings of Groote Eylandt and Chasm Island', p. 399.
44   Ibid.

white and pink—in a style combining silhouette, outline and infill. With its human figures, harpoon and flag, the prau is animated with movement and life. The X-ray perspective of the prau and detail of its contents are all the more impressive given the rock shelter's distance from the ocean.

Despite his groundbreaking efforts to link archaeology and art, and modernise the study of rock art in Australia, McCarthy's reliance on material culture was also a constraint on his interpretation. For example, he bases his chronological sequence for the rock art on the representation of a few unique objects. Such uncommon objects as metal axes of foreign origin become the key temporal markers of his sequence even though the rock art styles and superimposition relationships he documented provide a stronger pattern of change over time. It is hardly surprising, then, that despite the variability in content, colour and style evident at Angwurrkburna, McCarthy's three-phase sequence is not validated in our results.

Angwurrkburna Summary

The dates for Angwurrkburna show that use of the rock shelter began at least 2700 years ago and continued possibly until shortly after 1950 (as indicated by the modern date in H1). This is not to imply continuous occupation, more that the site remained part of a cultural landscape over a significant period.

Linking the art and archaeology, the evidence from Angwurrkburna indicates that between 2700 and 1700 years ago the rock shelter was a place where people went to paint, camp and to chip locally available stone. The lower part of the deposit contains a large amount of discarded ochre including partially used crayons and ochre of all different colours. This suggests that Indigenous people had access to a plentiful supply of ochre and did not need to curate it. From the evidence in the upper part of the deposit, which dates from 1700 years ago to the present day, it seems that stone-working activities decreased. Painting continued but only red ochres were discarded in any quantity. If we tie this to the art sequence, we can interpret this pattern in a number of ways. People might have been more carefully curating ochres because they had become harder to obtain, possibly because the seasonal presence of Macassans had disrupted access to particular ochre sources or affected existing processes of art production. It is also possible that art production was more intensive in this recent phase of occupation, inspired by the changes engendered by the presence of Macassans, and all available pigments were used up and little discarded. Given the evidence from the art sequence, this seems to be the most likely explanation.

The archaeology of Angwurrkburna demonstrates that the activities of painting, tool production and daily life were not carried out in isolation. Moreover, the rock paintings, ochre-stained grinding patch and presence of used ochre fragments in the dated deposit provide a clearer indication of the timing for rock art production and the relative chronology McCarthy first posed. Angwurrkburna shows, as McCarthy supposed but was unable to prove, that Groote Eylandters have probably been painting for several millennia.

Conclusions: Rock art, archaeology and the enduring legacy of Frederick McCarthy's research on Groote Eylandt

When Frederick McCarthy set out to investigate 'the cave paintings of Groote Eylandt and Chasm Island' his stated purpose was to ascertain the fundamental characteristics and chronology of Groote Eylandt and Chasm Island rock art.[45] Another objective was to provide a baseline study of the archipelago's rock art for comparison with art in the broader Arnhem Land region, and in turn the rest of Australia and the world. But McCarthy's work on Groote Eylandt reveals as much about the development of Australian archaeology as it does about the art and culture of Groote Eylandt peoples. Two particular features exemplify his approach and signal the emergence of the archaeology of art as a discipline of study. First was his systematic attention to recording rock art to scale and in its entirety. Second was his desire to link rock art to stratified archaeological deposits. McCarthy's comprehensive illustrations, tables and notes suggest that he was able to provide 'a complete record of the art represented in the groups recorded', but his second goal remained elusive. Despite this limitation, one of the enduring legacies of McCarthy's research on Groote Eylandt was in cementing a place for the scholarly investigation of rock art in Australia and in producing a record of the rock art on Groote Eylandt that still lends itself to analysis in the present day.

The archaeological research, on the other hand, has proved less robust over the decades since publication. From a historical perspective, the 12 years from fieldwork in 1948 to publication in 1960 can now be understood as a crucial period in the development of global archaeology. It was a time when the discipline underwent a rapid change, with the introduction of new analytical techniques and theoretical frameworks that produced very different explanations about cultural change than those used by McCarthy and Setzler. The now familiar methods of modern archaeology such as radiocarbon dating and the analyses of past environments and economic systems using shell, faunal and botanical remains were fast becoming integral to research projects in Europe and the United States of America. In Britain, for example, excavations at the Mesolithic

---

45   McCarthy and Setzler, 'The archaeology of Arnhem Land', p. 297.

site of Star Carr, Yorkshire, in the late 1940s and early 1950s were at the forefront of the new field of economic archaeology, reconstructing the seasonal hunting patterns of Mesolithic hunter-gathers from a range of faunal remains.[46]

Against this backdrop of radical transformation, 'The archaeology of Arnhem Land' is a curiously anachronistic account of the pre-European history of the region. It is more a reflection of a nascent antipodean discipline than a programmatic example of the research potential of Australian archaeology such as that set out by John Mulvaney in the following year.[47] It was only a short time after the publication of the Expedition report that Australian archaeology entered a key phase of intellectual growth and discovery, with Pleistocene dates for Indigenous occupation announced in 1962 by Mulvaney at Kenniff Cave in Queensland and by Carmel White (Schrire) in Kakadu.[48]

In many ways, the trajectory of our own research owes more to the dynamic developments in Australian archaeology from the 1960s and 1970s than to the research presented in the Expedition report. The ethno-archaeological research by Betty Meehan with the Anbarra on the Blyth River anticipated the developments in community-based archaeology in the 1990s and provided an example of how to do research embedded in a community context.[49] Campbell MacKnight's exhaustive research on the archaeology of Macassan sites and the history of the trepang industry across Arnhem Land provided the framework for examining, in contrast, the Indigenous archaeological record of that period and the process of cross-cultural engagement.[50]

The research carried out by the Expedition in 1948 represented a major sea change for Australian archaeology in a number of ways. First and most importantly, archaeology was included as a key discipline along with anthropology and the natural sciences. Second, the research questions that drove the archaeological and rock art research—questions about chronology, contact, stone technology and art sequences—are still debated today. Third, McCarthy's application of a systematic method for rock art recording moved the study of rock art away from selective description towards a more archaeological approach as developed by McMah (who later published as Maynard) for Sydney rock engravings.[51]

---

46   Clark, J. G. D. 1954, *Excavations at Star Carr: An early Mesolithic site at Seamer near Scarborough, Yorkshire*, Cambridge University Press, UK.
47   Mulvaney, D. J. 1961, 'The Stone Age of Australia', *Proceedings of the Prehistoric Society*, vol. 27, pp. 56–107.
48   Mulvaney, D. J. and Joyce, E. B. 1965, 'Archaeological and geomorphological investigations on Mt Moffatt Station, Queensland', *Proceedings of the Prehistoric Society*, vol. 31, pp. 147–212; White, C. 1976, Plateau and plain: prehistoric investigations in Arnhem Land, PhD thesis, the Australian National University, Canberra; White, C. 1967, 'The prehistory of the Kakadu people', *Mankind*, vol. 6, no. 9, pp. 426–31; White, C. 1967, 'Early stone axes in Arnhem Land', *Antiquity*, vol. 412, pp. 147–52; Schrire, *The Alligator Rivers*.
49   Meehan, B. F. 1982, *Shell Bed to Shell Midden*, Globe Press, Melbourne.
50   MacKnight, C. C. 1976, *The Voyage to 'Marege': Macassan trepangers in northern Australia*, Melbourne University Press, Carlton, Vic.
51   McMah, L. 1965, A quantitative analysis of the Aboriginal rock carvings in the district of Sydney and the Hawkesbury River, BA (Hons) thesis, Department of Anthropology, University of Sydney, NSW.

The innovative sea change our research is making is, we suggest, our focus on the art and archaeology of cross-cultural interactions from the perspective of the Indigenous archaeological record, rather than the material record left by the outsiders. In addition, our research was explicitly embedded for the duration of the fieldwork within a community-based approach. This moves the research process beyond describing Indigenous people as 'informants' or as the ubiquitous 'native' as framed by the archaeological discourse of the Expedition report,[52] to one where fieldwork methods, research questions and the everyday experience of doing archaeology as part of a family or community group are a negotiated process. While McCarthy worked closely with Indigenous people on Groote Eylandt,[53] his field research and published writing remain firmly within the realm of archaeology as colonial practice.[54] He shared the daily activities of camping, fishing and hunting with Indigenous families on Groote Eylandt, as we know from his diaries and his influential paper on food gathering, co-written with Margaret McArthur (see Altman, this volume).[55] These experiences, however, were kept at a distance in his published archaeological research. These observations are made not to denigrate his achievements on the Expedition but more to explain that contemporary archaeological practice has moved in a direction that seeks to break down those artificial dissonances between past and present, prehistory and history, and scientist and 'native', to a position where Indigenous knowledge and practice are as integral to the research process as systematic recording methods.

Like McCarthy's, our field survey was also guided by Indigenous knowledge and experience of place. The Groote Eylandt we came to know, however, was more than a suite of old camping places and artefacts to be 'collected'. The landscape of rock art and archaeology revealed to us by the Indigenous families with whom we worked was a living terrain shaped and enriched by the everyday activities and necessities involved in living on country. As a result of this engagement, we have been able to locate sites—of which Angwurrkburna is just one example—where there is both rock art and an archaeological deposit. This allowed us to begin the kind of integrated interpretation that McCarthy sought all those years ago.

---

52 Clarke, A. 1998, 'Engendered fields: the language of the American–Australian Expedition to Arnhem Land', in M. Casey, J. Hope, D. Donlon and S. Wellfare (eds), *Redefining Archaeology: Feminist perspectives*, Archaeology and Natural History Publications, Research School of Pacific and Asian Studies, the Australian National University, Canberra, pp. 13–18.
53 F. D. McCarthy, 1948, Field notes Groote Eylandt, Diary 1, Diary 2, Diary 3, Library of the Australian Institute of Aboriginal and Torres Strait Islanders Studies.
54 McNiven, I. and Russell, L. 2005, *Appropriated Pasts: Indigenous peoples and the colonial culture of archaeology*, Altamira Press, Lanham, Md.
55 McCarthy, F. D. and McArthur, M. 1960, 'The food quest and the time factor in Aboriginal economic life', in C. P. Mountford (ed.), *Records of the American–Australian Scientific Expedition to Arnhem Land. Volume 2: Anthropology and nutrition*, Melbourne University Press, Carlton, Vic., pp. 145–94.

8. Ecology and the Arnhem Land Expedition: Raymond Specht, a botanist in the field

Lynne McCarthy

This chapter explores the work of Raymond Specht, botanist on the 1948 American–Australian Scientific Expedition to Arnhem Land. In this chapter, I examine Specht's botanical collecting from two related perspectives. First, I consider the practical challenges of undertaking field-based plant ecology in the tropical environment of northern Australia, and second, I discuss Specht's ecological surveys (presenting a brief history of the development of ecology as a discipline) and his creation of an extensive botanical collection during eight months working in the field. The botanical collections from the Expedition illuminate Specht's training in plant ecology, and his skill, dedication and passion for field-based work. I explore how Specht's experience leading up to the Expedition affected the subsequent approach that he took to fieldwork in Arnhem Land. Specht was required to negotiate landscapes that were familiar in principle, and yet at the same time foreign to a plant ecologist from southern Australia. His botanical and plant ecology work shows how Specht had to actively adapt to, and translate, his field skills and knowledge when working in northern Australia. It is *place*—in this case, Arnhem Land—that is centrally implicated in the work of this botanist. Specht's reading of landscape was informed by taking a holistic approach to his fieldwork, recording accurate and detailed observations of complex Arnhem Land environments.

Ecology in the Early Days

Ecology has been described as a science of holism: an integrative science linking knowledge about the physical world with the study of living things.[1] Complexity, diversity and a lack of unity have characterised ecological theory and practice since the discipline emerged during the late nineteenth and early twentieth centuries. By the 1890s, ecology was regarded as a separate field of study from biological sciences and botany.[2] During the early twentieth century, the

---

1 Hay, P. 2002, *Main Currents in Western Environmental Thought*, UNSW Press, Sydney; Gibbons, W. 1993, *Keeping all the Pieces: Perspectives on natural history and the environment*, Smithsonian Institution Press, Washington, DC.
2 McIntosh, R. P. 1985, *The Background of Ecology: Concept and Theory*, Cambridge University Press, UK.

discipline began to address broader questions about the relationships between living things and their environment.³ Field studies were seen as essential to the practice of ecology, and early ecologists generally followed a holistic philosophy in the study of landscapes and dynamics of plant communities.⁴ The concept of ecosystem has changed in character over time within this discipline, with a shift of emphasis from 'place' and 'organism' to 'flux' and 'process'.⁵ Specht's work on the Arnhem Land Expedition in 1948 reflects this earlier concept of ecosystem. Eliciting and understanding connections and relationships between place and diverse plant communities across Arnhem Land were his primary goals.

Trends in the development of the discipline of ecology in American, British and Australian contexts are pertinent to understanding the approach and techniques used for Specht's botanical and plant ecology work on the Arnhem Land Expedition. Frederic Clements forged the discipline of ecology in the United States of America in the 1890s, with attention to the development of the concept of a plant community as both a dynamic and a complex entity interacting with its environment.⁶ Clements set the tone for ecological research among American botanists for approximately 40 years. British thinking on the discipline of ecology began with regional surveys of plants in the landscape, creating a systematic overview. This was further developed towards a focus on understanding patterns between different plant communities—akin to the American concept of dynamic communities. Ecology in Australia was influenced by American and British scientific thinking, emerging as a discipline of science in the 1920s.⁷ It was initially regarded as a 'science of exploration', a key to understanding new lands.⁸

The Botany Department at the University of Adelaide played a leading role in plant ecology research in Australia, particularly focusing on interactions of plant communities with the environment. Head of Department, Professor Joseph Wood, encouraged his staff and students to develop experimental research on the taxonomy (classification and naming of plants), ecology, and distribution patterns of plant communities, emphasising the importance of fieldwork as part of any ecological research. This approach to ecological studies was instilled in

---

3   Kingsland, S. 1993, 'An elusive science: ecological enterprise in the southwestern United States', in M. Shortland (ed.), *Science and Nature: Essays in the history of the environmental sciences*, British Society for the History of Science Monographs 8, Oxford, pp. 151–79.
4   Bowler, P. 1993, 'Science and the environment: new agendas for the history of science?', in Shortland, *Science and Nature*, pp. 1–21.
5   Allen, T. F. and Roberts, D. W. 1997, 'Foreword', in R. Ulanowicz (ed.), *Ecology, The Ascendant Perspective*, Columbia University Press, New York, pp. xi–xiii.
6   Nicolson, M. 1988, 'No longer a stranger? A decade in the history of ecology', *History of Science*, vol. 26, no. 72, pp. 183–200; Kingsland, 'An elusive science', pp. 151–79.
7   Robin, L. R. 1998, *Defending the Little Desert: The rise of ecological consciousness in Australia*, Melbourne University Press, Carlton, Vic
8   Robin, L. R. 1997, 'Ecology: a science of empire?', in T. Griffiths and L. R. Robin (eds), *Ecology and Empire: Environmental history of settler societies*, Melbourne University Press, Carlton, Vic., pp. 63–75.

Raymond Specht, a student in this department. As a second-year undergraduate in 1944, Specht gained experience as a field botanist by conducting a plant-collecting field trip for assessment. He travelled from Adelaide to Whyalla and Iron Knob via the lower Flinders Ranges in South Australia. One hundred plant specimens were collected, dried, pressed, identified, and prepared for the Adelaide Herbarium.[9] The most formative year of Specht's time in the Botany Department was his honours year in 1946 and work on the ecological survey of 260 sq km of the Adelaide Hills. Travelling on foot and by bicycle, he investigated distribution patterns of different eucalypt species in the landscape, which led to his lifelong study and interest in the structure, growth and biodiversity of ecosystems and plant communities (see Specht, this volume). These experiences as a field ecologist in southern Australia provided Specht with methods and techniques that he would soon draw upon when he joined the Arnhem Land Expedition as a botanist.

Specht's Recruitment to the Arnhem Land Expedition

The 1948 Arnhem Land Expedition was jointly sponsored by the National Geographic Society, the Smithsonian Institution and Australia's Department of Information. The Expedition party was eight months in the field, collecting more than 25 tonnes of specimens, which were intended as important contributions to science. Expedition members included people from the disciplines of archaeology, anthropology, ichthyology, ornithology, nutrition and medical sciences, and botany, as well as photographers and filmmakers (see May, this volume). The leader, Charles Mountford, reported that no previous scientific expedition in Australia had covered so many interlocking fields of natural history, medical science and ethnology.[10]

The Australian Government intended that the Expedition would generate large amounts of scientific and general information, provide a record of Aboriginal people in story, photograph and film, and provide favourable publicity for the nation. It would also foster good relations with the United States, and stimulate scientific cooperation between the two countries (see Beazley, this volume).[11]

Raymond Specht was initially invited to be part of the Arnhem Land Expedition in September 1946:

---

9 Specht, R. L. n.d., The development of environmental science policy in Australia, Unpublished manuscript.
10 Specht, R. L., in C. P. Mountford (ed.) 1956, *Records of the American–Australian Scientific Expedition to Arnhem Land. Volume 1: Art, myth and symbolism*, Melbourne University Press, Carlton, Vic., p. xxi.
11 Bonney, Director-General, Memorandum to The Secretary Department of Treasury, 1947, Publicity—Arnhem Land Expedition—C. P. Mountford, Series No. CP815/1–005.87, Part 1, National Archives of Australia (henceforth NAA), Canberra.

I was called into the professor's office…and Wood said to me 'you won't be getting any payment, you'll get your travel and your keep, but you'd better go'…I had to prepare all this mountain of equipment to get away in January…By the time we'd got everything ready…I was informed that they were going to delay the expedition for a year…so everything went into chaos and I went back to teaching.[12]

The Expedition was delayed until March 1948 to allow completion of American research work in the Pacific, and to enable the Smithsonian to form a more representative and distinguished team of scientists. Norman McCrae, the Chief Administration Officer at the Department of Information, wrote to Specht in January 1948 with a formal offer for the position of botanist, at an annual salary of £500, on the understanding that Specht was already willing to accompany the Expedition and was qualified for the work. The letter of offer noted that work would commence on 1 February and finish at the end of November.[13] Specht accepted the offer, formally joining the Expedition. The initial delay of the Expedition provided an opportunity for him to begin work on producing ecological maps of areas in northern Australia, drafted from aerial photographs. Mountford considered this to be valuable groundwork for the planning of research activities at each location to be visited.[14]

Three main camps were successively established across Arnhem Land, located in different types of landscape to maximise the diversity of scientific findings: Groote Eylandt, an island camp with stony hinterland; Yirrkala, on the coast; and Oenpelli (now Gunbalanya), with its stone country and floodplains, in Western Arnhem Land. As Charles Mountford wrote in his account of the Expedition, work for the botanist and other naturalists began after arriving in Darwin. During a 10-day delay prior to the Expedition party heading to Groote Eylandt, a sample of scientific specimens was collected along the coast and within the rainforest near Darwin. While working on Groote Eylandt, Raymond Specht collected and surveyed plants around the Umbakumba base camp and accompanied Margaret McArthur (nutritionist from the Australian Institute of Anatomy) to Bickerton Island to assist with nutritional studies and more botanical collecting. Yirrkala was an opportunity to collect along the coast, with its freshwater swamps and forests. At Oenpelli, Specht worked in open savannas, black-soil floodplains and sandstone plateau country.[15]

---

12 Specht, R. L. 2006, Oral history recording by Martin Thomas and Sally K. May, Oral TTC 5662, recorded 2 May 2006, National Library of Australia (henceforth NLA), Canberra.
13 N. McCrae to R. L. Specht, 21 January 1948, Publicity—Arnhem Land Expedition—Mountford, Series No. CP815/1–005.87, Part 1, NAA.
14 C. P. Mountford to Bonney, 6 February 1947, Publicity—Arnhem Land Expedition—C. P. Mountford, Series No. CP815/1–005.87, Part 1, NAA.
15 Mountford, *Records of the American–Australian Scientific Expedition to Arnhem Land*, vol. 1, p. xxiii.

8. Ecology and the Arnhem Land Expedition

A Botanist Working in the Tropical North

> [I]t was interesting to land on Darwin aerodrome, because the tips of the wings [of the aeroplane] were touching this tall grass…as we landed. Interesting to an ecologist of southern Australia where nothing grows more than about a foot or two.[16]

The Arnhem Land Expedition was Raymond Specht's first visit to northern Australia. Drawing on his previous experience as a southern plant ecologist, he prepared the necessary equipment for collecting plant specimens, including such items as mountains of newspaper, plant presses, secateurs, compass, notebook, axe and backpack. For the Expedition, Specht's brother, Gordon, an apprentice sheetmetal worker, provided 12 sets of galvanised-steel plant presses. Refrigerator trays were used, as they were the same size as a folded broadsheet page of the *Adelaide Advertiser* newspaper. Plant specimens were placed on sheets of newspaper and securely pressed between two metal grids with leather straps.[17]

A typical day for the Expedition botanist commenced before breakfast, checking and drying plant specimens previously collected. Then, with axe over one shoulder and backpack over the other, he would head out to collect five new specimens before lunch and five before dinner. Where possible, the whole of the plant was collected, including the flowers, leaves, fruits and bark. Considering the requirement for 10 sets of each plant specimen collected, 100 specimens per day for processing was not unusual. Evenings were for pressing and drying the ever increasing botanical collection.[18] Bessie Mountford would often help Specht change the papers for drying plants in the evenings. Diaries she kept about her experiences in Arnhem Land have many entries that mention these activities: 'After tea I helped Ray again with the paper changing…Ray has piles of specimens. He certainly is collecting as much as he possibly can.'[19]

As Specht was to discover, there were some added challenges for the botanist working in a tropical environment. During the drying of the more succulent plants, newspaper sheets in presses needed to be changed every day. Mangroves and rainforest plants presented an added challenge to a botanist not experienced in collecting these types of plants from the field. They required a longer time to dry, coupled with an additional problem of leaves and flowers breaking off from the stems. Prior to joining the Expedition, Specht spent

---

16 Specht, Oral history recording, NLA.
17 Ibid.
18 Mountford, C. P. 1949, 'Exploring Stone Age Arnhem Land', *National Geographic*, vol. 96, no. 5, p. 750.
19 Bessie Mountford, Unpublished diary 4, 1948 American–Australian Expedition to Arnhem Land, Entry written at Oenpelli 7 October 1948, PRG 487/1/2, Mountford-Sheard Collection, State Library of South Australia (henceforth SLSA).

some time at the Queensland Herbarium in Brisbane acquainting himself with collection techniques and drying methods for tropical species. The herbarium staff recommended using an ordinary four-gallon drum filled with formalin to soak succulent plants for 24 hours, prior to placement in plant presses. This additional step solved the problem of leaves and flowers breaking off stems, ensuring that a respectable herbarium specimen was collected and preserved. With each day of collecting, it became necessary to counter longer drying times, as there was a steadily growing mountain of plants needing to be pressed. Prior to the Expedition, Raymond Specht and his brother devised another mechanism to assist in the drying of plant specimens: a drying oven. Specimens were put into the oven (a tank encased in a water jacket) and the unit was placed over a campfire. Drying time for plant specimens was significantly reduced—from 10–15 days to an average of three or four.[20] Modifications in the processing and management of a growing botanical collection of tropical plants were integrated into the daily practice of the botanist. This was part of the challenge for Specht, working in a landscape unlike any he had encountered before.

Bickerton Island, west of Groote Eylandt, was a mix of mangrove swamp, eucalypt forest, black-soil plains and rocky tableland. Specht spent 21 days on the island and collected more than 200 plant specimens. A number of these were newly discovered species growing in rocky gorges and sandstone hills. At Yirrkala, another 288 species collected from along the coast, freshwater billabongs and eucalypt forests were added to the collection.[21] It was at Oenpelli, however, the final base camp, where botanical work proved most interesting. Mountford sent a telegram to the Department of Information stating: 'Expect Oenpelli to be rich field for all branches of scientific work for expedition stop rugged interior holds many rare specimens birds animals plants.'[22]

The stone country where a number of unknown species flourished was of immense interest to Specht.[23] He described the new plants in English and Latin, referring to field notes and the herbarium specimen. An example is *Acacia mountfordiae*, a species of wattle restricted to rocky sandstone habitat around Oenpelli. Specht named this plant after Bessie Mountford, following a request from Charles. There were also plant specimens collected earlier on the Expedition that were found growing in different environmental conditions at Oenpelli.[24] These observations provided an opportunity for the botanist to begin thinking about another dimension of plant ecology: the history of changes in composition and distribution of Arnhem Land plant life over time and space.

---

20   Specht, Oral history recording.
21   Mountford, 'Exploring Stone Age Arnhem Land', p. 758.
22   C. P. Mountford, Telegram to the Department of Information, 14 September 1948, National Archives Publicity—Arnhem Land Expedition—C. P. Mountford, Series No. CP815/1–005.87, Part 3, NAA.
23   Mountford, 'Exploring Stone Age Arnhem Land', p. 778.
24   Bessie Mountford, Unpublished diary 4, Entry written at Oenpelli, 6 October 1948, Mountford-Sheard Collection, SLSA.

Specht was very diligent in recording information for each specimen collected—13 500 in total. His Expedition field books listed a series of details including locality, habitat, life form (tree, shrub, herb, grass), date of collection, identification, and name of collector. There were additional notes on the colour and arrangement of leaves and flowers, and samples of bark taken from tree species. Every detail was needed, for, as Specht recalled, 'people might never have seen these things before'.[25]

Over eight months, Specht created a comprehensive botanical collection, and detailed ecological surveys with what Bessie Mountford described as a 'quiet persistence and continued interest in his chosen career [that was] most commendable'.[26] Forty-two crates of botanical specimens were transported from Darwin to the Queensland Botanic Gardens in Brisbane at the end of the Expedition.[27] The original collection was deposited in the Queensland Herbarium in Brisbane and replica sets went to institutions in Melbourne, Sydney, Canberra, Adelaide and Perth. Sets were also dispatched to Kew in the United Kingdom, Leiden in the Netherlands, and to the Arnold Arboretum and the Smithsonian Institution in the United States. Specht went to Brisbane for approximately five months to work in the Government Botanist's Office and complete work on the Arnhem Land collection. With assistance from a number of botanists from Australia and overseas, he completed identification of all the plant specimens.[28]

Arnhem Land: A venue for science

The idea of 'place' is central to Specht's work on the Expedition. Frank Vanclay defines three conditions that contribute to the idea of 'place': geographic location, physicality, and investment with meaning and value.[29] As I will discuss, these factors are demonstrated in Specht's holistic approach to understanding the landscape, resulting in the creation of ecological surveys and vegetation maps of different study sites. In his published report, Specht illustrated the interrelationships between plant communities and other components of a dynamic ecosystem including climate, soil, bedrock and topography.[30]

---

25 Specht, Oral history recording.
26 Bessie Mountford, Unpublished diary 5, 1948 American–Australian Expedition to Arnhem Land, Entry written at Oenpelli 13 October 1948, Mountford-Sheard Collection, SLSA.
27 Publicity—Arnhem Land Expedition—C. P. Mountford, Series No. CP815/1–005.87, Part 3, NAA.
28 Mountford, C. P. and Specht, R. L. (eds) 1958, *Records of the American–Australian Scientific Expedition to Arnhem Land. Volume 3: Botany and plant ecology*, Melbourne University Press, Carlton, Vic., p. 185.
29 Vanclay, F. 2008, 'Place matters', in F. Vanclay, M. Higgins and A. Blackshaw (eds), *Making Sense of Place: Exploring concepts and expressions of place through different senses and lenses*, NMA Press, Canberra, pp. 3–11.
30 Mountford and Specht, *Records of the American–Australian Scientific Expedition to Arnhem Land*, vol. 3.

During the Expedition, Specht wrote letters home to his family in Adelaide, describing features of the landscape in which he was working. Two examples illustrate the importance of understanding 'place' for the plant ecologist. The first letter provides a detailed description of the landscape as seen from the air:

> [T]he Arnhem Land scarp was the most interesting part. Huge and majestic, distorted and writhing in agony as the sandstone had cracked apart when the earth bent under some gigantic strain, this geological formation appeared. Cracks that had been deepened into gorges with silver streams at their bases and waterfalls with spray rising high above them. Huge desolate crags, grand and beautiful in the early morning sunlight. Vegetation was confined to isolated cracks and crevices in which soil had collected. I am looking forward to visiting this country from Oenpelli. Then after 60–80 miles we flew over the backbone of Arnhem Land…This country is like Darwin with Darwin stringybarks, woollybutts and bloodwoods, red ironstone soil but not very much spear grass (due to lower rainfall?). A few wet swamps and streams looked remarkedly [sic] green from the air…and finally Blue Mud Bay. I often wondered why they dotted the coastline here (on maps), but now I know. There is a vast area of saltwater swamps behind, and, of course, the sea here is a real blue mud.[31]

Specht makes sense of Arnhem Land unfolding below him as a function of time, geology and the dynamic nature of plant communities. He provides a geological location for this place in northern Australia. Attention to the physicality of the landscape is captured through his description of the dynamic nature of the Arnhem Land scarp, and the unique features found in this tropical landscape. This interpretation reflects his ecological training, taking a holistic approach to understanding the workings of Arnhem Land ecology.

A second letter provides a vivid description of another study site on the Expedition. Again, the botanist demonstrates his holistic understanding of place, interpreting changes in the structure and composition of plant communities in relation to different environmental features:

> The majority of the area was stringybark savannah forest developed on an undulating ridge of truncated lateritic earth, with occasional outcrops of quartzite. A coastal sand-dune covered with grasses and an occasional bush and Pandanus ran alongside most of the N–S beaches. Behind this, narrow belts of monsoon forest and paperbark swamps and billabongs occurred with a couple of streams lined with mangroves near their mouths. One paperbark lagoon impressed me beyond description.

---

31   R. L. Specht, Letter written home to family in Adelaide from Groote Eylandt, 11 April 1948.

It was clothed in lots of blue waterlilies and green sedges…the beaches were sandy, lined with Casuarina and merged into either reef of lateritic slabs of quartzite or just sandy beach.[32]

For the Expedition botanist, a survey was recognised as more than just collecting and recording an inventory of Arnhem Land plants. Work also included an investigation into the dynamics of plant communities growing in unique environmental conditions including sandstone hills, freshwater billabongs, undulating plains and extensive floodplains (see Figure 8.1). Specht's letters about the landscape reveal an increasing familiarity with Arnhem Land through an active engagement with the locations visited. It is exactly the kind of engagement that Jeff Malpas suggests develops a sense of place.[33]

Figure 8.1 Western Arnhem Land near Gunbalanya (formerly Oenpelli), 2009

Photograph by Lynne McCarthy

32   R. L. Specht, Letter written home to family in Adelaide from Umbakumba, Groote Eylandt, 17 May 1948.
33   Malpas, J. 2008, 'Place and human being', in Vanclay et al., *Making Sense of Place*, pp. 325–31.

A Living Collection

The botanical collections from the Expedition are of national and international significance. The collection is a diverse and rich assemblage of Arnhem Land flora that includes specimens of fungi, moss, lichen, ferns, algae (freshwater and marine), gymnosperms (non-flowering plants), and flowering plants. The collection included newly discovered species and new varieties of plants.

Sixty years after the Expedition, scientific research into the ecological workings of the tropical north continues.[34] Raymond Specht's work has been referred to as the earliest comprehensive description of flora from Arnhem Land, providing a valuable resource for continuing research across northern Australia including extensive surveys of plant communities, fire management, biodiversity studies, and vegetation-mapping projects. Specht's oral history in this volume—providing an insider's perspective on the legacy of the Arnhem Land Expedition—highlights the fact that many of the ecological questions he posed at the time formed the basis for his continuing national and international research as a plant ecologist. Species composition, structure and the formation of plant communities growing in different environmental conditions and locations could be further investigated through the analysis of the comprehensive botanical collections generated from his Arnhem Land fieldwork.

Individual specimens from the collection have been reviewed, reclassified and in some instances renamed. Some herbarium specimens now carry additional labels and annotations from recent botanists working with the collection, outlining changes to accepted scientific names and classification (see Figure 8.2). Specht named the plant shown in Figure 8.2 for his wife Marion, choosing *magnifica* to describe the most magnificent flower collected during the Expedition. In the Queensland Herbarium, the newly rediscovered plant specimens from 1948—the majority of which were collected from Bickerton Island and Oenpelli—are stored in a fire- and bomb-proof room within the main herbarium holdings (see Figure 8.3). This is testimony to the national significance of this botanical collection, ensuring secure storage and access to researchers for many years to come.

---

34 Woinarski, J., Mackey, B., Nix, H. and Traill, B. 2007, *The Nature of Northern Australia: Natural values, ecological processes and future prospects*, ANU E Press, Canberra.

Figure 8.2 Herbarium specimen *Melaleuca magnifica* collected from Bickerton Bay

Photograph by Lynne McCarthy, 2009. By permission of Queensland Herbarium, Brisbane Botanic Gardens Mt Coot-tha. American–Australian Scientific Expedition to Arnhem Land Collection.

Figure 8.3 Herbarium specimen *Cassia harneyi* collected from Bickerton Island

Photograph by Lynne McCarthy, 2009. By permission of Queensland Herbarium, Brisbane Botanic Gardens Mt Coot-tha. American–Australian Scientific Expedition to Arnhem Land Collection.

Concluding Remarks

For Raymond Specht—a young plant ecologist from southern Australia—the role of botanist on the Arnhem Land Expedition was an exciting and challenging prospect. A comprehensive botanical collection of 13 500 specimens and ecological surveys and vegetation maps provided the groundwork for investigations into the ecology of Arnhem Land plant communities. His skill, dedication and passion for fieldwork were driving forces in the completion of a significant body of work on the botany and plant ecology of Arnhem Land. The Expedition botanist embraced his work in northern Australia, maintaining a holistic approach to understanding the ecology of tropical landscapes.

9. Piecing the History Together: An overview of the 1948 Arnhem Land Expedition

Sally K. May

Friday, 2 February 1945 was a defining day in the life of Charles Mountford. The South Australian ethnographer stood nervously in front of a room packed to capacity with enthusiastic members of the National Geographic Society. They had come to be entertained with stories of the exotic Indigenous people of Australia by the adventurer who had 'captured' them in photographs and moving pictures. A handful of people in the audience that day had the power to further Mountford's ethnological collecting and research ambitions. Members of the National Geographic Society Research Committee approached Mountford and suggested he submit a proposal for a scientific research expedition.[1] This suggestion sparked the beginning of a planning process that culminated in a seven-month journey across the Northern Territory of Australia. The story behind the negotiations, preparations and final realisation of this Expedition is important for our understanding of its legacy, and it is clear that politics, propaganda and science became uneasy bedfellows for the 1948 American–Australian Scientific Expedition to Arnhem Land.

After 10 years of researching the Arnhem Land Expedition, I feel like an octogenarian trying to populate their family tree but finding that with each new person comes another 40 lines of possible investigation. The Arnhem Land Expedition is a never-ending, interwoven tree of people, places and events. ABC journalist Colin Simpson's much quoted reflection on the importance of this Expedition sums up the scale of the task. He states, 'What it accomplished is said to have been scientifically considerable, but is not measurable now, and perhaps never will be. Such findings take years to write and codify and publish and disseminate. When that is completed, the use of them is only at the beginning.'[2] When Simpson wrote these words in 1951 he obviously suspected that more than half a century later we would still be writing, codifying, publishing and disseminating the findings of their work.

---

1 Mountford, C. 1975, 'Report on expedition for the National Geographic Society', *Great Adventures with National Geographic*, National Geographic Society, Washington, DC, p. 225; Mountford, C. P. (ed.) 1956, *Records of the American–Australian Scientific Expedition to Arnhem Land. Volume 1: Art, myth and symbolism*, Melbourne University Press, Carlton, Vic., p. ix.
2 Simpson, C. 1951, *Adam in Ochre: Inside Aboriginal Australia*, Angus & Robertson, Sydney, p. 40.

In spite of that, while the collections are the tangible result of the Arnhem Land Expedition, they are not the only reason for its lasting, and perhaps increasing, significance. Interest in this Expedition comes from a much wider group than just museum workers and academics, and includes Indigenous Australians, descendants of the men and women who participated in the Expedition, members of the general public who grew up reading Mountford's popular books or seeing his films, the mums and dads who remember reading the latest update on the Expedition in newspapers throughout 1948, and much, much more. Our true understanding of the significance of this Expedition for many stakeholders is only just beginning to emerge.

In February 1948, a team of Australians and Americans came together in Darwin, Australia, to begin what was then one of the largest scientific expeditions ever to have taken place in this country. They travelled across Arnhem Land until November 1948, basing their work around three key Indigenous communities: Groote Eylandt, Yirrkala and Oenpelli (today Gunbalanya) (Figure 9.1). Before I go into more detail about the base camps and the nature of the research it is important to understand a little more of the origins of the Expedition and the people and organisations at the forefront of the planning.

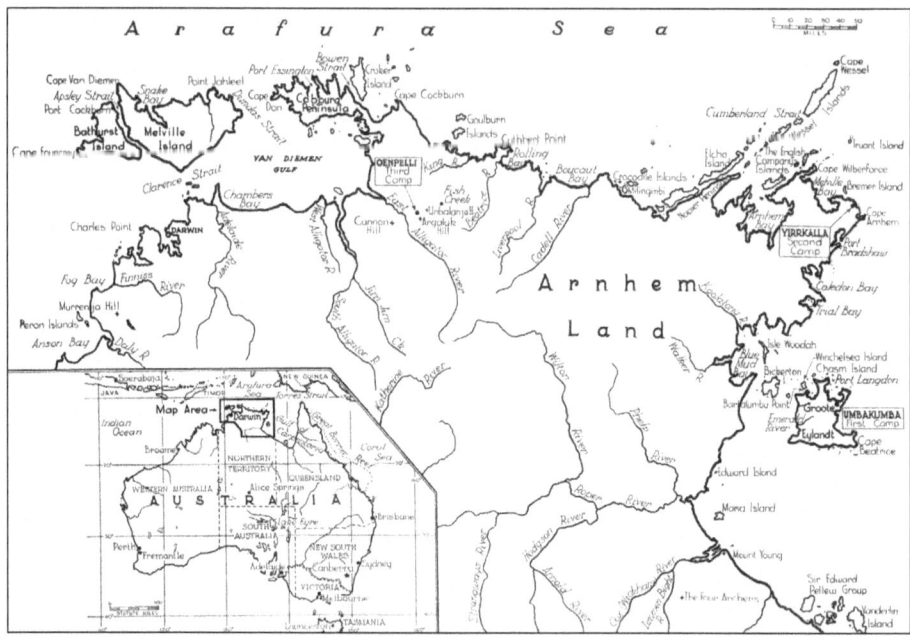

Figure 9.1 Map of the Northern Territory, Australia, showing regions visited during the 1948 Arnhem Land Expedition

From Charles P. Mountford (ed.) 1956, *Records of the American–Australian Scientific Expedition to Arnhem Land. Volume 1: Art, myth and symbolism*, Melbourne University Press, Carlton, Vic.

While on the surface the pursuit of science and knowledge would seem to be the key motivator for the Arnhem Land Expedition, in truth politics was central to its success in attaining funding and international collaborators. This can be better understood by looking at the leader of the Expedition and his work promoting and planning the Expedition prior to 1948 (Figure 9.2). Charles Mountford was born in 1890 to a family with Scottish and English heritage. Most of his family were farmers or general labourers who lived in South Australia. Mountford insisted to his biographer, Max Lamshed, that his family was 'poor, but it was a uniform poverty. Everyone was in the same boat, so we didn't notice.'[3] In his early life, Mountford lived in Adelaide working in jobs such as a stereoscope salesman, stable boy, blacksmith's striker, and tram conductor. By the age of twenty, he was undertaking a course in mechanics and engineering, which helped him to secure a position with the engineering department of the postal service. He married in 1914, and was posted to Darwin in 1920 as the mechanic in charge at the Darwin Post Office.[4] It was in Darwin that Mountford's interest in Indigenous Australian cultures is thought to have begun.[5]

Figure 9.2 Frank Setzler and Charles Mountford in Adelaide, 17 November 1948

By permission of the National Library of Australia. nla.pic-an24313084.

---

3 Lamshed, M. 1972, *Monty: A biography of C. P. Mountford*, Rigby, Adelaide, p. 10.
4 Ibid, p. 10.
5 May, S. K. 2009, *Collecting Cultures: Myth, politics, and collaboration in the 1948 Arnhem Land Expedition*, Altamira, Calif., p. 37.

After returning to Adelaide in 1922–23, and the death of his wife in 1925, Mountford took to travelling around South Australia with his father. They came across many Indigenous rock art sites during these adventures and made contact with Norman Tindale at the South Australian Museum to discuss their findings. Tindale, and others such as J. B. Cleland and T. D. Campbell, encouraged Mountford to continue exploring and documenting sites. Mountford participated in three anthropological research expeditions to Central Australia during the 1930s, with the assistance of these colleagues. This period is discussed in detail by Philip Jones, but it is important to note that by 1948 Mountford had attained certain knowledge relating to Indigenous art and, in particular, the Pitjantjatjara, Adnjamatana and Arrernte people.[6] He had produced short films including *Tjurunga* (1942) and *Walkabout* (1942), and collected and documented ethnographic artefacts, rock art sites and cultural stories from Indigenous communities in South Australia.[7] These films were what caught the attention of the then Federal Minister of Information, Arthur Calwell. This now notorious politician saw the potential of these films for international publicity for Australia.[8] Mountford was offered a position in Calwell's Department of Information and sent on a lecture tour to promote Australia in the United States.[9]

As mentioned earlier, Mountford was awarded funding for a new expedition to Arnhem Land.[10] His proposal to the National Geographic Society outlines his intentions and, in particular, his desire to record and collect Australian Indigenous art. He states: 'Knowing that the simple art of these people would be the first aspect of their culture to disappear, I have concentrated on the investigation and recording of all phases of their art.'[11] He goes on to claim that his previous work in Central Australia 'has saved the art of the Central Australian from extinction'.[12] The official 1945 research proposal submitted by Mountford[13] includes study of four main areas: a) the art of the bark paintings; b) the art of the body paintings; c) the general ethnology of the people; and d) music in secular and ceremonial life. Yet, there were also unpublicised aims for this Expedition. These aims were outlined 18 months later in a private letter from Mountford to the President of the National Geographic Society, Gilbert Grosvenor:[14]

---

6   Jones, this volume.
7   May, *Collecting Cultures*.
8   Arthur Calwell is remembered for championing the White Australia Policy.
9   Mountford, 'Report on expedition for the National Geographic Society', p. 225; Mountford, *Records of the American–Australian Scientific Expedition to Arnhem Land*, vol. 1, p. ix.
10 L. J. Briggs, 20 April 1945, Letter to G. Grosvenor, Accession file 178294, Smithsonian Institution Archives, Washington, DC.
11 Charles Mountford, 5 March 1945, Letter to the Chairman of the National Geographic Society Research Committee, Accession File 178294, Smithsonian Institution Archives, Washington, DC, p. 2.
12 Ibid.
13 Ibid.
14 Charles Mountford, 28 January 1947, Letter to Gilbert Grosvenor, Setzler Files, Box 7, Folder 4, Arnhem Land Correspondence 1948–1949, Folder 1 of 2, National Anthropological Archives, Washington, DC.

1. Establish a good neighbour policy and scientific cooperation between the United States of America and Australia.

2. Provide publicity for Australia through the publication of three, if not four, illustrated articles in the *National Geographic Magazine*. (Circulation 1,250,000. Estimated Readers 5,000,000).

3. Study and record the aborigine's pattern of life in relation to the terrestrial and marine fauna and flora.

4. Investigate seasonal movements and shelter of the aborigines, and, by examination of their foods determine how well, or otherwise, they are able [to] 'live off the land'.

5. Make a nutritional health survey of the natives and their food as a guide for future administration.

6. Collect and identify the plants, birds, animals and fish in the various environments of Arnhem Land.

7. Carry out a food fish survey along the coast of Arnhem Land.

8. Determine the food resources of land and sea as data for future military operations [this was urgently needed, but not available, during the previous war].

9. Produce, for the National Film Board, five coloured cine films on the ethnology and natural history of Arnhem Land.

International politics and propaganda were just as important (if not more important) as science for the Arnhem Land Expedition.

Calwell is today recognised for the role he played in the Arnhem Land Expedition; it could not have occurred without his backing. He saw the National Geographic Society's funding of an expedition as a wonderful opportunity for promoting political and scientific relations between Australia and the United States. Calwell arranged for the Commonwealth Government to pay Mountford his usual wage plus expenses for the Expedition and transport.[15] The Ministers for Air, the Army and Health all offered support including transport, food, and, importantly, three scientists from the Australian Institute of Anatomy were allowed to join the Expedition and study Indigenous health and nutrition (Figure 9.3). The Minister for the Interior also placed his organisation in the Northern Territory at their disposal.[16]

---

15 Mountford, Letter to the Chairman of the National Geographic Society Research Committee, p. 4.
16 Mountford, *Records of the American–Australian Scientific Expedition to Arnhem Land*, vol. 1, p. xxi.

Figure 9.3 Expedition members aboard flight from Adelaide to Darwin— left: Bessie Mountford, Margaret McArthur, Brian Billington, Peter Bassett-Smith, Charles Mountford (standing), Frank Setzler (standing). Right: Frederick McCarthy, Kelvin Hodges, Herbert Deignan, John Bray, Raymond Specht, Bob Miller, Dave Johnson, March 1948

By permisison of Raymond Specht.

Arthur Calwell was responsible for the massive expansion of the Arnhem Land Expedition and the associated publicity. He led negotiations for funding and personnel with the Australian Minister to the United States, Sir Frederic Eggleston, in Washington, DC, the Secretary of the Smithsonian Institution, Alexander Wetmore, and staff of the National Geographic Society.[17] As Wetmore wrote: 'We look forward with keen interest to this work, particularly to the close association that it brings between representatives of our two governments. We may, I trust, consider this a beginning to an even closer cooperation in future scientific matters than has existed heretofore.'[18] With the involvement of other institutions, including the Australian Museum and the Smithsonian Institution, the expedition Mountford had originally planned grew to 17 people and a diverse range of disciplines.

The Expedition was originally planned for 1947. The one-year delay was due to the Smithsonian Institution unexpectedly needing staff intended for the Arnhem Land Expedition for 'commitments in connection with the Bikini tests'.[19] In other words, the scientists intended for the Arnhem Land Expedition

---

17   Ibid., p. xxi; Mountford, 'Report on expedition for the National Geographic Society', p. 225.
18   Alexander Wetmore, 3 December 1947, Letter to Bridges, Accession File 178294, Smithsonian Institution Archives, Washington, DC, p. 3.
19   Arthur Calwell, 28 February 1947, Letter to J. J. Dedman, Series A 9816/4, 1947/89, Part 1, NADC, Arnhem Land Expedition, National Archives of Australia, Canberra.

were required for research relating to nuclear weapons testing in the Pacific. Calwell felt that without the Americans, the Expedition would not achieve the desired publicity, so, with little consultation, he decided to delay for one year. This alone is evidence of the power Calwell had over this team and process. Yet the delay provided Mountford and his team with more time to prepare for their ambitious research and schedule. The Expedition team now included Mountford as leader and Smithsonian Institution archaeologist Frank Setzler as deputy leader. It also included a botanist, mammalogist, ichthyologist, ornithologist, anthropologist, photographer, cine-photographer, and a team of medical and nutritional scientists plus support staff. Together these men and women embarked on an amazing journey.

After leaving Darwin, the Expedition team set up its first base camp on Groote Eylandt in the Gulf of Carpentaria. Three months later, they moved to Yirrkala on the Gove Peninsula and three months following that to Oenpelli (now Gunbalanya) in Western Arnhem Land. Mountford states that he chose these camps because they represented different environmental regions and research would therefore produce diverse outcomes. He also chose a camp at the Roper River but this was abandoned due to delays in starting work on Groote Eylandt.[20]

After two weeks in Darwin waiting for their supplies to arrive overland from Adelaide, the team made its way to the first base camp, Umbakumba, on Groote Eylandt. Most of the team arrived aboard an RAAF Catalina flying-boat, however, a few team members decided to make the journey by sea and were stranded when a storm pushed the *Phoenix* onto a reef near the mouth of the Liverpool River. The barge was stuck on the reef for five weeks as the crew attempted to save Expedition equipment and food. One of the stranded Expedition members was National Geographic Society photographer Howell Walker, who later documented this journey in the article 'Cruise to Stone Age Arnhem Land'.[21] The media had a field day, as this article illustrates:

Starving Scientists

A Catalina left Darwin at daylight today with emergency supplies for the American–Australian Scientific Expedition on Groote Eylandt, as the launch which was to have followed the expedition with supplies broke down. Until the aeroplane arrives the scientists will have a first-class chance of studying native food-stuffs.[22]

---

20 Mountford, *Records of the American–Australian Scientific Expedition to Arnhem Land*, vol. 1, p. xxiii; Mountford, 'Report on expedition for the National Geographic Society', p. 225.
21 Walker, H. 1949, 'Cruise to Stone Age Arnhem Land', *National Geographic*, vol. 96, no. 3, pp. 417–30.
22 'Starving scientists', *Daily Mirror*, 16 April 1948.

Cameraman Peter Bassett-Smith was one of those waiting on Groote Eylandt and he clearly had a bit of time on his hands, as he managed to pen an epic song about the experience. He titled his song 'The Phoenix Never Came In' and the following is a sample of his work:

> An expedition left the north one day,
> Flew by Catalina far away,
> All the stores were to have gone ahead
> On the barge Phoenix, instead.
> But the Phoenix never came in.
> While on Groote Eylandt they were near starvin'
> She hadn't even left Darwin.
> Oh! The Phoenix never came in.
> All was well on a clear blue sea,
> Eggs for breakfast, caviar for tea!
> Super service made the voyage fine,
> On that Capricornian Line,
> But the Phoenix never came in.[23]

Not to be outdone, Fred Gray also wrote a song, which he titled 'Shores of Umbukwumba':

> From the shores of Umbukwumba to the great Ung-oo-roo-koo,
> This place's so full of scientists, there's no room for me or you
> They were eating lots of tucker, and sitting in their tents,
> And waiting for the Phoenix in the cause of sci-i-ence.[24]

Mountford and his team had set up camp next to Fred Gray's so-called 'native settlement' at Umbakumba. Here Mountford thought he would have a better chance of becoming acquainted with the local people and access to facilities.[25] Setzler later recorded that the younger Indigenous men were keen to assist the Expedition with tasks such as moving equipment but the older men 'preferred to wait and see what this white intrusion might signify'.[26] The memories of Gerry Blitner, recorded shortly before he passed away, are enlightening, as they provide an insight into the Indigenous experience of the Expedition.[27] Gerry

---

23 This song is taken from the unpublished booklet of the fiftieth anniversary reunion of the Arnhem Land Expedition produced by and in the possession of Raymond Specht.
24 I have not reproduced the whole song here but rather just a selection. The full song is included in ibid.
25 Mountford, *Records of the American–Australian Scientific Expedition to Arnhem Land*, vol. 1, p. xxiii.
26 Frank Setzler, 13 January 1950, Lecture Notes, National Geographic Society presentation, Accession File 178294, Smithsonian Institution Archives, Washington, DC, p. 8.
27 M. Thomas, 2007, Gerald Blitner interviewed by Martin Thomas [sound recording], ID 4198706 (ORAL TRC 5851), National Library of Australia, Canberra; S. K. May, 2007, Gerald Blitner interviewed by Sally K. May [digital film recording], Research School of Humanities and the Arts, the Australian National University, Canberra.

was an Indigenous assistant to the Expedition on Groote Eylandt and provided valuable insights into the activities and the concerns felt by local community members.

Margaret McArthur (nutritionist) arrived by air into Groote Eylandt and began her research immediately. She had successfully established a nutrition camp at Hemple Bay by the time the *Phoenix* arrived. McArthur would later also work with Expedition botanist, Raymond Specht, and Native Affairs officer Howard Coate on Bickerton Island. Her aim was to investigate the food-gathering techniques and nutrition of the local people while Specht concentrated on the botany of the area.[28]

Specht's diary also gives an interesting insight into camp life during the Expedition's time on Groote Eylandt. He writes:

> Apart from two excellent cooks (helped by two Aborigines) who do wonders with tinned food, we have many other amenities. We each have a tent that serves as a laboratory as well…We have an open invitation to visit and use the Grays' homestead whenever we like. The Grays have put themselves out for us. They have even put electric light down to our mess tent, as well as water. Our work has definitely upset their routine; Fred Gray, in typical English style, doesn't deny it, but passes it off with a smile. His wife, Marjorie…appreciates the company. Her 'desert island disks'—gramophone records including 'I'm all so alone in a strange land'—haunts [sic] us at night.[29]

Another example of the work taking place includes the production of face casts by Frank Setzler. Setzler took plaster hand and face casts of people from the Umbakumba community using the Negaocol technique. These casts were intended to assist in producing life-size moulds of Australian Indigenous people to display in the Smithsonian Institution. His method was as follows:

> After becoming acquainted with some of the men and observing their craving for tobacco, I was able to induce Kumbiala to undergo a warm mud bath treatment. This mulage had to be dissolved in a double boiler, then allowed to cool so as not to burn, but applied as warm as possible. The first coat was put on with a stiff brush in order to fill the pores… after removing the masks, the natives' faces, as you will probably notice, will be a shade lighter and their pores lose years of accumulated dirt.[30]

---

28 Mountford, *Records of the American–Australian Scientific Expedition to Arnhem Land*, vol. 1, p. xxv.
29 Raymond Specht, 22 April 1948, Arnhem Land Expedition field diary, in possession of Raymond Specht, Brisbane.
30 Setzler, Lecture Notes, p. 8.

Some of these casts were made into bronze busts and are still held at the National Museum of Natural History in Washington, DC. Setzler also collected palm and fingerprints from more than 100 people. He undertook this work with the assistance of Bessie Mountford, the wife of the Expedition leader and honorary secretary for the team. He tested the tastebuds of the members of 60 families, collected hair samples, took photographs, collected artefacts, produced biological reports on Indigenous activities and took soil samples for pharmaceutical companies.[31]

While dozens of men and women assisted with the Expedition on Groote Eylandt, it was a man Mountford called Nangapiana who was singled out as an important assistant. Nangapiana was an artist and his work is represented in many collections that now exist from the Arnhem Land Expedition.[32] Most of the Expedition members kept journals during their adventures and, as a result, we know the names (or the names that the Expedition members used) of some of the people who worked with the Expedition.[33]

The Expedition moved to its second base camp, Yirrkala, on Thursday, 8 July. Yirrkala was a Methodist Overseas Mission station at this time, having been established in 1935, and it was again decided to set up camp near these existing facilities. A few days after arriving at this base camp, Expedition members received a wireless message informing them that Arthur Robert Driver, Administrator of the Northern Territory, Elvin Seibert, US Consul from Adelaide, and Kevin Murphy, Deputy Administrator of the Department of Information would be landing near Yirrkala at 9.30 am with the intention of visiting their camp.[34] Murphy and Driver requested a private audience with Mountford and Setzler and stated very clearly that the Department of Information was upset at the delays and poor transport arrangements they considered had been made by the leader to date. The result of this meeting was that Mountford was asked to relinquish leadership of the scientific aspects of the Expedition to Setzler and he was told to concentrate on producing films rather than undertaking anthropological research. Setzler was reluctant but did not immediately refuse the new position offered to him—something that Mountford found hard to forgive.[35] Setzler considered the offer and the next day discussed it with his American colleagues, who quickly advised him to refuse.[36] He sent a telegram

---

31 Frank Setzler, (n.d.), Memo to Mountford, Setzler Files, Box 7, Folder 2 of 2, p. 2, National Anthropological Archives, Washington, DC.
32 May, *Collecting Cultures*.
33 Ibid.
34 Frank Setzler, 12 July 1948, Letter to A. Wetmore, Accession File 178294, Smithsonian Institution Archives, Washington, DC.
35 Charles Mountford, 29 July 1948, Letter to A. Wetmore, Accession File 178294, Smithsonian Institution Archives, Washington, DC.
36 Frank Setzler, 12 July 1948, Letter to A. Wetmore, Accession File 178294, Smithsonian Institution Archives, Washington, DC.

to Kevin Murphy informing him that it was simply impossible for him to accept the position.[37] The fieldwork in Yirrkala was not off to a good start. There was, however, one good outcome from this meeting. Murphy arranged for Bill Harney to join the Expedition, stating, 'my only concern is that you and your colleagues be given ample opportunity for profitable scientific research. To this end [I] am sending [Bill] Harney as guide confident that his knowledge of terrain will give you what you want.'[38]

So what did the researchers concentrate on during their time at Yirrkala? Mountford and McCarthy were working with, and collecting paintings from, artists such as Mawalan Marika, Wandjuk Marika and Narritjin Maymuru. While Mountford's collection of objects, and especially paintings, remained constant during the Expedition, his record keeping slowly deteriorated at Yirrkala and Oenpelli. The same methods of ethnographic collecting were undertaken throughout the Expedition and Mountford remained primarily around the base camp for the three months they were camped at Yirrkala.

It was a different story for other Expedition members, who scattered themselves around the islands and mainland sites of Arnhem Land. For example, McArthur, Miller, Setzler, McCarthy and Harney travelled to Port Bradshaw, where they conducted their independent research including archaeological excavations. McArthur established a nutrition camp with two Indigenous companions— something that concerned Mountford greatly. McArthur claimed that she could get a truer picture of the local people in their natural environment if she was by herself,[39] however Mountford did not think it was appropriate for a woman to be alone in Arnhem Land. Nevertheless, he gave her permission to go.[40] Even as late as 1948, McArthur's ability to work independently in remote regions of Australia was considered daring and, to some, inappropriate for a woman, with one newspaper article labelling her 'gamer than Ned Kelly'.[41]

On their return from Port Bradshaw, Setzler and McCarthy travelled to Milingimbi Island to carry out archaeological research while the others concentrated their study around the camp. There was growing tension between some Expedition members by this stage, the worst of which appears to have been between Mountford and McCarthy. To give some idea of their feelings towards each other, I will offer this quote from McCarthy's diary: 'I told him [Mountford] that I was fed up with the bloody expedition on the basis of the constant jealousy of all the work that I was doing and the constant arguments about the number of and the distribution of the specimens.'[42]

---

37 Ibid.
38 Kevin Murphy, 14 July 1948, Letter to Frank Setzler, Accession File 178294, Smithsonian Institution Archives, Washington, DC.
39 Mountford, *Records of the American–Australian Scientific Expedition to Arnhem Land*, vol. 1, p. xxvii.
40 Mountford, 'Report on expedition for the National Geographic Society', p. 229.
41 'Scientist "gamer" than Ned Kelly', *Herald*, 22 September 1948.
42 Frederick McCarthy, 18 July 1948, Entry in diary 4, MS3513 Box 22, Item 269, AIATSIS Library, Canberra.

During their time on Milingimbi Island, Setzler and McCarthy undertook excavations and also collaborated to collect ethnographic artefacts. They seemed to prioritise their archaeological work but after they had finished each day they returned to their tent and began trading with whoever had brought materials to sell. McCarthy recorded that people were eager to trade and, as discussed by Hamby,[43] the number of artefacts obtained over a three-week period was substantial.[44]

Back at Yirrkala, the team continued to work with large numbers of local people in areas ranging from general camp maintenance and painting to string figures and medical research. One person who stands out as a central figure is Mawalan Marika (also spelt Mauwalun or Moalun by Expedition members). Born in 1908, Mawalan Marika was a highly regarded leader of the Rirratjingu people of north-east Arnhem Land. He was a significant artist and is represented in many museum collections. Many works of Mawalan's family members are also represented in the Arnhem Land Expedition collection, including his son Wandjuk Marika.[45]

Yirrkala was a productive camp for the group and all Expedition members made large collections. Before moving to Oenpelli, most of the team was taken to Darwin for one week to secure their collections and restock their supplies. They arrived at their new camp by 20 September 1948 (Figure 9.4).[46] Interestingly, on the way to Oenpelli, mammalogist David Johnson jumped ship at Cape Don and walked 260 km overland to Oenpelli (arriving on 19 October), on his way acquiring a significant collection of mammals for the Smithsonian Institution.

The final base camp for the Arnhem Land Expedition proved to be the hardest for most of the Expedition members. It was hot, the local mission did not really want them there, and the team members had been in the field for six months already.[47] There is no doubting, however, that this final base camp provided some of the most important scientific findings of the Expedition. The group set up camp at the edge of the Oenpelli billabong, surrounded by a dramatic landscape of rocky outliers and with the Arnhem Land Escarpment in the distance.

---

43 Hamby, this volume.
44 Frederick McCarthy, (n.d.), Report on scientific work, Series 10 1927–1956, 22/1948, p. 8, Australian Museum Archives, Sydney.
45 May, *Collecting Cultures*.
46 Setzler, Lecture Notes, p. 28.
47 May, *Collecting Cultures*.

Figure 9.4 *Phantom* and *Victory* being unloaded at Oenpelli Landing, 20 September 1948

Photograph by Robert Rush Miller. By permission of the National Library of Australia. nla.pic-vn4514017.

The township of Oenpelli sits in country belonging to the Mangerridji people, and, in 1948, it was a Church Missionary Society settlement with a history that included life as a buffalo shooting camp. In 1948, most of the Expedition members remained in or very near to Oenpelli throughout the three months they were conducting their research. Some Expedition members (including Howell Walker, Peter Bassett-Smith and Raymond Specht) suggested to me that at Oenpelli they had the least amount of contact with local people. This was due in part to the mission being unwilling to spare people from their normal jobs.[48]

The traditional owner of this region at the time of the Expedition was a man by the name of Nipper Marakara (Figure 9.5). During his remarkable life, he oversaw the movement of Paddy Cahill into this region in the early 1900s, and the establishment of the church in Oenpelli in 1925; he worked with Baldwin Spencer and Ronald and Catherine Berndt, and was still active when Mountford and his team turned up in 1948. Very little has been written on this important Indigenous leader and artist. Mountford records this traditional owner's name as Kumutun in his records from the Arnhem Land Expedition and also mentions

---

48   Ibid.

three artists by the names of Larida, Willirra and Wulkini. Visiting ABC journalist Colin Simpson reflected on the situation at Oenpelli in 1948 with the following statement:

> The old men Mountford brought back to the tent had been hoeing the mission's melon patch. They looked unimpressive, they looked dreadful in cast-offs of clothing and shapeless relics of felt hats. They sat down on the grass, folding themselves down in that slow and diffident way they have with white men, one wringing his nose out with his fingers, another coughing. I thought to myself, 'Nothing much can come of this'. I was judging on appearances, presuming that the old men had shed their validity as aborigines and put off their old culture because they had put on rags of white-man clothing and were taking hand-outs from the mission.
>
> It was these old men and others they mustered who, transformed with paint and fervour, gave us the unforgettable performance of the... corroboree a few days later.[49]

Herbert Deignan, Robert Miller and Raymond Specht were probably more excited about Oenpelli than any of the other researchers, as there they found abundant and diverse birds, fish and plants for their work and made some important discoveries. Miller claimed that the waterways surrounding Oenpelli were the richest he had ever fished and Specht discovered several new species of plants.[50]

During the time in Oenpelli, conditions were not ideal for medical research and the intense heat and the dust were a continuous trial.[51] As well as working with Setzler on archaeological excavations, McCarthy travelled with McArthur and John Bray to Fish Creek where they undertook an influential study of food gathering (see Altman, this volume).[52]

The fieldwork component of the Arnhem Land Expedition officially came to a conclusion in early November 1948, with a barge transporting the collections and the team members back to Darwin along the East Alligator River.[53]

---

49 Simpson, *Adam in Ochre*, pp. 6-7.
50 Mountford, 'Report on expedition for the National Geographic Society', p. 230.
51 Ibid.
52 McCarthy, F. and McArthur, M. 1960, 'The food quest and the time factor in Aboriginal economic life', in C. P. Mountford (ed.), *Records of the American–Australian Scientific Expedition to Arnhem Land. Volume 2: Anthropology and nutrition*, Melbourne University Press, Carlton, Vic., pp. 145–94.
53 Mountford, *Records of the American–Australian Scientific Expedition to Arnhem Land*, vol. 1, p. xxix–xxx.

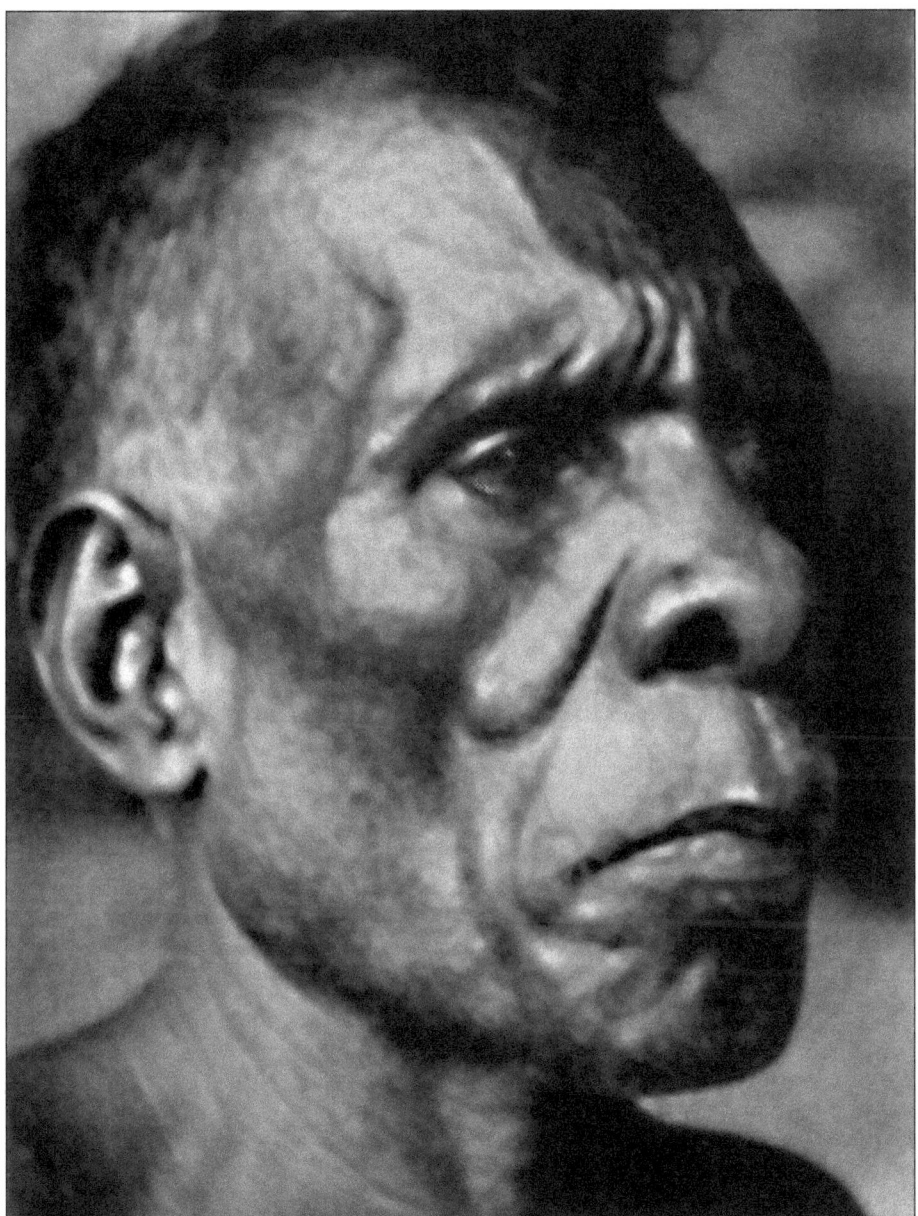

Figure 9.5 Portrait of Nipper Marakara (Kumutun) from Oenpelli (now Gunbalunya)

Photograph by Charles P. Mountford. From Charles P. Mountford (ed.) 1956, *Records of the American–Australian Scientific Expedition to Arnhem Land. Volume 1: Art, myth and symbolism*, Melbourne University Press, Carlton, Vic.

Rumours had leaked to the press that all was not well among the Expedition members, and as it began to reach its conclusion Mountford realised that in order to protect the reputation of the Expedition (and its stakeholders) he would need to ask his team to present a united front. He wrote to Alexander Wetmore on 5 November 1948, stating that he was afraid his letters might have created a wrong impression and that the camp was actually a very harmonious one. He *claimed* that he had not heard of a single argument between any of the members.[54] At the same time, he requested that Setzler not be allowed anywhere near the Australian ministerial or departmental heads for fear that he would not be discreet. Wetmore was receiving letters from many of the Expedition members and was probably better informed about problems in the camp than many of the people in the field. For example, the Expedition ornithologist, Herbert Deignan, wrote to him in August stating that Mountford wanted all of the party to arrive together in Adelaide at the end because of the Expedition's recent troubles.[55] After managing to direct an extended Expedition, Mountford now had to fight for his reputation, his legacy and his job.

This was clearly a politically complex and logistically daunting Expedition and Mountford's sacrifices to make it happen were extreme. On top of the pressure placed upon the leader from the government came the responsibility of satisfying museums in Australia and in the United States, as well as the National Geographic Society and individual members of the team. Eventually, these worries took their toll on Mountford's health and he suffered fainting spells. Setzler commented that 'our main hope now is to hold him down from worry and exhaustion, so that we can all safely return to Darwin'.[56]

There are many aspects of this Expedition that I have not touched upon. These include the relationships that were formed between particular Expedition members who continued to correspond for decades and the encouragement that McArthur received from many of her colleagues to continue and expand her research. I have also not touched upon the fact that some of the work undertaken in 1948 today causes distress for Indigenous communities.[57] This includes the removal of human skeletal remains from their place of rest without the permission of local community members (Figure 9.6). I have argued elsewhere that the people in the Aboriginal communities visited were recorded alongside

---

54 Charles Mountford, 5 November 1948, Letter to A. Wetmore, Accession File 178294, Smithsonian Institution Archives, Washington, DC.
55 Herbert Deignan, 26 August 1948, Letter to A. Wetmore, Accession File 178294, Smithsonian Institution Archives, Washington, DC.
56 Frank Setzler, 6 October 1948, Letter to A. Wetmore, Accession File 178294, p. 2, Smithsonian Institution Archives, Washington, DC.
57 May, S. K. with Gumurdul, D., Manakgu, J., Maralngurra, G. and Nawinridj, W. 2005, '"You write it down and bring it back…that's what we want"—revisiting the 1948 removal of human remains from Gunbalanya (Oenpelli), Australia', in C. Smith and H. M. Wobst (eds), *Indigenous Peoples and Archaeology*, Routledge, London.

the flora and fauna of the region.[58] They were photographed, their movements recorded, their artefacts collected, and the findings published primarily for the benefit of non-Indigenous people.

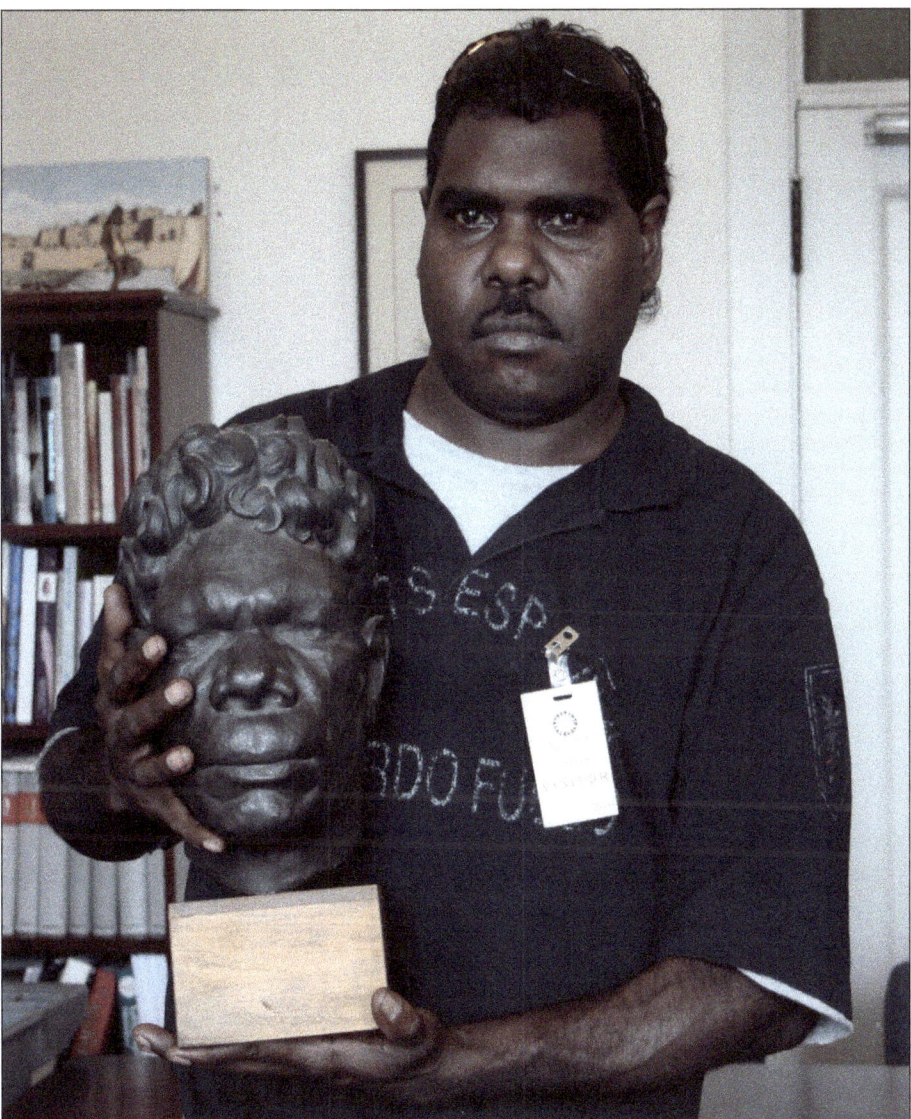

Figure 9.6 Thomas Amagula of Groote Eylandt at the Smithsonian Institution holding a bronze bust of one of his relatives, produced from a face cast taken in 1948 by Frank Setzler, 2008

Photograph by Sally K. May

---

58   May, *Collecting Cultures*, p. 192.

To a large extent, Indigenous people were caught up in a game being played by the Commonwealth of Australia. They were used to further political and social goals. The impact upon local communities appears not to have been considered. Yet, Indigenous community members were not simply victims of this political game. The Expedition provided a unique opportunity for trade, employment and skills acquisition. The wish for an ethnographic collection placed these communities in a situation of power and they made the most of these opportunities, gaining money, food and goods in return for services. Some community members had the opportunity to work with internationally renowned experts and learnt skills associated with their disciplines (such as botany, archaeology and medical science).

Today it is essential that museums consult with the communities visited by the Arnhem Land Expedition to contextualise their collections. The lack of Indigenous voices in the records and documentation of this Expedition must be addressed. In keeping these artefacts, institutions have entered into a contract of engagement with Arnhem Land communities—something that can be of benefit to both parties.

Part II
Collectors and Collections

10. The String Figures of Yirrkala: Examination of a legacy

Robyn McKenzie

Who's the painted cave man
Who lives in Arnhem Land
You'll find it's Fred McCarthy
Tying strings around his hand.[1]

— Anonymous

When the 1948 American–Australian Scientific Expedition to Arnhem Land was all but over and the party was taking stock in Darwin, Howell Walker, the National Geographic Society writer-photographer, asked each participant to respond to two questions: 'What did they consider the most significant contribution to their field that the Expedition had made possible?'; and 'What would their respective home institutions consider the most valuable work done by the Expedition?'

Frederick McCarthy, one of three ethnographic researchers on the Expedition (alongside Frank Setzler from the Smithsonian Institution and Charles Mountford, the Expedition leader), not surprisingly stated that the 'collection of specimens' of material culture and natural history would be most valued by his institution, the Australian Museum. For the most significant contribution to the field of anthropology, he nominated the archaeological survey he carried out in collaboration with Setzler (see Clarke and Frederick, this volume). He gave equal standing to the collection of string figures he made at Yirrkala: 'a record number…from one group of natives.' McCarthy described it as 'the most complete study of string-figures yet made in one area in Australia' and noted that it 'increases the total to three times as many [as] previously known in the whole of the continent'.[2]

McCarthy's collection of string figures—constituting by his estimate one-fifth of all 'known' string figures in the world at the time—remains the largest of

---

1   Author unknown, stanza of a ditty/song/poem, typewritten and pasted into McCarthy's diary on 24 July. F. D. McCarthy, 1948, Diary 4, Yirrkalla Diary No. 1 and Milingimbi, Papers of Frederick D. McCarthy, MS3513/14/4, Australian Institute of Aboriginal and Torres Strait Islander Studies (AIATSIS), Canberra.
2   The questions from Walker and McCarthy's response—both typewritten on separate sheets of paper—are pasted into McCarthy's diary opposite the entry for 12 November. F. D. McCarthy, 1948, Diary 5, Yirkalla Diary No. 2 and Oenpelli, Papers of Frederick D. McCarthy, MS3513/14/5, AIATSIS.

its kind collected from one community at one time.³ Commonly referred to as a game, amusement or pastime, string figures (also known by the name 'cat's cradle') are patterns or designs made with a loop of string 'by co-ordinated movements of the fingers of both hands, assisted by the teeth, neck, elbows, knees and toes when necessary'.⁴ While usually executed by a single person, some require two or more participants.

McCarthy's documentation consisted of three principal (separate but complementary) components: mounted figures, textual records and photographs. There are 193 mounted figures in the Cultural Collections of the Australian Museum. Made with lengths of industrially manufactured string (knotted to form a loop), the majority of the figures were fashioned by McCarthy's principal informant, Ngarrawu Mununggurr. The final design was slipped from her hands and fixed to a cardboard or brown-paper support with small pieces of tape. Ngarrawu had exceptional skill in string-figure making. She could perform figures 'step by step, in slow motion', which McCarthy found 'invaluable' for documenting the sequence of manipulations by which a figure was made.⁵ These 'instructions' were recorded in two dedicated notebooks.⁶ In the Australian Museum Archives, there are 159 photographs of Ngarrawu and two male informants, Mawalan Marika and his son, Wandjuk, demonstrating designs.

In assessing the significance of this collection as a legacy of the Expedition, it is important first to understand how it was seen within its original context. Why did McCarthy regard this collection one of the most significant anthropological achievements of the Expedition? Why did he consider it more important than the material culture collections—the bark paintings, for example—which have received the most attention?⁷

---

3   McCarthy, F. D. 1960, 'The string figures of Yirrkalla', in C. P. Mountford (ed.), *Records of the American–Australian Scientific Expedition to Arnhem Land. Volume 2: Anthropology and nutrition*, Melbourne University Press, Carlton, Vic., p. 422. See Martin Probert's survey of museum holdings of string-figure materials: 'Museum and other institutions with string figure artefacts—an inventory of string figures mounted on card, string figures on film, string figure photographs, and recordings of string figure songs' (last revised August 2010), <http://website.lineone.net/~m.p/sf/archives.html>, accessed 1 December 2010.
4   McCarthy, F. D. 1958, 'String figures of Australia', *The Australian Museum Magazine*, vol. 12, no. 9, p. 279.
5   McCarthy, 'The string figures of Yirrkalla', p. 415.
6   F. D. McCarthy, 1948, Arnhem Land Expedition Diary No. 6, String-figure techniques, Yirrkalla and Oenpelli, AMS515, Australian Museum Archives, Sydney; F. D. McCarthy, 1948, Arnhem Land Expedition Diary No. 7, String-figure techniques Yirrkala, Papers of Frederick D. McCarthy, MS3513/14/6, AIATSIS.
7   See Neale, M. 1998, 'Charles Mountford and the "bastard barks"—a gift from the American Australian Scientific Expedition to Arnhem Land', in L. Seear and J. Ewington (eds), *Brought to Light: Australian art 1850–1965*, Queensland Art Gallery, Brisbane, pp. 210–17; and May, S. K. 2010, *Collecting Cultures: Myth, politics, and collaboration in the 1948 Arnhem Land Expedition*, Altamira, Calif.

10. The String Figures of Yirrkala

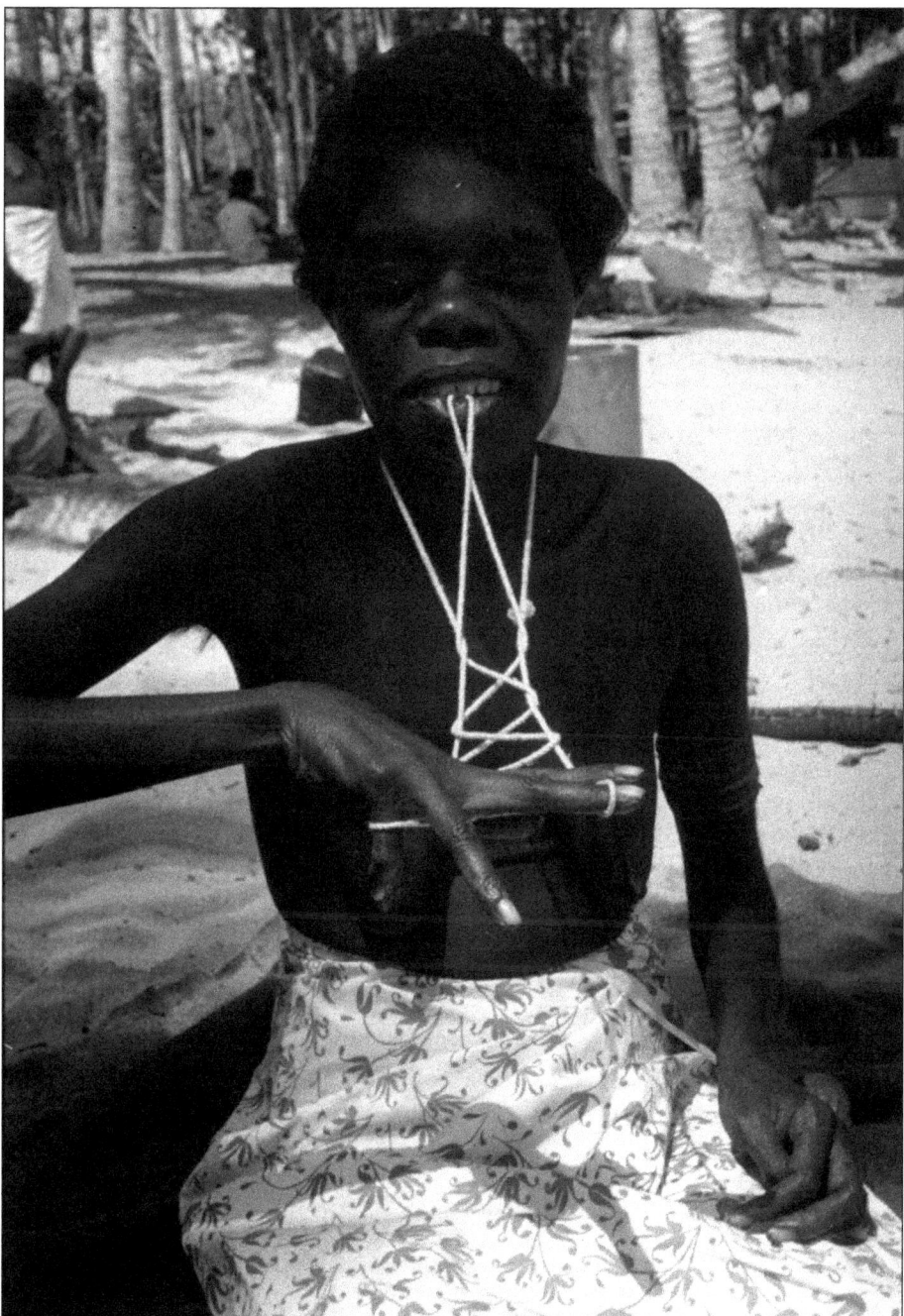

Figure 10.1 Ngarrawu Munuŋgurr making *Lightning/Bapa* string figure, Yirrkala Beach Camp, 1948

Photograph by Frederick McCarthy. By permission of Australian Museum Archives. AMS 353, Fred McCarthy Field Trip Photographs, V08961.32.

String figures do not lend themselves to being collected in the usual sense. The whole fun of string-figure making (and its foundational ontological premise) is that you always begin and end with the dumb and inert material: the loop of string. In contrast, the constituency or 'place of being' of the string figure is in the animation of the string, and its transformation through movement or manipulation. As Dinah Eastop, a contemporary commentator, has written: 'string figures exist only in the process of "making" them.'[8] We need to understand therefore what it was that McCarthy was collecting, and why. It is interesting to note in this regard that McCarthy recorded the Yolngu Matha term for string figures as *'maitka-uma'* (his transcription of *matjka-wuma*).[9] This is a compound term, combining *matjka*, meaning string and things made with string (including string figures and chest harnesses), and *wuma*, a verb meaning to do or make.[10] Anthropologists and ethnologists considered the examination of games to be within the broad purview of studying a culture in its entirety. Since games were not considered of serious import, they were, however, often not accorded much time or space. String figures, however, were a special case.

From Little Things Big Things Grow: Or a case of 'mild diffusionism'

> In ethnology, as in other sciences, nothing is too insignificant to receive attention.[11]
>
> — Alfred C. Haddon

Alfred C. Haddon was a major force in the development and promotion of the anthropological study of string figures. He first encountered them on his 1888 trip to the Torres Strait.[12] After returning from a second tour—the

---

8   Eastop, D. 2007, 'Playing with Haddon's string figures', *Textile*, vol. 5, no. 2, p. 197.
9   In this text, I use the accepted contemporary orthography for Yolngu Matha words and personal and place names. The variant original spellings of what McCarthy referred to as 'native names' are preserved in quotations from primary sources, such as his diaries and published writing. The term 'Yolngu Matha', meaning Yolngu language, is inclusive of the different languages spoken by the Yolngu people of North-East Arnhem Land. These languages are clan based, and individuals might speak a number of different languages, depending on their clan affiliations and the context. Many words are, however, similar across language groups. McCarthy's informants would have predominantly spoken the languages of their respective clans: Djapu, Rirratjingu and Manggalili.
10 McCarthy, 1948, Diary 6, AMS515, Australian Museum Archives. The function of *matjka-wuma* as a compound noun+verb form was explained to me by linguist Frances Morphy (Personal correspondence, 21 October 2010).
11 Haddon, A. C. 1906, 'Introduction', in C. F. Jayne, *String Figures*, republished in 1962 as *String Figures and How to Make Them: A study of cat's-cradle in many lands*, Dover, New York, p. xi.
12 Eastop, 'Playing with Haddon's string figures', pp. 192–5; Haddon, A. C. 1890, 'The ethnography of the western tribes of Torres Straits', *Journal of the Anthropological Institute of Great Britain and Ireland*, vol. 19, p. 361.

famous Cambridge Anthropological Expedition to the Torres Strait of 1898—Haddon co-wrote an article with W. H. R. Rivers (who accompanied him on that Expedition), which established a nomenclature and descriptive method for recording construction techniques for string figures. Addressing 'the paucity of the available information' on string figures, their object was 'to induce field workers to pay attention to the subject'.[13] By specifying standard terms for fingers, loops, near and far strings, and movements, they developed a systematic basis for the 'scientific' study of string figures, enhancing the potential for comparative analysis.[14] Their system of notation, with some modifications, remains the standard in use today.

In his introduction to Carolyn Furness Jayne's popular guide to *String Figures* (1906) (an inventory of research to that date), Haddon noted that in a number of cultures there were aspects of the practice that suggested a connection with religion and mythology. As he put it, 'we have here to do with some symbolism'.[15] He suggested that further research into this would be profitable. However, the primary motive of string-figure study—throughout its heyday in the first decades of the twentieth century—was determined by the 'scientific' course Haddon and Rivers had set. The recording of designs and the method of making them was the major preoccupation. The study of string figures was placed in the service of diffusionist theory, the goal of which was to map the spread of culture in time across geographic areas.[16] If the same string-figure design was found to occur in different places, it was inferred that some form of contact transmission between populations had taken place. As the same figure could be made by different means, the technique or order of manipulations was considered an essential factor in making such comparative analyses, rather than the focus being on final patterns alone.[17] As a later commentator explained: 'crucial affinities lie in style and procedure—distinctive openings, manipulations, extensions, and releases.'[18]

While anthropological debates about the value of diffusionist theory and between the adherents of different diffusionist hypotheses were most heated in Britain in the 1910s and 1920s, diffusionist thinking had a longer pedigree. The historian of anthropology George Stocking has argued that before the emergence

---

13   Rivers, W. H. R. and Haddon, A. C. 1902, 'A method of recording string figures and tricks', *Man*, vol. 2, pp. 146–7.
14   Haddon, 'Introduction', p. xii; Sillitoe, P. 1975–76, 'Why string figures?', *Cambridge Anthropology*, vol. 3, no. 1, pp. 18–20.
15   Haddon, 'Introduction', p. xxii.
16   For a succinct discussion of diffusionism, see Kuklick, H. 2008, 'The British tradition', in H. Kuklick (ed.), *A New History of Anthropology*, Wiley-Blackwell, Oxford, pp. 68–9.
17   Davidson, D. S. 1941, *Aboriginal Australian String Figures*, republished in 2006, Hesperian Press, Carlisle, WA, p. 783.
18   Lane, B. 1963, 'On string figures: a protest', [Letter to the Editor], *American Anthropologist*, vol. 65, no. 4, p. 911.

of functionalism in the 1930s, two models of thinking alternated in dominance—both taking a historical or diachronic perspective: 'a progressive developmental paradigm', which was evolutionist in nature; and 'a migrational or diffusionary paradigm'.[19] In this context, it should be noted that Haddon credited E. B. Tylor, who in 1879 gave an address on the geographical distribution of games, as the first to draw attention to the possible use of string-figure distribution to trace the migration of cultures.[20]

The one and only time McCarthy worked on string figures was on the Arnhem Land Expedition. This was the first of only two opportunities he had to work with living cultures in his career.[21] During 30 years as head of the Department of Ethnology at the Australian Museum, he explored a broad field of topics, which could be placed under the general heading of anthropology, but his primary area of interest was in the sub-field of archaeology—in particular, the typology of stone tools and the sequencing of rock art.[22] McCarthy came to the pursuit of 'the prehistory and archaeology of the Aboriginal past' through his work at the museum, where he started at a very young age. From 1932 to 1935, he undertook a part-time Diploma of Anthropology at the University of Sydney under A. P. Elkin.[23] His great strengths were the description, analysis and ordering of artefacts. *The Stone Implements of Australia* (co-authored with E. Brammell and H. V. Noone) was published in 1946 and for years remained an unsurpassed classic. Professor John Mulvaney considered it 'the most systematic and best documented handbook on implement classification on a continental scale'.[24]

---

19 Stocking, G. W. 1984, 'Radcliffe-Brown and British social anthropology', in G. W. Stocking (ed.), *Functionalism Historicized: Essays on British social anthropology*, University of Wisconsin Press, Madison, and London, pp. 135–6.
20 Tylor, E. B. 1880, 'Remarks on the geographical distribution of games', [paper delivered 14 March 1879], *The Journal of the Anthropological Institute of Great Britain and Ireland*, vol. 9, pp. 23–30. Notably in this address Tylor postulated a migration pattern from a centre of origin in South-East Asia 'westward into Europe, and eastward and southward through Polynesia and into Australia'. On Tylor's influence see, Haddon, 'Introduction', p. xx; and Sherman, M. A. 1992, 'Preface', in J. Averkieva and M. A. Sherman, *Kwakiutl String Figures*, University of Washington Press, Seattle, and London, p. xiv.
21 On the limited opportunities McCarthy had for this type of fieldwork, see Mulvaney, D. J. 1993, 'Sesquicentenary to bicentenary: reflections on a museologist', *Records of the Australian Museum*, supp. 17, pp. 17–24; and Khan, K. 1993, 'Frederick David McCarthy: an appreciation', *Records of the Australian Museum*, supp. 17, pp. 1–5.
22 For a discussion of the development and segmented interests of the profession, see Urry, J. 1993, 'The search for unity in British anthropology, 1880–1920', in *Before Social Anthropology: Essays on the history of British anthropology*, Harwood Academic Publishers, Chur, Switzerland, p. 8.
23 McBryde, I. 1998, 'Frederick David McCarthy 13 August 1905 – 18 November 1997', [obituary], *Australian Aboriginal Studies*, no. 1, p. 52. For a comprehensive account of McCarthy's career, see Attenbrow, V. 2008, 'Ethnographic and archaeological collections by F. D. McCarthy in the Australian Museum', in N. Peterson, L. Allen and L. Hamby (eds), *The Makers and Making of Indigenous Australian Museum Collections*, Melbourne University Press, Carlton, Vic., pp. 472–507.
24 Mulvaney, D. J. 1980, 'Two remarkably parallel careers', *Australian Anthropology*, vol. 10, pp. 96–101, at p. 99; and Mulvaney, 'Sesqui-centenary to bicentenary', p. 19.

Mulvaney has described McCarthy as having 'mildly diffusionist principles'.[25] In the thesis he submitted for the Diploma of Anthropology in early 1935, on Aboriginal material culture of Eastern Australia, McCarthy surveyed various theoretical arguments regarding the dynamics of cultural diffusion in Australia.[26] He discussed the work of the Vienna School theorist Fritz Graebner and the British diffusionist Rivers, but gave most space to the work of the American D. S. Davidson, a follower of Carl Wissler. McCarthy had a sustained and long-term engagement with Davidson's work and through it with a strain of diffusionist thinking that went under the name 'age and area theory' or 'geographical distribution theory'. In 1936, McCarthy reviewed a series of articles Davidson had published on Australian Aboriginal material culture. His review commenced with a slab of explanation of the theory, quoted from Davidson:

> This theory as its name implies, purports to reconstruct the historical development of a culture trait or complex by interpreting the chronological relationship between the relative geographical positions which the trait has successively occupied, or between the relative geographical distributions of the various differences which the trait has gone through in its historical development.

The quotation continues, giving more detail on the theory and its method. At the end, McCarthy sums up, not disapprovingly: 'From this statement of the aims of the theory, it is apparent that detailed and complete data, and a strict interpretation of the evidence are required.'[27]

McCarthy was sympathetic to the rigours of this approach and to its aim of tracking, in effect, continuity and change in the development of culture.[28] In this latter respect, his interests are not that distant from the concerns of current researchers.[29] In a major article based on work he did for his dissertation, 'Aboriginal Australian material culture: Causative factors in its composition',

---

25 Mulvaney, 'Sesqui-centenary to bicentenary', p. 23.
26 McCarthy, F D, 1935, The Material Culture of Eastern Australia: A Study of Factors Entering into its Composition, unpublished thesis submitted for the Diploma of Anthropology, University of Sydney, pp. 123–30. Papers of Frederick D McCarthy, MS3513/17, and MS283, AIATSIS, Canberra. (There are two copies of McCarthy's thesis in the AIATSIS library: MS3513/17 is an annotated typescript, the other MS283 is a copy of this typescript with reprints of articles he published in *Oceania* and *Mankind* based on the thesis inserted.) For McCarthy's later considered views on diffusionist theory see, McCarthy, Frederick D, 1974, 'Relationships Between Australian Aboriginal Material Culture, and South-East Asia and Melanesia', in Elkin, A. P. and MacIntosh, N. W. G. (eds) 1974, *Grafton Elliot Smith: The Man and His Work*, Sydney University Press, pp. 210–14.
27 McCarthy, F. D. 1936, 'The geographical distribution theory and Australian material culture', [review], *Mankind*, vol. 2, no. 1, p. 12.
28 For an assessment of differences in thinking between McCarthy and Davidson, see Konecny, T. 1993, 'Ethnographic artefacts: the iceberg's tip', *Records of the Australian Museum*, supp. 17, pp. 45–6.
29 See Attenbrow, 'Ethnographic and archaeological collections by F. D. McCarthy in the Australian Museum', p. 497: 'patterns of diffusion and patterns of chronological change…these are still questions and themes being addressed by today's researchers.'

published over two editions of *Mankind* in 1940, McCarthy wrote: 'the material culture of the aborigines has not remained static…The aborigines have experimented with many aspects of their culture, and in the adaptation to their environment have brought into play a great deal of ingenuity, resource and skill.' In his analysis of the 'causes of local variation', he recognised such factors as 'elaboration'—the development of locally unique forms (of a widespread feature, usually a customary way of doing something); 'invention'— the contributions made by individual craftsmen; and 'diffusion and trade'— the spread of influences between people within a local area.[30] The significant difference between McCarthy and contemporary researchers is primarily the product of the scale of the project—the big idea, the encyclopedic frame, the large map—which he and his colleagues were trying to fill. When it came to plotting external influences on the development of Australian Aboriginal culture—'the line of demarcation between introduced and indigenous traits'— he argued that there were problems that would not be 'satisfactorily settled' until 'a complete distributional analysis has been made of all traits in Australia and neighbouring cultures'.[31]

McCarthy was a late addition to the Expedition. His inclusion was not finally confirmed until early February 1948—a little more than one month before departure. In a letter to Mountford written at that time, he reported that he had been 'reading up the string figures' but was finding 'the technique extremely difficult to follow'.[32] It is possible, given this correspondence, that the idea of making a collection of string figures was first suggested by Mountford, who had previously done work on them.[33] But the project would have appealed to McCarthy's sense of professional purpose. As he told himself in his diary: 'There is no complete collection from Arnhem Land in existence.'[34]

On the Expedition, McCarthy was involved in collecting material culture artefacts, excavating archaeological sites, and documenting rock art as well as recording string figures. Opportunities for observational fieldwork (of 'the making and use of objects') were limited by the routines of life at the mission stations where the Expedition set up base camps.[35] No matter how we might wish to classify his various pursuits, there is a sense they were all one and the same

---

30   McCarthy, F. D. 1940, 'Aboriginal Australian material culture: causative factors in its composition', *Mankind*, vol. 2, no. 8, pp. 242, 244–50.
31   Ibid., p. 258.
32   McCarthy to Mountford, 4 February 1948, Papers of Frederick D. McCarthy, MS3513/14/8, AIATSIS.
33   McCarthy, 'The string figures of Yirrkalla', p. 422. In his published report in the records of the Expedition, in summarising the work done on string figures in Australia up until 1948, McCarthy includes reference to the 44 figures (without techniques) Mountford collected from the Adnyamathanha tribe in the northern Flinders Ranges in 1937 and 1938 (published in 1950). See: Mountford, C. P. 1950, 'String figures of the Adnyamatana tribe', *Mankind*, vol. 4, no. 5, pp. 183–9.
34   McCarthy, 14 July 1948, Diary 4, AMS515, Australian Museum Archives.
35   F. D. McCarthy, 1948, Arnhem Land Expedition, Report on Scientific Work, AMS10/22/1948, Australian Museum Archives.

thing for McCarthy: the gathering (collecting or describing) of ethnographic 'facts' for later analysis. The notable exception was the innovative ethnographic study of the hunter-gatherer economy done in collaboration with Margaret McArthur (see Jon Altman, this volume).

McCarthy left detailed descriptions of his process and procedures in the diaries he kept during the Expedition. Throughout these pages, his ambition of getting 'the complete' collection is apparent—the larger the number, the more complete a collection was deemed to be. His approach to collecting and recording was atomistic. He collected the bark paintings at a different time to recording their interpretations or stories; he collected the mounted figures separately from recording the techniques of making them. The objects were always collected first, and in quantity. They occupied the first column or row in his data table, providing the referent or master key for the other fields. That was their primary value. In the case of string figures, other data fields such as 'techniques of making' could be considered just as, or more, important.

In his answer to Walker's question regarding the most significant contribution made by the Expedition to the field of anthropology, McCarthy gave the reasons for his selection. He valued the archaeological survey because it was an 'untouched field' and produced 'type cultures hitherto unknown'. He valued the string figures because of the comprehensive nature of the collection: 'a record number…from one group of natives.' Interestingly, he felt the need to defend his position (which could have been seen as self-serving) with an aside as to why Mountford's collection of bark paintings and their interpretations did not rate. While finding fault with Mountford's collecting methods on Groote Eylandt, his basic argument was that collections of barks already existed from these areas. He pointed out that Ronald and Catherine Berndt had previously 'done more detailed and prolonged work' at Yirrkala and Oenpelli (now Gunbalanya).[36] The string figures, like the archaeological survey, filled in blanks on the map and made original additions to the database. The barks did not.

The Specimen Quest and the Time Factor: Collecting, recording and writing up

> I began collecting string-figure techniques as soon as we reached Yirrkala.[37]
>
> — Frederick McCarthy

---

36 McCarthy, 12 November 1948, Diary 5, AMS515, Australian Museum Archives.
37 McCarthy, 1948, Diary 6, AMS515, Australian Museum Archives.

Yirrkala, on the mainland coast, where the Expedition set up their second base camp, had been established as a Methodist mission in 1934. Most members of the 14 Yolngu clans living in the surrounding region were gradually drawn to the settlement in the following decades.[38] When McCarthy arrived, he noted that a significant proportion of the local population was living beyond the settlement. 'There are 100 natives here at present but as many again are out in the bush & at Pt. Bradshaw, Caledon Bay & Melville Bay because of a shortage of food on the Mission.' As he described it, the settlement consisted of 'the main building', occupied by the missionaries, while 'the natives live in corrugated iron huts set in three rows on a flat to the North, & there is an extensive garden...the site is beside a beautiful sea beach'.[39]

McCarthy had been 'anxious' to start collecting string figures early in the Expedition when they were on Groote Eylandt, but was prevented from doing so by not having cardboard 'to pin them down'.[40] At Yirrkala, he was conscious of the need to get off the mark quickly. He wanted to go to Milingimbi Island with Setzler to do archaeological excavations for at least a month, and to explore other sites around the hinterland of Yirrkala, so was planning to spend 'only five weeks at most' in the mission itself. McCarthy's diary for 14 July recorded his advance preparations for the work ahead. He made a list of the material culture items they required, set up the ethnographic store tent, and began to study the string figures.[41]

McCarthy's firsthand account of the process of his collecting—what he did when and where and with whom—is recorded in his diaries and notebooks. This commentary forms the basis for his published account in the records of the Expedition.[42] Another contemporary source is McCarthy's report to his superiors at the Australian Museum. In this, he acknowledged his debt to his principal informant, Ngarrawu: 'a positive genius with a piece of string. She produced one hundred and eighty figures, all of which were photographed, mounted on card, and the techniques recorded.'[43] This statement implies a logical order to the activity of collecting string figures: the person makes the figure, it is photographed on their hands, mounted on card, and then the technique of

---

38 Caruana, W. 1997, 'The past 100 years: a brief history of the artists and their art', in W. Caruana and N. Lendon (eds), *The Painters of the Wagilag Sisters Story 1937–1997*, National Gallery of Australia, Canberra, p. 12; Hutcherson, G. 1998, *Gong-Wapitja: Women and art from Yirrkala, Northeast Arnhem Land*, Aboriginal Studies Press, Canberra, p. 1.
39 McCarthy, 9 July 1948, Diary 4, AMS515, Australian Museum Archives.
40 It was probably delayed on board the *Phoenix* along with the rest of the party's non-essential supplies. The *Phoenix* did not arrive at Umbakumba until halfway through the party's 14-week stay, by which time McCarthy was absorbed in archaeological pursuits.
41 McCarthy, 14 July 1948, Diary 4, AMS515, Australian Museum Archives.
42 McCarthy, 'The string figures of Yirrkalla', pp. 415–511.
43 F. D. McCarthy, 1948, Arnhem Land Expedition, Report on Scientific Work, AMS10/22/1948, Australian Museum Archives.

making it is recorded. It did not, however, happen this way. The stages in the process and the three data types they relate to (photograph, mounted specimen, and textual record) were 'collected' at separate times.

McCarthy's activity can be divided into three phases. In the first of these—a two-week period from shortly after his arrival in Yirrkala to his departure for Milingimbi—he collected mounted specimens. He secured his first series (some six figures) from Mathaman Marika, one of the men with whom he had sustained contact during his time in Yirrkala. He found that Mathaman was not very good at making string figures—'a poor manipulator'—so the next day he approached the women at the Beach Camp. Working with a small group, he collected 20 figures. Archaeological diversions took up the next two days. When he returned to the task, he worked for the first time with Ngarrawu, who was to become his principal informant. Ngarrawu Mununggurr was a young Djapu woman in her twenties from the Caledon Bay area (a granddaughter of Wonggu). Married to Nanyin Maymuru of the Manggalili clan, she had one young child at the time. She was regularly employed as a domestic by the mission, and with her co-wife, Djunbiya, had been coopted by the Expedition to work as an assistant in the Nutrition Unit's testing lab, washing bottles and doing other tasks. Kelvin Hodges and Brian Billington, who ran the lab, first alerted McCarthy to the women's skill with string figures. While McCarthy appreciated the talent of both, Ngarrawu knew a greater range of designs.[44] He found her 'an ideal subject with whom to work'. Ngarrawu was, he records, 'shy in manner, but always happy & laughing' and 'a most obliging & cheerful person'.[45] After returning from another archaeological excursion, he spent three solid days working with Ngarrawu, at the end of which his collection of mounted string figures had grown to 90.

In collecting the mounted figures, after having 'exhausted those voluntarily performed' for him, McCarthy suggested subjects.[46] Once the figure was made and then mounted, the support was annotated with the name of the maker, the name of the subject in English, and its Yolngu Matha name. Relevant finger positions were marked in, and sometimes the general position of the hands was sketched. In many of the mounted figures, especially those relating to animals, parts of the design were identified as representing specific features, such as head, tail, belly, and so on. It is possible from McCarthy's diary entries to estimate the time he spent collecting the mounted figures, and from that to calculate that the average time taken to collect a single specimen was approximately 20 minutes. The concentration of this activity into three half-day and four full-day sessions made this a fairly demanding pace.

---

44   McCarthy, 'The string figures of Yirrkalla', p. 415.
45   McCarthy, 1948, Diary 6; McCarthy, 7 September 1948, Diary 5, AMS515, Australian Museum Archives.
46   McCarthy, 'The string figures of Yirrkalla', p. 415.

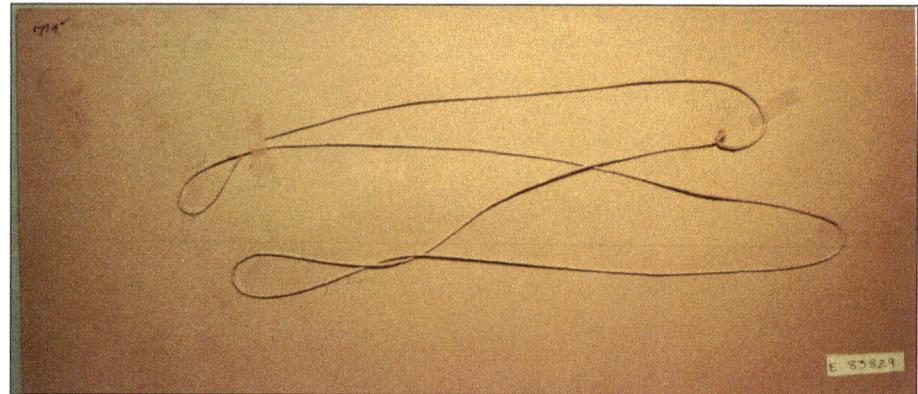

Figure 10.2 Ngarrawu Munuŋgurr, *Wawalik sisters standing up*, string figure mounted on cardboard, 1948

Photograph by Stan Florek. By permission of Australian Museum. Cultural Collections & Community Engagement, E. 83829.

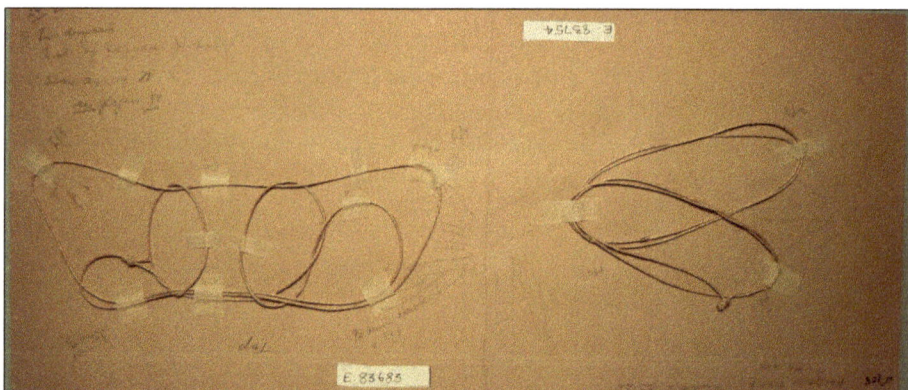

Figure 10.3 Ngarrawu Munuŋgurr, *Two Dingoes/Wungun* and *Kangaroo track/Mudbia luku*, string figures mounted on cardboard, 1948

Photograph by Stan Florek. By permission of Australian Museum. Cultural Collections & Community Engagement, E. 83683 and E. 83754.

After this, McCarthy spent approximately three weeks at Milingimbi (see Louise Hamby, this volume). When he returned to Yirrkala on 20 August, he learnt that the Expedition was due to depart for Oenpelli in less than two weeks, leaving 'very little time for recording the string figure techniques'.[47] McCarthy spent part of the next four days working with Ngarrawu recording instructions for making the string figures he had collected. During sessions that lasted two to three hours, they spent an average of 15 minutes on each figure. Ngarrawu's ability to accommodate the demands of McCarthy's 'methodology' was truly a feat. She could reproduce designs faultlessly, at random, on demand.[48]

47 McCarthy, 20 August 1948, Diary 4, AMS515, Australian Museum Archives.
48 McCarthy, 1948, Diary 6, AMS515, Australian Museum Archives.

During the run-up to his departure, McCarthy had competing demands on his time, including preparing the ethnological collection for transport and recording interpretations of the 70 or so barks collected from Yirrkala that he and Setzler had then to divide between their two institutions. He had obviously decided to call it a day on the string figures, with the 90 mounted specimens collected and the 65 techniques recorded, when, on Saturday, 28 August, he began to 'write-up' his findings into his notebook. It is telling that in his diary entry for that day he tallies up the numbers for the other members of the team (leaving spaces to fill for those he does not have at hand): 'Miller got his 201st fish species on the trip, Specht has 225 species of plants from Yirrkalla, Deignan has __ species of birds on the trip, & Johnson has __ species of mammals.'[49]

Number was a currency that all the researchers on the Expedition traded in. With the exception perhaps of the Nutrition Unit, the total numbers of things collected was the measure of their work both for themselves and others; it was always the thing cited to summarise the Expedition's achievements. The emphasis on number went beyond it being an easy way of thinking about their performance, or translating what they were doing in their particular fields to their masters, or to a lay public. It was both simpler and more complex than that. Collecting as many objects as possible was an overriding concern. Their research behaviour was acquisitive. In building these collections, they were literally gathering data, and, according to the paradigm in which they were working, building a base for furthering knowledge.

This concern with quantity was made explicit in McCarthy's diaries. When the party was advised that the boat coming to transport their gear to Oenpelli was delayed, the three activities of collecting, recording and writing up were now combined in a final spate of string-figure research. Working with Ngarrawu, he caught up on recording the outstanding techniques for the 90 mounted figures already collected, and documented new ones also. This continued for a little more than a week, by which time the new departure date was approaching. McCarthy's diary tells the story:

> 4 September: I continued working with Narau & got the total of string figures to 173.
>
> 5 September: In the evening I worked with Narau & took the total to 183 string figures.
>
> 7 September: The total now is 190…There are probably more to be got here & I shall try to get ten more to make the 200 should time permit.[50]

---

49 McCarthy, 28 August 1948, Diary 5, AMS515, Australian Museum Archives.
50 Ibid.

In this third and final phase of McCarthy's work on the string figures at Yirrkala, he began to gather and record a new and different kind of data: what he referred to as 'social background' or 'social tie-up' material. This information about customary aspects of string-figure making was told to him by male informants—principally, Wandjuk Marika, his father, Mawalan, and Mawalan's brother Mathaman. They described various prohibitions and lore concerning figure making, including regulations that applied differentially to men, women and children. This explained a number of McCarthy's observations—in particular, the greater expertise of women in this aspect of the culture. Whereas men used string figures in ceremony, they were an everyday activity for the women. The men and the women had different names for the figures, denoting their 'inside' and 'outside' significance, and there were a number of figures that were known and made by men or women only. The children were instructed according to these rules.[51]

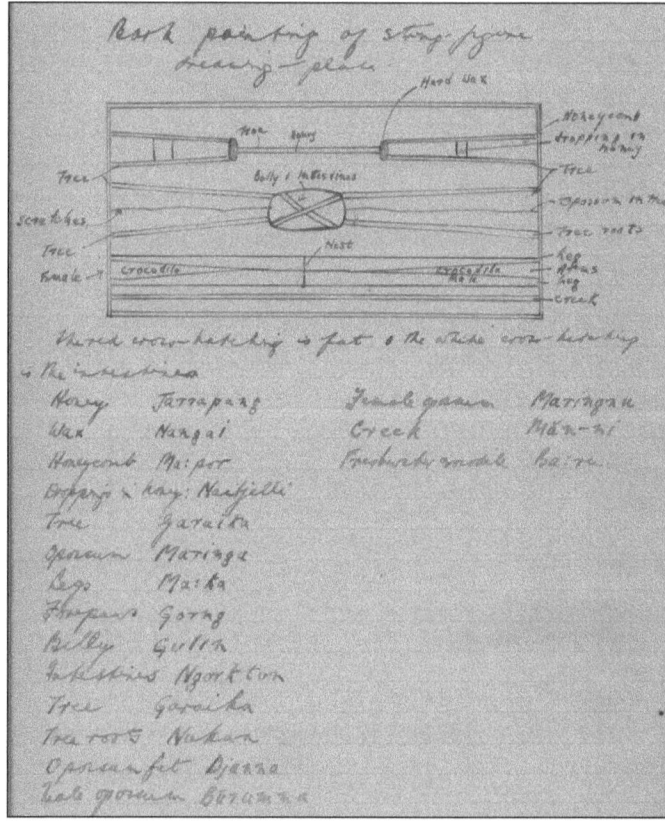

Figure 10.4 Frederick McCarthy, *Bark painting of string-figure dreaming-place*, documentation of a painting by Wandjuk Marika

By permission of AIATSIS, Canberra. Papers of Frederick D. McCarthy, MS3513/14/6, Arnhem Land Expedition, Diary No. 7, String-figure techniques, Yirrkala.

---

51   McCarthy, 1948, Diary 6, AMS515, Australian Museum Archives.

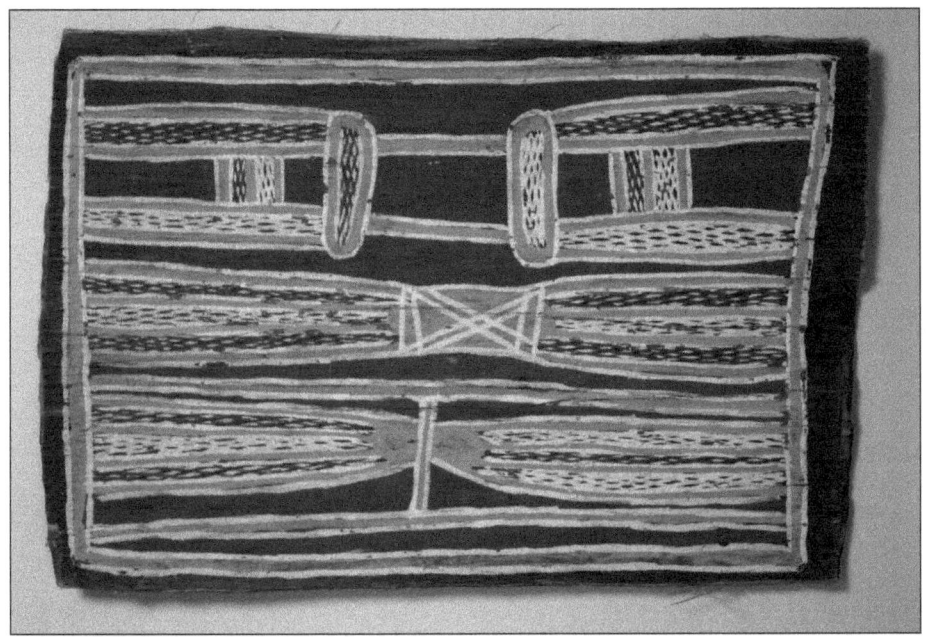

Figure 10.5 Wandjuk Marika, *String-figure dreaming-place*, earth pigments on bark, 1948

Photograph by Finton Mahony. By permission of Australian Museum. Cultural Collections & Community Engagement, E.53210.

At this time, Wandjuk made for McCarthy a bark painting of 'string-figure dreaming-place'. McCarthy made a sketch of the painting in his notebook, annotating it and recording an index of Yolngu Matha names identifying the various elements represented. He recorded a number of narratives or myths involving string figures that were told to him. One of these (which he reproduced in full in the Expedition records) was an origin or creation story. It related the making of string and string figures to the well-known Wagilag Sisters myth cycle: 'String was first made by the two Wawalik sisters…[who made] a record in string of all the animals, plants and other things they saw, as well as their own activities.' In the myth, as he records it, there are 92 string figures mentioned, of which he has collected all but 16.[52]

On his last day in Yirrkala, McCarthy escaped from packing up the camp to take photographs of the string figures. His approach to this was characteristically focused. He had planned to photograph various stages in the making of the designs, but no doubt due to the time constraint, he chose to record the final stage only of the complete series. In the three hours between 9 am and noon, Ngarrawu made 149 figures for him to photograph: 'she made the next one in

---

52 McCarthy, 'The string figures of Yirrkalla', pp. 425–7.

the time it took me to write down the name & number of the previous one.' In the hour after the lunch break, she made another 40 figures.[53] McCarthy then photographed Mawalan and Wandjuk making a number of the men's figures.

Tying Strings Around his Hand

> It's painfully obvious that McCarthy never made a single string figure [in] his whole life.[54]
>
> — Mark A. Sherman

The greater part of McCarthy's paper in the records of the Expedition consisted of instructions for making figures, accompanied by an illustration of the final form of each figure (based either on the mounted figure or on the photograph).[55] They were organised, as was standard practice, according to a typology based on method of construction. Those made from the same openings were grouped together.

In 1941, D. S. Davidson had published a book based on his own field research that summarised the current state of knowledge on Australian Aboriginal string figures. McCarthy took it with him on the Expedition, and he used aspects of it as a template when writing up his data. His discussion of the 'characteristics' of the Yirrkala string figures was based on the factors Davidson had defined as significant for analysis of string figures as a 'cultural trait'—in particular, the types of manipulation and their number.[56]

McCarthy also described the range of subjects evident in the naming of figures, noting that 'the most important source of motives lies in the natural environment, human and animal behaviour and material culture'. Under the heading of 'Landscape and natural phenomena', for example, he lists: 'waterhole (two figures), two waterholes, water in a river-bed, ripples on a pool, running creek, crab-hole, lightning, morning star, sun, rain, clouds, granite boulders.'[57] There were string figures for most things encountered in the Yolngu world. He noted that the resemblance of the designs to the subjects they represented varied considerably.

---

53 McCarthy, 7 September 1948, Diary 5, AMS515, Australian Museum Archives. McCarthy records in his diary taking photographs of Ngarrawu making approximately 190 figures. There are, however, only 159 photographs from this session in total in the Archives of the Australian Museum. From changes in location and the evident time of day recorded in these images, it is possible to establish the order in which they were taken, and that a roll of film (corresponding to the 40 images McCarthy records taking after lunch) is missing.
54 Mark A. Sherman to Stan Florek, 11 March 1995, Correspondence Files, Anthropology Department, Australian Museum. Mark Sherman, with Honor Maude, wrote a revision of McCarthy's instructions for making the Yirrkala figures, published in 1995.
55 Maude, H. C. and Sherman, M. A. 1995, 'The string figures of Yirrkala: a major revision', *Bulletin of the International String Figure Association*, vol. 2, p. 89. As they note: 'The drawings made from the mounted specimens typically *do not* show the hands, whereas those made from the photographs *do*.'
56 Davidson, *Aboriginal Australian String Figures*, pp. 786–91.
57 McCarthy, 'The string figures of Yirrkalla', pp. 420–1.

THE STRING FIGURES OF YIRRKALLA

54. Women's Crocodile

1. Opening A
2. Release thumb loops
3. Place right thumb over three strings, pick up near little finger string with thumbs and return to position
4. Pick up near right index finger string with left index finger
5. Pick up near little finger string with thumbs from below and return to position
6. Insert thumbs inside index finger loops and transfer
7. Navaho near thumb string with teeth on both hands
8. Release index finger loops
9. Extend
10. Pick up from below far thumb string with index fingers
11. Release thumb strings
12. Pick up from below near little finger string with thumbs
13. Insert both thumbs inside index finger loops
14. Navaho near thumb string with teeth on both hands
15. Pick up near index finger string with middle fingers
16. Release thumb loops
17. Extend to figure.
Size 12 by 6 inches

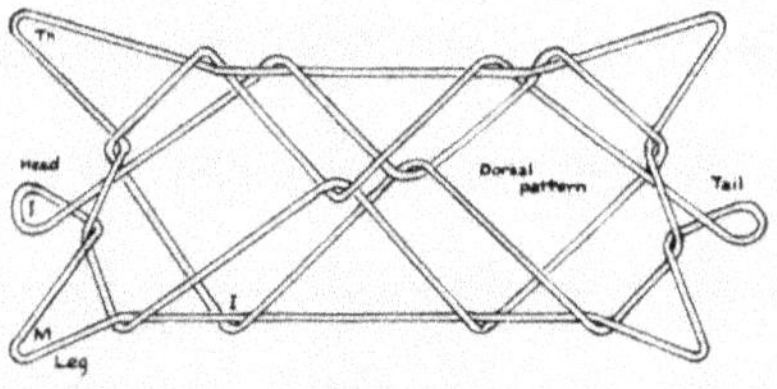

Fig. 60

55. Ripples on a Pool

1. Opening A
2. Release thumb loops
3. Place right thumb over three strings and pick up far right little finger string with right index finger
4. Pick up near right index finger string with left index finger
5. Extend
6. Pick up near little finger string from below with backs of thumbs and return to position
7. Insert thumbs under near upper index finger string
8. Navaho near lower thumb string with teeth
9. Insert index finger in thumb loop and transfer loops to index fingers
10. Extend (pindiki)
11. Pick up near little finger string with thumbs and return to position
12. Insert thumbs under near upper index finger loop
13. Navaho near lower thumb string with teeth on both hands
14. Pick up near lower index finger string with middle fingers
15. Release far little finger string
16. Extend to figure.
Size 7 by 4 inches

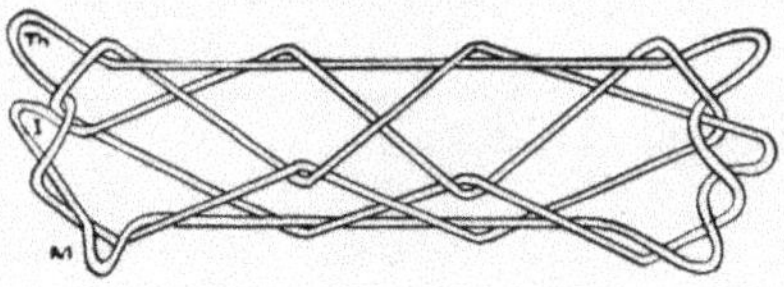

Fig. 61

56. Clouds

1. Opening A
2. Pull out from behind the right index finger loop with tips of left thumb and index finger
3. Repeat with left index finger loop
4. Insert left loop through right one
5. Pick up the two loops with index fingers
6. Extend to figure.

Size 11 by 5 inches

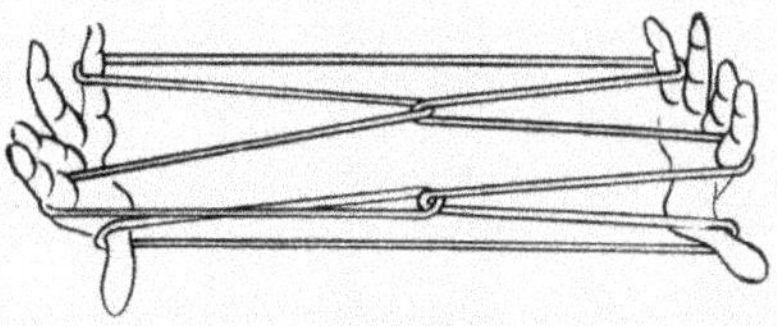

Fig. 62

465

Figure 10.6 Page from Frederick McCarthy, 'The string figures of Yirrkalla'

From C. P. Mountford (ed.) 1960, *Records of the American–Australian Scientific Expedition to Arnhem Land. Volume 2: Anthropology and nutrition*, Melbourne University Press, Carlton, Vic.

Davidson argued that 'the making of string figures in common with many other traits' had been introduced into Australia from Melanesia via Cape York in northern Queensland.[58] McCarthy was an advocate of Rivers' theory that Australia was probably visited by successive 'small bands of immigrant people arriving by chance at various points of the north Australian coastline', and that there were therefore 'a number of centres from which traits could diffuse'.[59] On the basis that only 24 Yirrkala figures, and three of the 78 collected from Central Australia, were duplicated in records from Queensland, he concluded that Arnhem Land formed a second point of diffusion (particularly into the Northern Territory and Central Australia). Based on the limited duplications he found between the Yirrkala figures and those collected in other locations, McCarthy argued, more radically, however, that the majority of Australian figures were in fact of 'local origin'. They represented local subjects and were made using local techniques, 'developed by a people from the common basic foundation'.[60]

Davidson had emphatically stated (while admitting it seemed strange given 'the complex social and totemic systems' in Aboriginal culture) that there was no evidence that designs had significant content or meaning. '[P]ractically no patterns have been given a social, totemic or magical connotation…it would seem that string figures in Australia serve almost entirely the purpose of amusement', he wrote.[61] What is singular therefore in McCarthy's report is the information he includes under the heading of 'Socio-magical regulation'—the data gathered in his last days in Yirrkala. He observed, for example, that the making of string figures provided 'a link between the women and the tribal mythology', from which they were customarily excluded when it was expressed in the form of ceremonial ritual. 'As they make the string figures the women are thinking not only of a particular animal but of its significance in the Wawalik sisters' saga,' he explained.[62]

While this kind of 'associated cultural data' was acknowledged as useful additional material, it seemed to be of little interest to McCarthy's contemporaries. Reviewers of McCarthy's work made no comment about it. Discussion fell rather to the import of his data, and the comparative analysis he undertook, for diffusionist hypotheses. The impact of his findings upon Davidson's assertion that string figures were a 'meaningless' pursuit was not addressed. A review by the American anthropologist Joseph Birdsell provoked an indignant letter from Barbara Lane at the University of Pittsburgh.[63] Birdsell proposed that

---

58   Davidson, *Aboriginal Australian String Figures*, pp. 783–6.
59   McCarthy, 'Dr Davidson and distribution', p. 71.
60   McCarthy, 'String figures of Australia', p. 283.
61   Davidson, *Aboriginal Australian String Figures*, p. 782.
62   McCarthy, 'The string figures of Yirrkalla', p. 427.
63   Birdsell, J. B. 1962, '*Records of the American–Australian Scientific Expedition to Arnhem Land, Number 2: Anthropology and nutrition*, Charles P. Mountford (Ed.) New York: Cambridge University Press, 1960', [review], *American Anthropologist*, vol. 64, no. 2, p. 412. Lane, 'On string figures', p. 911.

McCarthy's research, given the large sample size and the argument that the majority of figures were of local genesis, sounded the death knell for 'the little game of using string figures to trace cultural relationships'. An irony here is that in 1995 two contemporary experts on string figures, Honor Maude and Mark A. Sherman, having found that only 10 per cent of the Yirrkala designs could be made from McCarthy's instructions, published a 'major revision' of the techniques for making them.[64] There are a number of factors that could have contributed to the errors and inconsistencies in McCarthy's published data, but one assumption that can be safely made is that he was not practised in making string figures or recording how to make them. Both are recognised as difficult skills to master.

The written introduction to McCarthy's inventory of data starts with an acknowledgment of the role of his informants, in which they are all identified by name. He paid particular tribute to Ngarrawu, as he did also in an article on string figures in the *Australian Museum Magazine*:

> Na:rau…proved to be a golden goose, to coin a term; a genius with a loop of string. She set a world's record which may never be broken. Of the 212 designs that I collected at Yirrkala Na:rau made all but 10, and fashioned all but 6 of the 187 techniques (or series of manipulations secured). Whether she made the figures slowly for recording purposes or rapidly for photography, her errors were remarkable [sic] low. Her long slim fingers moved gracefully over the strings, like a pianist's over the keys of her piano. Her astoundingly wide knowledge of the designs, sequences of manipulations and subjects is, from the technical and quantitative points of view, proof of a mastery of her craft and of the possession of highly intellectual powers of mental and manual co-ordination. With Na:rau string-figure-making is an art.[65]

In Yirrkala, McCarthy's main Yolngu interlocutors belonged to two family groups, from two different clans: the Marika family of the Rirratjingu clan and the Maymuru family of the Manggalili clan. Mathaman Marika had provided the Yolngu Matha names for things on McCarthy's list of material culture items, and he accompanied McCarthy and Bill Harney on an excursion to Yalangbara where they documented a cave-painting site (of Mathaman's dreaming story). McCarthy was adopted by Wandjuk Marika as his classificatory 'brother'. He spent one particular morning with Wandjuk, Nanyin and Narratjin Maymuru getting interpretations of bark paintings. 'An interesting day,' he records in his diary. The larger discussion enabled him 'to get an insight into the artists [sic] approach & composition & use of colour'.[66] Another day he photographed the

---

64 Maude and Sherman, 'The string figures of Yirrkala'.
65 McCarthy, 'String figures of Australia', p. 281.
66 McCarthy, 26 August 1948, Diary 5, AMS515, Australian Museum Archives.

use of a pile house made by Mawalan Marika and his family. (McCarthy had identified Dadaynga or Roy Marika as a particularly skilful exponent of string-figure making among the men, but he was not able to work with him 'as he was employed by the mission all day'.)[67] These were the men from whom McCarthy gained his information about string figures and who later, as community leaders negotiating relations with the wider Australian society, saw 'educating Europeans about aboriginal culture' as a strategic tool.[68] Ngarrawu, through her marriage to Nanyin Maymuru, was part of this social grouping, but as a woman, working as the principal informant/collaborator with a male anthropologist, her role was unique.

For McCarthy, the collection of mounted figures was a way of recording the final design, to which the step-by-step instructions referred. Perhaps understandably, he did not value them as items of material culture in themselves. (Being made of industrially manufactured string, rather than the traditional type made from the inside bark of the kurrajong tree, they were obviously not the authentic artefacts of 'stone-age man'.) He did not include string figures in lists he made of the types of material culture items he wished to acquire.[69] He also did not include them in the Ethnology Register, made in the field, in which collected items were inventoried.[70] Most tellingly, he did not accession them into the Museum's collection on his return, as he did with the other artefacts.[71] They were kept, but ended up buried under a layer of other unregistered items in the Museum's stores, until unearthed by curator Stan Florek in 1988.[72]

The value of these objects today is different to what it was when McCarthy collected them. Their material status is now paramount. They can be recognised as genuine historical artefacts of cross-cultural encounter and exchange. The product of collaboration between two individuals with different skills, they are representative of an engagement between knowledge systems. They do provide an excellent historical record of the practice of string-figure making in Yirrkala. For the visual anthropologist, the collection invites a semiotic analysis. The representational mode of string figures—as made in any part of the world—has not been adequately fathomed. So the size of the collection, and the extent of the accompanying data, is valuable indeed. It offers the opportunity to understand how string figures function as an aesthetic meaning system—that is, as an art form.[73]

---

67 Ibid., 7 September 1948.
68 See Morphy, H. 1991, *Ancestral Connections: Art and an Aboriginal system of knowledge*, University of Chicago Press, Ill., and London, p. 17; and also Thomas, this volume.
69 Copies of these lists were kept in his diaries.
70 F. D. McCarthy, 1948, Diary 8, Ethnology Register, Papers of Frederick D. McCarthy, MS3513/14/7, AIATSIS.
71 Konecny, 'Ethnographic artefacts', p. 46.
72 Florek, S. 1993, 'F. D. McCarthy's string figures from Yirrkala: a museum perspective', *Records of the Australian Museum*, supp. 17, p. 117.
73 See Morphy, H. 2008, *Becoming Art: Exploring cross-cultural categories*, UNSW Press, Sydney, p. xi.

Figure 10.7 Susan Yunupingu demonstrating string-figure technique, Yirrkala, 2009

Photograph by Robyn McKenzie

Contrary to the expectations of McCarthy and his contemporaries, string-figure making continues in the Yirrkala community today. On my first six-week field trip in 2008–09, I recorded a contemporary repertoire of figures and tricks. McCarthy noted that his interest in *matjka-wuma* had stimulated enthusiasm for 'the making of them' within the community.[74] Ngarrawu also gained renown from being considered 'at Yirrkala by her people as the most skilful individual with maitka-uma'.[75] While still practised, string-figure making has not been highly valued as a cultural expression. Wherever it sat in the order of things within the semi-traditional society of 1948, its fate was tied to the community's increasing interaction with the values of a dominant mainstream Australian society. Just as the string figures were not objects that McCarthy could collect as such, it was explained to me that string figures are not something that you can buy and sell—unlike string bags or bark paintings.[76] After McCarthy, no-one wanted string figures from the Yolngu. Unlike other cultural activities, they have no commodity value in the contemporary economy.

What significance the collection holds for today's community is yet to be told. I hope my interest has the same catalytic effect as McCarthy's did—and not just for Yolngu. The final aim of my project is to work in collaboration with the Yirrkala community to bring the string figures 'out of storage' and reanimate them, including telling their story in an exhibition context in which they can be seen, appreciated and experienced as living culture.

Acknowledgments

I would like to thank my supervisors and other colleagues at the Research School of the Humanities and the Arts at the Australian National University for reading and providing comment on my chapter, as well as the editors of this volume; the staff of the Australian Institute of Aboriginal and Torres Strait Islander Studies Library, Cultural Collections at the Australian Museum and the Australian Museum Archives for their help with access to research collections; and to the Buku-Larrnggay Mulka Art Centre in Yirrkala for facilitating my stay and the Yolngu women I met there for assisting with my research through sharing their knowledge of string figures.

---

74 McCarthy, 1948, Diary 6, AMS515, Australian Museum Archives.
75 McCarthy, 7 September 1948, Diary 5, AMS515, Australian Museum Archives.
76 Nyalung Wunungmurra in conversation with the author, 12 January 2009.

11. The Forgotten Collection: Baskets reveal histories

Louise Hamby

The legacy of the 1948 American–Australian Scientific Expedition to Arnhem Land continues to be enhanced by analysis of the collections assembled by members of this unique enterprise. The assemblage of fibre objects—part of the bigger material culture collection—is, however, mainly forgotten. Due to the passion of the leader, Charles Mountford, much is known about the bark paintings but very little information has been published concerning fibre items. These pieces are made from fibres primarily from natural materials and are either worn on the body or used as containers. They can be for ceremonial or everyday use. Aboriginal women and men made these works at all the base camps—Gunbalanya (formerly Oenpelli), Groote Eylandt and Yirrkala—as well as on Milingimbi. This chapter brings together the dispersed group of fibre objects currently being held in the Australian Museum, the National Museum of Australia, the South Australian Museum and the National Museum of Natural History, a division of the Smithsonian Institution in Washington, DC, to reveal histories that connect people, place and time. The quantitative data concerning the fibre objects from all the base camps are used in the formation of general statements. It is, however, the collecting of Frederick McCarthy, from the Australian Museum, and Frank M. Setzler, from the Smithsonian Institution, that is integral to this study. Their collection of fibre objects from Milingimbi forms the core of this research. The examination of a smaller set of works from the overall ethnographic collection made by these men provides greater depth to the study by providing detailed analysis that can be applied to the objects from the other collecting sites. The fibre collection from Milingimbi can act as a metonym for the whole collection in the same way that Sally K. May has used the bark paintings.[1]

The material culture items collected from the Expedition are a valuable legacy for Aboriginal people and researchers. Many were made entirely from prepared or manipulated fibre. Fibre—such as hand-spun string made from plants, feathers, fur, human hair and wool—was also used as a binding component of other items collected such as spears. The fibre objects inform people today not only of what people were wearing but what they were doing and how

---

1 May, S. K. 2010, *Collecting Cultures: Myth, politics, and collaboration in the 1948 Arnhem Land Expedition*, Altamira, Lanham, Md, p. 14. See also May, S. K. 2000, The last frontier? Acquiring the American–Australian Scientific Expedition ethnographic collection 1948, BA (Hons) thesis, Department of Archaeology, Flinders University, Adelaide, p. xix.

they were making things in 1948. As Martin Thomas has written, '[o]ne would never guess from the bulk of the filmic evidence that the people depicted wore western clothes and lived in mission housing'.[2] In contrast with the image that the Expedition wished to portray, this was a transitional time when people wore some Western clothes as well as some traditional items such as armbands. Women carried metal tins and also had specifically constructed baskets for yam collecting, while men had special baskets for their day-to-day equipment and for ceremonial occasions. Although people now had metal hooks for fishing, they also were still using butterfly nets knotted from hand-spun string. Because other manufactured materials were available, some of these things made their way into some of the classic items being made at this time, particularly by women. For example, manufactured dyed wool was incorporated into string bags and armbands, while cloth found its way into baskets. The string figures collected by McCarthy are unique items, made from manufactured string that he brought with him on the Expedition (see McKenzie, this volume). Manufactured items are incorporated into collected items but there is no evidence that any members collected complete articles of European clothing or metal buckets, for example. The members were consciously collecting items they regarded as 'authentic' to past traditions, not necessarily what was in everyday use.

Men, women and children used fibre objects in many aspects of life. My research reveals that fibre objects form the highest percentage of items of a particular category in the ethnographic collections. The quantities demonstrate the importance of these objects in Aboriginal everyday life outside missions and their exchange value within missions. My analysis has brought forward differences in collecting methodologies and generally attitudes between members of the Expedition. Most importantly, this research is initiating a reconnection between these objects and community members, revealing stories about the Yolngu who were influential in the formation of these collections and what they mean to people today.

Distribution of Objects

Museum Numbers

Determining exactly how many ethnographic objects were collected for the American–Australian Scientific Expedition to Arnhem Land is a difficult task. A complete inventory was not made in 1948. The objects were distributed across many institutions. For various reasons they might not have been catalogued at

---

2 Thomas, M. 2007, 'Taking them back: archival media in Arnhem Land today', *Cultural Studies Review*, vol. 13, no. 2, p. 25.

11. The Forgotten Collection

the time, which increased the possibilities of errors. Equally difficult to establish is what items, and how many, went to which institutions. For this study, the interest lies with the distribution and complexities of the fibre objects.

Sally May has provided a baseline number of 2144 ethnographic items collected on the Expedition. She arrived at this number from museum register data.[3] The category 'other objects' in May's breakdown includes works such as spear-throwers and belts. Other items that would be included in this figure are fibre objects that have not been specifically identified elsewhere in her chart.

Based on my research to date, the total number of fibre objects from the Expedition is 655. I have used individual museum registers as a starting point for analysis. After visiting all of the museums, I have been able to locate only 90.5 per cent of the objects listed in the registers. These 593 objects have all been viewed and photographed. These figures are subject to change as new items are found and might differ from the original numbers listed in diaries and records of the Expedition members.

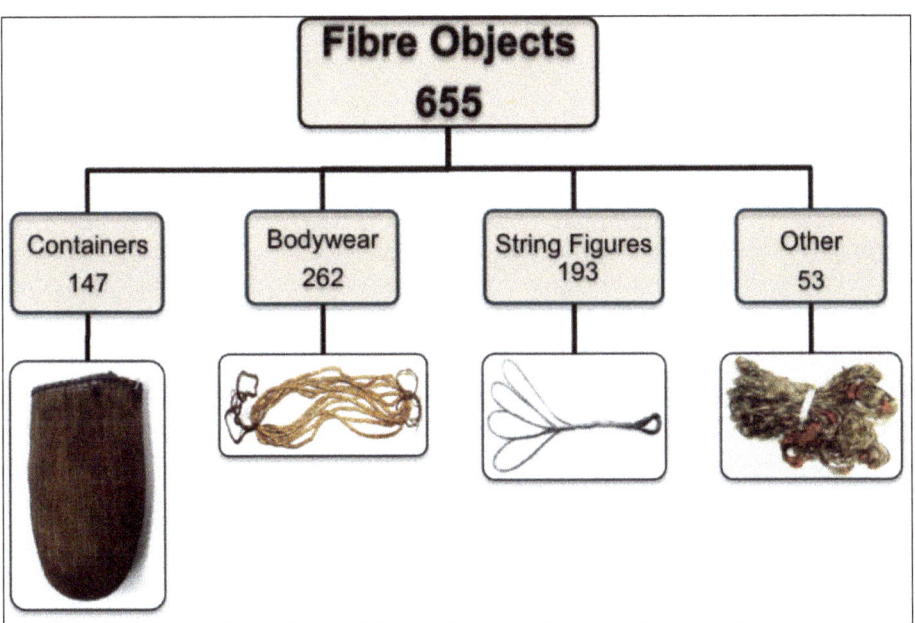

Figure 11.1 Number and type of fibre objects collected from all sites during the Arnhem Land Expedition

May's figures were obtained using the museum registers. In the past, museums would often give groups of items one registration number. With fibre objects, this most commonly occurred with armbands. A bundle of up to 30 could be

---

3 May, The last frontier?, p. 54; May, S. 2003, 'Colonial collections of portable art and intercultural encounters in Aboriginal Australia', *Before Farming*, vol. 1, no. 8, pp. 1–17, at p. 3.

given the same registration number. This practice did not usually occur for larger items such as bark paintings, so the count for those objects is likely to be more accurate. Observations about types and numbers of objects collected based solely on registers can be skewed and are unlikely to give an accurate representation of what was actually collected at the time. In this case, the proportion of fibre objects is shown to be far greater than has hitherto been recognised. This is also the case with the numbers of paintings on paper, as shown in recent research by Sarah Bunn and Annaliese Treacy.[4] In May's original figures, bark paintings represented 22.6 per cent of the ethnographic collection. By my reckoning, the fibre objects represent 30.5 per cent of May's total figure of ethnographic items.

Geographic Spread

The origins of the fibre items extended beyond the three base camps where they were collected, so the collection provides a broad picture of Arnhem Land fibre practice. Localities represented in the collection include Cape Stewart, Chasm Island, Delissaville (now Belyuen) and Elcho Island. One needs to take into consideration that some of the objects collected at a particular place were made by people who lived elsewhere. For example, Bessie Mountford describes a Milingimbi woman working at Yirrkala: 'Bali is making a basket, she says for me, in the coiled fashion. She is a Milingimbi woman, has been to school, and so versed in language and arts beyond the local women.'[5] It is not known if this particular basket is held in a museum collection; however, the Smithsonian does have one coiled basket from Milingimbi (E387541) that is discussed later in the chapter. If Bessie Mountford had collected this object, it would most likely be included in the Yirrkala grouping.

Milingimbi was an important collection site in 1948. It is an island less than 1 km from the mainland community of Ramingining. The island is at a low elevation, with mangrove and tidal mud flats dividing it into many sections. Pandanus and other small trees are common. Several clan groups live on the main island and nearby Mooronga Island in the Arafura Sea. Today's population is about 1500, but in 1948 there were around 400 people, 250 of whom regularly resided at the Methodist Mission. It is the collection site for the largest number of fibre items. For this study, Milingimbi has been selected for a variety of reasons, including my own knowledge base for the area, and the fact that more fibre objects were collected there than at the other sites. Other reasons include the collection rationale and methodology of Frederick McCarthy and Frank Setzler, who at this point were separated from the rest of the Expedition team.

---

4   Bunn, S. and Treacy, A. (Forthcoming), *Australian Institute for Conservation of Cultural Material Bulletin*, vol. 31.
5   B. Mountford, 1948, Diary 3, Saturday 14 September, p. 62, PRG 487/1/2, p. 60, Mountford-Sheard Collection, State Library of South Australia (hereafter SLSA), Adelaide.

11. The Forgotten Collection

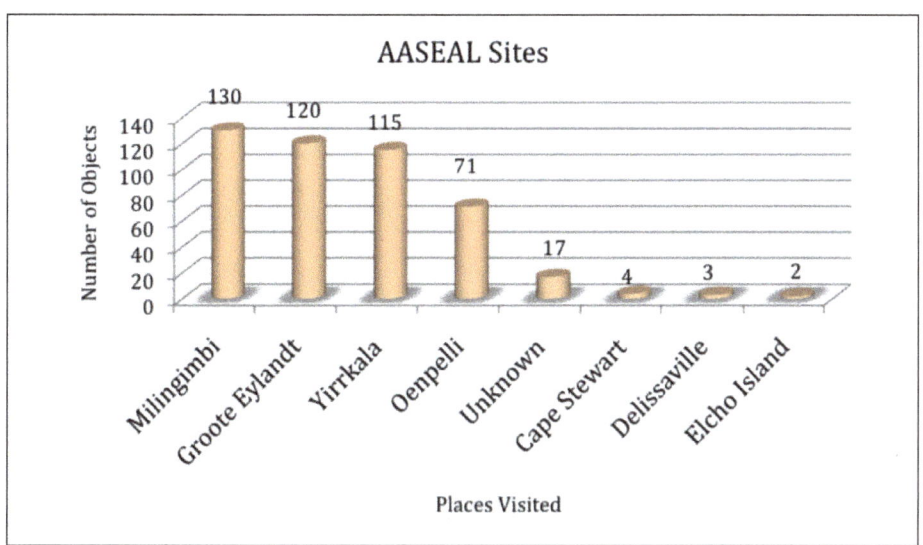

Figure 11.2 Distribution of fibre objects from sites visited by the Arnhem Land Expedition

Milingimbi Camp

Background

McCarthy and Setzler flew from Yirrkala to Milingimbi on 30 July 1948 in a RAAF DC3 Dakota plane. The Reverend Tom Hannah rode up on his horse and cart to collect them and their gear.[6] Hannah was the superintendent at the Croker Island Mission but had been relieving for Reverend Alfred F. Ellemor for the previous seven months. It was a friendly start to their three-week stay at the Methodist Mission, which ended on 20 August 1948. The men were pleased with their accommodation at the laymen's house, a small two-roomed house with a screened verandah. They were more than delighted with the arrangement of eating at the main mission house with Tom Hannah, his wife and daughter, and having the missionaries take over the rationing and pay of the workers.[7] This gave the men more time to concentrate on their archaeological excavations and ethnographic collecting.

---

6 F. McCarthy, 1948, Diary 4: Yirrkala Diary No. 1 F. D. McCarthy and Milingimbi, MS3513/14/4, Australian Institute of Aboriginal and Torres Strait Islander Studies (AIATSIS), Canberra.
7 F. M. Setzler, 1948, Groote Eylandt to Yirrkala to Milingimbi, vol. II, MS5230, National Library of Australia (hereafter NLA), Canberra.

At Milingimbi, the men were free from the direct and daily influence of Mountford, but still constrained by systems he had put into place. McCarthy, by the time he went to Milingimbi, was distrustful of Mountford's intentions regarding the ownership and dispersal of collections:

> [H]e is not really concerned whether we get a collection or not so long as he gets a private collection of bark paintings which I believe he wants for the purpose of exhibitions & lectures in the U.S. but I think he has cooked his goose and eaten it. It appears to be the general opinion in Darwin & amongst the Missionaries that Mountford has made a mess of the leadership.[8]

Mountford had set up an account with Ellemor for collection purposes at Milingimbi. This covered the purchase of bark paintings and payment of wages. McCarthy's distrust was reinforced when a telegram arrived on 16 August directing McCarthy and Setzler to leave all the bark paintings and pipes with Ellemor.[9] One outcome of Mountford's directive was that no bark paintings or pipes from Milingimbi reached the Smithsonian.

McCarthy and Setzler were happy to be at Milingimbi, despite the pressure of Mountford's demands. Their routine was quickly established, as it needed to fit with the operations of the mission and the Aboriginal men whom they employed. The mission cultivated a strong work ethic and Christian beliefs in the Aboriginal people. During the weekdays, work commenced about nine and finished at five, with a long lunch break. Friday was an exception. The Aboriginal men did not work on Friday afternoons because that was when the mission store was open. This was an opportunity for people to spend money on sweets, jam and tea. During working times, the two anthropologists were mostly engaged in archaeological work—mainly at the Macassan Well and Wallaby Mound. Apart from writing up results and marking specimens, the remainder of their time was mostly spent collecting ethnographic items.[10]

The lack of a stated collection policy for the ethnographic objects gave McCarthy and Setzler freedom to gather many types of objects.[11] The attitudes, beliefs and work of a particular group of men were important to the approach and methodology taken by McCarthy and Setzler at Milingimbi. The group consisted of the American anthropologist William Lloyd Warner (1898–1970), the clergymen Hannah and Ellemor, and key Aboriginal men including Harry Makarrwala, David Milngawurruwuy, Gingi, Peter Muntjingu, Bill Balarra and Binyinyiwuy.

---

8   F. McCarthy, Diary 4, 1 August 1948, MS3513/14/4, AIATSIS.
9   F. M. Setzler, August 16 1948, Groote Eylandt to Yirrkala to Milingimbi, vol. II, MS5230, NLA.
10 Ibid.
11 May, The last frontier?, p. 63; May, 'Colonial collections of portable art and intercultural encounters in Aboriginal Australia'.

The Legacy of William Lloyd Warner

Warner's pioneering work at Milingimbi in the period 1927–29 was a guide for collection building and archaeology at all the Expedition base camps. Warner was the first person to perform excavations in Arnhem Land. McCarthy and Setzler drew upon his work.[12] At Yirrkala, McCarthy used Warner's documentation of material culture from Milingimbi when directing Aboriginal people to make specimens. Setzler commented: 'McCarthy is feeling better and is checking types of material culture as reported by Warner. He will carry forward the directions for making those specimens. It all seems backwards, but that is our only method for obtaining ethnological specimens.'[13]

This dependence on Warner's research was evident at Groote Eylandt as well. They had men doing bark paintings and making material culture items, based on examples collected by Warner.[14] It is an oddity of the Expedition that Milingimbi's material culture from the 1920s was being reproduced by men in other communities whose styles were quite different. It demonstrates the influence and strength of the earlier work of Warner.

Mission Pricing

Milingimbi, since its establishment by the missionary James Watson, was known for its good reputation for dealing with Aboriginal people. In Watson's time, the mission became a place where fair trade was practised and men would travel for months with goods to trade.[15] Subsequent missionaries, including T. T. Webb and Harold and Ella Shepherdson, carried on in this spirit. Selling material culture items to the mission encouraged people not only to work but to gain an income while supporting the mission's endeavours. The fibre items and other objects from Milingimbi were exchanged for a combination of trade goods and cash. The missionaries at Milingimbi had established prices for material culture items, as McCarthy documented in his diary:

> They pay a basic price for each kind of article, sell it in Darwin, & give the native the total less 10%. Thus painted skulls are worth £1, bark paintings 10/- to £1 shovel-spears (iron) 4/- to 7/-, stone-headed spears 5-10/- baskets 5-10/- mats, 10-15/ & so on.[16]

---

12 McCarthy, F. D. and Setzler, F. M. 1960, 'The archaeology of Arnhem Land', in C. P. Mountford (ed.), *Records of the American-Australian Scientific Expedition to Arnhem Land. Volume 2: Anthropology and nutrition*, Melbourne University Press, Carlton, Vic., pp. 215–95.
13 F. M. Setzler, 30 July 1948, Groote Eylandt to Yirrkala to Milingimbi, vol. II, p. 159, MS5230, NLA.
14 Ibid., p. 156.
15 Trudgeon, R. 2000, *Why Warriors Lie Down and Die: Towards an understanding of why the Aboriginal people of Arnhem Land face the greatest crisis in health and education since European contact*, Aboriginal Resource and Development Services Incorporated, Darwin, p. 29.
16 F. McCarthy, Diary 4, 1 August 1948, MS3513/14/4, AIATSIS.

As the quotation makes clear, the mission's purchases included not only material culture items, but painted skulls—an issue to be discussed later. Mission pricing affected the trading of McCarthy and Setzler, who had at their disposal tobacco, a few combs, mirrors and razor blades, supplied by Mountford. Red combs were put to use, as can be seen in Howell Walker's photograph of Margaret McArthur and Aboriginal women at Oenpelli in the 1949 *National Geographic* article on the Expedition.[17] Of the trade items provided by Mountford, the most coveted was tobacco. McCarthy pointed out that it would have been far better if Mountford had provided other items that people wanted, such as knives, tomahawks, shorts, shirts and belts. McCarthy regarded this as yet another failure in Mountford's planning. McCarthy noted in his diary that trading by Setzler sometimes got them into difficult situations due to standards and prices previously set by Ellemor. The mission paid a more equitable price for objects and also recognised their value.

> In addition, Hannah points out (5 August) after Setzler had got some fine spears & baskets that we should be paying more than we are for these specimens. We are now in an awkward situation—we want a good collection, we will have to pay a lot for it because of the mission standards, & we will have to make up on the bark paintings.[18]

Aboriginal Men

In order to make their Milingimbi collection, McCarthy and Setzler needed the missionaries' assistance in finding men whom they could employ for archaeological excavations and to provide information about Aboriginal culture. Fortunately, the names of most of them are known. Setzler and McCarthy photographed them on 10 August 1948 and their names are noted on the sleeve housing the negative.[19] On a recent trip to Milingimbi in 2009, I was given the updated spellings and other names for the men as they are now remembered in the community by Ruth Nalmakarra Garrawurra and Joe Neparrnga Gumbula. They are David Milngawurruwuy (Djambarrpuyungu), Gingi (Wobukarra), Peter Muntjingu (Gupapuyngu), Bill Balarra (Liyagawumirr) and Binyinyiwuy (Djambarrpuyngu).[20] Both men mention, in addition to these workers, Harry Makarrwala and his son, Jackie, showing them sites and generally being helpful to them. These men's knowledge of English made work easier for McCarthy and Setzler. Makarrwala was the man who worked most closely with Warner during 1927–29. These named individuals would have brought material culture items to trade or would have told others to visit the researchers after work.

---

17 Mountford, C. P. 1949, 'Exploring Stone Age Arnhem Land', *National Geographic*, p. 766.
18 F. McCarthy, Diary 4, 1 August 1948, MS3513/14/4, AIATSIS.
19 F. M. Setzler, Photograph 36_milingimbi_22, Smithsonian Archives, Washington, DC.
20 Ibid; F. McCarthy, PhotographV08956.14.pcd4565.Img0051, Australian Museum Archives, Sydney.

Figure 11.3 David Milngawurruwuy, Gingi, Peter Muntjingu, Bill Balarra and Binyinyiwuy on Milingimbi, 1948

Photograph by Frank Setzler. By permission of the National Anthropological Archives, Smithsonian Institution. Frank Setzler Photographs, Photo Lot 36, Box 8, Image 22.

Ways of Collecting

Setzler was very disapproving of Mountford's method of obtaining material culture. At the Oenpelli base camp, there were not many artists available to produce paintings for Mountford due to the fact they were working at the nearby buffalo-shooting camp. Mountford hired eight young men from Goulburn Island, who walked to Oenpelli once on the mainland, to make paintings. Setzler called them 'kids': 'At this date, October 20, it looks as though we shall not obtain any real ethnological specimens. Monty has had the Goulburn Island natives drawing. Some of the younger men have never attempted to paint, so he is trying to teach them, having them practice on paper.'[21]

At Milingimbi, Setzler's ideas about the appropriate ways of collecting ethnographic items were made clear:

---

21 F. M. Setzler, 2 October 1948, Oenpelli, vol. III, p. 242, NLA.

> Many specimens coming in are not those made to order—so to speak—but the actual specimens which they use in their everyday life. This turns out by far the best procedure—to purchase or trade for the things of their culture we desire, rather than have a group of natives fed by us make new things as we direct, rather than get the objects they actually use. This is a more orthodox way of collecting, I feel.[22]

Their collecting practice at Milingimbi seems to have conformed to this model. Whether or not this was based solely on conscious decision or whether it came about because they had little time to engage people after their archaeological work is not clear. McCarthy and Setzler felt that collecting everyday items was a better method than setting up artificial situations to obtain 'real ethnological specimens'. At Milingimbi, there was no need to direct individuals to make particular items as was done at other sites, where Warner's materials from Milingibi were used as templates. People brought items to them and they made their selections. As noted from the diary excerpt, they felt this was a better way of collecting than directing people to make specific items.

Acquisitions

According to Setzler's diary, trade with men first took place on 4 August 1948: 'Native boys brought 3 woomeras, 2 stone spear points hafted, 2 steel shovel spears, 2 stone spear points unhafted, a basket, and polished ax [sic] head. Bought all of them for a stick of native tobacco a piece. Big business.'[23]

This passage shows us the variety of items coming in at an early date, as well as how Setzler was paying for the objects, mainly with tobacco. By 8 August, the collection was mounting. Concerning fibre objects, McCarthy stated they now had a dozen baskets and other ornaments. By this time, some disagreements were occurring between the two men in regard to the collecting process:

> His [Setzler's] attitude is to get specimens as cheaply as possible, such as a basket for one stick of tobacco, but I believe that these poor natives should be given some reasonable value for the great amount of work involved in making a netted bag, twined basket, & spear—we are paying more for bark paintings which take very little time, than for the objects which take a lot of time & trouble.[24]

---

22 F. M. Setzler, 5 August 1948, Groote Eylandt to Yirrkala to Milingimbi, vol. II, p. 183, MS5230, NLA.
23 Ibid.
24 F. McCarthy, Diary 4, 8 August 1948, p. 46, MS3513/14/4, AIATSIS.

Figure 11.4 Group of armbands from Groote Eylandt

Photograph by Louise Hamby. By permission of the National Museum of Natural History, Smithsonian Institution. ID No. E387420B.

Frederick McCarthy had a strong interest in the fibre objects and an appreciation of the time required in their construction. The fact that makers of bark paintings (the men) were getting far more money than the other makers of equivalent items had become a matter of concern for him. The women were the main producers of fibre objects. This could have played a part in the prices they were paid for their work. May points to the fact that bark paintings would also sell for more money than the less 'aesthetically pleasing' items.[25] Despite the anthropologists' disagreements and their lack of trade goods, collecting continued throughout the trip. Both men proved popular with people on the mainland, as well as with locals who came to trade with them. Mainland people and others came to Milingimbi to visit family, participate in ceremonies and trade. Some objects catalogued as being from Milingimbi have other place names written on them.

Most of the items in the Milingimbi collection were amassed by McCarthy and Setzler except for some works commissioned by Mountford and some that the anthropologists bought directly from the mission. These items included two tassel spear-throwers, two hafted stone axes, one necklet charm, four painted skulls, and three bone points.[26] Other than the charm, these items are not the focus of this chapter—although they do deserve more research. The painted skulls and other skeletal material have recently been the subject of repatriation claims.

---

25 May, The last frontier?, p. 67; May, 'Colonial collections of portable art and intercultural encounters in Aboriginal Australia'.
26 T. Hannah, 1948, List of goods bought from the Mission by McCarthy and Setzler, August 1948, PRG 12188/17/9, Mortlock Library, Adelaide.

McCarthy and Setzler were in agreement about the distribution of objects once they were collected. Setzler wrote in his diary while at Oenpelli how they shared bark paintings according to subject matter and took turns deciding who would have each one:

> After lunch Monty, Fred, and I began sorting the bark paintings made by the Goulburn Island 'artists' and the Liverpool River guys. These are the worst lot of bark paintings collected. Most of them were made by kids who had never painted before and they were trying to imitate the old Oenpelli X-ray technique. Monty had picked out twelve of the best, which he had wrapped up, so we never even had a chance to see them. Then he insisted on having first choice of the large group from which we selected. Fred and I continued our old method of taking turns for first selection. What a contrast!!![27]

After 10 days at Milingimbi, McCarthy was positive about the virtues of being there. He and Setzler were happy with their collecting and their work. He writes in his diary:

> Milingimbi should certainly have been a base camp instead of Yirrkala. There are more natives, two bush camps at Gatji & Cape Stewart within 30 miles, & we could have got a wonderful collection, good dance sequences for films, & sheltered...bases for the Nutrition Unit here. Preliminary inquiry by inspection would have revealed this to Mountford but he did not make a reconnaissance to properly investigate base camp sites—he picked them chiefly to study the bark painting art & allow the others in the Expedition to fit in as best they could.[28]

Discussion of Objects

Fibre Objects

I have grouped all the fibre items collected by the Expedition into categories: bodywear, containers, string figures and other items. Bodywear includes all the items that people could wear, from headdresses to pubic covers. Containers from the Expedition include baskets, string bags and bark and palm containers. The last category of 'other items' comprises works few in number such as a head ring, a mat, raw materials, pendants and cordage. Many of the items are

---

27 F. M. Setzler, 30 October 1948, Oenpelli, vol. III, p. 262, NLA.
28 F. McCarthy, Diary 4, 9 August 1948, p. 51, MS3513/14/4, AIATSIS.

made totally from a single plant fibre type such as pandanus for a basket, cane for an armband or unprocessed bark fibre for a head ring. Other items such as pendants contain multiple materials.

An examination of the representative types of objects collected during the Expedition provides a picture of items that were available for trade or purchase and that were in use in the communities at the time of the Expedition.

Bodywear

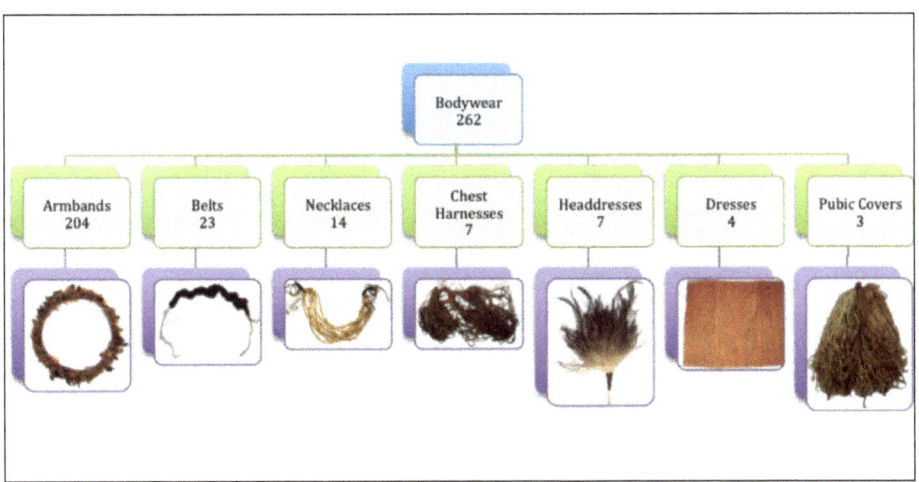

Figure 11.5 Items of bodywear collected at sites visited by the Arnhem Land Expedition

Most of the bodywear was made for everyday use, with armbands being the largest group. The most common type of armband is one that has an inner core of a strip of vine wrapped with plain, hand-spun string. The wrapped sort can be varied by the addition of small feathers, fur or wool wrapped or spun into the string. A variant has a wrapped band with attached feathered pendants. The other classic armband is interlaced from vine. Woven pandanus armbands, often painted with ochre, do not appear in major collections before the Expedition. Those from the Expedition come mainly from Groote Eylandt and Yirrkala.

Belts are the next largest category. They were made from hand-spun human hair or interlaced pandanus. Almost all of the necklaces are chokers made of grass stems threaded on hand-spun string. The remaining items—seven or less of which are represented in the collections—include pubic covers, bark dresses, headdresses and chest ornaments.

Figure 11.6 String bag from Yirrkala

Photograph by Louise Hamby. By permission of the National Museum of Australia. ID No. 1985.67.160.

Containers

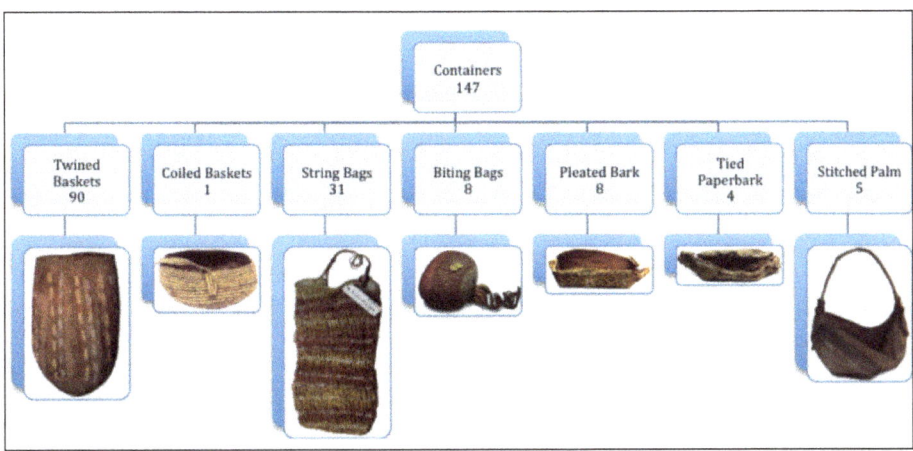

Figure 11.7 Containers collected at all sites visited by the Arnhem Land Expedition

Twined baskets made primarily from pandanus make up the largest group of containers. Included in the baskets is one exceptional coiled basket discussed later in the chapter. Some twined baskets are plain, while others are decorated with ochred feather pendants or rows of feathers woven into the body of the basket. About half of the looped and knotted string bags are biting bags, sometimes known as 'power bags' or 'spirit bags' and used in ceremony. They are stuffed with various materials and then tightly bound to make a rounded form. Bark containers include folded palm-leaf baskets, pleated stitched rigid bark containers and soft paperbark ones.

Figure 11.8 Shuttle from Yirrkala

Photograph by Louise Hamby. By permission of the National Museum of Natural History, Smithsonian Institution. ID No. E387479.

Other Fibre Objects

Some of the items in this category are raw materials or objects made from them, such as feathered string. They were subsequently used in the fabrication of bodywear or containers. The largest group consists of cordage, ranging in scale from heavy rope to delicate feathered string. Pendants are among the 'other items', as they could be used for armbands or attachments to baskets. The pendants from the Expedition all contain red-orange lorikeet feathers. Other works include fans, shuttles, toys, raw materials, a head ring, a mat, a coconut shell and a sail.

Milingimbi Quantities

Examples of most items listed above appear in the Milingimbi collections. Towards the end of his stay on Milingimbi, McCarthy noted in his diary that they had 15 bark paintings and 213 other specimens.[29] At the end of the trip, McCarthy and Setzler compiled an Ethnology Register that gives higher figures for items collected than those noted in the diary. The total number of ethnological items given in the register is 312. (The register did not include any of the bark paintings.)[30] Of the objects listed, 127 were fibre and the remaining 185 a mixture of weapons and other items. For the Milingimbi fibre objects, there is an anomaly in number: 53 baskets are listed, but I have found only 43. This means that 19 per cent of the baskets are not to be found in the museums. What has happened to them?

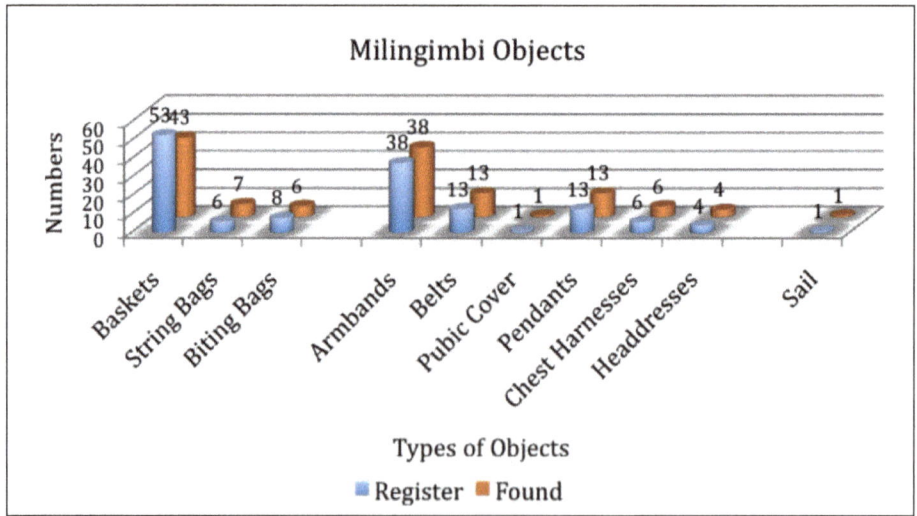

Figure 11.9 Comparison of fibre objects listed in McCarthy and Setzler's Ethnology Register with actual objects in the collections of the National Museum of Australia, the South Australian Museum, the Australian Museum and the National Museum of Natural History, Smithsonian Institution

---

29 Ibid., 14 August 1948, p. 57.
30 1948, Ethnology Register, Diary 8, MS3513, AIATSIS.

Works collected on the Expedition are held in institutions that were not part of the original distribution scheme. For example, the Kluge-Rhue Collection at the University of Virginia has one of the paintings on paper that appeared in Volume 1 of the *Records of the American–Australian Scientific Expedition to Arnhem Land*.[31] It was purchased by John Kluge in 1995 from Museum Art International.[32] It is not known where or how Museum Art International obtained the painting. Sally May's Table 6.1 in her honours thesis lists all the items missing from their home institutions. None of these is from Milingimbi.[33] She does provide information on two of the missing baskets from Milingimbi: one was stolen while on loan to the Commonwealth Department of Trade and one was exchanged. In September 1949, McCarthy started corresponding with W. W. Bowen, Director of Dartmouth College Museum, to arrange an exchange of North American baskets for Australian material.[34] In January 1951, the basket numbered E52808 arrived at the Hood Museum of Art.[35] This ochred basket has now been given a new registration number and is housed with other Australian objects that were exchanged.[36]

For the fibre objects there are a few possibilities to explain their absences. Some objects have been registered and have subsequently been lost in the years since the Expedition and are listed as 'missing' or 'location pending'. The collection managers and myself could have made mistakes in ascertaining whether certain objects are indeed from the Expedition. Some might have been incorrectly attributed or, as in the case of the painting, some might have been kept by Mountford or other Expedition members. May supports this idea, noting that 'unofficially, Charles Mountford was selling and giving away artefacts from the AASEAL ethnographic collection'.[37]

Exceptional Objects

All of the baskets in the various museums holding Expedition material are twined, with one exception: Smithsonian basket E387541. According to the accession cards, the donor for this object was Frank M. Setzler and it was collected at Milingimbi. The record is as follows: 'Bundle technique, strap handle coiled technique. This represents an introduced technique by the missionaries for trade purposes. Foreign to native techniques, similar to the weaving of mats which are sold by the missions.'[38]

---

31 Mountford, C. P. 1956, *Records of the American–Australian Scientific Expedition to Arnhem Land. Volume 1: Art, myth and symbolism*, Melbourne University Press, Carlton, Vic., plate 88A.
32 M. Smith, Personal communication to L. Hamby, 27 May 2009, Charlottesville, Va.
33 May, The last frontier?, p. 90.
34 D. Haynes, Personal communication to L. Hamby, 2009, Hood Museum of Art, Hanover, NH.
35 May, The last frontier?, pp. 89–91.
36 Basket 51.8.12669, Hood Museum of Art, Dartmouth College, Hanover, NH.
37 May, The last frontier?, p. 91; May, 'Colonial collections of portable art and intercultural encounters in Aboriginal Australia'.
38 Smithsonian, 2008, Accession 178294, Smithsonian Institution, Washington, DC.

Whether Ellemor sent the basket to Mountford before the division of objects, or whether Setzler or McCarthy obtained the basket personally, is unknown. The Smithsonian basket is most unusual, being the only coiled basket and one that Setzler acknowledges as being made for trade using a non-traditional technique. It is symptomatic of Setzler's methodology of collecting what people were making, rather than soliciting commissioned pieces.

I surmise that there is only one coiled basket in the Expedition collections because the men doing the collecting did not regard coiling as an authentic technique. Coiling had been practised in Arnhem Land since its introduction in the late 1920s on Goulburn Island.[39] This basket is similar in form to the five baskets, possibly from the Lower Murray River, offered in a 2009 Sotheby's auction in Melbourne.[40] These were obtained from the Sheard family—long-time friends of Charles Mountford—along with an Expedition painting from Oenpelli (see Chapman and Russell, this volume). By the late 1940s, many women would have made this style of basket in Arnhem Land.[41] Perhaps the rationale for not collecting them was that they did not fit into a paradigm of belonging to ancient traditions. That is to say, Mountford did not want them because they were not made using twining—the classic Arnhem Land technique for making baskets. Men and women were primarily making classic twined baskets but they were also making and selling coiled baskets.

In addition to this coiled basket, McCarthy collected fibre items that were classic in form but incorporated manufactured materials. These items would not have been considered 'real ethnographic specimens' by others on the Expedition. Martin Thomas has commented on the Expedition's tendency 'to obscure or overlook the historical conditions of the communities they visited'.[42] It is likely that the unwritten collecting policy created a bias towards objects with no outside influence or materials. The most commonly used non-traditional material was coloured wool, which appears in objects collected at Milingimbi and other sites. Some armbands have been wrapped with hand-spun string, overlaid with bright-red wool that is wrapped into place. At Milingimbi, red wool was spun into string. Objects such as the coiled basket support the idea that many of the works were not commissioned; they were everyday ones, complete with repaired handles.

Milingimbi baskets also incorporated red wool. It was used in outlining stitching in two twined baskets, held by the Australian Museum (E52811 and E52812). More than half of the string bags from Milingimbi incorporate red or other coloured wool. Many of the biting or fighting bags are made almost totally from mass-produced materials. Pieces of fabric also made their way into baskets. In basket E52798 from the Australian Museum, fabric replaces the usual string handle.

---

39 Allen, L. and Hamby, L. 2005, 'Links to the south', in L. Hamby (ed.), *Twined Together: Kunmadj Njalehnjaleken*, Injalak Arts and Crafts, Gunbalanya, NT, pp. 59–65.
40 Sotheby's 2009, *Aboriginal Art: Melbourne 2009*, Sotheby's, Armadale, Vic., p. 22.
41 Allen and Hamby, 'Links to the south'.
42 Thomas, 'Taking them back', p. 25.

Linking Objects and People

The objects collected during the Expedition contribute to a greater understanding of fibre-based practice in 1948, the biases of Expedition members notwithstanding. Examining the items and recording information from museums provide a range of data. When other archival information, such as documents and photographs, are included, a broader picture emerges. This expanded image, combined with information from Indigenous communities, leads to a more meaningful interpretation.

Discussions with people at Milingimbi indicate that the main groups present on the island in 1948 were the Djinang, Gupapuyngu, Djambarrpuyngu, Walamangu and Wangurri clans. They were the makers of most of the objects. Neither the names nor the clan affiliations of individual makers were recorded; however, a few older people can identify some objects. One such knowledgeable person is the Malarra woman Laurie Baymarrwanga. The late Reverend Joe Mawunydjil, the Milingimbi Shire Council Liaison Officer, listened to Baymarrwanga describe the baskets: 'She can tell. She can see the pattern differences.'[43] He was referring to the designs on baskets from the Expedition that she grouped into moiety divisions of Dhuwa and Yirritja. Some 60 per cent of the known twined baskets from Milingimbi have ochred designs.

The photographs taken at Milingimbi by McCarthy and Setzler have been an essential component of the research. Often they photographed the same scene of unidentified people. Martin Thomas writes about the loss of identities particularly in the 1948 Expedition. Thomas states that 'Mountford's documentation of artists' names is similarly patchy, and the identities of weavers, fibre workers and tool makers are, in many cases, lost forever'.[44] Fortunately, some Aboriginal people have very good memories and a strong knowledge base and are able to assist. By working closely with Joe Neparrnga Gumbula, a Yolngu researcher, and Ruth Nalmakarra Garrawurra from Milingimbi, identifications have been made of many individuals in the photographs. Both McCarthy and Setzler photographed three women carrying wood with bundles of pandanus on their heads. We can infer that the women they identified—Ngulurra, Djikanmurruwuy Garrawirrtja and Madowk, a Garrawurra woman, and others—made objects from pandanus and might have been the makers of some of the objects from Milingimbi. Other women are Ngulurra, a Djambarrpuyngu woman, and Djarrga. Other women identified in different photographs include Miningal (Wubulkarra), Mudaykala (Gupapuyngu), Djarrga and Lunpupuy.

---

43   J. Mawunydjil, Personal communication to L. Hamby, 4 April 2008, Milingimbi, NT.
44   Thomas, M. 2010, 'A short history of the Arnhem Land Expedition', *Aboriginal History*, vol. 34, p. 160.

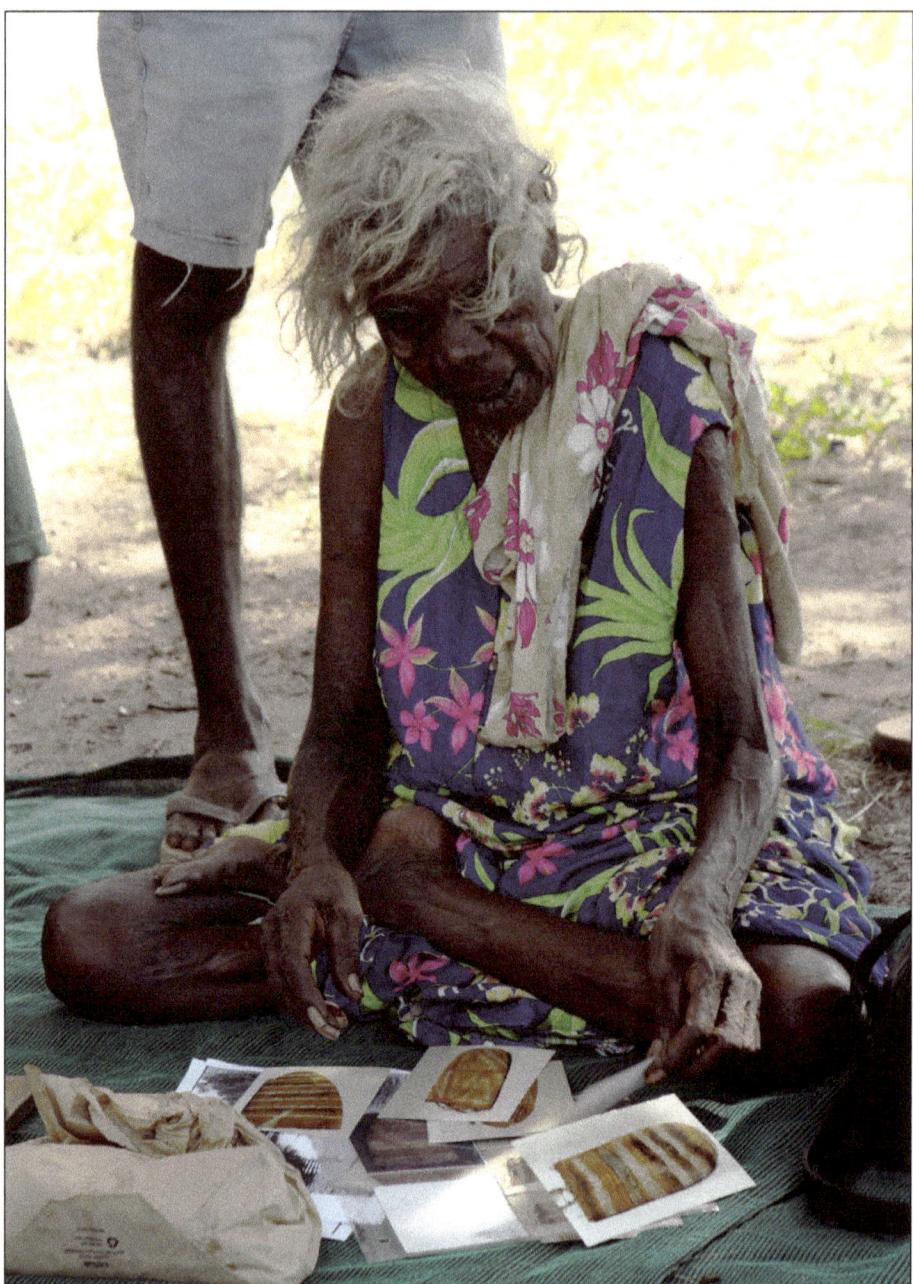

Figure 11.10 Laurie Baymarrwanga looking at baskets from the Expedition, Milingimbi, 15 April 2008

Photograph by Louise Hamby

Figure 11.11 Ngulurra (Djambarrpuyngu clan), Djikanmurruwuy (Garrawirrtja clan) and Madowk (Garrawurra clan) carrying pandanus on top of firewood, 1948

Photograph by Frank Setzler. By permission of the National Anthropological Archives, Smithsonian Institution. Frank Setzler Photographs, Photo Lot 36, Box 8, Image 18.

An exciting case study involves a basket from Milingimbi—item E52809—in the Australian Museum. The official records provide minimal information about it. This closely twined basket is distinctively painted, so is unlikely to be an everyday one. I had no other clues to its links with specific people or activities until I was able to connect the basket, diaries and photographs with information gained from Gumbula.

Figure 11.12 Mininyala (Wubulkara clan), Djakala (Garrawurra clan) and Ngulurra (Djambarrpuyngu clan) on the beach at Milingimbi, 1948

Photograph by Frank Setzler. By permission of the National Anthropological Archives, Smithsonian Institution. Frank Setzler Photographs, Photo Lot 36, Box 8, Image 11.

Early in my investigations, when I had access to a few of the photographs taken by Frank Setzler at Milingimbi, I showed his group photograph taken on the beach at Milingimbi to Gumbula. Setzler's description on the negative sleeve is: 'Native children on the beach in front of mission houses on Milingimbi. August 1948.'[45] As noted, McCarthy and Setzler frequently photographed the same scenes simultaneously. McCarthy, however, took more photographs of people creating fibre objects. In this case, he took two close-up images of one man who appears in Setzler's group shot on the beach.[46] On the right-hand side there is a man painting a basket. Gumbula was able to identify eight of the 16 individuals: Manuwa, Lunpupuy, Lityawuy, Fred, Yirrili, Mungunu Gaykamangu, Muntjingu and Banakaka. After documenting the baskets from the American–Australian Scientific Expedition to Arnhem Land and examining photographs, I thought it would be interesting to see if I could find the basket that was being painted

---

45 F. M. Setzler, 1948, Photo Lot 36, Image 9, Smithsonian Institution National Anthropological Archives, Washington, DC.
46 McCarthy, F. 1957, *Australia's Aborigines, Their Life and Culture*, Colorgravure Publications, Adelaide; and McCarthy, F. 1974, *Australian Aboriginal Decorative Art*, Australian Museum, Sydney.

by Mungunu Gaykamangu in the photograph. Only McCarthy and Setzler were at Milingimbi. I therefore felt that this basket, if it had been collected, would have gone to either the Smithsonian or the Australian Museum. A search of photographs of collected baskets revealed that the Australian Museum does indeed hold the basket, registered as E52809.

Figure 11.13 A group of people on the beach at Milingimbi. Known individuals, when counted from the left of the image: 3–5, Manuwa, Lunpupuy, Lityawuy; 12–16, Fred, Yirrili, Mungunu Gaykamangu, Muntjingu, Banakaka, 1948 (identifications by Joe Neparrnga Gumbula)

Photograph by Frank Setzler. By permission of the National Anthropological Archives, Smithsonian Institution. Frank Setzler Photographs, Photo Lot 36, Box 8, Image 9.

In February 2009, I met again with Gumbula to show him the photographs. He was convinced that we had located the basket depicted—a ceremonial one from his Gupapuyngu clan. Mungunu Gaykamangu was Gumbula's uncle on his father's side.

Figure 11.14 Twined basket from Milingimbi

Photograph by Louise Hamby. By permission of the Australian Museum. ID No. E52809.

In April 2009, Gumbula reflected further on this photograph, the process of identification, and what might become of the basket. There are three categories in Gumbula's system of classifying knowledge, images and objects: *garma* ('open'), *ŋärra'* ('restricted'), and a third broad-access category, *dhuni' makarr garma mirr* ('sheltered'). The last category is one open to public access, but images should be viewed only with guidance from an appropriate elder.[47] He draws an analogy between these protocols and the concept of a traffic light with its three colours. He describes this basket as orange, denoting caution. It would be used in special ceremonies. 'This is a very important basket. Only the elders can carry on.'[48] He and his family members are now interested in what the future of this basket might be. In October, he said that he wished to do more consultation with people at Milingimbi and would 'probably sign to get it back'.[49] Without doubt, there are many other baskets that fall into Gumbula's access category of orange and red items. In order to ascertain the orders of classification, much more research is required.

Conclusion

Research to date has demonstrated that the fibre collection from the Expedition is more significant than previously documented. There are more fibre objects than bark paintings, yet the latter have received much attention. Perhaps their reception would have been different if they too had been distributed at the same time as the division of paintings among gallery directors in Brisbane in 1956.[50] The numbers collected indicate their importance in the life of the people making and using them. Many were objects in use at the time; they were not made to fit outsiders' concepts of 'real ethnological specimens'. As May points out, McCarthy not only wished to fill gaps in the Australian Museum collection, he wanted 'to collect and record those objects that the expedition members observed being made and used'.[51] Milingimbi was a different collecting site from the others and is important in that the majority of the items were brought to the collectors, rather than being requested. The collected items represented a slice of life from a material culture view. They are representative of the materials available to their makers in 1948, which include fabric and wool, not just 'classic' materials such as bark fibre and pandanus.

---

47 Gumbula, N., Corn, A. and Mant, J. 2008, 'Matjabala Mali' Buku-Ruŋanmaram: implications for archives and access in Arnhem Land, The Fourth International Conference on the History of Records and Archives, University of Western Australia, Perth.
48 N. Gumbula, Personal communication to L. Hamby, 28 October 2009, Sydney.
49 Ibid.
50 Neale, M. 1998, 'Charles Mountford and the "bastard barks"', in L. Seear and J. Ewington (eds), *Brought to Light: Australian art*, Queensland Art Gallery, Brisbane, p. 210.
51 May, The last frontier?, p. 123.

McCarthy and Setzler collected most of the fibre objects, however Mountford might have collected some of these, as did his wife, Bessie. In August, she wrote in her diary, 'I collected one basket, bought a lovely bailer shell, and paid for everything including the mats'.[52] I have not found a basket attributed to her, or the mats. Indeed, there is only one mat in the entire collection. Her name might, however, in time be attached to other items that have not yet been studied. She also collected shell specimens and got her first 'cat-eye'—the operculum or foot-closure on a turban shell—on the same day that her husband bought his first painting at Groote Eylandt.[53] Perhaps if Bessie Mountford had also gone to Milingimbi we might have seen even more fibre objects. She gave much thought to the events happening around her in Arnhem Land and reflected on the collecting: 'The greed of the collector is understandable. One would have to keep a firm hand on oneself, and have a mind quite clear as to the why's [sic] and basic values of collecting.'[54] According to Craig Elliot, Margaret McArthur also collected baskets, bags and bark containers.[55]

It is unlikely that researchers now will ever know the origins and maker of every piece from the Expedition. The fibre objects will assist in bringing forward knowledge of the social and cultural practices of their era. The connection of people to the objects and photographs from the Expedition is one of the most direct and satisfying aspects of researching this subject. To discover more histories like those at Milingimbi requires additional time and resources, and a commitment to involving Indigenous researchers from the communities. The history of all the objects from the Expedition can be enhanced from collaborative research in the future. Individuals such as Joe Neparrnga Gumbula, an Australian Research Council Fellow, are already pursuing this objective.

Acknowledgments

I would like to thank the following people. At Milingimbi: Laurie Baymarrwanga, the late Joe Mawunydjil, Joe Neparrnga Gumbula and Ruth Nalmakarra Garrawurra. Museums and their staff: Australian Museum—Phil Gordon and Melanie van Offen; South Australian Museum—Keryn Walshe; National Museum of Australia—Claire Owens, David Kaus and Karen Peterson; Smithsonian—Felicia Pickering; the Australian National University—Maryam Rashidi, Martin Thomas and Sally May.

---

52 B. Mountford, 1948, Diary 3, Friday August 13, p. 17, PRG 487/1/2, SLSA.
53 B. Mountford, 1948, Diary 1, Tuesday April 20, p. 96, PRG 487/1/2, SLSA.
54 B. Mountford, 1948, Diary 3, Thursday September 2, p. 60, PRG 487/1/2, SLSA.
55 Elliott, C. 1992, American Australian Scientific Expedition to Arnhem Land, Unpublished cataloguing consultancy report, National Museum of Australia, Canberra, p. 96.

12. Hidden for Sixty Years: The motion pictures of the American–Australian Scientific Expedition to Arnhem Land

Joshua Harris

Introduction

> Fellow Members and Guests of the National Geographic Society: It is a great pleasure to give you a report on the Arnhem Land Expedition. 'Aboriginal Australia' represents a film originally three miles long, condensed to a mere three thousand feet.[1]
>
> — Frank Setzler

These words, spoken by Frank M. Setzler, opened his lecture and report on the Arnhem Land Expedition at Constitution Hall in Washington, DC, on Friday evening, 13 January 1950. The lecture's centrepiece were the sights and sounds recorded during 10 months in the field—a meticulously edited film taken from hours of raw footage shot by photographer Howell Walker as the representative of the National Geographic Society (NGS).

In early 2007, all that was known to us in the National Geographic Society Film Archives was the existence of the 'mere three thousand feet' of film from Setzler's lecture (roughly 75 minutes of footage). The extent of the archival materials relating to the moving images shot by Walker was the two original reels of the lecture film 'Project 73 Aboriginal Australia' and some scant notes in a slim file relating to it.

When contacted by Martin Thomas in early 2007, nothing was known about the whereabouts of any of the original raw footage captured by Walker (the 'three miles' Setzler mentions). It was certainly a possibility that additional footage existed, but locating and identifying such film would be a monumental task. Expedition films of this type were often passed around at will, cut, edited, re-edited and lost with little regard for their historical significance. Many times the 'outtakes' (footage not used in a final production) were discarded and considered 'useless' once the edited piece was finished. In addition, the cataloguing of film reels and footage was often non-existent, or so poor that no information could be garnered without intensive investigation. In many instances, even something

---

1 Transcription of introduction to speech of Frank Setzler given at Constitution Hall, Washington, DC, 13 January 1950, National Geographic Society Film Archives file 'Project 73 Aboriginal Australia', National Geographic Society, Washington, DC.

as simple as the labelling on the film can or the leader (the first several feet of a film reel, generally used to assist in the threading of film onto a projector or machine, but also used to label visual and audio information) of the film itself was absent, illegible or faded.

Supporting documentation was also slim, making any clues as to the footage's existence difficult. This is evidenced by the very slender file found in a 'lecture films' file cabinet kept in the archive. As was the case with the Arnhem Land project, the file contained very little information. The only real clue in the file, beyond Setzler's quote, which was contained in the file as a photocopy of only the first page of his speech, was a motion picture footage log. (Of unknown date, but most likely from soon after the Expedition, the log indicated that there was a total of seven cans of 'trims'. The term 'trims' was often used in the past to refer to footage cut out of its original camera roll and that was not part of a final motion picture—referred to elsewhere in this chapter as 'outtakes' or 'raw footage'.) This information certainly did not contribute much to the search effort, as it was already obvious from the practice of cinematography itself that Walker would have shot many hours of footage while in the field.

Figure 12.1 Howell Walker using his 16 mm camera at Umbakumba on Groote Eylandt, 1949

Photograph by Frank Setzler. By permission of National Anthropological Archives, Smithsonian Institution. Photo Lot 36, Box 7.

The NGS Film Archives consist of hundreds of thousands of elements of film, videotape, audio recordings, paper materials, photographs, artwork and other materials documenting society projects. A large collection holds the visual and audio portions of lecture and research reports given to NGS membership before the introduction of society documentary television production in 1965. Often these lectures were presented as silent films to which the narration was given by a scientist, researcher, journalist or photographer from an expedition. By the time of the talk on the Arnhem Land Expedition, society lectures were immensely popular public events given to large audiences at well-known venues. The Setzler lecture, delivered alongside Howell Walker's film footage at Constitution Hall—a venue of 3700 seats—is therefore the quintessential example of the society lecture film.

Contained within two on-site and three off-site storage vaults, the NGS film collections represent a vast array of film, video and audio formats and a wide range of preservation conditions. Following a theoretical model based upon 'preventative conservation', archive staff work to maintain and monitor optimal storage conditions that will ultimately preserve collections for extended periods, reducing the need for future intrusive conservation of individual items. Storing film in a cool, dry climate increases the life of the collections while also preventing and slowing the further deterioration of already damaged assets.[2]

The history of the film and audiovisual collections at the NGS is not unlike that of many other institutions housing similar materials. Film and video have generally not been well accepted as primary sources and historical documents, and thus the priority given to their preservation has been much lower than that of other collection types. The difficulty, expense and time-consuming processes involved in working with film have placed its preservation well behind that of other contemporary mediums of documentation, especially photographic collections.

Setting the Scene

The NGS film and audiovisual archives in its current state primarily serves the needs of the NGS television and documentary production departments as well as those of web-based production and stock-footage sales. Thus, the preservation, migration and usage of materials in the collections are determined by demand and their importance to the most current society ventures. In other words, in order for any type of reformatting, migration or preservation action to be undertaken or funded there must be an NGS documentary, new product or outside paying

---

2 Reilly, J. M. 1993, *IPI Storage Guide for Acetate Film*, Image Permanence Institute, Rochester, NY.

client with specific needs for the archival footage. These business decisions are the guiding force behind the priorities placed on collection management and the resources of the staff entrusted with caring for the archives. The consequence of this type of collection management is that many historically significant films are left behind, as well as those that might be more severely degraded or are in need of more intensive conservation actions. This 'on-demand' approach to media migration does not diminish the amount of preservation that has been accomplished and completed; by default, this method, given the age and subject matter held in the collection, does yield some positive results. While certain collections might be heavily utilised for their commercial and aesthetic value to the modern-day filmmaker or producer (the focus is often on more modern footage, often shot with the latest 'hi-definition' cameras or more easily reformatted for modern hi-definition broadcasting standards), other collections remain unknown and hidden far from sight.

Within this context, it is apparent how the possibility of locating any of the additional raw footage from Walker's camera seemed extremely slim. Not only was the film's physical existence in question, but also the resources—both human and otherwise—to put towards such an endeavour were not available. It should be pointed out, too, that the Arnhem Land Expedition films were not the first—and certainly will not be the last—about which queries as to their whereabouts have been sent to the archives. The material was put on the list along with a slew of other questionable, lost, orphaned or otherwise unknown films. An 'orphan work' is a broad term used to describe films that have no clear copyright holder, no commercial potential to pay for preservation or have in some way been neglected.[3] Historical, ethnographic and documentary film elements are some of the clearest examples of orphaned works: they have often been neglected, lack the background documentation to put them into context and are of unknown copyright or origin.

The Finding

The location of the Arnhem Land Expedition films was not a methodical or organised venture; rather, it was by chance and only through the search for other, more pressing assets that, one by one, the films began to emerge from hiding. Over the next year a total of 10 individual rolls of film were located in a variety of locations, both at the society's Washington, DC, headquarters and buried in boxes in the off-site storage locations. It was certainly the finding of the first can (containing two rolls labelled #5 and #6) in the basement cold vault

---

3   More information on orphan films can be found online at Duke University: <http://www.law.duke.edu/cspd/pdf/cspdorphanfilm.pdf> (viewed 28 October 2010); and the Library of Congress, National Film Preservation Board: <http://www.loc.gov/film/study.html> (viewed 28 October 2010).

in Washington that gave the hope that an entire set might be assembled. On trips to the off-site vaults outside Pittsburgh, Pennsylvania, other rolls slowly came to light. A simple look at the dusty cans with their faded labels made it probable that the footage contained within had been viewed or handled by only a few people since the Expedition.

A common practice in filmmaking is to assemble all of the 'camera rolls' of film taken in the field (often about 122 m each) onto larger reels of about 300–460 m. Therefore, the location of 10 reels (not including the two rolls of edited lecture films) could easily account for all the field footage shot by Walker. It is also probable that camera rolls were discarded before or shortly after processing— deemed by Walker to be of inferior quality or containing footage not worthy or possible of making it into the final lecture film or any other future edited piece.

The discovery of these films was a feat in and of itself. These were truly the 'needle in the haystack'; simply knowing the films existed, were identified and were being held in the proper storage conditions makes this a success story outright. The fact that the films had been kept in cool and dry storage conditions meant that some amount of 'preventive conservation' had been unknowingly taking place. 'Preventive conservation' is a term used by the museum and archive community to refer to storing and housing artefacts within the most optimal environmental conditions to prevent their further deterioration or the need for more intrusive techniques that involve physical handling of the item.[4]

We knew from the notes on file that Howell Walker used Kodachrome film stock in the field. Kodachrome was the most common film stock used by NGS cinematographers at the time. More specifically, the stock was Kodachrome Color Reversal, a film type by which a positive image is produced upon a transparent base. This became a very popular type of film in documentary and ethnographic filmmaking, as reversal film was cheaper and negated the need to process a negative to create a positive film print. The reversal film could be—and very often was—directly projected without need for processing. This certainly is proven by the number of times Setzler and others projected the final lecture film, which was made up of the camera originals. A footage projection log found in the film archive file indicates the final edited film was shown at least 28 times— including at universities, museums, conventions and other locales—over a five-year period.[5] Kodachrome itself is well known for its long-term colour accuracy and dark-storage longevity, which make it a very good archival film format in terms of the images themselves.[6]

---

4   More information specifically related to preventive conservation in film can be found at the Library of Congress, National Film Preservation Board: <http://www.loc.gov/film/storage.html> (viewed 28 October 2010).
5   Film archive file P73 Aboriginal Australia, Screening Footage Log.
6   National Film Preservation Foundation 2004, *The Film Preservation Guide: The basics for archives, libraries, and museums*, National Film Preservation Foundation, San Francisco, p. 11.

In order to determine if the films were in a state of extreme degradation and might need 'emergency triage', we had to first complete a simple visual inspection. At a minimum, this would add some amount of basic knowledge to our data on the film condition. Even if nothing could be done in the short term, any knowledge would add to our understanding of the collection.

One of the first signs of film decay is the pungent odour of vinegar emanating from the film can or box. 'Vinegar syndrome' is frequently encountered in films from the era in which the Arnhem Land Expedition films were shot, as it is a condition that primarily affects film stock made with a cellulose triacetate base; its progression is greatly affected by storage conditions. The symptoms of vinegar syndrome are the odour, followed eventually by shrinkage, embrittlement and buckling of the gelatin emulsion. Storage in warm and humid conditions greatly accelerates the syndrome's onset; once it begins in earnest, the remaining life of the film is short because the decay process speeds up as it goes along. Early diagnosis and cool, dry storage are the most effective defences. As vinegar syndrome can spread to nearby films, it is also necessary to segregate affected films from better-preserved assets.

Vinegar syndrome is not always easily observed by the sense of smell, as trace amounts might be undetectable to human senses. The film archivist can use certain tools to measure the amount of free acid in the film can. In the case of the Arnhem Land films, there was no noticeable odour upon opening the containers, and no visible damage was apparent. The Image Permanence Institute at the Rochester Institute of Technology has developed a product called A-D strips, which are used to measure the amount of free acid present in film containers. These strips change colour when exposed to acetic acid and are a very useful tool in determining the level of film deterioration.[7] A-D strips were immediately placed into the film cans in order to measure the true amount of acetate degradation occurring.

The films did appear to display common signs of age, such as warping and possibly some shrinkage. Over time a certain degree of shrinkage occurs due to the evaporation of solvents and other agents left over from the manufacture of the film base as well as decomposition reactions in the base.[8]

We also noticed that the rolls contained an extremely high number of 'splices'. Small pieces of film are joined together to form longer, continuous rolls, and splicing was a key technique used in film cutting and editing. A variety of materials have been employed in the past to join pieces of film together and create these 'splices'. During much of the twentieth century, various types of

---

7 Image Permanence Institute 1998, *User's Guide for A-D Strips*, Image Permanence Institute, Rochester, New York.
8 Ibid., pp. 12–15.

glues, adhesives, tapes and cements were used. Such materials can cause myriad problems when it comes to film degradation. Not only can splices become brittle and break apart, the adhesives can ooze onto images or remain stuck after tape is removed. Splices as crude as masking tapes, electrical tape or transparent 'office' tape have been observed in the NGS collections. These crude splices are seen primarily in films from the documentary genre, as opposed to those from 'Hollywood'-style narrative films, and are usually indicative of time constraints and budgetary concerns.

Figure 12.2 Archivists Joshua Harris and Bryce Lowe examine a reel of outtakes from the Arnhem Land Expedition films, 2008

Photograph by Martin Thomas

Thus, we knew shortly after their discovery and through the use of A-D strips and the bare minimum visual inspection that the films did exhibit some expected signs of age but were considered to be overall in 'fair' condition. Since no immediate action could take place, simply knowing of the films' existence, having the assets inventoried and placed in a 'known' location in the vault, and creating catalogue records in a database, were about as much as could be expected.

The Examination

As new formats emerge within broadcasting and technologies evolve, the human resources of a television archive are also shifted in that direction. As budgets tighten and production schedules become shorter, the time is not available for an archivist with limited resources to spend days scrolling through footage or meticulously repairing splices and damaged film. This is evidenced by the remarkable fact that National Geographic Television sold, gave away or discarded all of its traditional film editing, repair and viewing equipment more than 10 years ago to follow the swift-moving wave into digital video production. The only film bench left is in a cramped corner of the often-crowded projection booth of the Grosvenor Auditorium at the society headquarters in Washington, DC.

This situation made a full conservation effort of the Arnhem Land Expedition films fairly unlikely. As manager, I was unable to spare even a few precious man-hours for an archive staff member to examine the films in more detail. But, as we squeezed in time at night or on the weekend, we were able to at least do a cursory examination of the films and get a general idea of their condition. On initial examination, we were delighted that the film images themselves appeared to be excellent. Colour fading is one of the most noticeable and fast-acting chemical processes occurring in film over time. Films often take on a purple hue, due to the fading of less stable yellow and cyan dyes that make up colour images. The situation with the splices, though, was even worse than had at first been thought. The films in the Arnhem Land collection appeared to have been assembled hastily and with little regard to future usage. A variety of tapes not designed for film splicing were utilised, including masking tape and pieces of paper with glue applied to the surface. In several instances, film was joined together with overlapping images—that is, frames from one reel placed directly on top of frames from the next reel. We also noticed that there was no continuity within the outtakes and the films were assembled with disregard to subject matter or time line. For example, shots of Setzler examining artefacts were spliced to footage of Arnhem Landers fishing into which were interjected eight frames of unrelated scenes of ceremonial footage. A few glaring examples of the lack of care taken with the outtakes are shown by the fact that there are several sequences of 'flipped images', where a piece of film is spliced upside down to its adjoining piece. When displayed, this would show the clip upside down—evidence once again of the fact that little regard was placed on the raw field footage as a legitimate historical artefact or an asset that would be utilised in the future. Several other types of damage included warping, curling, emulsion scratches (which create visible blemishes on the image) and broken sprocket transport holes.

Some of the problems, such as shrinkage and colour fading, are irreversible. Modern technological advancements in digital film restoration provide some hope for addressing these issues, but it was clear that the film originals had undergone permanent damage. Other damage, such as splices and perforation breaks, can be repaired but only with a significant amount of meticulous time and effort. These film degradation issues are of concern because they also make the process of transferring the films to modern media problematic. Any type of film transfer or migration requires running the film through often complex and complicated equipment. A minimal amount of repair and preparation has ideally to be accomplished in order to run the film through modern film equipment without risking further damage to the original.

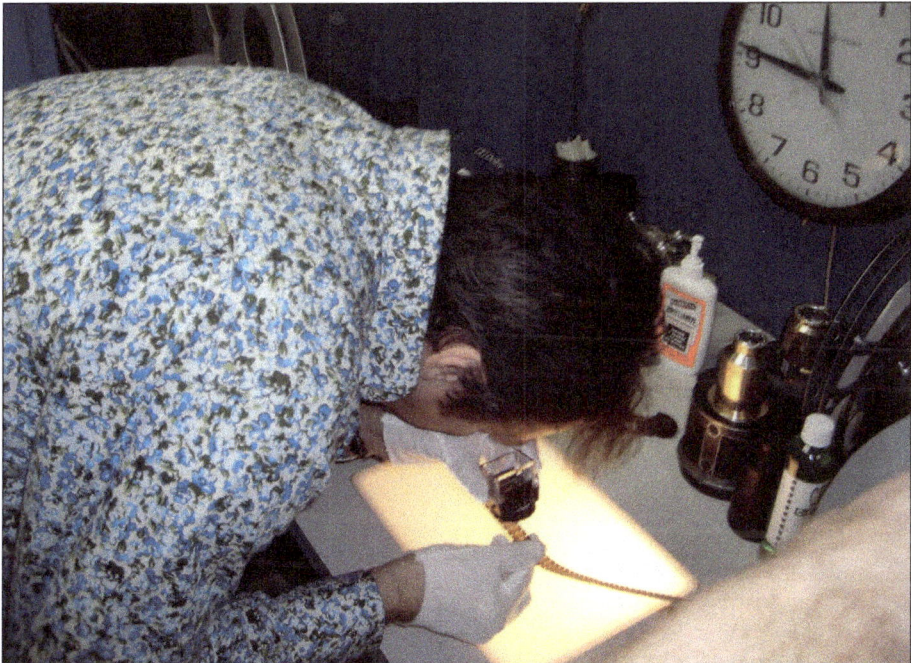

Figure 12.3 Historian Martin Thomas taking a close look at some footage frames from the Arnhem Land film collection, 2008

Photograph by Josh Harris

Thus, reel by reel, we managed to get a little better idea as to the true condition of the reels. These types of metadata are very important and were added to the catalogue records for these assets. If no immediate work could be done on the films, it was very important for us as archivists to capture whatever information we could (whenever we could!) to aid in future possible use, preservation or restoration efforts. Just knowing this type of information makes the process of applying for funding or preparing future proposals much easier. The more that is known about the asset's condition, the more precise is a price estimate that can be put together for a more intensive preservation project.

The timing was certainly right for the discovery of this 'lost footage'. Claims had been made and notices given by myself and several previous NGS archivists as to the number of historically significant films in the collections that needed some type of attention. The sheer volume of pre-1965 films that have never been transferred to a newer medium is staggering. But this is by no means a rare or unusual case within moving-image collections, and claims for preservation dollars typically become a yearly routine for most film archivists. The archivist finds him or herself fighting a constant battle against time and rapid technological changes while attempting to prevent the further decay of the artefact. The NGS is no exception to the general rule that the battle for precious dollars will always favour higher priorities, societal operations and more immediate business decisions. Given the recent global economic downturn, this holds true now more than ever.

Saving the Footage

Mid December 2007, however, brought excellent news with the potential to break this trend of neglecting older films; in fact, it had been more than 10 years since the last preservation project involving pre-1965 films. Some extra funds—not utilised during the fiscal year—were still available. But the time line was tight; these one-time budgetary items had to be used by the end of the calendar year. A proposal and project plan would have to be written up immediately and the project had to begin by the last day of 2007 in order to be accepted. From an archival perspective, where projects are often planned in the long term and take shape over a fairly lengthy period, this was not ideal, but it might have been our only chance to work on these collections. We wrote a simple yet comprehensive proposal in only a matter of days. To our amazement, the funding was approved, but the stipulations and demands put on the project were considerable: the greatest number of footage hours was to be transferred to the highest-quality format possible with the most minimal amount of physical film preparation and repair. This posed an extremely difficult challenge as we tried to plan and start this project in a matter of two weeks.

The archivists themselves—as the only few people in the society with any knowledge concerning the audiovisual collections—were offered the freedom to choose the majority of the films to be transferred. This was a rare case in an institution with so many conflicting ideas on the priority level given to certain subject matter. The films from 'Project 73' were given highest-level priority, and it was within this framework that the Arnhem Land films found their way into a shipping container destined for Crawford Communications in Atlanta, Georgia (the lab commissioned to assist in carrying out this project). All 10 rolls of outtakes were to be converted, including the two original lecture films, totalling almost 12 hours of footage.

There is no single, straightforward workflow for the preservation, restoration or migration of moving-image artefacts. Each film roll will have its own situation and will need to be treated as an individual case. A basic framework must be established and laid out with the laboratory, and parameters put on the type and nature of intervention to be taken on each film. There is not enough time to discuss the endless number of possibilities that arise from a project such as this. This is also not the forum to discuss the theory, techniques, criteria and ethical concerns for moving-image migration, duplication or restoration. But it should be noted that film archivists and those charged with caring for audiovisual collections do face an immense number of issues regarding any such project. This holds ever truer as digital technologies continually add to the ways in which images can be manipulated and altered.[9]

As the project came together, it was clear that given the budgetary, organisational and time restrictions placed upon us, a true 'restoration' project would not be possible. The goal, in effect, would be 'duplication'—the essential function of creating a facsimile of the films. The facsimile, used for access and preservation purposes, would negate the possibilities of having to touch the original films, thereby preventing further degradation due to physical handling.

We were adamant about maintaining as much of the authenticity of the films as possible. That is, the images would be exact replicas, blemishes and all; they would not be 'colour corrected' and would therefore maintain as much of the visual integrity, such as colour saturation and balance, as Howell Walker had captured. The films would be scanned, frame by frame, at a resolution of 4k— the highest resolution available at the time. Scanned footage would be output to a high-definition format known as D-5, with other very specific parameters placed upon 'frame rate'. Our guiding principle was to replicate the look and feel of the original film, in its current state. This would create a true historical document that would also show the ageing and decay that occurred to the original over time. No further digital 'touch-up' would occur. Digital tools would be used only to stabilise film that could not run through the scanner due to shrinkage, warping or other damage.

The transfer process was not without its issues and problems. Even with minimal intervention, films as fragile as these took a significant amount of time to duplicate. Most were too delicate to be cleaned properly because some of the chemical solvents used could break apart bad splices or further damage the originals. As the films went through the scanner, several broke in the machine and had to be repaired immediately. Shrunken film had to be slowly scanned and stabilised and the tapes and adhesives removed by hand if affecting the

---

9 Wallmuller, J. 2007, 'Criteria for the use of digital technology', *Moving Image Restoration*, vol. 7, no. 1, pp. 1–19.

transfer. Some of the limitations of technology and the large amounts of storage needed for digital files required some rescanning of the films. It is worthwhile to note here that communication and open dialogue with any lab doing such intensive work are vital. For example, we quickly realised that the technicians had flipped the upside-down images mentioned earlier and had taken other actions not agreed upon. The only way to fix these issues would be to rescan the film—a chance we did not want to take given its physical state. This again shows how professional laboratories—more accustomed to production than archival footage—might not fully understand the archivist's perspective and might be prone to decision making that does not adhere to the unique aspects of working with archival moving images.

The final steps of this story come with the footage returned to the society's headquarters. We placed the films in new archival film cans and accessioned the new film transfer masters, creating new catalogue records in the database. We created additional backup copies including standard-definition (not high-definition) copies and DVDs to be added to the NGS film library as loan copies. We ended by fully digitising each tape into our 'media asset management' system, creating a full-resolution preservation file, a medium-sized (Mpeg-2) file appropriate in many production settings and a low-resolution, highly compressed file (Mpeg-1), which can be used for Internet online access. While there are still many 'unknowns' in the world of digital moving-image preservation, we were able to utilise some digital tools in order to better preserve the Arnhem Land Expedition films and ensure their accessibility far into the future. We hope that the footage will be made available to a wider audience via the World Wide Web in the near future.

Conclusion

The discovery and preservation of Howell Walker's films from the 1948 American–Australian Scientific Expedition to Arnhem Land are a modern-day success story in film archiving. Despite the bumps in the road and some less-than-ideal situations, it is remarkable that the films have survived and have now found a new life, more than 60 years after the Expedition itself. Their survival is proof of the importance of proper storage conditions for film and audiovisual collections, but their discovery and conservation also demonstrate the difficulties and challenges faced by moving-image archives worldwide as they attempt to preserve and provide access to these artefacts. The time, funds and resources to work with these collections make them very difficult and expensive to care for. Knowing the global financial crisis began shortly after this project was finished makes it very clear now just how lucky we were to spend some time preserving this collection.

Film collections are still only gaining acceptance as important historical documents and artefacts. The work described in this chapter has presented the films of the Arnhem Land Expedition as a real-life example of the legitimate place of moving-image collections as a part of our global cultural heritage. It is clear that the hard work, effort and time-consuming processes needed to migrate and digitally preserve these films will deepen our understanding of the Arnhem Land cultures and the Expedition as a whole. Thus, the legacy of the Expedition will continue and the educational value of the materials it collected will increase long into the future.

13. The Responsibilities of Leadership: The records of Charles P. Mountford

Denise Chapman and Suzy Russell

In 1948 Charles P. Mountford led the American–Australian Scientific Expedition to Arnhem Land—one of the largest and most comprehensive scientific expeditions ever undertaken in Australia. A part-time ethnographer, Mountford worked consistently through the late 1930s into the early 1960s (something that was often possible only whilst on leave from his paid employment).

The Mountford-Sheard Collection of the State Library of South Australia (PRG 1218) holds the wealth of material gathered by Mountford throughout his career. Indeed, the Arnhem Land Expedition was the catalyst for the collection to be organised and donated. Like many of the Expedition members, Mountford was exhausted upon his return. To recover, he went to stay with his friend Harold Sheard in the coastal town of Port Elliot. During this stay, Sheard observed Mountford sorting through his Arnhem Land work, and became worried when he saw Mountford discarding papers that Sheard thought might hold future value. Sheard began a project to assemble Mountford's entire private archive, and sought a suitable repository for the collection. With the encouragement and collaboration of South Australia's State Librarian, Hedley Brideson, the bulk of the collection was donated to the State Library in 1957.

Brideson recounted in a 1998 interview that he first met Mountford when he invited him to give a presentation to a Sunday-school class. The two crossed paths again at various functions and in time they came to discuss Sheard's growing collection of 'Mountfordiana', with Mountford joking at one point that Sheard was soon going to be 'sleeping out on the lawn' and that he 'couldn't cope with it anymore'. To this Brideson responded, 'All right then, let us have it. We'll find somewhere to put it.'[1] An extensive bibliography prepared by Sheard accompanied the donation in 1958, and Mountford requested that the collection be named Mountford-Sheard to reflect his friend's substantial contribution.[2]

---

[1] B. M. Robertson and R. Starke, Interview with Hedley Brideson, 1998, OH 478, State Library of South Australia (hereafter SLSA), Adelaide.
[2] Sheard, H. L. 1958, *Charles Pearcy Mountford: An annotated bibliography, chronology and checklist of books, papers, manuscripts and sundries*, Stone Copying Company, Cremorne, NSW.

More material was donated in the following years, and the Mountford-Sheard Collection became the first of several ethnographic collections acquired by the State Library under Brideson's directorship.

While the South Australian Museum might have seemed a more logical home for Mountford's work, it is likely that the frosty relations between Mountford and Museum Director, Norman Tindale (to be expanded on below), made this impossible. According to Brideson, 'it was no good Mountford seeing the Museum', and if Mountford had taken the collection to Tindale, his response would have been 'throw the bloody lot out'.[3]

In this chapter, we will discuss the contents of the Mountford-Sheard Collection generated before, during and after the historic Expedition. Through these records, and through the diaries of Mountford's wife and honorary Expedition secretary, Bessie, we will highlight the work accomplished by Mountford as well as some of the many challenges he faced. This self-taught South Australian ethnographer was considered by many to be unqualified to assume the eminent role of Expedition leader. We will begin by exploring how Mountford came to be appointed to the position.

Mountford Makes the Grade: The origin of the Arnhem Land Expedition

The idea for the Arnhem Land Expedition originated in 1945 when Mountford was on a lecture tour of the United States, organised by his employer, the Commonwealth Department of Information. During this tour, which commenced just after Christmas in 1944, Mountford recorded an extraordinary 4000 pages in his journal, and described in detail the events leading to the suggestion of an expedition to Arnhem Land. The tour included a pivotal presentation to the National Geographic Society (NGS) at Constitution Hall in Washington, DC. Mountford referred to the crowd of more than 4000 as the 'intelligensia [sic] of Washington' and remarked that one could not buy a ticket to such a show.[4]

It is apparent from Mountford's journal that the presentation of his work to such an eminent audience was a major coup; his enthusiasm and sense of satisfaction are evident. He writes that although nervous, he tried to behave nonchalantly, as though speaking to such a large, illustrious group was an everyday occurrence. Despite an awkward moment when the film broke during the screenings, Mountford felt afterwards that he had 'made the grade', and Dr Alexander

---

3   B. M. Robertson and R. Starke, Interview with Hedley Brideson, 1998, OH 478, SLSA.
4   C. P. Mountford, 2 February 1945, Records relating to Charles Mountford's Journeys to America and to Melbourne, 1944–46, p. 19, PRG 1218/16/2, SLSA.

Wetmore, Secretary of the Smithsonian Institution, congratulated him after the show.[5] Mountford wrote that night, 'I don't think I need to bother about Tindale's innuendos from now on.'[6] This is one of many references to a career-long professional rivalry between the two men. Their working relationship began in 1925 when they collaborated on a paper about rock engravings rediscovered by Mountford at Morowie, in the mid-north of South Australia.[7] By 1945 the two had encountered each other innumerable times. Mountford was an Honorary Assistant in Ethnology at the South Australian Museum, and he travelled with Tindale during a 1935 field trip to the Warburton Range.

In a field deeply divided between 'professionals' and 'amateurs', Mountford felt that he was dismissed by Tindale and others—most notably A. P. Elkin—as insufficiently trained to have his scientific work taken seriously. This accounts for Mountford's mention of Tindale's 'innuendos' in his US journal. Mountford struggled against this perceived inferiority throughout his career and it troubled him to the end of his life. In a 1968 interview, Mountford, still harbouring these resentments, recounted how a funding application was undone by Tindale—he 'killed it, damned it out of sight'—and stated that 'everyone knew Elkin's opinion of me, because he'd been trying to down me for many many years'.[8] But the derision was not entirely one-sided. Throughout his notes, Mountford cast doubts on Tindale's findings. Pamphlets and articles collected by Mountford, by Tindale and other authors, are peppered with annotations in which he disagrees with the authors' findings.[9]

Tindale was working in military intelligence and stationed at the Pentagon at the time of Mountford's 1944–45 lecture tour of the United States. He was invited to attend a presentation given by Mountford on 18 January 1945 at the Department of the Interior. His presence unsettled Mountford, who recorded in his diary: 'I was sure that T[indale] would get up and give a sub-lecture, but curiously enough, he kept quiet.'[10] Later, following a lecture at Washington's exclusive Cosmos Club, on 5 February, the Secretary of the NGS suggested that Mountford approach the society for a grant to carry out more research.[11] Arnhem Land was purportedly chosen because it was perceived that little research had been done on the natural history and ethnology of the area (a suggestion disputed by anthropologists Elkin and Ronald and Catherine Berndt).[12] From the

---

5   Ibid., p. 23.
6   Ibid., p. 27.
7   Tindale, N. B. and Mountford, C. P. 1926, *Native Markings on Rocks at Morowie, South Australia*, Royal Society of South Australia, Adelaide.
8   Charles P. Mountford, Autobiographical Notes [sound recording], 1968, PRG 1218/39, SLSA.
9   Authors' personal observations of annotations present on a wide range of materials in the Mountford-Sheard Collection and Personal Library of C. P. Mountford.
10   C. P. Mountford, 18 January 1945, Records relating to Charles Mountford's Journeys to America and to Melbourne, 1944–46, p. 425, PRG 1218/16/1, SLSA.
11   Ibid., 5 February 1945, pp. 77–85.
12   Gray, G. 2007, *A Cautious Silence: The politics of Australian anthropology*, Aboriginal Studies Press, Canberra, pp. 191–4.

outset, the plans were dogged by political wrangling between the authorities and within the anthropological community. Mountford commented: 'All this intrigue, play and counter-play is rather awful when all I want to do is to collect this information for future generations, and to create a better understanding of the aboriginal people.'[13]

Mountford received approval for the work from the NGS whilst still in the United States, and then had to secure the support of the Australian Government, which he managed—tentatively—with help from Sir Frederic Eggleston, the Australian Minister to the United States. A second lecture tour of the United States in 1946 was used to further plan the Expedition. Once back in Australia, plans progressed rapidly for departure in March 1947, but the Expedition was postponed, finally getting under way in March 1948.

'Fools, rogues and bad fortune': The Groote Eylandt camp[14]

Mountford's personal journal—documenting the beginning of the Expedition and the Groote Eylandt camp—exceeds 600 pages. From the moment of take-off for the Top End, his writing was prolific. The prologue was a swipe at Elkin,

> who has caused me a great deal of trouble in the past, because of his extreme jealousy (he is angry because he was not placed in charge of this expedition), has been trying to underground me up here…It has been a remarkable battle against Departmental stupidity and the malicious underground attacks of Elkin.[15]

The journal's recurrent themes include Mountford's experience of responsibility, administrative and logistical issues, illness, observations of other participants, and personality conflicts. Mountford also wrote about aspects of the physical environment, including the weather, which heavily influenced transport arrangements, and recorded his interactions with Aboriginal informants and his opinions of the mission superintendents and their methods.

---

13   C. P. Mountford, 19 February 1945, Records relating to Charles Mountford's Journeys to America and to Melbourne, 1944–46, p. 271, PRG 1218/16/2, SLSA.
14   Charles P. Mountford, 3 May 1948, Expedition to Arnhem Land 1948, vol. 1, Personal Journal, p. 273, PRG 1218/17/12, SLSA.
15   Ibid., 18 March 1948, p. 13.

Figure 13.1 Charles Mountford filming from the blister of a Catalina seaplane en route to Groote Eylandt, 1948

By permission of the State Library of South Australia. PRG 1218/34/2841.

There were 47 tonnes of gear in need of transport and this more than any other issue haunted the organisation.[16] The workload put considerable strain on Mountford's health, yet he felt only *he* had the influence and ability to oversee the organisational matters. He perhaps felt that by handling these tasks alone, he could prove his capabilities as a leader. For instance, when the *Phoenix*, a supply barge, failed to arrive on Groote Eylandt, and radio communication also failed, Mountford, along with anthropologist Fred Rose, patrol officer Gordon Sweeney and a group of Aboriginal men, made a treacherous 60 km trek to Angurugu Mission station to use the radio and find out what had happened. Mountford was fifty-eight at the time, and in his journal he expressed frequently how his health issues were affecting him. During the journey to Angurugu, he described himself as 'long passed the "boy-scout" stage', of a 'mature age', and as having lived a 'soft life' for a number of years previously:

---

16 Mountford, C. P. (ed.) 1956, *Records of the American–Australian Scientific Expedition to Arnhem Land. Volume 1: Art, myth and symbolism*, Melbourne University Press, Carlton, Vic., p. xxiii.

> I would never have contemplated such a journey from choice, but the food situation is getting serious, the telephone does not work, and no-one but myself would be in the position to make the decisions. So there was nothing else to do but go. I was not happy about the matter.[17]

Waist-deep swamps extended for miles, and, before reaching the mission, Mountford was nearly swept away when he fell into a fast-running stream. He grabbed a tree branch and was rescued by some Aboriginal boys who were waiting nearby.[18]

Mountford also recorded in his journal an account of the fraught sea journey to Boucaut Bay near Milingimbi, where the *Phoenix* was stranded. Fred Gray, the superintendent of Umbakumba Aboriginal settlement, took them to the stranded barge in his 10-m launch, *Wanderer II*, which was buffeted by heavy seas for five days. They reached Milingimbi, relieved to find that the barge had floated off the reef and was resting safely in the mud. They loaded some of the scientific equipment onto their boat and, taking ornithologist Bert Deignan with them, set out for a six-day, equally fraught journey back to Umbakumba. Then, as Mountford wrote, 'on 24th May…five weeks after her scheduled time, the Phoenix entered Little Lagoon with the supplies for which we had waited so long'.[19] Now, with all of the scientists and equipment in one place, the work could at last get under way.

The party worked on Groote Eylandt and adjacent islands from 4 April until 8 July—about seven weeks longer than anticipated, due to the late arrival of the *Phoenix*. Mountford believed this was advantageous as it offered greater opportunity for study, although the delays necessitated the abandonment of planned work on the Roper River.

The next campsite was at the Yirrkala Methodist mission on the Gove Peninsula. Mountford said little about it in his journal. In fact, after the move, the first entry in his personal journal was made weeks after their arrival at Yirrkala, on 28 July: 'For a whole month I have not had time to write in my diary,' he wrote. He went on to record a summary of their trip from Groote Eylandt and arrival at Yirrkala on 8 July, writing 'we reached Yirrkala on the 8th and'—but he never finished the sentence.[20] It is interesting to note that although Mountford continued to record his ethnographic findings, and numbered another 82 pages in this final notebook, signalling his intent to continue writing, this was the final entry in his personal journal.

---

17   C. P. Mountford, 13 April 1948, Expedition to Arnhem Land 1948, vol. 1, Personal journal, p. 199, PRG 1218/17/12 SLSA.
18   Ibid., p. 213.
19   Mountford, *Records of the American–Australian Scientific Expedition to Arnhem Land*, vol. 1, p. xxv.
20   Charles P. Mountford, 28 July 1948, Expedition to Arnhem Land 1948, vol. 2, Personal journal, p. 651, PRG 1218/17/13, SLSA.

While we have found nothing that directly explains this cessation (neither Charles nor Bessie Mountford wrote specifically about the matter), it is hardly coincidental that this change in habit occurred about the time of the leadership discussion of 10 July (see Jones, this volume). Having been directed by the Department of Information, which oversaw the Expedition, to concentrate on filmmaking, photography and administrative matters, Charles Mountford was under pressure to squeeze the most out of every day.[21] The pressures of leadership left little time for personal note taking. The desire to continue with investigation of Arnhem Land painting took precedence over recording a personal journal. In his Yirrkala field notes, he wrote, with barely concealed frustration, 'I will not have time to gather the interpretation of more than a few [paintings] from this locality, because of other duties'.[22] Without any further narrative from Mountford, it becomes difficult to discuss the Mountford-Sheard Collection in a chronological fashion. Instead, the remainder of this chapter will discuss the collection thematically.

An Eye for Detail: Photography and fieldwork

Mountford was a keen and talented photographer, with an artistic eye that is evident in his portrait photography. The significance of his portraiture—often used in his and others' publications—lies in his ability to capture a shared humanity. While much ethnographic photography of his era focused on people as 'objects', Mountford's style produced images of both ethnographic and aesthetic appeal: the thoughtful study of a woman and infant or a child at play.

The Mountford-Sheard Collection contains almost 2500 photographs (1900 black-and-white negatives and 600 coloured slides) taken during the Arnhem Land Expedition. A portion of these has been reproduced in Mountford's personal and fieldwork journals and in photograph albums. The albums do not hold unique information, but do distil and present what Mountford thought to be his best images on a given topic.

Mountford photographed and described artworks at each of the three Expedition bases. The collection contains two large volumes of the analysis of Groote Eylandt artworks. For some of these, Mountford was able to record associated myths in writing, music and song. One journal contains typescripts of songs and their meaning.[23] He also described recording sessions, including the reactions of the local people when hearing their songs played back.

---

21   Bessie Ilma Mountford, 10 July 1948, Diary: Expedition to Arnhem Land, p. 258, PRG 487/1/2, SLSA.
22   Charles P. Mountford, Expedition to Arnhem Land, 1948: Art of Yirrkalla, p. 101, PRG 1218/17/20, SLSA.
23   Charles P. Mountford, Expedition to Arnhem Land, 1948: Art of Groote Eylandt, PRG 1218/17/18, SLSA.

Figure 13.2 Two Aboriginal children play in a wooden toy canoe, Groote Eylandt, 1948

Photograph by Charles P. Mountford. By permission of the State Library of South Australia. PRG 1218/34/2756.

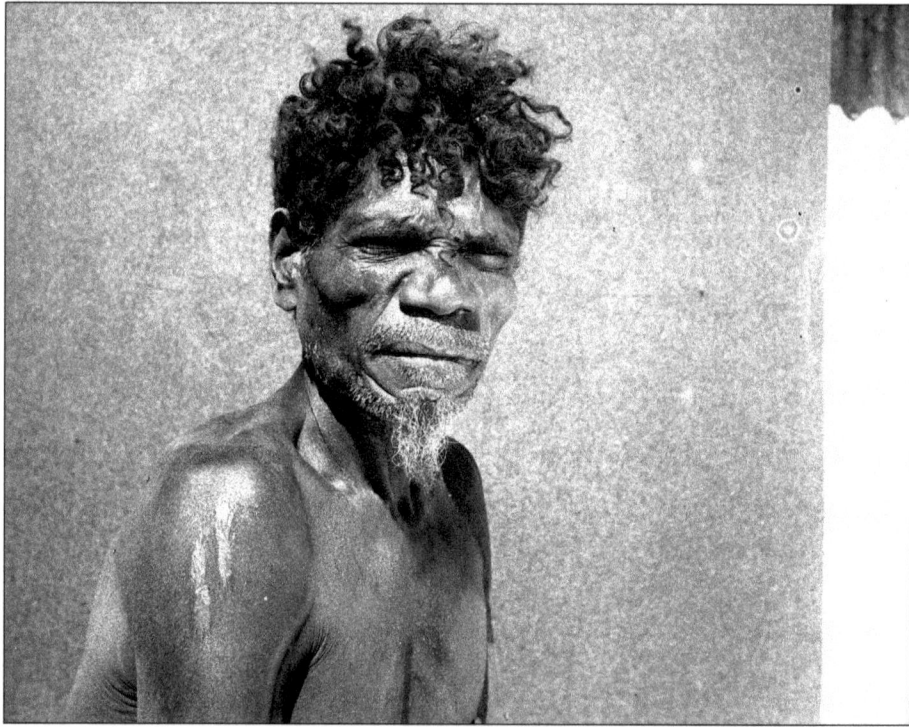

Figure 13.3 Portrait of Yirrkala artist Mawalan Marika, 1948

Photograph by Charles P. Mountford. By permission of the State Library of South Australia. PRG 1218/34/3350.

13. The Responsibilities of Leadership

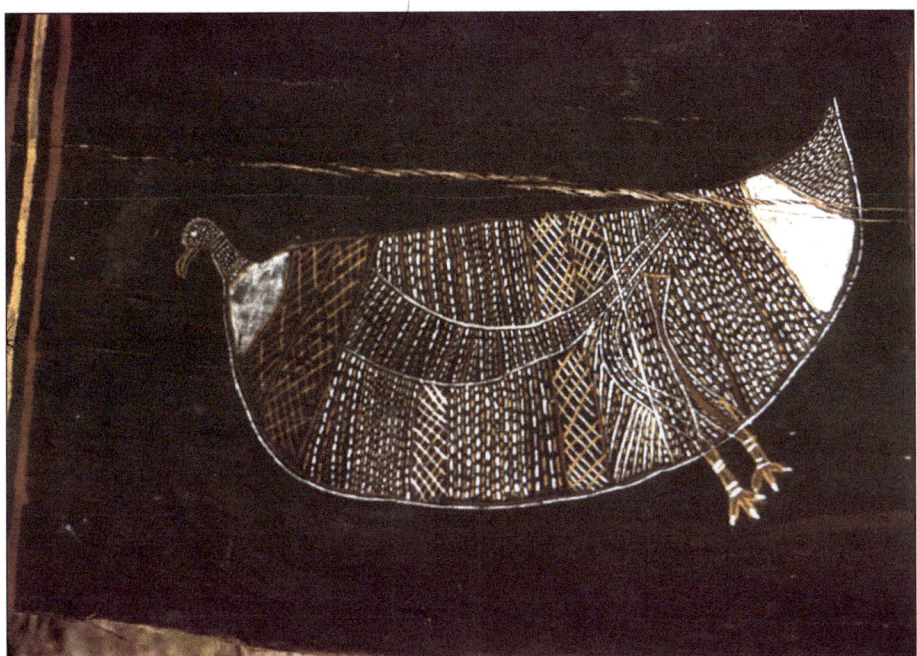

Figure 13.4 Bark painting created for Charles P. Mountford on Groote Eylandt (artist unknown). The painting depicts the mythical sea eagle Iniwakada (species *Haliastur indus*), 1948

By permission of the State Library of South Australia. PRG 1218/35/1574.

Mountford also recorded non-ceremonial music, bird calls and didjeridu. The State Library of South Australia holds approximately 50 minutes of original recordings, relating to Groote Eylandt, Delissaville (now Belyuen) and Oenpelli (now Gunbalanya).[24] The results of Mountford's fieldwork in Yirrkala are contained in the bound volume *Expedition to Arnhem Land, 1948, Art of Yirrkalla* [sic], which contains 176 pages of notes, photographs and drawings of bark paintings; woven, decorated and painted objects; and rubbings of engraved objects.[25] As in each of his fieldwork journals, here bark paintings are illustrated with a small photograph. Next to the photo, Mountford drew a mock-up of the artwork with descriptions and annotations pointing out important aspects of the design and its associated story.

---

24 Charles P. Mountford, National Geographic Society, Arnhem Land Expedition, Aboriginal songs recorded by C. P. Mountford, 1948, PRG 1218/17/49-54, SLSA.
25 Charles P. Mountford, Expedition to Arnhem Land, 1948: Art of Yirrkalla, PRG 1218/17/20, SLSA.

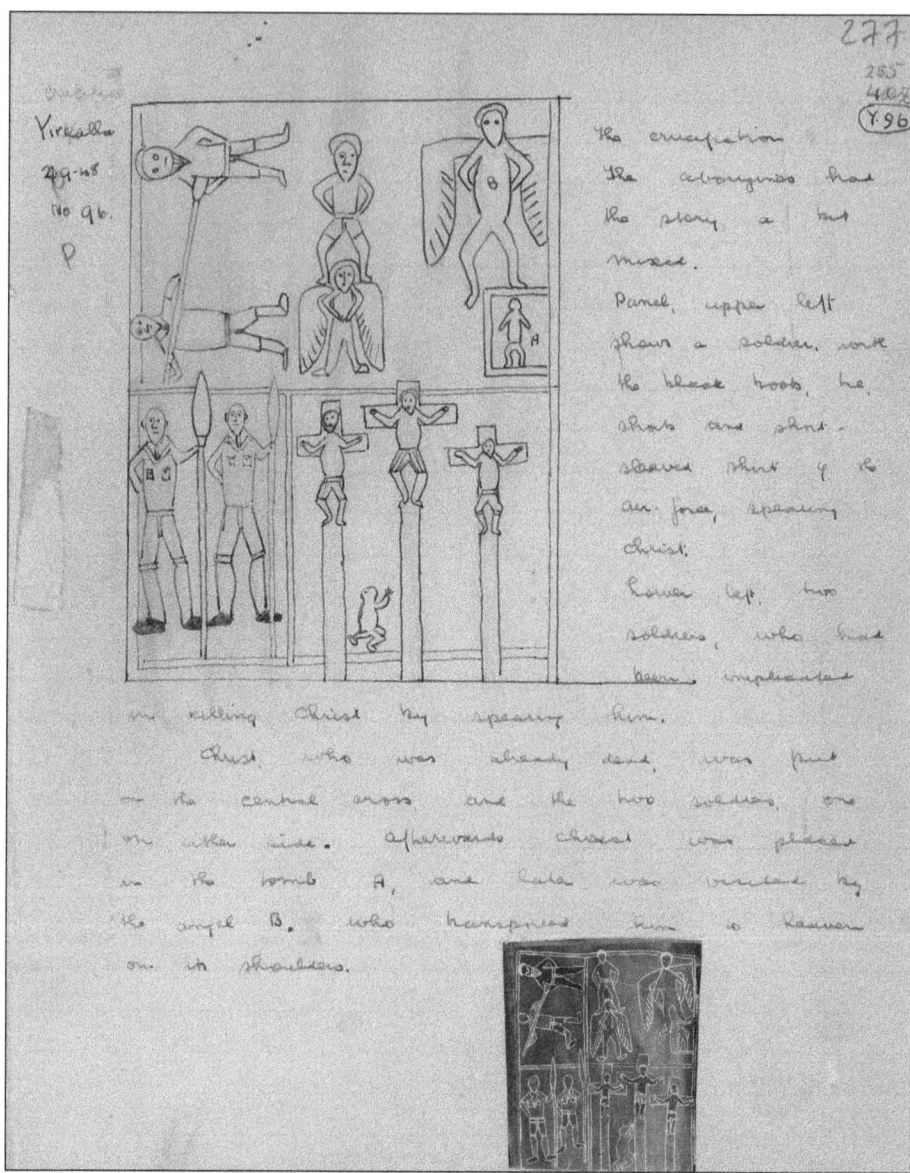

Figure 13.5 Field notes relating to a painting depicting the crucifixion, created by Mawalan Marika for Charles P. Mountford in Yirrkala, 1948

By permission of the State Library of South Australia. PRG 1218/17/20, p. 277.

During the Expedition's third and final camp at Oenpelli, Mountford spent most of his time documenting the rock art of the area, mostly around the massifs Injalak and Arguluk, with brief sojourns to Inagurdurwil, Cannon Hill and Obiri (now Ubirr). Mountford was advised of the best spots to see such artwork by Alf Dyer, the Church Missionary Society representative at Oenpelli. Dyer corresponded with Mountford before the Expedition's departure, describing the best sites for rock art. Dyer's letters include hand-drawn maps showing the distribution of paintings.[26] The cave paintings of Western Arnhem Land are acknowledged as some of the world's most significant, and thousands of sites have been located in the area. Mountford described them as 'the most numerous and beautiful series of cave paintings that we know of in Australia'.[27] Four large volumes in the Mountford-Sheard Collection contain highlights of the pictures Mountford took of rock art galleries in and around Western Arnhem Land.[28] Each figure is assigned a unique number and there is a record of its location and size plus a visual description. There is a photograph and/or a sketch of the figure, but generally little or no ethnological interpretation.

Figure 13.6 Marawana (Larry) sitting on top of Injalak Hill looking out over Oenpelli (now Gunbalanya), 1948

Photograph by Howell Walker. By permission of the State Library of South Australia. PRG 1218/35/1703.

Mountford returned to Oenpelli in 1949, and the Adelaide *Advertiser* reported that this trip led to the 'new' discovery of cave paintings at Obiri—a shelter 18 m long and 2.7 m high containing tens of thousands of figures. Mountford hoped the site could become a national reserve, so that the paintings could be

---

26   Alf Dyer to Charles P. Mountford, 4 February 1948, pp. 113–15a, PRG 1218/17/7, SLSA.
27   Mountford, *Records of the American–Australian Scientific Expedition to Arnhem Land*, vol. 1, p. 109.
28   Charles P. Mountford, Expedition to Arnhem Land, 1948: Art of Oenpelli, PRG 1218/17/21-24, SLSA.

properly protected as well as enjoyed.²⁹ (The area is now part of the Kakadu National Park.) Some of the colour photographs taken during this trip and the 1948 Expedition were later included in a book of Aboriginal art published for the United Nations Educational, Scientific and Cultural Organisation (UNESCO) in 1954.³⁰

'Dear Monty': Correspondence in the Mountford-Sheard Collection

In the extensive correspondence and administration files of the Expedition, Mountford's labour can be best appreciated. Mountford (with the assistance of wife, Bessie) was sending and receiving up to 10 letters and telegrams a day, covering every aspect of the Expedition. Overall the seven volumes of correspondence give a fascinating insight into the Expedition's administration, before, during and after its completion. It is remarkable to scan these pages and consider the many facets of the Expedition with which Mountford was occupied.

Evident in the correspondence files is the conflict that arose between Mountford and the administrative staff of the Arnhem Land missions, most notably the two Church Missionary Society (CMS) missions: Groote Eylandt and Oenpelli. J. Bruce Montgomerie of the CMS complained that it was 'extremely difficult to work in harmony and goodwill with him…he expected all work on the Mission to cease while he used the Aborigines for various works required to be done'.³¹ Whether this conflict was the result of Mountford's personal behaviour or whether as leader he shouldered the responsibility for the actions of the whole party and their stakeholders is difficult to know. Certainly, there were other anthropologists, such as Donald Thomson and the Berndts, who came into conflict with the CMS.³²

There is a continual stream of correspondence between the missions and Mountford, arguing about the payment of accounts and the compensation given for the use of Aboriginal labour. The final resolution of these matters came more than a year after the completion of the Expedition, with the Department of Information finally settling all payments. Mountford had kept comprehensive records of all transactions—to satisfy his own needs as well as those of the

---

29   Charles P. Mountford, Aboriginal Art Oenpelli, Manuscript, 1949, PRG 1218/17/47, SLSA.
30   New York Graphic Society 1954, *Australia: Aboriginal paintings, Arnhem Land*, New York Graphic Society by arrangement with UNESCO, New York.
31   Cole, K. 1975, *A History of Oenpelli*, Nungalinya Publications, Darwin, p. 61.
32   Ibid.; Gray, *A Cautious Silence*; Cole, K. 1980, *Dick Harris, Missionary to the Aborigines: A biography of the Reverend Canon George Richmond Harris, M.B.E., pioneer missionary to the Aborigines of Arnhem Land*, Keith Cole Publications, Bendigo, Vic.

budget-conscious department. A meticulous and stubborn person, he could never bring himself to agree with the missions' tally and he disputed the records they produced to support their claims.[33]

Another important event documented in the correspondence files is the previously mentioned attempt to oust Mountford from his position as leader soon after the party's arrival at Yirrkala. As the Mountford-Sheard Collection contains no diarised accounts from this time, it is only through correspondence files and Bessie Mountford's journal that we are able to gain insight into his perspective. In a letter to Alexander Wetmore written two weeks after the incident, Charles Mountford wrote that the visiting officials had

> accused me of mismanagement (though all their accusations were based on incidents caused by the stranded *Phoenix*), made insulting remarks about my status as a scientist, and forbade me to carry out research work…Mr. [Kevin] Murphy [of the Department of Information] then offered the control of the scientific personnel to Mr. [Frank] Setzler [the deputy leader]…to my surprise Setzler did not refuse the position.[34]

When Bessie Mountford asked her husband what the meeting had been about, he gravely replied, 'I have been demoted as leader. Frank is to take my place.'[35] Bessie Mountford noted that

> Murphy was anxious for film, and thought to secure more of Monty's work in film-making by demanding that Monty leave all research to the professionals. [He] emphasised that Monty was a film director, *not* a scientist, and was very rude in his emphasis. He had also been regaled with gossip through some channel or other.[36]

News of the visitors' agenda spread slowly at first, but Bessie Mountford wrote that when told, Herbert Deignan was 'shamed to sickness by the action of his colleague' and vowed to sort it out.[37] The next day, the American scientists met, and Bessie Mountford believed it was their influence that led Setzler to belatedly refuse the leadership offer. 'Never have I seen a man so utterly defeated as Frank S. He later confessed to Monty that never in his life had he been given such a drubbing: that he had never realised just how awful a thing he had done.'[38]

Shortly thereafter, Bessie typed a telegram from Setzler to Murphy at the Department of Information: '[A]fter conferring with my American colleagues

---

33   Charles P. Mountford, AASEAL Correspondence, Volume 7, 1949, PRG 1218/17/10, SLSA.
34   Charles P. Mountford to Alexander Wetmore, 29 July 1948, pp. 463–4, PRG 1218/17/8, SLSA.
35   Bessie Ilma Mountford, 10 July 1948, Diary, p. 254, PRG 487/1/2, SLSA.
36   Ibid., p. 258.
37   Ibid., p. 256.
38   Ibid., 11 July 1948, p. 260.

I find it impossible to accept the position you offered me. Regards Frank Setzler.' (Beneath this, Mountford added a cryptic 'No?')[39] Tensions eased in the following days and Bessie Mountford believed that some good might have come from the event, both in firming up loyalty for her husband and in helping him face some of his shortcomings. She noted he was 'adopting a less rigid manner in matters of control'.[40]

'She accepted discomfort and asked no favours': The diaries of Bessie Mountford

As indicated above, the diaries kept by Bessie Mountford (PRG 487/1) form a valuable counterpoint to the Expedition's scientific records. She was Mountford's second wife, and he usually referred to her as Johnnie, after her maiden name, Johnstone. She acted as honorary secretary throughout the Expedition. The couple was married in 1933, eight years after the death of Charles's first wife, Florence (née Purnell).

Prior to, and following, the Expedition, Bessie Mountford had an active political career, advocating for women's rights and political representation through organisations such as the League of Women Voters. This organisation promoted equal rights in marriage, divorce and in the workforce, and Bessie Mountford gave conference papers and wrote essays for the cause. In addition, she campaigned for the support of war widows, family endowment and other organised welfare assistance. She ran as an independent candidate for the seat of Hindmarsh in the 1938 and 1941 South Australian state elections, battling a political system geared against the success of women. During the 1960s, she served as Vice-President of the League of Women Voters of South Australia, and continued to campaign with associated national organisations such as the Australian Federation of Women Voters.[41] In addition to her considerable secretarial duties during the Expedition, Bessie assisted various members of the party with their work; she specifically mentions helping Setzler, Specht and Walker.

The journalist Colin Simpson, who joined the Expedition at Oenpelli, wrote of Bessie Mountford:

> Mrs. Mountford, when she was not busy with correspondence, bookkeeping, and the typing of her husband's notes, could always interest herself in her surroundings. She showed no chagrin at being left

---

39 Frank Setzler to Kevin Murphy, 12 July 1948, PRG 1218/17/16, SLSA.
40 Bessie Ilma Mountford, 14 July 1948, Diary, p. 268, PRG 487/1/2, SLSA.
41 Bessie Mountford, League of Women Voters of SA, SRG 116/28 1941–1965, SLSA.

behind when others went off to arduous, exciting places. She accepted discomfort and asked no favours. She never took rank to herself as the leader's wife, but she was always and admirably the wife of the leader.[42]

Bessie often drafted Expedition correspondence. It is unclear whether it was first dictated by Charles or whether the words were her own, with him acting as editor. Much of the correspondence in the bound volumes held by our library is typed, yet there are numerous handwritten annotations by Charles, which would suggest the latter.

In addition to hundreds of pages of notes, Bessie Mountford's diaries contain photographic inserts, the provenance of which is unclear. She described the particulars of her journeying, including travelling conditions, weather and landscapes, and reflected on interactions between the Expedition members, her husband's experiences, and the people she met. Her notes reveal her as observant, opinionated, intelligent and compassionate.

When Bessie first encountered the Aboriginal people of Umbakumba, she wrote: 'Like all other native people I have met they are quick to laugh.'[43] She described the women as very shy and commented on the people's Western form of dress, their way of working, and on how society and ceremony might have been affected by trade, war and other European contact. She set out to deliberately interact with Aboriginal women, when time off from her own work permitted:

> I tried to talk to some of the native women this morning, but…They do not speak my tongue…I did admire the construction of their carrying dishes, which, unlike the Central Aust. people, is made of bark. A long piece about a yard long is husked and cut into wide strips about a quarter of the way from each end. These are drawn together and tied with bark so as to give a carrying dish about 18 to 21 inches [46–53 cm] long.[44]

At Yirrkala, Bessie wrote of teaching two Aboriginal women, Bali and Bangara, to crochet, and recorded details of a traditional naming ritual, communicated by an Aboriginal woman.[45] Also at Yirrkala, she attended a religious sermon, and she remarked in exasperation about an unsuitable analogy the speaker used to impart a parable about recognising Jesus, which frightened and confused the Aboriginal congregation: 'the discourse of the young speaker was so illogical that I fear I finished up wanting to shake white people who presume beyond their knowledge, if not beyond their capacity.'[46]

---

42 Simpson, C. 1973, *Adam in Ochre: Inside Aboriginal Australia*, Angus & Robertson, Sydney, p. 64.
43 Bessie Ilma Mountford, 4 April 1948, Diary, p. 67, PRG 487/1/1, SLSA.
44 Ibid., 9 April 1948, p. 72.
45 Ibid., 30 August 1948, 4 September 1948, pp. 53, 62, PRG 487/1/3.
46 Ibid., 5 September 1948, p. 63.

She empathised with the circumstances of other non-Aboriginal women, removed from their familiar surroundings and coping with remote life on the settlements. She described Marjorie Gray, the wife of Fred Gray, as an Englishwoman from the city who 'feels the loneliness of this way of life...[is] not flexible of mind, but is kindly of heart and simple in manner'.[47] Of their goodbye, she wrote:

> [M]y heart ached for her. Ever since she reached Groote Eylandt the thought of the people of the expedition staying with them has been a beacon towards which she has carried on. Someone was coming! Now—it was no wonder she cried when I bade her farewell...it took me all of my self control not to sit down and weep with her.[48]

Bessie Mountford knew the Expedition's departure would be a sorrow for Mrs Gray, who had no prior knowledge of what to expect when she received Fred Gray's proposal by telegram in England. Eventually, Marjorie moved back to her home country, in 1967, to 'look after her father', where she remained permanently.[49]

It must have been difficult to separate the dual roles of secretary and wife, but we are able to observe Bessie's love and support for Charles (despite their sleeping in separate tents) in her personal journal. Following the attempt to oust him in Yirrkala, she writes:

> Of course I was quick to protect and, if possible, comfort, encouraging the poor hurt creature, to talk and ease himself...Whatever I have been curtailed by in the way of heat and insect pests were as nothing for the fact that I could be near Monty at so critical an hour.[50]

As Bessie was one of only two women on the Expedition, these diaries also serve as a rare and useful woman's perspective.

In addition to her Arnhem Land diaries, material donated by Bessie Mountford to the State Library includes genealogical information, letters, and a diary she kept on her husband's 1940 expedition to Central Australia.

A Continuing Legacy

The Mountford-Sheard Collection is a historically significant and valuable record of anthropological fieldwork of the mid twentieth century. The collection

---

47 Ibid., 4 April 1948, p. 65, PRG 487/1/1.
48 Ibid., 8 July 1948, p. 238, PRG 487/1/2.
49 Dewar, M. 2006, 'Fred Gray and Umbakumba: the 1930s and 1940s', *Picturing Relations: Groote Eylandt Barks Symposium*, Ian Potter Museum of Art, University of Melbourne, Vic., 23 September 2006, p. 4.
50 Bessie Ilma Mountford, 10 July 1948, Diary, p. 254, PRG 487/1/2, SLSA.

is of obvious cultural significance to the Aboriginal communities of Arnhem Land. Mountford kept erratic, yet detailed, notes on various aspects of art, religion and ceremony. Furthermore, the archive gives insight into the day-to-day joys and hardships of the ethnographer at work. While Mountford's detractors questioned his scientific credibility, scholars have subsequently acknowledged that much of his work, including that accomplished on the Arnhem Land Expedition, contributed to the popularisation of Aboriginal art both in Australia and overseas.[51]

The Expedition collected 25 tonnes of material including nearly 500 paintings on both bark and paper. In 1956, many of these were distributed to Australian state art galleries and museums. Tracey Lock-Weir has written that these were the 'first Aboriginal works collected in the field and accepted by public art galleries, not only for their ethnographic significance, but also for their aesthetic qualities'.[52] Philip Jones argues that Mountford 'achieved more success than any other individual in promoting Aboriginal art…during the 1950s and 1960s', and that the collection acquired during the Arnhem Land Exhibition 'formed the basis of Aboriginal collections in Australian art museums'.[53]

Aboriginal communities, scholars and authors continue to seek access to the Mountford-Sheard Collection, poring over old ground or finding new threads to spin out. While there might still be questions concerning Mountford's methods or his manner, there can be no disputing the continuing legacy of the collection he entrusted to the State Library of South Australia.

---

51 Lock-Weir, T. 2002, *Art of Arnhem Land 1940s–1970s*, Art Gallery of South Australia, Adelaide; May, S. K. 2000, The last frontier? Acquiring the American–Australian Scientific Expedition Ethnographic collection 1948, BA (Hons) thesis, Flinders University, Adelaide; Neale, M. 1998, 'Charles Mountford and the "bastard barks"—a gift from the American Australian Scientific Expedition to Arnhem Land, 1948', in L. Seear and J. Ewington (eds), *Brought to Light: Australian Art 1850–1965*, Queensland Art Gallery, South Brisbane, pp. 210–17.
52 Lock-Weir, *Art of Arnhem Land 1940s–1970s*.
53 Jones, P. 1988, 'Perceptions of Aboriginal art: a history', in P. Sutton (ed.), *Dreamings: The art of Aboriginal Australia*, Viking, Ringwood, Vic., pp. 171–3.

14. Beneath the Billabongs: The scientific legacy of Robert Rush Miller[1]

Gifford Hubbs Miller and Robert Charles Cashner

Robert 'Bob' Rush Miller was born in the state of Colorado on 23 April 1916, but he grew up in California, where from an early age he became interested in hot, dry places, and spent long hours in the desert southwest of the United States. Although his father, Ralph Gifford Miller, was a lawyer, as dictated by his own father, Ralph was more interested in natural history and took his sons on many backcountry trips, always wanting to go 'where the foot of man has never trod'. Bob was intrigued by the geology of the desert, and initially planned to be a geologist, but his discovery of tiny fishes living in the most remote and isolated desert springs galvanised his interest in zoology. Bob's fascination with fish began in earnest as an undergraduate on a Pomona College geology field trip to the Mohave Desert. There, in the lowermost permanent flow of the Mohave River, Bob saw small fishes. He questioned his professor about their identity and why they were present in the desert. The professor had no answers, so Bob collected some of the fish with his hat and took them back to Pomona for study. His passion for collecting in the most remote and inhospitable settings and his demand to understand the origin of tiny desert fishes won the attention of faculty at the University of California, Berkeley. He transferred from Pomona College to Berkeley after his sophomore year, and completed his undergraduate degree there in 1939. On one expedition looking for fish in Death Valley with his father while still an undergraduate, he sank his mother's Buick in mud. After collecting the fish he sought, Bob tried unsuccessfully for two hours to dislodge the car. By then it was 48°C, and, cautioning his father to stay under the car, he set forth to get help on the highway, about 3 km away. He collapsed of sunstroke and dragged himself to the road just as a rare car came by and rescued him from certain death. He quickly returned to save his father, and his mother's precious Buick.

These stories of dedicated fish collecting reached Carl Hubbs, renowned ichthyologist specialising in the fishes of the arid American west, who was then at the University of Michigan. Hubbs invited Bob to join his crew on a field expedition during the summer of 1938. He had been collecting fish in the western United States with his family for many years, and, to maintain enthusiasm for the arduous expeditions, Hubbs offered his three children a bounty of five cents

---

1 This chapter was greatly aided by research and details of Dr Robert Rush Miller's life compiled by his daughter, the late Frances M. Cashner.

a piece for each species collected, one dollar for a new species and five dollars for a new genus. Bob Miller first met Hubbs and his family at a campsite in Nevada, where he was shocked to see the famous ichthyologist dressed like a tramp. But he immediately fell in love with Hubbs' daughter, nineteen-year-old Frances, and proposed to her two weeks later. The following year, Bob accepted Hubbs' offer of graduate work at Michigan (see Figure 14.1), where he completed his PhD in 1944 and subsequently accepted an appointment as Assistant Curator of Fishes at the Smithsonian Institution's National Museum of Natural History. In those days, the saying was 'join the Smithsonian and see the world'. He began his tenure at the Smithsonian with an extended field expedition to Guatemala in 1946.

Figure 14.1 Miller at his microscope while finishing his PhD at the University of Michigan, 23 May 1944

By permission of the Estate of R. R. Miller.

When the Australian ethnologist and photographer Charles Pearcy Mountford was in the United States in 1945 on a lecture tour, sponsored by the Australian Government, the National Geographic Society offered to support a research project of Mountford's choosing (see Jones and May, this volume). As the plan for an expedition to Arnhem Land gained momentum, the Smithsonian decided to commit four members of staff. They were archaeologist Frank M. Setzler, mammalogist David H. Johnson, ornithologist Herbert G. Deignan, and Robert R. Miller—one of the Expedition's youngest members, as the ichthyologist. Bob left Frances and their two small children in California with her parents, Carl and Laura Hubbs. Carl had recently accepted a post at the Scripps Institution of Oceanography in La Jolla, California. In February 1948, Bob Miller departed from San Francisco for 10 months in Australia.

Figure 14.2 Miller just before departing San Francisco for Australia and the Arnhem Land Expedition in February 1948

Photograph by Frances Hubbs Miller. By permission of the National Library of Australia. nla.gov.au/nla.pic-vn4511010.

Already well known as a tenacious collector, Bob lived up to his reputation on the Arnhem Land Expedition. If there had been a contest to determine who could collect the most specimens, Bob Miller would have won, with more than 30 000 fish specimens—a number far higher than any other collector of 'things'. Bob's dedication to being certain that he had collected a complete record of all fish that lived within a specific habitat was caricatured by the well-known Australian artist Eric Jolliffe (see Figure 14.3), who joined the Expedition for 10 days in July 1948 during their stay at Yirrkala. Bob not only collected fish, he also had a life-long interest in herpetology, and was unable to resist collecting in that field as well (see Figure 14.4).[2]

Figure 14.3 Cartoon of Robert Rush Miller by Eric Jolliffe, which illustrates the persistent collecting style that characterised Miller's field research for his entire career

By permission of the estate of R. R. Miller.

---

2 Personal photographs taken by Robert Rush Miller during the Arnhem Land Expedition: <http://nla.gov.au/nla.pic-vn4473516> (viewed 20 October 2010). His personal diaries are archived as Papers of Robert Rush Miller, 1947–51, MS 10053, National Library of Australia, Canberra.

14. Beneath the Billabongs

Figure 14.4 Miller as herpetologist, Arnhem Land, 1948

Photograph by a member of the Expedition. By permission of the Estate of R. R. Miller.

Of course, Arnhem Land presented numerous challenges to the collection of its fish fauna. And to meet this challenge, Bob employed a wide range of strategies to ensure he acquired a representative sampling of the fishes living in the country, including what the locals were eating. Many of his collections involved the copious use of various poisons: 'collection made with 40 pounds of barbasco root'; 'collection made with 35 pounds of derris root'; 'pool…a few inches deep…collection made by one-fourth pound of derris root…water temperature 100°F'; 'collected in the billabong…with a total of 25 pounds of rotenone'. Other methods were also employed when the conditions were appropriate—'a few fish shot with dust pistol'; 'collection made by hand'; 'collection by three-prong spear'; 'collection by night light and dipnet'—and of course Bob used more conventional methods, too: 'collection made by hook and line and spear'; 'collected by trolling'; 'collected in the billabong…with a gill net 125 feet [38 m] long'.[3]

In his collecting, Bob was assisted by many helpers—from members of the Expedition to local Aboriginal people, including children tagging along for the fun (see Figures 14.5 and 14.6). But he was aided especially by Gerry Blitner, from Groote Eylandt, who accompanied him on many outings, and the two became firm friends (see Figure 14.7). In collecting fish by treating small water bodies with a poison that primarily kills fish and is harmless to humans, Bob quickly became popular with the local Aboriginal communities, because unwanted fish could be eaten (see Figure 14.8).

Figure 14.5 Miller, Frank Setzler and the men known to them as Kumbiala and Quartpot on Central Hill, Groote Eylandt, 25 May 1948

Photograph by Frederick McCarthy. By permission of the National Library of Australia. nla.pic-vn4494298.

---

3 All from field notes cited by Taylor, W. R. 1964, 'Fishes of Arnhem Land', in R. Specht (ed.), *Records of the American–Australian Expedition to Arnhem Land. Volume 4: Zoology*, Melbourne University Press, Carlton, Vic., pp. 45–307.

Figure 14.6 Bob Miller and Frank Setzler on the way to Second Reef near Port Langdon, Groote Eylandt, Northern Territory, 25 April 1948

Photograph attributed to Peter Bassett-Smith. By permission of the National Library of Australia. nla.pic-vn4494255.

Figure 14.7 Gerry Blitner with spear and fish, Emerald River, Groote Eylandt, 5 June 1948

Photograph by R. R. Miller. By permission of the National Library of Australia.nla.pic-vn4515154.

Figure 14.8 Aboriginal children and a man (names unknown) with their catch west of Yirrkala, 8 August 1948

Photograph by R. R. Miller. By permission of the National Library of Australia. nla.pic-vn4534255.

While Bob was in Arnhem Land, he received a letter from the University of Michigan offering him a position as Curator of Fishes in the Museum of Zoology—the position previously held by his PhD advisor, and now father-in-law, Carl Hubbs. Bob considered the offer seriously. He was never particularly interested in marine fishes. In Bob's mind, there was only one global ocean, and the ability for fish to move freely around the world led to what he considered a less interesting taxonomic and evolutionary story. Marine ichthyologists would quickly disabuse Bob Miller's idea of marine fishes moving to wherever they liked; there are only a handful of marine species that are truly cosmopolitan. But the real appeal to Bob and other 'freshies' is that 42 per cent of all fish species are obligate freshwater taxa, despite the fact that only 0.01 per cent of all unfrozen water on Earth's surface is fresh. To Bob this meant there were intriguing questions for him to tackle in the fresh waters of the North American west. Indeed, through his 60-plus-year career, he never ran out of new ideas and interesting projects involving freshwater fishes. And he loved the arid south-west of the United States and Mexico, with the oddities of tiny fishes incongruously populating isolated springs in the desert. While still in Arnhem Land, Bob accepted the University of Michigan's offer. This meant that he would never be able to work up the extensive collection of marine, estuarine and freshwater fishes he had worked so hard to acquire. Identifying and writing up the results of the fish fauna of the Arnhem Land Expedition was left to William R. Taylor, who was hired by the Smithsonian Institution specifically to work on the Arnhem Land fish collections made by Bob and the Expedition in 1948.[4]

---

[4] Ibid.

Although Bob Miller returned to Michigan and refocused his research efforts on the fish fauna of the western United States, Arnhem Land had exposed him to a moister environment than he had encountered in his earlier study of the deserts of the American south-west. He was impressed by the diversity of the rainforest fishes, which presented a stark contrast with the relatively small numbers of desert fish species. The Australian experience might well have motivated him to study the freshwater fishes of Mexico. Beginning in the mid-1950s, he led biannual field campaigns throughout Mexico, and he became the leading international expert on Mexican fishes. He wrote *Freshwater Fishes of México*, the definitive book on that large faunal region.[5] Although Mexico is only one-fifth the size of the continental United States, it is home to nearly two-thirds as many freshwater fishes as the United States and Canada combined. His book offers keys and distribution maps for more than 500 native species. The book and its accompanying illustrations and historical overview provide a synthesis of Mexican fishes and their current conservation status—similar in its goals in many respects to those of the Mountford-led Expedition to Arnhem Land 50 years earlier.

The Australian experience also imprinted on Bob the fragile relationship between the human enterprise and the distribution of plants and animals, especially the distribution of freshwater fishes. He was an early and ardent advocate for conservation, heralding the urgency in 1961 with a call to arms titled 'Man and the changing fish fauna of the American southwest'.[6] He was a founding member of the Desert Fishes Council (Figure 14.9), chairing the organisation from 1974 until 1976. With his wife, Frances, and brother-in-law, Clark Hubbs, he wrote in the book *Battle Against Extinction*:

> There are sound biological reasons for holding samples of virgin country in perpetuity. In time, most of the desert will be used by humans for one purpose or another—irrigation, grazing, mining, or playgrounds—but inevitably, scientists will need to know the original situation. A control is a basic part of every experiment. Retention of wilderness for the maintenance of biological diversity is a necessity for the survival of humans themselves. What we must avoid is a domesticated, homogeneous earth; for many it would be a far less fascinating place to live.[7]

---

5   Miller, R. R., Minckley, W. L. and Norris, S. M. 2006, *Freshwater Fishes of México*, University of Chicago Press, Ill. This was published posthumously with contributions from Minckley and Norris.
6   Miller, R. R. 1961, 'Man and the changing fish fauna of the American southwest', *Papers of the Michigan Academy of Science, Arts & Letters*, vol. 46, no. 365.
7   Miller, R. R., Hubbs, C. and Miller, F. H. 1992, 'Ichthyological exploration of the American west: the Hubbs–Miller era, 1915–1950', in W. L. Minckley and J. E. Deacon (eds), *Battle Against Extinction: Native fish management in the American west*, University of Arizona Press, Tucson, pp. 19–40.

Figure 14.9 Miller and Carl Hubbs in Tempe, Arizona, at the Desert Fishes Council meeting in November 1973

By permission of the Desert Fishes Council Archives.

And, in 1989, he documented the sad litany of fish extinctions in 'Extinctions of North American fishes during the past century'.[8]

The influence of the Arnhem Land Expedition was not limited to his professional life. It also rippled through his family, especially his two oldest children, Frances and Gifford, both of whom were small children when Bob was on the Expedition (four and two years of age, respectively). Tokens of Australia were conspicuously displayed in the Miller household until Bob's death in 2003, with stories of the Expedition common fare around the dinner table. These constant reminders made strong impressions on the children. There is no doubt that this contributed to both Frances's and Gifford's desires to travel to exotic places such as Africa, Alaska, Arctic Canada and, eventually, Australia. Frances, a zoologist specialising in primate behavioural studies, did her dissertation research in the forests of Equatorial Guinea. Gifford became a geologist, specialising in climate change of the Quaternary—the most recent

---

8   Miller, R. R., Williams, J. D. and Williams, J. E. 1989, 'Extinctions of North American fishes during the past century', *Fisheries*, vol. 14, pp. 22–48.

geological era, encompassing the past several hundred thousand years. And although his dissertation research was conducted in the Canadian Arctic, he eventually found a route to a research program in Australia.

In fact, Bob Miller's most enduring Australian legacy from the Arnhem Land Expedition might be that both Frances and Gifford spent extended times in Australia and became involved in Australian research. This legacy extended yet another generation. Bob Miller's granddaughter, Mollie Cashner, after accompanying her grandfather to the fiftieth Arnhem Land Reunion in Sydney in 1998, was inspired to study fish, and has recently completed her PhD in ichthyology. She has a postdoctoral position at Southeastern Louisiana University.

Robert and Frances Cashner (Bob's son-in-law and daughter) and their two younger daughters, Mollie and Emily, first came to Australia in late January 1991. An Australian colleague, Donald Gartside, helped arrange positions for both Robert and Fran at Southern Cross University, in Lismore, New South Wales. Fran taught introductory biology classes and oversaw the related laboratories, while Robert undertook a research project on the Nymboida–Mann River—a major tributary of the Clarence River basin. His study resulted in an honours thesis and a publication in the *Proceedings of the Linnaean Society of New South Wales*. The Cashner family's stay was over in mid-August; no-one wanted to go home. Mollie returned four years later to do an undergraduate research project on wattlebirds in Melbourne. Both Emily and Mollie have made return trips with their parents. Fran made at least 11 trips to Australia and Robert 16. During one of those return trips, an exchange program was established between undergraduate students at Southern Cross and the University of New Orleans, where both Robert and Fran taught. Although the havoc wreaked by Hurricane Katrina in New Orleans caused this very successful exchange program to be suspended, it could soon be re-established.

Gifford has visited Australia most years since the late 1980s, including three year-long sabbaticals at the Australian National University (ANU) with his wife, Midra. Although he is a geologist by training, his research in collaboration with John Magee of the ANU on the evolution of the Australian summer monsoon has developed into a broader research campaign that seeks to unravel the footprints of human colonisation on the Australian continent—in particular, to explain the demise of the Australian mega-fauna. The topic bridges his father's biological background and close association with Aboriginal groups during the Arnhem Land Expedition with the classical methods of geological investigation. In this research, Gifford continues the core thread of the scientific questions that motivated the original Arnhem Land Expedition. How did Aboriginal groups extract a living from the Australian landscape, especially in the early centuries after initial colonisation of the continent? And in the process, how did the Australian landscape respond to that activity? These questions remain alive in the contemporary world as we ponder how humans everywhere fit into their landscape and how we can manage a sustainable future. The published results of this research have revitalised the debate over the causes of mega-faunal extinction and climate change in Australia, including four articles in the two leading international scientific journals: *Science* and *Nature*.[9]

---

9   Miller, G. H., Magee, J. W. and Jull, A. J. T. 1997, 'Low-latitude glacial cooling in the southern hemisphere from amino acid racemization in emu eggshells', *Nature*, vol. 385, pp. 241–4; Miller, G. H., Magee, J. W., Johnson, B. J., Fogel, M., Spooner, N. A., McCulloch, M. T. and Ayliffe, L. K. 1999, 'Pleistocene extinction of *Genyornis newtoni*: human impact on Australian megafauna', *Science*, vol. 283, pp. 205–8; Johnson, B. J., Miller, G. H., Fogel, M. L., Magee, J. W., Gagan, M. K. and Chivas, A. R. 1999, '65,000 years of vegetation change in Central Australia and the Australian summer monsoon', *Science*, vol. 284, pp. 1150–2; Miller, G. H., Fogel, M. L., Magee, J. W., Gagan, M. K., Clarke, S. and Johnson, B. J. 2005, 'Ecosystem collapse in Pleistocene Australia and a human role in megafaunal extinction', *Science*, vol. 309, pp. 287–90.

15. An Insider's Perspective: Raymond Louis Specht's oral history

Edited and introduced by Margo Daly

This chapter is based on an oral history interview conducted by Sally K. May and Martin Thomas for the National Library of Australia (NLA ORAL TRC 5662) at Professor Specht's Brisbane home in May 2006. The extracts from this long interview have been updated and amended by Professor Specht, so they do on occasion differ from the original recording.

Biographical overview

Figure 15.1 Studio portrait of Raymond Specht taken prior to commencement of the Arnhem Land Expedition

By permission of the State Library of South Australia. PRG 1218/17/12.

In 1948, at the age of twenty-three, Raymond Specht became the second-youngest member of the American–Australian Scientific Expedition to Arnhem Land. He studied the botany, plant ecology and ethno-botany of Aboriginal communities, later collating this information to become part of the published four-volume report on the Arnhem Land Expedition.

Prior to his selection as an Expedition member, Specht attended Adelaide Teachers' College to train as a science teacher while concurrently completing his Bachelor of Science with Honours at the University of Adelaide. Professor Joseph Garnett Wood, head of the Botany Department and an international leading figure in plant biochemistry, became a mentor for Specht, and challenged his understandings of field-based plant ecology (see McCarthy, this volume).

During the early 1940s, Specht decided to specialise as a plant ecologist. Under the guidance of Professor Wood, he studied the ecologically complex Adelaide Hills region. This work illustrated a systematic and holistic approach to thinking about plant ecology—a characteristic Specht embraced throughout his scientific career, and which became a key feature of his botanical work in Arnhem Land.

Emeritus Professor Specht is regarded as one of Australia's eminent plant ecologists, internationally regarded for his work on heathlands and arid-zone communities in southern Australia and the chaparral lands and arid-zone vegetation in the south-western United States. He received Fulbright, Smith-Mundt and Carnegie grants in 1956, a Royal Society Nuffield Foundation Commonwealth Bursary in 1964 and became a Senior Fulbright Scholar in 1983. In 2000, Specht was named as an IBC Outstanding Intellectual of the Twentieth Century.

Specht has been an active member of scientific committees and published extensively in the areas of plant ecology and conservation. Some of his major publications include *Vegetation of South Australia* (1972), *Conservation Survey of Australia* (1974, 1995), *Heathlands of the World* (1979, 1981), *Mediterranean Ecosystems of the World* (1981, 1988), *Ecological Biogeography of Australia. Volume 1* (1981), and, co-authored with his daughter, Alison Specht, *Australian Plant Communities: Dynamics of structure, growth & biodiversity* (1999, second edition 2002). Specht was Professor of Botany at the University of Queensland from 1966 to 1989.

Career Formations

Raymond Specht loved flowers as a child. You could say botany was in the blood: his grandfather, who was born in Australia into a German family, had been interested in growing gladiolus since 1900 and, in his retirement, he wrote six 'erudite articles' for the *British Gladiolus Journal*. Yet at that time Raymond Specht had no desire to be a botanist. From early adolescence he had wanted to be a teacher of maths and physics—the subjects he excelled in at Adelaide High School.

Specht relates that his career trajectory could be defined by being 'pushed' into things and 'pulled' out of others—a career somewhat out of his own control, where 'luck' played a part. His former science teacher, Stan Edmonds, and other educators, including Professor Wood, encouraged him 'to promote biology in the secondary school syllabus' instead of just chemistry and physics; as Specht 'entered the Teachers College they said you're not going to be a physicist mathematician, you're going to be a biologist'. Specht found zoology, with its teaching by rote, 'terribly boring' but was fascinated and challenged by botany under the tutorship of the brilliant Wood.

By 1946, he was spellbound by plant ecology and became one of Wood's six honours students that year. The 'physicist mathematician' had turned botanist.

> Wood gave me the most difficult part in South Australia to survey and that was in the Adelaide Hills, ten miles by ten miles [16 km x 16 km] from Green Hill Road south to Cherry Gardens and east to Piccadilly Valley. I had to walk and bicycle up and down all those ridges and record the distribution of the eucalypts and the understorey vegetation. I was interested in the general patterns of the distribution of eucalypts, and, to a lesser extent, the distribution of the heathy sclerophyll and the grassy savannah understoreys. The rainfall gradient from the Adelaide Plain, about 20 inches per annum up to the summit of Mount Lofty, 45 inches per annum, with sunny north-facing aspects and shady south-facing aspects of ridges, gave a fascinating distribution pattern of eucalypt species.

Wood suggested that Specht make a model of this section for the 1946 Australian and New Zealand Association for the Advancement of Science (ANZAAS) Congress, the first science congress after World War II. The model 'was a great success' and remained in the Botany Department's foyer until the mid 1990s. At this stage, Specht was still expecting that he would become a biology teacher—the 'bright young buck' introducing the new subject. While Specht taught secondary school only briefly, he feels his education training gave him a valuable 'way of looking at the world':

> In teaching you should have an holistic overview and that was how I was trained. I looked at ecological research in an holistic sort of way, not just what happened to one species of plant or animal; I tried to integrate the various aspects of climate, geology, soils and vegetation in an ecosystem.

It is essential, if you're going to teach a subject or a section of a subject, to know a lot about it. That's the first thing. But you have to be able to see it in reality. I was thrust into ecology, in the field, and I became fascinated with the inter-relationships within the plant community, with its climate and geology, soils and interaction of animals. One must look at ecosystems, which are an integrated complex of environment, plant community and associated animals and decomposers, the fungi and such forth.

The study of ecology in South Australia 'was way ahead of the rest of the world'. The biologist and plant ecologist Robert Langdon Crocker and Professor Wood 'had recently published papers about the dynamics of vegetation in space and time'. An annual survey of the revegetation of overgrazed arid-zone vegetation had begun in Koonamore Vegetation Reserve in 1925 and was continuing in 1946. 'The whole thing as a holistic entity…was being pieced together: one could follow the changes because a group of students went every year to look at the vegetation, to map it and photograph it and see the changes that had occurred over the last fifteen years.' It was within this context that Specht was offered a place on the Arnhem Land Expedition.

Shortly after the ANZAAS conference in Adelaide in August 1946, Charles Mountford returned from the United States with the offer from the *National Geographic* to take an expedition into Arnhem Land in 1947. I was called into the professor's office…Wood always called us by our surname. He was very Australian, a real ocker Australian, but terribly nervous. He was a chain smoker; he would flick the butt of his cigarette into his mouth! Wood said to me, 'Oh, you won't be getting any payment. You'll get your travel and your keep, but you'd better go.' Crocker and Madigan had achieved fame by crossing the Simpson Desert. 'You will become a "legend" by being on such a fantastic expedition.'

Mountford wanted a botanical collector, an ecologist that was able to think about Aboriginal ecology. He'd been exploring and photographing the art of Aborigines in Central Australia many times, working out from Alice Springs. During the 1930s, he had led expeditions run by the Board of Anthropological Research at the University of Adelaide. Mountford indicated to me that he wanted to see how the Aborigines fitted in with the environment, plant communities and soils and climate, et cetera. How they were able to survive. He didn't express it in that way but that was roughly what he meant, or how I interpreted it. He knew enough about Aboriginal ecology and of the ecological papers of Wood and Crocker to understand the complexity of interrelationships.

Thus, Specht envisaged being part of a team of experts collaboratively putting the big ecological picture of northern Australia together: 'As I would have understood it, we'd be working as a team because at that point in time, in '46, '47, the war was over and Australia really didn't know anything about the North.' These expectations, however, were not fulfilled.

> There was no one doing a comprehensive ecological study of Aboriginal life in Northern Australia. To me it was an opportunity that we would have zoologists and archaeologists and anthropologists, and Mountford would be able to see Aborigines in their home landscape, how they worked. Of course, by the time the Expedition occurred in 1948, it had expanded from five to twelve scientists, plus support staff. And Mountford had all those logistics problems that were horrific, but I would have liked us to have all sat down and just had round-table conversations about what we should do, how we integrated, or tried to integrate with each other, but that didn't ever happen.

Preparing for the Expedition

Specht had 'never seen an Aborigine' and had 'never heard' of Arnhem Land prior to being invited to join the Expedition. In the four months after the initial offer, 'I had to do a lot of sleuthing'. In that time, he wrote an article for the teachers' college annual magazine about the 'Black War' in Arnhem Land. It was 'a crash course to learn about this place and get equipment organised in time for January–February'. 'Certainly I had to get some idea of what equipment would be necessary. I had to get mountains of paper, newspaper, which I got from the *Adelaide Advertiser* in offcuts.' A 'folded broadsheet' was just the right size to fit into the galvanised-steel plant presses that his younger brother, Gordon, an apprentice sheet-metal worker, had made for him.

> Plant specimens would be put between the newspaper. A set of plant specimens in newspaper would be placed between two grids either side and strapped up with a belt. The newspapers had to be changed daily until the specimens were dry.

> And by the time I'd got everything ready for the Expedition and I'd passed my Honours year in plant ecology as well as several education subjects, I was informed that the Expedition was to be delayed for a year because American scientists from the Smithsonian had to go down and survey Bikini Atoll before the hydrogen bomb was exploded. So everything went into chaos and I went back to teaching.

After three months, Specht was 'pulled out' of teaching when an offer came for him to join the Waite Agricultural Research Institute. The delayed start of the Arnhem Land Expedition gave him 'far more experience and it gave me many contacts with the most brilliant men in Australia in the environmental field'. Professor James Prescott, Director of the Waite, and also joint Director of the Soils Division of the CSIRO (then CSIR) in the same building, 'was a climatologist of note' who had been researching 'the possibility of agriculture in northern Australia'.

> I worked at the Waite Institute in January 1948 and made an ecological survey of the Bordertown–Keith area during that period, and then, in February 1948, I joined Mountford coming up here [to Brisbane].

> I was going to be honorary scientist on the Expedition in 1947 but by 1948 they agreed to pay me. Mountford got me employment, money, from the Department of Information and they allowed me to come up to Brisbane for a week, two weeks, beforehand. I visited the Queensland Herbarium, which had experience in New Guinea and Queensland of course, and Stan Blake had been into the Darwin–Katherine area on the CSIRO Land Systems Survey in 1946. So I was able to get a lot of know-how.

World War II was over and Australia was very interested in developing the north agriculturally. In 1946, 'the CSIRO Division of Plant Industry in Canberra appointed C. S. Christian at Gatton Agricultural College in Queensland to develop the land system survey of northern Australia and eventually Papua New Guinea'. The concept was to look at the land holistically. Employed in the field were a geologist, a geomorphologist, a soil scientist and a plant ecologist, while a soil chemist and climatologist worked in a laboratory. 'They had aerial photographs. They surveyed the Darwin–Katherine area, that included the Kakadu area, west of Arnhem Land.'

Through his contacts, Mountford was able to obtain oblique aerial photo-mosaics of Arnhem Land. These photo-mosaics, which Specht studied before the Expedition, were to prove very useful for Specht's collecting in Arnhem Land.

> I knew roughly what Arnhem Land was like before the Expedition in 1948. That was lucky because if the Expedition had gone out in '47, that wouldn't have been achieved. I had a good background at least and when we flew over Arnhem Land in the Catalina I could see roughly the whole place unfolding.

I was saying, 'Yes, I want to go to this mangrove stand or this sand dune stand, this swamp, this eucalypt forest or outcrop of granite.' I knew where I'd get diversity in plants.

The Americans

I was fortunate to come up to Brisbane with Mountford just before the Americans, two of them arrived—[ornithologist] Bert Deignan and [archaeologist and deputy leader] Frank Setzler. We went down to the Brisbane River where most of the ships came in. There were these people looking down at Mountford and myself and they said, 'Who's that little fellow down there? He must be Mountford's son.' I was 23. So that was my first introduction to the American side of the trip.

Specht 'didn't know quite what to think' of these two American scientists from the Smithsonian.

I knew they were pretty senior and important. They weren't big-noting themselves but Frank was a bit…I suppose you'd use the word 'ocker' American. He was one of those people that would enjoy singing around the piano at alumni reunions. He loved community activities, jovial banter. He brought out his horseshoes and he hoped that because there would be plenty of time in the day, especially for an archaeologist, he was going to have us all play tossing horseshoes. Which would have been a good thing if we had had time…

Bert Deignan had spent a couple of years in Thailand. He was an authority on the birds of Thailand and he was a very quiet, shy man, but a very educated man. He was an erudite man, an ornithologist. He would tell us all about the archer fish in the big river going through Bangkok. He'd be sitting there having a cigarette, a cocktail out on the balcony and the archer fish would shoot the cigarette out. It was fascinating.

We went down to Sydney, where mammalogist Dave Johnson and ichthyologist Bob Miller flew in from the United States. We must have been invited to New South Wales Government House. We flew to Canberra and we were adding more to the group. We went to see [Arthur] Calwell, who was the Minister with the Department of Information. Calwell was 'rough' in speech, but I wasn't in a position to make any value judgment of him. Mountford wanted him to come to the 25th Reunion [of the Expedition] because he obviously did a tremendous amount. He overrode Murphy, the Director of the Department of Information, when things went wrong because the Australian–American friendship was much

> more important than whether we overdid the budget. Then we went out to see Governor-General William McKell where we were ushered into the reception room. Apparently Frank Setzler got around to saying he'd heard about Cascade beer from Tasmania so the Governor sent a couple of bottles to Frank at the Canberra Hotel. I thought Menzies was going to add to it. We were staying at the Canberra Hotel and Robert Menzies was at the next table. He came across and I think he gave us some wine.

Specht remembers the functions as 'meet and greet' affairs. He was not singled out to be spoken to by the powerbrokers: 'I mean not to me, I was just a pipsqueak, [a] chicken.' He can remember little else from this time in Canberra, except the 'wonderful' sight of a platypus in the Molonglo River.

> Then we went down to Melbourne. We had a reception in that hotel opposite the Victorian Parliament House. But we also went to one in Government House and all these guests didn't know where Arnhem Land was. They thought we were going down to the Antarctic. A little embarrassing. I think the elite of Melbourne had no idea. No one knew where Arnhem Land was in those days, it was up the north somewhere. Dave Johnson had arrived because there's a photograph of Dave and myself with the curator of mammals of the Melbourne Museum.

The 'fish man', Bob Miller, whom Specht describes as 'a very friendly sort of soul', had also arrived (see Miller and Cashner, this volume). 'And then a number of us, including Bob Miller, went out to Sherbrook Forest to see the lyre birds with the Field Nats. So that was my first time to see a lyre bird.'

Specht describes Howell Walker, the *National Geographic* reporter and photographer, as a 'lovely man, a Princeton graduate in philosophy or something like that. All the Americans had high degrees and they'd had long careers behind them from the American side' (see Jenkins, this volume).

> Howell was up in Darwin, broke his arm or something, the day before the Japanese bombed Darwin, and he was evacuated down to Katherine and eventually back to Sydney. I don't know whether he had married his Australian girlfriend then. Subsequently, of course, he joined the photogrammetric service and flew over the Coral Sea. The photogrammetric unit was located in the foundation building of the University of Queensland where the Coral Sea Battle was planned—the turning point of the war. He wrote an article on the Top End for the *National Geographic* and then on the Coral Sea Battle. So probably Howell was twisting the arm of the *National Geographic* and saying get up to Arnhem Land, study these rock paintings and such forth…I think he was.

15. An Insider's Perspective

Figure 15.2 Raymond Specht (left) and Expedition mammalogist, David Johnson (right), with an unidentified official at the National Museum of Victoria (now Museum Victoria), 1948

By permission of the State Library of South Australia. PRG 1218/17/12.

Mountford

In Adelaide, 'people like Mountford and Tindale were kind of legends around the place'. Of Mountford, Specht 'knew about the films that he'd taken in the Centre. *Brown Men and Red Sand*, there were a couple of films. I didn't know much more about him than that.'

Getting to know Mountford later as a person, Specht admits that he was 'a difficult man':

> Mountford was not communicative as a leader. I was hoping, as an ecologist, [to know] what everyone else was planning to do. We could sit around the table and you'd get enough information on what people were trying to do, or aiming to do. So he was somewhat reticent. But he was a very kindly soul. He was to me, anyhow. He looked after me, and Mrs Mountford did the same. I was almost their child. When we got married he presented us with a couple of photographs. One of them of Uluru and one of the roosting tree at Oenpelli [now Gunbalanya].

Specht was unsure 'what may have gone on behind the scenes', but it was clear that 'everyone had their own agenda'.

> [I]n my case, if there was a catastrophe like there was with supplies, I could just go out and collect plants. Each of the plant communities would have at least fifty species. So to collect fifty plants in sets of ten kept me pretty busy. At Yirrkala, the Aborigines started burning the grasslands, which was characteristic, and Bert [Deignan] would have to go out beyond the burnt area and the birds were getting fewer and fewer. So it was frustrating. The fish man [Miller] would have to go and find a reef or something or a stream to put out his fish poison and collect, or have people to help him put them into pickle.

> Mountford was aloof. Organising, organising everything. The logistics of getting all these people to do their things, and by the time you got to archaeology and searching for cave paintings, or going to a special tribal ceremony, which they did at Lake Hubert, south of Umbakumba, they'd have to be organised with the Aborigines and with other individuals to get down there. I didn't have a clue what was going on, you see.

> We knew that they were having problems. I think Mountford was the leader 'God', as it were. Those problems were his problems. He did have a transport officer [Keith Cordon], he did have a cook [John Bray], he did have advisors like [Gordon] Sweeney and [Bill] Harney and eventually Mrs Mountford. We knew there were problems but we

didn't help him in the solution. Then of course they had the problems with the Department of Information saying, 'You're overstepping the mark with the Department of Civil Aviation, with the Navy'—all this. Then the army got in on the act. I don't know how he ever managed to pull puppet strings with all the things that were going wrong. You can criticise Mountford but he managed in spite of that to get these series of bark paintings done. And Fred Gray [at Umbakumba settlement] of course was a tremendous help in the logistics.

Specht points out that the eminent professor of anthropology A. P. Elkin looked down on Mountford:

He was not a university man and in those days there were people in Britain that if you'd worked like Mountford, you didn't have to go to the university. You got an MA. This was not considered an honorary MA but a real MA. But Australia was terribly rigid in its university system. If you didn't have a degree and didn't have overseas experience to get a PhD from Britain, you were really not regarded. Unfortunately, Elkin was a clergyman but he didn't have any charity as far as I could see.

Frederick McCarthy

Specht describes Australian Museum Curator of Anthropology, Frederick McCarthy, as 'a delightful person, a very charming but very friendly soul. Everyone got on well with him. He was very industrious.'

[T]hey wanted to get an anthropologist, because Mountford as leader, although he was interested in art and mythology and symbolism, couldn't deal with anthropology. Setzler was an archaeologist by interest. Fred had been interested in the rock paintings, the rock engravings in the Hawkesbury sandstone area in particular. I don't think he'd seen many Aborigines. But it was an ideal opportunity as either [Norman] Tindale but certainly Elkin would have pushed him. And rightly so. Because he was interested in rock engravings on the Hawkesbury sandstone, he was particularly interested in seeing the paintings that Flinders had recorded in 1803 on Chasm Island and other rock paintings. So he was probably, in some ways, crossing swords with Mountford by his interest.

Specht recalls that McCarthy's interests were indeed wide ranging: 'Fred was able to fit in with all sorts of things. He worked with Setzler on archaeological digs, with Margaret McArthur studying hunter-gatherer techniques of the men, he recorded string figures, about 180, 190 of them at Yirrkala', working with 'a wonderful girl' (see McKenzie, this volume).

Figure 15.3 The Expedition party dining at Umbakumba on Groote Eylandt. Margaret McArthur (left) and Frederick McCarthy (right) are nearest the camera, 1948

By permission of the State Library of South Australia. PRG 1218/1/3.

The Nutrition Unit: Brian Billington, Kelvin Hodges and Margaret McArthur

Specht formed a special bond with the members of the Nutrition Unit—Brian Billington, Kelvin Hodges and Margaret McArthur: 'They were all about my age. So we were kind of…a little club.'

> [T]hese young people would sit in the middle of the table and someone at the end would call, 'Pass something…', such as, 'pass the jam'; it would come past us and we all had bits before we passed it on. This was repeated when the jam was returned, so we got double feeding…
>
> Brian was [nicknamed] 'Good Tucker Darwin' by the Aborigines. He was a little overweight. In fact, he couldn't wear pyjamas, he had to wear a kind of sarong to go to bed because pyjamas would itch him. Brian had to work on taking medical surveys of all the people in the settlements, and so that kept him pretty busy. And when he got to

Oenpelli, quite a number of the Indigenous people had been taken to the leprosarium in Darwin, so he had a hard job. He'd register people to go and see him and they'd be out in the bush, fearing that they may be sent away to the leprosarium in Darwin. He had virtually to chase them out in the bush to get the full quota; it was impossible. But he was very gentle and tender and a wonderful man to have on the Expedition.

Billington was the doctor for the Expedition members, too, several of whom, including Specht, became sick or were injured in the field and needed his attention.

I got severe conjunctivitis in Groote Eylandt from the flies around the camp. Fred McCarthy got rather weak, tired between Yirrkala and Oenpelli. And Mountford got rather stressed at Oenpelli. His wife was also stressed because of the heat and the humidity that climbed during October before the start of the Wet Season. We were all stressed with that. This was mental rather than physical. Bob Miller got Dengue, breakbone fever, that was pretty grim. It was common. But Brian Billington managed to survive all the hookworms and things like that that the Aborigines suffered. We all survived those things.

Specht praises Margaret McArthur's ability to 'think laterally and integrate':

Margaret was a girl in an all-male camp with Mrs Mountford as chaperone. She was very capable. She'd worked in the Australian Institute of Anatomy. After the war they decided to undertake nutrition studies, which they did initially in a study of pregnant women in the slums of Sydney. And then the team went up to New Guinea and did nutrition studies from the Trobriands, the Sago culture, up to the Highland culture. Margaret was on the New Guinean team…But then in '48 they decided to study the nutrition of the Top End. Margaret was appointed as nutritionist on the Expedition. She had trained as a biochemist in Melbourne and then went into nutrition studies. Margaret studied nutrition in the settlements but she was anxious to study nomadic culture and do time-and-motion studies, which was the first and only time that it was done in Australia. Margaret could look after herself. She was very capable.

Exploring the Legacy of the 1948 Arnhem Land Expedition

Bill Harney

Figure 15.4 Portrait of Bill Harney taken during the Arnhem Land Expedition, 1948

Photograph by Charles P. Mountford. By permission of the State Library of South Australia. PRG 1218/17/12.

Specht remembers bushman Bill Harney, who joined the Expedition at Yirrkala, as 'an excellent talker' and collector of Aboriginal songs and lore.

> Bill was born in Charters Towers, he was Irish, obviously—Harney. His father died when he was about eight and I think he'd gone to about grade four [in school]. He headed out west cattle droving and that was the first step in Bill Harney's education. Because, every time they'd camp, all the youngsters like Bill would have to make the fire and do a bit of cooking, but they were all expected around the campfire to tell stories or sing. And then when they'd get to a centre like Longreach they'd all head down to the local pub.

Harney had told Specht 'that there were often remittance men in these outlying pubs' who had had Cambridge or Oxford educations, 'but they'd been gamblers, womanisers' who had then been dispatched to Australia 'on a retaining fee to keep them away from Great Britain'. Harney absorbed the talk 'about religion or Malthus or politics':

> Eventually he went off to the First War, served on the Somme. He came back and landed in Brisbane with his mate and said, 'I'm not going to be near any cities again.' So he and his mate headed up to Borroloola, where they set up a cattle station. But they didn't have enough cattle, so they borrowed some, as you do. And of course they caught up with them for rustling cattle.

Harney and his friend were 'put into the Borroloola gaol to await the arrival of the magistrate' from Darwin, who only came every six months. Borroloola, as 'the landing point' for tin miners, was 'reasonably large' with a town hall and library.

> Anyhow, the white ants got into the Town Hall and they had to shift the library into the gaol where Harney and his mate were able to peruse this large collection. And as well, there was a man called Jose, who was apparently a remittance man, but he had taken up residence in half a tank with an Aboriginal girl. He was exceedingly well educated. He taught Harney a tremendous amount.

Harney and his mate then 'decided they'd go trepanging and that got them out into the Groote Eylandt area, Caledon Bay', where they worked with Aboriginal people 'on the trepanging and so he had a very great first-hand understanding of Aboriginal protocol and culture'. Harney 'became very much part of that landscape. He learnt a lot about Aboriginal behaviour patterns'.

> During that time he decided he'd learn a bit about geology and mining. So in the light of the moon he'd be out the back of his trawler studying

for his diploma. He became quite a competent geologist. But then he just knew so much about the Aboriginal culture. He married a half-caste girl who had been brought up in the [Groote Eylandt] mission, she was a stolen generation person. So he kept in great contact with the Aborigines and eventually got to Katherine during the Depression.

It was at this time that Harney's son drowned while trying to save a friend in the Todd River at Alice Springs, and then his wife and daughter died of tuberculosis. 'Bill was then bereft, obviously. He got into working…making the road from Katherine to Victoria River Downs.' He was involved with other Aboriginal women and fathered other children, including Bill Harney junior.

Collecting and Classifying

Specht was asked to collect plant specimens for ten institutions, including every herbarium in Australia, Kew Gardens in England, Leiden Botanical Garden in the Netherlands (which was then beginning the Flora Malesiana project), the Arnold Arboretum (sponsor of the Archbold expeditions to the Solomon Islands and New Guinea), and the Smithsonian Institution in Washington, DC. 'It was a massive task. I tried to get ten sets of specimens every day in sets of ten.' This was easiest when they were small plants. Larger plants such as pandanus required collecting specific parts of leaf, sucker leaf and the fruit.

> At Yirrkala there was a little stand of Pandanus, so there were plenty of sucker leaves, plenty of trees to get samples up above and down below. But there were only six of these big fruits. So I got those and I had to wire them up, tighten them up as they dried out, but there were all these bits from last year's fruits broken up on the ground so I collected those. As far as I could see, they were all *Pandanus spiralis*.

> Several years later Harold St John from Hawaii decided to study the Pandanus of the Pacific and he included these specimens from Yirrkala. He found that sucker leaves were different from the tops and that these cones that I had wrapped up, which were the recent ones, were somewhat different in shape from the bits lying on the ground from the previous year. For several decades, I believed that St John had applied the species epithet, *spechtii*, to the old phalanges and sucker leaves of the Pandanus specimens that I had collected at Yirrkala. I liked to boast that I had a 'sucker' name after me.

The process of collecting and classifying was intensive:

> You take field notes. You had to record the colour of the flowers, the height. People might never have seen these things before. Now you don't worry about those things, they know enough about them, unless they're exceptional. There were different bark on eucalypt trees, you got samples of that. I had to collect wood samples of the trees for CSIRO Forest Products, who'd done a lot of work in New Guinea and the rain forests of Queensland. So every sample was recorded with the number. They were tagged and placed between sheets of newspaper and, if too large, you try to bend the specimen to fit in the newspaper. A Pandanus leaf, you'll bend up and down. And then you'd press them within newspaper.

During the short time Specht had spent at the Queensland Herbarium, he had developed knowledge of conserving tropical plants. Certain specimens from the mangroves and rainforests with succulent leaves were difficult to dry in the newspaper 'because they take a long time and by that stage the leaves break off from the stems'.

> The Queensland Herbarium had experience in north Queensland rain forest and the mangroves and New Guinea and they recommended that I take a four-gallon drum and add formalin and soak those plants in it for 24 hours. So you had this problem of just collecting ten sets of specimens, some of which were very complicated to represent the whole plant, other than the field notes, and then you had to deal with some of them to stop this loss of leaf and flower material.

> Under normal circumstances, admittedly, it's quite dry through much of the period of the dry season, but we were there in a cyclone. It still meant that every day I'd have a hundred sheets of specimens and the newspaper in which they were being dried had to be changed every night. You'd have a thousand before the first lot were dry.

> The Queensland Herbarium suggested that I get a special tank with a water jacket around it and this would steam up and dry the specimens. So at the last moment, fortunately, my brother was still at the latter stage of his sheet metal apprenticeship, and he was able to construct this drying-oven before I got back to Adelaide from Brisbane, after meeting the rest of the Expedition. This oven was taken in the field and used to dry the pressed specimens. We'd put them into the drying oven and this was stoked up.

Figure 15.5 Specimen of *Melaleuca magnifica* collected by Raymond Specht in June 1948, now in the collection of the US National Herbarium, Smithsonian Institution

By permission of the US National Herbarium, Smithsonian Institution. Sheet No. 02316992.

This meant that Specht had to change the specimens every three or four days, instead of every 10 to 15 days. 'The mountain of material was somewhat controllable.' The drying unit was large: 'the internal size of it would be half of a broadsheet of paper, newspaper, and we'd stack them up and put them on the end so that you got a somewhat upward draft. But it was just a water jacket around the side and I hoped that it wouldn't boil dry and the solder would melt. Which it didn't, thank goodness'.

Specht was not sure whether he would find many surprises in the botany of Arnhem Land:

> Initially Robert Brown with Captain Matthew Flinders had been around the coast during January, February of 1803 and they were botanical gentlemen, very avid, expert collectors. So the swamps and coastal stuff and the eucalypt forests were pretty well documented.

Specht did make some botanical discoveries, collecting 'about twenty-odd plant species that were new and a couple of others that have since been found to be new. Others have been modified with time.'

> On Bickerton Island I found a water plant called *Nymphoides* related to, not quite, the water lily family; it had floating leaves, but these were in the form of a little wishbone shape so I called it *Nymphoides furculifolia*. I got a couple of other new plants from Bickerton Island.

> I didn't get into the sandstone on Groote Eylandt. But I did get a bit of a chance to get, at the foot of the Oenpelli Waterfall, a small tree and that was *Blepharocarya*. The other known species was over in Cape York. I called that tree *Blepharocarya depauperata*—small in stature. I managed to get up to the top of the Waterfall, hardly there for more than a short time; Deignan came with me. We were together for four days, camped out there. Bert was able to get up on top of the sandstone where he found his spinifex bird *Amytornis woodwardi*. He patiently sat between the spinifex clumps and waited for that little bird to jump across.

> At the Oenpelli Waterfall I got quite a number of different plants, one of which was a *Pityrodia* but it didn't have enough material. Eventually I contacted Stuart James, Agricultural Advisor to the CMS Missions, and he got some examples. I called it *Pityrodia jamesii*. I collected an *Acacia* that I named after Mrs Mountford who, in the latter stages, came in every night and helped me with changing the newspapers. A good remedial thing for me as well as for her, especially in the steamy weather that was coming up, and Mountford said, 'Would you name a plant after Mrs Mountford?' I named an acacia after Mrs Mountford, *Acacia mountfordae* for the feminine, genitive. I collected a beautiful melaleuca

which had a giant flowering head. I managed to call that *Melaleuca magnifica* which impressed everyone. I did describe a *Cassia* after Bill Harney but this *Cassia* was later shown to be an introduced plant.

Aboriginal Contact

Specht's first encounter with Aboriginal people was shortly after arriving in Darwin when the party made a short trip to Delissaville (now Belyuen) (see Barwick and Marett, this volume).

> We were invited over to the other side of Darwin Harbour to a place called Delissaville. We had a fascinating weekend during which the Aborigines showed us 200-feet, accurate spear throwing. It was the first time I'd seen an Aborigine. I went out and collected with a couple of little boys and they told me the names of plants and so forth, directing me. But that was great fun, with young kids.

> The Superintendent of Delissaville, Tom Wake, had a big house. They put on a special dance, secret dance ceremony, which we attended and filmed…But Margaret McArthur was not allowed and of course Bessie Mountford was not allowed either. Margaret certainly was very upset. But that was just one of those things.

Specht talks about how he was 'on the periphery' in terms of working within Aboriginal protocol:

> Like the zoologist [Johnson] from the United States…you didn't trespass. I mean I think we were observers. I was a keen observer on ethnobotany, the use of plants. Dave Johnson was particularly concerned with the effect of fire and the hunting of animals. Deignan studied birds, but I don't know how he impacted with Aborigines…Bob Miller, of course, was concerned with fish in the reefs and out in depths where he must have been very conscious of Aboriginal fishing techniques. Dave Johnson was taking pelts and skinning them and getting skeletons sometimes, fighting against Aboriginal dogs, they used to pinch anything, dig under the tents and get everything. On Bickerton Island, we call them 'archaeologist dogs' as they were good at digging holes. I was the closest, of the naturalists, I suppose, with Aborigines, because of my interest in bush tucker and other uses of plants.

Specht wrote a paper on ethno-botany in the Expedition records. This was part of his interest in the cultural meanings of plants to Aboriginal people. 'It was certainly a change of culture because I'd never seen another culture before, other than the heritage of an ocker Australian.'

His introduction to ethno-botany came in his honours year at university:

> We had to read books on ethno-botany, the origins of wheat and rice and cotton and things like that throughout the world, just to have some experience of it. I had studied Australian ecology and world ecology—which was Britain and the United States—and a bit of work in Denmark and France, Switzerland. Ethno-botany was part of our experience and I expected that I was going to take notes on how plants were used if I had contacts with the Aborigines. Of course it became much more feasible when the nutrition unit, in particular Margaret McArthur, was out there in the bush.

Along with McArthur, Specht began to take notes on how the plants were being used and eaten. This differed among the various Aboriginal groups:

> You would get a plant on the sand dune like *Boerhavia* and Groote Eylandters would say, 'Yes, we dig up the root and eat it.' You'd get to Yirrkala and they'd say, 'What did they do that for? They must have been starving.'

> It was fortunate that I had, on Bickerton Island, Kumbiala seconded to me for collecting bark and wood specimens. He was good as an axe man. It was remarkable to have Kumbiala there and he was able to give names of plants.

Specht had learnt the International Phonetic Alphabet at Teachers' College, which helped him record the names of plants told to him by Kumbiala.

> But it was just lucky. Fortunately Bill Harney, when we caught up with him in Yirrkala, knew most of them and checked with the Yolngu people and we were able to get a reasonable interpretation of plant names, which stood the test of time.

In fact, it was only a few weeks before working with the bilingual Kumbiala that Specht had met his first non-English-speaking Aboriginal person:

> At Groote Eylandt the first time I went out, there was an old man scraping off the bark of the acacia wattle on the coastal dune, *Acacia torulosa*, and I said, 'What are you doing?' He didn't understand me and he pointed up. He had a string of bark, you see, but we just couldn't communicate…In fact, he was making a pubic tassel called *mapina* which was also the name of the tree.

Specht's informant and helper, Kumbiala, a Woodah Island man, had long been employed in trepanging by Fred Gray, superintendent of the Aboriginal settlement at Umbakumba. There were unsubstantiated rumours of Kumbiala's involvement with a murder: 'Kumbiala was put in charge of me and he gave a tremendous amount of help. I was a bit scared because of the murders. We were all a bit scared of that.'

Figure 15.6 Portrait of Kumbiala, who guided Specht on Groote Eylandt, 1948

Photograph by Frank M. Setzler. By permission of National Anthropological Archives, Smithsonian Institution. Photo Lot 36, Lantern Slide 40.

I gradually got to know Kumbiala only too well. I had to get wood samples and bark samples. I gave him the axe and I thought, oh gee. Anyhow, during that time, he said, 'Roy', as he called me, they all called me Roy, not Ray, 'I am making you a woomera and when I get back to Umbakumba, I'm going to paint it and give it to you.' That's the totem design for Woodah Island. So I feel that I am part of the Woodah Island tribe or clan. It's the Woodah Island clan that made a sorry ceremony in the Darwin Supreme Court about four years ago I think, or maybe five. They built two totem poles and decorated them. The descendants of the people that had murdered Constable McColl, they came across to the Supreme Court in Darwin and set them up. I gather they're in the foyer now. And they got the descendants of Constable McColl, who had been murdered accidentally, and they had a sorry ceremony. So it's interesting that Prime Minister Howard can't do it but Woodah Island people, who are my clansmen, can. But technically all those artefacts, we were not allowed to have them ourselves. They were technically Expedition property.

At the Umbakumba settlement, run by Fred Gray and his wife, Marjorie, where the Expedition camped, Specht began to learn about the effects of the recent child endowment system on Aboriginal children and their parents (see Thomas, this volume). Marjorie, a teacher, had come from England in 1946 to marry Fred, who had been her boyfriend prior to his departure for Australia in 1922.

I think it must have been the child endowment; they set up a school that received financial support from the government. The RAAF had left the sea plane base, so there was no other support to give the Grays money; it was a way in which they could get money to maintain the Umbakumba settlement.

When the Department of Civil Aviation sea plane base was established on Little Lagoon, Groote Eylandt, Fred was encouraged to bring his group over from Caledon Bay—and that's how Kumbiala came across—to work with the Indigenous people of Groote Eylandt. Gray built up gardens and orchards to supply the sea plane base.

When Marjorie Gray arrived in 1946 after the war, the Grays built a house, hut and so forth, a school. They had accommodation, 24-hour accommodation for the boys and girls. They had the orchard and garden and there was a wharf.

The point was that the child endowment had come as a federal bonus to all people and if these missions or settlements had children 24 hours a day, five years old and on, in their control, then they got their allowance of child endowment. The mission got it and the Umbakumba settlement got it. They would then have the children [all] day; they would look after them in dormitories. These were Aboriginal children that were technically, quote, 'stolen generation', and the parents would sit around the periphery of the settlement. At the missions, if they went to church on Sunday, they'd get a handout of flour, baccy and tea. So they stayed around.

So I think that the parents were likely to be more involved with the settlement at Umbakumba than they were at the CMS Mission. The CMS Mission on Groote Eylandt had been set up about 1920 and that was for half-castes who were brought in from the mainland. That's where

> Bill Harney eventually met his wife, who was half-caste, in the mission settlement. They were just taken away from their parents and brought up 24 hours a day in that settlement. But things had changed by 1948. In 1938, the Arnhem Land Aboriginal Reserve was created. This was really land tenure, Aboriginal land tenure, although the missions and the settlements had control of most Aborigines...It was their land and it was long before Mabo.

When Specht accompanied Margaret McArthur to Hemple Bay and again on Bickerton Island for two weeks in April and May, the child endowment issue threatened her research:

> We had a camp of four families. Because of child endowment regulations, we thought that kids five years old and under were allowed to be out with their parents in the camp.
>
> Mrs Gray somehow was interpreting the child endowment legislation and found that these five-year-olds should be back in the settlement. So halfway through the camp, Margaret was starting on her time-and-motion studies, 24 hours a day for six days. Aborigines from the settlement, I think Nangapianga came, and the leader of the group, I thought it was Kumbiala, had spears in their hands, yelling at each other. And Margaret said, 'Ray, you've got to do something'. With my heart in my mouth, I ran down between the feuding pair and tried to ask them what was the problem. Some of them could understand enough, [and they] told me that the five-year-old children had to be taken back to Umbakumba. I said, 'Well, no, you can't'—and wrote a note to Mrs Gray on a piece of toilet paper, the only paper available!
>
> I dismissed the idea of taking the kids away and upsetting Margaret's time-and-motion studies with this family, halfway through the critical part of the work.

Specht, however, felt sympathy for 'poor Marjorie'—obviously in culture shock after just two years in Australia. She was a great fan of the BBC's Desert Island Discs program. 'The song "I'm All So Alone in a Strange Land" would waft over our camp every night.' She 'was very lonely', and the four months the Expedition spent at Umbakumba were 'a wonderful time for her'. He also stresses that Gray attempted to 'achieve happiness, friendliness, amongst the Aboriginal group'.

> But eventually the government of the Arnhem Land group, the Federal government, worried about the missions and their impact and of course the Grays' settlement was rather an unusual one with its history. It wasn't religious in any way. Fred knew more about Aboriginal culture and tried

to maintain it, but he realised that the world was changing and that's why he was encouraging, as the Federal government was encouraging, white man's education. So I think he was caught. He had to do it but he wasn't quite sure whether it was the right thing. And of course he'd lost the original tribal inter-relationships.

Figure 15.7 Raymond Specht having his beard trimmed by a Royal Australian Air Force serviceman at Yirrkala, 1948

By permission of the State Library of South Australia. PRG 487/1/3.

After the Expedition

After the Expedition ended in November 1948, Specht's 'mountain of specimens' was packaged up in kerosene crates and shipped from Darwin to Brisbane. 'Mountford, through the Department of Information, got me money for another five months to go up to Brisbane and start identifying these 1300 sets of plants that I'd collected.'

> After a short Christmas holiday, I came up to Brisbane to work in the Government Botanist's office and sort out all this material that had been collected, and identify them.
>
> They were all in higgledy piggledy order and I had to spread them out to get them into some sort of order. Fortunately the botanist that had been on the Darwin/Katherine survey for the CSIRO [Stan Blake] was an authority on grasses and sedges so it was a wonderful boon to have him on site. He also was getting interested in the Northern Territory eucalypts and so he took over their identification.

The ferns were sent to Mary Tindale in Sydney, while Noel Lothian of the Adelaide Botanic Gardens 'was an authority on the *Wahlenbergia*s or bluebells'. All the rest Specht had to deal with himself:

> After sorting and identifying the specimens, you've got to label the specimens. Mountford got special label[s] showing Arnhem Land Expedition, *National Geographic*, et cetera, Smithsonian, and the location with the latitude and longitude. These labels were printed off so, you can imagine, we had to process about 1300 specimens in sets of ten so we had about 13,000–14,000 little labels. Then we had to get someone to type the identification, for example, *Melaleuca magnifica*, with Specht after it, because I was the describer; then the description, whether it was a shrub or a tree, and flower colour, and collecting date.
>
> There were still about twenty or so that didn't have any identification. And eventually those unknown plants had to be described in my dog Latin and I had to get black-and-white illustrations of each.
>
> I had to get all this stuff ready, sort it all out, and get it sent across to herbaria in Brisbane, Sydney, Canberra, Melbourne, to Perth and overseas. The Department of Information took the material to London and to Amsterdam, and the ambassadors presented the material. And similarly to the Smithsonian Institution and the Arnold Arboretum in the United States.

During all this 'slog', Specht met his future wife, Marion Gillies, on an excursion to Fraser Island, when she was a third-year science student with a group visiting from the University of Queensland. She 'changed from marine ecology—she was a fauna ecologist studying mangroves—to study the soil fauna in the Ninety Mile Desert' of South Australia after their marriage in 1952. They settled in Adelaide, where Specht took up a position as research fellow at the University of Adelaide, where he was eventually given a lectureship. Marion continued to do fieldwork while she was pregnant with daughter Alison—'still riding till eight months of pregnancy on the back of my motor bike', says Specht.

> After work on Friday, we'd hurtle down to Keith, 150 miles, and out into the desert. And we'd research there from dawn till dusk Saturday and Sunday and then hurtle back Sunday night and start work on Monday morning.

They would later take baby Alison, who herself became an ecologist, out into the field. 'There's a wonderful photograph of Alison in diapers, her first initiation to field work.'

After May 1949, any work on the Arnhem Land project was 'extracurricular', including the mammoth preparation of Volume 3 of the Expedition records, *Botany and Plant Ecology*, which Specht co-edited with Mountford.

> Being in Adelaide I saw Mountford every week at least and from my 120 negatives, we were able to print a reasonable set of photographs for illustration, including maps…

> Mountford got his Volume 1 [*Art, Myth and Symbolism*] out, I don't know how he ever did it with all the other things he was doing. He had all the material for Volume 2 [*Anthropology and Nutrition*]…but of course because I was going in 1956 to the United States, somehow I jumped the queue. So while we were away, they started processing Volume 3 before Volume 2. It came out in 1958. Because of that delay, the very valuable material that Frank Setzler, Fred McCarthy and the nutrition unit had done didn't come out until 1960, which was twelve years after the Expedition.

Specht ended up editing the fourth volume, *Zoology*, which was published in 1964. It had been held up by the long time it took for William R. Taylor at the Smithsonian—who had taken over Miller's position when he moved to Michigan—to complete the study of fishes (see Miller and Cashner, this volume). 'I was the only Expedition biologist in Australia, on the spot.' Mountford was by that time studying in Cambridge.

Specht felt that the results of the Expedition were to an extent submerged because the Expedition records rapidly became collectors' items and too expensive for scientists to buy. But above all, the 'impact' of the Expedition research was lessened because of the delay in publication.

It was Specht's idea to have the twenty-fifth and fiftieth anniversary Arnhem Land Expedition reunions, which occurred in 1973 and 1998. He also, however, met up with his former Expedition colleagues in the United States. Specht was encouraged 'to go to California and Arizona, etc. and to study mineral nutrition at University of California, Berkeley'. He took up a Fulbright award for this purpose in 1956. While visiting Washington, DC, he met Frank Setzler and Bert Deignan again and attended a National Geographic Society luncheon where the lecture film on the Expedition, shot by Howell Walker, was shown (see Harris, this volume). Some weeks later, he renewed his friendship with Bob Miller at Ann Arbor, Michigan.

Part III
Aboriginal Engagements with the Expedition

16. The American Clever Man (*Marrkijbu Burdan Merika*)[1]

Bruce Birch

A Note on the Recordings

At the time the first recording of the story of the 'American Clever Man' was made, none of those present realised that the central character in the story was based on David H. Johnson, mammalogist with the 1948 American–Australian Scientific Expedition to Arnhem Land.[2] In fact, the text remained untranscribed and only dimly grasped until early 2009, when art historian Sabine Hoeng made the link to Johnson. Hoeng (who coordinates a bilingual Iwaidja–English publishing project based on Croker Island) had recorded a brief reference to the same story in October 2008, and, when Archie Brown brought up the story again in a March 2009 recording, she was inspired to search the relevant literature for references to an American who had travelled alone through Cobourg Peninsula— soon locating the following note in Mountford's introduction to the records of the Expedition: 'On 19 October…Johnson reached Oenpelli [now Gunbalanya][3] after walking 160 miles [260 km] from Cape Don, without a native to guide him. He had been successful in making a collection of mammals which can be compared with that made by the naturalist Gilbert over a hundred years ago.'[4]

This matched the information from local Indigenous people that the man in the story was American, that he was practising taxidermy on small mammals, and that the events took place in the immediate aftermath of World War II. I then transcribed and translated the 2006 recording, and set up an interview

---

1   The Iwaidja term *marrkijbu*, which is often translated as 'clever man' or 'shaman', refers to a man who possesses, as a result of training and practice, an unusual capacity to manipulate aspects of both the natural and the supernatural worlds.
2   The story of the 'American Clever Man' was first recorded on 26 July 2006 as an oral text spoken by Archie Brown, a member of the Yalama clan, who is based on Croker Island and who was born and grew up on Cobourg Peninsula. This recording was made at Wanjurrk in Mountnorris Bay during a trip funded by the Dokumentation Bedrohte Sprache (DoBeS) program of the Volkswagen Foundation as part of a grant awarded to linguists Nick Evans (then at the University of Melbourne) and Hans-Jürgen Sasse (then at Cologne University) to document Iwaidja, a highly endangered language spoken now mostly on Croker Island and the Cobourg Peninsula.
3   The name 'Oenpelli' is an approximation of *Uwunbarlany*, which is the placename in Erre, the original language of the area, now no longer spoken. The cognate placename in Kuwinjku, which has now become the dominant language of the area, is *Kunbarlanya*, today typically written as *Gunbalanya*.
4   Mountford, C. P. (ed.) 1956, *Records of the American–Australian Scientific Expedition to Arnhem Land. Volume 1: Art, myth and symbolism*, Melbourne University Press, Carlton, Vic., p. xxix.

in September 2009 not only with Archie Brown, but also with David 'Cookie' Minyimak, who I had been told had accompanied Johnson on local hunting trips while he was based at Cape Don. I also invited two other men who had been based at Cape Don at that time—Charlie Mangulda and Khaki Marrala—who both knew the story well and could therefore help with filling out details. These additional recordings were then transcribed and translated with the help of Iwaidja-speaking language workers at Adjamarduku Outstation on Croker Island, forming the basis for a film I presented at the Barks, Birds & Billabongs symposium in November 2009.

Johnson at Cape Don

The story of the American Clever Man begins at Jamarldinki (Cape Don) at the western tip of Cobourg Peninsula, where a lighthouse settlement was established in 1918. Johnson was based there during September 1948, collecting animals, transforming them into museum objects using his skills as a taxidermist, and packing them in boxes ready for shipment to Darwin via the regular supply boat, *Sheena*. For his travels in the vicinity of Cape Don, Johnson employed the services of Buckley Darrarndarra, a man of the nearby Kamurlkbarn clan estate, and his canoe, the *Yinbi* (named, like all canoes, after the place where the tree from which it was made once grew). Darrarndarra took along two of his sons, David 'Cookie' Minyimak and the late Johnny Williams, on his trips with Johnson, and it is from Minyimak that we have a firsthand account of Johnson's travels on Cobourg.

The people living at Cape Don observed Johnson with growing amazement as he went about his business. It became increasingly obvious that Johnson was no ordinary 'Balanda' (as white people are known throughout Arnhem Land). Johnson went out at night alone into the bush, shooting bats and other small game (he was apparently an excellent shot),[5] and would spend the following day skinning them and then returning them to a life-like state by means of taxidermy. Adding to the unusual impression was Johnson's apparently immaculate appearance. He is said to have worn only pale-coloured (*bidbarran*) clothing and yet to have emerged from the bush as clean as when he set out. According to one informant, he was never seen to bathe, but was nevertheless always 'clean, no dirty' (see Interview Extract II below). This impression is confirmed by Expedition colleague Raymond Specht, who states that Johnson 'always seemed neatly dressed even after a hard day(s) in the field'.[6]

---

5   Ray Specht, Personal communication.
6   Ibid.

16. The American Clever Man

Figures 16.1 and 16.2 Views of Arnhem Land Expedition mammalogist, David H. Johnson, performing taxidermy, 1948

Photograph by Howell Walker. By permission of the State Library of South Australia. PRG 487/1/2/204/1 and PRG 487/1/2/204/2.

Figure 16.2

Photograph by Howell Walker. By permission of the State Library of South Australia. PRG 487/1/2/204/1 and PRG 487/1/2/204/2.

When local people looked for an explanation of Johnson's atypical abilities and behaviour, they came up, unsurprisingly, with the notion that he was a *marrkijbu*, a person with a heightened ability to manipulate aspects of both the natural and the supernatural realms—a 'shaman' or 'clever man'. Johnson did indeed fit this description well, at least in relation to his knowledge of, and control over, aspects of the natural environment. He not only had the professional training of a mammalogist, and therefore an advanced understanding of the animals on Cobourg and their behaviour, but was also a skilled 'backwoods man', accustomed to, and unafraid of, spending long periods alone in the bush. Johnson himself records that he was

> put ashore at Cape Don on 18 September…The following three weeks were spent on the Cobourg Peninsula with headquarters at the Cape Don lighthouse…Local trips were made by boat to Popham Bay on the north shore of the peninsula and to Black Rock Point on the south shore… From the latter locality a trip was made overland on foot to Knocker Bay on Port Essington.[7]

Johnson's description is in accord with the Indigenous account as far as the places he visited are concerned, although it diverges in terms of what occurred there. It was at a place called Madirrala in Knocker Bay that Johnson's status as a *marrkijbu*—if not already confirmed—was placed beyond doubt in the eyes of Indigenous observers. By this stage of his visit, we can assume that Johnson's unusual behaviour had already impacted strongly on the population at Cape Don. One imagines his daily activities being reported on and discussed around campfires at night. One event, however, that occurred during his period on Cobourg Peninsula stands out from all others. At Madirrala, the story goes that Johnson not only saw a *yumbarrbarr* (a gigantic malevolent spirit which feasts on human flesh, and of which local Indigenous people are naturally terrified), but was contemplating catching it.[8]

David Minyimak tells the story briefly the following way.

---

[7] Johnson, D. H. 1964, 'Mammals of the Arnhem Land Expedition', in R. Specht (ed.), *Records of the American–Australian Scientific Expedition to Arnhem Land. Volume 4: Zoology*, Melbourne University Press, Carlton, Vic., p. 429.

[8] The earliest mention in literature of the *yumbarrbarr* on Cobourg Peninsula occurs in John Lort Stokes' 1846 account. Stokes writes: 'The natives in the neighbourhood of Port Essington are, like all others on the continent, very superstitious; they fancy that a large kind of tree, called the Imburra-burra, resembling the Adansonia, contains evil spirits.' Stokes mistakenly interprets *yumbarrbarr* as the name of the tree, rather than the name of the malevolent spirits who are said to inhabit it. The tree alluded to could be the milkwood (*Alstonia actinophylla*), one of the trees that *yumbarrbarr* are said to inhabit, along with the banyan and the tamarind. Stokes, J. L. 1846, *Discoveries in Australia: With an account of the coasts and rivers explored and surveyed during the voyage of H.M.S. Beagle, in the years 1837–38–39–40–41–42–43. Volume 2*, T. and W. Boone, London.

Interview Extract I[9]

Madirrala.
[We arrived at] Madirrala.

Well, jarraran hunting. Mirrnayaj.
[My father, my brother and I] went looking for crocodiles.

Jumung jadnirrang barakbarda,
When we came back,

abiny ngartung, 'Ay!'
he [Johnson] said to us, 'Eh!'

'Artayang burrang warrkbi.'
'I saw a big man.'

'Nganduka?'
'Where?' [We asked him.]

'Balkbany barakbarda arlirr ari.'
'He appeared over there near that tree.'

'Kardayang? Nuyi?'
'You saw him? You?'

'Anamanyi, but...'
'I would have liked to have captured him, but...'

'too big.'
'[he was] too big.'

'Awardudban.'
'So I left him there.'

In this part of the country, *yumbarrbarr* are believed to inhabit trees—that is, to actually live inside them. Their presence can be diagnosed by certain signs, such as the accompanying presence of human remains in the vicinity—victims of the *yumbarrbarr*'s appetite for human flesh.

While the bulk of the Indigenous population lives in fear of *yumbarrbarr*, *marrkijbu* or 'clever men' do not. On the contrary, *marrkijbu* have the ability to 'tame' *yumbarrbarr*, and to use them as an extension of their own power, getting

---

9 All recordings excerpted and quoted here are stored with associated metadata and time-aligned annotations in the online Dokumentation Bedrohte Sprache (DoBeS) Archive based at the Max Planck Institute for Psycholinguistics, Nijmegen, the Netherlands. Interview Extract I, dvR_091112, Begin Time: 00:01:41.456, End Time: 00:02:06.805 (DoBeS Archive), Recorded at Adjamarduku Outstation, Croker Island, 12 November 2009, Narrator: David 'Cookie' Minyimak.

them to perform difficult or even mundane tasks. For example, Archie Brown and David Minyimak, in a separate text, have described an incident during a Kuwarr ceremony when one of the ceremonial leaders, Paddy Compass Namadbara, a *marrkijbu*, instructed 'his *yumbarrbarr*' to frighten them by throwing rocks at them as they sat around the campfire at night, as punishment for their perceived flippant attitude towards the Kuwarr ceremonial process.[10]

Thus, given both his apparent lack of fear of the *yumbarrbarr* and his statement that he wanted to catch it, Johnson's behaviour would have consolidated the already strong conviction in the minds of local people that he was indeed a *marrkijbu burdan Merika*—an 'American clever man'.

Johnson, on the other hand, mentions an encounter of a different kind at Knocker Bay:

> *Sambar deer* were seen twice, and tracks many other times on the western and southern shores of Port Essington. At Knocker Bay [known to the locals as Madirrala] a female and a half-grown fawn were startled from a stunted thicket of mangroves and ran out into the shallow water of the bay for a distance before turning back to shore and disappearing into other thickets.[11]

Given the potential for miscommunication across the cultural and linguistic chasm separating Johnson from his Indigenous support crew, and given the already mounting evidence of Johnson's special status in the minds of his hosts, it is plausible that Johnson recounted his sighting of sambar deer to Darrarndarra and Minyimak on their return from crocodile hunting, and that this was misinterpreted by them as a sighting of the *yumbarrbarr* which was believed to inhabit this locality.

The partial homonymy of the words '*yumbarrbarr*' and 'sambar' suggests the possibility that Johnson might have even mentioned the word 'sambar'—a term for the deer which was most likely not in general usage on Cobourg—and that this was misheard as a reference to the malevolent spirit. This particular mishearing would have been further encouraged by the developing understanding of Johnson as a 'clever man'. *Yumbarrbarr* are known to inhabit particular places. Madirrala was one such place, and therefore the sighting of a *yumbarrbarr* there was not unexpected. Thus, the conditions were conducive to the misunderstanding, and Johnson's sighting of deer was interpreted as a sighting instead of a local malevolent spirit with a similar-sounding name.

---

10 W_081001 (DoBeS Archive). For a discussion of the Kuwarr ceremony (known in the neighbouring language Kunwinjku as *Ubarr*) in the context of the Arnhem Land Expedition, see Garde, this volume.
11 Johnson, 'Mammals of the Arnhem Land Expedition', p. 432.

Figure 16.3 David 'Cookie' Minyimak, 2007

Photograph by Sabine Hoeng

The following edited extract from a recording made in September 2009 gives an impressionistic survey of some of the key elements of Johnson's stay at Cape Don. Present were Charlie Mangulda (CM), David 'Cookie' Minyimak (DM), Khaki Marrala (KM), and Archie Brown (AB).

Interview Extract II[12]

> CM: *Riwularrung ba war, ngabi nyirran from Kunbarlanya.*
> When the war finished, I came back from Gunbalanya.

---

12 dvR_090904, Begin Time: 00:00:09.690, End Time: 00:06:16.603, (DoBeS Archive), Recorded at Adjamarduku Outstation, Croker Island, 9 September 2009, Narrators: Charlie Mangulda; Archie Brown; David 'Cookie' Minyimak; and Khaki Marrala.

And we bin there Jamarldinki, and bingkung that Balanda.
We were all there at Cape Don when that Balanda [Johnson] arrived.

Cookie janad ijbanakaniny barakbarda. He know.
Cookie [and his father] went around with him [while he was] there. He knows.

[…]

AB: *Ngabi I was mightbe about a…fifteen or eighteen years old.*
I was about fifteen or eighteen.

AB: *Karlu, birta ngabi aburranymin [inaudible].*
Hang on, maybe I wasn't that old.

CM: *Ngabi I bin still young baraka Jamarldinki. Everybody bin young.*
I was still young when we were at Jamarldinki. We were all young.

AB: *Mightbe I was thirteen. Thirteen or fourteen.*[13]

CM: *We bin still young.*

[…]

DM: *What, I'm going to start from Cape Don?*
Do you want me to start the story from when he was at Cape Don?

When I'm going to start?
Where do you want me to start?

[…]

But I don't know his name. I forget.

AB: *Karlu, you don't know his name, but you just start it straight away.*

Ngabi I don't know.
I don't know.

[…]

DM: *Rimany warrkbi barakbarda.*
He captured that man there.[14]

---

13 According to AB himself, he was born at Minarri at the neck of Cobourg Peninsula about the start of World War II, in which case he would have been only eight or nine at the oldest.
14 DM refers here to the events believed to have occurred during Johnson's solo walk to Oenpelli. See Interview Extract III.

Ba wardyad bingkung. Bartuwa, he bin start right up to Inybarlmun.
When he got to the stone country. He started out [from Cape Don], and went straight to Inybarlmun.

Bingkung. From Inybarlmun,
He arrived there. From Inybarlmun,

barakbarda yabiny wal mana rtuwa wardyad.
he went like the wind down to the stone country.

AB: *Durr, durr!*
Go, go![15]

DM: *Barakbarda angmanamin start.*

That's where your part of the story starts.

CM: *Malany yungkudnakandung wurnbarran. Kurrurnbarrakan Kajaji, eh?*
Where did you go camping? You spent a night at Kajaji [Black Rock Point], didn't you?

First, kudbunbaning Kajaji yungkudnakaniny.
First, you went and stayed at Kajaji.

Kajaji yungkudnakaniny kudbunbaning arruman.
You and your father.[16]

DM: *Iyi, yinirrk Kajaji ngadbunbaning.*
Yes, we stayed at Kajaji first of all.

CM: *Lda janad Balanda.*
And that Balanda as well.

And yawaran Waladirra angbaharl.
And he went to the headwaters of Waladirra Creek.

DM: *Iyi yawaran Waladirra.*
Yes, he went to Waladirra.

CM: *Warang numiwang, all night.*
He went out [hunting] all night.

---

15 AB is encouraging DM to continue the story, but in the next line DM tries to hand it back to AB.
16 CM has stepped in to take over the narrative at this point, seeing that it was stalling.

DM: Rirrkbung kirrimul ba wukan.
He stuffed [those animals] and sewed them up so that they looked like they were alive.

CM: Anang all that kalakalak anang, bartuwalda anirrkbung.
He shot birds as well, then stuffed them and sewed them up.

Ringuldangung like real live one.
He made them look as if they were alive.

Ruka abiny.
That's what he did

He bin work all night.
He worked all night.

[…]

Mungardk.
Possums.

Marduny.
Bandicoots.

Animangung barakbarda all kind.
He collected lots of different kinds [of animals].

And anirrkbung, ayuwirrang kirrimul…
And when he sewed them up, they returned to…

like kijalk properly.
like they had a real body.

Nganduka kudbinminy? Yungkudnirran Jamarldinki, eh?
What did you do then? You went back to Cape Don, didn't you?

Yungkudnakaniny barakbarda, kurrubularrung, yungkudnirran Jamarldinki, kurrumbuldarukun.
You went there, and when you were finished, you went back to Cape Don and then he [Johnson] left.

DM: Jadnirran Jamarldinki, ba kabala yardirran Dawin kayirrk.
We went back to Jamarldinki, and the boat went back to Darwin.

[…]

AB: Nganduka ba jumung yumbarrbarr rayang?
Where did he see the *yumbarrbarr*?

[…]

KM: Rayang ba yumbarrbarr baraka Madirrala.
He saw the *yumbarrbarr* at Madirrala.

Baraka jambang aring raharrandung.
He was leaning against a tamarind tree.

DM: Jarrurakany wuka barangayirrak.
We went off looking for whatsitsname.[17]

KM: Raharrandung baka jambang.
He was leaning on that tamarind.

DM: Madirrala ba rayang barakbarda.
Madirrala. That's where he saw it.

CM: Madirrala, oh yeah.

DM: Walmurja ba jumung yumbarrbarr. Nanimiyardmanyi ngarrumbanawunbuni.
The *yumbarrbarr* lived in the monsoon vine forest there. If he had wanted to, he could have killed us.

[…]

DM: Iyi ngadnakandung kubuny.
Yes, we went by canoe.

AB: Old Buckley [Darrarndarra].

DM: And nother one, my brother, bin pass away Darwin.
And also my brother [Johnny Williams], who died in Darwin.

CM: Ruka ajaldi Budawin.
He's buried in Darwin.

DM: Iyi, ajaldi Budawin.
Yes, he's buried in Darwin.

DM: That Balanda from Jamarldinki ijanakaniny kubuny right up there.
That Balanda came with us by canoe [to various locations].

Yardirran Jamarldinki,
Then he came back to Cape Don,

---

17 'Whatsitsname' possibly refers to 'crocodile', as in DM's telling of the Madirrala episode, he and his father went hunting crocodiles, leaving Johnson by himself (see Interview Extract I).

and he start from Jamarldinki to there wardyad, Kunbarlanya.
and starting out from Cape Don, he went to the stone country, and then Gunbalanya [formerly Oenpelli].

CM: *First awaran kani.*
First, he came this way.

That one now, Knocker Bay.
That place we were talking about, Knocker Bay.

And baning there, buwularrung they bin go back Jamarldinki.
And he stayed there. When they finished there, they went back to Cape Don.

He bin long Kajaji artbung.
He also went to Kajaji.

AB: Robert Cunningham country.[18]

CM: *Yawaran barakbarda, alright yardirran kani Jamarldinki, before yabiny move yawaran.*
He went to those places, then came back to Cape Don before setting off.

He bin walk kani Inybarlmun.
He walked this way, to Inybarlmun.[19]

One night there, kuburr Mangulhan.
Spent one night there, the next day Mangulhan.

Only one day.

How that Balanda? Mightbe scientist properly.
How did that Balanda do that? He must have been a real scientist.

Mm.

[…]

CM: *Not bajubaju, but all in white, eh.*
Not just his shirt, he was dressed all in pale-coloured clothes.

DM: Tall!

---

18 The senior traditional owner (now deceased) of the Akarlda clan estate, the largest estate on Cobourg.
19 'This' is used deictically here—that is, towards where CM was located at the time of the recording.

CM: But yawarang bush, when he bin come out from bush ardirrang, clean!
But after being in the bush, he would come out as clean as when he started!

DM: He was in the bush.

CM: No dirty.
Not dirty.

CM: Like 'Ari Yurrngud', eh.
Like Jesus, eh.

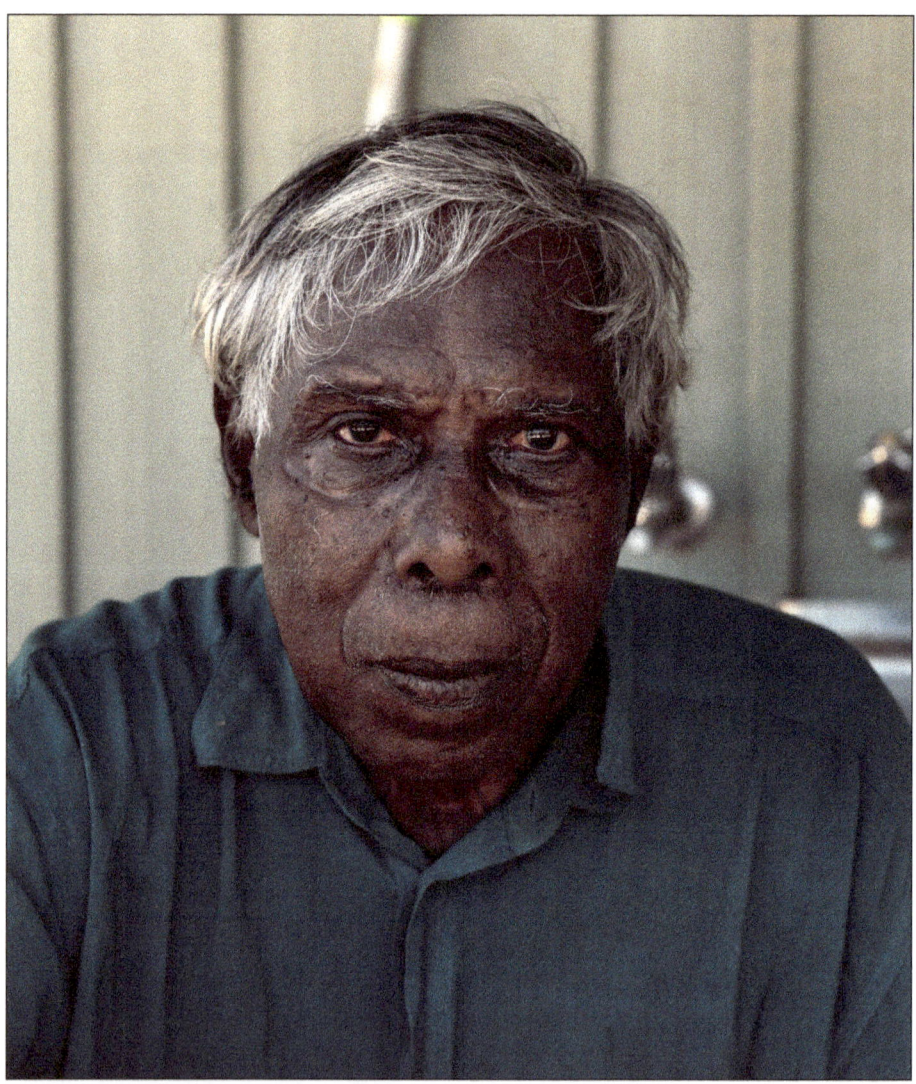

Figure 16.4 Archie Brown, 2009

Photograph by Adis Hondo

Johnson's Solo Walk to Oenpelli

On completion of Johnson's stay at Cape Don, his next action was perhaps, by this stage, no longer surprising to the locals. In Johnson's own words: 'On 8 October, I left Cape Don and walked overland to join the main party at Oenpelli…This twelve-day trip provided an intimate view of the entire length of the Cobourg Peninsula, with its remarkable fauna of large introduced mammals.'[20]

As far as we know, Johnson never wrote a detailed account of the trip, and our knowledge of it from the Balanda viewpoint is therefore sketchy. All we know at this stage is that Johnson made the trip alone, shooting game along the way, and that his passage was aided by the existence of a vehicle track for a large part of the journey. The Indigenous account, however, is far from lacking in detail. In this account, Johnson makes the trip of more than 200 km in an amazing two days, spending the first night at a sawmill settlement in the area known as Inybarlmun, on the neck of the Cobourg Peninsula, before heading south to the escarpment or 'stone country' north of Gunbalanya. On arriving there, he visits a dangerous ancestral site called Dilkbany. Here he captures the spirit of Marrarna, a man of the Alarrju clan, whose remains had been deposited there in the country of his paternal ancestors some years earlier.[21] From Dilkbany, Johnson takes Marrarna's remains first to Gunbalanya, where he joins the main party of the Expedition, though not informing them of Marrarna's capture, then via Darwin back to the United States, where Marrarna is resurrected as a strong young man. Johnson is said to have made a fortune as a result.

These extraordinary events went unwitnessed. Rather, knowledge of them is inferred on the basis of a letter and accompanying photograph that arrived in the settlement of Minjilang on Croker Island many years later, addressed to Marrarna's brother's daughter, Ada Brown. Ada reportedly burst out crying when she saw the photograph, recognising it as an image of Marrarna as a young man. The source of the letter, its actual contents and the date it arrived are not known at this stage. The photograph no longer exists. It is said to have been buried with Ada Brown when she died.

Encouraged no doubt by Johnson's established reputation as a 'clever man', the story of Johnson's solo trek to Gunbalanya, including the unusual events which happened along the way, and the ensuing resurrection event in the United States, has evolved as an explanation of the mysterious letter and photograph that arrived at Minjilang many years later. In the following interview extract, Archie Brown, the son of Ada, tells his version of the story.

---

20   Johnson, 'Mammals of the Arnhem Land Expedition', p. 429.
21   Marrarna's subsection name was *Nangila*. His semi-matrimoiety affiliation was *Yarriyarnkurrk*, specifically the *Kujurn* ('white clay') matrilineage, and his *nguya* 'patrilineal clan affiliation' was Alarrju. Hoeng, S. B. 2009, Northwestern Arnhem Land genealogical database, Unpublished ms.

Interview Extract III[22]

Abalduwunduwunma jumung ngabi babam. Old man.
I'm going to talk about my grandfather.[23] Old man.

Badbawarda. Burrang. Abalduwunduwunma ba jumung yawaran…
The other one. The elder [of the two brothers]. I'm going to talk about when he went…

ajikbiny, ajikbiny from Jamarldinki. Ba Balanda.
he set off from Cape Don. The Balanda.

Ngarri jadbaning Jamarldinki. Kirrk.
We were living at Cape Don. All of us.

Ajikbiny burdan Jamarldinki. Awaran warrin.
He set off from Cape Don. Overland.

Awaran warrin, balkbany…Inybarlmun.
He walked overland and came out at…Inybarlmun.[24]

Anadbung. Minarri.
He came across [people living] there. Minarri, actually.[25]

Anadbung. Sawmill aring barakbarda.
He found them. There was a sawmill there.

Mana wurnbarran barakbarda. Dirran kuburr,
He might have spent the night there. Next morning,

yajikbiny barakbarda, lda Mangulhan yabulakuny.
he set off from there, and headed down to Mangulhan.[26]

Mangulhan, barda yawurtiny yarimany alan ba jumung yawara alan
Mangulhan. He would have taken the road.[27]

---

22 dvR_060726_T1, Begin Time: 00:12:53.060, End Time: 00:17:44.310, (DoBeS Archive), Recorded at Wanjurrk, Mountnorris Bay, 26 July 2006, Narrator: Archie Brown.
23 *Babam* is a reciprocal kin term indicating a particular type of grandkin. The term refers: 1) to one's mother's father and his siblings, of both sexes; and 2) in the case of a man, to his daughter's children, and in the case of a woman, to her brother's daughter's children. In this case, the narrator is referring to his mother's father's brother—that is, Marrarna.
24 Inybarlmun was the site of a timber mill established by Reuben Cooper. Cooper died in 1942, and, at the time of Johnson's walk, the mill was run by the Ah-mat brothers. This was also a major base for Indigenous people of the region, so the news of Johnson's 'overnight' stay there would have been transmitted readily.
25 Minarri was the precise location of the timber mill in the Inybarlmun area.
26 Mangulhan is the name for a region within the estate of the Alarrju clan, to which AB's grandfather, Marrarna, belonged.
27 Bray records that Johnson had told him there had been 'an old motor track to follow most of the way'. J. E. Bray, 1948, Private Journal of John E. Bray, collection of Andrew Bray, Canberra.

Buwa alan. Wularrud. Wara mangawala.
There was a road there in the old days. It went right down there.

Rimany alan yawurtiny,
He took that road and headed inland.

Yawurtiny jumung Dilkbany. Yawurtiny Dilkbany, rayang baraka...
He went up to Dilkbany, and he saw that...[28]

Rayang wuka wardyad. Ngabi babam.
He [Johnson] saw him [Marrarna] among the rocks. My grandfather.

Darrkal. Darrkal ba jumung Dilkbany wardyad.
There was an opening. An opening in the rocks there at Dilkbany.

Rayang lda aring. Maju rayang lda yabarrkbungkuny yawurlhany.
He saw him standing there. When [Marrarna] saw him, he [Marrarna] must have taken off inside.

Yarakan wardyad. Rakan wardyad, ardirran arimalkbany.
So he [Johnson] threw a rock. By throwing that rock, he managed to bring that old man back out again.[29]

Abalkbany. Abalkbany barda rimany rildariny burruburrukang.
He came out. [Johnson] grabbed him and put him in a small bag.

Rildariny burruburrukang barda ijbanakandung.
He put him in that bag and the two of them left.

Ijbanakandung yarimandung.
He carried him off.

Warlmun janad, barakbarda. Warlmun, maju warlmun, ijalkud ba kijalk warrkbi janad.
It was his spirit that he took. It seemed like a spirit, but it must have been the actual body itself.[30]

Ijbanakandung. Yarildariny ijbanakandung. Kunbarlanya.
They headed off. He put him in the bag and they headed for Gunbalanya [Oenpelli].

Marrakarrak baning Kunbarlanya.

---

28 Dilkbany is the location of an *iyarliyarl*, a dangerous ancestral site. Transgressions committed at this place are believed to result in the release and spread of fatal disease.
29 The act of throwing a rock, when performed by a *marrkijbu* 'clever man', is commonly recognised as a method of exerting power over someone or something.
30 The narrator is going to some trouble to specify the state of his grandfather, presumably in order that it 'makes sense' in the context of his resurrection in the United States.

His son lived at Gunbalanya [Oenpelli].

Kani ngaldahardama ba jumung kani janad aju marrakarrak.
His son who is buried here where I'm talking now.[31]

Mana Kunbarlanya baning.
I think he lived at Gunbalanya [Oenpelli] then.

Aa...iyi. Kunbarlanya baning.
Ah...yes. He lived at Gunbalanya [Oenpelli].

But karlu rujiny. Yawaran. Ba Balanda.
But he didn't show him. He just left. The Balanda.

Karlu abiny wamung. Jamin janad wajuk.
He didn't tell the others [that is, his colleagues] either. He kept it to himself.

Jumung anakandung rimandung.
He was carrying it with him.

Yabingkung Budawin yawaran wuka Merika jumung burrang kunak ijalkud.
Back in Darwin, he took a plane to the United States, to a major city.

Lda rimalkbany. Bartuwa.
Then he took him out. OK.

Barakbarda ba bidbarran ba Balanda, jumung rimany,
That white man, that Balanda, the one who took [my grandfather],

barda kurljakbiny. Ringuldiny kalkirrirr burrang.
became rich. He made lots of money.

Abukung ba jumung mana baraka boss one, jumung yarildangakan wuka.
His bosses gave it to him, the ones who had sent him here.

Bartuwa. Rimalkbany rildakbirran.
OK. He opened the bag and took him out.

Rildakbirran, bumany...pija murrkud.
He took him out, and they took...lots of photos.

Well janad ruka babam imalda there abiny change.
At that point, my grandfather had already undergone a change.

---

31 The text was recorded at Wanjurrk, in Mountnorris Bay, where Namadbara is buried. Namadbara was the son of Marrarna's brother Jumu, and the kin term *marrakarrak* refers to him in this case.

Dirdan balkbany jumung kirrimul warrkbi kijalk.
He'd assumed the body of a living man.

Karlu artbung ba jumung kirrimul adbunudba, ayaldi nganduka ngamin.
He no longer resembled the bundle of human remains, the way we put them there.

Ba rtuwa balkbany kijalk aring. Rildakburliwan. Anildakburliwan.
He stood there as a living person. He spoke to [Johnson]. He spoke to all of them.

'Ngabi.'
'It's me.'

'Ngabi. Ngabi yarrumbilimany.'
'It's me. I'm the one you captured.'

'Ngabi yanbilimany.'
'You took me.'

Kijbungkun janad jirrak.
He identified himself.

'Ngabi Marrarna.'
'I'm Marrarna.'

'Ngabi ngangurnaj barakbarda.'
'That's my name.'

'Ngabi ayunmardyarrwuny…'
'My sons' and daughters' names are…'

'Ilarri; Nawarlaj; Mayabany.'
'Ilarri; Nawarlaj; Mayabany.'

Ringijbungkung barakbarda aju. Ruka jumung aju Wilyi kani.
He identified this man buried here. The one buried here at Wilyi [a reference to Namadbara (Paddy Compass)].

Barakbarda…lda wurduwajba, jumung janad aniwujban.
Him…along with his sisters.

'Ngabi nganduwurakbung.'
'My elder brother,' [he said].

'Ngabi aburakbung.'

'My younger brother.'[32]

'Jumu aniwujban. Wanadjanad.'
'Jumu fathered those two.'[33]

Barakbarda.
That's what he told them.

From there, bartuwa, barda ardirran arildangakan ngarrung pija.
After that, he sent that photograph back to us.

Bumany pija, riwularrung kirrk ringijbungkung.
They took photos, and when they'd finished he mentioned [his daughter's] name.

Ringijbungkung ngabi nganmingkang aju Minjilang.
He spoke the name of my mother, who is buried at Minjilang.

'Yangkabaldangan jumung pija barda janad.'
'You must send this picture to her.'

'Banangaman.'
'She can keep it.'

Ringijbungkung.
He spoke her name.

Ba ngabi ngandumany. Ringijbungkung.
My mother. He spoke her name.

Ardirran arildangakan jumung Balanda barda ngarrabilimany ba pija.
That Balanda sent the picture back [to Minjilang] and we got it.

Ardirran barlkbarrakan wuka youngfella.
That old man had resumed the body of a young man.

---

32 The narrator corrects himself here. Marrarna, as stated elsewhere in the text, was the elder of two brothers.
33 Jumu was Marrarna's younger brother. Jumu's children were Namadbara and the narrator's mother, Ada Brown.

Bartuwa, Ngarrabilimang that pija, kayang barda marrakarrak wiyu, bardalkany.
OK. We received that photo, and when she saw her own 'father', she burst out crying.

Barda ngarrarakinngurn…
So we asked her…

Barda ngarrarakinngurn ngabilijanad.
So we asked her, me and him [my younger brother].

Ngabi lda ruka aju Minjilang.
Me and the one now buried at Minjilang [my brother].

'Malany ba pija angbardalkany?'
'Why did you start crying when you saw the picture?'

'Ya, babam,' abiny.
'It's your grandfather,' she said.

'Ay, nga.'
'Ah, I see.'

Barda arrumbujiny.
Then she showed us.

'Nuwurri babam badbawarda burrang, riki abiny.'
'This is your other grandfather, the eldest one.'

'Jamin aniwujban wanad.'
'The father of [my cousins].'

'Ngarrumbayang wardad mayakbu.'
'My father and their father were brothers.'[34]

'Ngarrumbayang wardad aniwujban badbawarda babam ngarrimung ngadnduwujban ngabi lda…'
'His children have the same paternal grandfather as me and…'

'yaja ba…'
'your uncle [Namadbara]…'

---

34 The narrator's mother uses the term *wardad…mayakbu* 'one patriline', referring to the relation between herself, and her cousins, whose father had the same father as her own father.

'baning Kunbarlanya.' Kunbarlanya baning durdu. Wukany.
'who lives at Gunbalanya [Oenpelli].' He was still living at Gunbalanya [Oenpelli] at that time.

Ba ruka Wilyi aju.
This one who's buried here at Wilyi.

Bartuwa.
OK.

Kamandung ba pija.
She used to have that photo.

Mightbe jarrajurrkbang ngalaj pija yajaldi.
Perhaps we buried her together with that photo.

Baraka rimardyarrwuny.
That was her 'father'.

Ya.
Yes.

Bartuwa. That's the end of the story.
OK. That's the end of the story.

Conclusion

The story of the American Clever Man allows us a rare insight into how the Indigenous people of North-West Arnhem Land tried to make sense of the activities of an alien culture in their midst, as instantiated by the Arnhem Land Expedition, exposing the fact that observation and analysis during the course of the Expedition were inevitably reciprocal in nature, the result of the interaction of two distinct culturally reinforced world views.

Beyond this, the story demonstrates the nature of communication across a cultural divide. The sections of the Indigenous account involving Marrarna's capture and subsequent resurrection remind us that the act of interpretation is necessarily constrained by the culturally specific contextual knowledge brought to the task by those doing the interpreting, and that the details of the interpretation often tell us as much about the interpret*ers* as about the interpret*ed*, while at the same time expressing much about relations between the two. In the same way, non-Indigenous people have historically interpreted complex areas of Indigenous culture by situating them, inevitably, in a cultural context which was familiar to them. Many early British observers of Indigenous social organisation in the Cobourg region, for example, were convinced of the existence of a hierarchical caste system there, along the lines of that already known to exist in Hindu culture.[35] Such an interpretation might be explained by the fact that both the actual Hindu caste system and the imaginary Arnhem Land version resonated strongly with the class stratification of British society, which formed the cultural milieu of the observers and thus constrained their observations.

The story of the American Clever Man should not be read as a falsifiable account of historical events. Rather, it presents us with an example of how the art of storytelling can be used to communicate across a cultural gap, offering perceptive insights into the nature of relations between mainstream and Indigenous cultures in Australia. To take one example only, the fact that the Johnson character profits enormously and gains prestige in his own culture by capturing the spirit of an Indigenous person provides a powerful metaphor for what has been termed the 'Aboriginal industry' in Australia, whereby non-Indigenous people have historically been the main beneficiaries of funding for projects involving the Indigenous population, via their role in administration, evaluation, coordination, and so on.

Johnson is perhaps unfortunate in being characterised not only as a 'grave-robber', but as one who amasses great wealth on returning home with his 'prize', as there is no evidence that he personally exhumed or removed any human remains during his time in Arnhem Land, his focus being the collection of small mammals.

While the actions of Johnson's character in the story in removing human remains might not constitute an accurate description of events, they are, however, far from wild fantasies whose origin is only to be guessed at. Rather, they reflect one of the many activities undertaken by the Arnhem Land Expedition while based at Oenpelli, conducted chiefly by the physical anthropologist Frank Setzler, who removed skeletal material from the area around Oenpelli, placed it in boxes, and sent it ultimately to the Smithsonian Institution. Not until 2010 were the last of these human remains repatriated to descendant communities.

One theme of the story—perhaps the overriding one—is the denial of the anonymity of these remains, facilitated via Marrarna's resurrection. Marrarna's first act when he comes to life in America is to identify himself. 'It's me,' he tells his captors. 'My name is Marrarna.' His next act is to identify his family back home. In a sense, one could say that Marrarna's character in the story acts as 'spokesperson' for all of the 'anonymous' human remains now stored in

---

35 See, for example, Earl, G. W. 1853, *The Native Races of the Indian Archipelago: Papuans*, Hippolyte Bailliere, London, pp. 216–17.

museums around the world, and their 'anonymous' descendants who are now involved in attempts to repatriate the bones of their ancestors—sometimes in the face of opposition from the institutions who now claim ownership of them.

The story of the American Clever Man represents an unplanned but invaluable legacy of the 1948 American–Australian Scientific Expedition to Arnhem Land. It holds up a mirror for those who participated then, as well as for those who follow in their footsteps today.

17. Missing the Revolution! Negotiating disclosure on the pre-Macassans (Bayini) in North-East Arnhem Land

Ian S. McIntosh

By their own admission, members of Charles Mountford's 1948 American–Australian Scientific Expedition to Arnhem Land were motivated by a search for the primitive. It is no surprise, then, that the published records show a singular lack of awareness of the sorts of debate raging within Aboriginal circles at that time. For example, so-called missionised Yolngu (as the Aboriginal people of North-East Arnhem Land are known) were engaged in a major discussion about whether Christianity was an expression of the Dreaming and thus culturally mandated or whether God gave Yolngu the Dreaming as some missionaries insisted.

While the Expedition's point of entry into Aboriginal Australia was through the Christian missions, their focus was salvage anthropology, so it is not clear whether Expedition leader, Charles Mountford, was aware of or interested in this discourse taking place at the highest levels in Yolngu society.

In this chapter, I examine what was lost and what was gained by taking such a tack and not addressing the very real issues at play in Yolngu lives. To highlight this disconnect, I examine Yolngu disclosure relating to ethnographic material 'hunted and gathered' by Expedition members in North-East Arnhem Land pertaining to a curious, then-unidentified (and supposed) group of Asian seafarers known as the Bayini (or Baiini): the pre-Macassans. I then review the changing nature of this disclosure over time for the light it throws on the changing nature of relations between Yolngu and Balanda (non-Aborigines)—a subject that was not considered an Expedition research priority.

In the literature of North-East Arnhem Land, the identity of pre-Macassans as a historical phenomenon has always been something of a conundrum.[1] In Yolngu circles, while the mystery was also very real, the Bayini occupied centre stage in Yolngu cosmology. All things within the Yolngu realm can be explained by reference to the Dreaming, but to which deity did the stories of these foreign

---

1 McIntosh, I. S. 1995, 'Who are the Bayini?', *The Beagle: Records of the Museums and Art Galleries of the Northern Territory*, vol. 12, pp. 193–208.

visitors belong? Despite exhaustive anthropological research in North-East Arnhem Land, there was no reference to any overarching Dreaming figure or deity that spoke to the existence of non-Aborigines in the Yolngu world. Information regarding a 'Dreaming Macassan' was concealed by Yolngu for reasons that will become clear throughout this paper.

All visitors to Arnhem Land since the 'beginning of time'—including random and unplanned Indonesian visitors, Portuguese and Dutch explorers, trepanging Macassans, Japanese pearlers and Europeans (of all descriptions)—were explainable, in part, through the prism of Bayini narratives and the 'Dreaming Macassan'. But these narratives—known in the literature only in fragments through the extended captions associated with Yolngu drawings collected by Charles Mountford—provided only a glimpse into what is a very complex subject. And yet, even with the little information that was openly shared by Yolngu, it was apparent that the Bayini narratives were concerned—at a fundamental level—with Yolngu lives and Yolngu futures in a world that was increasingly being dominated by outsiders. Given the increased exposure of Yolngu to outsiders—including missionaries, anthropologists, and military personnel (during World War II)—a decision was made by Yolngu elders to send the Bayini narratives (and the 'Dreaming Macassan') further 'inside' into the non-accessible realm of the sacred and to restrict access to interpretations that might be construed as privileging the place of whites or other outsiders on Yolngu land. After all, the ancestors of the Yolngu, the Bayini, were white and all-powerful! How easy would it have been for the present-day non-Aborigines to assert some mythical connection to the land and further usurp Yolngu authority—as certainly happened in other parts of Australia in the colonial era when non-Aborigines perpetuated the notion that they, as whites, were the Aboriginal deceased come back to life to reclaim their rightful heritage. So this process of reinterpretation of a public story as a 'hidden transcript' was a priority in the mission setting where power lay not in traditional hands but in those of the select few missionaries and their appointed Aboriginal interlocutors.

For the purposes of public or 'outside' discussion with their interrogators, Yolngu would, post 1948, describe the Bayini as the predecessors of Macassans. They were indeed a historical group, Yolngu said, but they also possessed extraordinary supernatural powers. And yet their provenance and activities were shrouded in secrecy.

I will argue that an understanding of the changes taking place in Yolngu lives is understandable only through the prism of the Bayini and that the significance of the Bayini paintings and myths is not possible without reference to the aforementioned 'hidden transcript' or the broader struggle of Yolngu for their rights to the land and sea, and their right to practise the religion of their choice in a manner of their choosing. By not engaging with mission Yolngu on their efforts to integrate the traditional (including Islamic-inspired beliefs)² and the modern, and ending the great disparity in wealth between black and white, the Expedition missed a chance to document what was a remarkably dynamic period of Yolngu-directed change in the mid twentieth century. It might be argued that the team members were not in any one location long enough to elicit detailed information on the Bayini, but I would counter with the assertion that if Yolngu Christianity had been taken seriously, and the people treated with the respect and dignity that were owed them as landowners, the mystery of the Bayini would not have been a mystery at all. There would not have been any reason to conceal these narratives from the Expedition members or those researchers who came in their wake.

Figure 17.1 Munggurrawuy Yunupingu, *Bayini men and women of Port Bradshaw*. Painting collected by Charles Mountford and donated to the Art Gallery of New South Wales by the Commonwealth of Australia in 1956. Natural pigments on paper, 45.5 x 58.5 cm, 1948

Artist unknown. By permission of the Art Gallery of New South Wales. Accession No. 9270. © Estate of Munggurrawuy Yunupingu, courtesy of Buku-Larrnggay Mulka Centre. Photograph: Brenton Mcgeachie.

---

2 McIntosh, I. S. 1996, 'Islam and Australia's Aborigines? A perspective from north-east Arnhem Land', *Journal of Religious History*, vol. 20, no. 1, pp. 53–77.

The Shock of Disclosure

If the 1948 American–Australian Scientific Expedition to Arnhem Land appears today as a mere footnote in the history of northern Australia, it is a footnote that nonetheless still packs a punch in certain Yolngu contexts.[3] Perhaps the most significant legacy of the Expedition is the revolution that Ronald Berndt described in his groundbreaking monograph, *An Adjustment Movement in Arnhem Land* (1962).[4] A radical transformation was taking place in Yolngu lives from Milingimbi to Yirrkala and it was sparked, according to my close friend and confidant, the Yolngu leader David Burrumarra, by the shock that followed the disclosure on film of certain sacred works of Yolngu art collected by Expedition members. Berndt quotes Burrumarra, one of the instigators of the 1957 movement, about the chain of causation:

> They [Expedition members] took pictures of our sacred ceremonies and *raŋga* [ceremonial objects], and we got excited. Why do they do this? We understood when Warner, Thomson and the Berndts were here. But why do they come again and again to study us? They take photographs of sacred things and show them to all the people throughout Australia and other places…We got a shock. We're not supposed to show these *mareiin*, these *raŋga* to just anybody…All this made us think…Then we saw a film at the Elcho church. It was from the American-Australian Expedition, and it showed the sacred ceremonies and emblems. And everybody saw it…We've got no power to hide (these *raŋga*): they are taking away our possessions. Are we to lose all this? Our most precious possessions—our *raŋga*! We have nothing else: this is really our only wealth.[5]

Yolngu at the Elcho Island (Galiwin'ku) mission, in particular, had been searching for a way of satisfactorily adjusting or bringing together the very best of Aboriginal and Western ways of living without compromising the integrity of their own society and culture.[6] According to Burrumarra, as reported by Berndt, there was a strong sense that people were lost between two worlds, and things came to a head in the wake of the visits of the American–Australian Scientific Expedition to the Yolngu communities of Yirrkala and Milingimbi. The adjustment movement involved Yolngu taking the unprecedented step of publicly revealing their sacred objects, creating a memorial to a way of life that

---

3   Mountford, C. P. (ed.) 1956, *Records of the American–Australian Scientific Expedition to Arnhem Land. Volume 1: Art, myth and symbolism*, Melbourne University Press, Carlton, Vic.
4   Berndt, R. M. 1962, *An Adjustment Movement in Arnhem Land*, Mouton, Paris.
5   Ibid., (see Note vi), p. 40.
6   Burrumarra's nephew Wandjuk Marika from Yirrkala worked closely with Mountford in 1948 and was one of a number of Yolngu leaders from other Christian missions who opposed the adjustment movement and the very idea of the public revelation of sacred paraphernalia.

was changing forever. Yolngu would now follow two laws: Aboriginal and non-Aboriginal. They would be Christian in a Yolngu world and Yolngu in a Christian world, with each informing the other in an arrangement that Burrumarra would call 'membership and remembership'. While investigators such as Mountford were busily documenting a moiety and clan-based identity for Yolngu artists, a new pan-Yolngu Christian social order was being constructed by Yolngu themselves—one that was inclusive of selected non-Aborigines who were adopted into their kinship system.[7]

The Arnhem Land Expedition was not in itself the cause of this revolution, but the public presentation of those sacred images on film at Elcho Island certainly had an impact. Members of the Expedition, I imagine, would have viewed this as an entirely unanticipated consequence of their scholarly activity. Anthropologically speaking, they were on a 'search and rescue' operation and had no interest in the theological or cosmological ruminations of 'mission boys' such as Burrumarra or his nephew Wandjuk Marika (who provided paintings to the Expedition at Yirrkala) or the status of the Yolngu embrace of Christianity.

But team leader, Charles Mountford, did have a strong interest in the history and legacy of Yolngu contact with Macassans. These Muslim traders from the entrepot of Macassar on the island of Sulawesi in eastern Indonesia had been visiting northern Australia and interacting with Yolngu from at least 1780. They were in search of bêche-de-mer or trepang in the shallow Arafura Sea inter-tidal zone, in what is described as Australia's first international trade.[8] The legacy of this extended contact was substantial.[9] A considerable number of Yolngu rituals feature references to the artefacts of trade such as boats, anchors and flags, life in South-East Asian seaports, and the notion of a high god called 'Allah' (or Walitha'walitha). Pioneering anthropologist Lloyd Warner documented some of these rituals during fieldwork in North-East Arnhem Land in the late 1920s.[10] By the 1940s, however, Yolngu were guarded in their responses to Mountford's questioning on such topics, especially Islam, as evidenced in the largely cryptic information on the mysterious group of Islamic traders who had supposedly preceded the Macassan trepangers. These visitors, called the Bayini, were unknown to the literature prior to the 1940s.

---

7   McIntosh, I. S. 2000, *Aboriginal Reconciliation and the Dreaming, Warramiri Yolngu and the Quest for Equality*, Cultural Survival Series on Ethnicity and Change, Allyn and Bacon, Boston.
8   Macknight, C. C. 1976, *The Voyage to Marege': Macassan trepangers in northern Australia*, Melbourne University Press, Carlton, Vic.
9   Macknight, C. C. 2008, 'Harvesting the memory: open beaches in Makassar and Arnhem Land', in P. Veth, P. Sutton and M. Neale (eds), *Strangers on the Shore: Early coastal contacts in Australia*, National Museum of Australia, Canberra, p. 137; McIntosh, I. S. 2008, 'Pre-Macassans at Dholtji?: exploring one of north-east Arnhem Land's great conundrums', in Veth et al., *Strangers on the Shore*, pp. 165–80.
10 Warner, W. L. 1958, *A Black Civilization: A social study of an Australian tribe*, Harper and Row, New York.

There was a fundamental difference in the stories of these pre-Macassans or Bayini and the Macassan trepangers. The former had a sacred or 'hidden' dimension that spoke to the very essence of what it meant to be Yolngu in the world that now included others. The latter belonged to a profane dimension. These were the stories of a long history of trade and interaction of both a positive and a negative nature.

The concealment of the stories of the Bayini beyond fleeting references to them building boats, making pottery, growing rice, or weaving on their looms was quite thorough. But then there are those even more obscure references to Bayini 'flying fox' people creating sacred waterholes, or the story of the birth of the first light-skinned baby—obviously the result of a liaison between a Yolngu woman and an Indonesian man. These stories speak to an entirely different level of significance.

In the 1940s, it was not a simple matter of the Yolngu strategically forgetting anachronistic traditions or those in conflict with Christianity (or Islam) in order to facilitate the growth of the Christian mission, though this was certainly encouraged, as I have said elsewhere.[11] The sacred narratives of the Bayini—described by Burrumarra as his 'backbone'—speak to Yolngu feelings of self-worth and dignity at a time when their material poverty was most pronounced and when missionaries promoted guilt and shame as tools for Christian conversion. In the terminology of the American anthropologist and subaltern studies specialist James C. Scott, a 'hidden transcript' was concealed from the prying eyes of anthropologists and others determined to unlock every secret that Yolngu possessed, including—especially—those secrets that spoke of the increasingly problematic place of uninvited whites in a Yolngu world.[12]

Scott argued that all subaltern or subordinate peoples resist domination in similar ways, never consenting to their dominance. He uses the term 'public transcript' to describe interactions between the oppressor and the oppressed and 'hidden transcript' for the critique of power that goes on offstage and out of sight of power holders. In this chapter, rather than uncovering what must remain hidden, I review what lies beneath the surface of those public interactions—such as when Mountford and his team were in search of ethnographic minutiae, in which the oppressed appear to accept their domination and happily oblige the whims of the oppressor.

I spent a number of years in Arnhem Land living and working in close cooperation with Berndt's informant the late David Burrumarra MBE of Elcho Island (1917–94), and we spoke in considerable detail about the Yolngu response to the Expedition presence, the associated films, and the adjustment

---

11 McIntosh, *Aboriginal Reconciliation and the Dreaming, Warramiri Yolngu and the Quest for Equality*.
12 Scott, J. C. 1990, *Domination and the Arts of Resistance. Hidden transcripts*, Yale University Press, New Haven, Conn.

movement it helped to engender. While I was not privy to the details of the 'hidden transcript', Burrumarra was convinced that I understood its nature and purpose. It was at the very heart of our extended conversations on the history of black–white relations in Arnhem Land and indeed Australia.

Figure 17.2 David Burrumarra of Elcho Island, 2009

Drawing by Julia Blackburn

A short anecdote brings his reasoning to light. On one occasion, Burrumarra and I were witnessing the final stage of the Kunapipi ritual—that stage when the initiates present themselves to the community after a protracted absence journeying 'inside the belly of the snake' to reassure family members that they are still in the land of the living. It was dawn and we were both painted with red ochre—symbolic of the menstrual blood of the ancestral sisters 'swallowed' by the rainbow serpent. I recall asking Burrumarra various questions about the antiquity of the ritual—it looked so foreign and ancient—and he was disappointed that I would talk in such terms. This ritual was not about the past, he said. Didn't I have the red paint on me? The serpent was not separate from the collected peoples assembled on that cleared sandy performance space. I was a part of this ritual. It was not just the dancers. There was no category of outside observer!

In the same way, Burrumarra showed great interest in my attempts to decipher the deeper significance of the Bayini narratives. Volume after volume of field notes that I collected during our conversations (and later as part of my doctoral studies in anthropology) on every aspect of this legacy in song, dance, sites, personal names, totemic emblems, artefacts, and occupations, represent merely an outer layer, Burrumarra said. If I really wanted to comprehend the Bayini, Burrumarra added, 'Look at the way I act'. His lifelong battles to secure a better life for Yolngu, the endless fight in support of sea and land rights, are all central to an understanding of the Bayini.[13] The meaning of the stories and of the 'hidden transcript' was embodied in the very nature of these daily unequal public transactions between Yolngu and outsiders.

The History of Disclosure

Towards the end of his life, Burrumarra revealed much about the way in which Bayini narratives were withheld, not only from anthropologists and historians but also from younger members of the Yolngu community.[14] On a number of occasions, he told me that the narratives were too sacred, too complex and for many years had helped to define the nature of cross-cultural interaction. A clean break from the past was required in the interests of building new, strong and vibrant Christian communities.[15]

But Burrumarra also revealed deeper reasons for nondisclosure: the power imbalance between black and white Australians, which is a central theme in the Bayini narratives.[16] As far back as the 1920s, Burrumarra's close relative Harry Makarrwola, who was the chief informant for Lloyd Warner, was struggling with what to disclose on this topic. While there is no mention of pre-Macassans or Bayini in Warner's published account,[17] there is a strong suggestion from his data that there existed in Yolngu discourse some overarching belief associated with the power and prestige of the Other—a power that rightfully belonged to the Yolngu. Specifically, the notion of a 'Dreaming Macassan' appears to provide the nucleus for Yolngu thoughts on the origin and purpose of non-Aborigines—in particular, Macassan trepangers and then, later, Japanese and Europeans. This Dreaming entity (which encapsulates all the Bayini narratives) is known as Birrinydji and narratives associated with him provide Yolngu with

---

13 McIntosh, 'Pre-Macassans at Dholtji?'.
14 McIntosh, I. S. 1994, *The Whale and the Cross: Conversations with David Burrumarra MBE*, Northern Territory Historical Society, Darwin.
15 And yet, those rituals associated with the Bayini would continue to be performed on a regular basis across the region, especially during funerals. McIntosh, I. S. 2004, 'Personal names and the negotiation of change: reconsidering Arnhem Land's adjustment movement', *Anthropological Forum*, vol. 14, no. 2, pp. 141–62.
16 McIntosh, *Aboriginal Reconciliation and the Dreaming, Warramiri Yolngu and the Quest for Equality*.
17 Warner, *A Black Civilization*.

an understanding of who these outsiders were and why they were on Yolngu land, and also answer key questions about their own place in the world. For example, why did Yolngu work for the Macassans, and not the other way around? What must have gone wrong at the beginning of time for the influence of these outsiders to be so pervasive?

In the 1940s and 1950s, however, researchers Charles Mountford and Ronald and Catherine Berndt would make no reference to the existence of the deity known as Birrinydji.[18] A significant change was taking place in the nature of Yolngu accounts, a shift in emphasis from a mythical perspective with respect to outside visitation to a focus on the perceived historical nature of both pre-Macassans (or the Bayini) and Macassans. The concept of the 'Bayini' was born at this point—the choice of words indicative of the presence of a 'hidden transcript'. *Bayini* is a word that means woman—a golden-skinned woman married to Birrinydji, the Dreaming Macassan. As Burrumarra once said to me, in his conversations with Balanda, he and his peers would emphasise the exploits of Bayini women, revealing only those accounts that were suitable for Yolngu women and anthropologists to hear. The exploits of Birrinydji and Bayini men were not historical in nature and therefore not negotiable in the mission environment.

Right up to the late 1980s, nothing substantial was added to the scholarship on the Bayini, despite the investigations of a considerable number of anthropologists. The Macassan trepanging past had been definitively recorded by historian Campbell Macknight, and, for many, his book *The Voyage to Marege'* (1976) brought closure to this avenue of inquiry, despite its lack of deeper investigation into Yolngu perspectives on the Macassan past. The Bayini, in Macknight's classic work, are dismissed simply as a reflection of Aboriginal experiences in South-East Asia, transposed onto Arnhem Land shores. Macknight says: 'The idea of things which properly belong overseas has been transferred to familiar places in order to integrate this knowledge into the spatially oriented framework of Aboriginal thought.'[19] Importantly, however, he also says that the Bayini stories are a 'most remarkable instance of the need to distinguish between the account of the past current in a society and the actual events of the past'.[20] Yes, but with little or no access to data on the pan-Yolngu significance of the Bayini, it was impossible for Macknight to reach a more substantial conclusion as to their significance. Even by his own admission, Macknight's field references to the Bayini (following his visits to some of the most important Bayini—and Birrinydji—sites along the

---

18 Berndt, R. M. and Berndt C. H. 1954, *Arnhem Land: Its history and its people*, F. W. Cheshire, Melbourne.
19 Macknight, *The Voyage to Marege'*, p. 92.
20 Ibid., p. 161.

coast) are obscure to the point of incomprehensibility. Burrumarra, for example, told Macknight (in the wake of the Apollo moon landing) that the Bayini came from the moon!

The very noticeable absence of anthropological references to the Bayini post Mountford is curious because even today the principal distinguishing feature of North-East Arnhem Land communities is the presence of artefacts connected with the Dreaming Macassan—most noticeably the ubiquitous flagpole and flag, and the mast complete with rigging stationed in the centre of communities—all of which signal the presence of Birrinydji and his 'replacements', a people whom Yolngu in the 1940s called, in their own cryptic fashion, the Bayini. As I have described previously, the Bayini are understood to have sung certain Yolngu lands into existence and then lain down on the sand to rest.[21] While Birrinydji is associated most closely with a number of clans including the Warramiri, Lamamirri and Dhalwangu, all Yolngu in North-East Arnhem Land are understood to claim descent from the Bayini either through their mothers or fathers.

Comparing Transactions

When artworks (and their associated commentaries) were presented to Mountford and other Expedition members in 1948, the Yolngu had no idea what would become of them. Trust was implied as the transaction was being conducted in a controlled setting: a Christian mission. But there was little or no consideration given to how Yolngu might feel about the reproduction of their works in books or on film and there was certainly a lack of sensitivity towards issues of ownership regarding items of cultural significance (see also Garde, this volume). Expedition anthropologists were a long way, for example, from the ideal of 'stranger and friend' championed by Hortense Powdermaker.[22] The concept of participant observation played little part in the Expedition's methodology. Just a year after the Mountford Expedition, Ronald and Catherine Berndt's collection of sacred Bayini sculptures was displayed in Sydney's David Jones department store to a bemused shopping public.[23]

According to the Art Gallery of New South Wales Curator, Jonathan Jones, Mountford's approach to collecting artwork and the related narratives was unorthodox. Mountford said of his method: '[I would] ask the men to make bark

---

21   McIntosh, 'Pre-Macassans at Dholtji?'.
22   Powdermaker, H. 1966, *Stranger and Friend: The way of an anthropologist*, W. W. Norton & Co., New York.
23   Gray, G. 2009, 'Cluttering up the department: Ronald Berndt and the distribution of the University of Sydney ethnographic collection', *Recollections: Journal of the National Museum of Australia*, vol. 2, no. 2.

paintings for me, seldom suggesting a subject. At the end of each day, the artists bought [sic] their work to my tent, related the associated myth, and explained the meanings of the designs.'[24]

Team member Frederick D. McCarthy, as reported in Jones, was openly critical of this approach, recalling how at

> dusk or thereabouts he [Mountford] got [the Aboriginal artists] together near his tent…and hammered the interpretation out of them, sometimes in a friendly way, at others [in a] bullying style…His data is [sic] not the product of spontaneous work on the part of the native but has been got from a short-term 'pounding' of the informants.[25]

We know that the Yolngu artists were paid for their work with tobacco, food and sometimes coins, in transactions reminiscent of those of missionaries, when the amount of sustenance granted or withheld was based on how dutifully the Yolngu had completed their assigned tasks that week.[26]

Given the material poverty of mission residents, cooperating with Mountford was undoubtedly an attractive idea. And while disclosure of certain Dreaming-related themes by Yolngu was thorough, Mountford's bullying on the subject of the Bayini resulted in a curious collection of images and an enigmatic text—a perplexing picture of the past that has inspired wild speculation on the part of scholars who would follow. Some would argue, for example, that the Bayini were Portuguese while others believed them to be members of Zheng He's voyage of discovery—suggestions that have no merit.

In the 1940s, Yolngu were willing to freely share images of the Bayini and Macassans with non-Aborigines but what was being released by Yolngu in the form of narratives was very restricted and a product of considerable community discussion and negotiation.

If we compare the Mountford transactions with similar ones occurring 40 years later in North-East Arnhem Land, the role of the community in determining the extent of disclosure and concealment is readily apparent.

In the mid-1980s, Yolngu on Elcho Island would welcome the visits of Ramangining art advisor and scholar Djon Mundine. With chequebook in hand, he would stand on top of the council office stairs in company with various Yolngu elders (and in front of a considerable crowd) as various art objects were presented to him for sale. In consultation with those gathered, he would make his decisions on whether to purchase the item and what level of compensation

---

24 Jones, J. n.d., *Mountford Gifts: Work from the American–Australian Scientific Expedition to Arnhem Land 1948*, Art Gallery of New South Wales, Sydney.
25 Ibid.
26 McIntosh, *The Whale and the Cross*.

would be offered. Were the pandanus mats and dilly bags of sufficient quality? Was the artwork suitable for public release and distribution? Every so often a sacred painting would be presented for sale and the decision to proceed (or not) was often in the hands of certain selected members of the assembled body of Yolngu.

Very occasionally a painting would appear that was inappropriate for general viewing or sale, and, on more than one occasion, on the orders of elders such as Burrumarra, it was buried in the sand at some undisclosed location or sent to the waterhole's murky depths—the artist publicly shamed.

One can only imagine, then, the sorts of discussions that were taking place in the camps at Yirrkala and Milingimbi during the visits of Expedition members in the 1940s. What could be shared with outsiders, and what would remain untold, and why? What new interpretations of old stories were required in order to negotiate the changing nature of their world in ways that promoted their interests as Yolngu?

The Context of Disclosure

One example of the challenge of disclosure for Yolngu was made evident by Burrumarra in the late 1980s when he was describing, in elaborate detail, the nature of the 'public transcript' (as opposed to the 'hidden transcript'). In the public transcript, the Macassans might have developed close relationships with Yolngu but they were still the Other. In these stories, we can still see the proof of this past, the physical traces of the once prominent Macassan trepang industry: tamarind trees, stone lines and broken pieces of pottery lining the shores of North-East Arnhem Land. In the 'hidden transcript', in contrast, the Bayini are not the Other. They are Yolngu but with a language that comes from a place far away to the north of Australia. In these stories there is no trepang because the Bayini were not trepangers. They were the bringers of the law to the Yolngu, the law that described the injustice that Yolngu felt at the hands of the Europeans and the Macassans who came before them.

According to Burrumarra, the public transcript also sends a very powerful message about the history of cross-cultural encounters. He described to me various waves of foreign visitation to Arnhem Land, emphasising the changing skin colour of groups over the vast passage of time. The earliest visitors were black and they lived as Yolngu, respecting Yolngu laws. Reciprocity was a feature of their relationship. These visitors were the ones, for example, who cared for the souls of the Yirritja moiety dead in a paradise believed to exist somewhere to the north-east of Arnhem Land in a place called Badu or Nalkuma—the subject referred to in many images and explanatory notes in Mountford's Expedition report.

Next in this historical narrative came the gold-coloured Bayini, who introduced new laws and technology to the Yolngu. Their impact was both profound and problematic. According to Burrumarra, they were deficient in passing on their advanced skills to Yolngu, leading to all manner of chaos and despair.[27]

Finally there were Macassan trepangers, Japanese pearlers and then Europeans. The visitors in each new wave were ever lighter in skin colour—an expression of the lessening interest in reciprocity and respect in their dealings with Yolngu.

The important thing to remember, said Burrumarra, was that Birrinydji (the Dreaming Macassan) had drawn forth all of these seafarers—black and white and everything in between—onto the Arnhem Land coast by the strength of his *marr* or desire for the Yolngu and their future. This entity introduced Yolngu, in varying stages, to a new world of material riches and opportunity, but also, ultimately, to the inequality and dispossession that Yolngu were experiencing in their daily lives.

The old adage 'speaking truth to power', or standing up for your rights in a very unequal battle, Scott says, always has a utopian ring to it because it is so rarely practised.[28] How could the Yolngu even share this story with the Mountford Expedition or others? Like the hidden transcript, it was essentially a critique of the failure of those non-Aborigines who held dominion over Yolngu lives to value their history, laws or traditions. So what we therefore find in the Expedition report is a very detailed account in bark and narrative of the first wave of visitation of those people who ultimately care for the Yolngu in the 'land of the dead', but very scant information on all the other waves of visitors, such as the Bayini and Macassans.

The Christian Dimension

One of the most significant constraints on disclosure by Yolngu in Mountford's day was whether or not the narratives to be shared with Expedition anthropologists were consistent with, or had been superseded by (or absorbed into), Christian teachings. Mountford's report, as mentioned, reveals a very significant amount of information on the notion of a Yolngu 'land of the dead', so this topic was obviously unproblematic in terms of Yolngu disclosure. Biblical narratives took precedence in describing the nature of the soul's journey to this paradise. Public revelation of such details could only help to ensure the consignment of this Yolngu belief to the past. Burrumarra, for example, would openly speak of how sceptical he had been, even as a youth, about the stories he had heard from his

---

27 McIntosh, 'Islam and Australia's Aborigines?'.
28 Scott, *Domination and the Arts of Resistance*, p. 1.

older brother of a whale carrying the soul of the dead on its back to an unknown place called Badu. He was intrigued by these stories, but acknowledged that they had little bearing on his life or the lives of other mission Yolngu. More important to him was the belief that the final resting place of the soul was the sacred waterholes located on his homeland at Dholtji and Gulirra in places that he often described as paradise or heaven.

The partial and confused stories of the Bayini that were told to Mountford, however, were not so easily consigned to the past. One can see in hindsight that the jumbled mix of myth and history was sending forth a strong message that they were, at the very least, in conflict with the Christian message.

The 1940s and 1950s were a time when the foundational Dreaming deities for the two Yolngu moieties (Dhuwa and Yirritja) were being recast as Old Testament prophets—a process that was sped up following the adjustment movement. The significance of the God-figure 'Allah' that Yolngu had learned about through hundreds of years of interaction with Indonesians was also being reconsidered and reconfigured. As I have written elsewhere, mission elder Harry Makarrwola in the 1950s spoke of Allah in the new scheme of 'adjustment' thinking as a messenger of the God of Christians.[29] Even on Elcho Island today, funerary rites that invoke the will of Allah are still enacted, but they are inevitably followed by Christian prayers and hymns—evidence of the continued existence of a hidden transcript.

This transition in interpretations of the Bayini was a subject of serious debate in the 1940s right across North-East Arnhem Land missions, but it was not a mere reflection of the will of Christian missionaries. The Elcho Island Church, for example, is built on a sacred site associated with the totemic eagle's nest. The decision to locate it there was made by missionaries and Yolngu alike. Within the walls of the church were placed special rocks associated with the moiety deities, so the message was very clear: while Yolngu were now part of the greater Christian body, the law of the land was integral to their understanding of the new ways. As if in confirmation of this 'eternal truth', it is said that one of the stone 'bilma' or clap-stick rangga placed in the church wall replicated itself in the landscape of its own volition. As it was removed from the ground by Yolngu Christians another moved upwards to replace it. This was a powerful statement for Yolngu of Burrumarra's concept of 'membership and remembership'—the notion that the new was grounded in the old, and that the old could never vanish entirely from the world.

---

29 McIntosh, 'Islam and Australia's Aborigines?'.

A Startling Disclosure

The most startling disclosure regarding Birrinydji (and the Bayini) came in 1988 at the hands of Burrumarra when he revealed for the first time an image of this deity.[30] This painting was not created for sale, but rather as an extension of the adjustment movement 'revolution'. Burrumarra wanted a new flag (or series of flags) for Australia in which the most significant Dreaming elements of the land on which the flag was being flown would be represented alongside non-Aboriginal symbols such as the Union Jack—all in the spirit of Aboriginal reconciliation. For his clan, the Warramiri, the most significant symbols were the octopus, the whale, and the Dreaming Macassan—Birrinydji.

Figure 17.3 Flag treaty proposal featuring an image of Birrinydji, the Dreaming Macassan, painted by George Liwukang and David Burrumarra. Oil on masonite, 1988

By permission of the Faculty of Law, University of New South Wales.

In Burrumarra's view, Yolngu were still relying too much on the hidden transcript in the wake of the adjustment movement. Apart from the Birrinydji and Bayini narratives, all other major beliefs had been fully disclosed and documented at great length by anthropologists in numerous theses and texts. With this body of law becoming increasingly anachronistic in the growing Christian community, the time for the Dreaming Macassan's disclosure had arrived, according to Burrumarra. His rationale was simple. He wanted to remind his fellow Yolngu that white wealth came from Aboriginal land, and that indigenous Christianity had a long history, based as it was on a foundation that included hundreds of

---

30 McIntosh, *Aboriginal Reconciliation and the Dreaming, Warramiri Yolngu and the Quest for Equality*.

years of contact with Islam. Christianity was not the white man's religion at all. It was a Yolngu religion, for the Yolngu were Birrinydji's people, and the followers of Birrinydji were Christian.

But Burrumarra's desire for disclosure was met with considerable opposition. Many wanted this Dreaming to remain concealed from white eyes. For Burrumarra, Christianity was an expression of the will of the Dreaming Macassan. For others, however, it was also of continuing relevance in shaping private discourse (and negotiating relations) between black and white. Birrinydji and Bayini narratives were therefore not subjects that should be freely shared in the public domain. But Burrumarra persisted with his decision, and, as the senior spokesperson for this Dreaming law, he would not be dissuaded.

Very soon after this momentous interaction, and with Burrumarra's permission, the Dhalwangu clan produced an image of Birrinydji on a signboard at their outstation at Gurrumurru, to the south-east of Elcho Island on Arnhem Bay. As if overnight, entirely new interpretations of the Birrinydji and Bayini legacy began to emerge.[31]

In Burrumarra's narrative (also reflected in the account given by Makarrwola to Warner in the 1920s), Yolngu at one time believed themselves to have been white, rich and all powerful. But, as I have described in detail elsewhere, when the Dreaming Macassan, Birrinydji, left Arnhem Land after his creational exploits at the 'beginning of time', Yolngu were set on a course to become black, poor and subject to domination.[32] In the newly emerging Dhalwangu account, however, Birrinydji never left Arnhem Land, and the Bayini have been reinstated as a pre-Macassan presence whose real purpose is not, and perhaps never will be, open to the prying eyes of the Other. In the stories that have been shared, the Bayini are seafarers who, at the dawn of time, make their way from points south of Numbulwar in the Gulf of Carpentaria, around Dholtji and Cape Wilberforce, and into Arnhem Bay and Gurrumurru, where their journey ends as mysteriously as it began.

Reflections on Disclosure

When considering the legacy of the 1948 Arnhem Land Expedition, it is not enough to simply reflect on lost opportunities. A longer-term view of disclosure regarding the Bayini sheds light on the ways in which Yolngu were transforming their own worlds in unique ways—under the guidance of missionaries to be

---

31 Toner, P. 2000, 'Ideology, influence and innovation: the impact of Macassan contact on Yolngu music', *Perfect Beat*, vol. 5, no. 1, pp. 22–41.
32 McIntosh, *Aboriginal Reconciliation and the Dreaming, Warramiri Yolngu and the Quest for Equality*.

sure, but in ways that reflected their own specific interests and concerns. The Expedition's salvage focus made it blind to these transitions, but their presence, in hindsight, actually played into the hands of people such as Burrumarra who had an integrationist mind-set.

So complete today is the apparent transition from a mythological to a historical perspective with regards to the pre-Macassan past that the significance of the former hidden transcript seems to be lost in time. But such a conclusion is problematic at best, given the rapid reworking of the Dreaming Macassan legacy following the disclosure by Burrumarra in the late 1980s.

Mountford's bullying could in no way elicit such a nuanced reading of the Yolngu past. To share exhaustive information on the Bayini in 1948 would have been difficult at best, and undoubtedly also compromising for Yolngu. As Burrumarra detailed in discussions described by Berndt in *An Adjustment Movement in Arnhem Land*, the Yolngu were seeking to extract the very best from the non-Aboriginal world in order to strengthen their own society. In a political environment in which there was an enormous disparity in power between whites and blacks on Aboriginal land, to suggest to outsiders that they might actually hold some privileged place in Yolngu cosmology (because the Bayini were themselves white or golden coloured), would have been seen as counterproductive.

Beliefs associated with the Bayini are fluid, not static. Both the public and the hidden 'transcripts' exhibit considerable complexity. The challenge for Expedition anthropologists to salvage ethnographic data regarding pre-Macassans was very considerable. But in order to find answers to their questions, they should have also looked to the future, not just the past. If they had taken Yolngu Christianity seriously and not prioritised the search for the primitive, the dynamism of Yolngu religion, and the multifaceted role it plays in Yolngu lives in the intercultural arena, would surely have been showcased. In their search for a romantic past, they missed the revolution taking place before their eyes.

Mountford's interest in the sorts of debates circulating in Yolngu communities at the time was negligible. His ethnographic team had the ambition of bringing to light every possible detail of the past. But, as I have described, this was not going to happen. Arnhem Land was in a state of flux and there were major debates unfolding about Christianity and the Dreaming. Was God a product of the Dreaming, as many Yolngu elders believed, or did God give Yolngu the Dreaming? It was a pity that Expedition members were so little interested in this debate because they might have learned something of the inside view of the Bayini. They would have surely seen how actively the Yolngu were participating in making their vision of the future coincide with an idyllic image of the past embedded in the Bayini narratives—stories of black and white people living and working together in peace and harmony, sharing equally in the resources of the land and sea. That story is yet to be shared openly because the hidden transcript remains hidden, and it will remain so while injustice continues to be a feature of Yolngu lives in a Balanda world, and while the great disparity in wealth between white and black remains the defining feature of their relationship.

18. Aural Snapshots of Musical Life: The 1948 recordings

Linda Barwick and Allan Marett
In memory of our friend Kenny Burrenjuck, 1950–2008

In the original proposal for the 1948 American–Australian Scientific Expedition to Arnhem Land made by Charles Mountford to the National Geographic Society, the fourth proposed study area (after bark painting, body painting and general ethnology) was 'music in secular and ceremonial life', with the note: 'the recording of Aboriginal songs if equipment is available.'[1] As it turned out, with the involvement of the Smithsonian Institution and the Australian Commonwealth Government, the majority of personnel on the Arnhem Land Expedition came from scientific disciplines, rather than the humanities (see May, this volume). Although Mountford himself did significant research on bark paintings and ethnology (as reported in Volume 1 of the Expedition records),[2] the planned focus on songs became rather neglected, partly because Mountford's own research interests and expertise lay elsewhere, and partly because there were apparently problems with the Expedition's recording equipment, which meant that he was unable to record after Groote Eylandt, the first official stop on the Expedition. It appears that no sound recordings were made at Yirrkala, the Expedition's second stop. At Oenpelli (now Gunbalanya), the third stop, Colin Simpson from the Australian Broadcasting Commission (now Corporation; ABC) with recordist Ray Giles visited the Expedition camp and made a feature radio program, along with a number of sound recordings, which were drawn on by Mountford in the official published recordings of the Expedition.[3] (For further discussion of Simpson, see MacGregor, this volume.)

A review of the published and unpublished audiovisual recordings associated with the Expedition reveals that a substantial proportion of them did not emanate from any of the three official Expedition locations; rather, they were of performers then resident at Delissaville (now Belyuen), a government settlement established in the 1940s on the Cox Peninsula, on the southern side of Darwin Harbour.

---

1 C. P. Mountford, Application to Chairman of the Research Committee, National Geographic Society, 5 March 1945, Correspondence 1945–49, vol. 1 1945–47, American/Australian Scientific Expedition to Arnhem Land 1948 Records, PRG 1218/17/4, Mountford-Sheard Collection, State Library of South Australia (hereafter SLSA), Adelaide.
2 Mountford, C. P. (ed.) 1956, *Records of the American–Australian Scientific Expedition to Arnhem Land. Volume 1: Art, myth and symbolism*, Melbourne University Press, Carlton, Vic.
3 Simpson, C. 1948, *Expedition to Arnhem Land*, Radio Feature, first broadcast 30 November 1948, Australian Broadcasting Commission, Sydney; Mountford, C. P. 1949, *American–Australian Scientific Expedition to Arnhem Land 1948*, (nine 78 rpm discs), Australian Broadcasting Commission, Sydney.

Both Mountford and Simpson visited Delissaville on separate occasions in 1948: Mountford, along with most of the other Expedition members, in March, before the Expedition proper set out for Groote Eylandt; and Simpson later in the year, after he had visited Oenpelli in September.[4] Delissaville performers might also have been recorded by Expedition members elsewhere: silent colour-film footage taken by the National Geographic Society's Howell Walker shows identifiable Delissaville dancers apparently performing for a non-Aboriginal audience in a location that could be Darwin's Botanical Gardens.[5] Since Walker did not visit Delissaville with Mountford and other Expedition members in March 1948, it is possible that this footage was recorded during the brief break that Expedition members took in Darwin in the period 9–18 September 1948.[6] Perhaps this was the same performance by dancers from Delissaville, Milingimbi and Melville Island in the Darwin Botanic Gardens witnessed by Simpson 'before we went into Arnhem Land'.[7]

We have used the term 'snapshots' in our title to evoke the idea of something intimately tied to a particular moment, yet incomplete—a partial record constrained by the time, place and means of its capture, inevitably representing only one point of view, or a few particular details of a more complex phenomenon. Like a series of snapshots, these few audiovisual recordings need contextualising, with metadata to name their subjects and their provenance, linking them to each other and to other records. While we acknowledge the aspirations of the recordists to present a true and authentic picture of Aboriginal musical life at the time, many questions are also raised. What did these aural snapshots actually represent? Why were particular groups present in these particular places and why were particular repertories performed?

Although some questions remain about the history of the recordings, this chapter will focus on the content of the Delissaville and Oenpelli material—the repertories and song genres recorded, their performers and their provenance—with a view to exploring what the compilation of these snapshots can tell us about musical life in the Top End of the Northern Territory at the time. Then, through close consideration of one event—a Kapuk (rag-burning) ceremony recorded by Simpson at Delissaville—we will reflect on the reliability of the interpretations placed on the event by its non-Aboriginal observers, and on the significance of the recording for present-day descendants of those recorded.

---

4   C. P. Mountford, 1948, Expedition to Arnhem Land, vol. 1, 1948, Personal Journal, PRG 1218/17/12, Mountford-Sheard Collection, SLSA; Simpson, C. 1949, *Delissaville: Death rite for Mabalung*, Radio Feature, first broadcast 15 March 1949, Australian Broadcasting Commission, Sydney; Simpson, C. 1951, *Adam in Ochre: Inside Aboriginal Australia*, Angus & Robertson, Sydney.
5   Walker, H. (cine-photographer) 1950, *Aboriginal Australia*, (Lecture film), National Geographic Society, Washington, DC.
6   Mountford's diary for this period covers the break in Darwin but does not mention such a performance; nevertheless, the possibility that other Expedition members attended something similar cannot be excluded.
7   Simpson, *Adam in Ochre*, p. 135.

First, we turn to an overview of the known sound recordings. As was normal practice at the time, original wire recordings were transferred to 78 rpm discs for preservation and access purposes, and copies were distributed not only to the collector but also to various libraries in Australia and overseas.[8] EMI Australia's Columbia Graphophone plant at Homebush, New South Wales, which processed location recordings for the ABC and other organisations, created a set of four 12-inch 78 rpm discs under the title *Groote Eylandt and Port Darwin Aboriginal Songs, Annotated by C. P. Mountford* from Mountford's original wire recordings.[9]

The Groote Eylandt recordings (PRX2712–14) include approximately 30 minutes of music, covering 21 songs belonging to clans then resident on the west coast of Groote Eylandt whose traditional country included Bickerton Island (a smaller island west of Groote). These songs were recorded at Thompsons Bay, some 13 km from Umbakumba, where the Expedition was based.[10] We will not discuss these songs further here.[11]

The disc of Port Darwin Aboriginal songs (PRX2715) includes six cuts. These songs were described in Mountford's personal journal on Sunday, 28 March 1948. Mountford noted: 'Today, we were able to get the wire recorder going, and record some of the songs of the Worgait, or, I understand, Worgaitja.'[12]

For the disc, Mountford recorded a brief introduction to each song, such as: 'This is a Worgait song chanted by Nilku and Gumbuduk. It is known as the Winmala song, and when it is sung it prevents the evil spirits from the bush from hurting the Aborigines in the camp.'[13]

Mountford's field notes were evidently used as the basis for this introduction, as the notes from 28 March demonstrate:

> The second song was chanted by two men, Nilku, and Gumbuduk.

---

8   Ibid., p. 220. For further information about this practice, see Elkin, A. P. and Jones, T. 1958, *Arnhem Land Music (North Australia)*, Oceania Monograph 9, University of Sydney, NSW, pp. 173–84; and Moyle, A. M. 1966, *A Handlist of Field Collections of Recorded Music in Australia and Torres Strait*, Australian Institute of Aboriginal Studies, Canberra.
9   Moyle, *A Handlist of Field Collections of Recorded Music in Australia and Torres Strait*, pp. 209–14; and Mountford, C. P. 1949, *Groote Eylandt and Port Darwin Aboriginal Songs Annotated by C. P. Mountford*, (four 12-inch discs, PRX2712–15), Columbia Graphophone, Homebush, NSW.
10 For more information on the circumstances surrounding this performance, see Thomas and Jones, this volume.
11 Mountford gives lengthy explanations and interpretations of some aspects of this restricted ceremony in the records of the Expedition. See Mountford, *Records of the American–Australian Scientific Expedition to Arnhem Land*, vol. 1.
12 Mountford, 1948, Personal Journal, vol. 1, pp. 87–93, PRG 1218/17/12, Mountford-Sheard Collection, SLSA.
13 Charles P. Mountford, Recorded introduction to PRX2715, Cut 2, 'The Winmala', transcribed by Linda Barwick, 2009.

> The song was known as Winmala. When it was chanted, it had the effect of keeping the evil spirits in the bush at bay, and thus protecting the camp. Some six weeks previously, the aborigines saw a light in the bush, which they attributed to a mythical serpent that moves about in the night and attacks and kills the people.[14]

We will have more to say about this particular song and its significance later in the chapter.

There is some confusion about the provenance of two further discs in this series, titled *Oenpelli Aboriginal Songs* (PRX2716–17). In her 1966 *Handlist* of Aboriginal and Torres Strait Islander music recordings, the musicologist Alice Moyle credited the discs to Colin Simpson, but in various library catalogues, including that of the State Library of South Australia's Mountford-Sheard Collection, they are credited to Mountford.[15] As will be discussed below, although presented in a different order, all of the cuts on these discs can be matched with Simpson's Oenpelli recordings, four of which were published separately by Simpson as part of the 12-disc set *Aboriginal Music from the Northern Territory of Australia, 1948, with Annotations by Professor A. P. Elkin* (PRX2645–52 and PRX2708–11).[16] Other recordings in this set came from Simpson's travels to Delissaville and Melville Island in the same year (which were made independently of the American–Australian Scientific Expedition to Arnhem Land). Very useful background information on the circumstances of Simpson's travels with Postmaster General's Department recordist Ray Giles can be found in Simpson's 1951 book, *Adam in Ochre*.[17]

Table 18.1 summarises the contents of this 12-disc publication by Simpson. For unknown reasons, the recordings are presented out of chronological order. In the table, we have grouped them into the three main locations, retaining the spelling used in Elkin's notes, with a transliteration into present-day orthography in square brackets where appropriate.

---

14 Mountford, 1948, Unpublished Field Notes, p. 87, SLSA. Another disc in the Mountford-Sheard Collection of the State Library of South Australia, PRG 1218/17/55, *Aboriginal Songs of Delissaville, Oenpelli and Groote Eylandt*, contains an edited selection of the sound recordings, possibly prepared for a lecture, which also seems to be paraphrased from Mountford's field notes. The explanations, in a woman's voice, include the following for side 1, track 5 (Winmala song): 'That was the song Winmala. This is a magical song, which has the effect of keeping the evil spirits in the bush from injuring the people in the camp during the hours of darkness. One of the Aborigines said that a few months previously the people in the camp saw a flickering light in the bush, which they attributed to a mythical serpent that was known to travel at night and will attack and kill people. On this occasion the whole tribe assembled in the ceremonial ground whilst the men chanted the Winmala. No-one was attacked' (transcribed by Linda Barwick, 2010).

15 Moyle, *A Handlist of Field Collections of Recorded Music in Australia and Torres Strait*, p. 211.

16 Simpson, C. 1949, *Aboriginal Music from the Northern Territory of Australia, 1948, with Annotations by Professor A. P. Elkin*, (twelve 12-inch discs, PRX2809–10, PRX2645–52), Australian Broadcasting Commission (processed by Columbia Graphophone), Sydney. Elkin himself visited Delissaville in 1946, 1949 and 1952, and published extensive notes about his recordings, supplemented by musical transcription and analysis by Trevor Jones. See Elkin and Jones, *Arnhem Land Music*; and Elkin, A. P. 1950, 'Ngirawat, or, the sharing of names in the Wagaitj tribe, northern Australia', in I. Tönnies (ed.), *Beiträge zur Gesellungs- und Völkerwissenschaft*, Gebrüder Mann, Berlin.

17 See Simpson, *Adam in Ochre*.

Table 18.1 Summary contents of Simpson's 1948 recordings, sorted into rough chronological order

Index	Singer or group	Song genre	Location recorded
Side 1.1	Gunwinggu [Kunwinjku]	Jiwadja [Iwaidja] sea chant	Oenpelli
Side 1.2	'Sam or Joshua'	Gunbalang [Kun-barlang] sweetheart song	Oenpelli
Side 2.1	Djauan [Jawoyn]	Djauan [Jawoyn] trading and sweetheart song	Near Oenpelli
Side 2.2	Jiwadja [Iwaidja]	Jiwadja [Iwaidja] sea chant	Oenpelli
Side 5, 6		Ubar [Wubarr]	Oenpelli
Side 23, 24	Birds	-	Oenpelli
Side 3, 4.1	Tiwi	Tiwi mourning ceremony	Snake Bay, Melville Island
Side 4.2, 19.1	Wogaitj	Karaboga	Delissaville
Side 7.1–2, 8, 9.1	Brinken	Tjarada [Tjarrarta]	Delissaville
Side 7.3–4	Wogaitj	Mindarini [Mindirrini]	Delissaville
Side 12.4, 13, 14.1–2	Brinken	Mindarini	Delissaville
Side 9.2–3, 10, 19.2	Brinken	Balga style song about truck	Delissaville
Side 11, 12.1–3	Brinken	'songs without dancing'	Delissaville
Side 14.3, 15, 16	Alandi, man from SW Arnhem Land	N. Central Arnhem Land songs	Delissaville
Side 17, 18, 20	Wogaitj	Indi indi wonga [Nyindi-yindi Wangga]	Delissaville
Side 21, 22	Wogaitj (Mosek)	Mosek song	Delissaville

Source: Simpson, C. 1949, *Aboriginal Music from the Northern Territory of Australia, 1948, with Annotations by Professor A. P. Elkin*, (twelve 12-inch discs, PRX 2809–10, PRX 2645–52), Australian Broadcasting Commission (processed by Columbia Graphophone), Sydney.

Six sides in all (discs 1, 3 and 12) contain material recorded in Oenpelli (total duration: approximately 15 minutes). The first disc (sides 1 and 2) contains a selection of public didjeridu-accompanied songs in a variety of languages and styles, while disc 3 (sides 5 and 6) contains recordings of the restricted Ubar (Wubarr) ceremony, which we will not discuss further here. Disc 12 (sides 23 and 24) contains bird calls—some recorded by Ray Giles at dawn on the lagoon at Oenpelli, described in Simpson's chapter 'The morning of the birds'.[18]

A relatively small amount of Tiwi material (about 10 minutes in all) is published in this recording on side 3 and the first cut of side 4. From the account given of the recording session in Simpson's chapter 'Black opera', it seems that Ray Giles had a number of problems with his recording equipment that might have rendered some of the recordings unsuitable for publication.[19] Simpson's ABC radio feature *Island of Yoi* also drew on this material.[20] We will not discuss these recordings further here.

The Delissaville recordings constitute the bulk of Simpson's published collection: more than eight discs (sides 7–22 plus the second cut of side 4), constituting approximately 60 minutes of recorded sound. We will now discuss in more detail the known provenance of the various genres recorded at Delissaville.

First, we should explain that the term Wogaitj (also spelt Waugeit and Worgait) (from the Batjamalh word *wagatj*, meaning 'beach') generally referred to a grouping of people encompassing various language groups whose traditional country lay along the coast to the south of the Cox Peninsula, including speakers of Batjamalh, Kiyuk, Emmi/Mendhe and Marri Ammu/Marri Tjevin. Most residents of Delissaville, which was established on Larrakiya land in the 1940s, belonged to one of these language groups.[21] The grouping term Brinken (Brinkin) was used to describe language groups whose traditional country lay further south—from the Moyle River south to the Fitzmaurice—including speakers of Magati Ge, Marri Ngarr and Murrinh-patha, amongst others. Some people from these groups were resident in Delissaville, but other relatives lived in Daly River and Port Keats (Wadeye), and to this day there continues to be frequent ceremonial exchange amongst and between these groupings.[22]

Many of the Delissaville recordings are of Wangga—a public didjeridu-accompanied dance-song genre associated with the Wagatj (and, to a lesser

---

18 Ibid., pp. 69–73.
19 Ibid., pp. 143–8.
20 Simpson, C. 1949, *Island of Yoi*, Radio Feature, first broadcast 18 January 1949, Australian Broadcasting Commission, Sydney. For a contents listing of the Tiwi field recordings, see Moyle, *A Handlist of Field Collections of Recorded Music in Australia and Torres Strait*, p. 216.
21 For further details, see Povinelli, E. 1993, *Labor's Lot: The power, history, and culture of Aboriginal action*, University of Chicago Press, Ill.; and Marett, A. 2005, *Songs, Dreamings and Ghosts: The Wangga of north Australia*, Wesleyan University Press, Middletown, Conn.
22 Marett, *Songs, Dreamings and Ghosts*.

extent, Brinkin) language groups. Each language group held one or more named repertories composed and performed by known songmen for various public ceremonies.[23] Simpson's Delissaville recordings include extensive coverage of Wangga songs performed at a Karaboga 'final mourning' ceremony (side 4, cut 2, and side 19). This event, described in Simpson's chapter 'So Mabalang will lie down', formed the basis of the ABC feature *Delissaville: Death rite for Mabalung*.[24] Such ceremonies—performed to dispose of the belongings of the deceased person some time after their death—continue to be performed today, and later in this chapter we give a detailed analysis of various aspects of this performance.

The songs used in the Karaboga ceremony are from the Nyindi-yindi Wangga repertory today associated with the Burrenjuck family. The same repertory is performed in the Indi-indi 'trade' corroboree songs (sides 17–18 and 20). Several Wangga-style songs by the renowned dancer and composer Mosek were also recorded by Simpson (sides 21–22); according to Elkin's notes, one song composed by Mosek was received by him from the snake spirit of the waterhole Belyuen (after which the present-day community is named), and another was later given to Simpson by Mosek, probably in exchange for tobacco.[25] Mountford also recorded two Wangga songs on his trip to Delissaville; he too recorded Mosek (also known as Manbira or Manpurr) singing a song for Baluin (Belyuen) waterhole (Mountford, song 1), as well as the above-mentioned 'Winmala' song (song 2).

The Mindarini (Mindirrini) initiation chants (side 7, cuts 3–4; sides 12–13; side 14, cuts 1–2) recorded by Simpson—both from Belyuen residents and from visiting Brinkin performers—belong to a large pan-regional ritual complex (variously named 'naitpan', 'dingirri', 'kudjingka' or 'mandayala') that originates to the south, in the desert.[26] These songs are partially restricted and will not be discussed further here.

Two other genres recorded at Delissaville by Simpson from Brinkin men are the Tjarada (Tjarrarta) 'love magic' songs (sides 7–8; side 9, cut 1) and a Balga-style song cycle about a trip in a motor truck (side 9, cut 2; side 10; and side 19, cut 2). Like Mindirrini songs, Tjarrarta songs also originate in the desert (according to Mountford, these songs had been learned by a Delissaville resident when he was working at Newry Station in the eastern Kimberley).[27] In different areas,

---

23 Ibid.
24 Simpson, *Adam in Ochre*; and Simpson, *Delissaville*.
25 See Elkin's notes, in Simpson, *Aboriginal Music from the Northern Territory of Australia*, pp. 6–7. See also Simpson, *Adam in Ochre*, pp. 171–2.
26 Keen, I. 1994, *Knowledge and Secrecy in Aboriginal Religion*, Clarendon Press, Oxford, p. 142; Stanner, W. E. H. 1963 [1989], *On Aboriginal Religion*, Oceania Monograph 11, University of Sydney, NSW, p. 108.
27 See C. P. Mountford, 1948, Field Notes, p. 91, SLSA, and recorded explanation for cut 2: 'The Charada (1)' on disc 4, side 2 of Mountford, *American–Australian Scientific Expedition to Arnhem Land 1948*.

Tjarrarta songs may be kept more or less secret from the opposite sex, and they exist in both men's and women's versions.[28] There is no information in Simpson's book or Elkin's notes to suggest how private or otherwise these performances might have been, though Elkin notes that women were allowed to clap along with these songs. Of more certain public status is the song set about a trip in a motor truck (side 9, cut 2; side 10; and side 19, cut 2), which belongs to the Balga public genre (accompanied by either clap sticks or boomerang clap sticks) performed throughout the Kimberley region and traded into the Daly–Fitzmaurice region.[29] Like Wangga, Balga songs are individually composed songs used for public ceremony. There is a notable difference: unlike Wangga, Balga songs are commonly performed by mixed groups of men and women (though it seems that the group recorded by Simpson was entirely male). The Brinkin songs without dancing (side 11) also appear to be in Balga style, although this is not mentioned explicitly in the notes.

Mountford also recorded the Tjarrarta and Balga genres (songs 5 and 6, the Tjarada; and song 4, Bulga). Mountford's recording of a non-secret ritual song variously termed Djuraman, Duralamin or Djuralam (song 3) also appears to be in Balga style (that is, with cyclical isorhythmic text, and accompanied by clap sticks).[30] There are other correspondences with the Simpson recordings. Mountford's 'Song of the waterhole Balyuin by Manbira, a Worgeit man' ('Port Darwin Songs', cut 1) is the same song published in a different performance by Simpson (side 21, cuts 1–2) as 'Mosek's song' (Mosek's Aboriginal name was 'Manpurr', transcribed by Mountford as 'Manbira'). These similarities evidently arise from the same songs having been offered to visiting researchers on different occasions.

Finally, Simpson's recordings include a number of north-central or North-East Arnhem Land clan songs (Manikay) (side 14, cut 3; sides 15, 16) recorded from a Delissaville resident who, according to Elkin's notes, had been transferred there on parole from south-west Arnhem Land.[31]

Let us take a moment to reflect on the sources of the various songs recorded at Delissaville by Simpson and Mountford. We have at least two genres (Tjarrarta and Mindirrini) that originate in desert country far to the south, two or three

---

28 Berndt, R. M. 1976, *Love Songs of Arnhem Land*, Thomas Nelson, Melbourne.
29 Barwick, L. 1998, 'The Kimberleys area', in A. Kaeppler and J. W. Love (eds), *Encyclopedia of World Music (Oceania Volume)*, Garland Publishing, New York; Barwick, L. (Forthcoming), 'Musical form and style in Murriny Patha Djanba songs at Wadeye (Northern Territory, Australia)', in M. Tenzer and J. Roeder (eds), *Analytical and Cross-Cultural Studies in World Music*, Oxford University Press, Oxford, UK, and New York; and Moyle, A. M. 1968, *Songs from the Kimberleys: Companion booklet for a 12-inch LP disc, cat. no. AIAS/13*, Australian Institute of Aboriginal Studies, Canberra.
30 Mountford (1948, Personal Journal, p. 89, PRG 1218/17/12, Mountford-Sheard Collection, SLSA) has 'Djuraman'; the contents listing of the sound recordings have 'Duralamin'; and the anonymous female announcer on PRG 1218/17/55 pronounces the word 'Djuralam'.
31 See Elkin's notes to side 14, cut 3, on p. 5 of the notes to Simpson, *Aboriginal Music from the Northern Territory of Australia*.

repertories of Balga, a genre originating in the Kimberley region to the south-west, and one Manikay repertory from the north-east. Even the Wangga genre owned and performed by Delissaville residents had its historical origins not on the Cox Peninsula but in the traditional country of most of its residents: the Daly region to the south of Delissaville. Indeed, several Wangga repertories are represented in the recordings. Simpson's aural snapshot of Delissaville in 1948 reflects a remarkable diversity of language, affiliation to country and ceremonial practice.

A similar picture of underlying social and geographical diversity is suggested by the provenance of the 11 public songs recorded by Simpson and Giles at Oenpelli. For example, of the four Oenpelli songs published by Simpson in *Aboriginal Songs from the Northern Territory of Australia, 1948*, none actually belongs to the country around Oenpelli itself. Two sea songs are from the north coast (side 1, cut 1 and side 2, cut 2).[32] A Gunbalang (Kun-barlang) 'sweetheart' song (side 1, cut 2) originates from country to the north-west of Oenpelli, near Maningrida,[33] while the Djauan (Jawoyn) trading and sweetheart song (side 2, cut 1) comes from country to the south of Oenpelli.[34] Simpson recorded seven other public didjeridu-accompanied songs at Oenpelli, which are included in the ABC Radio Archives disc MA24; most of these are listed as unidentified Kunwinjku corroboree songs, tentatively identified by Iwaidja and Mawng informants in 2005 and 2007 as belonging to various public love-song or dance-song genres.

Seven of the 11 songs recorded by Simpson and Giles also appear, in a different order, in Mountford's *Oenpelli Aboriginal Songs*, discs PRX2716–[17] (PRG 1218/17/53-54, State Library of South Australia), and in a compilation disc probably prepared for a lecture by Mountford (PRG 1218/17/55, State Library of South Australia) (Table 18.2). Note that Simpson seems not to have provided Mountford with sound recordings of the restricted Wubarr songs he had recorded at Oenpelli, although members of the Expedition did film and photograph the ceremony (see Garde, this volume).

---

32 Although classified by Simpson's informants as 'Jiwadja' (Iwaidja) songs, these were identified by Iwaidja-speaking people in Minjilang in 2005 as probably a Nganarru song belonging to Manangkardi people and a Mirrijpu song belonging to Mawng people, both coming from Goulburn Island rather than Iwaidja country on the Cobourg Peninsula (Linda Barwick, field notes, 2005).
33 O'Keeffe, I. 2007, 'Sung and spoken: analysis of two different versions of a Kun-barlang love song', *Australian Aboriginal Studies*, vol. 2007, no. 2, pp. 46–62.
34 Merlan, F., Jacq, P. and Diwurruwurru-jaru Aboriginal Corporation 2005, *Jawoyn Topic Dictionary (Thesaurus)/Compiled by Francesca Merlan & Pascale Jacq*, Diwurruwurru-jaru Aboriginal Corporation, Katherine, NT.

Table 18.2 Correspondences between Simpson's Oenpelli recordings and Oenpelli songs in the Mountford-Sheard Collection

Summary description	Simpson 1	Simpson 2	Mountford [Simpson] 1	Mountford [Simpson] 2
Iwaidja corroboree by Kunwinjku men	Cut 1	Side 1, cut 1	Disc 5, side 1, cut 2	Side 2, cut 5 (part 1)
Unnamed [Kun-barlang]	Cut 2		Disc 5, side 2, cut 2	Side 2, cut 2
Jawoyn sweetheart	Cut 3			
Jawoyn sweetheart	Cut 4	Side 2, cut 1		
Iwaidja saltwater fish	Cut 5	Side 2, cut 2	Disc 6, side 1, cut 1	Side 2, cut 5 (part 2)
Sweetheart gossip song [Kun-barlang]	Cut 6	Side 1, cut 2	Disc 5, side 1, cut 1	Side 2, cut 4
Kangaroo Gulawubarra	Cut 7		Disc 5, side 2, cut 1	Side 2, cut 1
Kunwinjku corroboree 1.1	Cut 9		Disc 5, side 2, cut 3	Side 2, cut 3
Kunwinjku corroboree 1.2	Cut 10		Disc 6, side 1, cut 2	
Kunwinjku corroboree 2.1	Cut 11			
Kunwinjku corroboree 2.2	Cut 12			

Notes: 'Simpson 1' refers to the ABC Radio Archives disc MA24; 'Simpson 2' refers to Simpson, C. 1949, *Aboriginal Music from the Northern Territory of Australia, 1948, with Annotations by Professor A. P. Elkin*, (twelve 12-inch discs, PRX 2809–10, PRX 2645–52), Australian Broadcasting Commission (processed by Columbia Graphophone), Sydney; 'Mountford [Simpson] 1' refers to Mountford, C. P. [Simpson, C.] 1949, *Oenpelli Aboriginal Songs*, (two 12-inch discs, PRX2716 and FXS188 [PRG 1218/17/53-54, State Library of South Australia]), Columbia Graphophone, Homebush, NSW; and 'Mountford [Simpson] 2' refers to C. P. Mountford [Simpson] 1960, *Aboriginal Songs of Delissaville, Oenpelli and Groote Eylandt*, (one instantaneous 12-inch disc, compilation of previous recordings with spoken annotations, probably prepared for lecture presentations), PRG 1218/17/55, State Library of South Australia.

We can trace various reasons for the musical and linguistic diversity evidenced by these musical snapshots of Delissaville and Oenpelli. Each of these communities actually brought together people from a number of different language groups, providing a rich multilingual social fabric in which marriage laws maintained diversity by demanding that people married outside their own clan or language group. So the Wangga songs performed by Belyuen (Delissaville) residents still celebrate today, in their ancestral languages, their traditional country to the south, as well as creating ongoing attachments to their current residence through the sacred waterhole Belyuen (the inspiration for Mosek's song recorded by both Mountford and Simpson). Ceremonial exchange, too, has been—and continues to be—a means of maintenance and transmission of diversity. Wangga singers from Belyuen have been in constant demand to perform at circumcision ceremonies, funerals and other public events in Darwin and throughout the Top End, and Belyuen is visited in return by performance groups from Katherine, Beswick, Daly River and Wadeye. The Mindirrini songs are associated with a pan-regional ceremonial complex that tied together people across a large area of the Top End by regular visits to each other's country to perform ceremonies. On such occasions, more secular songs (such as Wangga or newly composed repertories such as the Brinkin truck song) may be performed and traded in addition to the sacred ceremonial songs. Delissaville residents working on cattle stations in the Kimberley formed relationships with other groups holding Tjarrarta and Balga songs, trading songs and perhaps brokering marriages and other social connections. Each of these groups in turn might hold songs that had been traded to them from yet further away. Finally, movements of individuals from one multilingual community to another might be motivated by any number of other extraneous social factors, including parole placements and work obligations.

In the course of the Barks, Birds & Billabongs symposium, it became clear that the 1948 Expedition provided a locus for interactions between Aboriginal and non-Aboriginal people—not just in 1948 but continuing right up to the present through the numerous records and outputs of the Expedition. Martin Thomas, for example, uncovered previously unseen dimensions of the Expedition in a series of recorded conversations in 2007 with Gerald Blitner, one of the guides and interpreters employed by the Expedition while it was on Groote Eylandt (see Thomas, this volume). Bruce Birch presented a local Indigenous story about mammalogist David Johnson's time at Cape Don and his solo walk to Oenpelli. This account included many elements not recorded by Johnson himself, including an encounter with a *yumbarrbarr* (a supernatural giant) at Port Essington on Cobourg Peninsula and, more remarkably, an encounter with the spirit of the man Marrarna, whose remains lay in a cave at Dilkbany, a dangerous *kuyak* or 'sickness' site north of Oenpelli (see Birch, this volume). Later in our chapter, we will briefly explore another contemporary interaction (from 2008), which occurred in ceremony between Marett and the son of one of the main dancers in the ceremony recorded by Simpson in 1948.

But first of all let us give some further details about the ceremony that was recorded by Simpson at Delissaville in 1948 and discussed in his book *Adam in Ochre* and the ABC documentary feature *Delissaville: Death rite for Mabalung*.[35] We will consider some problematic aspects of his account before comparing it with a version of the same ceremony performed in 2008 by the descendants of the people who performed 60 years earlier.

---

35 Simpson, *Delissaville*; Simpson, *Adam in Ochre*.

The ceremony recorded by Simpson at Delissaville in late September or October 1948 was a Kapuk or Karaboga ceremony, also known in English as a 'rag-burning' or 'burnim rag' ceremony. We know from numerous subsequent ethnographic accounts that the main purpose of this ceremony is to conduct the spirit of a deceased person away from the society of the living and into the society of the dead. This is done by burning the belongings, or 'rags', of the deceased in order to drive the spirit into the open and then conducting it away from the living through the performance of appropriate songs and dances. Marett recently described it as follows:

> In *Songs, Dreamings and Ghosts* I identified a number of functions for this ceremony: the removal of the pollution associated with death; the freeing of the spirit of the deceased from its attachment to the living; the comforting of those left behind; the enactment of reciprocal ceremonial responsibilities between different language groups; and the nurturing of a particular relationship between humans and the land, the latter of which is conceived of as living, sentient and the source of all human life…[36] [W]hen you burn a person's 'rags', his or her spirit, which at death has taken refuge in these particularly cherished belongings, is driven out by fire. Thus liberated, the spirit of the deceased must then be persuaded or coerced—the relative degree of coercion or persuasion depends a great deal on the character the deceased had when alive—to leave the company of the living and join the society of the dead, who are known variously (according to language) as *walakandha*, *ma-yawa*, *ngutj* or *wunymalang*. The way this is done is to sing the worlds of the living and the dead into alignment so that the deceased may cross over from one to the other. Living songmen, singing songs that have been given to them in dreams by their ancestral dead (who in many cases are their own deceased fathers), create a liminal space where the worlds of the living and dead interpenetrate. Dancing (where the living dance as the dead and the dead as the living) and other forms of ritual actions also assist.[37]

The primary deficiency of Simpson's account of the 1948 Kapuk was that to some degree he mistook the purpose of the ceremony, and this misapprehension rested on a mistaken view of the *wunymalang* (what he referred to as '*wingmalung*') spirits that formed the focus of the ceremony. Simpson, who was a journalist not a professional ethnographer, relied heavily on the testimony of the superintendent

---

36 Marett, *Songs, Dreamings and Ghosts*, pp. 60–9.
37 Marett, A. 2010, 'Vanishing songs: how musical extinctions threaten the planet', *Ethnomusicology Forum*, vol. 19, no. 2, p. 256.

of the Delissaville settlement, Tom Wake. This is particularly clear in the part of the ABC radio documentary *Delissaville: Death rite for Mabalung* in which they discuss *wunymalang*:

> TOM WAKE: The old man has now laid down on the blanket and the damper, which has been surrounded by some gifts. The idea of this is to absorb the evil spirit which caused the sickness of this girl and her death. He will get this sickness now, and then the man who is singing and the doctor blackfella will sing him better…The idea of [the] doctor blackfella, who is now marching around the arena, peering, gesturing, looking in all directions, is to try and round up and frighten or shepherd the *wingmalung* or malignant spirits into the man who is lying under the gifts and clothes. The reason for this is that the spirits, or *wingmalung*, are now aware that it is an old man that they have gone into, and therefore they want to leave him because an old man is of no use to them.
>
> COLIN SIMPSON: The malignant spirits, forced to leave the dead woman's clothes when the clothes were burnt, flew into the gift materials, and finding a man in the midst of the gifts transferred themselves to him. But he's an old man. He'll die soon anyway and they can't get out because they're being kept inside by the magic gestures of Mosek, who is also a *duworrabuk* [Batjamalh, *dawarrabörak*]. But the *wingmalung* are still fierce and fighting and even for such a famous *duworrabuk* as Aliong the old man, they can make it very uncomfortable.[38]

Wake and Simpson characterise the '*wingmalung*' as the malignant spirits that first caused the death of the young woman, Mabalung (written as Mabalang by Simpson), and then infected her belongings, from which they need to be exorcised by various ceremonial acts. It is as though *wunymalang* were some sort of pestilential agent—analogous perhaps to the *Tuberculosis bacillus* that, according to Western medicine, killed the young woman—but this is quite wrong. The *wunymalang* that provides the focus of the ceremony is in fact the spirit of the deceased. It is the form that the conception dream or *maruy* aspect of her being takes after death.[39] In the course of the ceremony, songs that have been given to a living songman by *wunymalang* are sung and living humans dance as *wunymalang*; indeed, the ceremony is about drawing the *wunymalang* dead into an intimate though temporary interaction with the living. This is what allows the spirit of the deceased to pass over into the company of the *wunymalang* dead. What the ceremonial performers are dealing with therefore is not some invasive pestilential agent, but the spirit of the deceased and the broad

---

38 Transcript from the sound recording by Allan Marett, December 2009. We preserve the spellings used in Simpson, *Adam in Ochre*.
39 See further Marett, *Songs, Dreamings and Ghosts*, p. 67.

company of the dead. True, the young woman's *wunymalang* could become malignant if the proper ceremonies are not performed in a timely way, and the other *wunymalang* that are invoked by the ceremony could become dangerous if not handled properly, but *wunymalang* are not inherently malignant—dangerous perhaps, but unless provoked in some way, not malignant. Most importantly, what Wake and Simpson failed to recognise in their account is that the focus of the ceremony is the young woman herself, not random demonic forces. Moreover, any suspicion that the account given by Wake and Simpson represented some older, now lost understanding of the nature of *wunymalang* and their role in the ceremony is repudiated by accounts of Kapuk ceremonies in the Delissaville community in the period immediately preceding and following the ceremony witnessed by Simpson. Writing of a ceremony performed two years earlier, A. P. Elkin makes it clear that the deceased's spirit is the focus of the ceremony:

> In 1946 I was present at a Delissaville corroboree: the Songman sang of his deceased wife: her spirit was reported in the song as saying that she was now finished (with the surroundings of the camp) and was going away. In the dance the men swayed gracefully and rhythmically…it was a swaying action—the action of a spirit, or 'shade' moving back and forth in the wind.[40]

Describing a Kapuk ceremony that took place at Delissaville some four years later than the one Simpson witnessed, Elkin again makes clear that we are dealing primarily with the spirit of the deceased, not with a host of malignant forces: 'an elder lies across the hole into which the ashes have been scraped and is covered with a rug so that the spirit can pass from the destroyed articles into him.'[41]

Another shortcoming of Simpson's account lies in its failure to grasp the significance of the kinship relationships between the ceremonial participants. This might have been a shortcoming of the Expedition as a whole, since Mountford has been criticised—not only by later commentators, but by his own contemporaries (such as Elkin)—for his failure to adequately record the kinship relationships of the artists whose work he collected. Philip Jones in this volume sees positive benefits flowing from this practice, in that it gave the artworks in Mountford's collection an autonomy that provided a foundation for the future development of the Aboriginal art movement, free of the 'relatively arcane data concerning kinship and social relations' (Jones, this volume). But there is a price to be paid when artistic products and processes are stripped of their original significance and are imbued with new meanings. In the case

---

40   Elkin and Jones, *Arnhem Land Music*, p. 153.
41   Ibid.

of the ceremony under consideration here, what Simpson failed to realise is that Kapuk ceremonies are very much family affairs. They are conducted for the family of the deceased, and the ceremonial participants all stand in strict kinship relationships to the deceased and one another. With the help of living members of the Belyuen community, we have been able to identify most of the key players in the 1948 ceremony and to establish their kinship relationships. The relationships set out in Figure 18.1 have been reconstructed by Barwick from a variety of sources including names and relationships mentioned in Simpson's account of the ceremony, put together with genealogical information collated by Marett and Barwick during their fieldwork at Belyuen.

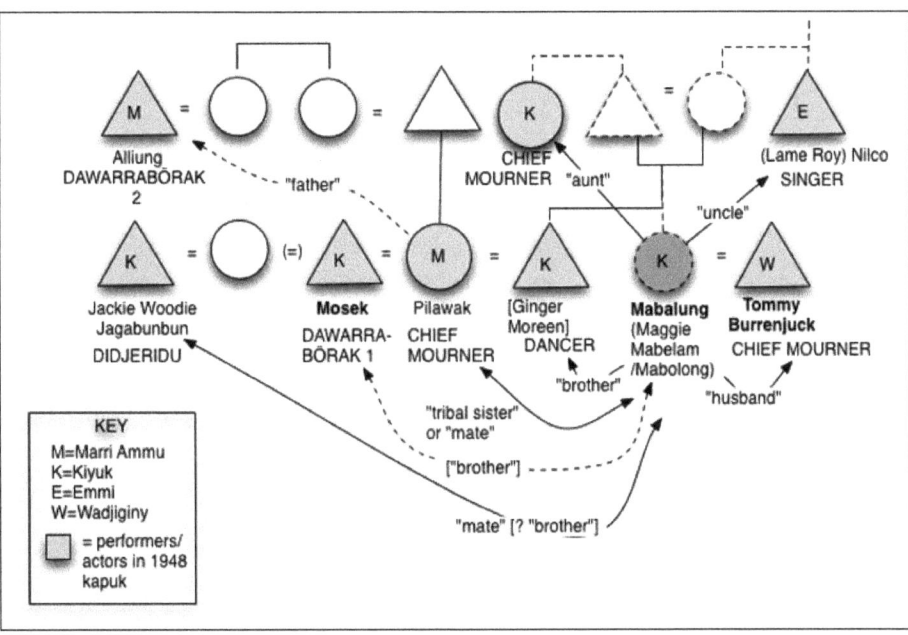

Figure 18.1 Relationships between the principal participants in the Karaboga ceremony, 1948

From Figure 18.1, we can see that the principal mourners for the deceased woman, Mabalung (Mabalang in Simpson's rendering, also known in other records as 'Maggie Mabelam' and 'Mabolong'), are her husband, Tommy Burrenjuck ('Burrajuk' in Simpson's rendering; Marett uses his original Aboriginal name, Barrtjap), and Pilawak (rendered 'Billawauk' by Simpson), wife of Mabalung's brother, Ginger Moreen, together with an unnamed aunt of the deceased. The deceased's husband, Tommy Barrtjap, was the principal songman and ceremonial leader at Belyuen/Delissaville until his death in the early 1990s. He was recorded by Elkin, by Alice Moyle and by Marett over a period of more than three decades, and his repertory forms the focus of a chapter in Marett's book *Songs, Dreamings and Ghosts*.[42] Pilawak went on to

---

42   Marett, *Songs, Dreamings and Ghosts*.

become one of the key ceremonial women at Belyuen. Marett saw her taking a leading role in a rag-burning ceremony held at Nadirri in 1988. Pilawak's other husband, Mosek Manpurr, was one of the two *dawarraböraks* (rendered as '*duworrabuk*' by Simpson) or 'doctor blackfellas' officiating at the ceremony. The other *dawarrabörak* was Alliung (rendered as 'Aliong' by Simpson), who stood in the classificatory relationship of 'father' to the deceased. The singer was Lame Roy Nyilco (Nilcoo), who stood in the correct relationship of 'mother's brother' to the deceased.

Having dealt with some of the problems with Simpson's account, let us turn to some of the significant similarities and differences between the 1948 Kapuk and a Kapuk performed very recently—in 2008—for members of the same family, since the latter not only sheds light on the former, but also shows the extent to which the traditions described by Simpson continue today. Figure 18.2 summarises the relationships of the participants in the 2008 ceremony. The key to the relationship between the two ceremonies is Tommy Barrtjap. The 1948 ceremony was for his second wife, Mabalung; the 2008 ceremony was for Tommy Barrtjap's eldest son and principal heir to his song tradition, Kenny Burrenjuck. Kenny was the son of Tommy and his third wife, Mabel Muluk (daughter of another great Belyuen songman Jimmy Muluk). The ceremony was organised by Tommy's fourth wife, Esther (the daughter of another leading songman Nym Mun.gi). This ceremony was even more of a family affair than the 1948 ceremony, in that Kenny's brother, Timothy, was one of the two singers, but Timothy felt aggrieved at having to sing for his brother: the relationship was too close. The other singer was Marett, who by then had been singing with Kenny for a number of years.

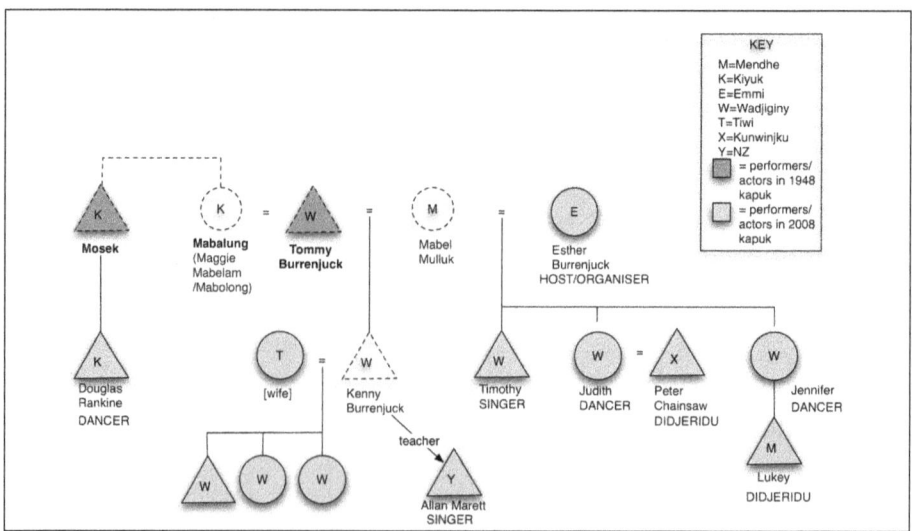

Figure 18.2 **Relationships between the participants in the ceremonies in 1948 and 2008**

As happened in 1948, the 2008 ceremony was conducted near the house of the family. In 1948 it was beside the hut of Tommy Barrtjap: 'The site for the ritual… is close to the ripple-iron hut of Burrajuk, the widower, where Mabalang lived.'[43] In 2008 the ceremony ground was constructed beside Esther Burrenjuck's house at the community of Fifteen Mile, on the outskirts of Darwin. This was not where Kenny lived (he had made his home for many years at Milikapiti—Snake Bay—on Melville Island), but it was one of the main residences of his patrilineal family, most of whom live at Belyuen or Fifteen Mile. It is common practice on the Daly River to perform ceremonies of this type either on the country of the deceased (this pattern is more common at Wadeye, where people have easier access to their country) or near the dwelling of the deceased's family (this has been the standard practice at Belyuen for more than half a century, because the country of most groups at Belyuen is far distant and relatively inaccessible).

The structure of the ceremony ground in 2008 was very similar to that in 1948. Basically, an area roughly in the shape of a square was enclosed by stretching cord between four posts located at each corner of the square. In 1948 the posts were made of rusty pipes and the cords were 'strong bush vine'.[44] Nowadays, the posts are usually made from cut saplings, and the cords or wire bought at a local shop. This was the case for the 2008 Kapuk. A hole is dug in the centre of the ground and kindling placed nearby. At Delissaville in 1948 and at Fifteen Mile in 2008 (and indeed in numerous other Kapuk ceremonies that we have witnessed at Belyuen) the belongings of the deceased are burnt outside the hole and then the ashes are pushed into the hole before it is filled in. In more southern Daly communities such as Wadeye, the belongings are put into the hole and set alight. This might be an innovation that derives from the availability of kerosene to ignite the fire. Whereas in 1948 spears and pearl-shell pendants were placed beside or on the corner posts, this was not the case in 2008, though it is not uncommon for spears to be located thus in modern ceremonies.

Let us turn now to the music and dance. As we have already said, the singer in 1948 was Lame Roy Nyilco ('Nilcoo'). A notable and unusual feature of this ceremony was that the same song was sung over and over throughout the whole ceremony. Typically Kapuk ceremonies use a variety of songs; the 2008 Kapuk, for example, used five different songs. At this distance in time, one can only speculate why this was the case. Perhaps Lame Roy Nyilco was not a very experienced singer; he is certainly not mentioned as a singer in any other records. In a work of popular non-fiction, John K. Ewers recorded that in 1947 the two main singers at Delissaville were Buntuck (Tommy Barrtjap's 'father'— father's brother—Jimmy Bandak) and Argok (Aguk Malvak, the father's brother

---

43   Simpson, *Adam in Ochre*, p. 173.
44   Ibid.

of another of the later Belyuen singers, Bobby Lambudju Lane).[45] Who knows why Jimmy Bandak did not perform for the Kapuk of his 'son' Tommy Barrtjap's wife. Perhaps he was simply elsewhere or perhaps he was deemed to be too close a relation. As already noted, in 2008 Timothy Burrenjuck complained vociferously on precisely these grounds at having to sing Kapuk for his brother, Kenny, and such matters were almost certainly observed more strictly in 1948.

Turning to the song itself, consultation with members of the Belyuen community suggests that the text is made up mainly of untranslatable vocables, which are regarded as the untranslated language of *wunymalang* spirits (since these are the spirits who give songmen songs in dreams). The vocables are interspersed with a few words in Batjamalh, including perhaps *nga-ve* (I go). Although this song is no longer sung—and indeed does not reappear in any of the later recordings of songs from Belyuen—it has many of the key characteristics that typify the Nyindi-yindi Wangga repertory owned and performed by the Burrenjuck family. The song is very similar (though not identical) to the song *Nyere-nye Bangany-nyaya* that Marett recorded Tommy Barrtjap singing in 1988, and which was also performed by Timothy Burrenjuck and Marett in the 2008 Kapuk. The similarities are striking.

The melodies of the two songs are almost identical and conform to the dorian series with an unstable third (C–D–E-flat/E–F–G–A–B-flat–C) that is typical of the Nyindi-yindi repertory.[46]

The structure of both songs consists of a series of vocal sections[47] (two in the case of the 1948 and 2008 recordings; four in the 1988 recording), followed by a coda, where the singer performs not text but didjeridu mouth sounds.[48] This last feature is almost unique to the Nyindi-yindi repertory.

Each vocal section consists of one or two melodic sections in which the text is sung isorhythmically, followed by a final melismatic vocal section.[49] Five other of Barrtjap's songs conform to this pattern.[50]

As mentioned above, the isorhythmic text sung in each vocal section comprises a mixture of vocables and Batjamalh words. The rhythm to which the isorhythmic text is performed is very similar in both performances.

---

45 Ewers, J. K. 1954, *With the Sun on My Back*, (Second edition), Angus & Robertson, Sydney, p. 25.
46 Marett, *Songs, Dreamings and Ghosts*, p. 158.
47 For a definition of 'vocal section', see ibid., pp. 18, 87–8 and passim.
48 'Didjeridu mouth sound' is a term coined by Alice Moyle to describe the vocalisation of didjeridu rhythms, often performed by a singer to indicate the next song's accompaniment rhythms to the didjeridu player; see Moyle, *Songs from the Northern Territory*.
49 For a definition of 'melodic section', see Marett, *Songs, Dreamings and Ghosts*, pp. 87–8 and passim.
50 See further ibid., pp. 174–5.

Each vocal section is accompanied by either fast, uneven quadruple beating or fast doubled beating (see Figure 18.3).[51] In the 1948 song, the first vocal section uses fast, uneven quadruple beating and the second vocal section and coda use fast doubled beating. In the 1988 performance of *Nyere-nye Bangany-nyaya*, the order is reversed: the first two vocal sections use fast doubled beating, and the third, fourth and coda use fast, uneven quadruple beating. In Timothy Burrenjuck and Marett's performance of *Nyere-nye Bangany-nyaya* in the 2008 Kapuk, fast, uneven quadruple beating was used throughout, but alternation between the two rhythmic modes was used for other songs belonging to the group of five mentioned in point 3 above.

Rhythmic mode	Repeating clapstick beating pattern
Fast uneven quadruple	 ♩ ♩ ♩ ♩
Fast doubled	 ♩ ♫ ♫ ♫ ♫

Figure 18.3 Repeating clap-stick beating patterns associated with the two rhythmic modes used in Nyilco's song

We can safely conclude that the song performed for the 1948 Kapuk belonged to the Nyindi-yindi repertory of the Burrenjuck family ('Barrtjap's Wangga').[52] Although the particular song performed by Nyilco appears not to have survived in the present-day repertory, it is clearly closely related to Barrtjap's *Nyere-nye Bangany-nyaya*.

Another key difference between the 1948 ceremony and that held in 2008 concerns the structure of the ceremony. In 1948, the ceremony clearly fell into two parts. In the first, the belongings of the deceased were burnt and the ashes interred. In the second, a native doctor, or *dawarrabörak*, Alliung, lay on the filled-in hole where the ashes were interred and was covered with a blanket. During this phase of the ceremony, Alliung also ate damper into which some of the ashes had been mixed. The point of this was to attract any residual power of the *wunymalang* spirit of the deceased woman into a spiritually powerful man, thereby protecting less powerful members of the community from any malicious intent the spirit might have. At the same time, the other *dawarrabörak*, Mosek, performed a grotesque dance that articulated some of the key properties of a *wunymalang*.

---

51   For a description of the rhythmic modes of *Wangga*, see ibid., pp. 203–6.
52   Ibid.

It is clear from Elkin's account that the two-part form of the ceremony was still being practised in 1952.⁵³ At some time prior to the 1980s, however, the second part of the ceremony was discontinued. We have been told that the reason for this was that after Alliung and Mosek died, there were no more *dawarrabōraks* at Belyuen with the power to carry it off. Certainly, we have never witnessed this part of the ritual, though elements of it survive. Marett has seen Frank Dumoo, the ritual leader for Wangga at Wadeye and the southern Daly, lying on the ground during a Kapuk and it has been reported that he sometimes also ceremonially eats damper on the dance ground. Even without this second part of the ceremony, however, circumspection about the power of the *wunymalang* persists in the truncated ceremony seen today. Normally, more senior men are the ones who first dance on the filled-in fire hole. Only later are the more vulnerable younger men and boys allowed onto this area. Indeed, in the 2008 Kapuk, some young boys initially rushed forward to dance on the hole just after it had been filled in, but they were quickly and quite roughly pushed away by the older men.

Yet another element of this ceremony might have survived from the now defunct second part, and some of its significance might, to some extent, rely on Simpson's description of the 1948 ceremony. At the very end of the 2008 ceremony, Douglas Rankin, the son of Mosek Manpurr (one of the two 1948 *dawarrabōraks*), announced that he wanted to dance. At that point, Marett was the principal singer, and Rankin danced directly and powerfully towards him, performing the grotesque movements associated with *wunymalang*—the sorts of movements that were described by Simpson as follows: 'He's a bent old man, a grotesque-looking figure…coming forward with stiff jerky movements. His eyes have a trance-like gaze in them…he holds out his crooked hands and then withdraws them.'⁵⁴

We are not suggesting that Rankin learnt to dance like this from hearing Simpson's recordings. It is more likely that as a young man he witnessed his own father and perhaps other *dawarrabōrak* dancing like this. But his decision to dance up to Marett in that way at the end of the Kapuk probably rested on his knowing that Marett knew precisely what he was invoking—namely, the *dawarrabōrak* dance. And the reason for this is because he knew about Simpson's ABC program, which has been lodged on a computer at the Belyuen Community 'Bangany Wangga' archive and widely circulated among community members in the form of CDs. And he knew that Marett also knew this program. That was the link that made this performative moment significant.

---

53 Elkin and Jones, *Arnhem Land Music*, p. 173.
54 Simpson, *Adam in Ochre*, p. 179.

We spoke earlier about the ways in which elements of the 1948 Expedition have continued to provide a locus for the generation of new stories and narratives. At Belyuen, it seems that Simpson's recordings and explanations probably played a part in generating the shared understandings that gave significance to Douglas Rankin's dance. The examples we cited earlier were primarily narrative in nature. In Aboriginal culture, however, dance is a more powerful but perhaps less easily accessed enactment of knowledge, and it behoves us to remain alert to such articulations of knowledge about the earlier recordings and other documents that are now the shared legacy of both Aboriginal and non-Aboriginal people.

Figure 18.4. Kenny Burrenjuck singing Wangga at Belyuen, 1997

Photograph by Linda Barwick

19. Unpacking the Testimony of Gerald Blitner: Cross-cultural brokerage and the Arnhem Land Expedition

Martin Thomas

The story begins at Umbakumba on the east coast of Groote Eylandt, the first base for the 1948 American–Australian Scientific Expedition to Arnhem Land. The party arrived there early in April 1948 and stayed three months. The position in the modern atlas of Umbakumba—an Aboriginal camping place for millennia—dates from the 1930s when it became a refuelling base for the Qantas Empire Airways flying boats that travelled the long-haul route between Sydney, Singapore and the south of England. Since World War II, Umbakumba had grown and morphed to the extent that officials in Darwin had come to cautiously recognise it as an Aboriginal settlement, intended in some indeterminate way for the betterment of the local population. Elsewhere in the Gulf of Carpentaria, Christian missionaries had been entrusted as the agents of this 'civilising' process. Umbakumba, in contrast, was effectively the initiative of a solitary individual: a self-styled superintendent named Frederick Harold Gray, who is said to have developed the settlement 'in protest of missionary methods'.[1] Gray had no religious agenda or affiliation, and there was no place of worship, at least in the Christian sense. The Expedition botanist, Raymond Specht, has described it as a 'secular mission'.[2]

Within days of getting there, the Australian Museum anthropologist, Frederick McCarthy, was expressing frustration and disappointment in his diary: 'I went to bed at 9 pm. Though tired out, couldn't sleep because of our situation. Here we are, 16 of us, backed by U.S. & Australian funds, but the natives are almost completely civilized, speaking English well and have dropped their ceremonial and hunting life.'[3]

The notion that Arnhem Land was a mysterious and pristine heartland—an Aboriginal enclave unpolluted by modernity—was not singular to McCarthy.

---

1 Rose, F. 1968, *Australia Revisited: The Aborigine story from Stone Age to space age*, Seven Seas Publishers, Berlin, p. 133.
2 Raymond Specht interviewed by Sally K. May and Martin Thomas, 2–4 May 2006, St Lucia, Queensland, Oral History Collection, ORAL TRC 5662, National Library of Australia (hereafter NLA), Canberra.
3 Frederick D. McCarthy, 1948, Diary 1: Groote Id, Papers of Frederick David McCarthy, Entry for 4 April 1948, MS 3513/14/1, Australian Institute of Aboriginal and Torres Strait Islander Studies (hereafter AIATSIS), Canberra.

It was one of the collective fantasies that gave rise to the 1948 Expedition.[4] As a newspaper of the period explained, the 'natives in Arnhem Land are particularly interesting to the American scientists as they have never developed beyond the Stone Age'.[5]

As much as the Expedition was constructed and promoted as a quest to discover antiquity, it is better thought of as a symptom of modernity. We see it in the Expedition photographs where Aboriginal performers have their voices recorded or watch with fascination as the visiting scientists go about their work, busy at the technological forefront. That juxtaposition of new ways and old ways is a formula repeated in image after image. This was the Expedition's comfort zone, the way it habitually declared its raison d'être—as is not surprising. The tradition of defining modernity by staging an encounter with a supposed antiquity is as old as modernity itself.[6] The Expedition properly began when it arrived at Umbakumba, expecting some fossil society where men (as they called people) lived in a state of nature. Instead, they found something considerably more complex: a dynamic community, which, although geographically isolated, was by no means quarantined from historical influences.

Umbakumba was the place where the Expedition met with Gerald, or Gerry, Blitner, whom I interviewed at his home in Darwin in 2007. I was referred to him by archaeologist Sally May, who met with him some weeks earlier and heard about his role in guiding the Expedition on Groote Eylandt. Sally and I had already worked together interviewing the two surviving Expedition members (botanist, Raymond Specht, and cine-photographer, Peter Bassett-Smith) for the National Library of Australia Oral History Collection. I was in Darwin shortly after Sally's initial meeting with Gerry and she suggested that I try to set up a formal interview, to be archived by the National Library. Although her excitement was infectious, I tried hard to suppress mine. It sounded too good to be true. A year earlier I had gone to the Expedition's three main bases to see what memories remained of its visit. While a few elders dimly recalled it, they had all been children at the time and no-one could offer substantial testimony. When making inquiries about events six decades earlier, one is confronted with the brutal reality of Aboriginal life expectancy. So few people survive into their seventies, let alone their eighties or beyond. It seemed that everyone who worked closely with the Expedition had passed away.

---

4 Charles P. Mountford's original grant application to the National Geographic Society described the Aboriginal population as largely uninfluenced 'by white civilization'. See his Application to Chairman of the Research Committee, National Geographic Society, 5 March 1945, AASEAL Correspondence Volume 2 (1945–1948)—Applications, PRG 1218/17/5, Mountford-Sheard Collection, State Library of South Australia (hereafter SLSA), Adelaide.
5 'Arnhem land expedition plans', *Northern Standard*, 12 March 1948.
6 The relationship between modernity and traditional cultures is the subject of an extensive literature. Examples include Muecke, S. 2004, *Ancient and Modern: Time, culture and Indigenous philosophy*, UNSW Press, Sydney; and Latour, B. 1993, *We Have Never Been Modern*, Harvard University Press, Cambridge, Mass.

19. Unpacking the Testimony of Gerald Blitner

Figure 19.1 Brian Billington using a microscope, watched by an unidentified boy, 1948

Photograph by Howell Walker. By permission of National Geographic Stock.

When I phoned Gerald Blitner, I was astonished when he told me his age. Born in 1920, he was twenty-eight when the Expedition came through—certainly no child. I was struck immediately by the commanding presence of this eighty-seven-year-old, even on the telephone. Although his health was poor and spells in hospital had been a troubling feature of his recent past, Gerald Blitner was still a captivating raconteur, deep-voiced and much prone to laughter. He asked me what I wanted to do with the recording and I told him that it would go to Canberra so that anyone could hear his story, told in his own words. He was checking me out, as was only appropriate. And I suppose I was checking him out too, trying to get a sense of where this might lead. He said that I could come round the next day and have a talk about it, signing off with a tantalising comment about the Expedition leader: 'And wait until you hear what I've got to say about Mr Mountford!'

After initial discussion and preparations, we began recording. Even after two days of interview—both exhaustive and exhausting—Gerry had more to say. He invited me back and we recorded for a third day a few weeks later. Since the recording is by far the most substantial commentary on the workings of the Expedition from someone of Aboriginal ancestry, the first objective of this chapter is to give some account of his testimony. In so doing, however, I hope to go somewhat further than simply reporting on Gerald Blitner's impressions, valuable (and at times provocative) as they are. In the first instance, I want to encourage a sympathetic *hearing* of Gerry's testimony; in the second, I want to facilitate a *reading* of it that will put it in dialogue with the larger body of evidence thrown up by the Arnhem Land Expedition. This body of evidence is truly an extensive dossier, remarkable for its plurality of perspectives and mixture of media. It is evidence that includes the diaries, notes and letters of Expedition members and associates; the 2000 pages of official reports; the vast cache of filmic, audio and photographic records; the collections of flora, fauna and objects of ethnological interest; as well as all that bureaucratic detritus, ranging from the texts of telegrams to financial paperwork. By setting the Blitner testimony in conversation with other sorts of records, it is possible to perform what I think of as a stereophonic audit of the Expedition's stay on Groote Eylandt. While keeping ears open to Gerry's story as it emerged in the process of interview, I will pick a somewhat haptic path through other evidence, evaluating how Gerry was mentioned or depicted—and scrutinising the very revealing ways in which he was overlooked or ignored.

The benefit of doing this is that it gets us closer to the messy business of cross-cultural interaction. Through this process, it becomes a little easier to think of the Expedition from multiple perspectives. Most noticeably, the early circumstances of Blitner's life—which inevitably shaped his particular slant on the Expedition story—dramatically expose the subject of race as one of the defining fault lines in the history of this research venture. The ways in which race and racism shaped his own destiny and self-image provide a compelling entree to the chequered history of Groote Eylandt in the twentieth century, so divergent from the cliché of a 'Stone-Age' culture expected by McCarthy and Mountford. By monitoring the friction that resulted from that glaring disparity between expectation and reality, we can scrutinise the pervasiveness of racial doctrines of the period.

Gerald Blitner's testimony does of course represent a subjective interpretation of the events it deals with—a caveat that must be attached to *all* historical evidence, whether it takes the form of written document, photograph, film or whatever. The crucial point is that his memories *were* substantial and that they were largely unmediated by published accounts of the Expedition, with which he seemed to be wholly unfamiliar. In the early stages of the interview, completely without prompting, he recalled the Expedition's arrival at Umbakumba and identified the roles of several personnel:

> Soon as the party all landed, we had all the tents up and all the water system up there with pipes, you know, running it along there, make it easier for them, and they started and, boy, the biggest humbug, you

know, big, big things to do. And Howell Walker wanted all the shots he could get and Frank Setzler, he wanted all the bones that he could find and all the Macassan heads that he could see, and Miller wanted every fish that he could see and an illustration about them and PC [sic] Mountford, I thought—I was told—by a couple of the people he was a self-proclaimed anthropologist and he acted that way…A tyrant, you know. He wanted it all his way, his way, his way.[7]

Figure 19.2 Frederick Blitner with Sarah, his second wife (name unknown), and their children Fred and Margaret (elder siblings of Gerald), 1919

Photograph attributed to C. E. Latham. By permission of Mitchell Library, State Library of New South Wales. PXA 1159, No. 44.

Even these few words reveal a nuts-and-bolts knowledge of the Expedition. Gerry's involvement, as he explained it, included guiding, translating and

---

7 Gerald Blitner interviewed by Martin Thomas, 27–28 August and 20 September 2007, Darwin, Oral History Collection, ORAL TRC 5851, NLA. Further Blitner quotes are from this source unless otherwise stated.

many other duties. He was already an accomplished navigator, and on many occasions he skippered Gray's boat, the *Wanderer*, ferrying the researchers. At nearly 2500 sq km, Groote (meaning 'great' in Dutch) Eylandt is the largest in an archipelago of mainly small islands and reefs. Bickerton Island, situated southeast of Blue Mud Bay and west of Groote, is the second largest, and sufficiently close to the continental mainland to allow a 'hop' between coast and islands. For centuries, people have been making this journey by canoe. The anthropologist Peter Worsley, who conducted fieldwork on Groote from 1952 to 1953, put the postwar population of the island at 450.[8] When Mountford and his colleagues were there, they conducted research on Groote and on several of the smaller islands. They were usually transported by Fred Gray or Gerry Blitner.

Gerry developed his sailing skills during his upbringing on the Church Missionary Society (CMS) mission, some 50 km from Umbakumba on the west coast of Groote. He was not originally an islander, but was born somewhere near the mouth of the Roper River on the Australian mainland. His mother, whom he knew only as Sarah, was an Aboriginal woman from the Vandalin Islands. With Gerry and her two older children, Margaret and Fred, she ended up at Roper River Mission (now Ngukurr), established in 1908 and also a CMS institution. The father of Gerry and his older siblings was Fred or Freddy Blitner, a white man involved in the trepang trade who Gerry said was of German background. He lived near Borroloola with Sarah and the children.[9] If the caption of a photograph of him dated 1919 is correct, Fred Blitner cohabited with both Sarah and a second Aboriginal wife. This was never mentioned in the interview. Shortly after Gerry's birth, Freddy Blitner abandoned the family and left the region. Gerry lived with his mother and siblings at Ngukurr until the age of four. It was then that the missionaries separated him from his mother and took him to the mission on Groote—at the time situated on Emerald River (though it had moved north to Anguguru, also on the west coast of the island, by the time of the Expedition). The CMS mission on Groote was conceived from the outset as an institution for the accommodation and upbringing of so-called half-caste children whom it was thought appropriate to protect from the 'degradation of the blacks' camps'.[10] Gerry had a mission upbringing, learnt to read and write in English, worshipped as a Christian, and acquired a large range of practical skills, ranging from spear fishing to sailing. He also formed connections with the

---

8   Cited in Rose, F. 1960, *Classification of Kin, Age Structure and Marriage Amongst the Groote Eylandt Aborigines: A study in method and a theory of Australian kinship*, Deutsche Akademie der Wissenschaften zu Berlin, Berlin, p. 12.
9   Freddy Blitner, also known as 'Freshwater Admiral', was a figure of some notoriety in the Gulf Country. A thumbnail sketch appears in Jose, N. 2002, *Black Sheep: Journey to Borroloola*, Hardie Grant Books, South Yarra, Vic., p. 35. Harney described an encounter with him in Harney, W. 1980, *Life Among the Aborigines*, Rigby, Adelaide, pp. 154–5.
10 Cited in Cole, K. 1984, *Fred Gray of Umbakumba: The story of Frederick Harold Gray, the founder of the Umbakumba Aboriginal settlement on Groote Eylandt*, Keith Cole Publications, Bendigo, Vic., p. 35.

Aboriginal people who lived near the mission. He learned about their culture and became fluent in Anindilyakwa, the language native to Groote. He was equally proficient in Kriol, which allowed him to communicate with Aboriginal people from other parts of Arnhem Land.[11] As the years passed, Gerry was incorporated into the local classificatory kinship system and acquired the host of adoptive 'fathers', 'mothers', 'brothers' and 'sisters' whom he referred to in the interview. Perhaps this helps explain his apparent success in navigating the trauma of separation from his birth parents so early in life.

Gerald Blitner was the 'Jerry' mentioned by Smithsonian Institution anthropologist, Frank Setzler, when he described their arrival at Umbakumba by Catalina. In his diary, Setzler wrote of Fred Gray's boat coming to meet them, towing a dinghy 'made by Jerry, a half-caste and Grays [sic] right hand man'.[12] Mountford's first mention of him occurred two days later, on 7 April, when 'Jerry the half-caste' ventured the opinion that the rock art on Groote had been painted not by the original Groote Islanders but by more recent arrivals from the mainland. Mountford wrote bluntly: 'Jerry's information totally unreliable.'[13] Some days later, however, he had risen slightly in Mountford's opinion. 'Jerry, the half-caste' gave 'some interesting information about burials'. But Mountford remained cautious because Gerry seemed to hold 'the Groote Eylandters in poor regard'.[14] When Gerry won a mention in the Expedition diaries, it was usually with the descriptor 'half-caste', always implying a lack of authority or authenticity. As a functionary of the Expedition—as a guide, translator or marine pilot—he was accepted and even taken for granted. But as someone of mixed race, he was of no use to Setzler's investigation of physical anthropology, presumably because Setzler also subscribed to his colleagues' notion of Arnhem Land being a Stone-Age society. As an ethnographic informant, Blitner was likewise seen as limited in value. In taking this course, the Expedition was turning its back on major discussions within anthropology. Since the interwar years, the desirability or otherwise of racial mixing had been a subject of theoretical and public interest. Racial purists were locked in debate with those who argued for the possible value of racial hybridity, especially in tropical environments. In 1926, the Harvard anthropologist Earnest A. Hooton had described miscegenation as 'perhaps the most important field of research in anthropology today'.[15] Hooton played a key role in initiating an earlier US–

---

11 Peter Worsley, who knew Blitner in the 1950s, confirms his proficiency in all these languages. Personal communication, 7 March 2010.
12 Frank M. Setzler, 1948, Diary kept on Arnhem Land Expedition, vol. 1, Papers of Frank Maryl Setzler, 1948–1973, MS 5230, NLA, p. 51.
13 Charles P. Mountford, 1948, Expedition to Arnhem Land, Personal Journal, vol. 1, p. 169, PRG 1218/17/12, Mountford-Sheard Collection, SLSA.
14 Ibid., pp. 188–9.
15 Cited in Anderson, W. 2009, 'Ambiguities of race: science on the reproductive frontier of Australia and the Pacific between the wars', *Australian Historical Studies*, vol. 40, no. 2, p. 151.

Australian research venture, the Harvard–Adelaide expedition run jointly by Norman B. Tindale and Joseph Birdsell in 1938–39. As Warwick Anderson points out, this 'Half-Caste Survey' was specifically motivated by an interest in the health and adaptability of 'the growing numbers of people in Australia claiming mixed European and Aboriginal ancestry'.[16]

Figure 19.3 Portrait of Gerald Blitner, 1948

Photograph by Frank M. Setzler. By permission of National Anthropological Archives, Smithsonian Institution. Photo Lot 36, Box 8, No. 88.

The Arnhem Land Expedition anthropologists never explained their lack of interest in mixed-race people, but it is fully evident in their attitude to Blitner. Even as a photographic subject, he was generally avoided as a waste of film. Mountford in particular kept him well outside the frame. My heart sank when, after the interview, I showed Gerry the 1949 *National Geographic* article on the Expedition, written by Mountford.[17] Given all he had done to support it, he expected to find a photo of himself. There was none, and his disappointment was palpable. Nor did he appear in Howell Walker's article on the Umbakumba settlement published four years later. Frank Setzler took just one photo of Gerry, which I found at the Smithsonian Institution: the final negative in a series of 88 that Setzler took on Groote. Even the numbering suggests that this was an afterthought. Unusually for Setzler, who was a more than competent

---

16 Ibid., p. 153.
17 Mountford, C. P. 1949, 'Exploring Stone Age Arnhem Land', *National Geographic* magazine, vol. 96, no. 6.

operator of his view camera, the photograph is technically poor, despite being a well thought-out composition. The challenge of photographing dark skin in harsh daylight is known to anyone who has used a camera in Arnhem Land. Setzler's task was made that much more difficult by the fact that Gerry was seated in the shade of the sail, which had the effect of heightening the contrast between him and the glare upon the water. The resulting image acquires what I suppose is an accidental symbolism: a darkening of Gerry to the point that his identity is obscured. Setzler must have rated the image a failure, for the negative was neither printed nor selected for inclusion in the set of lantern slides that he afterwards used in illustrated lectures. When asked about Gerry, Raymond Specht fondly described him as 'a power of strength' to Fred Gray and the Expedition members.[18] Yet in the visual record, he hovers at the edge of invisibility.

The Arnhem Land Expedition's absorption of racial ideology is never more explicit than in its treatment of Gerald Blitner. From the age of four, when, to the horror of his mother, he was catapulted into his new existence on the island, Gerry's mixed parentage had directed the course of his life. His marginality, his invisibility, his alleged 'unreliability' in the opinion of Mountford and others, must have been apparent to him, and I wonder whether his tendency to put himself centre stage in every story he told was not in some way an after-the-fact bid for compensation for the way his supposed racial hybridity had pushed him out of the picture in his dealings with the Expedition, as it did on countless other occasions during his life. People of mixed race were often portrayed as 'lost between two worlds', but this in no way approximated Blitner's experience or self-perception. For him, having mixed heritage was more like a form of dual nationality—an asset rather than a hindrance. According to his world view, it added to his authority as a worker and thinker. Since his was a knowledge rooted in two worlds, he had a greater pool of collective wisdom from which to draw. An altercation with incompetents in the air force that occurred during construction of a landing strip on the island illustrates the point:

> They couldn't even nail fibro. I said, 'Hey, stop doing that.' I went and told the superintendent, 'I'm the foreman of the—of the works. Tell 'em not to put anything anymore until I do it'…I said, 'This is the expert, Black Fella. Learn from two societies. Take it all off or get off the job.'

Gerry's linguistic talents, combined with building and carpentry skills, some mechanical know-how, and his willingness to work in almost any capacity, must have made him attractive to Fred Gray as a prospective employee. He never mentioned what year it was that he moved from the west coast to Umbakumba, but I suspect it was 1947. Superintendent Gray had been at him for years to come to work for him, and finally he accepted the offer. During the war, he had

---

18 Raymond Specht, Personal communication, 5 September 2007.

started working for the Royal Australian Air Force, and had taken up residence in military barracks. This marked his definitive break with the mission. He got out, he explained, because while he lived on mission premises his pay was kept in its entirety by the CMS. Economic independence was for Gerry a driving force, and that too can be connected with the sense of empowerment he drew from his white heritage.

Fred Gray (1899–1995) was a native of Worcestershire who migrated to Australia in his mid-twenties. Having lived mainly in the Gulf Country since 1932, he was, by 1948, considered a veteran of the region. An interest in trepanging brought him to coastal Arnhem Land where he developed a network of contacts with the local clans. Gray was close to several episodes of frontier violence in 1932, beginning at Caledon Bay, where five Japanese fishermen were fatally speared. The subsequent slaying of a sergeant on Woodah Island, and the deaths about this time of two imprudent sightseers in an unrelated incident, prompted media hysteria about murderous savages. Gray was involved in bringing the Yolngu elders Dhakiar and Merarra and three other men who admitted involvement in the violence to Darwin where they faced the justice system (a term I use loosely).[19] Gray's involvement in the incident greatly raised his profile with the Department of Native Affairs and the Northern Territory administration. The goodwill he won at that time would serve him in later years as he developed the settlement at Umbakumba.

Gray had visited Umbakumba, with its extensive lagoon, in the mid-1930s to harvest the sea slug known as trepang. In 1938, the Department of Civil Aviation identified it as an appropriate location for flying boats to land and refuel; 2832 ha were revoked from the Arnhem Land reserve and the construction of fuel tanks, a weather station and associated infrastructure commenced. Gray found employment organising an Aboriginal work force that numbered about 200. Construction ended, but the population that had built up at Umbakumba remained—and so did Gray. At what point he adopted the title 'superintendent' (a word favoured in missionary as well as asylum, prison and police circles) is difficult to tell, but as a white man among Aborigines he naturally saw himself in a position of leadership. By establishing gardens and bringing goats to the island, he maintained a trickle of income through the sale of meat and vegetables to the personnel who manned the Qantas base, among them Frederick Rose, a meteorologist, fervent communist and British-trained anthropologist, with whom Gray was friends for some years.

---

19   There are several accounts of the Caledon Bay killings. Examples include: Egan, E. 1996, *A Justice All Their Own: The Caledon Bay and Woodah Island killings 1932–1933*, Melbourne University Press, Carlton South, Vic.; Dewar, M. 1992, *The 'Black War' in Arnhem Land: Missionaries and the Yolngu 1908–1940*, the Australian National University North Australian Research Unit, Darwin; and McMillan, A. 2001, *An Intruder's Guide to East Arnhem Land*, Duffy & Snellgrove, Sydney, ch. 6. The 2004 film *Dhakiyarr vs the King* (dir. Tom Murray and Allan Collins) gives the perspective of contemporary Yolngu.

Before the war, Rose had been stationed at Umbakumba as a meteorologist and in his spare time he did a foundational study of Groote Eylandt kinship. He returned to the settlement with the Expedition party and stayed for some weeks, helping set up the anthropological research. Qantas services had been disbanded after the outbreak of the Pacific War, and the Umbakumba base was never again used for commercial aviation. Gray had remained at Umbakumba throughout the vicissitudes of the war years. He did not volunteer for military service, and instead carved out for himself a unique position on the island. Gerry cast Gray as an authoritarian figure whose offers of employment he had long resisted, partly because of reported violence on the settlement.

> I liked him but I still didn't like his—lot of his ways, like beating, molesting Black Fellas sometimes.
>
> Q. What do you mean molesting them?
>
> A. Belting them, hitting them with sticks just for the fun because he's a white man.

Gerry, who seemed to dislike speaking ill of anyone, had an ambivalent attitude to Gray, who by the time of his death at the age of ninety-five had become an iconic figure in the Northern Territory. He received the Order of Australia for his 'services to Aboriginal people'.[20] Amidst the memories of violence and disagreements, some sentimental feelings must have lingered, for a photograph of the two of them, taken years later at Gray's house outside Darwin, hung on Gerry's wall. He—and I gather most Aboriginal people on the island—addressed Gray as 'Dad', and sometimes Gerry referred to him as such in the interview. The familial language must to some extent have been modelled on the web of kinship affiliations indigenous to the island. Yet it also expressed his status as a patriarch. Gray's rule of the settlement was oppressive; Fred Rose later commented that 'Gray was no philanthropist and to implement his schemes he exploited the Aborigines', especially their ignorance of money.[21] Gerry would have agreed with this, and it is little wonder that he lasted only a few years in Gray's employ. Mountford's wife, Bessie, the Expedition secretary, expressed in her diary their collective bewilderment at the economic foundation of the settlement: 'Whence the finance we know not.'[22] But by careful if surreptitious observation, Gerry had figured it out. The income largely comprised revenue Gray received from the child endowment, a Commonwealth payment introduced in 1943 ostensibly for the purpose of supporting and strengthening the family unit. When the benefit was extended to the Aboriginal population, Gray exploited a loophole in the system that he might have learned about from the CMS missionaries who

---

20 Dewar, M. 1995, 'Fred Gray', (Obituary), *The Australian*, 4 August 1995.
21 Rose, *Australia Revisited*, p. 133.
22 Bessie Mountford, 1948, Arnhem Land Expedition Diary, vol. 1, Bessie Mountford Papers, p. 90, PRG 487/1/1, SLSA.

also made full use of it. This was a provision in the legislation that allowed any institution that kept children in dormitories to receive the child-endowment money and use it for their own ends. Gray—or rather his Aboriginal labourers—built dormitories where the children were compelled to sleep. As custodian, he could legitimately claim the allowance. Parents camped nearby to be close to the children and some took up work in the gardens. Gray was able to claim success in his civilising project on several fronts. He advertised the fact that thanks to his settlement, these former nomads were abandoning their wandering ways.[23] He explained to Bessie Mountford that the separation of children from their parents was justified because it gave him leverage in breaking up the tradition of polygamy on the island, where young brides were monopolised by older men.[24] The settlement numbered 163 inhabitants when the Expedition arrived.[25]

The constant pressure to demonstrate the usefulness of the settlement, and the lingering suspicion that a single white man in his position was on the lookout for sexual opportunities, might have contributed to his decision to propose by telegram to Marjorie Southwick, a schoolteacher he had known in England but had not seen for more than 20 years. Her decision to migrate from the south of England to marry Fred, and live with him on Groote Eylandt, is less explicable. In her memoir, *Life with the Aborigines* (1986), Marjorie said that she had always known that 'Fred was the only man for me'.[26] Bessie Mountford, whose diary best registered the emotional pulse of the Expedition, makes it plain, however, that Marjorie was abysmally unhappy. (Although they never divorced, Marjorie eventually returned to England and lived separately from Fred.) The bizarre world she had come to, and which she was keen to exit as soon as possible despite her affection for the Umbakumba residents, is apparent in film footage of the settlement, shot by Howell Walker.[27] Gray's propensity to unnerve the pen-pushers at Native Affairs is evident here in all its glory. Not for him the pith helmets and safari suits worn by Mountford and the likes. Rather than barrier himself against the tropics, Gray pared down his wardrobe to almost nothing. A loincloth or naga naga, as it is known in Aboriginal English, was his sole apparel. He wore it daily, as Gerry told me while we watched footage of Gray supervising a boxing match between two boys from the dormitory. As an agent of 'civilisation', Gray was at best unpredictable. He had a taste for music, and entertained the expeditioners with sessions around the gramophone, listening to his collection of classical discs. Yet these accoutrements of refinement never quite dispelled the bureaucratic suspicion that Frederick Gray had 'gone native'.

---

23   Gray's promotion of the settlement is apparent in Walker, H. 1953, 'From spear to hoe on Groote Eylandt', *National Geographic Magazine*, vol. 103, no. 1.
24   Bessie Mountford, 1948 Arnhem Land Expedition Diary, vol. 1, pp. 88–9, PRG 487/1/1, SLSA.
25   Cole, *Fred Gray of Umbakumba*, p. 99.
26   Gray, M. 1986, *Life with the Aborigines*, Regency Press, London, p. 9.
27   Walker, H. [as cine-photographer] 1950, *Aboriginal Australia*, (Lecture film), National Geographic Society, Washington, DC.

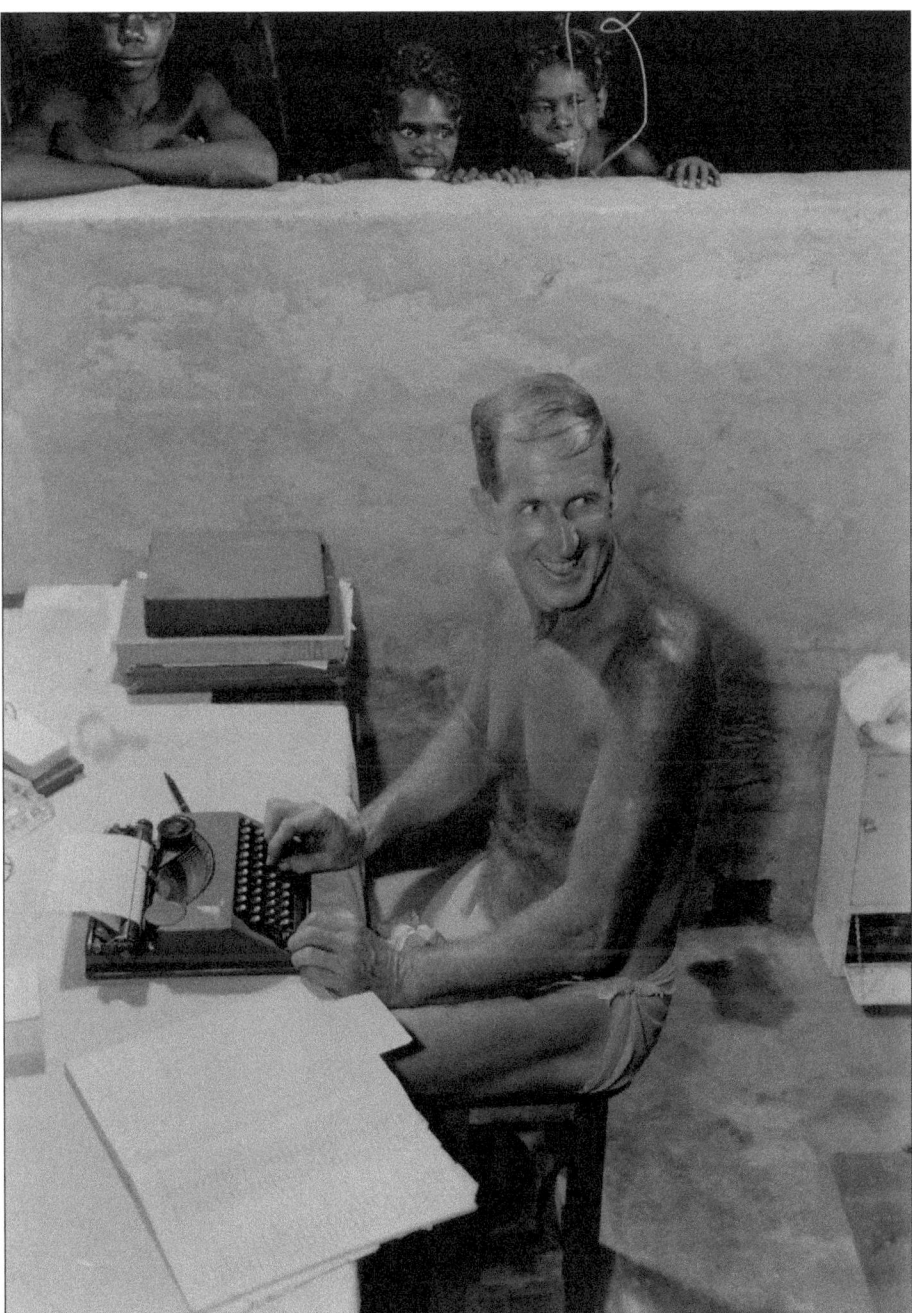

Figure 19.4 Fred Gray at Umbakumba, 1948

Photograph by Howell Walker. By permission of National Geographic Stock

Gerry claimed that the impending arrival of the Expedition was the reason Gray renewed pressure on him to come to work at Umbakumba. Knowing that the settlement would be under the spotlight, a makeover seemed appropriate. Gray had recently acquired a six-cylinder engine suitable for pumping water, and, with Gerry's energetic input and ability to mobilise the Umbakumba community, the gardens were greatly expanded to cover about 5 ha. 'The Mountford mob just come in at the right time,' he explained. The garden was flourishing and the whole place shipshape. Under Marjorie's tutelage, an enlarged school choir was ready to entertain the visitors. Gerry beamed proudly when he told of Mountford's effusive praise for the set-up. He said he regarded it as the best Aboriginal settlement he had ever seen. Privately, however, Mountford must have been reeling at this conspicuous display of 'civilisation', which McCarthy and others immediately identified as a failure in his planning. Landed in this imbroglio, the Expedition's three ethnological researchers pursued lines of inquiry that took them as far as possible from the queer spectacle that was Umbakumba. In the mode of physical anthropologist, Setzler searched for bones and other markers of racial uniqueness; McCarthy hunted for ancient rock art; and Mountford collected totemic symbols in the form of bark paintings and studied music and ceremony that seemed safely quarantined from historical influence.

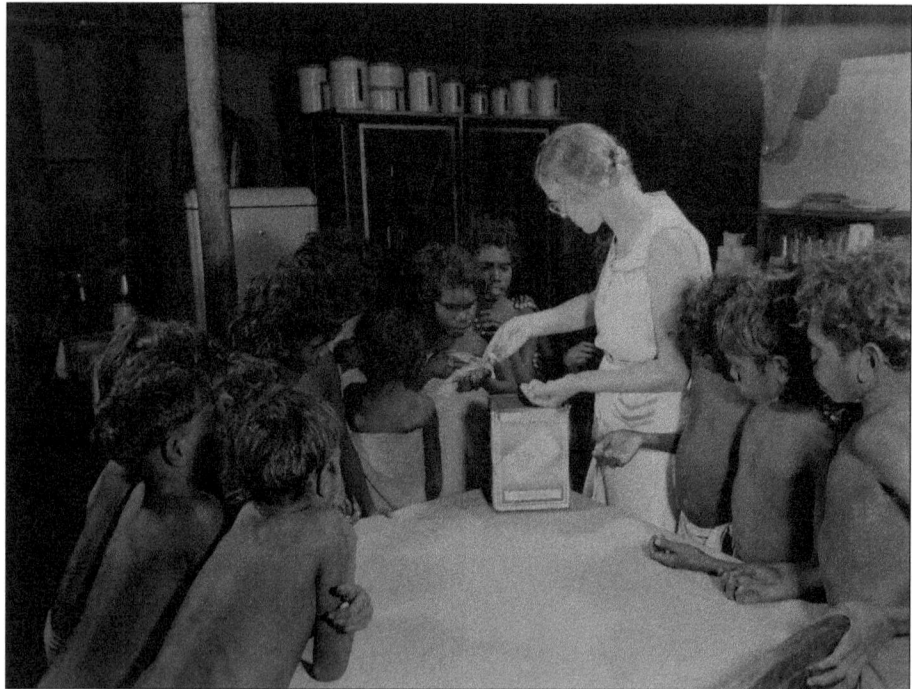

Figure 19.5 Marjorie Gray distributing food to children at Umbakumba, 1948

Photograph by Howell Walker. By permission of National Geographic Stock.

The role Gerry created for himself during the Expedition went far beyond his many acts of practical assistance. He became the unofficial go-between—a position that involved translation in the linguistic sense, and more. As we know from McCarthy, there were others at Umbakumba who spoke English, but most of them were young. The older people, who were most learned in law and culture, were the ones of greatest interest to the researchers. Gerry served as a conduit, moving back and forth between the scientists and the locals, articulating requests and delivering responses. He was party to both sides of the negotiations. His position is best thought of as a *cultural broker* or *intermediary*. The term 'cultural broker', which gained currency among North American historians in the 1990s, refers to a kind of specialist that emerged in nearly all situations of colonial contact and occupation. Motivated by necessity or opportunism—or frequently a combination of the two—cultural brokers played a central role in the two-way transmission of languages, ideas and commodities during the upheaval and confusion of the frontier experience. As the historian Margaret Connell Szasz explains it, cultural brokers devised ways of penetrating the borders between disparate peoples. Finding porosity in these boundaries, they forged 'pathways that link peoples rather than barriers that separate them'.[28] Trade, translation and diplomacy are among the roles assumed by such people. Szasz says of them:

> Of necessity, their lives reflected a complexity unknown to those living within the confines of a single culture. They knew how the 'other side' thought and behaved, and they responded accordingly. Their grasp of different perspectives led all sides to value them, although not all may have trusted them. Often they walked through a network of interconnections where they alone brought some understanding among disparate peoples. These mediators, therefore, have held a distinctive position in our past and into the present.[29]

The role of Gerry and other cultural brokers threw into question many of the claims to 'discovery' that were axiomatic to this large-scale scientific venture. For this and other reasons (including, in Gerry's case, his skin colour), their contributions are submerged to the extent that they are largely undetectable in official narratives such as the four-volume report on the Expedition. There is, however, sufficient evidence in other sources to build something of a picture of the young men who assumed roles of cultural brokerage in 1948. The social organisation of Arnhem Land is deeply gendered. The young men's age and gender were consistent with customary practice for dealing with visitors. Traditionally, it was the role of younger men to come forth as emissaries, negotiate

---

28   Szasz, M. C. 1994, 'Introduction', in M. C. Szasz (ed.), *Between Indian and White Worlds: The cultural broker*, University of Oklahoma Press, Norman, p. 3.
29   Ibid., p. 6.

with strangers, and report back to the senior men who wielded serious power. In 1948, the tendency towards male-to-male interaction, especially in the early meetings, was consolidated by the imbalance of the sexes *within* the Expedition party (representing as it did another highly gendered society).[30] Bessie Mountford, the honorary secretary, and nutritionist Margaret McArthur were the only women on a team that ultimately involved 17 researchers and support staff. The likelihood that younger Aboriginal men would assume positions as negotiators was increased by the widely variant education and life experience of mission residents in the immediate postwar era. The intergenerational mix included older people born and educated in the bush and younger folk schooled in English by missionaries or, at Umbakumba, by the Grays. Almost inevitably, young men made the opening gambits. In so doing, they were required to tread delicately around the factions and kin-based affiliations extant in their own communities. These are unlikely ever to have been straightforward, and in the mission era they were greatly complicated because a medley of sometimes rival clans, many of them bearing the grief of separation from their ancestral country, were concentrated together. This all added to the strain, indignity and confusion of negotiating the rules and expectations of Balanda (as white people are known throughout Arnhem Land).

In scenarios so fraught and complex, it stands to reason that the brokering of a successful relationship with the Expedition could enhance the status of the negotiator or of sectional interests with whom he was aligned. For Gerald Blitner, a relative newcomer to Umbakumba, the Expedition represented a considerable opportunity to consolidate his position within a settlement where he was still something of an outsider. The extent to which his skin colour marked him as different among the Umbakumba people is something I would have liked to ask about, but I never found a tactful way of phrasing the question. At times he spoke of being a 'yella fella'—a sometimes derogatory term in Aboriginal English. So I can only assume that he did at times experience a degree of discrimination from the Aboriginal side. His situation was thus very different to that of Wandjuk Marika, who performed an equivalent role when the Expedition was at Yirrkala. Wandjuk (1936–87) was the son of the esteemed artist and Rirratjingu clan leader Mawalan Marika. By dint of birth, he could expect a central place in the cultural and political life of Yirrkala—a position he certainly attained.[31] His closeness to the Expedition no doubt played a role in his family's high level of representation in the paintings collected and ceremonies performed during the Yirrkala sojourn of the Arnhem Land Expedition.

---

30 For discussion of gender and the Expedition, and the role of nutritionist Margaret McArthur within it, see Clarke, A. 1998, 'Engendered fields: the language of the 1948 American–Australian Expedition to Arnhem Land', in M. Casey, D. Donlon, J. Hope and S. Wellfare (eds), *Redefining Archaeology: Feminist perspectives*, ANH Publications, Research School of Pacific and Asian Studies, the Australian National University, Canberra.
31 See Marika, W. 1995, *Wandjuk Marika: Life story as told to Jennifer Isaacs*, University of Queensland Press, St Lucia.

For all the communities involved, the Expedition was both an opportunity and an imposition. The high level of cooperation it received makes little sense unless we grasp this prickly paradox. For the Arnhem Landers, the Expedition brought economic wealth: an influx of tobacco, trade goods, and a certain amount of cash. The economic reality of the Expedition, and the alternative it provided to the mission economies where tobacco and food supply were linked to church attendance and other disciplinary measures, explains much about the receptiveness of Arnhem Landers to the Expedition and the dislike of it on the part of missionaries.[32] Moreover, the Expedition provided occasion to study the ways of Balanda. This cannot be underrated, for at that postwar moment in Arnhem Land history, the need to come to grips with white Australia, and to convince it of the legitimacy of Aboriginal ways, was becoming ever more apparent. It is highly significant that later in their lives both Blitner and Marika entered the national stage as advocates for Aboriginal rights. Blitner served as deputy chairman of the Northern Land Council for 18 years, and was chairman from 1980 to 1983. In this, he built upon other experiences of cultural brokerage, including a period on Groote as an employee of the mining company GEMCO where he liaised between company officials and traditional owners.[33] Wandjuk attained distinction as an artist, musician, lawman and cultural ambassador. He was a founding member of the Aboriginal Arts Board of the Australia Council for the Arts and travelled internationally for festival and conference engagements. A great spokesman for his people, he was a bitter opponent of bauxite mining on the Gove Peninsula and contributed to that famed protest, the Bark Petition of 1963. To suggest that lessons from the Expedition, alongside many other interactions with Balanda, helped in formulating the ideas, the personal styles and political agendas of both these men is not being overly adventurous. To be efficacious, their campaigns for justice and recognition required knowledge of the society and political system that had long regarded them as Stone-Age curiosities.

There were members of the Expedition whom Gerry remembered with considerable fondness. He worked closely with the Smithsonian ichthyologist, Robert Miller, in developing his large collection of fish specimens from the island (see Miller and Cashner, this volume). The warmth between them is recorded in Miller's diary, recently acquired by the National Library of Australia, and is reflected in Miller's Kodachrome photographs.[34] In these images, Gerry does not lurk in the shadows as he does in the Setzler portrait. We see him as a family man, pictured at Umbakumba beside his wife, Jessie (nee Huddlestone), whom he married in 1946, and their first-born, Donald.

---

32 The corporal punishments meted out at Emerald River Mission are described in Dewar, *The 'Black War' in Arnhem Land*, p. 34.
33 I am indebted to Campbell Macknight for sharing these memories of Blitner in the 1960s. Personal communication, 26 March 2010.
34 R. R. Miller, 1948, Arnhem Land Expedition Diary, Papers of Robert Rush Miller, 1947–1951, MS 10053, NLA.

Figure 19.6 Gerald, Jessie and Donald Blitner at Umbakumba, Groote Eylandt, Northern Territory, 7 July 1948

Photograph by Robert Rush Miller. By permission of the National Library of Australia. PIC/12323/37.

Gerry's relationship with Mountford was not harmonious. He quickly became convinced that Mountford was personally hogging the resources of the settlement and the assistance of the Aboriginal people. To the frustration of the other members, he explained, Mountford 'was getting more trips than any other soul on board that expedition'. Gerry's alertness to rancour within the party is revealing, for it shows that the internal politics of the expeditioners were of interest and concern to the residents of Umbakumba, many of whom were forming their own relationships with particular researchers and who did not expect to be monopolised by just one of the visiting party. Blitner described an altercation involving Setzler and Miller, who complained to Mountford about the allocation of resources:

> 'We want more freedom with the boat and the use of Mr Blitner and some Aboriginals and we wanna see some of the islands too.' So I went and spoke to him [Mountford]. 'Dr Setzler and Miller and some English guys, doctors, it's their turn to go out and see something.' So I gave him merry hell, I gave Mountford merry hell, you know…I worked for those Americans—no, I mean I gave them more. I gave them more than I gave Mountford.

Gerry's admission that he tried to help other researchers more than Mountford suggests that ructions within the Expedition party were affecting the decision making of the Aboriginal hosts—and consequently influencing the path that the research was taking. Unlike the natural-history researchers, each of whom worked in his own clearly defined area of expertise, the crossover of interests among the three ethnological researchers made their situation on the island much more fraught.[35] Setzler and McCarthy fell into a sometimes uneasy alignment, while Mountford and McCarthy developed a hostility that lasted until the end of their lives. The stranding on a reef of the *Phoenix*, the dilapidated barge chartered to freight the supplies and equipment from Darwin to Groote, put strain on Gray with so many extra mouths to feed. As Gray's 'right hand man', Gerry was fully cognisant of the pressure it put on the community's resources—and on Gray's relationship with Mountford. On this matter, Gerry seems to have sided with Gray, whose feelings towards Mountford are made plain in his parting gift to the Expedition: an invoice for £307 for 'employment of Natives' during their time on the island. This could be read as a grab for cash on Gray's part, though it was also calculated to air his grievances. A memorandum accompanied the invoice, complaining that the 'deployment of natives to the Expedition completely upset the economy of this Settlement'.[36]

As newcomers to Arnhem Land, the ethnographic researchers tried to compensate for their lack of reference points within the local society. They sought help from the likes of Gray, Rose and Bill Harney who were more experienced than themselves, and they did their homework by reading the work of other scholars or travellers. The precedents set by earlier researchers greatly affected the perceptions of the visiting party. As much as the ethnologists were searching for 'new' data, the direction of their inquiries was profoundly influenced by earlier investigations. As a long-term associate of the South Australian Museum, Mountford had had plenty of time to study the writings and material culture collections of Norman Tindale, who worked on Groote in the early 1920s.[37] Gerry himself raised an intriguing example of this when we discussed Mountford's interest in secret-sacred ceremony. To paraphrase Gerry's position, he cast Mountford as something of a bull in a china shop in his approach. Gerry was deeply unnerved when Mountford listed a number of ceremonies that he hoped to witness during his residence on the island:

---

35 See May, S. K. 2010, *Collecting Cultures: Myth, politics, and collaboration in the 1948 Arnhem Land Expedition*, Altamira Press, Walnut Creek, Calif.

36 Invoice from F. H. Gray to Arnhem Land Expedition, 8 July 1948, AASEAL Correspondence, Volume 5, March–July 1948, Mountford-Sheard Papers, PRG 1218/17/8, SLSA.

37 Tindale, N. B. 1925–26 and 1928, 'Natives of Groote Eylandt and of the west coast of the Gulf of Carpentaria', parts I and II in *Records of the South Australian Museum*, vol. 3; part III in *Transactions of the Royal Society of South Australia*, vol. 53.

> I couldn't stand some of the stuff what Mountford kept on trying to initiate, you know, to make go. But he was after sacred things, very sacred: the Kunapipi, the Yabuduruwa, Lorrkon, Lilki, all those different dances, that we call 'em.
>
> Q. He wanted to make photos and things of them?
>
> A. Well, he wanted to make photos and things…And I said, 'You have to be very careful because these are not—not play dance, this is—this is the Kunapipi, you know. You must appreciate the Aboriginal sense of it all and bear holiness.

The revelation that Mountford asked to see these ceremonies struck me as odd. The rites mentioned are indigenous to the mainland, not to Groote Eylandt. Kunapipi, for example, is the large ceremony of male initiation, dedicated to the Rainbow Serpent, that spread widely across the Top End during the twentieth century, though even to this day it has never been held on Groote. When I probed Gerry about Mountford's wish list, he explained that it originated from a book by an American. The name of the author he had not thought about for years, and he first gave it as 'Walker', but then acknowledged it was wrong. Our discussions of Howell Walker had put him off the scent, though not by much. The American he was thinking of was not Walker, but *Warner*—as he quickly confirmed when I put forth the name. Despite the initial mix-up, it struck me as a rather stunning example of Gerry's attentiveness to the goings on of the Expedition and to the retentiveness of his memory. The diaries of Mountford, Setzler and McCarthy confirm that they each had a copy of *A Black Civilization* (1937) by W. Lloyd Warner. This classic monograph was based on fieldwork with the community known to Warner as the Murngin of North-East Arnhem Land. As the author of the most substantial ethnography so far published on Aboriginal life in the region, Warner was very much on their minds (see Hamby, this volume). Setzler had taken the trouble to visit him in Chicago prior to travelling to Australia. Not only did Gerry reveal that Mountford's reading of Warner was influencing the sort of data he hoped to film or in other ways document, he revealed that people on the island were comparing the approaches taken by the two researchers. Mountford, he said,

> thought he gonna get stuff like that, while Warner was doing things very quietly, you know, with man to man, but Mountford wanna be very, very abrupt and *the man*. He wanted to be *the man*: to find this, to give Australia that, you know, and I kept on talkin', 'Maybe you're tryin' to go too far.'

The proposition that Warner's methods were known and discussed on Groote Eylandt is not necessarily far fetched. As we know from the example of anthropologist and photographer Donald Thomson, researchers who lived among Arnhem Land communities for sustained periods became the subject of rich oral traditions. The twentieth century had seen the migration of mainland people, many from the Rose River region, to the western side of the island, and with them they brought a complex of ceremonies, one of which Mountford would eventually witness and document.

Gathering stories associated with sacred rock formations and other features of the landscape was high on Mountford's agenda. The eagerness with which he inquired into these subjects proved disconcerting to many of the men with whom he travelled around the island. Gerry remembered Banjo Nakwarrba, a senior man who dealt extensively with the researchers, being particularly aggravated at his persistence. He remembered Nakwarrba saying, '"By golly, you know, this fella, he wants to know about every jolly thing. We might as well make fib ones stickin' up in the air too, you know."' But Gerry counselled against outright fabrication:

> 'Well, I don't want to bully you mob. I don't want to bully the conversation here but you give him what you want him to know and—but don't tell him a lie, you know. It's—it's better to tell him a bit of the truth than a lie,' and they said, 'Yeah, you're right.'

In his manner and technique, Mountford created for himself some significant obstacles that had to be overcome in his quest to witness and document a major ceremony. The ritual life of Arnhem Land was for Mountford a subject of the highest interest. He was aware of the importance of ritual to social structure and cohesion, and to the maintenance of relationships between the people of today and the ancestral beings. He also knew from his experiences in Central Australia and elsewhere that ceremony was among the most dramatic aspects of Aboriginal culture. Mountford had attained elevation and celebrity within his own society through his adeptness in channelling Aboriginal content into the iconography of white Australia. Ritual, with its superb combination of dance and body painting, and its frequent use of sculptural objects, had particular cachet in this regard. The resulting imagery was as distinctively Aboriginal as you could get. Needless to say, it was highly photogenic (as long as it occurred in daylight hours). The musical dimension was also crucial, and Mountford, with a newfangled wire recorder as part of his kit, was well placed to capture technologically this ultimate signifier of a 'primitive' culture.

Given what Gerry said about Mountford's tactless and rather intrusive style, it is interesting that any ceremony was held at all. But after extensive negotiations, involving consultation with senior knowledge holders based at Rose River, the decision was made to hold an extended men's ceremony on the east coast of Groote Eylandt to which male members of the Expedition would be privy.

Mountford referred to it as the 'Arawaltja' and described it at length in Volume 1 of the Expedition records.[38] Gerry did not use this name for the ceremony, but he knew it well. At its heart is a beautiful sequence of dances that pays homage to the sea creatures that are totems to the major clans. Peter Worsley, who in 1957 published a highly critical assessment of Mountford's ethnography in MAN, has identified the use of the term *Arawaltja* as symptomatic of his 'amateurish' approach. The term *auwarawalja* (Worsley's spelling) is not the name of the ceremony but of the stringy-bark shelters that house sacred objects.[39] Mountford would make a similar blunder at Oenpelli (now Gunbalanya), where he gave the secret-sacred name of a ritual object as the name of the ceremony, rather than its proper title, the Wubarr (see Garde, this volume).

Mountford mentions that the ceremony he witnessed was performed only by 'those aborigines who live on the western side of Groote Eylandt'.[40] Blitner confirmed this when he watched the Expedition's footage of the ceremony on DVD. He said that he had first seen these dances when he was about fifteen and that the ritual had at that time been fairly recently introduced from the mainland by clans who had migrated there in recent generations. The performers of the ceremony were not the people of Umbakumba, with whom Mountford (according to Gerry) had rather burnt his bridges. Rather, visitors from the west of the island performed the 'Arawaltja'—much to the indignation of the locals, and to Gray as well. Mountford's diary records that Gray was 'somewhat opposed, because he is afraid of some old feuds breaking out afresh'.[41] His apprehension turned out to be justified, for when the delegation of performers arrived at Umbakumba from the west to commence the ceremony, tensions in the Umbakumba community were high and an ugly fight erupted (see Jones, this volume). Mountford, at some risk to himself, managed to break it up. They were forced to shift the ceremony from the outskirts of Umbakumba to Thompsons Bay—about 13 km distant. So Mountford did get to view and document a major ceremonial cycle, but he achieved this only by taking advantage of pre-existing divisions between the clans who inhabited the island. Gerry claimed to have had extensive discussions with the men who performed the ceremony. They reported that one of the reasons they went ahead with it was that Mountford was emphatic that he had been permitted to watch comparable men's ceremonies in Central and other parts of Australia and that this entitled him to the same level of access in Arnhem Land. When I questioned Gerry about the men's preparedness to allow cameras and a sound recorder into this secret ritual, he

---

38   Mountford, C. P. (ed.) 1956, *Records of the American–Australian Scientific Expedition to Arnhem Land. Volume 1: Art, myth and symbolism*, Melbourne University Press, Carlton, Vic., pp. 22–60.
39   Worsley, P. 2008, *An Academic Skating on Thin Ice*, Berghahn Books, New York, p. 90. The book review is item 241 in MAN, vol. 57 (December 1957), p. 186.
40   Mountford, *Records of the American–Australian Scientific Expedition to Arnhem Land*, vol. 1, p. 23.
41   Charles P. Mountford, 1948, Expedition to Arnhem Land, Personal Journal, vol. 2, p. 395, PRG 1218/17/13, Mountford-Sheard Collection, SLSA.

said that Mountford assured them that the documentation would be used only for research purposes and not shown publicly. If indeed Mountford made such a promise, he failed to keep it. Film and photographs of the Groote Eylandt ceremony were seen by men, women and children throughout the world.[42]

Figure 19.7 Gerald Blitner (left) and unidentified man with crocodile skin at Roper River, 1948

Photograph by Howell Walker. By permission of National Geographic Stock.

---

42 For further discussion of the documentation, see Thomas, M. 2007, 'Taking them back: archival media in Arnhem Land today', *Cultural Studies Review*, vol. 13, no. 2.

Figure 19.8 Gerald Blitner at home in Darwin, 2007

Photograph by Martin Thomas

Some four months after our interview, I was in Washington, DC, studying records of the Expedition at the Smithsonian. I had been there only a week when Sally May wrote with the sad news that Gerry had died in Darwin. It was February 2008. I heard that he was quickly flown to Groote and laid to rest on the island he loved. I was touched that his family, who did so much to encourage the interview going ahead, was anxious that I be advised of the news. With their support and permission, I have used their father's name publicly and reproduced these photographs of him.

Gerry's voice often came back to me during my time in Washington. I was thankful to think of him back on his island home, free of the pain and sickness of recent years. Even so, I yearned for a continuation of our conversation. How I would have loved to explore further the things we talked about, or to have shown him the beautiful black-and-white photographs taken by Howell Walker during their trip up the Roper, where Gerry's earliest years with his mother were spent. But such regrets—familiar to nearly all oral historians—by no means diminish the significance of Gerald Blitner's testimony. At the end of it all, he told me that he was deeply grateful he had done the interview, for he was himself surprised by the wealth of recollections it had prompted. The dialogue we enjoyed says much about the legacy of the Arnhem Land Expedition—still rippling and resonating 60 years later.

Acknowledgments

I am indebted to the family of Gerald Blitner for encouraging the interview and for allowing me to name and show photographs of their father in the wake of his passing. Thanks to Jon Altman, C. C. Macknight, Peter Worsley, Warwick Anderson, Rowena Dickins-Morrison, Amanda Harris and an anonymous peer reviewer for their comments on this chapter, and to Sally May for brokering the connection with Gerry. The interview was done as part of an Australian Museum Visiting Fellowship. The primary research in the United States was made possible by a Smithsonian Institution Fellowship. The National Geographic Society generously gave access to films, documents and photographs.

20. The Forbidden Gaze: The 1948 Wubarr ceremony performed for the American–Australian Scientific Expedition to Arnhem Land[1]

Murray Garde

They bin make im Ubarr, everyone bin go there, make that Ubarr, and they bin look that didjeridu.

'Hey! Ubarr alright!' And everyone they bin know…I went in front. They tell me…'This thing you can't tell im kid, you can't tell im friend, you can't tell im anybody, even your wife. You find your son…you can't tell im story about Ubarr, you got to tell im what I'm telling you now. This "outside" story. Anyone can listen, kid, no-matter who, but this "inside" story you can't say. If you go in Ring-place, middle of a Ring-place, you not supposed to tell im anybody…but oh, e's nice.' [2]

— Bill Neidjie

Introduction

Anthropology in Australia in the early twentieth century was dealing very much with the exploration and description of the unknown. The political and cultural underpinnings of the European project to colonise and document unknown peoples and places across the globe tell us as much about Western views of science and cultural development as they do about its colonial subjects of investigation. The *unknown* was in a process of being revealed, rationalised, classified and collected. In his preface to Charles Mountford's *Records of the American–Australian Scientific Expedition to Arnhem Land*, the Australian Minister of State for Information, Arthur Calwell, described Arnhem Land as

---

[1] Whilst this chapter discusses some aspects of ceremonial secrecy, it does not mention cultural information that is not in the public domain. In 1948, Aboriginal custodians of restricted Wubarr ceremonial knowledge had little idea that their treasured secrets were to be distributed in film and photographic form through mass media to those not entitled to view them. Even though the Wubarr ceremony is no longer performed, senior ceremonial custodians retain the right to decide which ceremonial matters or artistic depictions related to the ceremony can be made public. As a result, some artists paint Wubarr ceremony subjects from time to time, but do not make explicit in documentation details that are considered private.
[2] Bill Neidjie, in Taylor, K. (ed.) 1989, *Story About Feeling*, Magabala Books, Broome, WA, pp. 98–101.

'one of the least known parts of the earth's surface'.[3] In the early to mid twentieth century, anthropologists working in Arnhem Land such as Baldwin Spencer, W. Lloyd Warner, Herbert Basedow, A. P. Elkin, Donald Thomson and Ronald and Catherine Berndt had been working their way through a staggering array of complex systems of social organisation, religious traditions and extraordinary linguistic diversity, for which Aboriginal Australia is now famous.

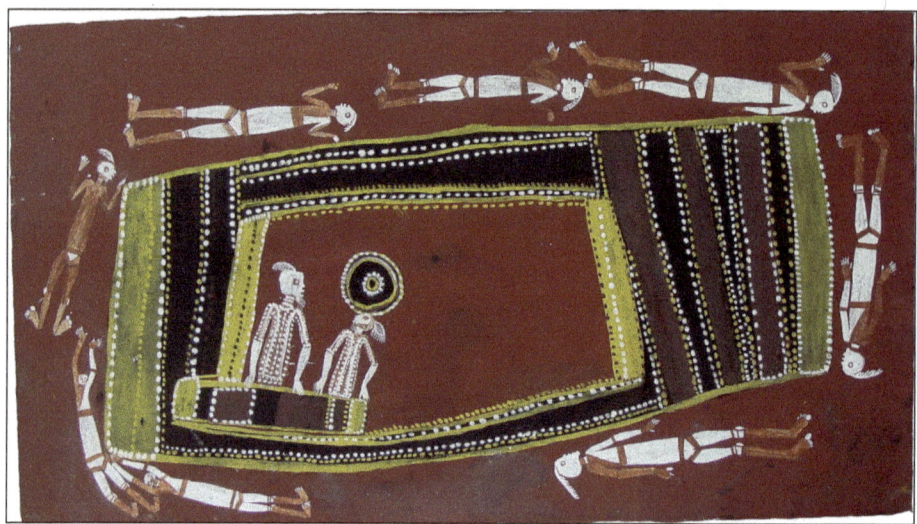

Figure 20.1 Lofty Bardayal Nadjamerrek, *The Wubarr Ceremony*. Earth pigment on paper, 2003

Private collection.

One of the more tangible expressions of Aboriginal religious and philosophical belief that attracted the attention of early anthropologists was the performance of religious rites and ceremonies. Major regional cult ceremonies in Arnhem Land encompass both public and secret domains of music, dance, ritual and visual arts. They celebrate and restate foundational mythologies that link the present with the origins of the cosmos and are spectacular expressions of many of the esoteric aspects of Aboriginal religion and art. Because the many religious ceremonies and rites they were witnessing were richly visual events, anthropologists in Arnhem Land frequently used still photography to document them. Until the late 1940s, ethnographic movie film was used less frequently, although both Spencer and Basedow made use of the cine-camera during their Arnhem Land expeditions.[4] Indeed, the world's first ethnographic film and the

---

3 Mountford, C. P. (ed.) 1956, *Records of the American–Australian Scientific Expedition to Arnhem Land. Volume 1: Art, myth and Symbolism*, Melbourne University Press, Carlton, Vic., p. vii.
4 Cantrill, A. and Cantrill, C. 1982, 'The 1901 cinematography of Walter Baldwin Spencer', *Cantrill's Film Notes*, nos 37 and 38 (April); Garde, M. and Kohen, A. 2004, 'Putting Herbert Basedow back in focus: the 1928 expedition to Arnhem Land', *Australian Aboriginal Studies*, vol. 2004, no. 1, pp. 126–36.

first ethnographic audio recordings made in Australia were those recorded by the Cambridge Expedition to the Torres Strait in 1898, led by anthropologist A. C. Haddon.

Film and the 1948 Arnhem Land Expedition

Charles Mountford's official Australian Government tours of the United States in 1945–46 involved the presentation of his Central Australian ethnographic films and photographs to large audiences. It was largely through the influence of these films, and the impression they left on American audiences, that National Geographic Society support for an expedition to Arnhem Land became possible. In his official proposal to the National Geographic Society, Mountford included 'the art of the body paintings, the general ethnology of the people [and] music in secular and ceremonial life' as areas of proposed anthropological research in northern Australia.[5]

Ethnographic film—either as unedited footage or as an assembled film documentary—had not yet developed into a fully functioning methodological tool of anthropology. Early ethnographic films were presented mostly to general audiences with the idea that they could offer an apparent transparency and immediacy beyond the abilities afforded by descriptive text. The idea, at least, was that complex rituals, dance and artistic accoutrement could be recorded in all their contextual detail for the very first time and revealed to a curious outside world. In the first half of the twentieth century, ethnographic film was frequently used for journalistic purposes. Such films operated as ethnographic reports for general consumption from the colonial front line.

Postmodern purges of anthropology have since exposed the illusion of the objective cinematographic eye, but this is not to say that ethnographic filmmakers of the mid twentieth century were always totally blind to the idea of their own culturally subjective perspectives. More recent contextualisations of early ethnographic photographic and film collections provide a better understanding of the layered meanings of these visual records.[6]

The 1948 Arnhem Land Expedition recorded performances of Aboriginal ceremony at Groote Eylandt and Gunbalanya (formerly Oenpelli). Ceremonial ritual and dance were recorded on movie film and still photography, and

---

5   Charles P. Mountford, 5 March 1945, Letter to the Chairman of the National Geographic Society Research Committee, Washington, DC, Accession File 178294, Smithsonian Institution Archives, Washington, DC.
6   For example: Batty, P., Allen, L. and Morton, J. (eds) 2005, *The Photographs of Baldwin Spencer*, Miegunyah Press, Carlton, Vic.; Peterson, N. 2003, *Donald Thomson in Arnhem Land*, (Second edition), Miegunyah Press, Carlton, Vic.; Poignant, R. and Poignant, A. 1996, *Encounter at Nagalarramba*, National Library of Australia, Canberra.

the accompanying music and speech were in some cases recorded on Pyrox magnetic wire recorders. At Groote Eylandt, the Expedition's first research location, Mountford arranged for what he termed an 'Arawaltja' ceremony to be performed near the Expedition camp (see chapters by Jones and Thomas, this volume). The ceremony was recorded on film and described and analysed in the first volume of the Expedition records.[7] Although the film documentation stands today as a rare and valuable record of complex ritual traditions, some of which are now defunct, members of the Expedition team were aware of the staged quality of their recordings, which flew in the face of their desire to record unadulterated 'primitives'. The 1948 Groote Eylandt ceremony was not performed in the usual location or at the usual time of the year. For convenience, Mountford arranged to have it performed within proximity of the base camp at Umbakumba and Expedition food was supplied to the performers.[8] For the Smithsonian archaeologist, Frank Setzler, this was a disappointment and rendered the ceremony 'artificial':

> How many dances were not put on that would have been used in their regular dance held at Amalipa we shall never know. One thing is certain and that is that no other Australian native ceremony has ever been recorded on cine film in color as this artificial corroboree has been. I say 'artificial' because all of it was put on for the benefit of the cameras. It would have been far better anthropologically if we could have been bystanders or photographers recording the dances and other activities during one of their annual dance ceremonies held in the regular sacred dance ground, Amalipa, during the fall [that is, late dry season] when the natives provide their own food, instead of the large tins of flour and other commodities supplied by Mountford. However, this film record is better than none.[9]

The 1948 Wubarr: Inception and performance

The Oenpelli ceremony recorded by the Expedition—known locally in various languages as *Wubarr*, *Ubarr*, *Uwarr* or *Guwarr*—is one of a number of major regional totemic cult ceremonies, and was in 1948 the most important in

---

7 Mountford, *Records of the American–Australian Scientific Expedition to Arnhem Land*, vol. 1, pp. 21–59.
8 Ibid., p. 39.
9 Frank M. Setzler, Diary, 1948, Papers of Frank M. Setzler, pp. 132–3, MS 5230, National Library of Australia (hereafter NLA), Canberra; also quoted in Thomas, M. 2007, 'Taking them back: archival media in Arnhem Land today', *Cultural Studies Review*, vol. 13, no. 2, p. 34.

Western Arnhem Land.[10] The ceremony was at one time also performed in North-East Arnhem Land, where it was referred to by the name *Ngurlmarrk*—an alternative term also used in Western Arnhem Land today, at least by the handful of old men who retain knowledge of the ceremony. Warner, who did fieldwork in the late 1920s, believed the Ngurlmarrk was recently adopted into the ceremonial repertoire of North-East Arnhem Land and at the time was 'still being learned by the older men'.[11] Warner's description of the ceremony and rituals makes it clear that this was a variation of the same ceremony performed in Western Arnhem Land. Also working in North-East Arnhem Land, Ian Keen confirmed the late adoption of the Ngurlmarrk, 'which probably originated from the *Wubarr* of Western Arnhem Land', but by the 1970s it was no longer being performed in the region.[12] Ronald Berndt, writing in 1962, noted that '[t]o the best of my knowledge the *ŋurlmag* has not been performed in full [in North-East Arnhem Land] for about 20 years'.[13] The last performance of the Wubarr in Western Arnhem Land is thought to have been about 1975 at Wulwunj near Mount Borradaile, 30 km north-west of Gunbalanya.[14]

A considerable amount of documentation of the Wubarr ceremony existed in 1948 when the American–Australian Scientific Expedition to Arnhem Land commissioned their ceremony at Gunbalanya.[15] I do not intend to discuss here the actual content of the 1948 film because senior custodians of the ceremony in Western Arnhem Land today regard most of this as restricted, as the Kundedjnjenghmi elders Bardayal Nadjamerrek and Jimmy Kalarriya explain:

> BARDAYAL: *Ubarr, daluk dja wurdurd kabarribekkan bad marrek kabarrinan. Marrek kabarringeybun, kabarriwakwan.*
> Women and children will hear the Ubarr [when the ceremony is performed], but they must not see it. They must not say the names [of certain ceremonial objects], they do not know about them.

---

10 The name of the ceremony varies depending on the language. The Alligator rivers languages around Gunbalanya, such as Mengerr, Erre, Urningangk and Gaagadju, called the ceremony *Ubarr*. The Kunwinjku people who moved into the Gunbalanya region from the east use the name *Wubarr*. The Iwaidja equivalent—from North-West Arnhem Land—is *Kuwarr*, and in Mawng on Goulburn Island it is *Uwarr*. Spencer also refers to the ceremonial ground as '*Goar*', which is most likely a cognate with *Kuwarr* (Spencer, B. 1914, *Native Tribes of the Northern Territory of Australia*, Macmillan, London, pp. 139–41). The fact that Frederick McCarthy records the Iwaidja name of the ceremony as *Gu:va:* (< *kuwarr*) in the title of his report on the ceremony might suggest that there were Iwaidja people present at the 1948 performance. See Frederick McCarthy, Gu:va: Ceremony at Oenpelli, 1948 typescript report, Folder 135, MS 5253, NLA.
11 Warner, W. L. 1969 [1937], *A Black Civilization: A study of an Australian tribe*, Harper and Row, New York, p. 301.
12 Keen, I. 1994, *Knowledge and Secrecy in an Aboriginal Religion*, Clarendon Press, Oxford, p. 142.
13 Berndt, R. M. 1962, *An Adjustment Movement in Arnhem Land*, Cahiers de L'Homme, Mouton, Paris and The Hague, p. 40.
14 †Mindabbarl Manakgu and Sam Namarulga, Personal communication, December 2006.
15 Spencer, *Native Tribes of the Northern Territory*, pp. 133–44; Spencer, B. 1928, *Wanderings in Wild Australia. Volume 2*, Macmillan, London, pp. 765–72; Warner, *A Black Civilization*, pp. 301–19.

KALARRIYA: *Nungan Wubarr ka-warlkayindi.*
The Wubarr ceremony is secret [literally, 'it stands hidden'].

Four performances of the Wubarr have been documented at Gunbalanya by anthropologists: Spencer in 1912;[16] Ronald and Catherine Berndt in 1947;[17] the Arnhem Land Expedition in 1948;[18] and the Berndts again in 1950.[19] In 1964, a Wubarr was also filmed on Goulburn Island (where the ceremony is called Uwarr)—a production made under the auspices of the newly established Australian Institute of Aboriginal Studies (now the Australian Institute of Aboriginal and Torres Strait Islander Studies: AIATSIS).[20]

In light of his comments about the perceived inauthenticity of ceremonies commissioned by non-Aboriginal visitors, Frank Setzler might have envied Baldwin Spencer, who had recorded the Wubarr (which he spelled *Ober*) near Oenpelli in July 1912. Spencer was visiting the buffalo shooter Paddy Cahill near the East Alligator River when the first stages of the ceremony were performed.[21] Being in the right place at the right time allowed Spencer to witness the rites performed by Gaagadju and neighbouring Alligator rivers language groups over a number of days. His documentation, including numerous photographs, song texts, diagrams and other descriptive material, makes it clear that this was indeed a Wubarr performance. In addition to Warner's and Spencer's descriptions of the ceremony, the Sydney University anthropologist A. P. Elkin mentions the Ngurlmarrk or Wubarr ceremony in his 1938 classic, *The Australian Aborigines*.[22] Mountford in 1948 was no doubt aware of this documentation and when the Australian Broadcasting Commission (ABC) radio journalist Colin Simpson joined the Expedition at Gunbalanya, the two men developed a plan to commission an 'aboriginal corroboree', as Simpson outlined in his book *Adam in Ochre*:

> Radio, this side of television, is non-pictorial and so was considered near to being non-competitive [with the *National Geographic* magazine's exclusive rights to cover the Expedition], and, by permission, we could go in and do a 'feature' on the expedition and gather whatever else seemed interesting to describe and record in sound, such as aboriginal

---

16   Spencer, *Native Tribes of the Northern Territory*, pp. 133–44; Spencer, *Wanderings in Wild Australia*, vol. 2, pp. 765–72.
17   Berndt, R. M. and Berndt, C. H. 1951, *Sexual Behaviour in Western Arnhem Land*, Viking Fund Publications in Anthropology, New York, pp. 114–38.
18   Frederick McCarthy, Gu:va: Ceremony at Oenpelli, 1948 typescript report, Folder 135, MS 5253, NLA.
19   Berndt, R. M. and Berndt, C. H. 1970, *Man, Land and Myth in North Australia: The Gunwinggu people*, Ure Smith, Sydney, pp. 128–32, plates between p. 86 and p. 87.
20   Holmes, C. (dir.) 1964, *Uwar of Goulburn Island* [The Uwar Ceremonies of Goulburn Island], Australian Institute of Aboriginal Studies, Audiovisual Collection, DAC00037_1-7, Australian Institute of Aboriginal and Torres Strait Islander Studies (hereafter AIATSIS), Canberra.
21   Spencer, *Native Tribes of the Northern Territory of Australia*, p. 765.
22   Elkin, A. P. 1938, *The Australian Aborigines*, Angus & Robertson, Sydney, pp. 257–8 and 260.

corroboree. For years the British Broadcasting Commission had been asking the A.B.C. for corroboree sound, and the A.B.C.'s face had been red with not having any to meet the B.B.C.'s requests.[23]

Simpson goes on to describe how he discussed local ceremonial traditions with Mountford and, in particular, the possibility of recording the sacred sounds of secret objects used in the Wubarr. Mountford tells Simpson: 'It would be really something if you could get that corroboree on your wire-recorder—and at the same time we could get it on ours.'[24]

Important regional ceremonies in Western Arnhem Land usually involve weeks of preparation and organisation. Various kinds of payments between people of particular social categories and ceremonial moiety groups are mandatory. They can involve food, trade goods and, most importantly, tobacco. Weeks before the rites commence, initiated youths are sent out as ceremonial messengers to invite distant groups to the ceremony. Simpson records that the 1948 Wubarr was organised by 'some old men of the Gunwinggu tribe' over a few days after he and Mountford conceived of the idea and put the request to them.[25] The ceremony was also paid for by Mountford with food and tobacco—this being in keeping with the Expedition practice of remunerating Aboriginal people for services rendered, as well as the local cultural practice relating to the commissioning of religious ceremonies.[26] The Wubarr rituals were usually held over a number of weeks. In August 1947, Ronald Berndt saw a Wubarr performed at Oenpelli over a period of six days. He noted that the rituals he saw 'normally extend over a much longer period'.[27] It is likely this 1947 ceremony had already been in progress for some days or weeks when Ronald Berndt and his wife, Catherine, arrived and conducted fieldwork (from 31 July to 12 August 1947).

The Wubarr ceremony commissioned by Mountford at Gunbalanya was reduced to a single day—Saturday, 23 October 1948—and was therefore greatly modified for the convenience of the non-Aboriginal audience. Many Wubarr rituals take place at night, but on the last day of the ceremony, the concluding rites in the public camp where women are present, occur in the morning.[28] To make it possible to photograph the ceremony, Mountford's 1948 condensed version of the Wubarr commenced in the morning and concluded in the afternoon after

---

23 Simpson, C. 1951, *Adam in Ochre: Inside Aboriginal Australia*, Angus & Robertson, Sydney, p. 6.
24 Ibid., p. 6
25 Ibid., pp. 6–7.
26 Colin Simpson, n.d., Footnotes: The [deleted restricted word] Corroboree, Papers of Colin Simpson, Folder 135, MS 5235, NLA.
27 Berndt and Berndt, *Sexual Behaviour in Western Arnhem Land*, p. 138.
28 Jimmy Kalarriya, Personal communication, 2009; Berndt and Berndt, *Sexual Behaviour in Western Arnhem Land*, p. 131.

the Expedition team had retired for a lunch break. As well as food and tobacco, Mountford went so far as to supply body paint for the ceremony. Frank Setzler's diary records the details:

> October 23, 1948—Saturday.
>
> This was the day planned for the corroboree. About 9:30 a.m. Walker and I took our cameras and walked over to the north side at the foot of Oenpelli Hill…About 10 a.m. the natives began to paint their bodies. The first dance was a sort of preliminary one to satisfy the spirits. Monty furnished them with some of his commercial paints…I took my 4 x 5 Speed Graphic and made 24 photos up to 12:00 noon. Used K-1 filter throughout and I hope they come out OK. We had an intermission at noon…After resting in the hot breezes blowing through the tent until 2:30, we went back to the corroboree…Fred got the description of the various dances. He has given me a copy.[29]

Setzler's 'Oenpelli Hill' is known by Aboriginal people as Arrkuluk—a hill on the southern side of the township, and a traditional Wubarr ceremony ground (see Figure 20.2). Wubarr ceremonies were usually performed at the base or on the top of elevated landscapes. This longstanding tradition is reflected even today—if not geographically, then linguistically—in the major regional ceremonies that have replaced the now defunct Wubarr, such as the Kunabibi and Yabbadurruwa. To enter the restricted men's ceremonial ground from outside, one says figuratively in the Bininj Gunwok dialects of Western Arnhem Land, *nga-bidbun*—'I'm going up'—regardless of whether the speaker will ascend, descend or walk across a flat area to get to the ceremony ground.

Setzler's interpretation of dances being performed to 'satisfy the spirits' is totally inconsistent with Aboriginal religion in general, let alone with what we now know about the Wubarr ceremony from other documentation.[30] Such interpretations have more in common with the trope of Hollywood voodoo than they do with the ethnographic realities of the Wubarr ceremony. Indeed, as historian Martin Thomas has already pointed out, Mountford's filming direction had its own touch of Hollywood in the way he staged aspects of these ceremonies.[31] Projecting an image of Aboriginal people in keeping with Mountford's primitivist views required a certain amount of stage management in the costume department. At Groote Eylandt, the performers wore too little or no clothing during ceremonial performance, so Mountford arranged for them to wear cotton loincloths that he had prepared and dyed with ink, thus creating

---

29   Frank M. Setzler, Diary, 1948, Papers of Frank M. Setzler, pp. 253–5, MS 5230, NLA.
30   For example: Berndt and Berndt, *Sexual Behaviour in Western Arnhem Land*, pp. 114–38; Berndt and Berndt, *Man, Land and Myth in Northern Australia*, pp. 128–32; Holmes, *Uwar of Goulburn Island*.
31   Thomas, 'Taking them back', pp. 25, 33.

the illusion of nakedness while still satisfying the sensitivities of his intended audiences.³² At the Oenpelli Wubarr performance, it was the opposite problem. Offending trousers had to come off in favour of loincloths, as anthropologist Frederick McCarthy recorded in his diary entry for the day of the ceremony: 'In the beginning [of the ceremony] one man appeared in a pair of long pants and Monty made him change into a Naga loin-cloth. He yelled out—Take them off, I'm paying for this.'³³

Figure 20.2 Arrkuluk, or 'Oenpelli Hill', where the 1948 Wubarr ceremony took place

Photograph by Murray Garde

The ceremonial performers, together with the group of Expedition photographers and onlookers, must have been quite a spectacle. From the diary and personal testimony of botanist Raymond Specht, who also witnessed the ceremony, we know that colour movie film was taken by cine-photographer Peter Bassett-Smith as well as by National Geographic Society photographer, Howell Walker. Mountford also took black-and-white movie footage of the ceremony, while Setzler and McCarthy took still photographs. One of McCarthy's images later appeared in the entry for 'Aborigines' in the 1958 edition of *The Australian Encyclopaedia*.³⁴ Ray Specht's letter home to his parents describes the photographic frenzy:

---

32 Letter from Expedition doctor, Brian Billington, to the Director of the Australian Institute of Anatomy, Frederick Clements, 18 June 1948, A2644, National Archives of Australia, Canberra. Billington says of the loincloths: 'Hollywood has nothing on C.P.M.' (that is, Mountford). Also quoted in Thomas, 'Taking them back', p. 25.
33 Frederick McCarthy, Papers of Frederick David McCarthy, Diary 5, Yirrkala Diary No. 2 and Oenpelli, 1948, MS 3513/14/5, AIATSIS.
34 McCarthy, F. 1958, 'Aborigines', in A. H. Chisholm (ed.), *The Australian Encyclopaedia. Volume 1*, (Second edition), Angus & Robertson, Sydney, p. 72a.

> Colin Simpson and Ray Giles have been out here doing an actuality broadcast for the A.B.C. Over the week-end, they recorded some corroborees. You have never seen anything like it—three movie cameras (Monty, Howell and Peter), two still cameras (Frank and Fred) and the A.B.C. However, in spite of this confusion, they all got some good material and appear quite happy with the results. I abandoned collecting plants on Saturday—for shame—and watched; it was a very interesting ceremony.[35]

Colin Simpson, replete with pith helmet and microphone, can be seen in some of the film footage as he darts in and around the Aboriginal performers making his audio recordings. The competition amongst the Expedition team members—all positioning themselves to get unimpeded photographic angles of the ceremony—is also revealed in McCarthy's descriptions of the melee:

> 23 Oct. An Ubar ceremony (see typed account) was held at Oenpelli Hill where the natives had a dancing ground, on the western side. Two young men were initiated. Colin Simpson made a wire recording, and bolted into the middle of the dancers all the time so spoiling the spectacle for the photographers—actually he spoilt a very beautiful and impressive performance for them…at another stage I was photographing when Bassett-Smith put his movie camera on a lower rock and spoilt my view—within a few minutes he fell off, with his camera, I said to Harney, 'Thank God, he's gone' forgetting that he might have injured himself and damaged his camera—Fortunately he didn't.[36]

Sacred Ceremonies, Secrecy and Politics

The recording of the 1948 Wubarr was a hybrid social scientific and journalistic endeavour that today raises the obvious issue of the cross-purposes of journalists and Aboriginal custodians of secret-sacred ceremonial knowledge. With the increasing visual and audio documentation of Aboriginal cultures, especially from the 1940s onwards, ethical issues relating to the publication of secret-sacred Aboriginal cultural and intellectual property developed momentum throughout Australia. One of the more egregious incidents involving the publication of culturally restricted photographs involved T. G. H. Strehlow and *Stern* magazine in 1978. In an attempt to raise funds for the maintenance of his extensive collection of Central Australian material culture, Strehlow sold highly

---

35 Raymond Specht, Letters of Ray Specht, Extract from letter to parents dated Oenpelli, October 25 1948. Extract communicated by email, 6 November 2009.
36 McCarthy, Papers of Frederick David McCarthy, Diary 5, Yirrkala Diary No. 2 and Oenpelli, entry for 23 October 1948.

sensitive and culturally restricted photographs to the German magazine *Stern*, which then—unbeknownst to Strehlow—sold them on to *People* magazine in Australia. To the shock and outrage of Central Australian communities, *People* published them in an article about Strehlow and Arrernte culture.[37]

In 1977, just a year before the *Stern* incident, Mountford himself was involved in a similar controversy with the publication of his book *Nomads of the Australian Desert*, which contained photographs of secret-sacred subjects and other information given to Mountford by Pitjantjatjara men on the condition that it remain confidential. The book was withdrawn from sale in the Northern Territory after a court injunction.[38]

In 1948, the Expedition team in Gunbalanya was aware of the secrecy of the Wubarr ceremony and that what they were recording was not in the public domain. Simpson in *Adam in Ochre* (1951) dedicates a chapter to the performance of the 1948 Wubarr, including colour photos of secret rituals and objects used in the ceremony. Details concerning the manufacture, secret names and use of these objects are fully divulged. He acknowledges that these are things that women and the uninitiated must never hear mentioned, let alone see.[39] The book sold more than 50 000 copies and the secrets of the Wubarr were secret no more. In addition to the publication of Simpson's book, Setzler later showed Wubarr film footage in public lectures across the United States. Whilst we have no evidence of the Aboriginal custodians of this material being consulted about this at the time, Thomas points out that Simpson did indeed explain to the Expedition's principal Aboriginal interpreter at Gunbalanya, Larry Marrawana, that the public didjeridu-accompanied songs that Simpson was recording on his Pyrox wire recorder (and unrelated to the Wubarr) would make their way into radio programs that would be broadcast across Australia.[40]

Simpson's main objective had been to produce an ABC radio documentary about the Wubarr for the series *Australian Walkabout* (see MacGregor, this volume). He produced a script and edited the audio for the production, but it was never broadcast—on the advice of Elkin. The issue at stake was not so much that the public revelation of the secret ceremonial material would distress the Aboriginal community, but rather that such distress might put future research at risk. Simpson's account of the incident can be found among his unpublished papers:

---

37 'Secrets of the Arandas', *People Magazine*, 3 August 1978, p. 22.
38 *Foster and Others v. Mountford and Rigby Ltd*. 14, *Australian Law Reports* (1977), p. 71.
39 Simpson, *Adam in Ochre*, p. 13.
40 Thomas, 'Taking them back', p. 32; Simpson, *Adam in Ochre*, p. 67. Larry Marrawana has been identified as a na-Kodjok subsection man of the Wurrik clan. His wife, Esther Maralngurra, and children (a son and a daughter) are still living at Gunbalanya and its outstations today.

> The recording of the [Wubarr]⁴¹ Corroboree has never gone on the air. The script was referred to Professor Elkin, head of the Department of Anthropology at the University of Sydney. He said we had recorded a 'secret' corroboree which should not be broadcast, as such a broadcast might embarrass further anthropological research in Arnhem Land if it became known to tribal leaders that such ceremonies, sacred to them, were being broadcast to the hearing of women and uninitiated young men. I never did see how that could happen and I never did agree with Professor Elkin's judgement on this matter, which the Australian Broadcasting Commission accepted and which amounted to a ban, except that Professor Elkin said he did not mind the feature being broadcast outside Australia.[42]

In the more recent postcolonial decades, when some anthropologists and journalists were slowly gaining awareness of the ethical implications of publishing culturally sensitive documentation, Aboriginal people themselves were gradually realising that books, photographs and films of their secret-sacred ceremonies had been circulated by anthropologists and journalists in the public domain, risking exposure of these private and ritually dangerous images to their women and children.[43] As Simpson's comments demonstrate, these concerns within Aboriginal communities were used as ammunition in the political rivalries amongst anthropologists and journalists in Arnhem Land and elsewhere. Mountford was unpopular, not only with many of his Expedition team members, but also with certain anthropologists of the day, particularly Elkin and his acolyte Ronald Berndt, who might have felt snubbed at being excluded from such a high-profile Expedition. Elkin often found opportunity to criticise and belittle the findings of the Expedition.[44] Likewise, Mountford took delight in attacking Elkin and the Berndts in the Expedition records, casting aspersions on Ronald Berndt's well-known preoccupation with sexuality in Aboriginal culture:

> Elkin and the Berndts casually mention cave paintings at Oenpelli... These writers, whose main interest appears to have been the eroticism of the cave paintings, saw little to interest them in the hundreds of colourful X-ray paintings, or the delightful groups of little *Mimi* running figures. The only cave paintings these writers specifically mention (already described by Spencer) is [sic] illustrated by a bark painting made by

---

41 The original word used here is restricted.
42 Colin Simpson, n.d., Supplement: [restricted word deleted]: Myths and a Ban, Papers of Colin Simpson, Folder 135, MS 5235, NLA.
43 Peterson, N. 2003, 'The changing photographic contract: Aborigines and image ethics', in C. Pinney and N. Peterson (eds), *Photography's Other Histories*, Duke University Press, Durham, NC, pp. 119–45.
44 For example, there are sniping exchanges in the correspondence between Elkin and Simpson in Simpson's personal papers, MS 5253/206, NLA.

a young aboriginal. Although the writers claim that this bark painting is a replica of the original cave painting…this claim is far from being correct.[45]

In return, Berndt, writing in 1962, identified the 1948 Expedition as instrumental in the collapse of traditional religious life on Elcho Island. As Ian McIntosh discusses at greater length in this volume, Berndt quoted one of the leaders of the Elcho Island 'adjustment movement', David Burrumarra, who criticised the publication of photographs and films of secret ceremonies and sacred ritual objects (known as *raŋga* in North-East Arnhem Land) by the Arnhem Land Expedition:

> They [anthropologists] took pictures of our sacred ceremonies and *raŋga*, and we got excited. Why do they do this? We understood this when Warner, Thomson and the Berndts were here. But why do they come again and again to study us? They take photographs of sacred things and show them to all the people throughout Australia and other places…We got a shock. We're not supposed to show these *mareiin*, these *raŋga* to just anybody…All this made us think…Then we saw a film at the Elcho church. It was from the American-Australian Expedition, and it showed the sacred ceremonies and emblems. And everybody saw it…We've got no power to hide (these *raŋga*): they are taking away our possessions. Are we to lose all this? Our most precious possessions…this is really our only wealth.[46]

Ronald Berndt's own publications on Aboriginal secret-sacred ceremony have, however, also caused distress in some Aboriginal communities in Arnhem Land over the years. The rock art archaeologist George Chaloupka recalls an incident in 1974 when he was visiting Warruwi on Goulburn Island in his capacity as an officer of the Museum and Art Gallery of the Northern Territory to investigate damage done to ceremonial sites:

> In 1974, John Gwadbu, a member of the National Aboriginal Consultative Committee, acting on behalf of the Goulburn Island Council asked the visiting Senator Jim Keefe of the Federal Government to arrange for a survey and protection of their island's sites of significance. A number of important localities including ceremonial sites were recently disturbed.
>
> The Department of Aboriginal Affairs approached the Museum and Art Gallery of the Northern Territory and on 15 December I left for Warrawi. On my arrival at Goulburn Island the Acting President of the Goulburn Island Council Phillip Magulnir told me of the people's anger on finding

---

45 Mountford, *Records of the American–Australian Scientific Expedition to Arnhem Land*, vol. 1, p. 111.
46 Berndt, *An Adjustment Movement in Arnhem Land*, p. 40.

the Berndts' 1970 publication *Man, Land and Myth in North Australia: the Gunwinggu People*, with its explicit illustrations of ritual and sacred objects and structures in the possession of a young European woman. Phillip Magulnir asked me to take their message of disapproval for the public use of such material to the Australian Institute of Aboriginal Studies. John Gwadbu, George Winungoidj and Frank Marrali were also present. I recorded their communication.

The tape recording survived Cyclone Tracy, and in late January 1975 while in Canberra visiting family, I gave the tape to Peter Ucko [Institute Principal at the time]. I learned that Peter Ucko mentioned the Goulburn Island message at the meeting of a Publications Committee of which Berndt was a member, which apparently caused him some embarrassment.[47]

Again, in 2003, a copy of Ronald Berndt's book *Kunapipi*,[48] which contains documentation and photographs of that secret cult ceremony, was discovered by Aboriginal visitors to the Jabiru town library in Kakadu National Park, which caused similar shock and concern among senior ceremonial leaders such as Jimmy Kalarriya, who asked that the book be withdrawn.[49]

Repatriation of the 1948 Wubarr Film

The recent repatriation of photographs and film of the 1948 Wubarr ceremony was carefully negotiated between Western Arnhem Land elders and Martin Thomas in 2005–06. Acting as an intermediary, I approached Urningangk-Kunwinjku language elder Jacob Nayinggul and Mengerrdji-Kunwinjku Gunbalanya traditional owner Donald Gumurdul, telling them about the existence of the film footage, which had now been transferred to DVD.[50] Both men were initially cautious, but for good reason, as they explained. Some five years previously, a delegation from a southern cultural institution arrived in Gunbalanya with copies of the 1948 Wubarr on video cassette. Without first checking, and apparently with no knowledge of the cultural sensitivity of the content, a public showing of the film was arranged in the Gunbalanya Sports and Social Club—that is, the local pub. An audience of Aboriginal men, women and children gathered to watch with no knowledge of what it was they were about to see. The video commenced displaying the secret-sacred images of the Wubarr

---

47 Personal communication, 24 July 2009.
48 Berndt, R. M. 1951, *Kunapipi*, Cheshire, Melbourne.
49 Jimmy Kalarriya, Personal communication, 2003.
50 The film footage first returned to Arnhem Land in 2006 was that held in the archives of the AIATSIS Audiovisual Collection: V2451, V2453, V2954 and V2955.

ceremony filmed half a century earlier. Donald Gumurdul told me that after about a minute of this, he rose from his seat, went to the video cassette player, ejected the cassette, and silently walked out of the room with the cassette in his hand. The remainder of the Aboriginal audience left the building in a state of shock and embarrassment.

Martin Thomas has detailed an account of some of the reactions of Aboriginal men in Western Arnhem Land to the 2006 film repatriation, which was handled with more caution and consultation than the Gunbalanya fiasco some years previously.[51] At Kabulwarnamyo Outstation on the Arnhem Land Plateau, Kundedjnjenghmi elder Bardayal Nadjamerrek asked to view the 1948 Wubarr film after he was told of its existence. Together with other men of the outstation community, a private viewing was held, with Bardayal Nadjamerrek explaining the ceremony to younger men who had not seen a Wubarr, but had been inducted into the Kunabibi, which in the past 50 years has replaced the Wubarr as the most important large regional ceremony in Western Arnhem Land.

Bardayal Nadjamerrek conducted a lucid commentary on the ceremony and the names of the various rituals, interspersing this with exclamations of sheer pleasure in the manner of an audience at an actual ceremonial performance. His emotionally charged comments in the Bininj Gunwok language contained the kind of expressions one uses when expressing affection for a person one holds dear. The Wubarr ceremony film footage and Simpson's sound recordings were replayed simultaneously a number of times at that first session, and, at Bardayal's request, it was repeated numerous times at further morning sessions on each of the following days. Bardayal Nadjamerrek's responses were recorded as he watched and a selection of these is transcribed below.

Commentary Extract 1

> BARDAYAL: *La yi-na na-ngamed Djawirdda, Ngabbard yo, yo la yi-na, that old man tharran now, that old ya!*
> Look here, it's what's-his-name, Djawirdda, [I call him] my [classificatory] father, yes, yes, look, that's the old man now, yes that old man.
>
> MG: *Djawirdda Balang na-Kurnumbidj?*
> Djawirdda, Balang skin of the Kurnumbidj clan?
>
> BARDAYAL: *Yoh, nakka yi-na!*
> Yes, that's him, look!

---

51 Thomas, 'Taking them back'. Refer also to the radio documentary: Thomas, M. (prod.) 2007, 'Return to Arnhem Land', *Radio Eye*, Radio National, 2 June 2007, Australian Broadcasting Corporation, Sydney.

MG: *Dja na-ngale?*
Who is that now?

BARDAYAL: *Kodjok! Kodjok. Oho ka-dedjbayeng Kodjok! Kodjok, na-rrankolo.*
Kodjok [subsection name]. Oh for goodness sake, that dear man, it's Kodjok! Kodjok of the Darnkolo clan.

Commentary Extract 2

BARDAYAL: *Oooo Wubarr...nakka yi-na kabani-koklewkke!*
Ohhh the *Wubarr*, look at those two moving their heads!

Wubarr nguni-bengka ba-yimeng...Wo:rro...Ooo ngaban-djorrhbayeng!
He's telling them 'you two know this Wubarr ceremony!' Oooh, I am so moved to see these dear people.

Commentary Extract 3

BARDAYAL: *Ohoho Wubarr nga-kornbayeng! Yo, ngandi-baldarrkidyo Wubarr ba ngandi-marne...yi-bekka?*
Ohoho, the Wubarr, how I love this wonderful ceremony! They have come back to life for me, they have given me the Wubarr again...can you hear it?

MG: *Ya.*
Yes.

BARDAYAL: *Ohoho...Hehe nga-djorrhbayeng Wubarr ane! Mani yi-na Wubarr ka-yo!*
Hehe oh this wonderful Wubarr ceremony, how it moves me! There it is there, the Wubarr!

Other equally moving responses from other elders who viewed the film, such as Jacob Nayinggul and Thomson Yulidjiri, give some indication of the value of repatriating such culturally sensitive archival material.[52] Despite the circumstances of the commissioning of the ceremony, its adaptation and manipulation for a non-Aboriginal audience and the history of the abuse of trust relating to the privacy of the film, I believe the Aboriginal community in Western Arnhem Land today still sees a place for the careful and negotiated use of restricted ceremonial film and photography.

---

52 Thomas, 'Taking them back', p. 35.

Conclusion

Whilst limited by their cultural sensitivity, other historical recordings of certain defunct ceremonial traditions will also become increasingly important to Aboriginal communities in the future. Such recordings were originally allowed because of an assumption that across the cultural divide, there were value and pride in sharing these ceremonial events with outsiders. In return, the expectation has always been that the privacy of the material recorded should be respected. Projects that involve the recording and archiving of the musical, ceremonial and linguistic traditions of Western Arnhem Land continue today, motivated by the same sentiments as those of the 1948 Wubarr performers: a desire to maintain certain cultural practices, teach others about them and preserve them where they are endangered.

The 1948 ceremony was clouded, however, by the cross-purposes of the groups involved. The Expedition team recorded the Wubarr ceremony in the context of scientific research and journalistic treasure hunting. As far as the Expedition team was concerned, the beliefs of the 'natives' in relation to the secret status of their rituals was at best viewed as 'quaint' and, at worst, as an impediment to scientific endeavour and career advancement. We have no record of what the senior Aboriginal organisers of the ceremony thought about the idea of performing a sacred cult ritual for a group of foreigners on a brief visit. Whatever their deliberations, they did decide to perform an attenuated version of the rites in response to the request. The Aboriginal residents of Gunbalanya usually had to deal with the disapproving attitudes of their missionary overseers when it came to ceremonial matters. In the eyes of the Aboriginal residents of Gunbalanya, the request must have clearly distinguished the Expedition team from the mission, particularly as the Anglican Church Missionary Society missionaries at Gunbalanya have always been rather intolerant of Aboriginal ceremonial ritual.

In fact, it appears that the missionaries at Gunbalanya had little idea about the nature of the Wubarr ceremony. The mission invoice issued to the Expedition for transport expenses includes the following entry for the day of the ceremony: 'Transport of personnel and gear to Oenpelli Hill for Chunday Corroboree.' The name 'Chunday' is clearly a linguistic reinterpretation of the Aboriginal pronunciation of the term 'Sunday' or 'Big Sunday', which at the time was an Aboriginal English term for large regional religious ceremonies.[53] The sibilant 's' phoneme does not exist in Australian Aboriginal languages, so English words with 's' tend to be assimilated to the Kunwinjku palatal stop. Thus, Sunday

---

53 In *Sexual Behaviour in Western Arnhem Land*, the Berndts identify the term 'Big Sunday' as a derivation of the 'Big Sandy' area cleared for the performance of ceremonial rituals: 'the term "Sandy" having suggested to the natives the appellation "Sunday", as being appropriate from a religious point of view' (p. 117).

is more commonly pronounced *Junday* [ɟande]. When interacting with the Expedition members, the Kunwinjku referred to the ceremony by its proper name, 'Wubarr/Ubarr', as recorded in documentation, but when interacting with the missionaries, the English word 'Sunday' was used. The Gunbalanya missionaries therefore recorded the name 'Chunday' as an Aboriginal word for the name of the 'corroboree' being performed.

Simpson records that on the day after the Wubarr—a Sunday—no-one seemed interested in attending the mission church service:

> The Corroboree performance was 'paid for' in food and tobacco. On the following day, Sunday, only one or two of the men who had taken part in it attended church at the Mission. They explained to Mountford that, for attendance at church, they received a tin disc, which entitled them to a ration of food from the Mission. Having received food from us, and having some of it still left, they did not see any point in going to church.[54]

In the 60 years since the Expedition visited Gunbalanya, the speed of cultural change in Arnhem Land has been all too disruptive and painful for most. The debate about the role of culture, change and wellbeing for Indigenous people in settler-colonial states is in full swing. In the midst of a developing openness to understand and discuss conflicting cultural values, however, it seems hardly necessary to remind ourselves that some continuity with the past can still sit positively with modernity (or ameliorate its burdens). Across much of Arnhem Land today, large regional ceremonial rites are regarded as important contributors to social cohesion. In my experience, such ceremonies represent important occasions for people from many disparate groups to work together for the purpose of achieving a sense of the 'corporate good'.

In the dry season of 2008, over a three-month period, a Kunabibi ceremony was performed at Gunbalanya. On the last evening of the ceremony, I counted more than 100 initiates from across Western Arnhem Land who were being inducted—an enormous number by usual standards. It was, however, the first Kunabibi ceremony at Gunbalanya for more than 10 years and was made possible, according to the influential and respected leader Jacob Nayinggul, only by the breathing space afforded by social policies (alcohol restrictions and welfare quarantining) instigated as part of the recent Federal Government Northern Territory National Emergency Response (commonly known as 'the intervention')—an unintended consequence perhaps. While the Wubarr will never be performed again in Arnhem Land, the future viability of the ceremonies

---

54 Colin Simpson, n.d., Footnotes: The [restricted word deleted] Corroboree, Papers of Colin Simpson, Folder 135, loose manuscript, MS 5235, NLA.

that have replaced it is also by no means assured. Such celebratory cultural practices, however, have the potential to make a significant contribution to the psychological wellbeing of people in troubled times.

Acknowledgments

I would like to thank Martin Thomas for guidance and assistance in sharing with me the relevant archival material he painstakingly retrieved from institutions in Australia and the United States, and who first brought to my attention the archival recordings of the 1948 Wubarr. Thanks also to the anonymous referee whose comments assisted in improvements to an earlier draft of the chapter. I am also indebted to †Bardayal Nadjamerrek, †Mick Kubarkku, †Thomson Yulidjiri and Jimmy Kalarriya for sharing with me their knowledge and experience of the Wubarr ceremony—*milhbayeng ngudberre!*

21. Epilogue: Sifting the silence

Margo Neale, Project Director,
Barks, Birds & Billabongs symposium

It is now more than 60 years since the American–Australian Scientific Expedition team embarked upon their pioneering adventure into Arnhem Land—a region that was still recorded on some maps at the time as 'largely unexplored'. Mounting this 17-person, seven-month odyssey in the postwar period, with 47 tonnes of equipment and provisions, was a herculean effort. Despite this—and the enormous media and scientific attention and support it received at the time—very little is known of this Expedition today. Few, if any, efforts had been made in the intervening six decades to revisit and re-evaluate its significance. It appears to have been mysteriously buried, or, as Yolngu people might say, it has gone 'inside'. While a small number of individuals connected to the event personally, professionally or institutionally might have had varying degrees of awareness or knowledge of the Expedition, many Yolngu and Bininj communities have an acute interest in it, kept alive through oral traditions. The Barks, Birds & Billabongs Symposium brought this overlooked moment in Australian history back into the light, to the 'outside'.

Figure 21.1 Sally May, Donna Nadjamerrek, Anthony Murphy, Jeffrey Dharramanydji, Lori Richardson, Steve Webb, Thomas Amagula, Wilfred Nawirridj and Wukun Wanambi on the Community Perspective panel at the symposium, 2009

Photograph by George Serras

Figure 21.2 Thomas Amagula, 2009

Photograph by George Serras

Embarking on the symposium was not unlike an archaeological dig. We dusted off layers of accumulated, quasi-institutionalised forgetting; revived the memories of the handful of remaining Expedition members and their relatives; retrieved the archival past; and gave voice to those who were largely unheard in 1948. The centrality of Indigenous voices directly or indirectly during this symposium provided a partial, but necessary, rectification of the marginalisation of Indigenous perspectives six decades ago. What made this symposium particularly exciting was that no-one could foresee what would be uncovered in the process of deep-coring that took place. Already, collections from the Arnhem Land Expedition were being rediscovered: film footage at the Smithsonian Institution; paintings on paper at the State Library of South Australia archived among manuscripts; orphaned objects at the National Museum of Australia in Canberra; as well as Indigenous accounts of the Expedition, previously unheard outside the community.

The salvage mentality that motivated these scientific and cultural explorers decades ago is having some unintended positive consequences today. The so-called passive subjects of study in 1948 (or at least their descendants) have now become beneficiaries of it in ways that were explored at the symposium. With the rise of knowledge centres in Arnhem Land communities, there has been a transfer of knowledge to the people whose culture and environment were the subjects of study. Images of objects collected in 1948 were received—not as relics of the past, but in a way that saw their reanimation as part of a continuing and changing contemporary culture. Attitudinal changes in research protocols, in social context, in the nature of history telling, and issues of who owns the past, were re-examined. A contingent of some 25 Arnhem Landers, representing each of the three official Expedition sites, participated in the event and conducted a number of Indigenous panels dealing with repatriation of objects and knowledge.

On the Politics of Repatriation panel, the community members made the brave decision to show sensitive footage of the collection of human remains by the American archaeologist Frank Setzler, from burial sites at Arrkuluk Hill in Western Arnhem Land. They wanted people at the symposium to see this disturbing footage so that they would know what actually happened and understand why Aboriginal people are distressed and need their 'old people' returned to country. As Wilfred Nawirridj said, 'nobody should interfere—no-one should muck around—with these bones. They've been through ceremony… We hold dear these practices.' He went on to say: 'It's very sad to us…that our ancestors…never sleep very well, these remains. Night and day…they used to keep moving upside down, scratching.'

Figure 21.3 Donald Blitner, 2009

Photograph by George Serras

21. Epilogue

Figure 21.4 Politics of Repatriation panel: Sabine Hoeng, Joy Williams and Anthony Murphy, 2009

Photograph by George Serras

Figure 21.5 Audience at the Politics of Repatriation panel discussion, 2009

Photograph by George Serras

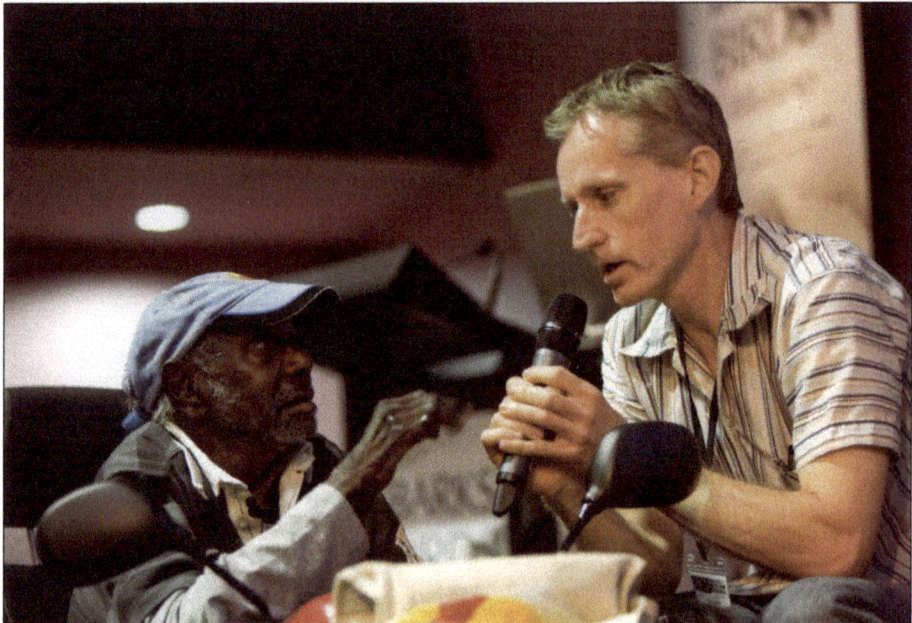

Figure 21.6 Jimmy Kalarriya Namarnyilk and Murray Garde, 2009

Photograph by George Serras

Joe Gumbula from Galiwinku, who has been active in lobbying the Smithsonian Institution, talked about how the clans feel responsible for not protecting their old people from being taken: 'It is a danger for us because of that thing and it's killing our people.'

Fears were also expressed about the cultural responsibilities they have when only some of the remains are returned; the anguish they feel when they have to leave other 'old people' behind. What do you do with the remains when they get back to the community? They have already gone through ceremony. What is the ceremony you do when you take them back, and where do you bury them?

Steve Webb, a physical anthropologist from Bond University, reflected the forward-thinking tone of the group when he emphasised the need to move on: 'This is not the time to condemn this institution or that institution. It's not the time to condemn people that took them…they were creatures of their own generation. But we're creatures of ours.'

Figure 21.7 Wilfred Nawirridj, Anthony Murphy and Jimmy Kalarriya Namarnyilk (seated) from Gunbalanya community, Martin Thomas and Expedition participant Raymond Specht pose in front of a display of objects from the Expedition, 2009

Photograph by George Serras

The day before the symposium launch there was a reunion of Aboriginal and non-Aboriginal descendants, and others closely involved with the 1948 Expedition in which a rare and electrifying engagement took place—an engagement in which history and memory intersected in the most human of occasions. Gathered together were one of the two surviving expeditioners, eighty-four-year-old Raymond Specht, and his family; the adult children of Gerald Blitner and other descendants from Groote Eylandt; the grandchildren of Charles P. Mountford; and relatives of many others—Indigenous and non-Indigenous—who intersected with the Expedition, including Joe Gumbulu from Galiwinku, Thomas Amagula from Groote Eylandt Jimmy Kalarriya Namarnyilk and Donna Nadjamerrek from Gunbalanya, and Naminapu Maymuru from Yirrkala. As a silent National Geographic Society film tracing the Expeditioners' exploits from community to community rolled, a microphone was passed around the room capturing a running commentary by those able to flesh out the story, put names to previously unnamed Aboriginal people and explain the 'old ways' depicted. Stories were heard through their fathers and grandfathers, which have not been recorded in history books, and connections were made and remade. What transpired over the afternoon was a remarkable, impromptu and dynamic piece of history telling from both sides of the 'frontier'. It was indeed history making.

So intent were the expeditioners on conducting a 'search and rescue' mission for an imagined static culture on the brink of extinction that they collected with rear-view vision. In hindsight, this has proven to be advantageous in many ways, providing baseline studies not only in the sciences and humanities, but also in the study of black/white relations, changing research protocols and museological practices. From the vantage point of the symposium in 2009, it became clear what they did not see—or at least could not understand: that Aboriginal people were already on the frontier of cross-cultural exchange and were not the remnants of the Stone Age they imagined. Furthermore, the expeditioners could not comprehend that they were themselves part of the narrative of outsiders who were active agents in the processes of accommodation and resistance that Arnhem Landers were engaged in. While the expeditioners themselves were trying to resist and adjust to 'natives who were becoming too civilised' for their studies, their 'subjects' were dealing with cultural preservation in a different way in the face of researchers, missionaries, adventurers and government personnel.

Figure 21.8 Annie Clarke, Donald Blitner, Thomas Amagula, Jabani Lalara and Brooke Rankmore, 2009

Photograph by George Serras

These and other intriguing narratives explored during the symposium provided new perspectives, interpretations and understandings. New growth rings were added to the Expedition and its legacy, such as an opportunity to acknowledge and celebrate the intellectual property, skills and Indigenous knowledge systems of the Arnhem Landers instead of only the ingenuity and expertise of the Western expeditioners, as was customary.

If the symposium was similar to an archaeological dig in relation to the past, in terms of the future, it was more akin to the opening of Pandora's Box, where new and unexamined ideas were inadvertently released to fertilise future ventures and collaborations, a number of which are already taking form and gathering momentum. These include collaboration with the Smithsonian Institution for an online research portal to unite the dispersed Arnhem Land Expedition collections and to share documentation. That is, to digitally reunite the significant holdings at the Smithsonian Institution in Washington, DC, the National Museum of Australia, the South Australian Museum, the Australian Museum and other places. This long-term project will not only enable researchers from around the world to access this hitherto inaccessible collection but, most significantly, it will enable Aboriginal communities to access their cultural heritage through the many knowledge centres that exist across Arnhem Land. It is a two-way process whereby access to the objects digitally will also stimulate Aboriginal people to augment the documentation that currently exists about this collection by humanising the objects with the names of makers, their clan associations and kinship relationships to living relatives—a big issue with older collections of this period. This reclamation process, through naming, was taking place at the symposium as archival images and footage were rolled out over the course of the week. Descendants were deeply moved at seeing their forebears and the way they practised culture 60 years ago. Some expressed this reconnection as 'bringing them [the people] back to life for us' or 'teaching us old ways again, which we can use to teach others'. The footage effectively became a training manual and a vehicle for remembering proudly. They expressed great pride in their cultural material and wanted copies of images from the Expedition archives for their knowledge centres. Another mooted collaboration is an international touring exhibition of the ethnological collection between the National Museum of Australia, the Australian National University, the Smithsonian Institution and possibly others.

Some years ago I planned to mount a collaborative touring international exhibition using collections from the 1948 Arnhem Land Expedition, with a particular focus on the ethnographic/art materials. I soon discovered that such a project would be an enormous and almost impossible enterprise, given the locations of diverse collections and the dissipation of knowledge and interest over the years. To undertake such a venture, and give due justice to the scale and significance of the Arnhem Land Expedition, and to recapture something of the collaborative spirit of the original project, I would need to pull together all the knowledge holders, in particular the original players and their descendants or current representatives—across cultures, across continents and across disciplines. This symposium was the beginning of that process. It was the opening conversation.

To facilitate this conversation, the symposium was kept relatively contained in terms of speakers and audience numbers. There were no parallel sessions, extraneous entertainment offerings, or keynote speakers. Instead, I aimed to stimulate dialogue between and amongst the speakers and the audience, to create an expanded workshop model. Speakers had already been talking to each other and their papers were exchanged in advance of the symposium to allow more informed discussions and new linkages to develop. Symposium delegates were in one venue throughout the three days of formal proceedings, which allowed continuity between sessions and an accumulation of knowledge over a full week of workshops, performances and meetings.

Figure 21.9 Manimawuy Dhamarrandji, Djombala Dhamarrandji, Djangirrawuy Garawirrtja and Joe Neparrnga Gumbula performing the Manikay *Currents from a Distant Shore: Birrkili Yolngu songs of Makassan contact in north-east Arnhem Land* at the National Museum of Australia, 2009

Photograph by George Serras

21. Epilogue

21.10 Djombala Dhamarrandji, Djangirrawuy Garawirrtja, Joe Neparrnga Gumbula and Manimawuy Dhamarrandji performing the Manikay *Currents from a Distant Shore: Birrkili Yolngu songs of Makassan contact in north-east Arnhem Land* at the National Museum of Australia, 2009

Photograph by George Serras

For the Museum, one of the greatest values in staging this symposium was to further our commitment to reconnecting Indigenous communities with overseas collections, to recovering voices and to stimulating future research. One of the most dramatic and unexpected results of the symposium was news that the Smithsonian was prepared to repatriate further human remains from Arnhem Land. Despite repeated lobbying by numerous delegations from Australian government and community organisations, the institution had remained trenchant in its determination to retain the final third of its original holdings. Yet within weeks of the symposium, they took the initiative, offering to release the remains. I believe this was a case of the power of soft diplomacy over political pressure. Representatives from the Smithsonian in the audience were able to experience the human dimension of the impact of missing ancestral remains, as community members spoke of their distress at the loss, and the shame they felt at not being able to save their 'old people'. Another unexpected outcome was the offer of a short-term placement at the Smithsonian for an Aboriginal trainee, Rebecca Richards, who was working on the National Museum's collection of paintings on bark and cardboard from the Arnhem Land Expedition. She continued this work on the Smithsonian's collection of paintings from the Arnhem Land Expedition. She has since gone on to become Australia's first Indigenous Rhodes Scholar.

Exploring the Legacy of the 1948 Arnhem Land Expedition

21.11 Manikay performance *Currents from a Distant Shore: Birrkili Yolngu songs of Makassan contact in north-east Arnhem Land* at the National Museum of Australia, 2009

Photograph by George Serras

Figure 21.12 Rita and Wukun Wanambi from Yirrkala and Brooke Rankmore from Groote Eylandt look over old photos at the National Library of Australia as part of the symposium's program for connecting communities with collections, 2009

Photograph by Chrischona Schmidt

An aspect of the symposium—widely noted by all involved—was the degree of respect shown to each other across generations and cultures. Given the highly sensitive subjects under discussion, the charged emotional atmosphere and the potential for political volatility, this was truly remarkable. Perhaps it was due to the quality of the human encounters that took place and the depth of engagement. Participants from such diverse fields, countries and age groups found that there was no place for disciplinary baggage, strategic allegiances and party lines. This was not a symposium about ideas or issues that could be held at arm's length for intellectual scrutiny.

When Charles P. Mountford was asked by the National Geographic Society in 1946 if he had an idea worthy of support, he replied, 'I've got more ideas than a dog's got fleas'. In a similar vein, Barks, Birds & Billabongs abounded with enough new ideas to satisfy even Mountford's expectations.

Figure 21.13 Djangirrawuy Garawirrtja, Renelle Buniyi, Margo Neale, Raymond Specht, Joe Neparrnga Gumbula, Djombala Dhamarrandji and Manimawuy Dhamarrandji at the symposium, 2009

Photograph by George Serras

Contributors

Jon Altman

Jon Altman is a Research Professor at the Centre for Aboriginal Economic Policy Research at the Australian National University. He has a disciplinary background in economics and anthropology. In 1990, he was appointed the foundation Director of the Centre—a position he held until 2010. In 2003, Professor Altman was elected a Fellow of the Academy of the Social Sciences in Australia.

Professor Altman undertook fieldwork for his doctorate in the Maningrida region, Western Arnhem Land, in 1979–81, residing with Kuninjku people at Mumeka outstation on the Mann River and collaborating on research about local livelihood options. These people share strong kinship, linguistic, economic and ceremonial ties with other groups in Gunbalanya (formerly Oenpelli)—one of the bases of the 1948 Arnhem Land Expedition. This research was published in the book *Hunter-Gatherers Today: An Aboriginal Economy in North Australia*. Since 1979, he has undertaken more than 40 field visits to Kuninjku country.

Professor Altman has regularly undertaken collaborative research with Kuninjku on the customary economy and wildlife harvesting, the arts, natural-resource management, and on the transformations of their unusual regional hybrid economy made up of customary, state and market sectors. His current research focuses on economic hybridity and critical development studies in remote Australia.

Linda Barwick

Linda Barwick is Associate Professor in the School of Letters, Art and Media at the University of Sydney and Director of the Pacific and Regional Archive for Digital Sources in Endangered Cultures (PARADISEC), an internationally acclaimed research facility established in 2003 by a number of Australian universities, led by the University of Sydney with support from the Australian Research Council (ARC).

Linda is an ethnomusicologist who has undertaken fieldwork in Australia, Italy and the Philippines, and is particularly interested in the uses of digital technologies for extending access to research results by cultural-heritage communities. Recent song documentation projects include the ARC-funded Murriny Patha song project, the Western Arnhem Land song project, funded by the Hans Rausing Endangered Languages Program (School of Oriental and African Studies, University of London), and the Iwaidja Documentation Project, funded by the Volkswagen Stiftung (based in the Max Planck Institute, Nijmegen).

Her many publications include multimedia CDs accompanied by extensive scholarly notes, produced in collaboration with Indigenous singers and their communities, and her work is cited in anthropology, cultural studies, linguistics and library science as well as within her own discipline.

She is a Deputy Director of the University of Sydney's Digital Innovation Unit, and has contributed to a number of other initiatives to develop awareness and capacity in the digital humanities, including the Australian e-Humanities Network and several projects funded under the ARC's e-research special research initiatives program.

Kim Beazley

Kim Beazley completed a Bachelor of Arts and Master of Arts at the University of Western Australia in 1970. He was awarded the Rhodes Scholarship for Western Australia in 1973, and completed an MPhil. at Oxford University in 1976. In February 2010, he took up an appointment as Australian Ambassador to the United States.

Ambassador Beazley taught at Murdoch University in the Department of Social Inquiry from 1976 to 1980. He was a Member of the Australian Parliament from 1980 to 2007. He was a minister from 1983 to 1996 in the Hawke and Keating Labor governments, holding at various times portfolios that included Defence, Finance, Transport and Communications, Employment, Education and Training, Aviation and Special Minister of State.

Ambassador Beazley was Deputy Prime Minister during 1995–96 under Prime Minister Paul Keating and was Leader of the Australian Labor Party and the Opposition from 1996 to 2001, and again from 2005 to 2006. While in Parliament, he served on a number of parliamentary committees, including Joint Intelligence and Joint Foreign Affairs, Defence and Trade.

Following his departure from Parliament in 2007, Ambassador Beazley was appointed Winthrop Professor of Political Science and International Relations at the University of Western Australia. He is Joint Chairman of the international advisory board of the Australian American Leadership Dialogue, and is a member of the advisory boards of Defence SA and the *Australian Army Journal*.

In July 2008, he was appointed Chancellor of the Australian National University—a position he held until December 2009. He was awarded the Companion of the Order of Australia for service to the Parliament of Australia through contributions to the development of government policies in relation to defence and international relations, as an advocate for Indigenous people, and to the community. In July 2009 he was appointed a member of the Council of the Australian War Memorial.

Bruce Birch

Bruce Birch is an anthropological linguist who has been based in the Cobourg region of North-West Arnhem Land for the past seven years, and is currently a Departmental Visitor in Linguistics at the Research School of Pacific and Asian Studies at the Australian National University. Bruce originally moved to the community of Minjilang on Croker Island to take up a position as principal field linguist for the DoBeS-funded Iwaidja Documentation Project in 2003. As a result of this project—which has recently received funding for a second phase—Iwaidja now has the largest online archive of annotated video and audio texts of any Australian Indigenous language.

Bruce has initiated and consulted on a number of projects in the area of Indigenous ecological knowledge, particularly marine knowledge, and is also consulting linguist for the Minjilang-based *Iwaidja Inyman*—a project committed to the publication and maintenance of the Iwaidja language and associated cultural knowledge, initiated and coordinated by his partner, Sabine Hoeng.

Robert C. Cashner

Robert C. Cashner, son-in-law of Robert Rush Miller, is an Emeritus Research Professor of Biological Sciences at the University of New Orleans. He received his doctoral degree from Tulane University and joined the faculty at the Louisiana State University in New Orleans (now the University of New Orleans) in 1973. Over the next 35 years, he advanced in the faculty ranks to Professor and was selected for the honour of Research Professor in 1993. He served as Chair of the Department of Biological Sciences from 1993 to 1996, before moving into the central administration. He was Dean of the Graduate School from 1996 to 2008 and Vice-Chancellor for Research from 2001 to 2008. He was awarded the Mackin Medallion in 2008 for Outstanding Service to the University.

His research area is ichthyology, with primary interests in freshwater fishes in the species-rich south-eastern United States and the stability of estuarine fish assemblages along the US Gulf Coast. He has conducted ichthyo-faunal studies throughout most of the continental United States, Mexico and Australia. He was appointed as a Visiting Scientist to Australia's Northern Rivers University (now Southern Cross University) in 1991 and 2001 and conducted a study of fish assemblages of the Nymboida River. He has served as major advisor for more than 30 masters of science and PhD students and has published more than 70 research articles and book chapters on fish diversity, ecology and assemblage stability.

He is an associate of the Sam Noble Natural History Museum at the University of Oklahoma and has current research projects with several colleagues. He has garnered more than $2 million in extra-mural funding. In 1997, he was elected President of the American Society of Ichthyologists and Herpetologists (ASIH); he continues to serve the ASIH as a permanent member of the Board of Governors. He has also been involved in Darwin Day events at the University of New Orleans and in the New Orleans community. In 2007, he received a Friend of Darwin Award from the National Center for Science Education.

Denise Chapman

Denise Chapman began work at the State Library of South Australia in 2003. She has contributed to the management of collections with Indigenous content, including photography, manuscripts, audiovisual pieces and artworks. The work has involved managing access to collections, policy development, digitisation priorities, research inquiries, and coordinating tours and training. During the past four years, she has been involved in processing the Mountford–Sheard Collection, which was listed on the United Nations Educational, Scientific and Cultural Organisation (UNESCO) Australian Memory of the World register in 2008.

Before joining the State Library of South Australia, Denise worked in the public library environment for two years, following the completion of a Graduate Diploma in Information Studies in 2001. She also has a Bachelor of Arts in Geography and History. She is a member of the Aboriginal and Torres Strait Islander Library and Information Resource Network.

Anne Clarke

Anne Clarke is a Senior Lecturer in Heritage Studies in the School of Philosophical and Historical Inquiry at the University of Sydney. She has carried out archaeological research in the Northern Territory since 1982. Anne has held teaching appointments in archaeology and heritage management at Charles Sturt University and the Australian National University. She has also held postdoctoral research fellowships at the ANU at the North Australia Research Unit, Darwin, and in the Department of Archaeology and Anthropology, Canberra.

Margo Daly

Margo Daly is a writer, editor and educator currently working as a researcher at the University of Sydney on an Australian Research Council-funded study of the 1948 Arnhem Land Expedition. She has a BA (Communications) from the University of Technology, Sydney (UTS), and an MA (Writing) from Sheffield Hallam University in the United Kingdom.

Travel writing is Margo's chief area of interest. She has authored guidebooks to Australia, Sydney and Tasmania for the Rough Guides series (Penguin, UK), and, during a decade based in London, researched destinations including northern Thailand, Morocco, France (Paris, the north, Poitou-Charentes and the Atlantic coast) and Brussels. Margo has published travel fiction in *Wild Ways: New Stories about Women on the Road* (Sceptre, 1998), which she co-edited with Jill Dawson. Travel memoirs appeared in *Gas and Air: Tales of Pregnancy, Birth and Beyond*, also co-edited with Jill Dawson (Bloomsbury, 2002), in *Meanjin* and *Women Travel* (Penguin, 1999).

Margo has taught travel writing for many years, at Sydney University's Centre for Continuing Education and more recently at the NSW Writers' Centre. She has taught narrative writing and creative non-fiction at UTS and creative writing in schools, community centres, adult education and to home-school students. She is currently undertaking a Bachelor of Teaching (Secondary) at Charles Sturt University to teach English and history.

Ursula Frederick

Ursula Frederick is an archaeologist with a special interest in art, archaeology, cross-cultural exchange and the contemporary past. Her expertise lies in the area of rock art research and visual arts. Her honours thesis (University of Western Australia) examined the ways in which Indigenous artists based at Cairns TAFE in far north Queensland incorporated rock art imagery into their contemporary artworks. Her master's thesis (ANU, 1997) was the first in-depth archaeological investigation of contact rock art undertaken in Australia and was based on an analysis of charcoal drawings in rock shelters in Watarrka National Park. In 1995 and 1996, Ursula carried out archaeological fieldwork with Dr Anne Clarke on Groote Eylandt, recording rock art sites with traditional owners and their families.

Ursula is currently enrolled in a PhD at the School of Art, and is employed by the Research School of Humanities, the Australian National University. She presents and publishes in the areas of art, archaeology, and visual-culture research. Her first book, *Women Willing to Fight: Essays on the Fighting Woman in Film*, co-edited with Silke Andris, was published in 2008. The volume included an exploration of popular representations of archaeology through the character of Lara Croft, thus combining Ursula's interests in archaeology, visual media and popular culture. Ursula is currently finalising *Cruising Country: Automobilities in Non-urban Australia*—a special issue of *Humanities Research*.

Murray Garde

Murray Garde is currently Research Fellow in the School of Archaeology and Anthropology at the Australian National University. From 1988 to 1999, he lived in the north-central Arnhem Land community of Maningrida and also on outstations in the Liverpool and Mann rivers districts of Western Arnhem Land. During this time, he first worked as a visiting homeland centre teacher and then as Curator of the Djómi Museum in Maningrida, and Cultural Research Officer for the Bawinanga Aboriginal Corporation. He enjoyed close friendships with the Kuninjku people who lived on outstations at the eastern margins of the Arnhem Land Plateau, and it was these people who first introduced him to some of the great regional cult ceremonies of the area in the tradition of those witnessed by members of the 1948 Arnhem Land Expedition.

In 1993, Murray instituted a rock art documentation project that focused on recording the cultural significance of rock art for the traditional Aboriginal owners in the Mann and Liverpool rivers districts. Much of this work also allowed him to study the dialects of Bininj Kunwok spoken across Western Arnhem Land, and, eventually, he became fluent enough to work as an interpreter in legal, medical and cultural contexts.

Louise Hamby

Louise Hamby is a Research Fellow at the Research School of Humanities and the Arts at the Australian National University in Canberra. She received an MFA degree from the University of Georgia in textiles. *Containers of Power*, her PhD from the School of Archaeology and Anthropology at the Australian National University, focused on fibre container forms from North-East Arnhem Land. Her previous position was an ARC Postdoctoral Fellow (Industry) working with Museum Victoria on the project 'Anthropological and Aboriginal Perspectives on the Donald Thomson Collection: Material culture, collecting and identity'.

Material culture—particularly fibre forms and bodywear from Arnhem Land—is the main content of her work. The interconnections between historical and contemporary forms are part of ongoing research with Aboriginal people from the region. This often involves working with dispersed collections of different types. She has curated and co-curated numerous exhibitions, most recently *Women with Clever Hands: Gapuwiyak Miyalkurruwurr Gong Djambatjmala*, which opened at Wagga Wagga Art Gallery. Her most recent publication is *Containers of Power: Women with Clever Hands*. Louise's expertise in historical Aboriginal material culture resulted in a consultancy for costume and set design for the Baz Luhrmann film *Australia*.

Her current Australian Research Council Discovery Grant, 'Contexts of Collection', examines the role of Indigenous people in the formation of collections from Arnhem Land. The collection from the 1948 Arnhem Land Expedition plays an integral part in mid-century relationships between collectors, institutions and the makers of the objects.

Joshua S. Harris

Joshua S. Harris is the former Archives Manager of the Film and Audiovisual Archives of the National Geographic Society. An archaeologist and historian by training, Joshua has been involved in collections management, preservation and research within a diverse array of museum, archive and university collection settings.

Josh began his career as an archaeologist with the Illinois State Museum, participating in prehistoric site identification and excavation throughout the American Midwest and South, with a primary focus on the processing and analysis of prehistoric botanical collections. Josh joined the University of Tennessee as an archaeologist in 2000 for large-scale excavation of multiple Native American prehistoric sites in the Smoky Mountain National Park. In 2001, he joined the Smithsonian Institution National Museum of Natural History in the Department of Invertebrate Zoology. He participated in and managed a large preservation project to design, re-curate and prevent the degradation of the mollusc collection (the world's largest). In addition, he was involved in digital imaging and multimedia catalogue development of invertebrate collections with a focus on Antarctic biological collections.

Josh moved to the National Geographic Society Film and Audiovisual Archives in 2004. In his time with the Society, he participated in a diverse range of activities, managing a collection representing more than 100 years of film and recorded sound history. He concentrated on preservation and preventative conservation, digital asset migration and management, access to moving-image collections and the use of archival moving-image collections across diverse platforms. In addition, he has worked on outreach, guidance and training to collections managers throughout the world, including in South-East Asia, Greece, Mexico and Central America, and has published numerous papers in the field. Josh recently joined the University of Kentucky Libraries in the Electronic and Digital Resources Division, where he is the lead designer of a new electronic resource-management system for use across the university library system.

Exploring the Legacy of the 1948 Arnhem Land Expedition

Mark Collins Jenkins

Mark Collins Jenkins is a writer, editor and historian, who, for many years, was on the staff of the National Geographic Society. His books include *Vampire Forensics: Uncovering the Origins of an Enduring Legend* (2010); *The Book of Marvels: An Explorer's Miscellany* (2009); *The Image Collection* (2009); *Odysseys and Photographs: Four National Geographic Field Men* (2008); *Worlds to Explore: Classic Tales of Travel and Adventure from National Geographic* (2006); and *High Adventure: The Story of the National Geographic Society* (2004).

Jenkins has also written for National Geographic Society products ranging from the Genographic Project—an attempt to map prehistoric migrations via traces left in the genetic code—to articles for the Society's award-winning web site. During his 22 years as a historian with the Society's Archives, Jenkins was creator, editor and principal writer of an electronic encyclopedia of society history comprising more than 1200 entries. He also helped establish an oral-history program and served as one of the curators of the museum exhibit *Latitudes, Lenses, and Lore: The World of Luis Marden* (November 2000 – March 2001). Alongside his colleagues, he was profiled in the 'Behind the Scenes' section of the February 2002 *National Geographic*.

A graduate of St Christopher's School in Richmond, Virginia, Jenkins studied at Washington and Lee University, where he was awarded a Bachelor's degree in English. After receiving a Master's degree from the University of Virginia, he joined the Geographic staff in 1987. Presently living in Fredericksburg, Virginia, he is a former trustee of the Historic Fredericksburg Foundation, where he helped start its long-running oral-history program and edited the *Journal of Fredericksburg History*.

Philip Jones

Philip Jones has worked as a Curator at the South Australian Museum since the mid 1980s. During that time, he has curated about 30 exhibitions dealing with Aboriginal art, history and material culture, anthropological and expeditionary history, and, more recently, the ethnography and history of Australia's 'Afghan' cameleers. He is a graduate in law and history from the University of Adelaide, where he also completed a PhD thesis titled '"A box of native things": Ethnographic collectors and the South Australian Museum, 1830s–1930s' (1996).

Philip has undertaken fieldwork in the Simpson Desert and Birdsville Track region, particularly in collaboration with linguist Dr Luise Hercus. As well as a series of publications dealing with the history and ethnography of the region, this fieldwork has involved a site-recording project with descendants of the Wangkangurru and Yarluyandi people of the region.

His particular interest in the provenance of artefacts and in the history and context of their collection underpins much of his exhibition research and writing. In 2007 he published *Ochre and Rust: Artefacts and Encounters on Australian Frontiers*, which won the 2008 Prime Minister's Literary Award for Non-Fiction. The book traces the paths artefacts follow—from their makers to their collectors—as a means of re-examining frontier history.

Philip Jones is currently engaged in an investigation of the respective roles of Francis Gillen and Baldwin Spencer in anthropological history, a history of the South Australian Museum, the social and economic contribution made by the 'Afghan' cameleers, a biography of the colonial artist George French Angas, and an analysis of the distribution and significance of red ochre.

Lynne McCarthy

Lynne McCarthy was a Research Fellow in the Centre for Historical Research at the National Museum of Australia from 2008 to 2010. Her doctoral research in the Flinders Ranges, South Australia, developed from her training in the disciplines of environmental science and palaeoecology. This research reconstructed vegetation and climate histories of the Flinders Ranges over the past 10 000 years, based on the analysis of pollen and plant macrofossil material preserved in native stick-nest rat deposits. This work—analogous to well-established research on packrat nest deposits in the United States—was a first for this type of palaeoecological study in semi-arid environments in South Australia.

Lynne joined the National Museum of Australia in 1999 as a Curator in the People and the Environment section. This provided an opportunity for contributing a deep-time perspective to the development of the *Old New Land* exhibit—the permanent gallery exploring environmental histories of Australia. Other curatorial work in the Museum has included the development of exhibits for another permanent gallery exhibition, *Australian Journeys*, and extensive work on the research and documentation of collections in the National Historical Collection. Prior to joining the Centre for Historical Research, Lynne worked more broadly across the Museum, including a period as an Exhibitions Coordinator and Senior Curator in the field of environmental history.

Lynne's interest in the botanical and ecological work from the 1948 Arnhem Land Expedition stems from her passion for fieldwork, and the opportunity to explore the complexities of the scientific and cultural dimensions of plant ecology and landscape histories of tropical environments across Arnhem Land. In addition, the honour of working with eminent Australian plant ecologist Raymond Specht has proved invaluable in capturing personal insights of his experiences on the 1948 Expedition as well as his other contributions to plant ecology in Australia.

Tony MacGregor

Tony MacGregor is the National Arts Editor for ABC Radio National, and has more than 20 years' experience as a documentary maker, sound artist and broadcaster. In 2008 he won a Walkley Award for Excellence in Radio Documentary Production. His radio documentary features have been broadcast in Europe, the United States and Australia, and he has created sound designs for galleries, museums and performance works in Australia, Germany, Austria and the United Kingdom, including collaborating in the creation of major works for the Biennale of Sydney, the Melbourne International Festival of the Arts, the Adelaide Biennial, Open Art Munich, the Steirischer Herbst (Graz) and Fotofeis, Edinburgh.

Among his writing credits is the libretto for the opera *Cosmonaut*, with music by David Chesworth, which premiered at the Melbourne International Festival of the Arts in 2002.

Tony has an MA in History and Cultural Studies from the University of Technology, Sydney (2001). His thesis, 'Sympathetic vibrations: effecting sound histories', used a set of early sound recordings as an entry point into a series of highly original critical readings of significant cultural relationships and experiences.

Ian S. McIntosh

Ian S. McIntosh is the Director of International Partnerships at Indiana University Purdue University at Indianapolis (IUPUI) and an Adjunct Professor of Anthropology in the IUPUI School of Liberal Arts. He is also an Associate Director of the Confucius Institute in Indianapolis. At IUPUI, he teaches a class on truth and reconciliation and also runs the Global Crossroads lab, which facilitates cross-cultural communication between diverse academic and activist populations.

An applied anthropologist, Ian is a former Managing Director of the Harvard-based indigenous-rights organisation Cultural Survival Inc., and is Senior Editorial Advisor for the *Cultural Survival Quarterly*—the premier journal focusing on the rights, voices and visions of the world's indigenous peoples. He is also a former Deputy Country Director of the Armenia Tree Project, for which his work in the Caucasus was recognised with a 2008 Energy Globe Award for Sustainability.

Ian has published two books and more than 100 articles and has worked on human-rights projects in a number of countries, including Mali, Kenya, Armenia and Australia. His greatest interests, however, are the religions and cultures of

Aboriginal Australia. He worked in a number of Indigenous communities in the Northern Territory and Queensland in the 1980s and 1990s and has written extensively on the historical and spiritual dimensions and legacy of Yolngu (North-East Arnhem Land Aboriginal) relations with Macassan (Sulawesi) seafarers who frequented the northern Australian coast from the early eighteenth to the early twentieth centuries.

Robyn McKenzie

Robyn McKenzie is a PhD candidate in the Interdisciplinary Cross-Cultural Research Program at the Research School of Humanities and the Arts, the Australian National University. Having trained as an art historian in the Fine Arts Department at the University of Melbourne, she taught in academic art history departments and in history/theory units in art schools. In this environment, an early focus on avant-garde modernisms was superseded by an interest in the neo-avant-garde conceptual art movements of the 1960s and 1970s and their influence on contemporary art making and criticism.

In the late 1980s and early 1990s, she directed a number of public programs under the auspices of the gallery 200 Gertrude Street in Melbourne, among them *The Present and Recent Past of Australian Art & Criticism*, in 1988. Robyn has published extensively in contemporary art magazines (both local and international) and exhibition catalogues. From 1995 to 1997, she was art critic for *The Age* newspaper in Melbourne, and from 1996 to 2002 she was Editor of *LIKE, Art Magazine*. She has also practised as a curator. Her most recent exhibition, *A Bird in the Hand: Paintings by Tony Clark and John Wolseley*, was held at the Art Gallery of New South Wales' Contemporary Project Space in 2006–07.

Robyn's PhD study on the string figures of Yirrkala marks a departure from— but also continues aspects of—her previous research and professional interests in the visual arts. A major objective of her research—focused on the Australian Museum collection made by Frederick McCarthy during the 1948 Arnhem Land Expedition—will be realised through an exhibition. Working in collaboration with the Yirrkala community, her aim is to reanimate the links between the collection and the intangible heritage of knowledge, practice and belief systems that it reflects, thinking through the ways in which contemporary audiences might read and interact with the collection today. In 2008 she received an Australian Museum Postgraduate Award allowing her to work closely with the collection and the Museum's expert staff.

Allan Marett

Allan Marett is Emeritus Professor of Musicology at the University of Sydney, where he was Professor until 2007. Previously, he was Professor of Music at the University of Hong Kong. He was the founding Director of the National Recording Project for Indigenous Performance in Australia—an initiative that aims to record and document the highly endangered traditions of Australian Indigenous music and dance.

His book *Songs, Dreamings and Ghosts: The Wangga of North Australia* won the 2006 Stanner Award, and the CD *Rak Badjalarr: Wangga Songs by Bobby Lane, Northern Australia*, which he co-authored with Linda Barwick and Lysbeth Ford, won a Northern Territory Indigenous music award. Together with Linda Barwick and others, he has edited a number of anthologies of writing on Australian Indigenous music and endangered cultures, including *The Essence of Singing and the Substance of Song: Recent Responses to the Aboriginal Performing Arts and Other Essays in Honour of Catherine Ellis* (1995), *Researchers, Communities, Institutions, Sound Recordings* (2003) and *Studies in Aboriginal Song: A special issue of Australian Aboriginal Studies* (2007).

His current research focuses on the classical song traditions of Western Arnhem Land as well as the music and culture of the Daly region, where he has worked for more than 20 years. Together with Linda Barwick and Lysbeth Ford, he is completing a new book on Wangga entitled *Wangga Songs of Northwest Australia: Recordings, song-texts and translations in their historical and ethnographic contexts*.

Marett is also active in the field of Sino–Japanese music history. Since the 1970s, he has been a member of the Cambridge-based Tang Music project, which has produced the series *Music from the Tang Court*—now in its seventh volume. Marett is a past President of the Musicological Society of Australia and past Vice-President of the International Council for Traditional Music.

Sally K. May

Sally K. May is Lecturer in the School of Archaeology and Anthropology at the Australian National University. She is also was Convenor of the Cultural and Environmental Heritage stream of the Graduate Program in Liberal Arts. Sally was previously also an ARC Postdoctoral Fellow based at Griffith University (Queensland) and a Lecturer in the Department of Archaeology at Flinders University (South Australia). Sally works closely with Indigenous communities around Australia on projects relating to museum collections, repatriation, archaeology, anthropology, cultural heritage management and rock art.

Since 1999, Sally has undertaken historical research relating to the 1948 Arnhem Land Expedition, producing numerous articles, book chapters and the 2009 book *Collecting Cultures: Myth, Politics, and Collaboration in the 1948 Arnhem Land Expedition*. Sally also worked with the Groote Eylandt and Gunbalanya (formerly Oenpelli) communities to help bring home a large percentage of the human skeletal remains taken during this Expedition and held for 60 years at the Smithsonian Institution.

Currently, Sally is working on a major ARC Discovery Project: 'Picturing Change: 21st century perspectives on recent Australian rock art.' In this five-year project, contact-period rock art from across Australia is being documented, with fieldwork in Western Arnhem Land (NT), Wollemi National Park (NSW), the Pilbara (WA), and Central Australia, west of Alice Springs (NT). Working closely with Australian Aboriginal colleagues, Sally and her collaborators are documenting the cultural significance of recent rock art sites. Sally May was an academic advisor for the Barks, Birds & Billabongs symposium.

Gifford Miller

Gifford Miller is a Professor of Geological Sciences and a Fellow of the Institute of Arctic and Alpine Research (INSTAAR) at the University of Colorado, Boulder. He uses the record of the recent geological past to gain a better understanding of Earth's climate system. His early research was predominantly in the cold deserts of the polar regions, with a focus on the eastern Canadian Arctic, and later the European Arctic (Svalbard), Russian Arctic (Franz Josef Land) and Greenland. He currently has active polar research programs in Iceland and Baffin Island, Arctic Canada. Recognising the need for improved tools to date events of the recent past, Miller established a laboratory for amino acid racemisation dating, and it was through this tool that he was caught up in the climate and human histories of the world's hot deserts, beginning with the Sahara Desert. Involvement in the history of climate and human colonisation of the Australian deserts was a natural extension of this work, as his late father, Robert Rush Miller, was a member of the 1948 Arnhem Land Expedition.

Miller's involvement in Australia began in the late 1980s, with an active research campaign since the early 1990s, focusing on the pacing of the Australian summer monsoon, causes of megafaunal extinction, and the footprints of human colonisation. This research is connected with the Research School of Earth Sciences at the Australian National University. Recently, Miller's research group, building on the Australian experience, expanded their fieldwork to Madagascar, where they are evaluating causes for the extinction of the elephant bird.

He has published more than 200 scientific papers and is a Fellow of the Geological Society of America and the American Geophysical Union. In 2006 he was granted the Geological Society of America's Easterbrook Distinguished Scientist Award and in 2008 was elected to the Norwegian Academy of Science and Letters as a foreign member. He also chaired the Department of Geological Sciences from 1993 to 1998, and was featured in two recent made-for-television documentaries about Australia: *The Bone Diggers* (2007) and *Death of the Megabeasts* (2009).

Margo Neale

Margo Neale is a Senior Research Fellow at the Centre for Historical Research, a Senior Curator and Principal Advisor (Indigenous) at the National Museum of Australia. She was inaugural Director of the Aboriginal and Torres Strait Islander Program at the Museum for opening, after previously working at the National Gallery of Australia, the Art Gallery of New South Wales and the Queensland Art Gallery.

She is also an Adjunct Professor in the History Program of the Australian Centre for Indigenous History at the Australian National University. Since 2004, Margo has been involved in numerous interdisciplinary projects, including the investigation of frontier narratives through non-text-based history telling in collaboration with Yale University, films such as *Frontier Conversations*, and exhibitions on multicultural communities and Indigenous urban identity.

Margo is a co-recipient of seven Australian Research Council grants, a judge on the Prime Minister's Prize for Australian History and was a participant in the 2020 Summit. She has lectured and published widely across disciplines including social history, art and culture in the Asia-Pacific region and co-edited *The Oxford Companion to Aboriginal Art and Culture* (2000). Her 2008 international touring exhibition, *Utopia: The genius of Emily Kame Kngwarreye*, was shown in Japan and won the Manning Clark House National Cultural Group Award 2008. In 2010 she organised and curated *Rituals of Life: The spirituality and culture of Aboriginal Australians through the Vatican Collection* to coincide with the canonisation of Mary MacKillop.

Margo, of Aboriginal and Irish descent, is originally from Victoria. She lived and worked in Arnhem Land in the 1970s and on Christmas Island in the 1980s before joining the National Museum of Australia in 2000. She was Director of the National Museum of Australia's Barks, Birds & Billabongs symposium.

Suzy Russell

Suzy Russell completed a Graduate Diploma in Information Studies in 2000, and has a Bachelor of Arts in Anthropology and Women's Studies.

Since joining the State Library of South Australia in 2003, she has worked on various aspects of the library's Indigenous collections, with a special focus on the Mountford–Sheard Collection. Her work entails reference and research, cataloguing, developing policy and staging events, as well as supplying content for online and physical exhibitions. She is a member of the Aboriginal and Torres Strait Islander Library and Information Resource Network and edits the network's quarterly newsletter.

Martin Thomas

Martin Thomas is an Australian Research Council Future Fellow in the School of History at the Australian National University and an Honorary Associate Professor in PARADISEC at the University of Sydney. His main interests are the perception of landscape, the history of cross-cultural encounter and inquiry, and the impact of technologies such as sound recording and photography that have transformed attitudes to space and time.

Martin is an oral-history interviewer for the National Library of Australia and has had long experience as a radio producer and broadcaster. His radio work began in New York in 1991 when interviews with homeless people became the basis for the ABC documentary *Home Front Manhattan* (1991)—a reflection on the First Gulf War. Since then he has made more than a dozen documentaries, including *This is Jimmie Barker* (2000), a study of the Aboriginal sound recordist, which was awarded the NSW Premier's Audio/Visual History Prize.

Martin's publications include *The Artificial Horizon: Imagining the Blue Mountains* (2003), winner of the Gleebooks Prize for Literary and Cultural Criticism in the NSW Premier's Literary Awards, and (as editor) *Culture in Translation: The Anthropological Legacy of R. H. Mathews* (2007). He is a leading authority on Mathews' pioneering contribution to cross-cultural research in Australia and is author of a biographical study, *The Many Worlds of R. H. Mathews* (2011).

Martin became interested in the 1948 Arnhem Land Expedition when he heard recordings from 1948 in the archives of the Australian Broadcasting Corporation. This was the stimulus for ongoing fieldwork in Arnhem Land that involves study of historical film, audio and photography with senior traditional owners. In 2008 he was awarded a Smithsonian Institution Fellowship to study Arnhem Land collections and archives in Washington, DC. He is part of a team (including Linda Barwick and Allan Marett) that is studying the history and impacts of the Expedition, funded as a five-year Discovery Project by the Australian Research Council. Martin was an academic advisor for the Barks, Birds & Billabongs symposium.

Index

A

A Black Civilisation (book) 396
Aboriginal art
  art historians' interest 44
  cultural significance 42
  international recognition 44
  official 1945 research proposal 174
  renaissance of 40
Aboriginal artists 44
Aboriginal languages
  language groups 26, 29, *115*, 123, 360–1
  no sibilant 's' 419–20
Aboriginals Ordinance (1918) 116–17
'aborigines' use of term 98
acquisitions 222–4
A–D strips 244
Adam in Ochre (book) 91, 96, 98, 99–100, 358
  bird recording experience 107–9
  recording buffalo hunt 101–5
Adelaide Hills
  plant ecology study 285
adjustment movement 22, 340–1, 350, 351, 415
advertisement for 1945 film and lecture tour of the US *12*
Allah, new scheme of adjustment 350
ALP (Australian Labor Party) 56–7
Amagula, Thomas *22,* 191, *423, 424, 430*
American Clever Man (Marrkijbu Burdan Merika) *see* Johnson, David H.
American Clever Man story
  interpretation 334–6
American–Australian Scientific Expedition (1948)
  see Arnhem Land Expedition
Americans, Specht's memories of 289–90
Anderson, Sheila Gordon 81
Anglo-Japanese relations
  pre-World War II 61

Angoroko, rock art 135
Angurugu Mission station, trek to 257–8
Angwurrkburna rock shelter
  artefacts and raw material types *147, 148*
  preliminary exploration 142–8
  preliminary explorations 142–8
  rock art 148–9
  site contents 145–7
  usage and chronology 152–3
Angwurrkburna rock shelter view *144*
  fragments artefacts and *145,* 146
  radio carbon dates *145*
  site plan and section drawing *145*
anthropologists
  early to mid twentieth century 404
anthropology
  combined with environmental study 14
anthropomorphs in rock art 148–9, *150, 151*
anti-communists, middle-of-the-road stance 68–70
ANZUS (Australia, New Zealand, United States Security) Treaty xii, 57, 60–4
'Arawaltja' ceremony 398, 406
archaeological research
  historical perspective 153–5
archaeological sites
  low numbers of artefacts 137
archaeology
  of art 153
  culture-historical framework 137
  Groote Eylandt 1948 138–9
  Groote Eylandt 1990s and beyond 141–53
armbands 225, *225*
Arnhem Land
  1932 frontier violence 386
  location unknown 290
  Specht's description 164
  Stone Age fantasy 377–8
Arnhem Land Aboriginal cultures xii

Arnhem Land Aboriginal Reserve 306
Arnhem Land art
　categories 44
Arnhem Land Expedition xi–xii
　60 years of hindsight 423
　Aboriginal commentary 379
　anthropological guidance 50
　archaeological team 136
　archaeology 136–8
　Calwell's commitment to 66–7
　customary economy at Kunnanj, Fish Creek 115–22
　delayed for one year 176–7
　discovery of films 242–3
　distribution of specimens 20–2
　as source of economic wealth 393
　first documentary aired 12–13
　lasting significance 172
　leadership conflict 265–6
　nine-point agenda 115
　origin 4, 14-15, 254-5
　overview 171–88
　planning 273
　political context 70–1
　positive PR 64–8
　reunion of non-Aboriginal and Aboriginal descendants 429–30
　viewed as anachronistic 1–2
　wide interest in 172
　see also Expedition team
Arnhem Land Reserve
　1931 declaration 116–17
Arrkukluk *411*
art, myth and symbolism, testing propositions 38–40
art historians
　interest in Aboriginal art 44
art objects
　mid-1980s purchasing method 347–8
art supplies
　bark sheets 41
　pigments 41–2

artists
　Yolngu, with Mountford *46*, 47
artwork
　artistic attribution 45, *46*, 47
assimilation 97–8
Australia
　1947 five-year defence budget 57
　American strategic purposes 57–8
　development of the north 67
　geographic value 58
　post-World War II 56–60
　US lecture presentation tour 66–7
Australia, New Zealand, United States (ANZUS) Security Treaty 57
Australian Broadcasting Commission (ABC)
　commission an 'aboriginal corroboree' 408
　Features Department 88, 105
　first documentary on the Expedition 12–13
　meeting national needs 91
　participating in Expedition 91
　radio documentary *Delissaville: Death rite for Mabalung* 367
　radio dramas 88
Australian Government
　aim for the Expedition 159
　joint sponsorship 159
Australian Security Intelligence Organisation (ASIO) 55
Australian Walkabout (ABC)
　inaugural airing 92
　inauguration 88
　Island of Yoi (radio documentary) 91
　name choice 93–4, 95
　radio documentary 87–9
　stated objective 92
authenticity, culturally determined 96–9

B
Bailey, David 4–5
Balanda
   cultural brokerage 393
   term for white people 3
Balarra, Bill (Liyagawumirr) 220, *221*
Balga songs 361–2
Balga-style song cycle 361
Balma site 3
Bark painting of string-figure dreaming-place 204
bark paintings
   documentation 45
   fetch more money 223
   McCarthy's collection brief 48
   Mountford documenting 42
   Mountford's collection 218
   sea eagle *261*
bark sheets 41
Barks, Birds & Billabongs Symposium
   Aboriginal participation in 26–7, 425
   degree of respect 435
   initiators' individual interests xi
   international touring exhibition plans 431–2
   new and unexamined ideas 431
   organisation 432
   process of uncovering and remembering 423–4
   running commentary on silent movie 429–30
barramundi and feral pig *130*
barramundi drive *129*
Barrihdjowkkeng *124*
Barrtjap, Tommy 369, 370
base camp sites
   reason for choices 177
baskets
   coiled technique 229–30
   styles and uses 227, *227*
   twined *236*
Bassett-Smith, Peter (film-maker) *176*
   demonstrating Expedition radio *17*
   equipment 81
   new to documentary genre 10–11
   role and background xiv
bauxite mining 393
Bayini
   associated beliefs fluid 353
   birth of concept 345
   claims of descent from 346
   Macknight's dismissal of the concept 345
   post-Expedition references 346
   pre-Macassan traders 337–9, 341
   sculptures publicly displayed 346
Bayini men and women of Port Bradshaw (painting) *339*
Bayini narratives
   conflicted with Christian message 350
   'hidden' dimensions 342, 347
Bayini natives, deemed sacred 338
Baymarrwanga, Laurie 231, *232*
Beazley, Kim 19
Bell, Alexander Graham, 76–8
belts 225, *225*
Belyuen (see Delissaville)
Berndt, Ronald
   preoccupation with Aboriginal sexuality 414–15
   publishes secret material 415
   senior leaders request withdrawal of book 416
Berndt, Ronald and Catherine 24
Bickerton Island
   food-gathering techniques 179, 382
   nutritional studies 160, 179
   plant specimens 162
Billington, Brian *176*
   Nutrition Unit 294–5
   role and background xiv
   using a microscope *379*
Bininj Gunwok language *115*, 123
Binyinyiwuy (Djambarrpuyngu) 220, *221*
Birch, Bruce 365

'Bird life on a swamp on Arnhem Land 1948' (recording) 88, 90, 107–11
bird recording experience 107–9
Birdsell, Joseph 208–9
Birrinydji (Dreaming Macassan) 344, 346, 349, *351*, 352
black–white relations in Arnhem Land, history 343
Blitner, Donald *394*, *426*, *430*
Blitner, Frederick *381*, 382
Blitner, Gerald (Gerry) *384*, *394*, *399*, *400*
   childhood life 382–3
   comes to Umbakumba 390
   cultural broker 391
   death 400
   employable talents 385
   first impressions 379
   fish collection methods 275–6
   involvement with Expedition 381–2
   lack of photographs 384–5
   memories of Gray 387
   memories of team members 385
   mentions by Expedition members 383
   Mountford's memories 383
   Mountford's style of fieldwork 396–7
   provided Indigenous insights 178–9
   relationship with Miller 393
   relationship with Mountford 394
   spear fishing *277*
   uncovers dimensions of the Expedition 365
   view of racial hybridity 385
   'yella fella' comment 392
Blitner, Jessie *394*
Board for Anthropological Research expeditions 40
bone collecting *see* skeletal material
botanical collection
   distribution of deposited sets 163
   significance and scope 166
botanical survey, scope of work 165
Botany Department, University of Adelaide
   leading role in research 158–9
Bray, John E *5*, 95, *176*
   role and background xiv
Brideson, Hedley 253
Brinkin songs 362
bronze bust *187*
Brown, Ada 327
Brown, Archie 314, 320, *326*
   story of removal of Marrarna's remains 327–34
brown paper drawing *36*
Bryce, Quentin *x*
buffalo hunt recording 101–5
Buniyi, Renelle *436*
Bureau of American Ethnology 15
'burnim rag' ceremony 365–74
Burrenjuck, Kenny 370, *375*
Burrenjuck, Timothy 372
Burrumarra, David *343*, *351*
   criticised secret materials made public 415
   discloses Dreaming Macassan 351–2
   explains disclosure 344–5
   meaning of stories 342–4
   reasons for nondisclosure 344
bush diet 125

C
Cahill, Paddy 117
Calwell, Arthur 4
   bonds with Setzler 58–9
   correspondence with Setzler 68–71
   delays expedition for one year 177
   describes Arnhem Land 403–4
   dislike of Evatt 60–70
   film potential for international publicity 174
   historical 64–8
   role in Arnhem Land Expedition 175–6
   Setzler's description 55
Cape Don
   indigenous memories 320–6

Cape Stewart
  fibre object distribution *217*
Cashner, Frances 281
Cashner, Mollie 281
Cashner, Robert 281
Cassia harneyi specimen *168*
caste system 335
cave paintings 263–4
ceremonial exchange 364–5
ceremonies
  future role 420–1
  importance today 420
  Kapuk (Karaboga) 366–74
  Karaboga 'final mourning' ceremony 361
  major regional cult 404
  male initiation 396
  photography 404
  preparation and organisation 409
  regional totemic cult 406–12
  stage management 410–11
  staged for cameras 406
  tensions associated with performance 51–2
  Umbakumba fight 398
Chaloupka, George 415
Chasm, Island, rock art site 135
chest harnesses *225*
Chifley government
  1946–49 period 61
  Cold War 62
  population growth benefits 63
  post-World War II policies 60–4
  suppressing miners' strike 58
child endowment legislation 305–6, 387–8
children
  separation from parents 388
  'stolen generation' 305–6
China, emerging threat 63–4
Christian missions 19
Christianity
  the Dreaming 337–8
  indigenous 351–2
  Yolngu beliefs 349–50
  Yolngu social order 341
church attendance, food payment for 420
Church Missionary Society
  conflict with team members 264
  Oenpelli settlement 117, 183
cinema, silent film with commentary 11
citizenship 97–8
clan songs (Manikay) 362
clans, Yolngu 3
clap-stick beating patterns *373*
Clarke, Annie *430*
Clements, Frederick 157–8
Clever Man, American *see* Johnson, David H.
Coate, Howard 7, 48–9, 53, 179
Cobourg Peninsula 317
  Johnson's trek 313
Cold War 55, 58, 60–4
  correspondence between two liberal anti-communists 68–71
collecting policy 230
collecting practice
  acquisitions 222–4
  Mountford 221, 224
  Setzler 221–2, 230
collection size
  equated to success 16, 191
colour photography 77, 82–3
Community Development Employment Projects (CDEP) scheme 130
Community Perspective panel *423*
containers 227, *227*
Coon, Carleton S. 14
cordage 228
Cordon, Keith
  role and background xiv
corroborees
  Katherine River *43*
Cosmos Club lunch 14
crayon drawings
  delineating tribal territories 37

significance 36
technique 38
Crocker, Robert Langdon 286
cross-cultural encounters 397, 398, 430
  history 348–9
crucifixion, painting of *262*
cultural brokerage
  Balanda 393
  roles of 391
culture recognition, Aboriginal 98
customary economy
  Fish Creek 127–8
customary sector
  hunter-gatherer tradition 127
  post-colonial transformation 127
  pre-colonial times 127–8

D
dance
  enactment of knowledge 375
Darrarndarra, Buckley 314
Davidson, D. S. 197
deceased's spirit
  focus of ceremony 368
Deignan, Herbert G. 6, *176*, 184, 186, 273, 289
  role and background xiv
Delissaville (also known as Belyuen)
  audiovisual recordings 356
  fibre object distribution *217*
  recordings 360–3, 362–3
  sound recordings 364
  source of recordings 355
Dhalwangu clan 352
Dhamarrandji, Djombala x, *432, 433, 436*
Dhamarrandji, Manimawuy x, *432, 433, 436*
Dharramanydji, Jeffrey *423*
diaries 396
dietary analysis
  research methods 123–4
diffusionist theory
  Arnhem Land string figures 208

debates about 195–6
McCarthy's approach 197–8
study of string figures 195
disclosure
  community role 347–8
  context of 348–9
  history of 344–6
  reflections on 352–4
  sacred objects 340–4
Djakala *234*
Djanbarrpuyungungu 220
Djauan (Jawoyn) trading and sweetheart song 363
Djikanmurruwuy carrying pandanus *233*
documentary as emerging genre 10–11
domination, subaltern resistance of 342
Dreaming
  Christianity 337–8
Dreaming Macassan 338, 344, 345
  artefacts connected with 346
  disclosure 351–2
dresses *225*
Driver, Arthur Robert 19, 52, 180
Dunkley, Aub 103–4
Dyer, Alf 262–3

E
ecology
  early theory and practice 157–8
  trends in the discipline 158
ecological study
  South Australia 286
economy *see* customary sector; hybrid economy; market sector
Eden, entering, analogy 99–100
Edmonds, Stan 285
Elcho Island
  challenges to traditional religious life 415
  fibre object distribution *217*
  funerary rites 350
Elcho Island Church 350
Elcho Island mission 340

Elkin, A.P.
  banned Australian broadcast of Wubarr 414
  campaign against Mountford 8, 35
  fieldwork methods 9–10
  Specht's view of 293
Ellemor, Reverend Alfred F. 217
ethno-botany 303
ethnographic archives
  digitisation 25
ethnographic holdings 20
ethnographic records, visual 24–5
ethnologists 395
Ethnology Register *228,* 228–9
ethnographic film 404–6
Evatt, communist takeover in China 63–4
expedition, concept of 2
Expedition records
  publication delay 309–10
Expedition team
  anniversaries 25–6
  anthropologist, McCarthy xiv
  archaeologist, Setzler xiv
  biochemist, Hodges xiv
  Blitner's memory of politics 394–5
  botanist, Specht xiv
  cine-photographer, Bassett-Smith xiv
  cook, Hollow and Bray xiv, 4, *5*
  corresponding with Wetmore 186
  deputy leader, Setzler 4
  doctor, Billington 294–5
  entomologist, honorary, Bray xiv, 4, *5*
  Ethnologist, Mountford xiv
  growing tension 181
  herpetologist, Miller *275*
  ichthyologist, Miller xiv
  internal tensions 25
  mammalogist, Johnson xiv
  nutritionist, McArthur xiv
  ornithologist, Deignan 289
  represented gendered society 392
  Specht's recruitment 159–61
  see also entries for individual team members

Expedition to Arnhem Land (radio documentary) 13, 87–9
expeditions
  conflict between members 48
  NGS sponsored 78
  old idea/new media 10
  published studies 23
  uniquely Western 18
experimental dairy farm 117

F
fair trade
  Milingimbi 219–20
Fenton, William N.
  cultural anthropologist 14–15
feral pig carcasses *131*
fibre objects
  armbands *223, 225, 226*
  baskets 229–30
  bodywear 225, *225*
  categories 224–5
  containers 227, *227*
  cordage 228
  daily uses 213–14
  distribution 214–16
  distribution between sites *217*
  exceptional 229–30
  geographic spread 216, *217*
  making *234*
  missing items *228,* 228–30
  number and types 214–16, *215*
  pendants 228
  registered and found *228*
field recordings 101
  content 90
  including 'wild sounds' 106–7
fieldwork
  community-based approach 155
  Mountford 346–7
fieldwork methodology
  A.P. Elkin 9–10
  benefits of working alone 36
  McCarthy 154, 155

459

film footage
  unapproved public use 21
films 24–5
  archival arrangements 250
  cataloguing of film reels and footage 239–40
  condition of 244–7
  duplication process 249–50
  examination of 246–8
  'flipped images' 246
  motion picture footage log 240
  original raw footage 239
  'orphan work' 241–2
  'outtakes' 239, 240
  preservation project 247–50
  splicing methods 246
firewood, women carrying 233
Fish Creek
  bush diet 125
  gendered work ethic 125–6, 126
  time gathering food 119
flag treaty proposal 351
food consumption
  dietary content 118
  Fish Creek group 117–22
  relationship to work effort 120
foreign visitation, various waves 348–9
freshwater fishes 278
freshwater fishes, Mexican 279
funeral rite, Delissaville 25

G
Garawirrtja, Djangirrawuy x, 432, 433, 436
Garde, Murray 428
Gartside, Donald 281
Gaykamangu, Mungunu 234
gendered society 391–2
'Geographic man' image 83–4
geological investigation, ongoing 281–2
Giles, Raymond 89, 89, 355
  field recordings 90
Gillies, Marion 309

Gingi (Wobukarra) 220, 221
God, Yolngu debate about 353
'going walkabout' 92–3
Goldberg, Frank 66–7
Gray, Frederick Harold
  honorary Aboriginal protector 19
  no religious agenda or affiliation 377
  Umbakaumba settlement 305, 389
    life-style 388
    pre-Umbakumba life 386
    proposes by telegram 388
Gray, Marjorie 268, 305, 306, 390
Groote Eylandt
  archaeology 138–9
  excavation sites map 143
  fibre object distribution 217
  postwar population 382
  relationship terms 50
  rock art recordings 135
  songs, recordings of 357
Grosvenor, Dr Gilbert Hovey 4, 10, 77–9, 84
Grosvenor, Melville Bell 84
Gumbula, Joe Neparrnga 22, 233–5, 235, 237, 238, 432, 433, 436
Gumurdul, Donald 416–17
Gunbalang (Kun-barlang) 'sweetheart' song 363
Gunbalanya 263
  appearance of old men 184
  camp site 182
  experimental dairy farm 117
  feature radio program 355
  fibre object distribution 217
  most difficult camp 182, 183
  photographic sessions 82
  plant specimens 162
  program of audio recording 10, 89, 363, 364
  rich and abundant 184
  rock art areas 262–4
  township 183

H

Haddon, Alfred C.
   string figure making instructions 194
'Half-Caste Survey' 384
Hannah, Reverend Tom 217
Harney, William E (Bill) 49, 181, 296
   role and background xiv
Harris, Joshua *245*
headdresses *225*
Hemple Bay, work effort 119
'hidden' (sacred) dimension 342
hidden transcripts
   explained 342
   the Other are Yolngu 348
   reinterpretation of a public story 338
   significance seems lost 353
Hodges, Kelvin *176*, 294–5
   role and background xiv
Hoeng, Sabine 313, *427*
Hollow, Reginald
   role and background xiv
homelands movement 123
Hooton, Earnest A. 383–4
Hubbard, Gardiner Greene 76
Hubbs, Carl 271, *280*
human figures
   in rock art 148–9, *150*
human remains *see* skeletal material
'humanised geography' 83
hunter-gatherer tradition
   gender work divisions 119–20
   postwar transition 114
   'the original affluent society' 120
hunter-gatherers
   now hunter fishers 132
   twenty-first-century society 132
hybrid economy
   Mumeka, Mann River (1979–1980) 122–6, 128
   21st century Australia 132–3
   transformation 130

I

identities, loss of 231
immigration program 65
'India,' recording of ceremonies *51*
Indigenous art *see* Aboriginal art
Indigenous authenticity 96–9
Indigenous communities
   caught up in political and social goals 188
   distress over some 1948 work 186–8
Indigenous memories
   Cape Don 320–6
Indigenous Rhodes Scholar, first 433
Indi-indi 'trade' corroboree songs 361
initiation chants, Mindarini 361
Iniwakada (mythical sea eagle) *261*
Injalak Hill *263*
'inside' story 403
institutional speech 105–6
international trade, Australia's first 341
interpretation 152
Islamic traders 341–2
Island of Yoi (radio documentary) 91

J

Johnson, David H. *176*, 182, 273, 289, *291*
   appearance 314
   at Cape Don 314–17
   mammalogist 313
   performing taxidermy *315, 316*
   role and background xiv
   solo walk to Oenpelli 327
   status as a *marrkijbu* 317
   stay at Cape Don 320
Jolliffe, Eric (cartoonist) 47, 274, *274*
Juduruna, rock art 135

K

'Kakadu naked' (novella) 99–100
kangaroo being butchered 125–6, *126*
Kapuk (Karaboga) ceremony 366–74
   second part discontinued 373–4

similarities and differences 1948–2008 *370*, 370–4
song structure and content 372–3
Karaboga 'final mourning' ceremony 361
kinship relationships
   inadequately recorded 368
   positioning in 369, *369*
Kodachrome 82–3, 243
Kumbiala 303, 304, *304*
Kunabibi (Kunapipi) ceremony 2008, Gunbalanya 343, 396, 420
Kuninjku (Kunwinjku) people
   move to Maningrida settlement 120, 123
Kunnanj, Fish Creek 113, 117
   customary economy 115–22
Kuwarr ceremony 319

L
labour force participation rate 125–6
Lalara, Jabani *430*
'land of the dead,' Yolngu 349
land system survey, northern Australia 288
language distribution map *115*
language groups 123, 360–1
   Arnhem Land 26
   Iwaidja 29
   marriage laws 364
Lanyipi, Gordon *x*
Legislative Council (Northern Territory) 19
liberal internationalism 56
linking objects and people 231
Liwukang, George *351*
loss of identities 231
'love magic' songs 361
Lowe, Bryce *245*

M
MacArthur, General Douglas 58, 65
Macassan contact, estimated inception of contact 151
Macassan prau painting *149*, 151–2
Macassan trepangers 3, 344
Macasser Well, excavation 136
Macknight, Campbell 345–6
Madowk carrying pandanus *233*
Madsen, Virginia 88
Magee, John 281
magpie-goose hunt *129*
Makarrwala, Harry 220
Makarrwala, Jackie 220
Malaleuca Magnifica 167
Mangulda, Charlie 314, 320
Manikay *434*
Manikay performers *x*
Mann River 113
Marakara, Nipper (Kumutun) 183, *185*
Marawana (Larry) *263*
Marett, Allan (as singer) 370
   functions for Kapuk 366
Marika, Mathaman 201
   provided Yolngu names 209
Marika, Mawalan 182, 192, *260, 262*
Marika, Wandjuk 3–4, 181, 192, 204-206, 209, 341, 392-3
Marika, Wandjuk, string figures *204, 205*
marine fishes vs freshwater fishes 279
market sector 128
Marrala, Khaki 314, 320
Marrarna 335
   remains moved to US 327–34
marriage laws 29, 364
marrkijbu 317, 319
Material culture 20, 35, 54, 137, 140, 152, 192, 197-8, 213, 219-221, 237
May, Sally K. xi, 378, *423*
McArthur, Margaret 176, 294
   alone with local people 181
   background 116
   collecting material culture 238
   Fish Creek dietary results 118–19
   food-gathering techniques 179
   living with Aboriginal group 113
   method influence Meehan 125

nutrition of local people 116–17
Nutrition Unit 294–5
research disregarded 120
research methods 116–17
role and background xiv
McCarthy, Frederick D. *176*, 347
  brief to collect bark paintings 48–9
  collection of string figures 191
  coup against Mountford 53
  diary entry for string figures 203
  diffusionist theory 192–8
  Diploma of Anthropology studies 196–7
  disappointed natives too 'civilised' 377
  distrustful of Mountford's intentions 218
  fieldwork methodology 154, 155
  Groote Eylandt aims and achievements 135
  Groote Eylandt rock art 140–1
  late addition to team 192–8
  material culture specialist 116
  Nutrition Unit *294*
  page from string figure notes *207*
  purpose of rock art research 153
  recording and documenting string figures 198–9
  reliance on material culture 152
  resided with Aboriginal group at Kunnanj 113
  rock art classificatory scheme 140
  rock art interpretations 140–1
  role and background xiv
  Specht's view of 293
Meehan, Betty 125
Melaleuca magnifica specimen *300*
men's work
  hunting and gathering 119
  Mumeka, Mann river 124–5
Menzies, Robert G. 55, 57
Mexican freshwater fishes 279
migrants, United States 65, 67
Milingimbi 182

Aboriginal workers 220, *221*
basket design 233
basket styles 230, 231
camp environment 217–18
collecting practice in 222
collection quantities 228
fair trade 219–20
fibre object distribution *217*
important collection site 216
objects collected 237–8
reason not a base camp 224
shell mounds 136
twined basket from *236*
Miller, Frances 280
Miller, Gifford 280–2
Miller, Robert R. *176, 272, 273, 274, 276, 277, 280*
  advocate for conservation 279–80
  early life 271–2
  expert on Mexican freshwater fishes 279
  family legacy 280–1
  first time in bush 290
  fish collection
    size 274
  Gerry Blitner 276
  Gerry Blitner's memories 381
  gets Dengue 295
  joins Expedition 273, 289
  Oenpelli, rich source of specimens 184
  relationship with Blitner 393
  role and background xiv
  University of Michigan job offer 278
Milngawurruwuy, David 220, *221*
Mindarini initiation chants 361
Mindarini songs 365
Mininyala *234*
Minyimak, David 'Cookie' 314, 320, *320*
missionaries 19–20
mixed-race people
  lack of interest in 384
Mosek [Manpurr] (dancer and composer) 361, 362, 363

motion pictures 239–51
Mountford, Bessie *176*
  assisted Setzler 180
  describes Milingimbi basketmaker 216
  diary entries
    documents tensions 52
    invaluable records 266–8
    thoughts on collecting 238
    Umbakumba people observed 267
  duties 45
  economic foundation of Umbakumba 387
  Expedition activities 266–8
  helped Specht preserve specimens 161
  interaction with Yirrkala women 267–8
  as diarist 161
  leadership conflict 265–6, 268
  on Marjorie Gray 268
  marriage 266
  Milingimbi 217
  plant named after her 162
  political activities 266
  role and background xiv
Mountford, Charles Pearcy 4, *33*
  1945–46 US tour 405
  Aboriginal art
    obtaining and documenting 45
    understanding of 42–4
  accepts imminent demise of traditional culture 40
  in Adelaide *173*
  allows removal of human remains 21
  anthropological expeditions to Central Australia 174
  approach to anthropology and art 35
  art supplies provision 41
  art-collecting methodology 53–4
  artwork, artistic attribution 47
  asks for team unity 186
  awarded funding for expedition 174
  background 8, 293
  characterisation of 34
  collecting practice 45, 47, 221, 224
  collection method unorthodox 346–7
  condensed Wubarr ceremony 409
  correspondence
    Mountford–Sheard Collection 264–6
    to NGS President 174–5
    to W. Lloyd Warner 37
  discarding papers 253
  disposing of artefacts 229
  explains purpose of expedition 13, 95
  fieldwork journals 261, *262*
  filming from a Catalina *257*
  films and records secret men's ceremony 398–9
  Gerry Blitner's memories 381
  health 186, 295
  interest in secret-sacred ceremonies 395–6
  knowledge of Indigenous art 174
  leader of Expedition 177
  leadership
    asked to relinquish 6, 53, 180
    Specht's view 292–3
  lecture tour of the US (1944–5) 66–7, 81, 174, 254–5, 273
  lecture tour of the US (2nd 1946) 256
  memories of Gerry Blitner 383
  methodology 35
  next to Gray's 'native settlement' 178
  no expedition as comprehensive 159
  official 1945 research proposal 174
  organisational challenge 40
  personal journal 256–9
    recording ceremonial songs *51*
    with Yolngu artists *46, 47*
  popularisation of Aboriginal art 269
  presentation to National Geographic Society 171
  purpose of Expedition 13–14
  reasons for appointment 49
  relationships
    A.P. Elkin 8
    Blitner 394
    Tindale 254, 255

rock-art motif interpretation 39–40
role and background xiv
self-taught ethnographer 254
size of collection 16
sound recordings 259–60
criticism of Australian anthropology 14–15
writings
  Groote Eylandt Journal 45
  newspaper articles 42
  through Board for Anthropological Research 42
Yirrkala 181
early life 173
Mountford–Sheard Collection of the State Library of South Australia 253–354
  correspondence 264–6
  legacy 268–9
  Oenpelli songs *364*
  photographs 259
  rock art galleries 263
Mulka Centre (community digital knowledge centre) 25
Mundine, Djon 347–8
Munn, Nancy 34
Muntjingu, Peter (Gupapyngu) 220, *221*
Mununggurr, Ngarrawu
  demonstrates string figures 192
  examples of string figures *202*
  mission and Expedition work 201–2
  recording instructions 202
  string figure skill 192
Murphy, Anthony *423, 427, 429*
Murphy, Kevin 52, 180, 181
museum collections, objects from Expedition 214–16
music
  credit for recordings 358
  in secular and ceremonial life 355
mythological trajectories
  placed in context 37

N
Nadjamerrek, Bardayal *404*, 417
Nadjamerrek, Donna *423*
Nakwarrba, Banjo 397
Namarnyilk, Jimmy Kalarriya *428, 429*
Namatjira, Albert 44
Nangapiana 180
nation building 56
National Geographic magazine
  broadened membership 77
  cover presentation change 79
  exclusive rights 408
  foreign editorial staff 80
  funding scientific expeditions 78
  pioneer publication 10
  specialised editorial staff 84
  use of colour photography 77
National Geographic Society
  cultivated image 79
  deportment of editorial staff 73–4
  endorse Mountford's leadership 53
  foundation and roles 74
  geography broadly construed 78
  membership base 76–8
  name selection 75
  offer Mountford support 273
  presentation by Mountford 66
  1960s and 1970s directions 84
  sponsorship of expeditions 78
National Geographic Society Film Archives 239, 241
  collection management 241–2
  lecture films 241
National Geographic Society lectures
  Setzler lecture film 241
National Geographic Society Research Committee 171
national security issues 67
national-history writings 23
nationhood
  changing sense of 97
'native chants' recording of 9–10
natural-history specimens 20

Nawirridj, Wilfred *423*, 425, *429*
Neale, Margo xi, *436*
necklaces *225*
Ngarrawu 200
   McCarthy notes her assistance 209
Ngularra *234*
Ngulurra *233*
Ngurlmarrk see Wubarr ceremony
Nineteen Forty-Eight time line 1
non-Aborigines
   Yongu thoughts on origin and purpose 344–5
North-East Arnhem Land Aboriginal People *see* Yolngu
North-West Arnhem Land
   insight into culture 334
Nutrition Unit 294–5
   dietary recommendations 121–2
Nyilco (Nilcoo), Lame Roy 369, 371
Nyindi-yindi repertory 372–3

O
Obiri cave paintings 263–4
Oenpelli *see* Gunbalanya
Oenpelli Hill *411*
original affluent society theory 126, 132, 133
Orwell, George 1
Other or 'the Other'
   who is considered 348
'outside' story 403
outstations 123
outstations, state support 133
ownership issues, lack of sensitivity towards 346

P
pandanus, women carrying *233*
pandanus collecting 298
paper drawings 49
past chronologies, measuring 137
pendants 228
performance at National Museum of Australia *423*, *433*, *434*

Peterson, Nicolas 24
Petrov affair 65–6
Phantom supply vessel 183
Phoenix supply barge 3, 47, 82, 177, 178, 257, 258
photographic equipment 81
photographs 24–5, 259
photography
   challenge of dark skin 385
   landscape shots 83
   shot lists 82
   Wubarr ceremony 411–12
   see also colour photography
pigments 41–2
Pilawak 369–70
'place,' idea of 163–5
plant specimens
   collecting and classifying 298–9, *300*, 301–2
   collection and care 161
   drying methods 161–2, 287
plaster hand and face casts 179–80
Poignant, Roslyn 24–5
Politics of Repatriation panel 425, *427*
population base
   growth benefits 63
Port Darwin Aboriginal songs 357
pottery shards, Macassan 139
pre-colonial transformation
   customary sector 127–8
pre-Macassans (Bayini)
   described 28
   hidden transcript 337–9
Prescott, Professor James 288
'preventive conservation' 243
pricing
   disagreement regarding 222
   Mission 219–20
pubic covers *225*
public songs, didjeridu-accompanied 360
'public transcripts' 342
Pyrox Wire Recorder *89*

Q

Qantas base 386, 387
quantitative data collection 122, 128

R

radio, demonstrated *17*
radio documentary feature 12, 87–9, 96, 355
'rag-burning' ceremony 365–74
Rankin, Douglas 374
Rankmore, Brooke *430, 435*
recording equipment 94
   problems with 355
recordings
   question of authority 105–6
   Tiwi material 360
regional Aboriginal economy 127
regions visited during 1948 Expedition *172*
Richards, Rebecca 433
Richardson, Lori *423*
ritual *see* ceremonies
rock art
   archaeological research approach 154
   cave paintings 263–4
   domestic scenes 149
   figurative motifs 148–9, *150*
   human figures 151
   marine and terrestrial fauna 149
   McCarthy's classificatory scheme 140-1
   McCarthy's interpretation 152
   motif interpretation 39–40
   rock engravings at Panaramittee *39*
   silhouettes and line paintings 149, *150*, 151
   stencils 151
   techniques 148–9, 151–3, *153*
rock art galleries, pictures of 263–4
Rose, Frederick 50, 386–7
Roth, Walter Edmund 23–4

S

Sahlins, Marshall 114, 120–1, 132
salvage mentality, later benefits of 425
sambar deer 319
Scott, James C. 342
sea eagle, mythical (Iniwakada) *261*
secret-sacred ceremonies 412–16
   made public 414, 416
Seibert, Elvin 180
Setzler, Frank M. 4, *173, 176,* 273, *276, 277*
   1950 Washington lecture opening 239
   archaeologist by disposition 6, 15
   arrival at Umbakumba 383
   bond with Calwell 55, 58–9
   Cascade beer 290
   collecting practice 221–2, 230
   correspondence with Calwell 68–71
   deputy leader 6, 177
   describes Wubarr ceremony 410
   Gerry Blitner's memories 381
   Groote Eylandt aims and achievements 135
   leadership role 7
   Milingimbi photography 234
   Mountford's collecting practice 224
   offered leadership 52–3
   offered Leadership role 180–1
   plaster hand and face casts 179–80
   recorded 2400 rock art 135
   recorded interviews 100–1
   relationship with McCarthy 48
   removes human remains 21
   role and background xiv
   Specht's memories of arrival 289–90
   staged ceremonies 406
   younger Indigenous men keen to assist 178
shaman 313
Sheard, Harold
   project to archive Mountford's collection 253
'shot lists' 82
shuttles *227*
silhouettes, dominant style 151

silhouettes and line paintings 149
Simpson, Colin
  ABC Features Department 105
  Aboriginal culture recognition 98
  Australian Walkabout series 87–9
  on Bessie Mountford 266–7
  credit for music recordings 358
  inaugurated *Australian Walkabout* series 88
  initiated audio recording 10
  mistook purpose of Kapuk 366
  Mountford–Sheard collection of recordings 362
  Oenpelli feature radio program 355
  Oenpelli, description of 184
  Oenpelli sound recordings 363
  post-ABC career 111
  presentation style 95
  professional habits 92
  public broadcast of songs 413–14
  public revelation of secret material 413–14
  recording session *89*
  recordings 358, *359*, 360
    summary contents 359
  reflection on importance of the expedition 171
  writing for recording 100–1
skeletal material
  distresses caused by removal 186–8
  departure from Smithsonian Institution 22, *22*
  no permit required to collect 21–2
  omitted from inventory of collections 21
  repatriation 425, 428
Smithsonian basket E387541 229–30
Smithsonian Institution 15
  delay expedition 176–7
  endorsement of Mountford's leadership 53
  importance of Expedition 6
  interest in Expedition 4

online research portal 431
  return of human remains 21–2, *22*, 433
snapshots, use of term 356
Snowy Mountains Hydro-Electric Scheme 56
social anthropology
  use of new media 9–10
songs
  Balga 361–2
  Balga public genre 362
  Brinkin 162
  ceremonial exchange 364–5
  didgeridu-accompanied 363
  Djauauan (Jawoyn) trading and sweetheart song 363
  Groote Eylandt recordings 357
  Gunbalang (Kun-barlang) 'sweetheart' song 363
  Manikay 362
  men's and women's versions 362
  Port Darwin 357
  private and public status 362
  provenance of 11 public songs 363
  public ceremony 362
  Wangga 360–1, 363
  Winmala 357, 358
  Worgait 357
  see also ceremonies
sorry ceremony 304–5
Sound Effect (SFX) 87
sound recordings
  authenticity of actuality 100–1
  radio documentary features 87–9
South Australian Museum 254
Southwick, Margaret 388
Specht, Alison 309
Specht, Raymond L. 176, 283, *291*, *307*, 429, *429*, 436
  Aboriginal contact 302
  after the Expedition 309–10
  bonds with Nutrition Unit members 294–5
  camp diary 179

career achievements 284
career trajectory 284–7, 288
collecting and classifying plant
    specimens 298–9, *300*, 301–2
Expedition members, discipline 159
holistic understanding of place 163–5
joins Expedition 159–60
memories of Mountford's leadership
    292–3
memories of the Americans 289–90
naming plants 303
Oenpelli prolific with specimens 184
preparing for the expedition 287–9
publications 284
recording methods 163
recruited to team 286–7
remembers Bill Harney 297–8
role and background xiv
sorting, identifying and labelling
    specimens 308
teacher training 285–6
view of McCarthy 293
view of Mountford 292–3
specimens
    natural-history 20
    transcontinental distribution 20–1
    volume equates to success 16
Spencer, Baldwin
    Wubarr performance 408
Spender, John 60
splicing
    materials used 244–5, *246*
    methods *246*
'starving scientists' article 177–8
State Library of South Australia
    Mountford–Sheard Collection 253–354
    original recordings 261
stencils 151
'stolen generation' 305–6
'Stone-Age' world 19–20
Strehlow, T.G.H.
    sold restricted photographs 412–13
string bag *226*

string figures 192
    an 'untouched field' 199
    existence in process of making 194
    instructions for making 194
    Lightning/Bapa 193
    link to tribal mythology 208
    material value 210, 212
    motive for study 195
    mounting and documenting 201–3
    notes from McCarthy's book *207*
    photographing designs 205–6
    representing environment 206, *207*
    'social background' 204
    of Yirrkala 191–212, *207*
superimposed paintings
    ceiling detail *150*
    family group *150*
'swaggie' image 94
Szasz, Margaret Connell 391

T
Taylor, William R. 278
team members *see* Expedition team
'Territory Growth Towns' 134
'The call of the wild' (essay) 88
Thomas, Martin xi, 231, *247*, *429*
    visited three main bases to check on
        memories 378
Thompson, John 9, 89, 95
Thomson, Donald 24, 397
Tindale, N.B. (Norman)
    crayon drawings 37
    encouraged Mountford to continue
        Central Australia exploration
        174
    field trip with Mountford 255
    intensive team methodology 35
    no interest in Mountford's papers for
        the Museum 254, 395
    tribal boundary and mapping project
        37
Tjarrata songs 361–2

469

tobacco as currency 4, 220, 222, 347, 361, 393, 409-10
tradition and transformation, 1948–2009 127–31
tribal boundary and mapping project 37

U
Ubar *see* Wubarr
Umbakumba *240*
   Bessie Mountford's observations 267
   community 305
   display of 'civilisation' 390
   first base camp 160, 177, 377
   flying boat 386
   uses from 1930s 377
United States
   Australia's relationship with 55-71
   Mountford's lecture tours 66–7, 81, 174, 254–5, 273
   Mountford's 2nd (1946) lecture tour 256
University of Michigan 278

V
Victory supply vessel 183
vinegar syndrome 244

W
Wake, Tom 367
'walkabout,' term 92–3
Walker, Harrison Howell Dodge 75, 240
   assigned to Australia 81
   films Coral Sea 290
   first position 80
   Gerry Blitner's memories 381
   hired by *National Geographic* 80
   impression made 73
   later life 84
   NGS photographing *74*
   photographic equipment 81
   representative of NGS 239
   retirement 84
   role and background xiv
   roving NGS reporter 74
   stranded on *Phoenix* 177
   surveys team members 191
   unconventional appearance 83–4
   writing style 80–1
   young life 80
Wanambi, Rita *435*
Wanambi, Wukan *423*
Wanambi, Wukun *435*
Wanderer II (ketch) 82
Wangga songs 360–1
   cultural exchange 364
   historical origins 363
Warner, William Lloyd 136, 219, 396
Webb, Steve *423*, 428
Western Arnhem Land
   white contact 117
   near Oenpelli *165*
   economic activity and food consumption 113
Wetmore, Alexander 4, 6–8
   correspondence
     to Setzler 6
     from team members 186
   ensured NGS's funding support 81
white authority 19
'wild sounds,' recording 87–9, *88*
wildlife harvesting 128
   key continuities 130
Williams, Joy *427*
Winchelsea Island
   Macassan artefacts 139
Winmala song 357, 358
wire recorder 94–5
women's work
   food gathering 119
   Mumeka, Mann river 124–5
Wood, Professor Joseph 158, 284, 285, 286
Woodah Island clan 304
wooden toy canoe, children play with *260*

Worgait
  songs 357
  term explained 360
work effort
  Hemple Bay 119
  Mumeka, Mann River 124–6
  time measurement 118
workforce participation
  Fish Creek 117–22
  Hemple Bay 125–6
workforce participation rate 125–6
  Fish Creek/Hemple Bay 121
Working on Country program 130
Worsley, Peter 382
Wubarr ceremony
  1948 location *411*
  ceremonial ground 410
  clothing 410–11
  commentary on viewing footage 417–18
  context of team's recording 419
  film footage shown in US 413
  four performances documented 408
  'hidden story' 407–8
  inception and performance 406–12
  modified for non-Aboriginal audience 409
  performance history 407
  public showing of video cassette 416–17
  published in public domain 413–14
  recordings 360
  repatriation of 1948 film 416–18
  rituals 409
  Seltzer's diary 410
Wubarr Ceremony, The (painting by Bardayal Nadjamerrek) *404*
Wubarr songs 363
wunymalang spirits 366, 367–8

Y
Yattalunga rock shelter paintings *38*
Yirrkala
  second base camp 3
  shuttle *227*
  string bag *226*
  two different clans 209
Yirrkala
  Bessie Mountford's observations 267
  camp set up 160
  fibre object distribution *217*
  fieldwork 182
  mission conditions 200
  Mountford's journal entry 258
  plant specimens 162
  second base camp 180
Yirrkala cemetery 3
Yolngu
  Christianity of 351–2
  Christianity/Dreaming discussion 337
  contact with Macassans 341
  cosmology 337–9
  'hidden transcript' 338
  response to non-Aborigines 338–9
  seeking best of non-Aboriginal world 353
  vision of future 353–4
Yolngu beliefs
  Christianity 349–50
Yolngu clans 3, 200
Yolngu rituals
  legacy from Macassans 341
yumbarrbarr (malevolent spirit) 317–19
Yunupingu, Munggurray *339*
Yunupingu, Susan, string figure technique *211*

www.ingramcontent.com/pod-product-compliance
Lightning Source LLC
Chambersburg PA
CBHW041248240426
43669CB00034B/2987